Philosophical Perspectives on Sex and Love

Philosophical Perspectives on Sex and Love

EDITED BY

ROBERT M. STEWART

New York   Oxford
OXFORD UNIVERSITY PRESS
1995

Oxford University Press

Oxford   New York   Toronto
Delhi   Bombay   Calcutta   Madras   Karachi
Kuala Lumpur   Singapore   Hong Kong   Tokyo
Nairobi   Dar es Salaam   Cape Town
Melbourne   Auckland   Madrid

and associated companies in
Berlin   Ibadan

Library of Congress Cataloging-in-Publication Data
Philosophical perspectives on sex and love/edited by Robert M. Stewart.
p.   cm.
Includes bibliographical references and index.
ISBN 0-19-508031-9
1. Sexual ethics.
2. Love.
3. Feminism.
4. Sex customs.
I. Stewart, Robert Michael, 1952–
HQ32.P49   1995   306.7—dc20   94-6158

9   8   7   6   5   4   3   2   1

Printed in the United States of America
on acid-free paper

PREFACE

Questions about human sexuality, love, and friendship are central to moral and social philosophy, yet few of the great philosophers have addressed them in a detailed and systematic way. Plato is one of the exceptions, for eros is a key to understanding the relationship between the mind of the individual and the eternal Forms or Ideas in his philosophy. Aristotle writes extensively about friendship love and its importance to personal happiness and the good of a polis. But if he had a theory of eros, it is unknown to us, perhaps never written down or lost with the bulk of his work. Neither Plato nor Aristotle has much to say about sexuality, certainly not in a positive vein.

Medieval philosophy, particularly the works of Saint Augustine and Saint Thomas Aquinas, includes many discussions of sexual morality and the various forms of love, but nearly always in a context of orthodox Christian theology. It is not until the moderns that secular treatments of these subjects reappear in the works of major philosophers—Descartes and Spinoza, Hume and Kant. But there again, the treatments are often brief and unsystematic. Nineteenth-century philosophers, particularly the French and Germans, seem more comfortable with the subjects of love and sexuality, no doubt due in part to the earlier writings of Rousseau and the influence of the romantic movement. The three great German philosophers of that century, Hegel, Schopenhauer, and Nietzsche, had important things to say about them; and Fichte's discourse on the moral relationships of the family is considered to be historically important. The English utilitarians Bentham and Mill addressed questions about homosexuality and the equality of the sexes in essays that are very relevant to our present-day concerns.

Recent work in the philosophy of love and sexuality begins, essentially, with the writings of the existentialists. Kierkegaard's *Either/Or*, Sartre's pessimistic investigations of the Self and its relations to the Other in *Being and Nothingness*, and de Beauvoir's classic feminist work *The Second Sex* are brilliant and provocative. Anglo-American philosophers, in contrast, have come rather late in this century to apply their analytic tools to questions of sex and love. Thomas Nagel's article "Sexual Perversion" stimulated considerable discussion, leading to many articles by other philosophers in the 1970s. Irving Singer's monumental trilogy, *The Nature of Love*, was published, and important books by Roger Scruton, Russell Vannoy, Richard Taylor, and other British and American philosophers appeared, along with several anthologies. Feminist philosophers contributed substantially to this growing body of work, forcing attention to broad questions of social structure and policy.

The present collection of readings does not attempt to provide a complete historical survey of writing on philosophical issues of sex and love, nor does it pretend to cover all the significant topics that philosophers have taken up. The emphasis is on selections that have moral or sociopolitical content, and an attempt is made to present material that is relevant to the concerns of students and likely to stimulate classroom discussion. The volume is intended for use in courses that survey topics in applied moral and social philosophy as well as for specialized courses on the philosophy of sex and love. The readings represent some of the best and most influential classical and contemporary work in this area, and can serve as an effective introduction to the basic questions of philosophy that concern human life and values.

A lengthy and up-to-date bibliography, necessarily selective, is included for the benefit of students and others who wish to pursue further investigation into what is a rapidly growing literature. The first part of the bibliography lists anthologies, and care has been taken not to list articles in the second part that appear unedited in those collections.

A number of friends and colleagues have helped in the creation of this text. Particular thanks go to James Conlon, Tony Graybosch, J. Roger Lee, and Linda LeMoncheck for their original essays. Professors Laurie Shrage and Neera Badhwar were especially helpful with the bibliographical references in their areas of special interest; Dan Barnett's word-processing skills and determination in tracking down references were invaluable. Tatiana Strishak's assistance in assembling the selections was also much appreciated. Finally, it is a pleasure to work with Oxford University Press's philosophy editor, Angela Blackburn, her editorial assistant, Robert Dilworth, and associate editor Paul Schlotthauer. Their patience, encouragement, and suggestions have been very welcome at crucial stages in this project.

March 1994
Chico, California   R. M. S.

CONTENTS

Introduction, 3

I Sex Roles, Equality, and Social Policy

JOHN STUART MILL
from *The Subjection of Women*, 11

ELIZABETH RAPAPORT
On the Future of Love: Rousseau and the Radical Feminists, 18

LINDA LEMONCHECK
Feminist Politics and Feminist Ethics: Treating Women as Sex Objects, 29

MICHAEL LEVIN
What Is Feminism?, 39

MELINDA VADAS
A First Look at the Pornography/Civil Rights Ordinance: Could Pornography Be the Subordination of Women?, 56

WILLIAM PARENT
A Second Look at Pornography and the Subordination of Women, 66

LAURIE SHRAGE
Should Feminists Oppose Prostitution?, 71

ROBERT STEWART
Moral Criticism and the Social Meaning of Prostitution, 81

II Sexual Norms and Ethics

JEROME NEU
Freud and Perversion, 87

THOMAS NAGEL
Sexual Perversion, 105

MICHAEL RUSE
Is Homosexuality Bad Sexuality?, 113

J. ROGER LEE
Sadomasochism: An Ethical Analysis, 125

DAVID HUME
   Of Chastity and Modesty, 138

IMMANUEL KANT
   Duties Towards the Body in Respect of Sexual Impulse, 140

   Crimina Carnis, 144

FREDERICK ELLISTON
   In Defense of Promiscuity, 146

RICHARD A. WASSERSTROM
   Is Adultery Immoral?, 159

JOHN H. BOGART
   On the Nature of Rape, 168

III   Erotic Love

PLATO
   from *Symposium*, 183

ARTHUR SCHOPENHAUER
   from The Metaphysics of the Love of the Sexes, 190

SØREN KIERKEGAARD
   Don Juan's Secret, 197

JEAN-PAUL SARTRE
   First Attitude Toward Others: Love, Language, Masochism, 202

SIMONE DE BEAUVOIR
   from The Woman in Love, 213

IRVING SINGER
   Appraisal and Bestowal, 217

ALAN SOBLE
   Reconciling Eros and Agape, 227

ROBERT NOZICK
   Love's Bond, 231

ROBERT C. SOLOMON
   The Virtue of (Erotic) Love, 241

IV   Friendship and Familial Love

ARISTOTLE
   from *Nicomachean Ethics*, 259

NEERA KAPUR BADHWAR
   The Circumstances of Justice: Pluralism, Community, and Friendship, 266

ELLEN FOX
Paternalism and Friendship, 283

JAMES CONLON
Why Lovers Can't Be Friends, 295

JANE ENGLISH
What Do Grown Children Owe Their Parents?, 300

JEFFREY BLUSTEIN
The Duties of Grown Children, 304

ANTHONY GRAYBOSCH
Parents, Children, and Friendship, 313

Select Bibliography, 323

Philosophical Perspectives on Sex and Love

INTRODUCTION

SEX ROLES, EQUALITY, AND SOCIAL POLICY

Pervading most recent work in the philosophy of love and sexuality is the influence of the contemporary feminist movement, a manifestation of the egalitarian currents of modern social and political thought. Liberal and radical thinkers of the nineteenth century laid the groundwork for present-day theorizing about the unequal roles of men and women in most societies, an inequality that goes beyond matters of civil liberty and economic opportunity to the mutual expectations of marital partners and our very conceptions of what it means to be male or female. John Stuart Mill's classic essay *The Subjection of Women* is a sustained and reasoned presentation of the essential elements of liberal feminism, emphasizing the untapped potential of half the human race; the social benefits of extending equal rights and opportunities to women would be immeasurable, he argues, and whatever case might have been made in earlier times for inequality of the sexes, it is in many respects comparable to slavery. The greater physical strength of men, socially transformed into custom and politically solidified by law, in no way legitimates the oppression and created dependency that typifies the lives of women in even the most advanced societies. As slavery has been abandoned by these nations, Mill insists, so must the subjection of women, for the sake of their self-development and the greatest good of humanity.

The emergence of contemporary feminism in the late 1960s, represented most notably in the writings of Shulamith Firestone, Ti-Grace Atkinson, Betty Friedan, and Gloria Steinem, is commonly linked to the civil rights movement in the United States and the "liberation" ideologies of the New Left. In the subsequent decades other feminist writers have gained prominence, some of the most radical—Mary Daly and Andrea Dworkin among them—bringing together ideas from philosophy and theology, Marxism and environmentalism, literary criticism and the study of popular culture. A French feminist tradition, going back to Simone de Beauvoir, flourishes today at the intersection of philosophy and literary theory.

Elizabeth Rapaport examines the radical feminism of Atkinson and Firestone in her essay, "On the Future of Love: Rousseau and the Radical Feminists." The analyses of love given by these two writers, who share the belief that heterosexual love is a means by which men maintain control over women, are interestingly compared by Rapaport to the theory of love put forth by Jean-Jacques Rousseau. Although Rousseau asserts precisely

3

the opposite view of the function of "moral" (as distinct from "physical") love in his *Discourse on the Origin of Inequality*—it serves to keep men in thrall to women—there are significant points of similarity to the feminist analyses in his account of the negative aspects of erotic love, particularly its tendency to undermine individual personality through a mutual, destructive dependency.

Linda LeMoncheck surveys different interpretations of the thesis that men in patriarchal societies commonly treat women as sex objects, relating these interpretations to distinct currents in feminist thought in her contribution to this volume. Michael Levin, a well-known philosopher and critic of the feminist movement, attacks feminists in a selection from his book *Feminism and Freedom* for ignoring or attempting to explain away empirical evidence of innate sex differences that would undermine their arguments for radical egalitarian social engineering.

The remaining selections in Part I concern a frequent theme in current feminist arguments against pornography and prostitution: that they perpetuate attitudes and behaviors that defame, degrade, and subordinate women—indeed, that they *are* the subordination of women. This view is most evident in the work of Catharine MacKinnon, an influential feminist activist and legal scholar, and collaborator with Andrea Dworkin on antipornography legislation (with more success in Canada than in the United States), who labels pornography a "form of female sexual slavery" and advocates banning even softcore publications such as *Playboy* and *Penthouse*. Philosopher Melinda Vadas offers a defense of the odd-sounding claim that pornography can be subordination, an argument challenged by William Parent in his reply. Laurie Shrage, a philosopher who has done extensive research on prostitution, argues in her article that the practice reinforces certain false and pernicious beliefs or attitudes about human sexuality and relations between men and women. Robert Stewart challenges some of her assumptions in his reply, questioning the relevance of social meaning in the moral assessment of actions.

SEXUAL NORMS AND ETHICS

The concept of perversion is a complex one, both descriptive and normative. Its use presupposes the validity of certain lawlike generalizations or norms that define human nature and set broad requirements for human flourishing. The natural law tradition in moral theory, particularly as developed in the writings of Aristotle and Thomas Aquinas, provides the context in which the more specific notion of sexual perversion makes sense; if we reject that theoretical background, an alternative—such as psychoanalysis—is needed in order to give the term a meaning. However, there is no guarantee that the ethical content will be preserved if the natural law theoretical context is abandoned in favor of a more "scientific" one.

Sexual perversion, as most comprehensively understood, involves at least three different kinds of properties. First, there is the idea of deviation from a norm—biological, social, psychological, or moral. The belief that the perverted is the unnatural has its basis here. Second, distinct from but related to the idea of abnormality is that of unhealthiness, which can be physical, mental, or moral-spiritual, corresponding to the various norms that perverted sexual behavior is thought to violate. Third, there is the implication that perverted sex is in some sense or respect bad sex. This can be a matter of its striking people as disgusting or unfulfilling, or—judging from a moral perspective—wrong or degrading.

The readings in this section represent a range of approaches to understanding sexual perversion and its ethical implications. Jerome Neu interprets and reconstructs Freud's theory in the light of recent philosophical developments and concerns. Thomas Nagel, influenced by Sartre's observations on sexuality, sketches an account of sexual perversion that relies on certain psychological norms of human sexual arousal. Normal desire, Nagel insists, passes through stages of "mutual sensing," when prospective partners become aroused at the awareness of one another's arousal, and "embodiment," when one feels most fully physical, present in one's body. Deviations from this pattern, as in most cases of fetishism, bestiality, voyeurism, and necrophilia, fail the test of normality, lacking a kind of completeness. Nagel's analysis has the implication that homosexuality is not a perversion, in view of the fact that gay males and lesbians experience mutual sensing and embodiment as regularly as do heterosexuals. Sadomasochistic activity, however, is a perversion in Nagel's view, since he believes that these normal stages are typically absent in sexual interactions between sadist and masochist.

Michael Ruse considers various ethical objections to homosexuality in a selection from his book, the most thorough and wide-ranging treatment of the topic by a philosopher. Ruse concentrates his attention on the claim that homosexuality is biologically unnatural, arguing that there is no sense in which this contention is true and also provides a basis for moral condemnation or other negative evaluations. J. Roger Lee, in his original contribution to this volume, addresses the topic of sadomasochism from the perspective of a moral philosopher influenced by Aristotelian virtue ethics and the psychoanalytic tradition. Sadomasochistic sexual behavior, he maintains, can be seen to be incompatible with human excellence when its psychological roots are properly understood.

Ruse's survey of the views of Kant and the English utilitarians on the morality of homosexuality is indicative of the persisting influence of these philosophers' opposing points of view. The account provided by the young David Hume of the reasons for regarding chastity and modesty in women as virtues contrasts sharply, in its detached consequentialism, with the grounds put forth by Kant in his early writings on ethics for exercising sexual restraint outside of marriage. Hume's broadly utilitarian theory of morality in Book III of his *Treatise of Human Nature* emphasizes the personal benefits and social advantages of conventional virtues (save certain religiously based qualities of character that serve no useful purpose). In his explanation of the desirability of feminine sexual continence—which anticipates sociobiological theory—Hume points out the need for men to have assurance that they are the father of their wife's children; otherwise they would be less prone to stay with the mother and provide care and protection. The immorality of licentious behavior, according to Kant, consists primarily not in the harm to which it often leads but in its intrinsic nature, for it involves the dishonoring of human beings by reducing them to mere objects of appetite. Persons are not things, Kant reminds us; we are not our own property or that of others. Only when two persons give themselves entirely to each other in monogamous marriage is it permissible to indulge in sexual intercourse, he argues, since then each wins himself back, the reciprocity or mutuality of the commitment preventing the one-sided domination of concubinage. Kant also attempts to explicate the moral wrongness of incest, adultery, masturbation, homosexuality, and bestiality in the selections from his *Lectures on Ethics*.

Three contemporary philosophers contribute selections to Part II that concern nonperverted behaviors thought by many to be immoral: promiscuity, adultery, and rape. Frederick Elliston's essay is a sustained argument for the benefits of sexual freedom, of sexual experiences with many different partners. Richard A. Wasserstrom considers the various reasons why adultery can be regarded as morally wrong; but he also raises difficult questions about the practice of committing to sexual exclusivity in marriage—might not open marriage be a better alternative? John H. Bogart's article surveys different definitions of the offense of rape and presents an argument for a strong conception based on the idea of voluntary and effective consent.

EROTIC LOVE

The theory of love developed and presented by Plato in his *Symposium* and other dialogues is the first systematic treatment by a philosopher that exists. Its historical influence has been immense, particularly upon early Christian and Renaissance thought. Eros is not, Plato tells us, to be identified with the Form of the Good or Beauty itself. Rather it is a seeking after the Good and the Beautiful. There is a ranking of the different kinds of human love, physical or sexual love being the lowest; above it is the love of the soul of a particular person, for example, the love of a man for the spirit of a boy. At more abstract levels, there is the love of just social institutions and, still higher, the love of theories and ideas themselves. The love of the Forms is the most noble and pure. In the selection from the *Symposium* included here, Socrates addresses a group of friends at a banquet (including the playwright Aristophanes and the younger Alcibiades, who loves Socrates). Having listened patiently to their speeches about the nature of eros, Socrates proceeds to relate a story about his youthful encounter with the priestess Diotima and its import for his understanding of erotic love.

If Plato's theory of love is too rationalistic, that of Arthur Schopenhauer—a theory that had considerable influence on the thinking of Freud—will strike many as unduly pessimistic. Ultimate reality for Schopenhauer was not Plato's intellectual realm of the Forms but rather the unconscious, striving Cosmic Will, a metaphysical force that manifests itself, at the level of Appearance, as ourselves and the world we perceive. The love between the sexes, Schopenhauer asserts, is but a kind of trick, in a sense, played on us by the Will, in order that we will be motivated to reproduce most effectively. Sexual desire alone can be gratified by innumerable members of the opposite sex, but love leads us to believe—mistakenly—that we must possess one particular individual. This can lead to the creation of unique and superior offspring, thus continuing the existence of the Cosmic Will, but it does not serve to promote human well-being, which is at best a temporary cessation of the pain and frustration that characterize the greater part of the lives of all creatures on this planet. Erotic love is a tragic illusion, for no one can live up to the expectations that it generates. Once sexual desire is satisfied, Schopenhauer maintains, we lose interest in the former object of our love and sink back into unhappiness. The selections from his masterwork, *The World as Will and Idea,* present the essentials of Schopenhauer's account of love.

In the writings of Kierkegaard, Sartre, and de Beauvoir on sex and love we find elegant prose—along with Plato and Schopenhauer, they are among the finest writers in the history of philosophy—and existentialist perspectives. Kierkegaard's portrayal of the motivations and character of Don Juan (as he appears in Mozart's *Don Giovanni*) is a fascinating and insightful picture of the seducer, the man in love with love. Simone de Beauvoir describes in exquisite detail the thoughts and emotions of a woman in love, her outlook and values shaped by a male-dominated society that promotes weakness and dependency among women. Jean-Paul Sartre, influenced by Hegel's master–slave dialectic, explores what he takes to be a paradox in erotic love: the lover wants to relate to another free subject, as he conceives himself to be, and yet in the very reality of his desire he cannot but objectify the person whom he loves. A union of free subjects is impossible, it appears, and so we are bound to be frustrated in love.

Irving Singer's analysis of love rests on a critical distinction between two kinds of value, which he terms "appraisal value" and "bestowal value." The former is a matter of objective qualities that a discriminating judge can determine to be possessed by a person or thing. Bestowal value, however, is a kind of gift that the lover gives to the object of his or her love, making him or her individually and uniquely worthy of that love in a way that cannot be explained simply in terms of objective merits. Following the French writer Stendhal in his emphasis on the lover's psychological contribution to the loveliness of the beloved, Singer insists that we cannot truly understand erotic love if we utilize only the idea of appraisal value. (For Singer's more recent thoughts on love, readers are directed to the third volume of *The Nature of Love,* especially chapter 10.) Alan Soble critically examines Singer's theory in an excerpt from his book, *The Structure of Love.*

The essays by Robert Nozick and Robert C. Solomon that conclude this section deal with the significance of love and its ethical value. Nozick distinguishes different forms of love and their importance for human well-being and identity. Solomon explains how love, despite its many pitfalls, can be a virtue.

FRIENDSHIP AND FAMILIAL LOVE

The classic discussion of friendship love is that of Aristotle in Books VIII and IX of the *Nicomachean Ethics,* selections from which are included here. Men cannot be truly happy, that is, self-realized and in possession of the full range of human excellences or virtues, unless they have friends. But we must distinguish three different types of friendship: that of utility (the lowest form), where persons maintain a relationship for its concrete benefits; that of pleasure, in which each enjoys the company of the other; and the friendship of esteem or virtue (the most valuable and complete type), where the friends share a conception of the good and help one another to become happier individuals. Aristotle believes that civic friendship is the basis for a just society. Yet contemporary communitarian critics of liberalism have argued that the individualism of modern capitalist society, grounded in libertarian values, undermines friendship and the values of community. Neera Kapur Badhwar defends liberalism against these allegations in her essay, "The Circumstances of Justice: Pluralism, Community, and Friendship."

Ellen Fox discusses an aspect of friendship that is often overlooked in her essay, "Paternalism and Friendship." She points out that friends can be justified in doing things that would otherwise constitute an unwarranted interference with another person's freedom. Fox argues in detail for special status of this kind within the context of close friendships. James Conlon addresses the common question of whether lovers in the erotic sense can be friends. He maintains that they cannot, on the ground that erotic love and friendship are two distinct genres of intimacy, and that the attempt to combine them is, he argues, "a seriously misguided ideal."

The remaining three selections concern love between members of a family and the moral obligations and ties that exist between parents and grown children. Jeffrey Blustein presents a careful analysis of the moral relationships between adults and their parents in an excerpt from his book, *Parents and Children*. Jane English argues in a similar vein that grown children do not, strictly speaking, *owe* things to their parents, for example, in repayment for sacrifices their mother and father made in raising them. The proper relationship between adults and their parents, when it is possible, should be one of friendship; what one ought to do for them, then, is akin to what one ought to do for other close friends—not a matter of paying back a debt that was not voluntarily incurred. Anthony Graybosch considers certain obstacles to parent–adult child friendships in his essay, distinguishing the kind of love that can obtain between parents and children from other kinds.

I
Sex Roles, Equality, and Social Policy

JOHN STUART MILL

The Subjection of Women

The generality of a practice is in some cases a strong presumption that it is, or at all events once was, conducive to laudable ends. This is the case, when the practice was first adopted, or afterwards kept up, as a means to such ends, and was grounded on experience of the mode in which they could be most effectually attained. If the authority of men over women, when first established, had been the result of a conscientious comparison between different modes of constituting the government of society; if, after trying various other modes of social organization —the government of women over men, equality between the two, and such mixed and divided modes of government as might be invented—it had been decided, on the testimony of experience, that the mode in which women are wholly under the rule of men, having no share at all in public concerns, and each in private being under the legal obligation of obedience to the man with whom she had associated her destiny, was the arrangement most conducive to the happiness and well-being of both; its general adoption might then be fairly thought to be some evidence that, at the time when it was adopted, it was the best: though even then the considerations which recommended it may, like so many other primeval social facts of the greatest importance, have subsequently, in the course of ages, ceased to exist. But the state of the case is in every respect the reverse of this. In the first place, the opinion in favour of the present system, which entirely subordinates the weaker sex to the stronger, rests upon theory only; for there never has been trial made of any other: so that experience, in the sense in which it is vulgarly opposed to theory, cannot be pretended to have pronounced any verdict. And in the second place, the adoption of this system of inequality never was the result of deliberation, or forethought, or any social ideas, or any notion whatever of what conduced to the benefit of humanity or the good order of society. It arose simply from the fact that from the very earliest twilight of human society, every woman (owing to the value attached to her by men, combined with her inferiority in muscular strength) was found in a state of bondage to some man. Laws and systems of polity always begin by recognizing the relations they find already existing between individuals. They convert what was a mere physical fact into a legal right, give it the sanction of society, and principally aim at the substitution of public and organized means of asserting and protecting these rights, instead of the irregular and lawless conflict of physical strength. Those who had already been compelled to obedience became in this manner legally bound to it. Slavery, from being a mere affair of force between the master and the slave, became regularized and a matter of compact among the masters, who, binding themselves to one another for common protection, guaranteed by their collective strength the private possessions of each, including his slaves. In early times, the great majority of the male sex were slaves, as well as the whole of the female. And many ages elapsed, some of them ages of high cultivation, before any thinker was bold enough to question the rightfulness, and the absolute social necessity, either of the one slavery or of the other. By degrees such thinkers did arise: and (the general progress of society assisting) the slavery of the male sex has, in all the countries of Christian Europe at least (though, in one of them, only within the last few years) been at length abolished, and that of the female sex has been gradually changed into a milder form of dependence. But this depen-

From John Stuart Mill, *Three Essays*. Oxford: Oxford University Press, 1975.

dence, as it exists at present, is not an original institution, taking a fresh start from considerations of justice and social expediency—it is the primitive state of slavery lasting on, through successive mitigations and modifications occasioned by the same causes which have softened the general manners, and brought all human relations more under the control of justice and the influence of humanity. It has not lost the taint of its brutal origin. No presumption in its favour, therefore, can be drawn from the fact of its existence. The only such presumption which it could be supposed to have, must be grounded on its having lasted till now, when so many other things which came down from the same odious source have been done away with. And this, indeed, is what makes it strange to ordinary ears, to hear it asserted that the inequality of rights between men and women has no other source than the law of the strongest.

That this statement should have the effect of a paradox, is in some respects creditable to the progress of civilization, and the improvement of the moral sentiments of mankind. We now live—that is to say, one or two of the most advanced nations of the world now live—in a state in which the law of the strongest seems to be entirely abandoned as the regulating principle of the world's affairs: nobody professes it, and, as regards most of the relations between human beings, nobody is permitted to practise it. When any one succeeds in doing so, it is under cover of some pretext which gives him the semblance of having some general social interest on his side. This being the ostensible state of things, people flatter themselves that the rule of mere force is ended; that the law of the strongest cannot be the reason of existence of anything which has remained in full operation down to the present time. However any of our present institutions may have begun, it can only, they think, have been preserved to this period of advanced civilization by a well-grounded feeling of its adaptation to human nature, and conduciveness to the general good. They do not understand the great vitality and durability of institutions which place right on the side of might; how intensely they are clung to; how the good as well as the bad propensities and sentiments of those who have power in their hands, become identified with retaining it; how slowly these bad institutions give way, one at a time, the weakest first, beginning with

those which are least interwoven with the daily habits of life; and how very rarely those who have obtained legal power because they first had physical, have ever lost their hold of it until the physical power had passed over to the other side. Such shifting of the physical force not having taken place in the case of women; this fact, combined with all the peculiar and characteristic features of the particular case, made it certain from the first that this branch of the system of right founded on might, though softened in its most atrocious features at an earlier period than several of the others, would be the very last to disappear. It was inevitable that this one case of a social relation grounded on force would survive through generations of institutions grounded on equal justice, an almost solitary exception to the general character of their laws and customs; but which, so long as it does not proclaim its own origin, and as discussion has not brought out its true character, is not felt to jar with modern civilization, any more than domestic slavery among the Greeks jarred with their notion of themselves as a free people.

The truth is, that people of the present and the last two or three generations have lost all practical sense of the primitive condition of humanity; and only the few who have studied history accurately, or have much frequented the parts of the world occupied by the living representatives of ages long past, are able to form any mental picture of what society then was. People are not aware how entirely, in former ages, the law of superior strength was the rule of life; how publicly and openly it was avowed, I do not say cynically or shamelessly—for these words imply a feeling that there was something in it to be ashamed of, and no such notion could find a place in the faculties of any person in those ages, except a philosopher or a saint. History gives a cruel experience of human nature, in showing how exactly the regard due to the life, possessions, and entire earthly happiness of any class of person, was measured by what they had the power of enforcing; how all who made any resistance to authorities that had arms in their hands, however dreadful might be the provocation, had not only the law of force but all other laws, and all the notions of social obligation against them; and, in the eyes of those whom they resisted, were not only guilty of crime, but of the worst of all crimes, deserving the most cruel chastisement which human beings could inflict. The first small vestige of a feeling of obligation in a superior to acknowledge any right in inferiors, began when he had been induced, for convenience, to make some promise to them. Though these promises, even when sanctioned by the most solemn oaths, were for many ages revoked or violated on the most trifling provocation or temptation, it is probable that this, except by persons of still worse than the average morality, was seldom done without some twinges of conscience. The ancient republics, being mostly grounded from the first upon some kind of mutual compact, or at any rate formed by an union of persons not very unequal in strength, afforded, in consequence, the first instance of a portion of human relations fenced round, and placed under the dominion of another law than that of force. And though the original law of force remained in full operation between them and their slaves, and also (except so far as limited by express compact) between a commonwealth and its subjects, or other independent commonwealths; the banishment of that primitive law, even from so narrow a field, commenced the regeneration of human nature, by giving birth to sentiments of which experience soon demonstrated the immense value even for material interest, and which thenceforward only required to be enlarged, not created. Though slaves were no part of the commonwealth, it was in the free states that slaves were first felt to have rights as human beings. The Stoics were, I believe, the first (except so far as the Jewish law constitutes an exception) who taught as a part of morality that men were bound by moral obligations to their slaves. No one, after Christianity became ascendant, could ever again have been a stranger to this belief, in theory; nor, after the rise of the Catholic Church, was it ever without persons to stand up for it. Yet to enforce it was the most arduous task which Christianity ever had to perform. For more than a thousand years the Church kept up the contest, with hardly any perceptible success. It was not for want of power over men's minds. Its power was prodigious. It could make kings and nobles resign their most valued possessions to enrich the Church. It could make thousands, in the prime of life and the height of worldly advantages, shut themselves up in convents to work out their salvation by poverty, fasting, and prayer. It could send hundreds of thousands across land and sea, Europe and Asia, to give their lives for the deliverance of the Holy Sepulchre. It could make kings relinquish wives who were the objects of their passionate attachment, because the Church declared that they were within the seventh (by our calculation the fourteenth) degree of relationship. All this it did; but it could not make men fight less with one another, nor tyrannize less cruelly over the serfs, and, when they were able, over burgesses. It could not make them renounce either of the applications of force; force militant, or force triumphant. This they could never be induced to do until they were themselves in their turn compelled by superior force. Only by the growing power of kings was an end put to fighting except between kings, or competitors for kingship; only by the growth of a wealthy and warlike bourgeoisie in the fortified towns, and of a plebeian infantry which proved more powerful in the field than the undisciplined chivalry, was the insolent tyranny of the nobles over the bourgeoisie and peasantry brought within some bounds. It was persisted in not only until, but long after, the oppressed had obtained a power enabling them often to take conspicuous vengeance; and on the Continent much of it continued to the time of the French Revolution, though in England the earlier and better organization of the democratic classes put an end to it sooner, by establishing equal laws and free national institutions.

If people are mostly so little aware how completely, during the greater part of the duration of our species, the law of force was the avowed rule of general conduct, any other being only a special and exceptional consequence of peculiar ties—and from how very recent a date it is that the affairs of society in general have been even pretended to be regulated according to any moral law; as little do people remember or consider, how institutions and customs which never had any ground but the law of force, last on into ages and states of general opinion which never would have permitted their first establishment. Less than forty years ago, Englishmen might still by law hold human beings in bondage as saleable property: within the present century they might kidnap them and carry them off, and work them literally to death. This absolutely extreme case of the law of force, condemned by those who can tolerate almost every other form of arbitrary power, and which, of all others, presents features the most revolting to the feelings of all who look at it from an impartial position, was the law of civilized and Christian England within the memory of persons now living: and in one half of Anglo-Saxon America three or four years ago, not only did slavery exist, but the slave trade, and the breeding of slaves expressly for it, was a general practice between slave states. Yet not only was there a greater strength of sentiment against it, but, in England at least, a less amount either of feeling or of interest in favour of it, than of any other of the customary abuses of force: for its motive was the love of gain, unmixed and undisguised; and those who profited by it were a very small numerical fraction of the country, while the natural feeling of all who were not personally interested in it, was unmitigated abhorrence. So extreme an instance makes it almost superfluous to refer to any other: but consider the long duration of absolute monarchy. In England at present it is the almost universal conviction that military despotism is a case of the law of force, having no other origin or justification. Yet in all the great nations of Europe except England it either still exists, or has only just ceased to exist, and has even now a strong party favourable to it in all ranks of the people, especially among persons of station and consequence. Such is the power of an established system, even when far from universal; when not only in almost every period of history there have been great and well-known examples of the contrary system, but these have almost invariably been afforded by the most illustrious and most prosperous communities. In this case, too, the possessor of the undue power, the person directly interested in it, is only one person, while those who are subject to it and suffer from it are literally all the rest. The yoke is naturally and necessarily humiliating to all persons, except the one who is on the throne, together with, at most, the one who expects to succeed to it. How different are these cases from that of the power of men over women! I am not now prejudging the question of its justifiableness. I am showing how vastly more permanent it could not but be, even if not justifiable, than these other dominations which have nevertheless lasted down to our own time. Whatever gratification of pride there is in the possession of power, and whatever personal interest in its exercise, is in this case not confined to a limited class, but common to the whole male sex. Instead of being, to most of its supporters, a thing desirable chiefly in the abstract, or, like the political ends usually contended for by factions, of little private importance to any but the leaders; it comes home to the person and hearth of every male head of a family, and of every one who looks forward to being so. The clodhopper exercises, or is to exercise, his share of the power equally with the highest nobleman. And the case is that in which the desire of power is the strongest: for everyone who desires power, desires it most over those who are nearest to him, with whom his life is passed, with whom he has most concerns in common, and in whom any independence of his authority is oftenest likely to interfere with his individual preferences. If, in the other cases specified, powers manifestly grounded only on force, and having so much less to support them, are so slowly and with so much difficulty got rid of, much more must it be so with this, even if it rests on no better foundation than those. We must consider, too, that the possessors of the power have facilities in this case, greater than in any other, to prevent any uprising against it. Every one of the subjects lives under the very eye, and almost, it may be said, in the hands, of one of the masters—in closer intimacy with him than with any of her fellow subjects; with no means of combining against him, no power of even locally overmastering him, and, on the other hand, with the strongest motives for seeking his favour and avoiding to give him offence. In struggles for political emancipation, everybody knows how often its champions are bought off by bribes, or daunted by terrors. In the case of women, each individual of the subject-class is in a chronic state of bribery and intimidation combined. In setting up the standard of resistance, a large number of the leaders, and still more of the followers, must make an almost complete sacrifice of the pleasures or the alleviations of their own individual lot. If ever any system of privilege and enforced subjection had its yoke tightly riveted on the necks of those who are kept down by it, this has. I have not yet shown that it is a wrong system: but every one who is capable of thinking on the subject must see that even if it is, it was certain to outlast all other forms of unjust authority. And when some of the grossest of the other forms still exist in many civilized countries, and have only recently been got rid of in others, it would be strange if that which is so much the deepest-rooted had yet been perceptibly shaken anywhere. There is more reason to wonder that the protests and testimonies against it should have been so numerous and so weighty as they are.

Some will object, that a comparison cannot fairly be made between the government of the male sex and the forms of unjust power which I have adduced in illustration of it, since these are arbitrary, and the effect of mere usurpation, while it on the contrary is natural. But was there ever any domination which did not appear natural to those who possessed it? There was a time when the division of mankind into two classes, a small one of masters and a numerous one of slaves, appeared, even to the most cultivated minds, to be a natural, and the only natural, condition of the human race. No less an intellect, and one which contributed no less to the progress of human thought, than Aristotle, held this opinion without doubt or misgiving; and rested it on the same premises on which the same assertion in regard to the dominion of men over women is usually based, namely that there are different natures among mankind, free natures, and slave natures; that the Greeks were of a free nature, the barbarian races of Thracians and Asiatics of a slave nature. But why need I go back to Aristotle? Did not the slave-owners of the Southern United States maintain the same doctrine, with all the fanaticism with which men cling to the theories that justify their passions and legitimate their personal interests? Did they not call heaven and earth to witness that the dominion of the white man over the black is natural, that the black race is by nature incapable of freedom, and marked out for slavery?—some even going so far as to say that the freedom of manual labourers is an unnatural order of things anywhere. Again, the theorists of absolute monarchy have always affirmed it to be the only natural form of government; issuing from the patriarchal, which was the primitive and spontaneous form of society, framed on the model of the paternal, which is anterior to society itself, and, as they contend, the most natural authority of all. Nay, for that matter, the law of force itself, to those who could not plead any other, has always seemed the most natural of all grounds for the exercise of authority. Conquering races hold it to be

Nature's own dictate that the conquered should obey the conquerors, or, as they euphoniously paraphrase it, that the feebler and more unwarlike races should submit to the braver and manlier. The smallest acquaintance with human life in the Middle Ages shows how supremely natural the dominion of the feudal nobility over men of low condition appeared to the nobility themselves, and how unnatural the conception seemed, of a person of the inferior class claiming equality with them, or exercising authority over them. It hardly seemed less so to the class held in subjection. The emancipated serfs never made any pretension to a share of authority; they only demanded more or less of limitation to the power of tyrannizing over them. So true is it that unnatural generally means only uncustomary, and that everything which is usual appears natural. The subjection of women to men being a universal custom, any departure from it quite naturally appears unnatural. But how entirely, even in this case, the feeling is dependent on custom, appears by ample experience. Nothing so much astonishes the people of distant parts of the world, when they first learn anything about England, as to be told that it is under a queen: the thing seems to them so unnatural as to be almost incredible. To Englishmen this does not seem in the least degree unnatural, because they are used to it; but they do feel it unnatural that women should be soldiers or members of Parliament. In the feudal ages, on the contrary, war and politics were not thought unnatural to women, because not unusual; it seemed natural that women of the privileged classes should be of manly character, inferior in nothing but bodily strength to their husbands and fathers. The independence of women seemed rather less unnatural to the Greeks than to other ancients, on account of the fabulous Amazons (whom they believed to be historical), and the partial example afforded by the Spartan women; who, though no less subordinate by law than in other Greek states, were more free in fact, and being trained to bodily exercises in the same manner with men, gave ample proof that they were not naturally disqualified for them. There can be little doubt that Spartan experience suggested to Plato, among many other of his doctrines, that of the social and political equality of the two sexes.

But, it will be said, the rule of men over women differs from all these others in not being a rule of force: it is accepted voluntarily; women make no complaint, and are consenting parties to it. In the first place, a great number of women do not accept it. Ever since there have been women able to make their sentiments known by their writings (the only mode of publicity which society permits to them), an increasing number of them have recorded protests against their present social condition: and recently many thousands of them, headed by the most eminent women known to the public, have petitioned Parliament for their admission to the Parliamentary Suffrage. The claim of women to be educated as solidly, and in the same branches of knowledge, as men, is urged with growing intensity, and with a great prospect of success; while the demand for their admission into professions and occupations hitherto closed against them, becomes every year more urgent. Though there are not in this country, as there are in the United States, periodical Conventions and an organized party to agitate for the Rights of Women, there is a numerous and active Society organized and managed by women, for the more limited object of obtaining the political franchise. Nor is it only in our own country and in America that women are beginning to protest, more or less collectively, against the disabilities under which they labour. France, and Italy, and Switzerland, and Russia now afford examples of the same thing. How many more women there are who silently cherish similar aspirations, no one can possibly know; but there are abundant tokens how many *would* cherish them, were they not so strenuously taught to repress them as contrary to the proprieties of their sex. It must be remembered, also, that no enslaved class ever asked for complete liberty at once. When Simon de Montfort called the deputies of the commons to sit for the first time in Parliament, did any of them dream of demanding that an assembly, elected by their constituents, should make and destroy ministries, and dictate to the king in affairs of State? No such thought entered into the imagination of the most ambitious of them. The nobility had already these pretensions; the commons pretended to nothing but to be exempt from arbitrary taxation, and from the gross individual oppression of the king's officers. It is a political law of nature that those who are under any power of ancient origin never begin by complaining of the power itself, but

only of its oppressive exercise. There is never any want of women who complain of ill usage by their husbands. There would be infinitely more, if complaint were not the greatest of all provocatives to a repetition and increase of the ill usage. It is this which frustrates all attempts to maintain the power but protect the woman against its abuses. In no other case (except that of a child) is the person who has been proved judicially to have suffered an injury, replaced under the physical power of the culprit who inflicted it. Accordingly wives, even in the most extreme and protracted cases of bodily ill usage, hardly ever dare avail themselves of the laws made for their protection: and if, in a moment of irrepressible indignation, or by the interference of neighbours, they are induced to do so, their whole effort afterwards is to disclose as little as they can, and to beg off their tyrant from his merited chastisement.

All causes, social and natural, combine to make it unlikely that women should be collectively rebellious to the power of men. They are so far in a position different from all other subject classes, that their masters require something more from them than actual service. Men do not want solely the obedience of women, they want their sentiments. All men, except the most brutish, desire to have, in the woman most nearly connected with them, not a forced slave but a willing one; not a slave merely, but a favourite. They have therefore put everything in practice to enslave their minds. The masters of all others slaves rely, for maintaining obedience, on fear; either fear of themselves, or religious fears. The masters of women wanted more than simple obedience, and they turned the whole force of education to effect their purpose. All women are brought up from the very earliest years in the belief that their ideal of character is the very opposite to that of men; not self-will, and government by self-control, but submission, and yielding to the control of others. All the moralities tell them that it is the duty of women, and all the current sentimentalities that it is their nature, to live for others; to make complete abnegation of themselves, and to have no life but in their affections. And by their affections are meant the only ones they are allowed to have—those to the men with whom they are connected, or to the children who constitute an additional and indefeasible tie between them and a man. When we put together three things—first, the natural attraction between opposite sexes; secondly, the wife's entire dependence on the husband, every privilege or pleasure she has being either his gift, or depending entirely on his will; and lastly, that the principal object of human pursuit, consideration, and all objects of social ambition, can in general be sought or obtained by her only through him—it would be a miracle if the object of being attractive to men had not become the polar star of feminine education and formation of character. And, this great means of influence over the minds of women having been acquired, an instinct of selfishness made men avail themselves of it to the utmost as a means of holding women in subjection, by representing to them meekness, submissiveness, and resignation of all individual will into the hands of a man, as an essential part of sexual attractiveness. Can it be doubted that any of the other yokes which mankind have succeeded in breaking, would have subsisted till now if the same means had existed, and had been as sedulously used, to bow down their minds to it? If it had been made the object of the life of every young plebeian to find personal favour in the eyes of some patrician, of every young serf with some seigneur; if domestication with him, and share of his personal affec-tions, had been held out as the prize which they all should look out for, the most gifted and aspiring being able to reckon on the most desirable prizes; and if, when this prize had been obtained, they had been shut out by a wall of brass from all interests not centring in him, all feelings and desires but those which he shared or inculcated; would not serfs and seigneurs, plebeians and patricians, have been as broadly distinguished at this day as men and women are? and would not all but a thinker here and there have believed the distinction to be a fundamental and unalterable fact in human nature?

The preceding considerations are amply sufficient to show that custom, however universal it may be, affords in this case no presumption, and ought not to create any prejudice, in favour of the arrangements which place women in social and political subjection to men. But I may go farther, and maintain that the course of history, and the tendencies of progressive human society, afford not only no presumption in favour of this system of inequality of rights, but a strong one against it; and that, so far as the whole course of human improvement up to this time, the whole stream of modern tendencies, warrants any inference on the subject, it is, that this relic of the past is discordant with the future, and must necessarily disappear.

ELIZABETH RAPAPORT

On the Future of Love:
Rousseau and the Radical Feminists

INTRODUCTION

Love can make people happy or miserable. It
can be mutual or one-sided. It can be symmetrical, two people loving each other in the same
way, or asymmetrical. Love can express itself
in the sharing and fusing of lives or in pathological dependence one upon another. Radical
feminists tend to portray love as we know it as
a one-sided pathological dependency of women
on men. Can there be, could there be, mutual,
symmetrical, nonpathological love between
men and women?

Feminism, even a moderate feminism, is a
doctrine with very radical implications. It is all
the more surprising that radical feminist ideas
have gained very large numbers of more and
less unreserved adherents. It seems that virtually everyone now understands and agrees
with the feminist slogan that "The personal is
political." Nowhere is the political more personal than in sexual love between men and
women. I have been surprised to find therefore
that radical feminists tend to have temperate,
even conservative views, on the possibility of
love between men and women. Radical feminists for the most part present variants of a
common analysis and critique of love. The
analysis supports the conclusion that love between men and women is extremely difficult if
not impossible in the present. But it also supports the conclusion that in a future in which
women's liberation has been effected through
radical economic and social reorganization, especially of our sexual, familial and childrearing
institutions, love between men and women will

be possible. Not only will it be possible but it
will be one of the principal, if not *the* principal
supports and expressions of human happiness.
It is striking that while feminists stigmatize
love as we know it as a central cultural mechanism though which women's oppression operates and by which it is mystified and legitimated, love retains in the society of the future
that same place at the pinnacle of valuable human experience that our culture ascribes to it.

The analysis of love as we now know it,
which I'm calling the radical feminist analysis,
pictures love as a destructive dependency relationship. Or rather women's love is pictured as
a destructive dependency upon men; men are
pictured as neither harmed by nor dependent
upon the women they love, if they love at all.
Love is not seen as a structurally symmetrical
relationship in which men and women love
each other in the same way and have a similar
or identical experience of love. Why don't radical feminists make their quietus with love present and future? There seem to be features of
the experience of love which would incite a flat
denial that love could lead to anything but
heartbreak or suffocation.

My aim in writing this paper is to vindicate
radical feminist optimism about the future of
love. I want to compare three theories: that of
Rousseau with that of two radical feminist writers, Ti-Grace Atkinson and Shulamith Firestone. Atkinson presents a rare truly denuncia-
tory radical feminist rejection of love now and
forever. Firestone is perhaps the most influential contemporary American radical feminist to
have written on love. Her views are representa-

From *Philosophical Forum* 5 (1973–74): 185–205. Reprinted with permission of the publisher.

tive of that combination of optimism for the future and condemnation of the present possibility of love which I attributed to most radical feminists above.

Rousseau, that arch-wallower in sentimentality, author of two best-selling blockbuster love stories, *La Nouvelle Héloïse* and *Emile,* in which the love of Emile and Sophie is chronicled, had despite these credentials a theory of love which vividly elaborates the negative features of love. He depicts love as an inherently pathetic or perhaps tragic loss of personality and destructive dependency relationship for both men and women. Yet love has for him precisely that feature of mutuality, of symmetry of quality or character for men and women the lack of which the radical feminists claim is a chief flaw of love as we know it. Mutuality is apparently not enough for the rehabilitation of love, unless landing men and women in the same soup is sufficient for its reclamation.

ATKINSON ON LOVE

It is not easy to imagine a more extreme view of sexual love than Atkinson's.[1] Yet she argues from some premises which are the common ground of radical feminists. Allow me to present a reconstruction of her argument in schematic form:

1. There is no basis in essential or essentially different biological or psychological traits for the differences in social role and personality between men and women save one: women can bear children and men cannot. Otherwise, male and female roles and traits are cultural, not natural.

2. Culturally acquired sexual roles and traits have a political origin. Very early in human history "men" took advantage of the one biologically different aspect of "women," childbearing, and the relative weakness and vulnerability that pregnancy entails to impose a differentiation of social function of "women." "Women" were forced to accept confinement and social definition in the ramified role of reproducing the species—childbearing, childtending and familial service. This political imposition created men and women.

3. Since male and female roles and traits are wholly the product of political oppression they can and should be eliminated in favor of a sexu-

ally undifferentiated human personality, culture, and social system. "Men" and "women" must be destroyed.

4. The politics and culture of sexual oppression is made possible by the sexual reproduction of the human species. A necessary step in extricating men and women from their present conditions of oppressor and oppressed is to eliminate sexual reproduction in favor of extrauterine conception and incubation, now technically feasible. Sexual intercourse is not a human need but a social institution. Allegedly natural or biological sexual drives or needs would disappear with the elimination of their reproductive and political functions. "Sexual 'drives' and 'needs' would disappear with their functions."[2]

5. Sexual love is wholly and inextricably bound up with the pathological deformations of human personality and its potentialities for realization associated with the humanly deplorable conditions of being a man or a woman. When sex goes, sexuality and sexual love go with it, and good riddance.

Atkinson says of sexual love, which for her has no human future:

> The most common female escape (from their imprisonment in the female role and the denial of their humanity) is the psychopathological condition of love. It is a euphoric state of fantasy in which the victim transforms her oppressor into her redeemer: she turns her natural hostility towards the aggressor against the remnants of herself—her Consciousness —and sees her counterpart in contrast to herself as all powerful (as he is by now at her expense). The combination of this power, her self-hatred, and the hope of a life that is self-justifying—the goal of all living creatures—results in a yearning for her stolen life—her Self—that is the delusion and poignancy of love. "Love" is the natural response of the victim to the rapist.[3]

What gives Atkinson's argument an air of the incredible is her attack on sexual intercourse itself.[4] She speculates that in a human future there may be some human value in "cooperative sensual experience" whose function and value would be a social and public expression of approval of the sensually gratified subject. She says that "the outside participant expresses by its presence an identification with the recipient's feelings for itself. This could serve as a reinforcement to the ego and to a generalization from the attitude of the agent towards the recipient to the attitude of the public as a whole toward the recipient."[5] Note that she is speculating not about the sexual future but the sensual future and that the kind of experience she envisions is not reciprocal but the gratification of one subject by another who represents the social community. Although Atkinson does not banish sensuality, this cannot be construed as a rehabilitation of love.

1–3 are common ground for many feminists. Atkinson's uniqueness is her insistence that all aspects of sexuality including sexual intercourse itself are humanly eliminable, destructive cultural constructs. The question arises, why do not all feminists who share the view that maleness and femaleness are oppressive social constructs share the view that with the elimination of these constructs must come the elimination of if not human sexual contact then at least sexual intercourse between "men" and "women"? Can sexuality and sexual love be separated from "maleness" and "femaleness" as they have been socially constructed?

Atkinson's remarks about "cooperative sensual experiences" suggest the following theory about that complex emotional and sexual relationship we call romantic or sexual love. Sexual love is a destructive dependency relationship. It is incompatible with human autonomy, with the recognition by the self and others of the independent worth of the individual for that human individual to be dependent upon any other particular individual or individuals for the fulfillment of its needs or the affirmation or conferral of its value. A human individual may need, however, or be enhanced in its sense of worth by, the generalized social recognition of its worth and the legitimacy of its needs. Therefore in an androgynous human future it would be wrong to expect what would formerly have been identified as "men" and "women" to want or have experiences of sexual love for people of the same or the opposite "sex." There is something wrong with love in addition to sexual oppression. It is a dependency relation which robs the lover of its autonomy, something that will be no more desirable when we are freed from the pathology of sexuality than it is now. Fortunately we will have no inclination for love once freed of the political and cultural compulsion to act out the roles of male and female, oppressor and oppressed.

This seems to me to be a not implausible theory for anyone who holds that love is a destructive dependency relationship and that "men" and "women" should be superceded. It certainly does induce shudders in anticipation of a world even more bereft of intimate contact than the isolation we presently endure and before which the contemporary spirit already quails.

I now want to turn to the kind of view of love which has more preponderant radical feminine support. We will see that it is Firestone's willingness to see dependency relationships rehabilitated that permits her to be both a good feminist and a partisan of a future for love.

FIRESTONE ON LOVE

I said in my introduction that for the radical feminist love is now impossible, but will be possible in a liberated human future. This is not quite accurate. The radical feminist thesis is that love as we now know it is a culturally pathological dependency relationship but that love can be a healthy and enriching dependency relationship in the revolutionary future. The distinction is really between healthy and destructive love, not between love and no love. In the section on Rousseau below, we shall see a challenge to the claim that dependency relationships can be rehabilitated. Rousseau, like Atkinson, holds that all dependency relationships are destructive. Let us examine both the bad love of the present and the good love of the future as portrayed by Firestone.[6] I will begin by setting forth what I take to be Firestone's requirements for healthy love and then show why and how she thinks love as we know it differs from healthy love.

Mutuality

"Love between two equals would be an enrichment. . . . "[7] The love relationship must be symmetrical in that both man and woman love each other in a similar or identical fashion. But another sort of mutuality is required if this is to be possible. Both man and woman must be and recognize themselves and each other as free-standing independent beings possessing equal and unqualified human worth as persons. Love has a precondition of self-respect and respect for the beloved's status as a free and equal human being.

Vulnerability, Openness, Interdependency

"Love is being psychically wide-open to another. It is a situation of total emotional vulnerability."[8] An individual cannot be open, not to say wide-open, to another unless he or she respects himself. To be vulnerable is to recognize our need and desire for the other person. It is also caring for or prizing the other as much as ourselves because of his or her unique value for ourself. Love is thus both selfish and unselfish,[9] a feature of love founded in the recognition of our vulnerability. In healthy love dependency is not merely tolerable. It is essential.

Idealization

"The beauty/character of the beloved, perhaps hidden to others under layers of defenses is revealed."[10] Firestone emphasizes that the vulnerability of love makes it possible for lovers to reveal the best of themselves to each other, permitting an idealization more in the sense of a prizing of what is really there for each other rather than an over-estimation of the qualities of the beloved. Others have noticed another possible aspect of a not unrealistic or falsifying idealization of the beloved. Love may provide an opportunity for the recognition by the self of qualities he or she did not know he or she possessed before the lover discovered them and revealed them. Love may also occasion the growth and positive development of personality.[11]

The Fusion of Egos, the Exchange of Selves

Love between two equals would be an enrichment, each enlarging himself through the other: instead of being one, locked in the cell of himself with only his own experience and view, he could participate in the existence of another—an extra window on the world. This accounts for the bliss that successful lovers experience: Lovers are temporarily freed from the burden of isolation that every individual bears.[12]

Firestone argues that love as we know it does not satisfy any of these conditions. She claims that women love pathologically and men don't love at all. Firestone is in essential agreement

with points 1–3 set forth in my reconstruction of Atkinson's argument above. We may therefore take 1–3 as the first installment of Firestone's analysis of love as we know it. The remaining crucial stages of the argument which provides the context for Firestone's critique of love are these:

4'. The political origins of the oppression of women by men have long been forgotten by both sexes. It is generally believed that the politically conditioned sexually differentiated social roles and statuses of men and women are essential or natural features of the two roles. This is expressed as the ideology of male supremacy. Men are seen as powerful, active, self-sufficient and fully human; women as weak, passive, and dependent—support players in the essentially male human drama. Male nature is human nature, female nature is to be helpmeet of man.

5'. The ideology of male supremacy corresponds to the real economic, social and political condition of men and women in the present and through most of human history. Women *are* dependent on men. For the most part whatever women may achieve socially and economically in the real world of oppression in which we live is through their acceptance by and associations with men.

6. Many of the changes introduced by modern industrial society have tended to undermine the power of men over women as well as the ideology of male supremacy—e.g., birth control technology, the possibility and the desirability of women having fewer children, women entering the paid labor force in massive numbers. "Romanticism develops in proportion to the liberation of women from their biology."[13] The love of women for men has the function of mystifying and reinforcing patriarchal hegemony. The function of romantic love is therefore the reinforcement of an otherwise weakened male hegemony.

7. In the modern industrial world it is possible for women, by acting in concert politically and to a much lesser extent through individual action, to establish lives for themselves as independent, active social and economic beings. Love induces them to try to live for and through men instead. Love robs them of the will, strength and insight into political realities and human possibilities necessary to attempt to overthrow male hegemony.

Firestone argues that under such conditions the love of woman for man can only be pathological and that men cannot love women at all. The mutual self-respect which is necessary for healthy love is impossible where neither men nor women regard women as genuine and autonomous persons. They cannot, therefore, be mutually wide open to each other. Men do not see a person worthy of the effort. Women's self-contempt precludes seeing themselves as having any personal substance and worth to reveal. They hope to gain substance and worth through the love of men.

Firestone claims that it is not generally the case that women idealize the men they love, although men tend to idealize the women they fall in love with. ("Falling in love" is very different from "loving" for Firestone, as I shall momentarily explain.) "Idealization occurs much less frequently on the part of women. . . . A man must idealize one woman over the rest in order to justify his descent to a lower caste. Women have no such reason to idealize. . . ."[14] They regard themselves as defective and men as full human beings. All men are in a sense idealized in female eyes. They all possess the value of being self-sufficient, authentic, human subjects which women concur in believing is not true of themselves. However, it is not true that any woman can love any man. Social and economic status make some men more lovable than others.

Men, Firestone claims, don't love, they fall in love. They see special virtues in one woman, which she for her part knows are not there and so lives in terror of his disillusionment, which comes often enough. Firestone accepts the Freudian thesis that men at least are seeking an ego-ideal and substitute for the forbidden mother in the women they fall in love with. Freud himself seems to support Firestone. He holds that the satisfaction of love's desire lessens or leads to the cessation of love. Firestone claims men fall in love rather than love both because they undervalue all women and unrealistically idealize the woman they fall in love with. Both prevent the intimate and open interaction with women that love requires. Women on their side prevent real contact by desperately trying to shore up men's illusions about them in order to hold their love.

Firestone has another reason for claiming men do not love and why when they fall in love

they are wont to fall out of love soon after: Men fear dependency. Their model of vulnerability is not the openness of genuine love but the dependency-love of women as they know them. They associate dependency with weakness and insufficiency. They have good cause to fear the love women offer them as well. Women are after all seeking to devour men's independent substance. Without openness or respect on either side there can of course be no fusion of egos. In no way is love as we know it the genuine article.

I find Firestone's stigmatization of love as we know it as serving the function of legitimating and reinforcing male hegemony convincing. I also believe that there is much to be said for her distinctions between destructive and healthy love. Her account does not however deal adequately with the social psychological issue of the possibility of non-destructive dependency relationships. Rousseau's account of destructive love locates the pathology of love precisely in the destructive character of all dependency relationships. It is a critique of this sort of psychology which partisans of love's future must provide. Rousseau's account of destructive love also supplies a needed corrective to the radical feminist claim that men do not love. The pathology of destructive love engulfs both men and women.

ROUSSEAU ON LOVE

Rousseau's theory of love might be captured by the traditional adage of husbands, "I can't live with her and I can't live without her," were the adage not so wry. The climate of love for Rousseau is bathed in intense feeling. Sexual love is portrayed by Rousseau as mutually destructive to men and women. Sexual love is at the center of Rousseau's account of social relations. It is the first other-regarding emotion that the developing human individual experiences and the paradigm of social relations with others. Sexual love is an inescapable human need. But the pursuit of love inevitably leads to frustration and unhappiness. The way we love inevitably defeats the ends of love. Defeat in love engulfs our whole personality. It destroys not only love but the lovers as well. For Rousseau man's love is like his sociality. Man is naturally social. But social living, the condition of human development and self-realization, is the irredeemable cause of human misery. To be happy we must be self-sufficient. But because we are human we need others. We are therefore happy neither in isolation nor in company.

Love, according to Rousseau's psychology, is a natural but not an original human need or desire. The distinction between original and nonoriginal elements in the human constitution is crucial in Rousseau's psychology. For Rousseau ontogeny recapitulates phylogeny. The nature of the human species and the human individual can only be understood in terms of their identical developmental courses. Savage man is not natural man but natural man at the beginning stages of human development. He has the potential to develop intellectual and moral capacities which will carry the human race from the savage to the civilized state. The development of these capacities is necessary for the full realization of human possibilities. Savage man is an isolate, a self-sufficient creature, with minimal, peaceful and uneventful interactions with others of his kind. He develops the characteristic and essential human capacities of reason and conscience as his world becomes social. As human life becomes social, he comes to need and depend upon others. He gains his humanity but loses his self-sufficiency. The quality of his life depends on the quality of his society. The human personality requires social living for its development. Its contours and contents vary with different sorts of society, some of which suit the inborn features of human personality very much more comfortably than others. A bad fit produces much avoidable misery. But societies cannot be torn off and replaced like ill-fitting suits of clothes. Tragically the best fit is not nearly good enough to prevent human misery. Why this is so can be seen by tracing out the parallel ontogenetic development course.[15]

The human child like the human savage is an essentially asocial creature. Rousseau sees the human adult as ruled and motivated by two "sentiments" which organize and color his affective structure, *Amour de soi*—rendered in English as "self-preservation," "self-love" or "proper self-love"—and *amour propre*, rendered in English as "pride," "selfishness" or "egotism." *Amour propre* is not yet an active principle in the infant and child. He is wholly a creature of self-love. *Amour de soi*, in savage

and child, Rousseau regards as a benign principle. *Amour propre* is regarded as a pernicious principle that always leads to personal unhappiness and interpersonal conflict. The whole strategy of childhood education that Rousseau sets out in his *Emile* revolves around allowing the child to develop the powers to satisfy the desires of self-love in such fashion as to be as far as possible autonomous and self-sufficient. Both the powers and desires are naturally given and naturally develop commensurately so that the powers are adequate for the satisfaction of desire. Of course the child will need adult help and guidance. But adult help and guidance should be aimed at increasing his autonomy as well as perhaps the illusion of a greater autonomy than he really has. "True happiness consists in decreasing the distance between our desires and our powers, in establishing a perfect equilibrium between power and will."[16] Happiness will therefore be possible for the well-educated child as it never will be for the man in any possible human society.

If the child is made to feel dependent on the will of others, whether they are generous with him, over-generous, or whether they deny him, he will develop hostile feelings towards those around him. Worse, his personality structure will be adversely affected. He will be by turns servile and domineering in his attempts to gain his will through those on whom he is forced to depend. Rousseau's doctrine is that both tyranny and servility stem from impotence and breed hatred for those with the power to satisfy and withhold satisfaction of our desires. Tyrannical or servile, the frustrated child is equally miserable.[17]

Amour propre, sexual desire and the capacity for sexual love, all develop at the same time, at puberty, and bring in their train the development of genuinely other-regarding emotions and social interactions which go beyond an awareness of others as simply helps or obstacles to the child's own ends.

As soon as man needs a companion he is no longer an isolated creature, his heart is no longer alone. All his relations with his species, all the affections of his heart, came into being along with this. His first passion soon arouses the rest.[18]

Sexual love is a natural but not an original desire. The sexual desire is original but can be satisfied indifferently by any one of the opposite sex. Savages meet and couple in passing. They form no sexual relationships which endure beyond the desires of the moment. Sexual love involves choice of a lover. This choice involves comparison and preference. These preferences require standards of beauty and virtue. These standards of beauty and virtue are products of social living and culture.

All women would be alike to a man who had no idea of virtue and beauty, and the first comer would always be the most charming. Love does not spring from Nature, far from it; it is the curb and law of her desires; it is love that makes one sex indifferent to the other, the loved one alone excepted. [19]

But the lover desires to be loved in turn. And here is where *amour propre* enters, like the snake into the Garden of Eden.

We wish to inspire the preference we feel; love must be mutual. To be loved we must be worthy of love; to be preferred we must be more worthy than the rest, at least in the eyes of our beloved. Hence we begin to look around among our fellows; we begin to compare ourselves with them, there is emulation, rivalry and jealousy. [20]

The lover wants his love to be reciprocated. She must see him as preeminent in virtue and beauty, if he is to succeed. This necessarily activates the human capacity for *amour propre,* for jealousy, rivalry and the desire to gain an invidious esteem. He must strive to be or at least appear to be in her eyes the preeminent possessor of the qualities she prizes most. His child's autonomy, were he lucky enough to have achieved it, falls away. It is perilous to human autonomy to need another. But love, were it possible, would more than fully compensate. The lover loses his autonomy in a deeper sense. He must give up a life guided by *amour de soi,* by the pursuit of the natural desires that his heart has and which would realize the potentialities of his personality, and assume the straightjacket of being or appearing to be the man of her heart's desire. So it is with love and so it is in all other human relations in which the affections and esteem of others are courted. They necessarily make rivals of men, force us to give up independent standards of self-esteem for socially imposed standards of our worth. We lose touch with our natural feelings, forfeit the chance for self-actualization. We lose ourselves and present a false self in the lists of social competition. While it does not prevent feelings of affection or continual growth of sympathy for others, it does neutralize or prevent affection and concern for others whenever one's own desire for the affection and esteem of others is active. *Amour propre* haunts and destroys all our attempts to reach out and make genuine contact with others.

With these psychological doctrines as necessary background, let us look at Rousseau's theory of love, at what a benign and happy love would be like and of what love must become in the irremediable circumstances of human social living.

Natural Attraction, the Fusion of Egos

Rousseau emphasizes the affective aspects of love. The goal of love is the fusion of two personalities. For this union to occur there must first be an initial attraction founded in like sensibility. This initial recognition of one's male or female counterpart provides the sentimental basis and the pull which draws us into union. Julie writes to her lover, Saint-Preux, "Our souls touch, so to speak at all points, and we feel an entire coherence . . . hence forward we shall have only mutual pleasures and pains; and like those magnets of which you were telling me that have, it is said, the same movements at different places, we shall have the same sensations though we were at the two poles of the earth." [21]

Dependency

Love begins with the recognition of a need for another, with the discovery of the radical insufficiency of the self and one's own powers for self-realization. The lover recognizes and feels his lack of or loss of autonomy. Saint-Preux writes to Julie, "I am no longer master of myself, I confess, my estranged soul is wholly absorbed in yours." [22]

Mutuality

Love would be mutual. Saint-Preux wants to possess as well as be possessed by Julie. If love is to be returned both man and woman must regard each other as worthy of love. Rousseau is certainly a male supremacist. He holds male and female natures are essentially different. Woman was made for man. The essence of womanhood was to serve, to please and to nurture man. Yet men value and respect the complementary and alien submissive virtues of women despite the defectiveness of female nature when judged by the standard of male nature. All the intellectual and moral inequalities of the sexes are neutralized by the mutual recognition of the need for love. Men do not respect women as full persons in the male sense. But they respect the terrible power women have to give or withhold the love they need. Men and women are equal in love. They are equally vulnerable and equally powerful.

Idealization

Love begins with the attraction and recognition of a like sensibility which seems to hold out the possibility of fusion of personalities. But love also requires that we see in the other and continue to see features of personality radically different from our own. The lover must find the perfections of the other and alien sex in the beloved, the perfections he or she necessarily lacks. Since love involves choice and standards of compassion between members of a sex, love's choice is for the man or woman pre-eminent of their sex. The standard of perfection will be a mixture of the personal and the public. It will be public insofar as canons of male and female beauty and virtue are cultural norms. It will be personal insofar as it involves placing a high value on the possession of certain qualities which may be found in either sex and which the lover finds in both himself and the beloved. These make possible the natural affinity of particular men and women for each other.

Exclusivity

If one man or woman is found perfect and finding perfection is a requirement for loving, there must be exclusive, complete fusion with and absorption in another. A multiplicity of love relations is precluded.

Rousseau holds that the achievement of love is illusional or delusional. To see why we must look at one more feature of love.

The Logic of Dependence

The lover is dependent, entirely, terribly dependent on his beloved for something he needs, the reciprocity of his love. Therefore loving falls under the domain of *amour propre*, not *amour de soi*. The lover cannot achieve love's desire, reciprocity, by the exercise of his own powers. He will only be loved if she finds him pre-eminent. He must present himself in the guise in which she would see her beloved. This leads to a false presentation of the self and the chronic fear of exposure and loss of love. Along the way the lover loses himself and necessarily the opportunity to gain love for this lost self.

But what of the fortunate possibility that a pair of lovers actually possess the very virtues that they seek and find in each other? Might not fortunate couples each rich in personal merit not escape the predicament of self-falsification and self-loss in love? The answer, I think, must be no. Love operates in the domain of *amour-propre*, not *amour de soi*. The reciprocity of need and dependence cannot prevent the disastrous working out of the effects of dependence in the human personality. To be happy we must be autonomous. But we are not autonomous in love. Therefore we cannot be happy in love. Love operates in the domain of *amour-propre*. Human beings can only act in a fashion not self- and mutually destructive when they are motivated by desires whose satisfaction is within their own powers. If we need another, the terrible possibility remains that their gratification of our need will be withdrawn. Even if love has been met with complete responsiveness, there is the future to dread. It is not within our power to secure the future love of our beloved against surfeit, disillusionment, or a rival found more worthy. Therefore, the lover is in a position of weakness, of impotence. Impotence forces him to employ tyrannical or servile means in futile attempts to secure what cannot be secured. The lover becomes a tyrant or a slave because of his impotence. In so doing he must both become and reveal a personality lacking in the perfections the lover sought and that he or she had found. In his weakness he confirms or creates the very doubts about his worthiness he feared his beloved was entertaining. Even if the doubts and fears that consume lovers and the jealous and craven responses they make do not result in the withdrawal of love, these feelings themselves, together with the sense of impotence they spring from, make the lover miserable. Such is certainly the case with Saint-Preux, who is given to depressive fits of jealous rage against his friend and protector, Lord Edward. Love is an illusion or a delusion. Or if you prefer, love is a genuine enough human experience, but a miserable one. Lovers may possess each other and consume each other, but they lose themselves.

I believe that Rousseau's two great fictional accounts of love, the story of Emile and Sophie and of Saint-Preux and Julie, support my interpretation of Rousseau's theory of love if properly read. Despite the undeniable aspects of the sentimental celebration of romantic love characteristic of these works and which largely account for their tremendous popular success, love is portrayed as a tragic disappointment in both. Rousseau had what has been called a bourgeois conception of love.[23] The ideal is married love. In one of his two great love stories the hero marries the girl and loses her. In the other he simply loses her. Both losses propel the male lovers, whose side of the story Rousseau identifies with and treats more fully, into massive depressions and sends them off on years-long travels to try to forget and heal their wounds. Both Emile and Saint-Preux are depicted as men of unusual pasts of merits. Emile is unusual in that he has been carefully educated for the attainment of happiness and virtue despite, and in the midst of, what Rousseau regarded as a deplorable social environment. Saint-Preux is portrayed as a man of unusual talents and qualities. Both, as a result of loving, succeed in doing nothing of any note in the world, more significant in Saint-Preux's case, and feeling nothing but intense misery, more significant in Emile's case.

Julie writes to her lover Saint-Preux:

Love is accompanied by a continual uneasiness over jealousy or privation, little suited to marriage, which is a state of enjoyment and peace. People do not marry in order to think exclusively of each other, but in order to fulfill the duties of civil society jointly, to govern the house prudently, to rear their children well. Lovers never see anyone but themselves, they incessantly attend only to themselves, and the only thing they are able to do is love each other.[24]

Despite his bourgeois ideal of love, it seems to be Rousseau's opinion that even the slight re-

quirements for the fulfillment of women's social role are incompatible with love, while potentially great and virtuous men have their capacity to act in the world as well as their happiness destroyed by love. In the little read and as far as I know untranslated sequel to *Emile, Emile et Sophie,* the tragic dissolution of Emile's marriage is portrayed. Emile's marriage falters because that paragon of virtue is distracted by Parisian pleasures and neglects his wife. It seems that when a social evil is not introduced as an obstacle to love's desire (Saint-Preux's low birth prevents his marriage to Julie), and even when the best of men and women have the best of chances for success love fails. His desire realized, Emile loses interest in his wife until her unfaithfulness revives the fires and torments of love.

THE FUTURE OF LOVE: SEXUAL LOVE AND SOCIAL PSYCHOLOGY

I have been writing about love as if there were one kind of experience of love that was uniform for all people or among all people of the same sex. This is almost certainly not the case. No doubt there are very different sorts of sexual love. But the theories I have been considering focus on certain core features of sexual love that reflect either psychological invariance or the differential impact on men and women of social conditions and cultural norms. These features permit considerable latitude for talking about the experience of men and women in love in a univocal way without inadmissible abstraction or distortion.

There is something to be learned from both Firestone's and Rousseau's account of love. We can make at least a beginning to identifying the causes of the pathologies that disfigure sexual love and point the way to its rehabilitation. Radical feminism need not lead to the excesses of Atkinson or to the denial that men as well as women are the victims of love as we now know it.

It seems to me that Firestone's account of the pathology of women's love is essentially accurate. Without self-respect and the respect of men grounded in the social and economic equality of the sexes, men and women cannot meet on the terrain of mutual openness and appreciation which love requires. Although Firestone claims that men can't love, her account of man's sexual and romantic encounters with women and Rousseau's are in fact much closer than this startling claim would seem to suggest. Firestone traces male inability to love to the fear of dependency. Rather than inability to love, we should follow Rousseau in identifying the distinctive pathology of male love as precisely that fear of dependency which he claims is the explanation for the dysfunctional character of love for *both* men and women. We should retain however a Firestonean perspective on the distinctiveness of male and female experience of love and their roots in the social inequality of the sexes.

If love is to be rehabilitated, something must be very wrong with the Rousseauvian thesis that dependency relationships are always self- and mutually destructive. Something *is* very wrong with this thesis. The radical feminist Thesis I, which explains the pathology of love as we know it as the product of sexual inequality, must be supplemented by an elaboration and substantiation of Thesis II. Dependency relations need not be destructive if our social psychological natures and the social conditions which they reflect are transformed.

There is a paradox at the heart of Rousseau's account of social relations. To be humanly happy we need others. But if we need others we are lost. Rousseau wanted to repudiate the kind of psychological egoism which regarded human beings as wholly selfish and as having purely instrumental interactions with each other, interactions whose goal was the satisfaction of the self, a self which was only in peripheral ways effected by or a product of its society and culture. But he was too deeply mired in individualism to make more than a very partial break with its social and psychological theory. He was able to project the essential effects of social living on the individual's personality structure only as threats to the integrity and happiness of the self. The result is a theory which posits the insufficiency of the human individual to achieve his or her self-realization in society. But what is really wanted is a theoretical critique of the insufficiency of individualism. This is a very large and a very difficult theoretical task which it goes without saying I cannot undertake here. But a few remarks will show the relevance of this critical task to the rehabilitation of love.

If autonomy from the need for others is pos-ited as a necessary condition for human happiness, all dependency relations are necessarily pernicious. Add that they are unavoidable and you have the plight of Rousseauvian love. But suppose that the just fear of dependency of men on women and women on men that now obtains is the product of dysfunctional economic and social relations not just between the sexes but throughout social life, not the product of some deficiency in human nature. Suppose that the fear of dependency is a variable feature of human personality attributable to social conditions which drive them into invidious competition for the social status and esteem which could be accorded everyone in a society where cooperative institutions supported fruitful and healthy interdependency. Suppose that the thesis is false, that love, respect, and esteem are only given to him who is so pre-eminent in the eyes of others as to scarcely seem to require the further perfection of being loved by others. Suppose we could grant our love on some basis other than the supposed absolute pre-eminence of the beloved. Under conditions in which lovers did not seek pre-eminence according to social norms of attainment in those whom they loved, dependency would not have the terrible aspect of courting almost certain exposure and failure. Love's eye could still seek and find the special qualities that lead to preferment, draw affection and nourish the growth of personality in lovers. Human differences and variety in sensibility and qualities would still guide and motivate love-choices. Such encounters would still be fraught with the perils of rejection and failure but not hopelessly and inevitably so. What I am proposing is a socialist theory of social psychology, of which we have now only the barest sketch. Love may be rehabilitated if the just fear of dependency relations we learn from love as we know it turns out to be grounded not in fear of ourselves but the pathological distortions of human personality produced by an unjust, destructive and successfully alterable social order.

Radical feminists have forced an admission on the part of many socialists that traditional socialist programs are insufficient for achieving women's liberation. The insufficiency of a feminist program alone to give love a future shows that this most personal of political problems requires more than sexual equality for its solution.

NOTES

My thanks to Joseph Agassi and Alice Jacobs for discussions we had about love; and to editors Carol Gould and Marx Wartofsky.

1. Ti-Grace Atkinson, "Radical Feminism" and "The Institution of Sexual Intercourse," both in *Notes from the Second Year: Women's Liberation* (Boston: 1969).

2. Atkinson, "The Institution of Sexual Intercourse," p.45.

3. Atkinson, "Radical Feminism," pp.36–37.

4. Atkinson's attack on sexual intercourse is part of her contribution to the debate about female sexuality and in particular, the vaginal orgasm. She writes, "The theory of vaginal orgasm was created quite recently to shore up that part of the foundation of a social institution that was being threatened by the increasing demand by women for freedom for women. The political institution I am referring to is the institution of sexual intercourse. The purpose, i.e., the social function, of the institution is to maintain the human species" (Ibid., p. 42).

5. Atkinson, "The Institution of Sexual Intercourse," p. 47.

6. Cf. *The Dialectic of Sex* (New York: Bantam Books, 1970), especially Chapters 5 and 6, "Love" and "The Culture of Romance."

7. Ibid., p. 128.

8. Ibid., p. 128.

9. Cf. J. O. Wisdom, on the paradoxically selfish and unselfish quality of love, "Freud and Melanie Klein: Psychology, Ontology and Weltanschauung," in *Psychoanalysis and Philosophy*, ed. C. Hanley and M. Lazerowitz (New York: 1970), pp. 349–54.

10. Firestone, p. 132.

11. Cf. Wisdom, p. 383. See also Simone de Beauvoir, *The Second Sex* (New York: Bantam Books, 1953).

12. Ibid., p. 128.

13. Ibid., p. 146.

14. Ibid., p. 131.

15. Cf. Rousseau's *A Discourse on the Origin of Inequality*, for his phylogenetic account.

16. *Emile*, Everyman Library, p.44

17. Cf. *Emile*, Part II.

18. Ibid., p. 175.

19. Ibid.

20. Ibid., p. 176.

21. *La Nouvelle Héloïse* (University Park: Pennsylvania State University Press, 1968), p. 47.

22. Ibid., p. 83.

23. Denis de Rougemont, *Love in the Western World* (New York: Pantheon, 1956).

24. *La Nouvelle Héloïse*, pp. 261–62.

LINDA LeMONCHECK

Feminist Politics and Feminist Ethics: Treating Women as Sex Objects

Socrates' assertion that the unexamined life is not worth living defines for many philosophers the essence of the philosophical enterprise. Socrates spent a lifetime asking his Athenian students and friends to question their beliefs about what constitutes a good life, so that they might better understand human nature and human needs. If the Socratic method is taken as one paradigm of philosophical inquiry,[1] then it is the practical duty of the philosopher to expose and question our most basic beliefs about the nature of the world around us. This task includes exposing and questioning the presuppositions that we may not realize we have about the way we, as well as other people, think and act.

Philosophy defined in this way suggests that philosophical inquiry is at the very heart of feminism. Whether liberal or radical, socialist or postmodern, feminists wish to expose and question our most basic beliefs about women and men, because it is our often unexamined presuppositions about the way women think and act versus the way men think and act that create the oppressive environment for both sexes that feminists seek to eradicate.[2] Feminists differ on what we mean by the term "oppression," on the causes of that oppression, and on the way we might rid our society of it. The liberal feminist is convinced that the way to eradicate women's oppression lies in passing federal and state laws that would grant women equality of opportunity in the home and in the workplace. The Marxist feminist regards capitalism as the root of women's oppression, while the radical feminist points to the oppressive nature of the heterosexual relationship itself. The socialist feminist believes that both economic and heterosexual institutions nor-

malized under conditions of male dominance define the gender roles that are the source for unfairly restrictive sex stereotypes. The psychoanalytic feminist asks us to examine those structures of the unconscious mind that associate the narcissistic wounds inflicted by female mothering with hatred and rejection of women. The postmodern feminist asks us to question whether moral justification for any feminist platform is either possible or necessary. Yet I think all feminists would agree that if we can clarify how we typically expect women as a group versus men as a group to think and act, we can better examine those expectations for their role in undermining the creation of an ultimately fulfilling and nurturing environment for both sexes.[3]

Is it ever appropriate to treat a woman as a sex object? The issue of what I shall refer to as "sex objectification" is of immediate interest to feminists, since one of our general claims is that the domination of women through heterosexual sex is essential to maintaining an unjustly patriarchal society, and treating a woman as a sex object is regarded as one form of the sexual domination of women by men.[4] Given my claim that philosophical inquiry is at the heart of feminism, how might philosophy help us examine the issue of sex objectification? The philosopher as semanticist will ask us to question the presuppositions of our *language:* what do we *mean* by the expression "sex object"? The overtly physical act of raping a woman as well as the mental act of merely fantasizing about having sex with her have both been called treating her as a sex object. Whistling at a shopper in a supermarket, whistling at a prostitute on a street corner, and whistling at a striptease performer have all been cited as instances of treating a woman as a sex object. Any definition of sex objectification will have to account for this variety.

The philosopher as moralist will ask: What moral principles, if any,[5] underlie the judgments we make about treating a woman as a sex object? If a woman says she enjoys heterosexual sex but hates being treated as a sex object, what are her reasons for disliking one kind of sexual encounter but not the other? If a man says he wishes *more* people would treat *him* as a sex object, does he *mean* something different than the woman who complains, or does he disagree only with her dislike of identical treatment that he happens to find enjoyable? Is the sex object's complaint of a moral nature, asking us to question the virtue of the objectifier? Or is the treatment simply in poor taste, an offence to one's aesthetic sensibilities, the way slurping one's soup or having bad breath is offensive?

Such questions only begin to touch upon the complexity of any thorough philosophical analysis of treating women as sex objects. The following discussion outlines some of the ways in which feminist politics and feminist ethics can contribute to our understanding of sex objectification. The first section offers an examination of how three different voices within feminist political theory might answer the question: Is it ever appropriate to treat a woman as a sex object? My claim is that the way each theorist describes and evaluates sex objectification reveals some of her distinctive presuppositions about the metaphysical relationship and moral value of the mind and the body. The second section suggests how one kind of feminist ethic, an ethic of care, can enhance our understanding of the nature and scope of sex objectification in a way that a more traditional ethic of justice cannot. The overall aim is to use the considerable variety and disagreement within feminist theory, as well as differences between feminist ethics and competing ethics, to help us better understand and evaluate treating a woman as a sex object.

I

The liberal feminist is someone who believes that if women wish to be truly liberated, they must recognize that their role as housewife and mother shackles them to a life in which they are all too often merely the domestic slaves and sexual objects of their husbands.[6] The liberal feminist's agenda is to encourage women to eradicate this oppressive environment by lobbying for changes in state and federal legislation that would give women access to the economic and political power that men have. Equal opportunity in the workplace written into law would no longer make women dependent upon men for women's economic survival, and so change the power differential that has heretofore kept them in a kind of domestic and sexual slavery. The liberal feminist's point is that women are more than just *bodies* to be exploited and abused; women also have *minds,* that is, they can also do the things that beings with minds can do, and be the sorts of productive members of society that beings with minds can be, such as nuclear physicists, university presidents, gourmet chefs, and astronauts. The domestic sphere is viewed as a trap in which women are valued primarily—if not solely—in terms of their bodies, so that the task for the liberal feminist is to show the world that women can perform as well or better than men at what men believe only men can do. Women can then be valued and become valuable to society in the way men are valued, as inventive, intelligent, and rational beings.[7]

Notice the metaphysical dualism of mind and body at the core of the liberal feminist's agenda: when the liberal feminist says that women should be valued for their minds and not merely for their bodies, she is saying that the mind is a fundamentally different kind of thing from the body; when the liberal feminist says that women should start being astronauts and stop being house drudges, she is saying that mental tasks are of a fundamentally different type than physical ones. Furthermore, the mind is to be *valued* over the body, for it is in the world of the mind that economic and sexual freedom from men lie.

For the liberal feminist, then, it is never appropriate to treat a woman as a sex *object* when she ought to be treated as the mentally active and autonomous *subject* of her experiences. The National Organization for Women (NOW), which has its roots in this kind of liberal feminism, has often been quoted as saying that treating women as sex objects is degrading to them and is objectionable on these grounds alone. When the woman-as-nuclear-physicist-as-mind gets a slap on the rump from her male colleague, she has been degraded from her status as *thinking* thing to the status of mere thing, to be petted and pawed at the behest of someone else. She has been treated not like a woman with a mind, but as a mere sex *object*.

The socialist feminist agrees with her liberal counterpart that treating a woman as a sex object is objectionable if it involves her sexual domination; but sex objectification need not be objectionable if the complaint is based solely on the fact that a woman is being treated "merely as a body." When my husband hides behind me at our class reunion to avoid the class gossip, he may be treating me "merely as a body" in this context, but I have no obvious reason to complain. Or suppose that, knowing that I am five feet, seven inches tall, my sister stands a ladder next to me in order to determine how tall the ladder is. In this context, I am, for her, a measuring stick, "merely a body" against which she can compare the length of the ladder. Examples of this type suggest to the socialist feminist that we should reconsider how we evaluate the mental versus the physical. The socialist feminist points out that the traditional dualism that the liberal feminist adopts has its roots in the writings of such philosophers as Plato and Descartes, philosophers whose views of women reflect the chauvinism of their era.[8] According to Plato, a woman can be a political ruler *in principle* because, given his distinction between the mind and the body, there is nothing about her *physical* sex that makes it impossible for her to rule with the *mind* of a philosopher. But a close reading of Plato suggests that he does not regard women as capable of the mental discipline required of the best rulers. Intelligent women were needed to reproduce potential philosopher kings and other genetically favored women with which to pair kings, but a philosopher queen was at best a second-rate ruler.[9] For Descartes, women are like animals, complex machines without their ghosts, bodies without rational intellect; it is "man," that is, *men* who are the "thinking things."[10]

Furthermore, in the traditional dualist's model, the world of the mind is not only the world of men, it is where anything of real and lasting *value* is found. For Plato, contemplating the world of the intangible and immutable Forms can offer a kind of wisdom that no experience of this transient world can match.[11] For Descartes, the essence of a man, that without which he would not be who he is, is thinking: I think, therefore, I am.[12]

The association of women with the body is not in and of itself objectionable. Certainly, Michelangelo's sculpture has shown us that a woman's body can be perceived by a man as a thing of beauty. The association acquires moral significance when women are associated with something that is not valued as highly as that with which men are associated. Thus, the socialist feminist argues, by accepting the traditional dualism of mind and body, the liberal feminist not only accepts the metaphysical distinction between the mind and body, but also accepts the moral evaluation made by men that the mind is more valuable than the body, that the mental is to be prized over the physical. Since men are associated with the mind and women with the body, men are simply more valuable than women. Traditional dualism's explicit credo is that men are better than women. If one accepts such a dualism and one wishes to be valued by and valuable to society, one has no choice but to think and act *like a man*.

The socialist feminist asks the liberal feminist to examine the way she attempts to eradicate her oppression: the liberal feminist puts on a business suit (a process labeled "man-dressing" by some feminists) to pursue a career in a world of careers determined by men in order to earn enough money to wield enough power to promote legislation whose parameters and language are defined by men. Her oppression continues, the socialist feminist argues, because she will still be expected to see to the needs of hearth and home (thus the notorious Superwoman syndrome of the emotionally and physically exhausted career woman/wife/mother), and because she has failed to define herself *in her own terms*. According to the socialist feminist, only by re-evaluating both the metaphysical and moral implications of the traditional dualism of mind and body can any woman hope to liberate herself from the oppressive environment of a male-defined world.

The socialist feminist also argues that by accepting the traditional dualism of mind and body, we miss some of the more subtle but important features of sex objectification. Sometimes what I *want* to be is a sexy body, an "object of sexual desire" or "sex object" in this broader sense. This does not imply that I do not also want to be treated with sexual kindness and care. It is simply that I do not want to discuss Cartesian dualism during foreplay; I do not want to be treated like a philosopher in bed. I want to *have sex*. So valuing the world of the mind over the body is no liberation for the woman who enjoys physical sex. In the sense of "sex object" just mentioned, a woman can like being treated as a sex object without liking sexual domination or control. Furthermore, a man's appreciating a woman's mind is no guarantee that she will not be "degraded," using the liberal feminist's term, from mental subject to sex *object*. The male boss who sexually harasses his female employee may say, without contradiction, "Baby, your brains are a turn-on!" The socialist feminist notes that keeping mind and body metaphysically separate may be important to making sense of racial minority civil rights issues, where it is often cited that the content of one's character and not the color of one's skin should determine social value; but even here the waters become muddied by the fact that many racial minority groups identify themselves in large part in terms of their race, their biology, their *bodies*. For the socialist feminist, the key is to reject, if not the metaphysical distinction between mind and body, the moral and aesthetic evaluation we place on the former at the expense of the latter. The mind is a thing to be treasured; but we must also celebrate the body, in particular the female body as women experience both the pain and the pleasures of the intensely physical process of childbirth, the pleasures of sex with either other women or men, and the pleasure of being the subject of aesthetic beauty whether fat or thin. Such a program is part of the socialist feminist's general program for re-evaluating the sex roles of our culture to determine the extent to which they encourage the domination of women by men.[13]

While the socialist feminist's concern is to *construct* new social values for a distinctly feminist culture, one kind of postmodern feminist of the past decade is an advocate of the *deconstruction* of social values. According to this postmodernist, the belief that there is some best moral and aesthetic environment in which women will thrive is simply mistaken. The world is not a place where definitive moral

judgments exist, yet we are fooled into believing they exist by the delimiting power of language. When a woman complains about being treated as a sex object, she mistakenly assumes that the language is somehow expressive of a moral truth. But, according to the feminist deconstructionist, Wittgenstein was wrong; the limits of our language are not the limits of our world. When we depend upon language to tell us what the world is really like, we are the proverbial blind men who seek to define the elephant by the length of its tail. Language is vital to express who we are and what we do. But language does not define moral truth or establish epistemological certainty; on the contrary, it allows us to tell stories, to describe the context of our experience. When a woman complains that she is treated as a sex object, she can tell us the story of how she feels— disgusted, angry, fearful, embarrassed—but, according to the feminist deconstructionist, we have no business evaluating her treatment as degrading, dehumanizing, insensitive, or lacking in good taste, as if to say, "This is a fact of the matter." Feminists can continue to make recommendations for what they consider to be the ideally liberating community, but the feminist deconstructionist will argue that such recommendations must ultimately be recognized for what they are, namely, as pieces of the story in a *description* of a feminist community that is itself one of many desirable communities. Feminist recommendations are not to be regarded as *prescriptions* for political and economic justice. Indeed, the feminist's program of deconstruction demands the rejection of all traditional binaries such as right/wrong, true/ false, fact/fiction, masculine/feminine, and mind/body; the feminist deconstructionist sees such binaries as representing the rigid categorization and dogmatic thinking that have kept women from living fulfilling lives. Was it not the liberal feminists's traditional dualism that left her with the Superwoman syndrome? Is not the socialist feminist's sex-role re-evaluation still an evaluation from within the very patriarchal conceptual and moral scheme from which she wishes to escape? The feminist as deconstructionist *de*-evaluates the way women and men treat each other, which is to say that she rejects moral or aesthetic justifications for accepting one kind of treatment over another; according to the deconstructionist feminist, her aim is a morally neutral one: to accurately describe and celebrate the variety in human experience.[14]

One of the chief difficulties with the feminist's program of deconstruction, however, is that while it acknowledges women's feelings of anger and frustration at being treated as sex objects, it deprives women of any justification for grounding those complaints in the kind of moral conviction that promises change. If the feminist agenda is an agenda for changing the status quo, the deconstructionist gives women neither moral, nor political, nor any ideological platform upon which they can justify the changes they wish to make. No moral program is more just than another, no political agenda is less oppressive than another, when all programs and agendas are merely texts to be described, stories to be told, and not issues to be fought for and won. One wonders with what force the feminist deconstructionist can press her own postmodern agenda when by definition such an agenda has no more claim on our moral or aesthetic sensibilities than any other.

While no single brand of feminism I have discussed captures all that is required for a thorough philosophical analysis of sex objectification, or for a more general account of women's oppression, we can identify some of the strengths of each feminist agenda. The liberal feminist points out that women are tired of being victimized, dominated, and bullied by men at home and at work, men who make every effort to define women in terms of men's values, needs, and interests. Women are intelligent, creative, and passionate individuals who want to feel and express their zest for life. This means that, for many women, work other than housework—work other that of the cook, the caretaker, the social director, the volunteer, even the helpmate—that is, work other than that of a stereotypic wife and mother, will be a vital part of who she is. The socialist feminist reminds us, however, that it is a patriarchal culture that has historically defined not only what roles women *do* play in society, but what roles they *ought* to play. We must be certain that in refusing to fit out culture's sex stereotypes that we also refuse to adopt the dominant value base that created them. The socialist feminist believes that feminism must define a new moral vision. The postmodern feminist's concern is that unless we reject the concept of a feminist moral vision, indeed any and all value-based strategies for liberation, we will invariably find ourselves limited by the dogmatic thinking and rigid categorization implied by moral principles of any sort. The very idea of "sticking to one's principles" is anathema to the deconstructionist agenda. The narrow-mindedness and stridency with which feminism is often associated, even by those with feminist sensibilities, suggest that we must take the deconstructionist's warnings seriously. The deconstructionist reminds us that the feminist community is itself merely a linguistic label for a community of human and humane beings. The question remains for all of us: To what extent can we construct a human and humane community in an environment that continues to congratulate men and condemn women for being treated as sex objects?

II

Feminists not only disagree about the nature, scope, and resolution of women's oppression, they disagree as to what, if anything, constitutes a distinctly feminist ethics.[15] There is agreement that such an ethics should describe a conceptual framework and provide a normative strategy for moral problem solving that does not stifle, trivialize, or marginalize a woman's voice. However, the most effective means of celebrating that voice, what Carol Gilligan has called a distinctly "different voice" from that of many, if not most men,[16] remains a matter of considerable debate.

For my purposes, I can briefly sketch one version of what has been called a feminist ethic of care and contrast it with the ethic of justice found in the rights-based, Kantian tradition of modern political theory.[17] By noting some of its theoretical presuppositions, we can approximate what an ethic of justice would say about the morality of sex objectification. My claim is that an ethic of care can tell us even more than an ethic of justice can about why women complain about being treated as sex objects, why the treatment remains so pervasive, and what we need to do to eliminate it. The requirements of justice are strong and compelling ones, and I do not want to dismiss them. Rather, I see my task as using an ethic of care to enhance what a more traditional ethic of justice has to tell us about the meaning and morality of sex objectification, in order to situate an ethic of care not merely within the realm of feminist aims and ideals, but squarely within a framework for thinking about moral problems in any context.[18]

A feminist ethic of care is an ethic that advocates making moral decisions based upon a recognition of the particularity and connectedness of the persons whose lives that decision affects. It is first and foremost an ethic of empathy, requiring the moral agent to take up the particular perspective of concrete others in deciding how to act with regard to them. It is an ethic of responsibility that defines moral agents as caretakers of those in need and as moved by sympathy and sentiment in determining what is right. This ethic is in marked contrast to an ethic of justice or an ethic of rights grounded in the moral philosophy of Immanuel Kant whose requirement that moral judgments be made by autonomous agents unhindered by personal sentiment or eccentricity has provided modern political philosophers such as John Rawls with the justification for rationality and impartiality that Rawls regards as essential to making fair judgments.[19] An ethic of justice identifies moral agents as rational, mutually disinterested individuals for whom impartiality precludes using one's sympathies or emotional attachments to decide what is right, and for whom moral rights are essential to claim what would otherwise be appropriated by those with greater power or authority. Moral agents under an ethic of justice are also self-determining in their capacity and willingness to impose moral obligations freely upon themselves.[20] While an ethic of care recommends judging each moral dilemma on its own merits, the moral principles that underlie an ethic of justice are unconditional, universalizable, and abstract in the sense that, once articulated, they are meant to justify moral conduct without qualification, in any and all moral contexts, for any and all moral agents.[21] In short, an ethic of care advocates making empathic connections among concrete others to create a caring community; an ethic of justice presupposes a relationship of empathic distance between isolated moral agents whose primary aim is to ensure, using the force of abstract moral authority, that others respect their rights.

Feminists who value an ethic of care have joined previous critics of rights-based ethics in arguing that an ethic that is based solely on claims of competing moral rights paints a picture of morality so detached and impersonal, if not outrightly antagonistic, that it cannot account for doing what is right out of love or compassion, or from a desire to improve one's moral character, nor can it account for supererogatory or altruistic behavior in which claims of moral rights seem superfluous or out of place.[22] Furthermore, feminists point out that women have historically been regarded by moral philosophers as primarily emotional, not rational or impartial, beings, and that women have seldom been afforded the self-determination required of autonomous moral agents under an ethic of justice. On this basis, women have traditionally been found to be deficient moral agents or have been denied moral agency altogether. Yet researchers such as Gilligan have found that, even when we acknowledge in women their capacity for impartiality and self-determination, many of them approach moral problems from a fundamentally different perspective, a perspective I have been calling an ethic of care. The American women in Gilligan's study live in a culture in which their gender is socially constructed around nurturance and caregiving as mother, wife, helpmate, volunteer. It is a gender that is encouraged by Western culture to approach situations from a perspective of partiality for loved ones, connectedness with community, and empathy for those in need. Feminists have argued that if this perspective is of value to the culture, then this perspective must be accorded its proper moral worth. Instead of rejecting their Western gender identity, feminists who advance an ethic of care have appropriated it in the belief that an ethic of justice based upon a rejection of moral sentiment or Kantian inclination cannot reflect a woman's different moral voice, nor can it foster the kind of sympathetic moral imagination required to resolve everyday moral problems.[23]

Given the above distinctions between the two ethics, what would an ethic of justice say about the morality of treating a woman as a sex object? Immanuel Kant's second formulation of the categorical imperative is instructive here: "Act in such a way that you always treat humanity, whether in your own person or in the person of any other, never simply as a means, but always at the same time as an end."[24] This imperative provides the groundwork for the ethic of justice I described above in so far as it is intended by Kant to be an unconditional and universalizable moral principle, applicable "in the abstract" to any moral context. Furthermore, the imperative defines a deontology of rights and duties carried out by moral agents whose autonomy, that is, their rationality and impartiality, not their moral sentiment or sympathy, define the proper moral motive.[25] Kant's moral imperative demands that all persons, in virtue of their common humanity, treat themselves and other persons with respect for their capacity for autonomous choice, a capacity that defines human beings as "ends in themselves" who can freely, rationally, and impartially determine how they ought to act, thus distinguishing human beings from animals or objects. Someone who is treated "simply as a means" is someone whose own interests, needs, or desires are subordinated to those of another, one whose capacity for making life choices free of the dominance or intimidation of another is severely limited. Thus, someone who is treated "simply as a means" is someone whose humanity, defined by one's capacity for autonomous choice, has been reduced to that of exploitable and expendable object.

When a woman complains that being treated as a sex object is humiliating, demeaning, degrading, even dehumanizing, she is invoking the Kantian ethic described above. For example, the sex object who is the victim of an employer's sexual harassment is not free of the domination and intimidation of her objectifier. She is being treated "simply as a means" to his own sexual ends. She is not being treated as someone whose common humanity makes her worthy of respect, but as an object worthy only of appropriation and exploitation by someone morally superior to her. Using my body to avoid the class gossip or as a convenient measuring stick is not treating me inappropriately when I am treated as an object *but also at the same time* as a person whose capacity for autonomous choice has not been sacrificed for another's gain.[26]

Not only does Kant's second formulation of the categorical imperative explain the experience of degradation the woman as sex object feels, it also legitimizes her demand that she be treated with respect for her capacity for autonomous choice. According to an ethic of justice,

the victim of sexual harassment has a right to be free of the domination or intimidation of her harasser, and the imperative upon which such a right is based establishes a moral minimum below which her harasser has a duty not to fall.[27] As such, an ethic of justice provides an extremely compelling prescription for right action. Furthermore, the unconditional, universal, and abstract nature of the prescription allows a woman to make this demand in any and all contexts in which sex objectification might occur, the bedroom as well as the boardroom, in relations involving sexual intimates as well as those involving strangers. In theory, at least, she can demand her right to respect by invoking an ethic of justice whenever and wherever her sexual autonomy is threatened.

The reality, however, is that the very demands that are her right under an ethic of justice ironically appear to perpetuate the misunderstanding, insensitivity, and antagonism that are the hallmarks of sex objectification. Women who are the victims of sexual harassment often say that men "just don't get it." The Western world's tradition of paying homage to an ethic of justice can tell us why. Bolstered by an ethic describing self-determined and sympathetically distant individuals in moral competition when their claims on each other conflict, men who subscribe to this ethic have no incentive to view personal relationships, much less sexually charged relationships, as vehicles for making strong empathic connections. On the contrary, an ethic of justice would seem to encourage them to regard sex as a means to retain and enhance an autonomy under constant siege, and so regard sex as a vehicle for the dominance and control of those whose autonomy might threaten their own, even at the expense of violating their own Kantian imperative. Women are viewed as competitors in a dangerous game of sexual politics whose rights to be treated as "ends in themselves" stand in direct, adversarial relation to those of men. As a result, women's rights in sexual relations are respected only in so far as they do not impinge on men's perceptions of themselves as initiators of the encounter and dominators of the action. From such a moral perspective, sexual harassers "just don't get it" because they are not encouraged by the ethic of justice described above to use their moral imaginations or moral sympathies to try to see the situation from the perspective of the harassed. If the proper moral motive is one of abstract and unconditional duty alone, then men will only grudgingly accord women the respect they desire without any real understanding of the pain and humiliation that are so much a part of the sex-objectifying process. Thus, the process is perpetuated by an ethic that not only provides no incentive for moral empathy in matters of sex, but whose requirements on the nature and relationship among moral agents would seem to preclude it.

An ethic of care, on the other hand, requires of moral agents that they take up the perspective of others in order to understand and respond to their needs. Therefore, it is an ethic that asks of any man considering treating a woman as a sex object that he first try to imagine what it would be like to be *this woman* treated *this way* in *this context*. Such empathy requires that he recognize what personal or professional relationship he bears to her, and what specific responsibilities to respond to her needs those relationships require, even in the face of his own sexual agenda. Furthermore, an ethic of care recognizes that sex objectification in the boardroom may raise significantly different moral questions than sex objectification in the bedroom, in virtue of the different personal relationships and social propriety of the sexual encounters that are involved.

Part of the demand for particularity requires that the would-be objectifier try to see the importance of the *sexual* component of his behavior. He would be asked to recognize that because women's sexual history in a Judeo-Christian culture is a history of being soiled and corrupted by fornication, to treat *this woman* with *this history* as nothing more than a sexual plaything is degrading in its Kantian dehumanization *and* in its sociocultural defilement.[28] An ethic of care also recognizes that because the objectification is sexual in nature, it raises issues of power and dominance in a patriarchal society that other forms of treating someone "simply as a means" may not raise. Because *this woman* is a member of a gendered class for whom the threat of sexual oppression in *this culture* is constant and real, the would-be objectifier will be required to try to imagine what it must feel like to be a woman in a patriarchal society, a society in which the fear of sexual harassment and rape define women's sexual psychology and undermine their sexual

lives.[29] Such moral requirements for empathy and connectedness are worlds apart from the demands for autonomy defined by an ethic of justice in which competing rights help create an environment of mutual antagonism and alienation. An ethic of care is an ethic whose value in moral sympathy and moral particularity would make the pain and humiliation the sex object feels especially real for her objectifier. Such an ethic would thus provide no incentive to assert his sexual power or to protect his sexual ego by treating her as a sex object.

In short, while women deserve to be treated with the respect required by an ethic of justice, their complaints about sex objectification go well beyond complaints about violations of their rights. Their complaints speak to the lack of care, lack of sensitivity, and the failure of empathy or understanding that sex objectifiers so frequently display. Many men fail to see how upsetting a pat on the fanny or a hand on the thigh can be because they are neither morally required to sympathize with any particular woman's desire to be free of her sex objectification, nor to understand the pain women as a gender suffer from living in a male-identified culture in which power is in large part derived from women's oppression through sex. Men sexually force themselves on women because they are not morally required to come to know the sexual needs of any particular woman, but instead are morally encouraged by an ethic of justice constantly to assert their own sexual autonomy and defend it from potential moral battery.

My claim is that by advocating an ethic of care, we will feel morally obligated to create a community of persons that is respectful of the sexuality of others *because* it is sympathetic to that sexuality. Rights against one another translate into responsibilities to one another in which a sensitive understanding of the sexual needs and interests of particular persons in specific contexts is given high moral value. There will be much less incentive for sexual intimidation because we will be morally obligated to understand what it feels like to be treated *this* way in *this* context by *this* person. In turn, a caring community will feel morally obligated to educate both men and women regarding each gender's unique social and sexual history, as a way of recognizing the effects of our social construction of gender on any particular man's or particular woman's goals and ideals. Only after we have tempered the crucial yet potentially alienating demand for autonomy with an equally strong requirement for empathy can we hope to establish the kind of moral community in which, together, both men and women can lead sexually fulfilling and satisfying lives.[30]

This is not to suggest that an ethic of care is problem-free. It has been suggested by a number of feminist and nonfeminist critics alike that an ethic of care only reinforces an oppressive stereotype of women as nurturing and selfless that has been the ruin of their economic independence and social self-esteem, that an ethic of care does not distinguish between constructive and destructive caring, and that an ethic of care requires a sympathetic imagination for people too physically or emotionally remote to be the practical objects of moral concern.[31] What these criticisms suggest is that we need some way to combine both the strong moral minima defined by an ethic of justice with an equally strong commitment to care that is circumscribed by our limited human capacity for responding to the needs of others and by the long-term interests of those we choose to care about. The task for feminist theorists is to continue to challenge prevailing notions of the valued and the valuable in human conduct. However, we must also remember that because such challenges are necessarily made from within the context of women's oppression, we must question our own theoretical presuppositions about that oppression before we can be free of it.

NOTES

1. Feminist philosophers have begun to question whether the Socratic method of inquiry is either necessary or well-suited to the task of doing good philosophy. For criticism of philosophy as a defense against attack by counterexample, see Janice Moulton, "A Paradigm of Philosophy: The Adversary Method," in *Discovering Reality: Feminist Perspectives on Epistemology, Metaphysics, Methodology, and Philosophy of Science*, eds. Sandra Harding and Merrill B. Hintikka (Boston: D. Reidel, 1983).

2. Whether the goals of feminist inquiry are consistent with the goals of philosophical inquiry is explored in Susan Sherwin, "Philosophical Methodology and Feminist Methodology: Are they Compatible?" in *Women, Knowledge, and Reality*, eds. Ann Garry and Marilyn Pearsall (Boston: Unwin Hyman, 1989); also see Jean Grimshaw, *Philosophy and Feminist Thinking* (Minneapolis: University of Minnesota Press, 1988); and Moira Gatens, *Feminism and Philosophy: Perspectives on Difference and Equality* (Bloomington: Indiana University Press, 1991).

3. For an excellent discussion and analysis of the variety within feminist theory, see Rosemarie Tong, *Feminist Thought: A Comprehensive Introduction* (Boulder, Colo: Westview Press 1989).

4. See my detailed analysis of sex objectification in *Dehumanizing Women: Treating Persons as Sex Objects* (Totowa, N. J.: Rowman & Allanheld, 1985).

5. Traditional Western moral philosophy requires that moral judgments be made by appeal to moral principles that are abstracted from particular cases to apply to all persons equally and without exception. Recently, however, feminists have challenged this moral tradition by arguing that moral decisions are made on a much more personal and context-specific basis in which abstract moral principles play little if any role in the justification of right conduct. On the superiority of moral judgments considered as claims of competing rights justified by abstract principles of fairness, see Lawrence Kohlberg, *The Philosophy of Moral Development* (New York: Harper & Row, 1981). A direct feminist challenge to Kohlberg, in which his ethic of justice is criticized as male-biased, can be found in Carol Gilligan's *In a Different Voice* (Cambridge, Mass.: Harvard University Press, 1982). For a further fleshing out of Gilligan's feminist ethics, see Nel Noddings, *Caring: A Feminine Approach to Ethics and Moral Education* (Berkeley and Los Angeles: University of California Press, 1984); and Rita Manning, *Speaking from the Heart* (Lanham, Md.: Rowman & Littlefield, 1992).

6. For some examples of the liberal feminist model, see Betty Friedan, *The Feminine Mystique* (New York: Dell, 1963), and Gloria Steinem, *Outrageous Acts and Everyday Rebellions* (New York: Holt, Rinehart & Winston, 1983). For a review of the liberal feminist movement in the United States, see Zillah Eisenstein, *Feminism and Sexual Equality: Crisis in Liberal America* (New York: Monthly Review Press, 1984).

7. Reducing women to their bodies in order to deny them economic or political power has ancient historical and philosophical roots. For excellent surveys of classical to modern philosophers' traditional attitudes toward women and "female nature," see Nancy Tuana, *Woman and the History of Philosophy* (New York: Paragon House, 1992), and Susan Moller Okin, *Women in Western Political Thought* (Princeton, N. J.: Princeton University Press, 1979). Also see Elizabeth V. Spelman's discussion of Aristotle's politics in her *Inessential Woman: Problems of Exclusion in Feminist Thought* (Boston: Beacon Press, 1988), chap. 2.

8. For an exciting history of what women did contribute to philosophy during Plato's and Descartes's time, see Mary Ellen Waithe, ed., *A History of Women Philosophers*, 3 vols. (Boston: Dordrecht, 1987–1989).

9. For a feminist analysis of Plato's views on women in the polis, see Spelman, *Inessential Woman*, chap. 1, and Lynda

Lange, "The Function of Equal Education in Plato's *Republic* and *Laws*," in *The Sexism of Social and Political Theory*, eds. Lorenne M. G. Clark and Lynda Lange (Toronto: University of Toronto Press, 1979).

10. For a feminist critique of Descartes's philosophical methodology, see Genevieve Lloyd, *The Man of Reason: "Male" and "Female" in Western Philosophy* (Minneapolis: University of Minnesota Press, 1984).

11. See Plato's *Republic* in *The Dialogues of Plato*, trans. B. Jowett (New York: Random House, 1920).

12. See René Descartes, *Meditations on First Philosophy*, trans. Elizabeth S. Haldane and G.R.T. Ross (London: Cambridge University Press, 1931), esp. Meditation II.

13 See Alison Jaggar's extended analysis of the socialist feminist agenda in *Feminist Politics and Human Nature* (Totowa, N. J.: Rowman & Allanheld, 1983).

14. For a variety of philosophical essays in feminist postmodernism, see Linda J. Nicholson, ed. *Feminism/Postmodernism* (New York: Routledge, 1990); Elaine Marks and Isabelle de Courtivron, eds., *New French Feminisms* (New York: Schocken Books, 1981); and Jeffner Allen and Iris Marion Young, eds., *The Thinking Muse: Feminism and Modern French Philosophy* (Bloomington: Indiana University Press, 1989).

15. For a review of the variety of approaches within feminist ethics, see Eva Feder Kittay and Diana T. Meyers, eds., *Women and Moral Theory* (Totowa, N. J.: Rowman & Littlefield, 1987); Eve Browning Cole and Susan Coultrap-McQuin, eds., *Explorations in Feminist Ethics* (Bloomington: Indiana University Press, 1992); and Claudia Card, ed., *Feminist Ethics* (Lawrence: University Press of Kansas, 1991).

16. Gilligan, *In a Different Voice*, 2.

17. An excellent selection of articles that elaborate on the debate between an ethic of care and an ethic of justice can be found in Section I: "The Question of Different Voice: Care, Justice, and Rights" in *Feminism and Political Theory*, ed. Cass R. Sunstein (Chicago: Chicago University Press, 1990); also see the articles listed under "The Care Debate" in Cole and Coultrap-McQuin, eds., *Explorations in Feminist Ethics*.

18. Some feminists reject an ethic of justice outright as too blatantly male-biased to give an accurate view of moral deliberation; see Noddings, *Caring*. Susan Moller Okin thinks the presuppositions and principles of Rawls' justice as fairness can be interpreted to include an ethic of care. See her "Reason and Feeling in Thinking about Justice," in Sunstein, ed., *Feminism and Political Theory*. Others see the two ethics working in tandem, depending upon the moral psychology of the deliberator and the context of deliberation. See Annette Baier, "What Do Women Want in a Moral Theory?" *Nous* 19 (1985): 53–63; and Owen Flanagan and Kathryn Jackson, "Justice, Care and Gender: The Kohlberg–Gilligan Debate Revisited," in Sunstein, ed., *Feminism and Political Theory*. Rita Manning regards care as the primary ethic, with justice informing a moral minimum below which no one should fall; see Manning, *Speaking from the Heart*.

19. John Rawls, *A Theory of Justice* (Cambridge, Mass.: Harvard University Press, 1971), 11–17. For a discussion of how Kantian moral philosophy figures in Rawls's account of justice as fairness, see Okin, *Women in Western Political Thought*. Also see Immanuel Kant on duty versus "inclination" in his *Groundwork of the Metaphysic of Morals*, trans. H. J. Paton (New York: Barnes & Noble, 1948), 63ff.

20. Rawls, *Theory of Justice*, 13.

21. Kant, *Groundwork*, 80.

22. See, for example, G. E. M. Anscombe, "Modern Moral Philosophy," *Philosophy* 33 (1958): 1–19; Alasdair MacIntyre, *After Virtue* (Notre Dame, Ind.: University of Notre Dame Press, 1981); and Bernard Williams, "Persons, Character, and Morality," in *Moral Luck* (Cambridge: Cambridge University Press, 1981.) For some contemporary feminist criticism of a traditional, rights-based ethic, see Lawrence Blum, *Friendship, Altruism and Morality* (London: Routledge & Kegan Paul, 1980), and John Hardwig, "Should Women Think in Terms of Rights?" in Sunstein, ed., *Feminism and Political Theory*.

23. On the nature and importance of the moral imagination in moral problem solving, see Martha Nussbaum, "Finely Aware and Richly Responsible: Literature and the Moral Imagination," *Journal of Philosophy* 82 (1985): 516–29. On the dangers of appropriating a stereotyped feminine identity in order to advocate an ethic of care, see Patricia Ward Scaltas, "Do Feminist Ethics Counter Feminist Aims?" in Cole and Coultrap-McQuin, eds., *Explorations*.

24. Kant, *Groundwork*, 91.

25. For an excellent analysis of the meaning of Kantian Autonomy, see Thomas E. Hill, Jr., "The Importance of Autonomy," in *Autonomy and Self-Respect* (Cambridge University Press, 1991).

26. See LeMoncheck, *Dehumanizing Women*, 26–30.

27. Rawls' maximin solution to determine his two principles of justice establishes just this kind of moral minimum; see *A Theory of Justice*, 15ff. Also see Manning, *Speaking from the Heart*, 73–82, on the importance of such minima for ensuring that an ethic of care is of appropriate prescriptive force.

28. See LeMoncheck, *Dehumanizing Women*, 48–50; Ann Garry, "Pornography and Respect for Women," in *Philosophy and Women*, eds. Sharon Bishop and Marjorie Weinzweig (Belmont, Calif.: Wadsworth, 1979), 134–35.

29. See Sandra Lee Bartky, "Toward a Phenomenology of Feminist Consciousness," in *Femininity and Domination* (New York: Routledge, 1990).

30. Thomas E. Hill, Jr., describes how at least one sense of autonomy is not only valuable but consistent with the moral prescription to be compassionate; see *Autonomy and Self-Respect*, 50–51.

31. For a systematic critique of an ethic of care by a feminist philosopher, see Claudia Card, "Women's Voices and Ethical Ideals: Must We Mean What We Say?" *Ethics* 99 (1988): 125–35. For a review of the most serious criticisms as well as directions for a line of defense, see Scaltas, "Do Feminist Ethics Counter Feminist Aims?"; Manning, *Speaking from the Heart*, chap. 7; and Joan C. Tronto, "Beyond Gender Difference to a Theory of Care," *Signs* 12, no. 4 (1987): 644-63.

MICHAEL LEVIN

What Is Feminism?

CHARACTERIZING FEMINISM

An adequate characterization of feminism should meet four conditions. First, it should be acceptable to those who call themselves feminists and consistent with the understanding of feminism held by sympathetic outsiders. Second, it should construe feminism, which presents itself as a critique of some of the broadest features of society, as comprehensive and systematic. Third, it should construe feminism as more than a platitude which no reasonable person would dispute but which has no practical consequences. Fourth, it should construe feminism as a view that is taken seriously by a significant number of people.

The third and fourth conditions present certain difficulties. The ban on triviality rules out the most commonly offered definitions of feminism, such as "justice for women" and "opposition to sexism," insofar as the crucial term *sexism* is in turn defined as "failure to give equal consideration on the basis of sex alone."[1] Consider "justice for women." The pure principle of justice, that similar cases are to be treated similarly, is empty and tautological, its meaning entirely dependent on the criterion used to determine the similarity among cases and the evidence considered relevant to whether men and women satisfy the criterion chosen. Thus, to determine whether history textbooks emphasizing male statesmen are just, it must first be decided whether justice is the distribution of equal shares to all, to the equally needy, to those faring equally well in laissez-faire competition, or perhaps some other standard altogether. It must then be determined empirically whether men and women are equal in the sense specified, and if they are, whether andro-centric history textbooks fail to provide shares equal in the sense specified. To demand just treatment for women is to demand nothing in particular about how women should be treated; this platitudinous demand therefore cannot be what anyone has in mind by "feminism." For similar reasons it is unavailing to characterize feminists and their critics as agreeing about ends—the equitable treatment of women—and disagreeing (only) about means. Equity is too vacuous to be anybody's goal; it is a goal given substance by the means chosen to it. Disagreement about such matters as quotas, textbook censorship, and comparable worth are disagreements about the feminist conception of equity itself, hence disagreeing about ends.

The fourth condition creates difficulties inasmuch as it seems to imply that feminism cannot be absurd, for much that feminists say seems too absurd for anyone to take seriously. Thus Richard Wasserstrom endorses an "assimilationist ideal" for society in which sex "would be the functional equivalent of the eye color of individuals in our society today": "Just as the normal, typical adult is virtually oblivious to the eye color of other persons for all major interpersonal relations, so the normal, typical adult in this kind of non-sexist society would be indifferent to the sexual, physiological differences of other persons for all interpersonal relationships."[2] One is reluctant to attribute to a distinguished legal philosopher the view that in an ideal society many people would not know the sex of their spouses, but if what Wasserstrom is saying does not imply this, what is he saying? When considering feminism, it is useful to balance the charitable maxim that no one should be saddled with a belief that is too silly, with Hobbes's observation that "men believeth many times impossibilities." Satisfying the third and fourth conditions simultaneously presents further problems since, as we will see, any substantial criticism of sex roles risks commitment to unviable empirical assumptions.

Mindful of these difficulties, let us begin with selections from the full range of feminist thought: two texts historically central to anything deserving to be called feminism, a more contemporary classic source, a radical feminist, aphorisms from two mainstream activists, documents of the U. S. government and the United Nations, and the work of seven academic feminists writing for serious publishers.[3]

What is now called the nature of women is an eminently artificial thing—the result of forced repression in some directions, unnatural stimulation in others. . . . [N]o class of dependents have had their character so entirely distorted from its natural proportions by the relation with their masters. [John Stuart Mill, 1869]

The great danger which threatens the infant in our culture lies in the fact that the mother to whom it is confided in all its helplessness is almost always a discontented woman: sexually she is frigid or unsatisfied; socially she feels herself inferior to men; she has no independent grasp on the world or on the future. . . . [In a world] where men and women would be equal, [a girl] will be brought up from the first with the same demands and rewards, the same severity and the same freedom, as her brothers, taking part in the same studies, the same games, promised the same future, surrounded with women and men who seemed her undoubted equals. [Simone de Beauvior, 1948]

[T]he standards of femininity, however suitable they may have been in the past, may now be dysfunctional. They are not standards of good mental health. [Jessie Bernard, 1971]

The sexes are inherently in everything alike, save reproductive systems, secondary sexual characteristics, orgasmic capacity, and genetic and morphological structure. [Kate Millertt, 1970]

If there were another word more all-embracing than *revolution,* I would use it. [Shulamith Firestone, 1970]

We're talking about a revolution, not just reform. It's the deepest possible change there is. [Gloria Steinem, circa 1972]

I want to have a part in creating a new society. . . . I have never reached my potential because of social conditions. I'm not going to get the rewards. I've been crippled. [Member of NOW, 1974]

When we ask why girls and women come to choose courses of study and occupations that lead them to a segregated and disadvantaged role in later life, part of the answer is "socialization." Somehow, the social environment conveys the message that some activities are appropriate and some inappropriate, that girls and women possess certain capabilities and lack others. [U.S. Department of Health, Education, and Welfare, 1980]

The States Parties to the present Convention, *Aware* that a change in the traditional role of men as well as women in society and in the family is needed to achieve full equality between men and women, *have. agreed* to adopt appropriate legislative and other measures, including sanctions where appropriate, to modify the social and cultural patterns of conduct of men and women, with a view to achieving the elimination of prejudices and customary and all other practices which are based on the idea of the inferiority or the superiority of either of the sexes or on stereotyped roles for men and women. [United Nations Convention on the Elimination of All Forms of Discrimination against Women (signed by the United States 1978)]

A sexually egalitarian society is one in which virtually no public recognition is given to the fact that there is a physiological sex difference between persons. This is not to say that the different reproductive function of each sex should be unacknowledged in such a society nor that there should be no physicians specializing in male and female complaints, etc. But it is to say that, except in this sort of context, the question whether someone is male or female should have no significance. [Alison Jaggar, 1974]

Change in women's roles means change in every aspect of society. [Judith Long Laws, 1979]

Feminism is in its nature radical. . . . It is the social institutions of which we complain primarily. . . . If you consider the past there is no doubt at all that the whole structure of society was designed *to keep women entirely in the power of men.* This no doubt sounds like pure feminist rant, but it is not. [Janet Richards, 1980]

Whatever sex differences in behavior now exist and whatever their origins we have no reason to assume that they would be barriers to any egalitarian society we may want to build. [Marian Lowe, 1983]

[B]ecause the sexual division of labor around childbearing prevails and defines women's position, a policy emphasizing material benefits and services to encourage childbearing may ease the material burdens of motherhood; but it may operate to perpetuate the existing sexual division of labor and women's social subordination. . . . A feminist and socialist transformation of the existing conditions of reproduction would seek . . . a new set of social relations. . . . The changes we require are total. [Rosalind Petchesky, 1984]

If we could imagine a culture free of values and constraints concerning sexuality, human beings would probably express their sexuality, physicality, friendship, and loving emotions in a variety of ways that would not be necessarily influenced by others' biological sex. . . . In particular, the institutions and ideologies of heterosexuality (i.e. heterosexism) are the primary force in the maintenance of patriarchal rule and the social, economic and political subordination of women. [Ruth Bleier, 1984]

The Lowe and Bleier citations are particularly noteworthy for being taken from works in Pergamon's Athene Series, "An International Collection of Feminist Books," described as follows by the publisher: "The ATHENE SERIES assumes that all those who are concerned with formulating explanations of the way the world works need to know and appreciate the significance of basic feminist principles." Anyone who dismisses Lowe or Bleier as typical of feminism must deny that the editors of the Athene Series know what feminism is.

As it emerges from these sources, feminism in its contemporary form has four central tenets:

1. Anatomical differences apart, men and women are the same. Infant boys and girls are born with virtually the same capacities to acquire skills and motives, and if raised identically would develop identically.
2. Men unfairly occupy positions of dominance because the myth that men are more aggressive than women has been perpetuated by the practice of raising boys to be oriented toward mastery and girls to be oriented toward people. If this stereotyping ceased, leadership would be equally divided between the sexes. Sexist socialization harms boys as well as girls by denying both the full range of possible aspirations, but on the whole boys get the better of the deal because they grow up to run everything.
3. True human individuality and fulfillment will come about only when people view themselves as *human* repositories of talents and traits, and deny that sex has any signifi-

cant effect on one's individual nature. Traditional femininity is a suffocating and pathological response to women's heretofore restricted lives, and will have to be abandoned.
4. These desirable changes will require the complete transformation of society.

Clause 1 may appear too sweeping, in light of the verbal assent to innate nonanatomical sex differences given by a number of writers who call themselves feminists. These writers say merely that any differences which may exist are irrelevant to extant rigid sex roles, which are produced by conditioning as per clause 2. Some of the passages cited above are consistent with this seemingly less extreme environmentalism, as is "stage two" feminism to be considered presently. It might seem that a view of this sort could be accommodated by replacing clause 1 by 1a: *None of the observed traits of human beings can be explained as manifestations of innate sex differences. These differences, while perhaps real, are irrelevant to the nature of society and the possibilities of social change.*

In fact, however, 1 and 1a are equivalent. Clause 1 obviously entails 1a—non-existent differences cannot explain anything—and, together with the principle of parsimony used elsewhere in science, 1a implies 1. If innate sex differences do not affect the individual and group behavior of human beings, they do not affect the only phenomena they are likely to affect, and positing such differences is pointless. Nothing distinguishes a world with an inefficacious cause from a world without it. Thus, whether someone genuinely accepts innate sex differences depends entirely on whether he believes they help to explain general features of society. Anyone who says he grants innate sex differences but goes on to deny that they are explanatory is merely giving lip service to them. We will have occasion later to catalogue the protean forms this lip service can take; for now we may continue to identify feminism with the original four tenets.

This account of feminism is explicit in the writings of feminists themselves and informed observers. One figure who has had participant observer status is Alice Rossi, at one time a feminist and also a past president of the American Sociological Association. She may be presumed to speak with authority. In 1964 she wrote:

It will be an assumption of this essay that by far the majority of the differences between the sexes which have been noted in social science research are socially rather than physiologically determined. . . . It will be a major thesis of this essay that we need to reassert the claim to sex equality. . . . By sex equality I mean a socially androgynous conception of the roles of men and women, in which they are equal and similar in such spheres as intellectual, artistic, political and occupational interest and participation, complementary only in those spheres dictated by physiological differences between the sexes. [It includes] equivalence and substitutability [as] part of the general definition of the parental role. . . . [The liberated woman's] intellectual aggressiveness as well as her brother's tender sentiments will be welcomed and accepted as *human* characteristics, without the self-questioning doubt of latent homosexuality that troubles many college-age men and women in our era when these qualities are sex-linked. . . . If a social movement rests content with legal changes without making as strong an effort to change the social institutions through which they are expressed, it will remain a hollow victory.[4]

Note that Rossi took the social causation theory to be an "assumption" not worth questioning, and the sex differences themselves to be findings of "social science research" rather than part of the lore of every culture. By 1977 Rossi had developed serious doubts about her proposal, and with considerable intellectual courage published a partial recantation in which she described feminism in more objective language as "an egalitarian ideology that denies any innate sex differences and assumes that a 'unisex' socialization will produce men and women that are free of the traditional culturally induced sex differences" and which shares with much social science "an extreme emphasis on cultural determinism."[5]

Muriel Carden, a sociologist commissioned by the Ford and Russell Sage foundations to study feminism, summarized it similarly:

Far too much has been made of the biological differences between men and women. Different socialization processes account for a larger part of the observed differences in men's and women's behavior, while biology plays only a minor part. Thus their [feminists'] argument for equality is based upon the belief that the biologically derived differences between the sexes are relatively minor and that a most

inequitable system has been built upon the assumption that such differences are basic and major. . . . [A]lmost everyone co-operates in this "oppressive" socialization or conditioning. Parents, teachers, toy manufacturers, and writers of children's books encourage girls to be "feminine."[6]

The claim that feminism functions as an ideological belief system has been empirically tested by Claire Fulenwider.[7] Following standard social scientific usage, she defines an ideology as a system of beliefs (as opposed to a set of attitudes) which "describe present reality . . . explain present reality—that is, show how it has developed historically [and prescribe] in what ways it is good or bad [and] posit a plan for changing present reality."[8] Minimizing the differences between radical, socialist, and reform feminism, Fulenwider finds all feminist writers agreeing that

Women are unjustly treated, that they are maintained in subordinate roles and positions, and that they are consistently removed from most vital decision-making opportunities of society. Furthermore, this discrimination against and exploitation and oppression of women are seen by feminists as rationally justified by a dominant sexist ideology. . . . Overall, however, [despite differences in emphasis by reform, socialist, and radical feminists], values and goals of the women's movement show fairly widespread agreement. The eradication of sexism—in practice and in attitude—is probably the most basic goal. Commitment to expanding options for women in all spheres of society is another shared aim, as is freedom from oppression and from gender-role stereotyping. . . . Feminists concur that major social structural changes —in the economy, in politics, and in social practices and expectations—are essential.[9]

To test this hypothesis, Fulenwider first asked over 2,000 respondents to score their agreement with eleven statements, including: "Women should have an equal role with men in running business, industry, and government"; "Our society, not nature, teaches women to prefer homemaking"; "men have more of the top jobs because society discriminates against women [rather than because] men have more drive"; and "Women must work together to change laws and customs that are unfair to all women"—essentially tenets 1 through 4. A panel of judges concurred that strong agreement with these statements is a criterion of commitment to feminism. Fulenwider then predicted that if feminism is an ideological framework for interpreting social reality, a high combined score on the criterion should constrain views about other political issues, a high score on one criterion statement should predict high scores on the others, and finally, that scores on the criterion should depend on a single underlying variable. Fulenwider's data bore out these predictions and, especially for women, scores on the criterion variable correlated highly with self-positioning along the single "abstract ordering dimension" of "role equality."[10] The "overriding conclusion" was that feminism "gives clear evidence of centrality, rationality, and constraint," and serves as a "political ideology."[11]

Once all nonanatomical sex differences are taken to be social in origin, an analogy between women and racial minorities is inevitable. The supposed powerlessness, confinement, and poverty of women, and the prevalence of stereotypic beliefs about them, must be caused in much the way that the similarly inferior social position of American Blacks is caused. That the condition of women is universal while that of American Blacks is temporary and local— Blacks run everything in Black African countries—is taken to show the very pervasiveness of sexist conditioning. To forestall further verbal disputation, I will use this analogy in an operational definition of "feminist": A feminist is anyone who takes seriously the analogy between Blacks and women. Anyone who compares the present status of women to that of Blacks in the antebellum South, and the outlook of nonfeminist women to the slave mentality, is a feminist. So too is anyone who thinks that raising children to disregard gender is as easy and important as raising children to disregard skin color. Here are three feminists, one self-described, one a legal scholar engaged in popular debate, and one a philosopher writing for his peers in a professional periodical:

The kind of feminine self-image which lowers aspiration and permits the acceptance of a dependent status [is] similar to the defeatist attitude of other minority groups.

Not so many years ago, black probationary firemen were looked on with disdain and fear. And when Jews, some with college degrees, turned to firefighting during the Depression, their value in action was

seriously questioned. . . . Are women really in such a different position?

The treatment of our western European ancestors accorded North American Indians, blacks, and the native people of Mexico remains the barbarous deed that it always was. The systematic exploitation of women in our (and other) societies is not any less wrong.[12]

The dissent in *Frontiero v. Richardson* written by Justice William Brennan and joined by three other justices is feminist in this operational sense: "The position of women in our society was, in many respects, comparable to that of blacks under the pre–Civil War slave codes."[13] Four of nine positive scores from the Supreme Court indicates an operational test sensitive to an important social phenomenon.

REFINEMENTS

The four central tenets of feminism must be expanded in a number of ways. First, it must be emphasized that the inequity of the sexual division of labor is said to be two-fold. The horizontal division of tasks into male and female, overlap notwithstanding, largely confines women to domestic tasks while allowing males to do everything else. The vertical division of tasks into subordinate and superordinate reserves for men the topmost positions of prestige and authority in all spheres, including those in which men and women participate jointly. In the United States, men are chief executives and women secretaries; in the Kalahari desert, men do the high-status hunting while women do the low-status gathering. A specific task may be considered male in one society and female in another, but it always enjoys high status when it is male.

A second refinement, or perhaps gap, that needs filling, concerns the process by which sex roles have come to be assigned. Many feminists treat the present order as a male conspiracy. Others, who recognize the unlikelihood of a universal conspiracy, argue that sex stereotypes perpetuate themselves: Each generation, having been raised to accept conventional sex roles, raises its own children to those same roles. But this more sophisticated theory merely postpones the problem, which reemerges in the following form: If women originally wanted power just as badly as men, how did sex stereotyping *begin?* Did patriarchy emerge independently many times, or did it radiate to all societies from a single central source?[14] However often it happened, how did prehistoric women as well as men come to be convinced that women do not want power as much as men do, and how did power come to be monopolized by men? As we will see, any noncircular version of feminist environmentalism must posit a historical moment at which men used their superior physical strength to wrest control.

The third salient feature of feminism is its attention to the family. The attribution of inequalities to socialization naturally generates suspicion about the chief instrument of socialization, the family, and its accompanying emotions. Juliet Mitchell and Nancy Chodorow reject love between men and women "enculturated in patriarchal society" as an inauthentic product of "social ideology."[15] For Mill, the family was "a school of despotism" (a judgement that may reflect Mill's own unhappy upbringing by a tyrannical father). Chodorow again:

The social organization of parenting produces sexual inequality, not simply role differentiation. It is politically and socially important to confront this organization. Even though it is an arrangement that seems universal, directly rooted in biology, and inevitable, it can be changed. . . . The elimination of the present organization of parenting [so that] children could be dependent at the outset on people of both genders . . . depends on the conscious organization and activity of all women and men who recognize that their interests lie in transforming the social organization of gender and eliminating sexual inequality.[16]

Simone de Beauvoir yokes the family with private property as the two chief sources of human misery:

Since the oppression of women has its cause in the will to perpetuate the family and to keep patrimony intact, woman escapes complete dependence to the degree to which she escapes from the family; if a society that forbids private property also rejects the family, the lot of women in it is found to be considerably ameliorated.[17]

Letty Pogrebin urges "action on all fronts" from "the first millisecond of birth" on:

everything we do with, to, for and around children— our speaking habits, living styles, adult relationships, chores, academic standards and our way of dealing with punishment, privilege, religion, television, sex, money and love . . . words, actions, reactions, gestures, attitudes and patterns of behavior— your own, your children's, and everyone else's— until you become, almost without trying, proudly and irresistibly antisexist.[18]

The allusion to speaking habits is prompted by research indicating that parents address male and female babies differently. Pogrebin advises parents to cancel this effect by practicing their full vocal ranges in talking to infants of either sex, "to learn to *hear* sexism before it rises in our throats."[19]

Simone de Beauvoir, like the vast majority of feminists, regards the radical alteration of parenting as more than a utopian fantasy. She finds it "easy to visualize" a world "where men and women would be equal,"

for that is precisely what the Soviet Union promised: women trained and raised exactly like men. . . . [M]arriage was to be based on a free agreement that the spouses could break at will; maternity was to be voluntary; pregnancy leaves were to be paid for by the State, which would assume charge of the children, signifying not that they would be *taken away* from their parents, but that they would not be *abandoned* to them.[20]

De Beauvoir is so far from alone among feminists in admiring Marxist-Leninism that this admiration, together with hostility to "capitalism," can be considered virtually a further distinguishing mark of feminism. The main criticism offered of the Soviet Union is that it has not gone far enough. Kate Millett sides with Trotsky against Lenin because "there was no realization [on Lenin's part] that while every practical effort should be made to implement a sexual revolution, the real test would be in changing attitudes."[21] To be sure, feminists are attracted primarily to the ideas that the Soviet state proclaims itself as embodying, rather than to the Soviet regime itself, but with that understood, a great many well-known feminists, including de Beauvoir, Millett, Firestone, Bleier, Mitchell, Chodorow, MacKinnon, Steinem, Sheila Rowbotham, Margaret Benston, Angela Davis, Eli Zaretsky, Evelyn Reed, Barbara

Ehrenreich, Vivian Howe, and Rayna Rapp identify themselves as socialists or Marxists of some sort. According to Germaine Greer, "The forcing-house of most of the younger women's liberation groups was the university left wing."[22] Catharine MacKinnon explains the link between feminism and Marxism in more general terms:

As the organized expropriation of the work of some for the benefit of others defines a class—workers—the organized expropriation of the sexuality of some for the use of others defines the sex, woman. Heterosexuality is its structure, gender and family its congealed forms, sex roles its qualities generalized to social persona, reproduction a consequence, and control its issue. [Marxism and feminism] argue, respectively, that the relations in which many work and few gain, in which some fuck and others get fucked, are the prime moments of politics.[23]

There is no doubt that the founders of Marxism were feminists. In *The Origin of the Family*, Engels wrote:

It will be plain that the first condition for the liberation of the wife is to bring the whole female sex into public industry and that this in turn demands the abolition of the monogamous family as the economic unit of society. Monogamous marriage comes on the scene as the subjugation of the one sex by the other. . . . The emancipation of woman will be possible only when . . . domestic work no longer claims anything but an insignificant portion of her time.

Now, there is nothing in Marxist *moral* theory that demands identical treatment of the sexes. If each is entitled to what he needs and owes what he can produce, men and women have different entitlements and obligations if they differ biologically in their needs and abilities.[24] At the same time, the Marxist axiom that economic factors are the sole cause of social and personal relations, by precluding any biological factor, does lead immediately to the factual assumptions of feminism. Marxists must, in logical consistency, be feminists.

FEMINISM AND FREEDOM

The claim by feminists to be proponents of liberation, together with widespread feminist sympathy for a tradition hostile to individual liberty, raises the question of just what feminists mean by freedom. The notion of freedom assumed in everyday expressions like "a free afternoon" and "freedom of speech" is noninterference: Speaking freely is saying what one wants to without constraint. This is also the idea of freedom behind everyday ascriptions of responsibility. It has been developed by a long philosophical tradition, and seems to me correct. More pertinently, it is also the idea of freedom implicit in the feminist demand that women be given power and control over their lives. Like all demands for power and control, this one is directed against forces thought to prevent women from doing what they want. Women are unfree under patriarchy because patriarchy prevents them from doing what they want.

One may wonder how women can be said to be unfree in this sense when so much characteristically female behavior is, as it seems to be, quite voluntary. In reply, some feminists straightforwardly deny that women like doing most of what they do, and claim that women do it because they are made to. Ruth Bleier maintains that in the past "for many (most?) heterosexual women sex was either to be neutrally endured or painful or forced and obligatory."[25] Female compliance with male demands is extorted by the threat of rape, wife-beating, and other forms of violence.

An answer somewhat more faithful to the realities of experience (but still a radical answer) is that, while women under patriarchy may be doing what they want, the conditions under which their wants were formed were constrained. Women have had no chance to acquire different wants. Now, that women have not chosen their wants is insufficient reason to deny that women are free, since no one, male or female, chooses his wants. Everyone's wants would have been somewhat different had he been raised differently. If a woman doing what she wishes to do is nevertheless unfree because her wishes were influenced by factors beyond her control, then no one is free. (Some philosophers have drawn precisely this conclusion, but the conclusion that free will is completely illusory is obviously irrelevant to whether women *alone* are unfree, or less free than men). Still, there are cases in which, because of the nature and origin of the motivating want, doing what one wants is nonetheless unfree, and it is to these cases that the ostensibly free actions of women are compared. A brainwashed prisoner does not sign a confession freely, although he may have come to believe in his country's guilt and wish to expose it, because his willingness to sign was forced on him. An Epsilon docilely carrying out his duties in Huxley's *Brave New World* is unfree because someone engineered his personality. Women are said to be similarly unfree when they "voluntarily" subordinate themselves to their husbands: They have been brainwashed to want to.

In a review of the mechanisms for constructing a "difference" and dominance relations between males and females, it becomes clear that such an effort can be effective only if an entire society, particularly the parents, is in agreement with the ultimate goals. Whether there are or are not biological, psychological, or genetic differences, as defined by the "average" male versus the "average" female, is really irrelevant to the task of rearing specific individuals to serve specific functions. A society has the infinite capacity for flexibility, and the socialization of its members can maximize or minimize any differences that might exist. One is reminded of Huxley's *Brave New World,* in which differential treatment is carried to any extreme: where individuals are born and bred to specific tasks and are isolated from any alternative life style. They have no option to choose. Value systems can be designed to promote acceptance of the difference and roles. Value systems can isolate individuals of different groups from one another. We are not approaching a brave new world. We have been living in it, although it is not quite as efficient as Huxley's nor as complex in its groups and role projections.[26]

Before the brainwashing hypothesis can be examined directly, its empirical and conceptual presuppositions must be extracted. Several factors distinguish a victim of brainwashing from ordinary people, whose preferences have also ultimately been caused by external forces. The most salient factor is the contrast between his posttreatment personality and his considerably richer original personality which, but for the treatment, he would still have. Had things been different, the prisoner would not be confessing, zombie-like, to imaginary crimes. The zombie-like manner is itself a major element in the popular idea of brainwashing. Huxley's Epsilons are less than autonomous not primarily because someone limited their preferences by

impoverishing their prenatal environment, but because their range of activities is abnormally narrow. If the prisoner emerges clear-eyed and responsive from the brainwashing session, *a new personality* has been created, and the uncoerced acts of this new personality are fully free.[27] Even metaphorically calling the average woman brainwashed, therefore, attributes to her an underlying personality far richer than the one she displays under patriarchy, and assumes that she, along with the average man, could have developed a range of preferences far wider than those she actually exhibits. Both attributions assume, in turn, that the human personalities currently on view are not significantly determined by biological factors, an assumption inconsistent with Mintz's dismissal of biological factors as irrelevant. (It should anyway be apparent that Mintz is making strong environmentalist assumptions when she speaks of society as infinitely flexible and capable of minimizing sex differences to any extent.)

The idea that voluntary sex-typed behavior is inauthentic explains the readiness to call for state action that is prominent in the feminist political agenda. The inauthentic preferences now enslaving people will change when, but only when, people stop acting in ways which perpetuate them. Reform therefore requires that people temporarily act against their own preferences and those of others until everyone's new behavior generates more authentic preferences. The problem is starting the process, since no one will wish to adopt the meritorious but unorthodox practices before they are adopted by everyone else. In the language of economics, feminist reform presents a coordination problem: how to get people to adopt a practice that benefits all when all follow it, but disadvantages anyone who follows it when others do not.[28] The first children raised nonsexistly will be subject to environmental countercues like their playmates' ridicule; as few pioneers will subject their children to ridicule in the name of an ideal, nonsexist childrearing will not work unless everyone does it. Worse, freeloaders can take advantage of local antisexist behavior. An employer who continues to hire on merit and pay market wages will outcompete any business rival who hires female role models without regard to merit and pays them their "comparable worth" without demanding increased productivity. An employer who establishes in-house day-care to accommodate female employees may suffer if his competitors choose to attract the cheapest labor force without regard to the convenience of females.

The accepted solution for coordination problems is to have the state *make* everyone act in the individually adverse but collectively beneficial way. Everyone wants a lighthouse, but private parties cannot finance one by renting its light to seafarers, since freeloaders need only sail near a lessor to catch the free spillover light. Everyone is waiting for everyone else to subscribe to the lighthouse fund, and to everyone's regret, the lighthouse is not built. At this point the government, able to exact payment from everyone, steps in to build the lighthouse with taxes or user's fees. There is no longer room to try to outmaneuver suckers, and all the would-be maneuverers are better off.

The various antisexism scenarios we will examine suggest a parallel resolution: avert the adverse consequences of antisexism by denying people the liberty to refuse to go along with antisexist reforms. Feminists are prone to look to the government not because they like to see other people pushed around, but because their plans require a coordinating mechanism. As this is being written,[29] for instance, Congress has before it a proposal to require all employers to grant four months' maternity leave to pregnant employees, on the grounds that many employers now replace women who leave their jobs to have children. Such a law is needed, if it is, precisely because employers who do not automatically grant maternity leave enjoy a competitive advantage over those who do, and will act to gain that advantage if not forbidden by law.

There is of course no *logical* link between feminism and advocacy of state intervention. Just as a libertarian can consistently regret the failure of private action to secure the advantages of a lighthouse, all the while insisting that construction of a lighthouse exceeds the bounds of permissible state action, so a libertarian feminist can consistently hold sex roles to be unjust artifacts while insisting that the co-ordinating mechanisms needed to eliminate sex roles—such as mandatory maternity leave—exceed the bounds of permissible state action. Still, the libertarian feminist remains committed to the same empirical theory about society that actuates her more statist sisters, and the ranks of libertarian feminism are bound in any event to remain thin, since it is psychologically difficult to regard a situation as extremely unjust without wishing to deploy the power of the state against it. In point of logic feminists' aims cannot be achieved without state coercion, and in point of fact those who subscribe to feminist theory will tend to endorse state action.

The need to start anew with a clean slate also explains the readiness to misrepresent reality. Like a concern with every facet of life and the conviction that expressed preferences are inauthentic, the impulse to suppress discordant empirical facts is a trait common to all totalitarian ideologies. This impulse is rooted in two fears. One is the fear that persisting memories of the old ways may prove attractive to those embarked on the initially difficult new ways. The second is the fear that reality itself amounts to a validation of sorts; the old ways cannot be all that bad if people are demonstrably getting along while following them. Legitimation by reality is best opposed not by an outright denial of the facts—which only calls them to people's attention—but by the pretense that they never existed. A major goal of totalitarian education thus becomes the creation of a new order by making it seem already in place. In 1964 Alice Rossi advocated ending "class excursions into the community . . . to introduce American children to building, construction, airports or zoos," because "going out into the community this way, youngsters would observe men and women in their present occupational roles." She recommended instead "having children see and hear a woman scientist or doctor; a man dancer or artist; both men and women who are business executives, writers and architects."[30] While Rossi has developed second thoughts about the feasibility of these ideas, they remain central to the thinking of other feminists.

INNATE SEX DIFFERENCES AGAIN

The average person familiar with the public debate would unquestionably include complete environmentalism in any definition of feminism, and feminists themselves have repeatedly proclaimed this tenet.[31] This inclusion is correct on logical as well as textual grounds. So far as feminist plans go, it is pointless to aspire toward an ideal of sexual equality that biology renders impossible. The goal of releasing personalities far richer than those people now possess is likewise pointless if people have their present personalities courtesy of biology and lack any underlying personalities to be released. But it is in its evaluative role that feminism depends most crucially on environmentalism. If the broad features of human society flow from innately programmed preferences of men and women, these features are not products of oppression, and the feminist indictment of them as such is in error. Whether the assignment of sex roles is a device to keep women in thrall depends on how this assignment came about and how it is sustained. It is not an oppressive device if it came about because men and women for the most part innately prefer things the way they are, or as an unintended consequence of preferences. (Compare: The bridge of the nose is not a device *for* keeping eyeglasses in place unless the bridge of the nose came into existence because it supports eyeglasses and continues to exist because it supports eyeglasses.) Like any finding of wrong, the feminist critique of society rests on a prior theory of fact, in this case a factual theory about the causes of the relations between the sexes. Legal verdicts are based on factual findings; after instructing the jury as to what sort of act counts as a crime, the judge asks them to decide whether an act of that sort was committed. A charge of theft is rebuttable by the factual showing that the accused robber received the wallet as a gift. By the same token, a charge of discrimination is rebuttable by showing (for instance) that the numerical preponderance of men in positions of power came about through individual choices.

It is precisely because the legitimacy of the position of men depends on the way in which men got their position that feminists argue that men have gotten where they are because women have been prevented from reaching (or aspiring to) those same positions, i. e. that women *would have gotten* those positions but for being interdicted. It is not a desire for rhetorical effect but the logic of the argument that leads Janet Richards to say that "all social arrangements . . . *were designed to ensure that women should be in the power and service of men,*"[32] and Kate Millett to describe sex as "an arrangement whereby one group of persons is con-

trolled by another."[33] The case against patriarchy cannot allow that men run things because men are more interested than women in running things. The case hinges on a question of fact, and we must heed the injunction of Mao Zedong: "No investigation, no right to speak!"

However, because it is possible to *say* that one recognizes innate sex differences without really doing so, this investigation must await a survey of common evasions—a survey also intended to verify that environmentalism is indeed the *nervus probandi* of feminism in all its forms.

Perfunctory Acknowledgement Followed by Silence

For instance, while the HEW document cited above seems to admit the possibility of nonsocial causes of sex segregation ("part of the answer is 'socialization'"), this possibility is not mentioned thereafter in the document, or in any of the dozens of references it cites. At other times, the concession that there are *some* innate nonanatomical sex differences is followed, inconsistently, by denial of the innateness of any specific sex difference that is brought up in context.

A variant form of pseudoconcession is covered by tenet 1a and illustrated by the citation from Marian Lowe: Sex differences exist but are irrelevant to any actual or possible society. It is sometimes difficult to see that this is what an author is up to, since one way to treat a factor as *ir*relevant is simply to fail to treat it as relevant. Thus Jessie Bernard begins *Women, Wives, Mothers* with the statement: "Men and women are different. A highly sophisticated corpus of research documents biological, psychological, social and cultural differences between them."[34] However, after a review of the evidence documenting the "inferior status of women" (in which the corpus of research cited at the outset is heavily criticized), Bernard concludes that a "new society" based on an "information net" will soon coalesce around "the values characterizing women up to now." Since Bernard neglects to consider the possibility that the sex differences conceded initially might bear on the possibility of this new order, she has in effect withdrawn her concession. Once again, a difference assumed to make no difference is assumed to be no difference.

Describing Innate Sex Differences as Small

This tactic figures prominently in discussions of the difference between male and female mean scores on mathematics aptitude tests, which Ruth Bleier (along with a great many others) dismisses as "small" and "almost trivial."[35] Calling this or any other sex difference small carries the implication that it is *too* small to explain any socially observed sex difference, and perhaps that the innate difference is too small to *deserve* to play a significant causal role.

The trouble with this idea is the absence of any standard for the size of a sex difference apart from the extent of its influence on the structure of society. One cannot first decide that a sex difference is small and conclude therefrom that it cannot be responsible for some given social phenomenon; one must first determine what phenomena can be explained by the difference in question and from that determination decide whether the difference is large or small. It is easy to see in the physical sciences that the importance of a factor cannot be assessed a priori. Even though the difference between the two natural isotopes of uranium is "only" three neutrons (about 1 percent of the atomic weight of uranium), those three neutrons determine whether an explosive chain reaction can be sustained—a large difference indeed. The same holds in the biosocial world. A small mean difference in mathematical aptitude also means small discrepancies at the extremes of the bell curve—it means, for instance, that 99.9 percent of the population above a certain percentile will be male. If mathematical creativity should turn out to require an aptitude drawn from that percentile, then virtually all important mathematical discoveries will be made by males, the general population will perceive mathematics as a male activity, relatively able girls will not aspire to success in mathematics—and the "small" mean difference will have had a major social effect.

It might seem doubtful to someone unfamiliar with automobiles that the twenty gallons of gasoline an automobile carries in its fuel tank is a big enough part of the automobile to be what makes it go. And no doubt the gasoline could not make the car go without the intervening mechanisms of combustion chamber, drive shaft, and axles. Still, it is the combustion of gasoline that makes cars go; no further causal variable is required. There is no way to estimate the importance of gasoline a priori; you have to determine its role in the system to which it belongs. Nor can you decide in advance that a sex difference is small. To do so is to assume that it is causally irrelevant to the system to which it belongs, and hence, in effect, nonexistent.

Appeal to the Fact/Value Gap

This is probably the most frequently cited reason for waving aside the question of sex differences. It begins from the truism that the way people *are* does not dictate how they *should* be. In particular, it is argued, the appropriate attitude to take toward sex differences, whatever they may be, is that they are raw material to be shaped in accordance with our values. It is the values that should be the object of primary concern. Maccoby and Jacklin conclude their survey of sex differences on this note:

We suggest that societies have the option of minimizing rather than maximizing sex differences through their socialization practices. A society could, for example, devote its energies more toward moderating male aggression than toward preparing women to submit to male aggression. . . . It is up to human beings to select those [institutions] that foster the life styles they most value.[36]

Christine Pierce holds that nothing follows if men are instinctively more aggressive than women: "Perhaps women are needed to rescue men from being caught up in their own anatomical destiny."[37] Janet Richards compares male dominance to rape:

Even if men are naturally inclined to dominance it does not follow that they ought to be allowed to run everything. Their being naturally dominant might be an excellent reason for imposing special restrictions to keep their nature under control. We do not think that men whose nature inclines them to rape ought to be given free rein to go around raping, so why should the naturally dominant be allowed to go around dominating? . . . If women are weak and need protection, it should have been the men who were controlled.[38]

This argument is often supplemented with a dilemma constructed by Mill: If sex roles are biologically unalterable, feminist reforms will not change them; and if sex roles *are* alterable, feminist reforms must be judged on their merits. Either way, there is no need to worry about what is biologically inevitable.

But the question of innate sex differences is not so easily evaded. Once again, since it is irrational to try to do what is known to be impossible, it is irrational not to try to determine whether biology precludes some envisioned reform. What is more, "impossibility" has a somewhat different meaning when applied to physical systems than when applied to homeostatic social systems. The internal state variables of homeostatic systems tend to converge to a relatively small number of values which can persist stably over time. There are states through which a society can temporarily pass which are nonetheless impossible in the sense of being unstable; they are states that no society can occupy permanently. By contrast, a mechanical system like a galaxy cannot even temporarily occupy a mechanically impossible state. It must not be assumed, therefore, that a social innovation possible in the sense that it can be instituted in the short run is also possible in the sense of corresponding to a condition that a society could stably occupy. Indeed, homeostatic systems like societies can occupy physically possible states beyond their elastic limits. These are not unstable states from which the system must rebound, but states from which the system cannot evolve back into stability, and which lead to the system's disintegration. It is obviously possible for all fertile women in a society to refuse to bear children, so that a childless society is possible for one generation, but after that the society will cease to exist.

To put the latter point in different but equivalent terms, "necessary" is meant conditionally in assertions like "sex roles are biologically necessary." To say that sex roles are biologically necessary is to say that there will be sex roles in any existing society. However, no law says that there must be sex roles no matter what—as there is a law that says that any two bodies will attract each other no matter what—since no law says that there must be any societies. It hardly follows, as Mill assumes, that feminist reforms will change nothing if sex roles are biologically necessary. Feminist re-

forms could not, by hypothesis, bring about a society with no sex roles, but the effort to destroy sex roles could in principle destroy society. (It is impossible to drive a car through a brick wall; does this mean that it is all the same whether one tries to drive through a brick wall or not?) I am not here sounding the alarm about any damage that feminism might or might not do; I am simply observing that Mill's argument does presuppose that sex roles are not biologically necessary features of a stable society.

Once it is granted that the mechanism that propels society toward and maintains it in stable states is individual preferences, the question naturally arises as to the *point* of manipulating sex differences in accordance with values. Let it be agreed for a moment that there might be arrangements consistent with biological laws that produce more sexually equal outcomes. Why are those arrangements preferable to the present one, if the present one arose under conditions of equal opportunity? While there is a tradition in social theory which finds equality valuable in itself, most egalitarians value equality because of a presumed causal connection between equality and other valued factors. Thus, when the question is pressed as to what is wrong with the present inequality of results, the reply almost inevitably is that *this inequality could not have come about under conditions of equal opportunity for men and women.* In other words, the wish to see sex differences manipulated toward more equal outcomes is virtually always (if not always clearly) premised on the denial that the present order really is the product of innate preferences. This denial amounts to an empirical theory about the origins of the present order. We may thus expect the ostensibly prospective citation of the fact/value gap to yield sooner or later to the theory that present reality involves the subjugation of women. Richards so yields when she talks of men being "allowed to dominate" under things as they are. Appeal to the fact/value gap as an argument for radical change assumes environmentalism after all.

The final lacuna in feminist appeal to the fact/value gap is obliviousness to the question of who is to select and control the institutions to be fostered if it is decided that male impulses need more controlling than they currently receive. If males really are naturally more dominant, it will always be males who are in charge. The only agency that can prevent males in a human group from dominating it is a more powerful human group. However, one group's intervention in the affairs of another to strip its males of power does not transfer power to the females of the subject group; the real power goes to the dominant members of the dominant group—who will be males if males are more interested in dominance than females. (In forcing a private firm to hire more female managers, the government does not transfer power to the women in the firm; it transfers power to the males running the government.) Talk of controlling male aggression and imposing values on facts is incoherent without the assumption that women are innately as prone to seek power as men.

It is possible to miss this point if individual and collective choice are conflated. Human beings are undeniably capable of making reflective decisions, but this capacity is almost always exercised by individuals in individual circumstances. Institutions are not chosen by anybody; they emerge unintended from those individual decisions. No child is socialized by society. Every child is individually socialized by his parents, and from these private practices evolve shared norms which are logically and causally derivative. Collective decisions can be made by governments—"collective decision making" is no more than a grandiose name for state action—but governments generally concern themselves with sharply defined goals rather than overall social structure. Totalitarian governments have not been able to change social structure appreciably, and democratically enacted social reforms generally codify antecedent unwilled changes in mores.

That societies may differ in their emphasis on "masculine" or "feminine" traits, the status accorded women, and similar variables does not suggest that the character of a society is up to its members. The Swiss did not decide to acquire a reputation for precision. Nor does the variance that has existed in the assignment of sex roles show that significantly greater variation awaits only the will to create it. The variation that is possible is, once again, an empirical question that must be answered before one even begins to ask which variants are desirable.

Appeal to the fact/value gap is often more confusing than clarifying. Once the question of innate sex differences is recast as the question of the best collective response to innate sex differences, the option of letting private individuals do as they please tends to sink from sight. Maccoby and Jacklin take up the significance of sex differences in visual–spatial ability by asking: "If girls are, on the average, less skilled in visual–spatial tasks, does this mean that fewer of them should be admitted to graduate schools in engineering, architecture, and art?"[39] Maccoby and Jacklin cite no advocate of such a proposal, and I have been unable to find any; they frame this issue in this needlessly contentious way because they have fused the question of what sex differences mean for society with the quite different question of what people should do about them.[40] Maccoby and Jacklin fail to consider the possibility that people "should" do nothing beyond allowing students to choose subjects on the basis of their own interests and aptitudes, recognizing that in all likelihood fewer girls than boys will choose architecture if indeed a difference in visual–spatial ability does exist.

The tendency to see every fact as grist for evaluation also fosters misunderstanding about the implications of evolution. It is very frequently argued that, because drives once adaptive may no longer be so, these drives should no longer count. Thus Nancy Chodorow concedes that a hunter–gatherer past selected for aggressiveness in human males and nurturance in human females, but replies that "the [evolutionary] argument is allowed to stand for industrial societies like ours which do not need the division of labor for physical reproduction."[41] Chodorow does not see that the point of the evolutionary argument is not to *justify* sexual dimorphism, but to *establish its existence*. This dimorphism may prompt behavior that is maladaptive in our present environment, but it is silly to criticize evolution as if it were a purposive agent that had slipped. If the question is whether women feel responsible for child care because of conditioning or because of drives which were selected as mankind evolved (and this is the question Chodorow is concerned to answer), it does not matter whether those drives have since become maladaptive if they, not socialization, explain the institution of motherhood.

The Treatment of Innate Drives as Obstacles

Thus Betty Friedan:

Even if it were true that all societies so far have been patriarchal and dominated by men, and even if that dominance is based on biological differences, it is irrelevant to the situation forcing women to demand equal opportunity in America and Britain today. Even if they are sorely handicapped by lack of testosterone it is inescapably necessary for women at this stage in human evolution to move to equality in society.[42]

This is less a denial of innate sex differences than sheer muddle. Since a handicap is anything that prevents someone from getting what he wants, it is logically impossible for not wanting something to be a handicap to its pursuit. A would-be competitor in a race may be handicapped by external factors like a muddy track or weak hamstrings, but he cannot be handicapped by his own indifference to winning. To treat a person's lack of desire as something that gets in his way is to draw an unreal distinction between *him* and his preferences and personality. If a woman's preferences and personality interfere with her, who is the *she* they interfere with? This abstract self must be conceived as a characterless monad, devoid of desires but nevertheless capable of autonomy. Such a view makes no literal sense, but it makes a kind of emotional sense for those who see so much value in male pursuits and so little value in female pursuits that they cannot believe that women do not want what men do.

"Women Are Better Than Men"

A familiar theme in feminist writing, particularly in the second stage said to have emerged after 1980, is that the world would be a better place if women were leaders because women are less belligerent than men.[43] Whatever its other merits, this idea would seem to involve a strong commitment to innate sex differences.

That commitment, however, is most equivocal because the critical point is left unclear: Is the greater cooperativeness of females innate, or is it the product of female socialization? The overall idea faces difficulty on either interpretation. If female cooperativeness is innate, how are women to reach positions of leadership whose attainment requires competitiveness? If female cooperativeness is learned, how did oppression produce moral superiority? And if oppression does produce morally superior beings, using female cooperativeness to ensure peace requires the perpetuation of the oppressive apparatus that produces it—a requirement at odds with the goal of liberation. The more popular second-stage writers, like Ehrenreich and Dowling, never explicitly contest environmentalism and so far as I can tell would be loath to attribute the female's superior moral nature to an innate program. But the ambivalence of the second stage surfaces very clearly in Carol Gilligan's work on sex differences in moral thinking. Gilligan received much attention for arguing that female moral judgement is distinguished by "an overriding concern with relationships and responsibilities . . . a world composed of relations rather than of people standing alone, a world that coheres through human connection rather than through systems of rules."[44]

This finding would seem to amount to no more than the common sense of the matter, which would have been derided as sexist stereotyping had it not been published by a woman. It certainly would not have surprised Freud, who held that the male superego must impose stricter, more impersonal rules to control the male's greater aggressiveness. The only interesting question raised by the cognitive-affective sex differences Gilligan identifies is their origin, and Gilligan firmly distances herself from any nativist interpretation: "No claims are being made about the origins of the differences described. . . . Clearly, these differences arise in a social context in which factors of socialization and power combine with reproductive biology."[45] Gilligan stresses the cooperative character of the games girls play as a contributor to the female moral style—without asking why girls choose cooperative games in the first place—and she leaves the overall impression that the female moral style is inculcated through early training. Separated from a nativist interpretation, Gilligan's conclusions come to little more than the triviality that groups raised in different environments, as boys and girls are said to be, develop different norms. It is not, after all, surprising that nomadic Arabs living on a harsh desert should value death in combat more than do contemporary Chicagoans. There is no distinctive female moral voice if men would have spoken in the same tones had they been raised as women are.

As it emerges, Gilligan's ultimate aim is less to explain the female voice than to chide society for ignoring it: "Sex differences in aggression are usually interpreted by taking the response as the norm, so that the absence of aggression in women is identified as the problem to be explained."[46] She cites no-one who regards female lack of aggression as a problem (Betty Friedan and Germaine Greer[47] come to mind), but Gilligan's use of sex differences is perhaps the distinguishing trait of "second-stage" feminism. To the very uncertain extent that innate sex differences are recognized, they become vehicles for expressing dissatisfaction at society's failure to accommodate the female nature—now described as complementary or superior to men's. The diabolization of men continues, with men now being blamed for the mistakes of first-stage feminism. If first-stage feminists imposed an impossible "superwoman" ideal on women, the tensions experienced by women trying to "have it all" are laid to their copying male standards.[48] Men are blamed for a high divorce rate. Taking a position indistinguishable from the first stage, Barbara Ehrenreich explains that a marriage in which the woman depends on a man to earn a living is inherently unstable. The existence of female nurturance, regarded as a new discovery, is seen as opening new possibilities for rapprochement between men and women, the tapping of long-ignored nonmasculine thoughts and feelings, a new appreciation for the female world view, a new emphasis on the feminine in men, and dismay at what has been lost through the universal dominance by men of extrafamilial pursuits and female domination of child-rearing.

Dissatisfaction with the present social order, moreover, leads second-stage feminists to the same practical recommendations as were advocated by first-stage feminists on environmentalist grounds. In *The Second Stage* Betty Friedan develops the view of testosterone as a handicap into a call for the total reorganization of society around women's "beta consciousness." Friedan remains adamant about quotas, an expanding female presence in the military, public funding for abortion, comparable worth, and along with Benjamin Barber, the "unfinished business" of the Equal Rights Amendment.[49] Other second-stage feminists continue to call for special preferences for women and for a statistical equality of outcome which, one would have thought, made sense only on environmentalist grounds. Elizabeth Wolgast begins *Equality and the Rights of Women* by stating: "We need an alternative to egalitarian reasoning" because "society does not create all the differences" between men and women.[50] It is better, she says, to "allow for various differences between the sexes,"[51] but the provisions she suggests are oddly atavistic:

Such a bivalent view provides a justification for affirmative action policies because it rejects a neutral perspective from which the concerns of both sexes can be seen "objectively." [Society] should not adopt linear scales for distinguishing all individuals regardless of sex. It suggests that men and women of talent, for example, will not generally match on the same set of parameters, and therefore, if a single standard is assumed and if that should be drawn from a sample of males, the comparison with a sample of women may be invidious. Without awareness of the possible range of differences between the sexes, this linear approach to merit must be treated with suspicion.[52]

Does the use of innate sex differences as a stick for continuing to beat society and demand special treatment at least imply recognition of innate sex differences? Not at all, for, so far as I can tell, second-stage feminists agree with first-stage feminists that the organization of sex roles is to no significant extent the result of innate sex differences. To say that marriage must be changed to accommodate female needs is precisely to assume that female needs have nothing to do with the shape of marriage as it presently exists. It is this refusal to see social institutions as connected to the innate sex differences they say they recognize that accounts for the felt propriety of the term *feminist* to describe the authors I have cited.

It will not do to pretend that second-stage feminism is entirely coherent. While many one-time feminists are no longer able to deny altogether the existence of biologically based sex differences, they are at the same time unwilling to admit that women *lack* any of the traits that men have. Naturally, no social institution can accommodate creatures who are amalgams of men and women, so much social reconstruction remains to be done: "Justice in social relations preserves (or creates) political and economic equality in the face of different roles, distinctive gender needs. . . . [T]he challenge of third stage feminism is how to make "different but equal" a reality, not because differences are ineluctable, but because equality is valuable only when it encourages rather than destroys them."[53]

NOTES

1. Peter Singer, "Ten Years of Animal Liberation," *New York Review of Books* (January 17, 1985): 52.

2. Richard Wasserstrom, "On Racism and Sexism," in *Today's Moral Problems,* 2nd ed., ed. Richard Wasserstrom (New York: Macmillan, 1981), pp. 96–97.

3. John Stuart Mill, *The Subjection of Women* (1869), ch. 1; Simone de Beauvoir, *The Second Sex,* trans. H. M. Parshley (New York: Knopf, 1953), p. 513; Millett, *Sexual Politics,* ch. 1, sec. 2, p. 2; Shulamith Firestone, *The Dialectic of Sex* (New York: Morrow, 1970), p. 1; Steinem (cited by Carol Felsenthal), "How Feminists Failed," *Chicago* (June 1982): 139; Member of NOW, cited in Muriel Carden, *The New Feminist Movement* (New York: Russell Sage, 1974), p. 12; Jessie Bernard, "The Paradox of the Happy Marriage," in Gornick and Moran, *Woman in Sexist Society,* p. 159; National Institute of Education Request for Proposal RFP-NIE-R-80-0018, Department of Health, Education, and Welfare, National Institute of Education (Washington, D. C.: April 30, 1980), p. 1; Alison Jaggar, "On Sexual Equality," *Ethics* 84 (July 1984): 276; Judith Long Laws, *The Second X* (New York: Elsevier, 1979), p. 372; Janet Richards, *The Sceptical Feminist* (Boston: Routledge & Kegan Paul, 1980), pp. 273–84; Marion Lowe, "The Dialectics of Biology and Culture," in *Women's Nature,* ed. Marian Lowe and Ruth Hubbard (New York: Pergamon, 1983), p. 56; Rosalind Petchesky, *Abortion and Women's Choice* (New York: Pergamon, 1984), pp. 176–82; Ruth Bleier, *Science and Gender* (New York: Pergamon, 1984), pp. 176–82.

4. Alice Rossi, "Equality between the Sexes: An Immodest Proposal," *Daedalus* 93 (1964): 608–10.

5. Alice Rossi, "A Biosocial Perspective on Parenting," *Daedalus* 106 (1977): 1–2.

6. Carden, p. 11. The parochial reference to toy manufacturers and authors of children's books—factors irrelevant to the vast majority of societies—illustrates the difficulty of interpreting feminism charitably.

7. Claire Fulenwider, *Feminism in American Politics* (New York: Praeger, 1980), p. 56.

8. Ibid., p. 23.

9. Ibid., pp. 30–35.

10. Ibid., p. 47.

11. Ibid., p. 56.

12. Helen Hacker, "Women as a Minority Group," in *Who Discriminates against Women?,* ed. Florence Denmark (Beverly Hills, Ca.: Sage, 1974), p. 134; Ralph Stern, letter, *New York* (January 31, 1983): 5; Christopher W. Morris, "Existential Limits to the Rectification of Past Wrongs," *American Philosophical Quarterly* 21 (April 1984): 177.

13. *Frontiero v. Richardson,* 411 US 677 (1973).

14. Anne Fausto-Sterling considers this possibility in *Myths of Gender.*

15. Nancy Chodorow, *The Reproduction of Mothering* (Berkeley, Ca.: University of California Press, 1978), p. 81; Juliet Mitchell, *Psychoanalysis and Feminism* (New York: Pantheon, 1974), cited in Chodorow, p. 81.

16. Ibid., pp. 214–19.

17. *The Second Sex,* p. 89.

18. Letty Pogrebin, *Growing Up Free* (New York: McGraw-Hill, 1980), pp. 516–17. Miss Pogrebin describes herself as a "moderate" situated midway between "traditionalists" and "radicals."

19. Ibid., p. 130.

20. *The Second Sex,* pp. 724–26.

21. *Sexual Politics,* p. 85.

22. See Germaine Greer, *The Female Eunuch* (New York: McGraw-Hill, 1970), pp. 313–29.

23. Catharine MacKinnon, "Feminism, Marxism, Method, and the State: An Agenda for Theory," *Signs* 7 (1982): 516–17.

24. The Soviet government for its part continues to move away from unisex equality. In 1981 it barred women from 460 jobs, apparently in response to health problems caused by women working under the same conditions as men. See Alexandra Biryukova, *Soviet Women: Their Role in Society, the Economy, the Trade Unions* (Moscow: Profizdat Publishers, 1981), pp. 31–41.

25. *Science and Gender,* p. 180.

26. Ellen Mintz, "The Prejudice of Parents," in Denmark, pp. 21–22.

27. But what became of the old personality? Has murder been done? These questions are obscure, but only because the suppositions that raise them are so contrary to fact. It is seldom helpful to assimilate ordinary behavior to abnormal behavior understood by its contrast with the normal. The position I defend in *Metaphysics and the Mind–Body Problem* (Oxford: Oxford University Press, 1979) is that free action is based on preferences one at least tacitly approves of. Thus, brainwashing victims do not act freely because nobody wants to have his preferences produced by brainwashing.

28. See R. Duncan Luce and Howard Raiffa, *Games and Decisions* (New York: Wiley, 1957), ch. 5.

29. May 1986.

30. "Immodest Proposal," p. 643.

31. "Biology is not enough to answer the question: Why is woman the *Other?*" (de Beauvoir). Elizabeth Janeway finds "little need to believe that men and women are born with psychological differences built into their brains because the workings

of society and culture, by themselves, are perfectly capable of producing all the differences we know so well" (*Man's World, Woman's Place* [New York: Morrow, 1971], p. 10); Letty Pogrebin's list of the "*real* differences between the sexes" comprises "voice, appearance, size and feel" (*Growing Up Free,* p. 315). Anne Oakley has her doubts about Kate Millett's "difference in orgasmic capacity"; she takes anatomical research to show that "the ultimate sexual response, the orgasm, is physiologically identical in male and female, except for the minor difference of organ and secretion" (*Sex, Gender, and Society* [New York: Harper & Row, 1972], p. 128). Feminists with impeccable scientific credentials say the same things. Here is Estelle Ramey: "As an endocrinologist, I think virtually all the differences in male and female behavior are culturally, not hormonally, determined. . . . It is said, for instance, that men are innately more aggressive than women. But conditioning, not sex hormones, makes them that way. Anyone seeing women at a bargain-basement sale—where aggression is viewed as appropriate—sees aggression that would make Atilla the Hun turn pale."

32. Richards, p. 138.

33. Miss Millett contends that there were prehistoric societies in which men did not "control" women, but admits (p. 27ff.) that there is no evidence for them.

34. Chicago: Aldine, 1975.

35. *Science and Gender,* p. 109.

36. Eleanor Maccoby and Carol Jacklin, *The Psychology of Sex Differences* (Stanford: Stanford University Press, 1974), p. 374.

37. "Natural Law Language and Women," in Gornick and Moran, p. 255.

38. *The Sceptical Feminist,* p. 44. Maccoby and Jacklin observe that the one message communicated to children more than all others combined is that boys should not fight. Their unawareness of how much socialization is devoted to controlling male aggression suggests that feminists like Pierce and Richards are unfamiliar with raising children.

39. *The Psychology of Sex Differences,* p. 366.

40. Maccoby and Jacklin attribute to Steven Goldberg the view that "where a biological basis exists, it behooves societies to socialize their children in such ways as to emphasize and exaggerate the difference" (ibid., p. 373). Goldberg argues only that societies *will* end up emphasizing sex differences, and he explicitly disavows the view Maccoby and Jacklin attribute to him: "I suspect that I shall also be criticized as having suggested that society *should* emphasize sex differences in its socialization. What society *should* do is a question that cannot be answered on scientific grounds and it is one that I do not concern myself with here." (*The Inevitability of Patriarchy,* 2nd ed. [London: Temple-Smith, 1977], p. 107).

41. *The Reproduction of Motherhood,* p. 21.

42. Betty Friedan, review of Goldberg, *New Statesman* (September 23, 1977): 44.

43. See e.g. Gloria Steinem, "What Would It Be Like if Women Win," in *The American Sisterhood,* ed. Wendy Martin (New York: Harper & Row, 1970), pp. 184–88. On the "second stage," see Betty Friedan, *The Second Stage* (New York: Simon & Schuster, 1981); Susan MacMillan, *Women, Reason, and Nature* (Princeton, N. J.: Princeton University Press, 1983); Janet Sayers, *Biological Politics* (New York: Methuen, 1982); Elizabeth Wolgast, *Equality and the Rights of Women* (Cornell: Cornell University Press, 1981); Barbara Ehrenreich, *The Hearts of Men* (New York: Doubleday, 1983); Colette Dowling, *The Cinderella Complex* (New York: Summit, 1981); Carol Gilligan, *In a Different Voice* (Cambridge, Mass.: Harvard University Press, 1983); Jean Bethke Elshtain, "Feminism, Family and Community," *Dissent* (November 1982): 442–49.

44. *In a Different Voice,* p. 29.

45. Ibid., p. 2.

46. Ibid., p. 43.

47. Thus Greer in *The Female Eunuch:* "What happens to the Jewish boy who never manages to escape the tyranny of his mother is exactly what happens to every girl whose upbringing is 'normal.' She is a female faggot. Like the male faggots she lives her life in a pet about guest lists and sauce bernaise, except when she is exercising by divine maternal right the same process that destroyed her lusts and desires upon the lusts and desires of her children. . . . She is a vain, demanding, servile bore."

48. See Suzanne Gordon, "The New Corporate Feminism," *The Nation* (February 5, 1983): 143–47.

49. Benjamin Barber, "Beyond the Feminist Mystique," *The New Republic* (July 11, 1983): 26–32.

50. *Equality and the Rights of Women,* pp. 16, 126.

51. Ibid., p. 126.

52. Ibid., p. 127.

53. "Beyond the Feminist Mystique," p. 32. "Not ineluctable" betrays the lingering tendency to deny sex differences in the crunch. In cataloguing evasions of innate sex differences, I have omitted simple inconsistency, as practiced for instance by Mill. At various junctures in *The Subjection of Women* he says: "There will never prove to be any natural tendencies common to women, and distinguishing their genius from men," "no-one is thus far entitled to any positive opinion on the subject," and "in accordance with the best general conclusions which the world's imperfect experience seems as yet to suggest, the general bent of their talents is toward the practical." It is ironic that contemporary feminists should disdain the reforms Mill argued for and helped win, while embracing his confused arguments.

MELINDA VADAS

A First Look at the Pornography/Civil Rights Ordinance: Could Pornography Be the Subordination of Women?

For a philosopher immersed in the analytic tradition, the "pornography issue" may be puzzling. This issue has been subjected, as the years of its tenure *as* an issue have increased, to a more and more complex analysis. The very definition of pornography has expanded, almost geometrically, from a few words to a few paragraphs to a few pages.[1] Early in the literature—a literature which now seems as quaint as the cosmological visions of the pre-Socratics—the general motivation for discussion and analysis seemed to be to explain why "dirty pictures," though perhaps not everyone's cup of tea, were not particularly harmful,[2] and were certainly nothing that a sane, liberal-minded society would restrict *by law*[3] (Lord Devlin's model society not being sane in its reliance on subjectivism and certainly not liberal-minded in its legislation of the good[4]).

In those dear dead days of simplicity, to have suggested that pornography itself (and not its censorship or actionability) had a direct relation not to questions of mere value or virtue but to questions of *justice*—and justice in the strictest deontological sense, not some utilitarian simulacrum—would have been seen as confused, irrational, or duplicitous.[5]

Then feminists began looking at pornography, most of them writing outside the analytic tradition and many writing outside of any (academic) philosophical tradition whatever.[6] Articles were written, definitions abounded, these were criticized and (usually) expanded; pornography was examined from every (as it were) angle. On some accounts, pornography started

to look pretty bad.[7] (Of course, in the intervening years, pornography itself had got worse, more violent, more "sick," and so on.) Still, the question of what all this—"this" representing perhaps a state of extreme disvalue—had to do with *justice* was not made clear.

THE ANALYSIS OF PORNOGRAPHY: A HISTORY THAT ENDS IN A CATEGORY MISTAKE?

Now we have, as I see it, the conceptual culmination of this newer feminist investigation into pornography encoded in what is most often referred to as the Dworkin/MacKinnon ordinance.[8] The ordinance was written by Andrea Dworkin, a feminist writer, and Catharine MacKinnon, a feminist lawyer. Dworkin and MacKinnon had been hired by the city of Minneapolis to develop an ordinance that would help the city control the problems related to "adult" material. The ordinance they wrote was passed by the city council, but vetoed by the mayor. It has since gone through various court battles at various levels of the American legal system, being most recently summarily dismissed by the Supreme Court. No doubt some form of it will surface again. In any case, it is not the ordinance's legal status that interests me here. I am interested rather in its status as containing a possibly meaningful philosophical claim. "Pornography," the ordinance states, "is the graphic sexually explicit subordination of women. . . ." This definition of pornography

From *Journal of Philosophy* LXXXIV (1987): 487–511. Copyright © 1987 The Journal of Philosophy, Inc. Reprinted with permission of the author and publisher.

should make any English speaker sit bolt up-right. Note the use of the "is" of identity between "pornography" and ". . . subordination." Now that is peculiar. And the peculiarity is not, as is usually the case in law, a function of mere legal jargonizing—the party-of-the-first-part sort of talk—but is *conceptual*.[9] And because the peculiarity is conceptual, it is, I think, philosophically interesting.

A befuddled reader might sensibly react to the Dworkin/MacKinnon definition of pornography as she would, say, to the claim, "Green is where the post office can be found." This statement (or "statement) is also conceptually "off," but not *horribly* so. In fumbling with its near-sense, the mind, being the mind, tries to revive the claim, as in, "Well, the remark must here refer to a board game, like Monopoly, and it is upon the green square that the game's post office is situated." Now the mind can rest, having made complete sense of the remark. In the Dworkin/MacKinnon case, the reader striving for sense might translate the given definition by mentally adding a few words, as in "Pornography is the graphic sexually explicit *depiction of the* subordination of women." Now the definition makes perfect sense. But this amended definition is not what the ordinance provides. The ordinance says that pornography is the subordination of women. Has the analysis of pornography ended, thanks to these feminists, with something like what Gilbert Ryle[10] called a category mistake or, to use A. C. Baier's term, a "semi-sentence"?[11] Surely, according to what I call the "reasonable view" of pornography, it would seem so.

PORNOGRAPHY: THE REASONABLE VIEW

The reasonable view of pornography remains straight and strong, the bones beneath the pile of paper flesh generated on this issue. The reasonable view has an incredibly deep and tenacious hold on our common sense and its near relative, our common moral consciousness. This may be because the reasonable view is true or because, though it is not true, it is conceptually welded to something else which is, and we cannot see the point of separation between this coin's true head and its false tail.

Like all moral views, the reasonable view is not unrelated to an epistemology and a metaphysic,[12] though these are not (as they usually are not) directly stated. The reasonable view is simply this: "Pornography is sexually explicit material—pictures on paper or film, or words on a page. Some people enjoy looking at this material; others do not. To forbid by law the production and dissemination of this material[13] is an act of moralistic piety gone unconscionably governmental—or outright tyranny. If you don't like the words, citizen, just don't read the words. If you don't like the pictures, friend, just don't look at the pictures." With some minor adjustments for principles of public offense[14] and property devaluation,[15] pornography on the reasonable view is rather quickly found to be something outside the area of deontological note.[16] The *ease* with which this conclusion is reached might itself give us pause. We might reflect on this ease and we might recall one of Ludwig Wittgenstein's many suggestive remarks: "The decisive moment in the conjuring trick has been made, and it was the very one that we thought quite innocent."[17] So, on the one hand, we have the simple and reasonable view of pornography and, on the other hand, what looks to be a conceptually bizarre view, the Dworkin/MacKinnon view—something coming, almost, from another form of life. And here we may recall another dark saying of Wittgenstein's: "If a lion spoke, we could not understand him" (§7). If Dworkin/MacKinnon is any indication of the radical feminist form of life, some might be tempted to ascribe the same leonine inscrutability to its opaque practitioners.

THE LAW OF NONCONTRADICTION APPLIED TO OUR CASE

Now I assume that, unless we adopt some kind of fashionable relativism,[18] if one of these views of pornography is correct—the reasonable view or the Dworkin/MacKinnon view—the other is not. Either pornography is, at worst, a bad thing[19] which we would rather not have about but which justice requires us to tolerate, or it is, in addition to being a bad thing, something whose production or dissemination is an actual injustice of some particular sort in that it violates the rights of (usually) women.

Although I am, like, I imagine, almost everyone else, strongly attracted to the reasonable view (because it *is* reasonable), the bizarre view expressed by Dworkin/MacKinnon is to me of greater philosophical interest, because and not in spite of its conceptual peculiarity. This peculiarity suggests an entirely new paradigm, a virtually different world—or extreme mental confusion. Leaving open the possibility that it might be the former, I have begun an investigation. Naturally, one cannot examine this "different world" and its plausibility as a conceptual map all at once. In what follows below, I begin, in typical, analytic, immoderately small-potatoes way, to begin to try to determine the answer to what seems to me to be a precedential question, viz., Under what conditions, if any, can a representation (here, a pornographic representation) *literally do*[20] what Dworkin/MacKinnon claims pornography does, that is, subordinate women? Whether or not these conditions of subordination do or could hold in this or any other possible world is, naturally, a subject for another time.

AN EQUIVALENCE

If, as Dworkin/MacKinnon claims, "Pornography is the . . . subordination of women," then I do believe it follows that pornography subordinates women. (If x is the subordination of y, then x subordinates y.) And the reverse entailment is also true; that is, if pornography subordinates women, it follows that pornography is the subordination of women. (If x subordinates y, then x is the subordination of y.) Thus, pornography subordinates women if and only if pornography is the subordination of women. (x subordinates y if and only if x is the subordination of y.) My reason for pointing out this equivalence is heuristic, since it seems that the "shallow" or ordinary grammatical structure of English makes the "x subordinates y" formulation more linguistically ordinary, more idiomatic, than the "x is the subordination of y" formulation. . . .

DIRECT AND PREPOSITIONAL TRANSFER OF VALUE PREDICATES

A *value* predicate is a predicate that ascribes moral or nonmoral goodness or badness itself (where goodness and badness are inclusive of rightness and wrongness) or ascribes that which is morally or nonmorally good or bad to some practice (or nonpractice) object, event, or action. Some value predicates transfer directly from "original" to depiction, and some transfer only prepositionally. An example of a direct transfer of a value predicate from an object to its depiction would be the predicate "is beautiful" as applied to a rose. This value predicate transfers directly from the rose to a photograph of the rose, since the predicate may apply to the depiction in the same sense in which it applies to the rose, and may apply to the depiction because it applies to the rose. On the other hand, the predicate "is a valuable floral specimen," transfers only prepositionally to the depiction of the rose. The depiction is not a valuable floral specimen, rather, it is a depiction *of* a valuable floral specimen.

This direct transfer of value predicates may take place between many practice constituents and their depictions. For example, consider the practice of social etiquette. Within this practice, certain actions shame or disgrace the agent of those actions, whereas others bring the agent social approval or even honor. Mistakenly drinking the water in one's fingerbowl, for example (especially if one slurps it loudly and exclaims, "Great soup!") is an action that would surely disgrace the foolish dinner guest. In describing this incident, we might say, e.g., "Clara was disgraced by this action," or, alternatively and equivalently, "This action disgraces Clara." Does the predicate "disgraces Clara" transfer, though, to a depiction of this unfortunate event? (Let us say that the host's nephew, Elwood, was videotaping the party.) And, if the predicate, "disgraces Clara," does transfer, does it transfer directly or prepositionally? Is Elwood's videotape footage of Clara slurping the water in her fingerbowl a depiction that disgraces Clara? Or is it merely a depiction *of* an action that disgraces Clara? (Again, if the predicate transfers directly, it also transfers prepositionally.) It goes without saying that drinking water in one's fingerbowl is a practice action; its meaning and significance are a function of its practice membership. In another practice, it might represent the height of sophistication and good manners, a point irrelevant here. I believe that critical reflection reveals that the predicate in the above instance transfers directly from the practice action to the depiction of it. Elwood's videotape footage disgraces Clara. The predicate "disgraces Clara" is used with the same meaning when applied to both action and depiction, and it applies to the depiction because it applied to the action. It is not the case that Clara is literally disgraced by the actual drinking and only metaphorically disgraced by Elwood's videotape.

The same direct predicate transfer would occur if the fingerbowl-slurping episode were part of a movie, and Clara a character in that movie. The character would be shamed or disgraced by her actions as revealed in the movie. Here the predicate transfers from this constituent of the practice of social etiquette as an extant material and conceptual construct, rather than from a particular, real-life finger-bowl slurping. (Transfers, we might say, from slurping as a type, rather than a token, to a token.) There may be no value-predicate transfer from the material scene of actress Jane Smith pretending to drink water in a fake fingerbowl to the depiction on the screen.

Let us consider another example of direct predicate transfer of a value predicate. A baseball player has the fans standing in the bleachers, applauding his record-breaking home run. Given the conventions of the practice of baseball—given this ovation's practice identity—this group applause is an action that honors this player. A photograph, taken by a local newspaper reporter, which depicts the standing ovation also honors this player. The predicate "honors this player" transfers directly from the practice constituent (the ovation) to a depiction of it. Again, there is no change in the meaning of the predicate, and the photograph honors the player because the original action honored him.

The following final example of direct predicate transfer of a value predicate is instructive because it illuminates the relationship between the performative power of certain utterances within certain practices (here, "I award you this medal") and the process of predicate transfer.

In an honor-awarding ceremony in the military, the utterances made are performative; that is, the utterances themselves accomplish the task of bestowing honor. The medal wearer is then honored, or continues to be honored, by wearing the medal bestowed in this ceremony. We might say that the "power" of the bestowal of honor moves, in this practice, from the performative utterance to the related object, the medal itself. The soldier so honored now continues to be honored by wearing his medal. A depiction of the soldier wearing his medal also honors the soldier. "Honors this soldier" is here a directly transferring value predicate. The picture honors the soldier in precisely the same sense in which the medal does, and it honors him because the medal does. However, both the medal itself and the photograph honor the soldier in virtue of their relationship to the honor-awarding ceremony of his practice and to the performative utterances of that ceremony.

Generally as the above examples bear out, the value predicates that directly transfer from practice constituents to depictions are those which have a strong notional component—*not* that we can mentally assign the predicates or not, as we might with equal facility think of a red or of a green triangle—but that the practice's assignment of the predicate to the practice constituent is locked within and constrained by the real and interrelated meanings of experience rather than, say, constrained by physical laws or logical impossibilities. Put another way, we can say that these directly transferring value predicates are more closely related to the real social meanings that create our experience than to the material edges of reality, though it *should not be forgotten* that these material edges do have a bearing on this predicate assignment as well (and that the meaning/material distinction is ultimately specious). Reflection and example might reveal these directly transferring value predicates to include "shames," "honors," "degrades," "defames," "exalts," "elevates," and—significantly for the case under examination—"subordinates." . . .

THE IRRATIONAL ASSIGNMENT OF VALUE PREDICATES TO PRACTICE CONSTITUENTS

Suppose that, as may in fact sometime be the case, those who receive medals in the military —and that is to say those who are honored— are men who should not, ideally speaking, be honored. (Suppose that they are Nazi soldiers being honored for killing Jewish civilians.) Can we then say, The photo of this Nazi soldier with his medals is not a photo that *really* honors the soldier, because those medals are *really* a sign of dishonor? This claim, like the claim that the baseball player on his third strike is not really striking out, because it would be objectively better if four strikes were out, is a confusion. It is a misleading way of saying that the practice that awards medals for killing Jews should be abolished. We *can* say that the practice, through its constituent (the medal), presents what is evil as good, and that a depiction of the practice constituent also presents what is evil as good. Indeed, it is this axiological transposition that makes a morally unacceptable practice morally unacceptable.[21] In presenting the dishonorable as honorable, the Nazi practice condemns itself. A photo of a Nazi wearing all his medals for killing Jews is a photo that honors what is evil and dishonorable. The photo honors what it should not because the medals honor what they should not. To say this is not to say that the photo does not *really* honor the soldier, because it does. We could say that those who are honored by practices that honor the dishonorable are thereby and in fact dishonored by being honored in this way, but the locution "not *really* being honored" remains misleading, and it in fact *makes inexplicable* our proper value judgment of the depiction. If the Nazi is not really being honored by this photo, then why is this picture contemptible? In looking at the photo of the Nazi with all his medals, we do *not* say, "Ah, finally this swine has received his just deserts," but rather, "How terrible that anyone would choose to honor such a man."

In sum, when a practice makes this type of axiological transposition (viz., presenting evil as good or good as evil) to say that the given practice constituent is not *really* good or not *really* evil is a confused way of saying that the practice has performed an axiological transposition, and that no practice should perform such a transposition. We cannot go on to suggest either that *this* abhorrent practice should not have performed the given axiological transposition or to suggest that the transposition be undone. We cannot suggest that *this* practice should not have performed the transposition because such a statement implies that the transposition is inessential to the practice's identity, when that is not in fact the case. Axiological

assignments, transposed or not, are part of what sketch out a practice's identity; e.g., part of what gave Nazism its practice identity just was its axiological perversity. And neither can this transposition be undone. The practice's presentation of evil as good or good as evil presents us with a compound meaning for the given constituent which, like all meanings, can never be erased, though, if the transposition is noted within the context of a morally perspicacious society, we may hope that the presentation of this constituent's perverse meaning will fall into disuse.[22]

THE MEANING OF "SUBORDINATION" AS THIS TERM IS USED IN THE PORNOGRAPHY/CIVIL RIGHTS ORDINANCE

Not every action that harms women subordinates women, and not all representations that portray women in a negative light—e.g., representations that make women look foolish or stupid or vain—subordinate women. To subordinate an individual or group of individuals—using the term "subordinate" as I believe it is used within the context of the Pornography/Civil Rights Ordinance[23]—is to place that person or group of persons socially in the class of those whose intrinsic or inherent moral worth or standing is not of the first rank, and whose rights are thereby of lesser scope, importance, or weight than the rights of others. Such a social placement of women into the class of intrinsic moral inferiors would indeed, as the ordinance also says, represent "a substantial threat to . . . the equality of citizens in the community."[24] The social establishment of a group's intrinsic moral inferiority quite naturally leads to their political oppression, and so close is this relationship between the social stamp of intrinsic moral inferiority and political oppression that it is more illuminating to see these disvalues as twin aspects of a single social coin, rather than as held together by a cause-and-effect relationship.

The social assignment of intrinsic moral inferiority to a group of persons—and, that is to say, their subordination—is quite other than a mere assertion of such inferiority, as would be made by the statement, "Women are morally inferior to men," or as might be entailed or implied by the assertion, "Women should be sexually abused by men."[25] The social assign-ment of intrinsic moral inferiority to women, the placement of women in the class of intrinsic moral inferiors, the subordination of women, is an actual, empirical, and not merely or essen-tially linguistic placement, though it is not of course a *physical* placing or moving. One may be assigned a social place without one's body being moved. One may, for example, actually, empirically place or be placed at the bottom of one's graduating class without thereby chang-ing one's spatial–temporal location. One can be subordinated without leaving the house. This fact does not make one's subordination "symbolic" or "metaphorical" any more than the above-mentioned scholastic placement is symbolic or metaphorical.

Although the social assignment of intrinsic moral inferiority to women cannot, by its very nature, be father to the *fact* of women's intrin-sic or inherent moral inferiority (that would re-quire some effort of patriarchal genetic engi-neering in which women were, say, turned into tobacco plants), the assignment to the class of intrinsic moral inferiors is nevertheless a real assignment to a real social category. Such a claim for the existence of an actual social cate-gory of intrinsic moral inferiority raises many questions beyond the scope of this article. One question would be that of the ontological or metaphysical status of the entity (society) that allegedly has these categories. We might ask whether or not it would be illuminating to at-tempt a reduction from the paradigm that speaks of a metaphysically real society to one that speaks only of individuals and their beliefs and attitudes. Briefly, I do not believe that this notion of society and the social can be illu-minatingly explained by reference only to indi-viduals and their mental states even if, as is surely the case, society is in some sense made up of individuals. Reductionistic schemes or paradigms are unwelcome if we lose predictive and explanatory power through the reduction—which is to say, if the adoption of the reductive scheme causes us to lose the *desired* epistemic access to the phenomenon under examination, the reductionistic scheme cannot be recom-mended.[26]

Whether or not a paradigm that has no room

for a metaphysically real notion of society does in fact cause us to lose desired epistemic access to some phenomenon (here, the phenomenon of subordination) cannot be decided, one way or the other, by pointing to the odd falls from validity which occur if we reason across para-digms. From "It is certain that the social place-ment of some group into the class of moral inferiors is unjust" we cannot infer "It is certain that x-x_n's false belief in y-y_n's intrinsic moral inferiority is unjust." The inference will not hold even if we drop the modal operator, "it is certain that," since to believe falsely in anoth-er's moral inferiority is not unjust, but only bad. This fall from validity only illustrates the problem of choosing a paradigm, but does not decide the outcome of that choice.[27]

COULD PORNOGRAPHY BE THE SUBORDINATION OF WOMEN?

If to subordinate someone, in the sense ex-plained, is to place that person socially into the class of intrinsic moral inferiors, then "subordi-nate" is a value predicate. It is among those predicates which may transfer directly from a practice constituent to a depiction of such a con-stituent, provided of course that the conditions for such direct transfer are met. Thus, porno-graphic depictions could subordinate women, if the predicate "subordinates" transfers with-out change of meaning from constituent to depiction and if the predicate applies to the depiction because it applied to the practice con-stituent.[28] As argued above, a predicate may apply to a practice constituent or to a depiction of a practice constituent, even though the as-signment of the predicate is a function of an irrationality that has infected the practice. Just as the Nazi's medals honor what are in fact a despicable man's despicable actions—but hon-or him nonetheless—so constituents in our practice of sexuality and their pornographic de-pictions may subordinate, in the sense of plac-ing the subordinated into the class of moral inferiors, those who are in fact moral equals—but subordinate them nonetheless. Of course, it is as irrational to subordinate moral equals as it is to honor despicable actions, but we cannot, on the grounds of this irrationality, say either "the medals do not honor" or "the depictions do not subordinate."[29]

So it seems that we have an affirmative answer to the precedential question of our investigation into the conceptual structure of the Dworkin/MacKinnon Ordinance, i.e., an affirmative answer to the question, Could pornography be the subordination of women? The seeming conceptual oddity of the ordinance's definition of pornography as "the graphic sexually explicit subordination of women" is revealed as neither odd nor uniquely generated, given the fairly common phenomenon of direct predicate transfer from practice constituents to their depictions.

A BRIEF OUTLINE OF SOME NORMATIVE ENTAILMENTS OF THE ABOVE ANALYSIS

What is wrong with the reasonable view quoted above is that it fails to allow for direct predicate transfer from practice constituents to their depictions, a failure which is compounded by the reasonable view's implicit adoption of a reductionistic paradigm which destroys epistemic access to the phenomenon of subordination, as such subordination is referred to within the context of the ordinance. Thus, the reasonable view does not have conceptual room for naming the production or dissemination of pornography as an injustice, but can at most see such actions as producing a state of mere disvalue. Since there is a morally relevant difference between producing a state of mere disvalue and bringing about an injustice, as well as a morally relevant difference between the additional and further harm engendered by producing a state of mere disvalue and the harm engendered by bringing about an injustice, the reasonable view will have different normative entailments from the civil-rights view.

On the civil-rights view, the additional harm related to producing or disseminating pornography (such as the harm represented by sex crimes) is directly and relevantly related to the producer's or disseminator's contribution toward the creation of women as a subordinated class, a contribution and creation which is itself an injustice. On the reasonable view, any further harm that is causally related to producing or disseminating pornography is related to the permissible, if devalued, action of producing or disseminating this merely depictionary material. On the civil-rights view, the additional harm is akin to that harm caused by a bank robber's pistol waving, which causes a frightened customer to die of a heart attack. The robber may be held responsible for this death, even though he did not intend it, because it is a causal consequence of a certain faulty and risk-creating aspect of his action. On the reasonable view, the harm caused by pornography is akin to that harm caused by my rude rebuff of a fellow bank customer's friendly greeting, which rebuff causes him to die of a heart attack. I cannot be held responsible for this death because, even though it is causally related to my faulty action, the faulty aspect of my action (its rudeness) did not create the risk of death or the realization of that risk. Rude actions do not ordinarily create such risks; and, if we find them faulty, that is not *why* we find them faulty. In the case of the bank robber, however, we can say that his pistol-waving action violated the rights of the bank customers to (among other things) personal safety in a public place, and it was just this faulty aspect of his action which created the risk and the realization of that risk.[30] Unjust actions often, though not always, create such additional risks. On the civil-rights view, it is the sexual subordination of women that is pornography which grounds and explains the faulty aspect of producing or disseminating it, and this faulty aspect creates an additional and further risk, the risk that members of this subordinated class will become the victims of sex crimes. *Why* the initial act of production or dissemination is faulty (because of its contribution to the creation of a subordinated class of persons) and *how* the additional harm (produced by sex crimes) comes about are linked by the faulty aspect of the original act. Actually to contribute to the creation of a class of subordinated people is concomitantly to create the foreseeable risk that they will be victimized by those who are acting in response and relation to this actual subordination. Contributing to the actual creation of such a subordinated class of people is relevantly different from suggesting or recommending that others engage in certain illicit behavior—although the latter may be within the bounds of just action, the former is not.

On the reasonable view, pornography is merely depictionary material, and, though it may be bad or faulty to produce or disseminate such material, in that the material depicts or recommends the subordination of women, the material does not literally or actually subordinate women, and therefore the producers and disseminators of this material are not bringing about a state of affairs in which women are actually subordinated, but are only bringing about a state of affairs in which women are depicted as subordinated. Therefore, these parties are not responsible, on the reasonable view, for what might happen if they *were* to bring about such a state of affairs of actual subordination, for they have not brought about such a state of affairs. On the reasonable view, mere depictions, as such, do not contribute to the creation of the practice identity of women as a subordinated class; thus, in producing or disseminating such depictions one is not engendering either a state of injustice or even a direct risk for others. Of course, those who hold the reasonable view recognize that agents acting upon the information or recommendations provided by pornographic depictions might harm others. If this occurs, however, the agents of harm are themselves responsible for the harm, not the creators or disseminators of the depictions. One who holds the reasonable view will naturally say that the agents simply should not have acted on the information or recommendations imparted. On the civil-rights view, pornography not only provides information and recommendations, but contributes to the actual and literal creation of women as a subordinated class, a class whose members may then be additionally victimized by those acting in response to this preestablished subordination.

NOTES

1. An example of a fairly standard (medium-length, too) definition of pornography would be Longino's: "Pornography . . . is verbal or pictorial material which represents or describes sexual behavior that is degrading or abusive to one or more of the participants *in such a way as to endorse the degradation.*" Helen Longino, "What Is Pornography," in Laura Lederer, ed., *Take Back the Night* (New York: William Morrow, 1980), p. 43. Some problems with this idea of "endorsement"—problems tangential to my inquiry—are noted by Alan Soble in "Pornography: Defamation and the Endorsement of Degradation," *Social Theory and Practice*, XI, 1 (Spring 1985): 61–87.

2. And of course some claim these representations are socially and personally helpful, sexually liberating, and so on. See, for example, G. L. Simon's, "Is Pornography Beneficial?" in Thomas A. Mappes and Jane S. Zembaty, eds., *Social Ethics* (New York: McGraw Hill, 1977), pp. 243–248.

3. This is not to say that otherwise sane and liberal-minded societies have not restricted pornography by law, for of course they have. The arguments of liberal theorists—see, for example, Ronald Dworkin's *Taking Rights Seriously* (Cambridge, Mass.: Harvard, 1977), especially ch. 10, "Liberty and Moralism"—stress that restrictions against such material, under the aegis of legislating the good, are inconsistent with liberal political theory.

4. See his *The Enforcement of Morals* (New York: Oxford, 1965), ch. 1.

5. Again see Dworkin, especially ch. 11, "Liberty and Liberalism," p. 262, on which page Dworkin states that showing the movie *Deep Throat* is not a threat to any principle of justice.

6. See, for example, Susan Griffin's fairly high-flying *Pornography and Silence* (New York: Harper and Row, 1982).

7. The by-now classic investigation and analysis of pornography is Andrea Dworkin's *Pornography: Men Possessing Women* (New York: Perigee, 1981). See also the chapter "Anti-Feminism," in her *Right-Wing Women* (New York: Perigee, 1982). *Take Back the Night, op. cit.,* is an anthology of women, all self-identified as feminists, writing about and criticizing pornography.

8. The title "Pornography/Civil Rights Ordinance" is preferred by the ordinance's supporters, whereas the title "Dworkin/MacKinnon Ordinance" is preferred by its detractors. I use the two titles interchangeably.

This ordinance implies that there is a connection between pornography and justice, in that producing and selling pornography (as well as other pornographically related activities) is seen as a violation of the rights of (usually) women. I will touch only tangentially upon this question of justice in this essay, since I believe other questions having to do with the possible conceptual status of pornographic representations come first.

The ordinance defines pornography as follows (This is taken from the version—the Ordinance has several versions—reprinted in *Ms. Magazine* (April 1985):46).

1. Pornography is the graphic sexually explicit subordination of women through pictures and/or words that also includes one or more of the following: (i) women are presented dehumanized as sexual objects, things, or commodities; or (ii) women are presented as sexual objects who enjoy pain or humiliation; or (iii) women are presented as sexual objects who experience sexual pleasure in being raped; or (iv) women are presented as sexual objects tied up or cut up or mutilated or bruised or physically hurt; or (v) women are presented in postures or positions of sexual submission, servility, or display; or (vi) women's body parts—including but not limited to vaginas, breasts, or buttocks—are exhibited such that women are reduced to those parts; or (vii) women are presented as whores by nature; or (viii) women are presented being penetrated by objects or animals; or (ix) women

are presented in scenarios of degradation, injury, torture, shown as filthy or inferior, bleeding, bruised or hurt in a context that makes these conditions sexual.

2. The use of men, children, or transsexuals in the place of women in (1) above is pornography for the purposes of this law.

9. As evidence of the ordinance's conceptual difficulty, one can look to the sympathetic, but adverse, opinion of Judge Frank Easterbrook [quoted in *Off Our Backs* (April 1986): 6]: "Depictions of subordination tend to perpetuate subordination. The subordinate status of women in turn leads to affront and lower pay at work, insult and injury at home, battery and rape on the streets . . . (but) this simply demonstrates the power of pornography as speech." Clearly, Easterbrook mentally translated the ordinance's definition of pornography into a more sensible form, ignoring the copula of identity between "pornography" and "subordination." The ordinance does not merely say that, in depicting subordination, pornography causes subordination. The ordinance says that pornography *is* subordination.

10. *The Concept of Mind* (New York: Barnes & Noble, 1949).

11. "To make a new point it may be necessary for the philosopher, as much as for the poet or the scientist, to speak in a new form of words not simply translatable into any of the old forms. But the philosopher who speaks too often in semisentences runs the risk of semiunderstanding from only a semiaudience." See "Nonsense," in Paul Edwards, ed., *Encyclopedia of Philosophy* (New York: Macmillan, 1967).

12. In both "Feminism, Marxism, Method, and the State," in *The Signs Reader* (Chicago: University Press, 1983), pp. 227–256, and "Not a Moral Issue," *Yale Law and Policy Review*, II, 321 (1984): 321–345, Catharine MacKinnon maintains that objectivity, in the sense of aperspectivity, is the way in which gender males both create and describe the world. From the point of view of such "aperspectivity" only direct, John-hits-Mary causal harm is recognized as the harm that creates injustice. Thus, if no such harm is connected with producing pornography, such production cannot be unjust.

13. Or—which is different—to make it actionable in the manner of the Pornography/Civil Rights Ordinance.

14. See Joel Feinberg's "The Offense Principle," in Mappes and Zembaty, *op. cit.,* pp. 252–257.

15. See the case of *Young v. American Mini Theaters, Inc.* described in Archibald Cox's *Freedom of Expression* (Cambridge, Mass.: Harvard, 1981), p. 34.

16. Again, I think that obscenity law, in legislating matters related to the good, is a deontological aberration. The just act/good act distinction is severely sketched by Charles Fried in *Right and Wrong* (Cambridge, Mass.: Harvard, 1979): "But while the demands of justice are implacable within their proper domain, it is . . . inappropriate and unnecessary to extend them outside of that domain. [There] the scale of judgment is marked, if at all, in degrees of praise only" (173 and 176). In other words, as long as what we do is within the bounds of just action, it is no one else's business adversely to judge, much less to prohibit or restrict, what we do. The production of pornography—as pornography is ordinarily defined by obscenity laws—falls into this realm of personal discretion.

17. *Philosophical Investigations*, G. E. M. Anscombe, ed. (New York: Macmillan, 3rd ed., 1958), §308.

18. A sensible non-Platonic defense of normative realism is given by Thomas Nagel in *The View from Nowhere* (New York: Oxford, 1986), especially in the section "Realism and Objectivity," pp. 138–143.

19. Again, some claim it is a positively good thing.

20. Of course, the notions of the literal and the metaphoric are problematic. I am working here with our intuitive and imperfect understanding of these concepts. Unless one wants to stack one's philosophical deck, it is important not suddenly to move the line between what counts as literally subordinating someone (versus metaphorically subordinating her) when examining the case of pornography. Cf. Nan Hunter's comment on the metaphoric nature of pornographic subordination in "Is One Woman's Sexuality Another Woman's Pornography?" *Ms.* (April 1985): 123.

21. The words from Isaiah (5:20–23) are apposite here: "Woe unto you who call evil good, and good evil, who turn darkness into light and light into darkness, who make bitter sweet and sweet bitter. Woe unto you!"

22. It seems to be possible for some practice constituents, especially practice objects, to be claimed and re-identified by new practices. For example, the naturally "kinky" hair of Black Americans, along with their very skin color, was seized from its racist presentation as shameful and made into a sign of pride and honor. This change in meaning was made possible, however, not by a mere collective mental act but by the (partial) abolition of the practice of racism and the birth of the social practice of antiracism. It is significant that other practice constituents of racism such as lynching and insulting forms of address, could not become transformed or re-identified. There is probably no hard and fast rule determining which practice constituents can be re-identified and which not (could the Nazi swastika ever become a symbol of Jewish self-affirmation?) and the impossibility of re-identifying most practice constituents is certainly not a logical one.

23. See Andrea Dworkin's "A Word People Don't Understand," in *Ms.* (April 1985): 46. Also Catharine MacKinnon in "Coming Apart," *Off Our Backs* (June 1985): 6.

24. The Pornography/Civil Rights Ordinance, Section One, reprinted in *Ms.* (April 1985): 46.

25. In "The Minneapolis Ordinance and the FACT Brief." *Women's Review of Books* (May 1986): 8, Rosemary Tong indirectly reveals the irreducibility of such social placement to perlocutionary effect. This particular irreducibility is just a specific instance of the difficulties that follow from the sort of paradigm shifts discussed below.

26. Of course, whether or not the access is desired is the question. It is axiomatic that change of one's paradigm destroys a certain type of explanatory power, viz., that of the old paradigm. We cannot, for example, explain the moves of a chess player *as chess moves* by describing the movement of the molecules of her body, even though, as is surely the case, the chess player is made up of molecules. The switch from the "Chess Game Paradigm" to the "Physics Paradigm" destroys the possibility of that old explanation being given. In the new paradigm, chess players assume the status of the metaphoric, and to speak of them as real is a reification. Similarly, we cannot explain the phenomenon of the social placement of women into the class of intrinsic moral inferiors *as subordination* by describing the mental states of individuals, even though society is as surely composed of individuals as the chess player is composed of molecules. The switch from the "Social Paradigm" to the

"Individual Paradigm" destroys the possibility of the social subordination explanation being given. In the new, reductionistic paradigm, society assumes the status of the metaphoric, and to speak of it as real is a reification.

A good account of the general debate between methodological individualists and holists is given in Simon, pp. 41–55. For a discussion of the relationship between feminism and various forms of individualism, see "The Critique of Individualism" in Jean Grimshaw's *Philosophy and Feminist Thinking* (Minneapolis: Minnesota UP, 1986), pp. 162–187.

27. This paradigm-related fall from validity is, *qua* fall from validity, like that generated by our inability to substitute in extentionally equivalent expressions in certain contexts. (E.g., John believes that Mark Twain wrote *Tom Sawyer*, but it does not follow that he believes that Samuel Clemens wrote *Tom Sawyer*.) But the opacity of beliefs does not place any object of knowledge beyond our reach (John could come to know that Samuel Clemens wrote *Tom Sawyer*), whereas a change of paradigms does do so. Paradigm changes destroy (and create) epistemic objects: "[T]hough the world does not change with a change of paradigm, the scientist afterward works in a different world" [Thomas Kuhn, *The Structure of Scientific Revolutions* (Chicago: University Press, 2d ed., 1970), p. 121.] In the case under discussion, the phenomenon of subordination, and its attendant and obvious injustice, can be lost in a paradigm change.

28. Since, as I have noted above, the representational arts are themselves practices, it can be the case that the identity of one of their practice constituents (e.g., a picture of a chess game) is doubly practice informed, and thus that identity is not entirely a function of the nonrepresentational practice (here, chess). Although it is clear that some value predicates of *non*practice objects can be generated by the representational practice alone (e.g., a beautiful picture of rotting fruit), it is not clear that nonaesthetic value predicates relating to a nonrepresentational practice constituent (e.g., a home run) can be so generated, much less gainsaid, by the representational practice, especially if one posits the existence of an overlapping ideology that both the representational and nonrepresentational practice share. Specifically, we might ask if it would be possible for pornographic representations to subordinate women even though the identity of the nonrepresentational practice constituents so represented contributed not at all to women's subordination. [If I follow her correctly, Susanne Kappeler's point in the *The Pornography of Representation* (Minneapolis: Minnesota UP, 1986) is that the subordination of women may occur through the mechanism of the representational practice alone, regardless of the nonrepresentational practice identity of that which is represented.]

It is certainly the case that the identity of a *depiction* of someone performing practice action *x* is other than the identity of someone performing practice action *x*, the depiction and the doing being informed by two different practices. It seems to me, however, empirically unlikely, if not impossible, that these identities would not influence each other, though the influence of the nonrepresentational practice is not necessarily the greater. [For an account of general representational to nonrepresentational influence on identity, see Robert Schwartz's "The Power of Pictures," this journal [*Journal of Philosophy*], 1.XXXII, 12 (December 1985): 711–720.]

29. And we could not truthfully make these negating statements about the medals that honor or the depictions that subordinate until such time as these practices have been abandoned as socially real, active practices *and* have either been entirely forgotten, obliterated from human memory, with such total erasure giving their constituents less social meaning than a blade of grass, *or* until they have been entirely replaced by new practices that would generate radically new social meanings. But this entire replacement of one practice by another is problematic. It would require the death of the institutions and ideology of the old practice as well as the complete abandonment of its illegitimate but nevertheless familiar and rewarding (to some) elements. The difficulties here are that, as long as human beings exist, the destruction of practice-generated meaning through social amnesia is a practical impossibility, and the replacement of one practice by another, in that it requires giving up what is perceived by some as familiar and good, is unlikely to occur except through a massive social cataclysm—and the degree of the massiveness of this required cataclysm would be a function of the degree and importance of that perceived good. Given these difficulties, it is more often the case that the "new" practice is not so new after all.

30. I draw this distinction between that which may and may not be imputed to the agents of faulty actions from Joel Feinberg's "Sua Culpa" in his *Doing and Deserving: Essays in the Theory of Responsibility* (Princeton, N. J.: University Press, 1970), pp. 187–221.

WILLIAM PARENT

A Second Look at Pornography
and the Subordination of Women

Feminist writer Andrea Dworkin and feminist lawyer Catharine MacKinnon recently proposed a new definition of "pornography" as "the graphic sexually explicit subordination of women" (henceforth D/M).[1] They introduced this definition as a part of an ordinance which was designed to help the city of Minneapolis control its burgeoning adult entertainment industry. The ordinance has not met with much legal success. (The Minneapolis city council barely passed it, but the Mayor vetoed it. And the United States Supreme Court summarily dismissed it.) Nonetheless, its conception of pornography is philosophically intriguing and worthy of analysis.

Melinda Vadas[2] attempts an ingenuously, highly original defense of the Dworkin/MacKinnon definition. She concedes that her task will not be an easy one. To equate pornography with the graphic, sexually explicit subordination of women "should make any English speaker sit bolt upright" (489). Would it not be much more reasonable, she asks, to conceive of pornography as the graphic, sexually explicit *depiction* of the subordination of women?

On this reasonable view (as Vadas herself calls it) pornography is not an intrinsic injustice. It may be highly offensive to many, and producing it may be a bad thing to do. But we can go no further in our moral condemnation of it. In Vadas's words: "the reasonable view does not have conceptual room for naming the production or dissemination of pornography as an injustice, but can at most see such actions as producing a state of mere disvalue" (510). D/M, on the other hand, construes pornogra-

phy as a species of sexual, and sexist, subjugation which by its very nature does injustice against women.

Vadas's attempt to defend D/M utilizes a distinction between what she calls direct predicate transfers and prepositional predicate transfers. A predicate transfers directly from an object, event, or action to a depiction of that object, event, or action if it applies both to the object, event, or action and to its depiction without equivocation or other change in meaning, and if it applies to the depiction because it applies to the action, object, or event (498). On the other hand, there are predicates which make this transfer only with the aid of a preposition like "of" or "about." These predicates transfer prepositionally. Some value predicates —e.g., "good," "bad," "ugly," "beautiful"— transfer directly, others only prepositionally. Vadas's object is to show that "subordinates" falls into the former class and that as a consequence D/M is logically defensible.

Let us look carefully at her examples of direct predicate transfer:

1. The predicate "is red" applies to a red rose and may also apply, in the same sense of "is red," to a depiction of the rose. And it applies to the depiction because it applies to the rose. The picture of the rose is red because the rose itself is. Vadas contrasts "is red" with "is sweet-smelling." The latter obviously transfers only prepositionally. A photograph of a rose is not itself sweet-smelling. Of course, perfume could be spilled on it, but then the predicate would

From Journal of Philosophy LXXXVII (1990): 205–11. Copyright ©1990 The Journal of Philosophy, Inc. Reprinted with permission of the author and publisher.

not apply to the photo because it applies to the rose (499).

2. The value predicate "is beautiful" transfers directly from a rose in nature to a photograph of the rose. The term applies to both the rose and its picture without equivocation or change in meaning, and it applies to the picture because it applies to the rose (502).

3. Clara mistakenly drinks the water in her finger bowl and then exclaims, before all the guests at a party, "Great soup!" This action disgraces Clara. Elwood videotapes Clara's gaffe. The predicate "disgraces Clara" transfers directly from the action itself to its depiction on film, since Vadas's two criteria are met. Or so she asserts (502).

4. A baseball player has the fans applauding his home run. Their applause honors him. A photograph taken of the applause also honors the player. The predicate "honors the player" transfers directly from the action of applauding to its depiction. There is, Vadas claims, no change in the meaning of the predicate, and the photo honors the player because the action of applause honored him (503). Similarly, the military honors a soldier by awarding him a medal. A depiction of the soldier wearing his medal also honors him (503).

The most striking, and discouraging, aspect of Vadas's treatment of these cases is the prevalence of assertion over argument. Perhaps she thinks that the phenomenon of direct predicate transfer is so incontrovertible that it requires no argument. But she is wrong.

Regarding case 1, all that we are warranted to say is that the predicate "is red" applies both to the real rose and to the rose-as-it-appears in the picture. To say that the pictured rose is red, or that the rose appearing in the picture is red, is much different from claiming that the picture itself of the rose is red. How odd it would be to hand someone a photograph of a rose and say that it, the photograph, is red. (If I took a picture of a red rose and dipped it in black paint, would we want to aver that the picture itself was red?) On the other hand, it is quite proper and intelligible to say that the picture is *of* a red rose. The difference between "is red" and "is sweet-smelling" lies not in the fact that the former transfers directly to photographs of roses while the latter transfers only prepositionally.

Rather, the difference is that the picture can directly capture visual but not olfactory qualities.

With regard to 2, "is beautiful" does not transfer to a picture of a rose because the pictured rose is beautiful. The aesthetic criteria pertinent to the evaluation of a photograph's beauty involve much more than the beauty of the objects photographed. They include such technical matters as lighting, angle, shadow, and background. Hence, Vadas's second condition of direct predicate transfers is not satisfied in 2.

Vadas fails to provide an argument in 3 for believing that Elwood's videotape of Clara itself disgraces her. Were Elwood to show the tape to a group of friends, he might well succeed in humiliating Clara. But then it would be the use to which he put the tape and not the tape itself that disgraces her. It is difficult to understand how a videotape that is never shown to anyone could disgrace anyone. Therefore, it is difficult to understand how "disgrace" transfers directly from Clara's action to the film of it.

As for 4, the photograph of the applause can certainly be used as a means for honoring the player. Thus, I might pass the picture around to an admiring audience as part of my tribute to his batting power. But here it is not the photo itself but my use of it in the appropriate circumstances which does the honoring. Inanimate objects do not intelligibly function as subjects for verbs like "disgrace" and "honor." It makes no logical sense to claim that films, pictures, statues, books, etc., honor or disgrace people. People honor or disgrace people, sometimes by using or taking pictures, sometimes by building statues, sometimes by writing books. Likewise, the picture of the soldier wearing his medal cannot by itself honor him, though once again it can be used in the act of honoring him.

Examples 1–4, then, offer no support for the thesis that some predicates transfer directly from actions, objects, or events to depictions of those actions, objects, or events. Vadas's argument in support of D/M depends crucially on the claim that "subordinates" is a value predicate that transfers directly to pornographic depictions. Unfortunately, she does not furnish an argument on behalf of this claim. Instead she is content to point out that "subordinates," in the sense of "placing a person into a class of intrinsic moral inferiors," unquestionably constitutes a value predicate and as such can function in direct predicate transfers. Accordingly, pornography can subordinate women (508–9). D/M is not logically incongruous.

The first point to emphasize here is that we have yet to be given any reason for supposing that pornography in fact does contribute to the creation of women as a subordinated people. Consequently we have as yet no reason to accept the Dworkin/MacKinnon account of the wrongness of producing pornography, namely "it is the sexual subordination of women that *is* pornography which grounds and explains the faulty aspect of producing or disseminating it" (511—the emphasis is mine).

But does it even make any sense to say that pornographic depictions subordinate women? Of course, it is easy to think of cases where pornography might be used to facilitate such subordination. For example, a man gets excited watching a violent rape depicted graphically in an adult film and then proceeds to subdue forcibly his wife. But it is not easy to understand how books, magazines, or films can by themselves "place a person into the class of intrinsic moral inferiors." Subordination is, after all, an action or a practice engaged in by human beings and directed against other beings. In other words, the logic of "subordinates" requires that it have some human action or actions as a subject.[3]

It also precludes characterization by the adjectives "graphic" and "sexually explicit." Depictions of human behavior are often quite meaningfully called graphic and/or sexually explicit. Pornographic films and literature, by virtue of their representative content, are aptly so described. The acts they depict, however, while sexual, are not themselves sexually explicit or graphic. These words apply only to the way in which these acts are described or portrayed. Thus, we watch an adult film that shows everything in vivid color, or we read an adult novel that is replete with explicit language.

Vadas's effort to defend D/M commits several times over what Gilbert Ryle[4] famously and felicitously dubbed a category mistake. These are mistakes which arise from the inability to use correctly certain words in our vocabulary. Ryle writes, "the theoretically interesting category mistakes are those made by people who are perfectly competent to apply concepts, at least in the situations with which they are

familiar, but are still liable in their abstract thinking to allocate these concepts to logical types to which they do not belong" (ibid., p. 17).

Vadas's assertions about photographs honoring ballplayers and videotapes disgracing guests are logically odd in just the way that Ryle describes. Honor and disgrace do not belong, logically, to pictures or tapes. Similarly, books, magazines, and films are not the kinds of things that can meaningfully be said to subordinate.

Rejecting D/M, must we then agree with Vadas's claim that, on the reasonable view, pornography comprises just a "mere disvalue"? Let us for the sake of argument accept a narrow conceptualization of pornography as consisting of verbal or pictorial material that depicts the coerced or violent subordination of women. (This is narrow because it rules out by definition pornography in which men are shown as victimized as well as so-called erotic pornography in which explicit sexual relations are depicted as expressions of love and caring between consenting partners.) What makes this species of pornography morally bad?

Some feminists claim that it is condemnable as anti-female propaganda.[5] But there is, to my knowledge, no research data indicating that exposure to pornography produces a contemptuous attitude toward women. Nor is there good reason to believe that the producers of pornography are determined to propagate such an attitude in their customers as opposed to exploiting an already existing misogynism for commercial gain. Explicit depictions of women being raped, beaten, tortured, hung from ceilings, and in other ways brutally subjugated are not likely to acquire entertainment or educational value in persons who like or respect women. On the contrary, these persons will be repulsed by such pornography.

Does exposure to pornography beget violence against women? Empirical studies of this question run up against the intractable problem of distinguishing causal claims from claims that watching or reading pornography simply reinforces preexisting negative attitudes toward women. Again, the idea that a man who harbors no disdain for women will become disposed to harm them after reading or viewing pornography invites the skeptical response: Why would utter disgust and disdain for pornographers not be his natural response to this kind of material? The causal argument also has to explain the fact that in Denmark, Sweden, and the Netherlands anti-women violence is relatively uncommon despite the widespread availability of pornography, while in Ireland and South Africa such violence is relatively common even though pornography is unavailable.[6]

So the reasonable view will abjure the suggestion that the major disvalue of pornography consists of either sexist propaganda or the incitement of violence against women. Instead it construes the main function of pornography, in the narrow sense under discussion here, to be misogynist pandering. And it identifies this function as the principal source of pornography's disvalue.

"To pander" means "to minister to the baser passions of another." The baser passion to which pornography ministers is not an interest in sex per se. Mature sexual behavior free of duplicity, coercion, and violence is not morally objectionable. Violent subordination through sex is morally objectionable, though, and it is precisely an interest in this kind of debasement to which pornography panders.

The use of "subordination" in this context should not cause a conceptual difficulty, but Vadas's conceptualization of it does. She avers that subordination involves placing a person or group of persons socially in the class of those whose intrinsic moral worth is not of the first rank (506). Unfortunately, the idea of intrinsic moral worth Vadas deploys here needs clarification, particularly in light of her view that bearers of this worth can be ranked in some kind of hierarchy. Ordinarily, the appeal to intrinsic worth serves to rule out any such ranking.

A more common and perspicuous account of subordination equates it with the practice of regarding a person as inferior to others in some respect(s) and as a consequence placing him/ her in a lower position, group, or class. There is nothing intrinsically wrong with this practice. Among its justifying purposes are greater technical knowledge, wider experience, and proven maturity of judgment. Still, many forms of subordination are morally unjust, and prominent among these is the arbitrary, brutal exercise of power by men over women depicted and endorsed in pornography.

The most appropriate and most forceful characterization of materials which describe or portray sexist subordination is that they are morally evil. "Moral evil" is a strong term of moral condemnation. Vadas claims that the reasonable view of pornography can at most criticize it as a "mere disvalue" (510). But moral evil is much more than a mere disvalue.

According to the *Oxford English Dictionary,* "evil" means first and foremost "morally depraved." "To deprave," in turn, means "to debase, vilify, or disparage." And "to debase" means "to lower in dignity, to depreciate, to bring into contempt." So there is an inextricable connection between the ideas of evil and the contemptuous treatment of persons. John Rawls[7] is right on the conceptual and moral mark when he writes: "What moves the evil man is the love of injustice. He delights in the impotence and humiliation of those subject to him, and he relishes being recognized by them as the wilful author of their degradation" (ibid., p. 439).

The most insidious evil actions are those which target a specific group for systematic devaluation and humiliation: Nazi terrorism against Jews, white supremacists' propaganda against blacks, social discrimination aimed at the old and sick, misogynists' abuse of women. But moral evil need not involve the actual exercise of unjust power. It is also found in the practice of profiting from such exercise—e.g., slave ownership. "Moral evil" also properly applies to the activity of producing verbal or pictorial representations of evil acts for the sake of others' amusement. Thus, it would be morally evil to make a film celebrating Nazi atrocities for the viewing pleasure of anti-Semites. Finally, the pleasure taken in depictions of human debasement is most appropriately described as evil, and is integral to the evil person's character (Rawls's point).

The application of "moral evil" to pornography is clear enough. Materials that depict in a favorable light the arbitrary debasement of women are intrinsically contemptuous of women and as such are morally evil. Likewise, the pleasure a person takes in reading or watching pornography is evil. Hence, pandering to this pleasure for the sake of commercial gain is an evil practice. So the business of pornography, which I equated earlier with a form of ignoble pandering, is on the reasonable view condemnable in very strong terms. It thrives by exploiting the profoundly pernicious enjoyment too many men find in pornographic images of demeaning subordination. Opponents of pornography should focus on this important point instead of proferring new but philosophically indefensible definitions of "pornography."

NOTES

1. The full statement of the definition is as follows:
   1. Pornography is the graphic sexually explicit subordination of women through pictures and/or words that also includes one or more of the following: (i) women are presented dehumanized as sexual objects, things, or commodities; or (ii) women are presented as sexual objects who enjoy pain or humiliation; or (iii) women are presented as sexual objects who experience sexual pleasure in being raped; or (iv) women are presented as sexual objects tied up or cut up or mutilated or bruised or physically hurt; or (v) women are presented in postures or positions of sexual submission, servility, or display; or (vi) women's body parts—including but not limited to vaginas, breasts, or buttocks—are exhibited such that women are reduced to those parts; or (vii) women are presented as whores by nature; or (viii) women are presented being penetrated by objects or animals; or (ix) women are presented in scenarios of degradation, injury, torture, shown as filthy or inferior, bleeding, bruised or hurt in a context that makes these conditions sexual.
   2. The use of men, children, or transsexuals in the place of women in (1) above is pornography for the purposes of this law.

2. "A First Look at the Pornography/Civil Rights Ordinance: Could Pornography Be the Subordination of Women?" in this journal [*Journal of Philosophy*], LXXXIV, 9 (September 1987): 487–511.

3. Dworkin and MacKinnon at times recognize this fact. During the Minneapolis hearings, for example, they stated that pornography is a systematic *practice* of exploitation and subordination based on sex which differentially harms women. See MacKinnon, *Feminism Unmodified* (Cambridge: Harvard, 1987), p. 212. See also Paul Brest and Ann Vandenberg, "Politics, Feminism, and the Constitution: The Anti-Pornography Movement in Minneapolis," *The Stanford Law Review,* XXXIX (February 1987), p. 619.

4. *The Concept of Mind* (New York: Barnes & Noble, 1949).

5. See, for example, Susan Brownmiller's *Against Our Will: Men, Women, and Rape,* excerpted in Laura Lederer, ed., *Take Back the Night* (New York: Morrow, 1980), p.33.

6. Joel Feinberg discusses this point in his *Offense to Others* (New York: Oxford, 1986), p. 149.

7. *A Theory of Justice* (Cambridge: Harvard, 1971).

LAURIE SHRAGE

Should Feminists Oppose Prostitution?

> Because sexuality is a social construction, individuals as individuals are not free to experience *eros* just as they choose. Yet just as the extraction and appropriation of surplus value by the capitalist represents a choice available, if not to individuals, to society as a whole, so too sexuality and the forms taken by *eros* must be seen as at some level open to change.
>
> Nancy Hartsock, *Money, Sex and Power*[1]

INTRODUCTION

Prostitution raises difficult issues for feminists. On the one hand, many feminists want to abolish discriminatory criminal statutes that are mostly used to harass and penalize prostitutes, and rarely to punish johns and pimps—laws which, for the most part, render prostitutes more vulnerable to exploitation by their male associates.[2] On the other hand, most feminists find the prostitute's work morally and politically objectionable. In their view, women who provide sexual services for a fee submit to sexual domination by men, and suffer degradation by being treated as sexual commodities.[3]

My concern, in this paper, is whether persons opposed to the social subordination of women should seek to discourage commercial sex. My goal is to marshal the moral arguments needed to sustain feminists' condemnation of the sex industry in our society. In reaching this goal, I reject accounts of commercial sex which posit cross-cultural and transhistorical causal mechanisms to explain the existence of prostitution or which assume that the activities we designate as "sex" have a universal meaning and purpose. By contrast, I analyze mercenary sex in terms of culturally specific beliefs and principles that organize its practice in contemporary American society. I try to

show that the sex industry, like other institutions in our society, is structured by deeply ingrained attitudes and values which are oppressive to women. The point of my analysis is not to advocate an egalitarian reformation of commercial sex, nor to advocate its abolition through state regulation. Instead, I focus on another political alternative: that which must be done to subvert widely held beliefs that legitimate this institution in our society. Ultimately, I argue that nothing closely resembling prostitution, as we currently know it, will exist, once we have undermined these cultural convictions.

WHY PROSTITUTION IS PROBLEMATIC

A number of recent papers on prostitution begin with the familiar observation that prostitution is one of the oldest professions.[4] Such "observations" take for granted that "prostitution" refers to a single transhistorical, transcultural activity. By contrast, my discussion of prostitution is limited to an activity that occurs in modern Western societies—a practice which involves the purchase of sexual services from women by men. Moreover, I am not interested in exploring the nature and extension of our moral concept "to prostitute oneself"; rather, I want to examine a specific activity we regard as prostitution in order to understand its social and political significance.

In formulating my analysis, I recognize that the term "prostitute" is ambiguous: it is used to designate both persons who supply sex on a commercial basis and persons who contribute their talents and efforts to base purposes for some reward. While these extensions may overlap, their relationship is not a logically

From *Ethics* 99 (1989): 347–361. Copyright ©1989 By The University of Chicago. Reprinted with permission of the author and publisher.

necessary one but is contingent upon complex moral and social principles. In this paper, I use the term "prostitute" as shorthand for "provider of commercial sexual services," and correspondingly, I use the term "prostitution" interchangeably with "commercial sex." By employing these terms in this fashion, I hope to appear consistent with colloquial English, and not to be taking for granted that a person who provides commercial sexual services "prostitutes" her- or himself.

Many analyses of prostitution aim to resolve the following issue: what would induce a woman to prostitute herself—to participate in an impersonal, commercial sexual transaction? These accounts seek the deeper psychological motives behind apparently voluntary acts of prostitution. Because our society regards female prostitution as a social, if not natural, aberration, such actions demand an explanation. Moreover, accepting fees for sex seems irrational and repugnant to many persons, even to the woman who does it, and so one wonders why she does it. My examination of prostitution does not focus on this question. While to do so may explain why a woman will choose prostitution from among various options, it does not explain how a woman's options have been constituted. In other words, although an answer to this question may help us understand why some women become sellers of sexual services rather than homemakers or engineers, it will not increase our understanding of why there is a demand for these services. Why, for example, can women not as easily achieve prosperity by selling child-care services? Finding out why there is a greater market for goods of one type than of another illuminates social forces and trends as much as, if not more than, finding out why individuals enter a particular market. Moreover, theorists who approach prostitution in this way do not assume that prostitution is "a problem about the women who are prostitutes, and our attitudes to them, [rather than] a problem about the men who demand to buy them."[5] This assumption, as Carole Pateman rightly points out, mars many other accounts.

However, I do not attempt to construct an account of the psychological, social, and economic forces that presumably cause men to demand commercial sex, or of the factors which cause a woman to market her sexual services.

Instead, I first consider whether prostitution, in all cultural contexts, constitutes a degrading and undesirable form of sexuality. I argue that, although the commercial availability of sexuality is not in every existing or conceivable society oppressive to women, in our society this practice depends upon the general acceptance of principles which serve to marginalize women socially and politically. Because of the cultural context in which prostitution operates, it epitomizes and perpetuates pernicious patriarchal beliefs and values and, therefore, is both damaging to the women who sell sex and, as an organized social practice, to all women in our society.

HISTORICAL AND CROSS-CULTURAL PERSPECTIVES

In describing Babylonian temple prostitution, Gerda Lerner reports: "For people who regarded fertility as sacred and essential to their own survival, the caring for the gods included, in some cases, offering them sexual services. Thus, a separate class of temple prostitutes developed. What seems to have happened was that sexual activity for and in behalf of the god or goddesses was considered beneficial to the people and sacred."[6] Similarly, according to Emma Goldman, the Babylonians believed that "the generative activity of human beings possessed a mysterious and sacred influence in promoting the fertility of Nature."[7] When the rationale for the impersonal provision of sex is conceived in terms of the promotion of nature's fecundity, the social meaning this activity has may differ substantially from the social significance it has in our own society.

In fifteenth-century France, as described by Jacques Rossiaud, commercial sex appears likewise to have had an import that contrasts with its role in contemporary America. According to Rossiaud:

By the age of thirty, most prostitutes had a real chance of becoming reintegrated into society. . . . Since public opinion did not view them with disgust, and since they were on good terms with priests and men of the law, it was not too difficult for them to find a position as servant or wife. To many city people, public prostitution represented a partial atonement of past misconduct. Many bachelors had compassion and sympathy for prostitutes, and finally, the local charitable foundations of the municipal authorities felt a charitable impulse to give special help to these repentant Magdalens and to open their way to marriage by dowering them. Marriage was definitely the most frequent end to the career of communal prostitutes who had roots in the town where they have publicly offered their bodies.[8]

The fact that prostitutes were regarded by medieval French society as eligible for marriage, and were desired by men for wives, suggests that the cultural principles which sustained commercial exchanges of sex in this society were quite different than those which shape our own sex industry. Consequently, the phenomenon of prostitution requires a distinct political analysis and moral assessment vis-à-vis fifteenth-century France. This historically specific approach is justified, in part, because commercial sexual transactions may have different consequences for individuals in an alien society than for individuals similarly placed in our own. Indeed, it is questionable whether, in two quite different cultural settings, we should regard a particular outward behavior—the impersonal provision of sexual services for fees or their equivalent—as the same practice, that is, as prostitution.

Another cross-cultural example may help to make the last point clear. Anthropologists have studied a group in New Guinea, called the Etoro, who believe that young male children need to ingest male fluid or semen in order to develop properly into adult males, much like we believe that young infants need their mother's milk, or some equivalent, to be properly nurtured. Furthermore, just as our belief underlies our practice of breast-feeding, the Etoro's belief underlies their practice of penis-feeding, where young male children fellate older males, often their relatives.[9] From the perspective of our society, the Etoro's practice involves behaviors which are highly stigmatized—incest, sex with children, and homosexuality. Yet, for an anthropologist who is attempting to interpret and translate these behaviors, to assume that the Etoro practice is best subsumed under the category of "sex," rather than, for example, "child rearing," would reflect ethnocentrism. Clearly, our choice of one translation scheme or the other will influence our attitude toward the Etoro practice. The point is that there is no practice, such as "sex," which can be morally evaluated apart from a cultural framework.

In general, historical and cross-cultural studies offer little reason to believe that the dominant forms of sexual practice in our society reflect psychological, biological, or moral absolutes that determine human sexual practice. Instead, such studies provide much evidence that, against a different backdrop of beliefs about the world, the activities we designate as "sex"—impersonal or otherwise—have an entirely different meaning and value. Yet, while we may choose not to condemn the "child-rearing" practices of the Etoro, we can nevertheless recognize that "penis-feeding" would be extremely damaging to children in our society. Similarly, though we can appreciate that making an occupation by the provision of sex may not have been oppressive to women in medieval France or ancient Babylon, we should nevertheless recognize that in our society it can be extremely damaging to women. What then are the features which, in our culture, render prostitution oppressive?

THE SOCIAL MEANING OF PROSTITUTION

Let me begin with a simple analogy. In our society there exists a taboo against eating cats and dogs. Now, suppose a member of our society wishes to engage in the unconventional behavior of ingesting cat or dog meat. In evaluating the moral and political character of this person's behavior, it is somewhat irrelevant whether eating cats or dogs "really" is or isn't healthy, or whether it "really" is or isn't different than eating cows, pigs, and chickens. What is relevant is that, by including cat and dog flesh in one's diet, a person may really make others upset and, therefore, do damage to them as well as to oneself. In short, how actions are widely perceived and interpreted by others, even if wrongly or seemingly irrationally, is crucial to determining their moral status because, though such interpretations may not hold up against some "objective reality," they are part of the "social reality" in which we live.

I am not using this example to argue that unconventional behavior is wrong but, rather, to illustrate the relevance of cultural convention to how our outward behaviors are perceived. Indeed, what is wrong with prostitution is not that it violates deeply entrenched social conventions—ideals of feminine purity, and the noncommoditization of sex—but precisely that it epitomizes other cultural assumptions—beliefs which, reasonable or not, serve to legitimate women's social subordination. In other words, rather than subvert patriarchal ideology, the prostitute's actions, and the industry as a whole, serve to perpetuate this system of values. By contrast, lesbian sex, and egalitarian heterosexual economic and romantic relationships, do not. In short, female prostitution oppresses women, not because some women who participate in it "suffer in the eyes of society" but because its organized practice testifies to and perpetuates socially hegemonic beliefs which oppress all women in many domains of their lives.

What, then, are some of the beliefs and values which structure the social meaning of the prostitute's business in our culture—principles which are not necessarily consciously held by us but are implicit in our observable behavior and social practice? First, people in our society generally believe that human beings naturally possess, but socially repress, powerful, emotionally destabilizing sexual appetites. Second, we assume that men are naturally suited for dominant social roles. Third, we assume that contact with male genitals in virtually all contexts is damaging and polluting to women. Fourth, we assume that a person's sexual practice renders her or him a particular "kind" of person, for example, "a homosexual," "a bisexual," "a whore," "a virgin," "a pervert," and so on. I will briefly examine the nature of these four assumptions, and then discuss how they determine the social significance and impact of prostitution in our society. Such principles are inscribed in all of a culture's communicative acts and institutions, but my examples will only be drawn from a common body of disciplinary resources: the writings of philosophers and other intellectuals.

The universal possession of a potent sex drive.—In describing the nature of sexual attraction, Schopenhauer states:

The sexual impulse in all its degrees and nuances plays not only on the stage and in novels, but also in the real world, where, next to the love of life, it shows itself the strongest and most powerful of motives, constantly lays claim to half the powers and thoughts of the younger portion of mankind, is the ultimate goal of almost all human effort, exerts an adverse influence on the most important events, interrupts the most serious occupations every hour, sometimes embarrasses for a while even the greatest minds, does not hesitate to intrude with its trash interfering with the negotiations of statesmen and the investigation of men of learning, knows how to slip its love letters and locks of hair even into ministerial portfolios and philosophical manuscripts, and no less devises daily the most entangled and the worst actions, destroys the most valuable relationships, breaks the firmest bonds, demands the sacrifice sometimes of life or health, sometimes of wealth, rank, and happiness, nay robs those who are otherwise honest of all conscience, makes those who have hitherto been faithful, traitors; accordingly to the whole, appears as a malevolent demon that strives to pervert, confuse, and overthrow everything.[10]

Freud, of course, chose the name "libido" to refer to this powerful natural instinct, which he believed manifests itself as early as infancy.

The assumption of a potent "sex drive" is implicit in Lars Ericsson's relatively recent defense of prostitution: "We must liberate ourselves from those mental fossils which prevent us from looking upon sex and sexuality with the same naturalness as upon our cravings for food and drink. And, contrary to popular belief, we may have something to learn from prostitution in this respect, namely, that coition resembles nourishment in that if it cannot be obtained in any other way it can always be bought. And bought meals are not always the worst."[11] More explicitly, he argues that the "sex drive" provides a noneconomic, natural basis for explaining the demand for commercial sex.[12] Moreover, he claims that because of the irrational nature of this impulse, prostitution will exist until all persons are granted sexual access upon demand to all other persons.[13] In a society where individuals lack such access to others, but where women are the social equals of men, Ericsson predicts that "the degree of female frustration that exists today . . . will no longer be tolerated, rationalized, or sublimated, but channeled into a demand for, inter alia, mercenary sex."[14] Consequently, Ericsson favors an unregulated sex industry, which can respond spontaneously to these natural human wants. Although Pateman, in her response to Ericsson, does not see the capitalist commoditization of sexuality as physiologically determined, she nevertheless yields to the assumption that "sexual impulses are part of our natural constitution as humans."[15]

Schopenhauer, Freud, Ericsson, and Pateman all clearly articulate what anthropologists refer to as our "cultural common sense" regarding the nature of human sexuality. By contrast, consider a group of people in New Guinea, called the Dani, as described by Karl Heider: "Especially striking is their five year postpartum sexual abstinence, which is uniformly observed and is not a subject of great concern or stress. This low level of sexuality appears to be a purely cultural phenomenon, not caused by any biological factors."[16] The moral of this anthropological tale is that our high level of sexuality is also "a purely cultural phenomenon," and not the inevitable result of human biology. Though the Dani's disinterest in sex need not lead us to regard our excessive concern as improper, it should lead us to view one of our cultural rationalizations for prostitution as just that—a cultural rationalization.

The "natural" dominance of men.—One readily apparent feature of the sex industry in our society is that it caters almost exclusively to a male clientele. Even the relatively small number of male prostitutes at work serve a predominantly male consumer group. Implicit in this particular division of labor, and also the predominant division of labor in other domains of our society, is the cultural principle that men are naturally disposed to dominate in their relations with others.

Ironically, this cultural conviction is implicit in some accounts of prostitution by feminist writers, especially in their attempts to explain the social and psychological causes of the problematic demand by men for impersonal, commercial sex. For example, Marxist feminists have argued that prostitution is the manifestation of the unequal class position of women vis-à-vis men: women who do not exchange their domestic and sexual services with the male ruling class for their subsistence are forced to market these services to multiple masters outside marriage.[17] The exploitation of female sexuality is a ruling-class privilege, an advantage which allows those socially identified as "men" to perpetuate their economic and cultural hegemony. In tying female prostitution to patriarchy and capitalism, Marxist accounts attempt to tie it to particular historical forces, rather than to biological or natural ones. However, without the assumption of men's biological superiority, Marxist feminist analyses cannot explain why women, at this particular moment under capitalism, have evolved as an economic under-class, that is, why capitalism gives rise to patriarchy. Why did women's role in production and reproduction not provide them a market advantage, a basis upon which they could subordinate men or assert their political equality?

Gayle Rubin has attempted to provide a purely social and historical analysis of female prostitution by applying some insights of structuralist anthropology.[18] She argues that economic prostitution originates from the unequal position of men and women within the mode of reproduction (the division of society into groups for the purpose of procreation and child rearing). In many human cultures, this system operates by what Lévi-Strauss referred to as "the exchange of women": a practice whereby men exchange their own sisters and daughters for the sisters and daughters of other men. These exchanges express or affirm "a social link between the partners of the exchange . . . confer[ing] upon its participants a special relationship of trust, solidarity, and mutual aid."[19] However, since women are not partners to the exchange but, rather, the objects traded, they are denied the social rights and privileges created by these acts of giving. The commoditization of female sexuality is the form this original "traffic in women" takes in capitalist societies. In short, Rubin's account does not assume, but attempts to explain, the dominance of men in production, by appealing to the original dominance of men in reproduction. Yet this account does not explain why women are the objects of the original affinal exchange, rather than men or opposite sex pairs.[20]

In appealing to the principle that men naturally assume dominant roles in all social systems, feminists uncritically accept a basic premise of patriarchy. In my view such principles do not denote universal causal mechanisms but represent naturally arbitrary, culturally determined beliefs which serve to legitimate certain practices.

Sexual contact pollutes women.—To say that extensive sexual experience in a woman is not prized in our society is to be guilty of indirectness and understatement. Rather, a history of sexual activity is a negative mark that is used to differentiate kinds of women. Instead of being valued for their experience in sexual matters, women are valued for their "innocence."

That the act of sexual intercourse with a man is damaging to a woman is implicit in the vulgar language we use to describe this act. As Robert Baker has pointed out, a woman is "fucked," "screwed," "banged," "had," and so forth, and it is a man (a "prick") who does it to her.[21] The metaphors we use for the act of sexual intercourse are similarly revealing. Consider, for example, Andrea Dworkin's description of intercourse: "The thrusting is persistent invasion. She is opened up, split down the center. She is occupied—physically, internally, in her privacy."[22] Dworkin invokes both images of physical assault and imperialist domination in her characterization of heterosexual copulation. Women are split, penetrated, entered, occupied, invaded, and colonized by men. Though aware of the nonliteralness of this language, Dworkin appears to think that these metaphors are motivated by natural, as opposed to arbitrary, cultural features of the world. According to Ann Garry, "Because in our culture we connect sex with harm that men do to women, and because we think of the female role in sex as that of harmed object, we can see that to treat a woman as a sex object is automatically to treat her as less than fully human."[23] As the public vehicles for "screwing," "penetration," "invasion," prostitutes are reduced to the status of animals or things—mere instruments for human ends.

The reification of sexual practice.—Another belief that determines the social significance of prostitution concerns the relationship between a person's social identity and her or his sexual behavior.[24] For example, we identify a person who has sexual relations with a person of the same gender as a "homosexual," and we regard a woman who has intercourse with multiple sexual partners as being of a particular type—for instance, a "loose woman," "slut," or "prostitute." As critics of our society, we may find these categories too narrow or the values they reflect objectionable. If so, we may refer to women who are sexually promiscuous, or who have sexual relations with other women, as "liberated women," and thereby show a rejection of double (and homophobic) standards of sexual morality. However, what such linguistic iconoclasm generally fails to challenge

is that a person's sexual practice makes her a particular "kind" of person.

I will now consider how these cultural convictions and values structure the meaning of prostitution in our society. Our society's tolerance for commercially available sex, legal or not, implies general acceptance of principles which perpetuate women's social subordination. Moreover, by their participation in an industry which exploits the myths of female social inequality and sexual vulnerability, the actions of the prostitute and her clients imply that they accept a set of values and beliefs which assign women to marginal social roles in all our cultural institutions, including marriage and waged employment. Just as an Uncle Tom exploits noxious beliefs about blacks for personal gain, and implies through his actions that blacks can benefit from a system of white supremacy, the prostitute and her clients imply that women can profit economically from patriarchy. Though we should not blame the workers in the sex industry for the social degradation they suffer, as theorists and critics of our society, we should question the existence of such businesses and the social principles implicit in our tolerance for them.

Because members of our society perceive persons in terms of their sexual orientation and practice, and because sexual contact in most settings—but especially outside the context of a "secure" heterosexual relationship—is thought to be harmful to women, the prostitute's work may have social implications that differ significantly from the work of persons in other professions. For instance, women who work or have worked in the sex industry may find their future social prospects severely limited. By contrast to medieval French society, they are not desired as wives or domestic servants in our own. And unlike other female subordinates in our society, the prostitute is viewed as a defiled creature; nonetheless, we rationalize and tolerate prostitutional sex out of the perceived need to mollify men's sexual desires.

In sum, the woman who provides sex on a commercial basis and the man who patronizes her epitomize and reinforce the social principles I have identified: these include beliefs that attribute to humans potent, subjugating sex drives that men can satisfy without inflicting self-harm through impersonal sexual encounters. Moreover, the prostitute cannot alter the political implications of her work by simply supplying her own rationale for the provision of her services. For example, Margo St. James has tried to represent the prostitute as a skilled sexual therapist, who serves a legitimate social need.[25] According to St. James, while the commercial sex provider may be unconventional in her sexual behavior, her work may be performed with honesty and dignity. However, this defense is implausible since it ignores the possible adverse impact of her behavior on herself and others, and the fact that, by participating in prostitution, her behavior does little to subvert the cultural principles that make her work harmful. Ann Garry reaches a similar conclusion about pornography: "I may not think that sex is dirty and that I would be a harmed object; I may not know what your view is; but what bothers me is that this is the view embodied in our language and culture. . . . As long as sex is connected with harm done to women, it will be very difficult not to see pornography as degrading to women. . . . The fact that audience attitude is so important makes one wary of giving whole-hearted approval to any pornography seen today."[26] Although the prostitute may want the meaning of her actions assessed relative to her own idiosyncratic beliefs and values, the political and social meaning of her actions must be assessed in the political and social context in which they occur.

One can imagine a society in which individuals sought commercial sexual services from women in order to obtain high quality sexual experiences. In our society, people pay for medical advice, meals, education in many fields, and so on, in order to obtain information, services, or goods that are superior to or in some respect more valuable than those they can obtain noncommercially. A context in which the rationale for seeking a prostitute's services was to obtain sex from a professional —from a person who knows what she is doing —is probably not a context in which women are thought to be violated when they have sexual contact with men. In such a situation, those who supplied sex on a commercial basis would probably not be stigmatized but, instead, granted ordinary social privileges.[27] The fact that prostitutes have such low social status in our society indicates that the society in which we live is not congruent with this imaginary one; that is, the prostitute's services in our society are not generally sought as a gourmet item. In short, if commercial sex was sought as a professional service, then women who provided sex commercially would probably not be regarded as "prostituting" themselves—as devoting their bodies or talents to base purposes, contrary to their true interests.

SUBVERTING THE STATUS QUO

Let me reiterate that I am not arguing for social conformism. Rather, my point is that not all nonconformist acts equally challenge conventional morality. For example, if a person wants to subvert the belief that eating cats and dogs is bad, it is not enough to simply engage in eating them. Similarly, it is unlikely that persons will subvert prevalent attitudes toward gender and sexuality by engaging in prostitution.

Consider another example. Suppose that I value high quality child care and am willing to pay a person well to obtain it. Because of both racial and gender oppression, the persons most likely to be interested in and suitable for such work are bright Third World and minority First World women who cannot compete fairly for other well-paid work. Suppose, then I hire a person who happens to be a woman and a person of color to provide child care on the basis of the belief that such work requires a high level of intelligence and responsibility. Though the belief on which this act is based may be unconventional, my action of hiring a "sitter" from among the so-called lower classes of society is not politically liberating.[28]

What can a person who works in the sex industry do to subvert widely held attitudes toward her work? To subvert the beliefs which currently structure commercial sex in our society, the female prostitute would need to assume the role not of a sexual subordinate but of a sexual equal or superior. For instance, if she were to have the authority to determine what services the customer could get, under what conditions the customer could get them, and what they would cost, she would gain the status of a sexual professional. Should she further want to establish herself as a sexual therapist, she would need to represent herself as having some type of special technical knowledge for solving problems having to do with human sexuality. In other words, experience is not enough to establish one's credentials as a therapist or professional. However, if the industry were reformed so that all these conditions were met, what would distinguish the prostitute's work from that of a bona fide "sexual therapist"? If her knowledge was thought to be only quasilegitimate, her work might have the status of something like the work of a chiropractor, but this would certainly be quite different than the current social status of her work.[29] In sum, the political alternatives of reformation and abolition are not mutually exclusive: if prostitution were sufficiently transformed to make it completely nonoppressive to women, though commercial transactions involving sex might still exist, prostitution as we now know it would not.

If our tolerance for marriage fundamentally rested on the myth of female subordination, then the same arguments which apply to prostitution would apply to it. Many theorists, including Simone de Beauvoir and Friedrich Engels, have argued that marriage, like prostitution, involves female sexual subservience. For example, according to de Beauvoir: "For both the sexual act is a service; the one is hired for life by one man; the other has several clients who pay her by the piece. The one is protected by one male against all others; the other is defended by all against the exclusive tyranny of each."[30] In addition, Lars Ericsson contends that marriage, unlike prostitution, involves economic dependence for women: "While the housewife is totally dependent on her husband, at least economically, the call girl in that respect stands on her own two feet. If she has a pimp, it is she, not he, who is the breadwinner in the family."[31]

Since the majority of marriages in our society render the wife the domestic and sexual subordinate of her husband, marriage degrades the woman who accepts it (or perhaps only the woman who accepts marriage on unequal terms), and its institutionalization in its present form oppresses all women. However, because marriage can be founded on principles which do not involve the subordination of women, we can challenge oppressive aspects of this institution without radically altering it.[32] For example, while the desire to control the sinful urges of men to fornicate may, historically, have been

part of the ideology of marriage, it does not seem to be a central component of our contemporary rationalization for this custom.[33] Marriage, at present in our society, is legitimated by other widely held values and beliefs, for example, the desirability of a long-term, emotionally and financially sustaining, parental partnership. However, I am unable to imagine nonpernicious principles which would legitimate the commercial provision of sex and which would not substantially alter or eliminate the industry as it now exists. Since commercial sex, unlike marriage, is not reformable, feminists should seek to undermine the beliefs and values which underlie our acceptance of it. Indeed, one way to do this is to outwardly oppose prostitution itself.

CONCLUSIONS

If my analysis is correct, then prostitution is not a social aberration or disorder but, rather, a consequence of well-established beliefs and values that form part of the foundation of all our social institutions and practices. Therefore, by striving to overcome discriminatory structures in all aspects of society—in the family, at work outside the home, and in our political institutions—feminists will succeed in challenging some of the cultural presuppositions which sustain prostitution. In other words, prostitution needs no unique remedy, legal or otherwise; it will be remedied as feminists make progress in altering patterns of belief and practice that oppress women in all aspects of their lives. Yet, while prostitution requires no special social cure, some important strategic and symbolic feminist goals may be served by selecting the sex industry for criticism at this time. In this respect, a consumer boycott of the industry is especially appropriate.

In examining prostitution, I have not tried to construct a theory which can explain the universal causes and moral character of prostitution. Such questions presuppose that there is a universal phenomenon to which the term refers and that commercial sex is always socially deviant and undesirable. Instead, I have considered the meaning of commercial sex in modern Western cultures. Although my arguments are consistent with the decriminalization of prostitution, I conclude from my investigation that feminists have legitimate reasons to politically oppose prostitution in our society. Since the principles which implicitly sustain and organize the sex industry are ones which underlie pernicious gender asymmetries in many domains of our social life, to tolerate a practice which epitomizes these principles is oppressive to women.

NOTES

I am grateful to Sandra Bartky, Alison Jaggar, Elizabeth Segal, Richard Arneson, and the anonymous reviewers for *Ethics* for their critical comments and suggestions. Also, I am indebted to Daniel Segal for suggesting many anthropological and historical examples relevant to my argument. In addition, I would like to thank the philosophy department of the Claremont Graduate School for the opportunity to present an earlier draft of this paper for discussion.

1. Nancy Hartsock, *Money, Sex and Power* (Boston: Northeastern University Press, 1985), p. 178.

2. See Rosemarie Tong, *Women, Sex, and the Law* (Totowa, N.J.: Rowman & Allanheld, 1984), pp. 37–64. See also Priscilla Alexander and Margo St. James, "Working on the Issue," National Organization for Women (NOW) National Task Force on Prostitution Report (San Francisco: NOW, 1982).

3. See Carole Pateman. "Defending Prostitution: Charges against Ericsson," *Ethics* 93 (1983): 561–65; and Kathleen Barry, *Female Sexual Slavery* (New York: Avon, 1979).

4. For example, see Gerda Lerner, "The Origin of Prostitution in Ancient Mesopotamia," *Signs: Journal of Women in Culture and Society* 11 (1986): 236–54; Lars Ericsson, "Charges against Prostitution: An Attempt at a Philosophical Assessment," *Ethics* 90 (1980): 335–66; and James Brundage, "Prostitution in the Medieval Canon Law," *Signs: Journal of Women in Culture and Society* 1 (1976): 825–45.

5. Pateman, p. 563.

6. Lerner, p. 239.

7. Emma Goldman, "The Traffic in Women," in *Red Emma Speaks*, ed. Alix Kates Shulman (New York: Schocken, 1983), p. 180.

8. Jacques Rossiaud, "Prostitution, Youth, and Society in the Towns of Southeastern France in the Fifteenth Century," in *Deviants and the Abandoned in French Society: Selections from the Annales Economies, Sociétés, Civilisations*, ed. Robert Forster and Orest Ranum (Baltimore: Johns Hopkins University Press, 1978), p. 21.

9. See Gilbert H. Herdt, ed., *Rituals of Manhood* (Berkeley and Los Angeles: University of California Press, 1982). Also see Harriet Whitehead, "The Varieties of Fertility Cultism in New Guinea: Part 1," *American Ethnologist* 13 (186): 80–99. In comparing penis-feeding to breast-feeding rather than to oral sex, some anthropologists point out that both involve the use of a culturally erotic bodily part of parental nurturing.

10. Arthur Schopenhauer, "The Metaphysics of the Love of the Sexes," in *The Works of Schopenhauer*, ed. Will Durant (New York: Simon & Schuster, 1928), p. 333.

11. Ericsson, p. 355.

12. Ibid., p. 347.

13. Ibid., pp. 359–60.

14. Ibid., p. 360.

15. Pateman, p. 563.

16. Karl Heider, "Dani Sexuality: A Low Energy System," *Man* 11 (1976): 188–201.

17. See Friedrich Engels, *The Origin of the Family, Private Property and the State* (New York: Penguin, 1985); Goldman; Alison Jaggar, "Prostitution," in *The Philosophy of Sex*, ed. Alan Soble (Totowa, N.J.: Rowman & Littlefield, 1980), pp. 353–58.

18. Gayle Rubin, "The Traffic in Women: Notes on the 'Political Economy' of Sex," in *Toward an Anthropology of Women*, ed. Rayna Reiter (New York: Monthly Review Press, 1975).

19. Ibid., p. 172.

20. In his attempt to describe the general principles of kinship organization implicit in different cultures, Lévi-Strauss admits it is conceivable that he has over-emphasized the patrilineal nature of these exchanges: "It may have been noted that we have assumed what might be called . . . a paternal perspective. That is, we have regarded the woman married by a member of the group as acquired, and the sister provided in exchange as lost. The situation might be altogether different in a system with matrilineal descent and matrilocal residence. . . . The essential thing is that every right acquired entails a concomitant obligation, and that every renunciation calls for a compensation. . . . Even supposing a very hypothetical marriage system in which the man and not the woman were exchanged . . . the total structure would remain unchanged" (Claude Lévi-Strauss, *The Elementary Structures of Kinship* [Boston: Beacon, 1969], p. 132). A culture in which men are gifts in a ritual of exchange is described by Michael Peletz, "The Exchange of Men in Nineteenth-Century Negeri Sembilan (Malaya)," *American Ethnologist* 14 (1987): 449–69.

21. Robert Baker, "'Pricks' and 'Chicks': A Pleas For 'Persons,'" in *Philosophy and Sex*, ed. R. Baker and F. Elliston (Buffalo, N.Y.: Prometheus, 1984), pp. 260–66. In this section, Baker provides both linguistic and nonlinguistic evidence that intercourse, in our cultural mythology, hurts women.

22. Andrea Dworkin, *Intercourse* (New York: Free Press, 1987), p. 122.

23. Ann Garry, "Pornography and Respect for Women," in Baker and Elliston, eds., p. 318.

24. In "Defending Prostitution," Pateman states: "The services of the prostitute are related in a more intimate manner to her body than those of other professionals. Sexual services, that is to say, sex and sexuality, are constitutive of the body in a way in which the counseling skills of the social worker are not. . . . Sexuality and the body are, further, integrally connected to conceptions of femininity and masculinity, and all these are constitutive of our individuality, our sense of self-identity" (p. 562). On my view, while our social identities are determined by our outward sexual practice, this is due to arbitrary, culturally determined conceptual mappings, rather than some universal relationship holding between persons and their bodies.

25. Margo St. James, Speech to the San Diego County National Organization for Women, La Jolla, California, February 27, 1982, and from private correspondence with St. James (1983). Margo St. James is the founder of COYOTE (Call Off Your Old Tired Ethics) and the editor of *Coyote Howls*. COYOTE is a civil rights organization which seeks to change the sex industry from within by gaining better working conditions for prostitutes.

26. Garry, pp. 318–23.

27. According to Bertrand Russell: "In Japan, apparently, the matter is quite otherwise. Prostitution is recognized and respected as a career, and is even adopted at the insistence of parents. It is often a not uncommon method of earning a marriage dowry" (*Marriage and Morals* [1929; reprint, New York: Liveright, 1970], p. 151). Perhaps contemporary Japan is closer to our imaginary society, a society where heterosexual intercourse is not felt to be polluting to women.

28. This of course does not mean we should not hire such people for child care, for that would simply be to deny a good person a better job than he or she might otherwise obtain—a job which unlike the prostitute's job is not likely to hurt their prospects for other work or social positions. Nevertheless, one should not believe that one's act of giving a person of this social description such a job does anything to change the unfair structure of our society.

29. I am grateful to Richard Arneson for suggesting this analogy to me.

30. Simone de Beauvoir, *The Second Sex* (New York: Vintage, 1974), p. 619. According to Engels: "Marriage of convenience turns often enough into the crassest prostitution—sometimes of both partners, but far more commonly of the woman, who only differs from the ordinary courtesan in that she does not let out her body on piecework as a wage worker, but sells it once and for all into slavery" (p. 102).

31. Ericsson, p. 354.

32. Pateman argues: "The conjugal relation is not necessarily one of domination and subjection, and in this it differs from prostitution" (p. 563). On this I agree with her.

33. Russell informs us that "Christianity, and more particularly St. Paul, introduced an entirely novel view of marriage, that it existed not primarily for the procreation of children, but to prevent the sin of fornication. . . . I remember once being advised by a doctor to abandon the practice of smoking, and he said that I should find it easier if, whenever the desire came upon me, I proceeded to suck an acid drop. It is in this spirit that St. Paul recommends marriage" (pp. 44–46).

ROBERT STEWART

Moral Criticism and the Social Meaning of Prostitution

In her recent article "Should Feminists Oppose Prostitution?" Laurie Shrage maintains that prostitution cannot be understood apart from a given cultural context. Its significance for us—there being no universal idea—is partly determined by a set of widespread beliefs that, she asserts, are oppressive and damaging to all women. She contends that these beliefs legitimize and provide the sole support for prostitution as we know it. Shrage cites four of these general opinions:

First, people in our society generally believe that human beings naturally possess, but socially repress, powerful, emotionally destabilizing sexual appetites. Second, we assume that men are naturally suited for dominant social roles. Third, we assume that contact with male genitals in virtually all contexts is damaging and polluting to women. Fourth, we assume that a person's sexual practice renders her or him a particular "kind" of person, for example, "a homosexual," "a bisexual," "a whore," "a virgin," "a pervert," and so on.[1]

Shrage's argument raises important questions about moral justification and relativism that extend far beyond the specific issue of the morality of tolerating prostitution. I hope to clarify some of these fundamental questions in the course of assessing her views. Though I will begin by briefly pointing out weaknesses in her case for rejecting two of the above beliefs, my central purpose is to challenge the assumption that the social meaning of a practice is decisive in determining its moral status or the moral rightness of condoning it—that is, that unjustifiable but common beliefs about the practice (at least when leading to harm or offense) can make what would otherwise be a morally permissible activity unacceptable.

I do not doubt that all four of the general beliefs mentioned are, at least implicitly, widely held in our society. But the first two, at least, might be partly true and worthy of acceptance if formulated more precisely. With regard to the first general belief Shrage asserts that the sexual preoccupation characteristic of our society is "excessive" and the belief is but a "cultural rationalization" for it. But we need not be Freudians to recognize that humans in comparison with many other mammals have a *potential* for strong sexual appetite, where that is understood in terms of affect, frequency, willingness to sacrifice other goods, and so forth. Certainly, it is also true that the degree of its actualization will vary among cultures. Shrage cites as her sole example of a society dramatically different from ours in this respect a small tribe in West New Guinea, the Grand Valley Dani, whose level of sexual interest is very low, as evidenced, for instance, in their apparent observance of a four- to six-year postpartum abstinence period. The research to which she refers is that of Karl Heider,[2] who notes that the Grand Valley Dani are "quite exceptional" if not "unique" in this respect among cultures with which he is acquainted, including other Dani tribes. Interestingly, Heider explains that low sexual interest is only one facet of a general lack of energy, enthusiasm, and excitement in the tribe members' lives; they are also remarkably unintellectual and manifest no interest in artistic achievement apart from body adornment. He speculates about the causes of this low energy level and suggests that lack of contact with other cultures and the absence of stress and stimulation in the lives of tribal children could partly account for it. In any event, if the causes are indeed social and not biological, we should be struck not only by the oddity of the low level of sexual interest among members of this tribe, in comparison with most peoples, but by the obvious suggestion that a level of sexual interest closer to that of our society is inseparable from the general level of motivation and creativity characteristic of advanced cultures.

The second widespread belief—that men naturally dominate—is impossible to assess without further clarification and refinement. Shrage asserts that male dominance in society is "naturally arbitrary and culturally determined." Yet is it so obvious from the standpoint of our present-day, imperfect understanding of social structures and processes that one sex is not, on the average, due to innate characteristics, more suited than the other for at least some social roles? The likely truth of the matter is that men are best suited for dominant roles in some areas of life, women in others. Rejection of the broad, unqualified, and unanalyzed assertion of male dominance is as meaningless as its affirmation. If we focus only on the issue of dominance in sexual relations, further distinctions are still necessary. For example, it might be true that men are, for biological reasons, more inclined on the average than women to initiate sexual contact, direct activity, seek variety, and so forth (perhaps due to a more intense and concentrated sexual need); but this is compatible with female dominance in other respects. Indeed, feminist critics of prostitution tend to ignore the ways in which female prostitutes dominate their clients in many, if not most, encounters.[3]

Shrage provides no real grounds for the implausible claims that prostitution perpetuates beliefs of the sort mentioned, and that these beliefs are in turn the sole support of the practice as we know it today. It is also very doubtful that greater condemnation and discouragement of prostitution in our society would have any substantial effect on either its prevalence or that of the beliefs and values to which Shrage objects. Sometimes, however, she seems to claim a symbolic connection rather than a causal one between the practice and the beliefs, saying that society's tolerance implies general acceptance of those beliefs and values, as does active participation in the practice of prostitution itself as provider or client.[4] Here again, she fails to substantiate the assertion. What tolerance or

participation "imply" will ultimately be a matter of what individuals intend by their acts or forebearance, and there is no reason to think that support of oppressive and false beliefs is typically among their motivations. One is reminded of similar claims—equally mistaken— that those who remain in their country or vote in its elections "imply" consent to all of its laws or to the authority of politicians.

Shrage's fundamental argument, however, rests on an assumption not about the moral relevance of what people mean by what they do but rather about how others interpret their actions (or misinterpret them). She offers an analogy between prostitution and eating dogs and cats in a society such as ours. What is mainly relevant to assessing the moral and political character of the latter practice is not its healthfulness or the similarities of these animals to cows, pigs, and chickens, she insists:

What is relevant is that, by including cat and dog flesh in one's diet, a person may really make others upset and, therefore, do damage to them as well as to oneself. In short, how actions are widely perceived and interpreted by others, even if wrongly or seemingly irrationally, is crucial to determining their moral status because, though such interpretations may not hold up against some "objective reality," they are part of the "social reality" in which we live.

Prostitution as it presently exists "epitomizes," "testifies to and perpetuates" the widespread beliefs that give it the particular social meaning it has in our culture and "oppress all women in many domains of their lives."[5] Thus, Shrage suggests, its social meaning renders it and its support or toleration immoral.

There is an objectionable form of relativism implicit in this assumption about moral relevance, one which is quite apparent when we apply it to some other examples. Since I find Shrage's example of eating dogs and cats unconvincing—it is distasteful but not immoral, even if it upsets the neighbors—let us consider two cases about which most of us will agree. Interracial sex is widely disapproved of in our society, though perhaps not nearly as much as it once was, due to irrational or at least unsupported beliefs about the races held by many whites. Similarly, in our society, and to a much greater degree in some other cultures (Islamic societies such as Pakistan), women who are victims of rape are sometimes blamed or at least disvalued on the basis of unjustifiable beliefs about the sexes. Whether these phenomena are viewed as occurrences in our society or others—the social meaning is negative in either case—there is nothing morally wrong with interracial sex or being a victim of rape, regardless of the senseless beliefs that color many people's perceptions of them. That many people are offended by interracial relationships or disgusted by rape victims is irrelevant. A third example, more analogous to the case of prostitution, is homosexual behavior in our society. Such behavior by some practitioners, for example, drag queens marching in Gay Pride parades, serves to reinforce stereotypical beliefs detrimental to homosexuals as a group. Yet we should tolerate this behavior, even if it offends many; it is immoral only if it is intended to harm others in certain substantial ways, and in fact does. As I noted earlier, this has not been shown to be generally true of prostitution in our society, however offensive it is to many.

I do not mean to suggest that selling one's sexual services is, in most circumstances, a desirable way to make a living, only that it is not morally wrong per se.[6] My aim has been to question the general claim that the social meaning of a mode of conduct is of primary relevance in assessing its moral status. I have argued that if people are offended (not truly harmed in serious, identifiable ways) by actions which they misinterpret or misunderstand in virtue of false beliefs or unreasonable attitudes, that fact does not constitute a basis for moral criticism, at least not beyond judgments of insensitivity. Shrage does not establish the causal claim about the harmful results of condoning or even participating in prostitution required by her argument. Were it the case that these harms did occur, that is, that a substantial number of women were denied opportunities they would otherwise have, and so forth, as a result of mistaken beliefs partly reinforced by prostitution as it exists, the appropriate strategy would be to find other ways to change those beliefs or attitudes without whose prevalence the harms would not result. Shrage does not advocate the legal prohibition of prostitution—only its reform, decriminalization, and regulation.[7] But I would argue that there is nothing wrong with prostitution as it is, apart from bad consequences that are largely the result of legislation. The abolition of these laws and advocacy of the moral position that commercial sex is permissible are the better approach. This moral position becomes more defensible when we realize that it is the individual meaning, that is, how actors view themselves, their motives, and their partners, not the social meaning, of conduct that is most relevant morally.[8]

NOTES

1. Laurie Shrage, "Should Feminists Oppose Prostitution?," *Ethics* 99 (1989): 352.

2. Karl Heider, "Dani Sexuality: A Low Energy System," *Man*, n. s., 11 (1976): 188–201.

3. Apart from the cases in which male clients desire the sexual dominance of the prostitute, the latter will need to be in control of the situation generally for her own safety, especially if she is an independent agent.

4. Shrage, "Should Feminists Oppose Prostitution?," 356–57.

5. Ibid., 351–52.

6. Since I reject the concept of moral obligation to oneself, considerations of self-inflicted harm, for example, loss of self-esteem or respect, degradation, erosion of the sense of one's privacy and identity—being variable and subjective—are entirely prudential ones. That they lack moral import is not to say that they are not often good reasons to avoid prostitution; for the same reasons one might want to avoid promiscuity. We should not lose sight of the fact, however, that these psychological cost factors—for example, guilt feelings—are frequently due to irrational beliefs or attitudes.

7. At least, this is the position presented in her more recent paper, "Is Sexual Desire Raced?: The Social Meaning of Interracial Prostitution," *Journal of Social Philosophy* 23 (1992): 42–51.

8. Shrage almost concedes this point in discussing marriage (see "Should Feminists Oppose Prostitution?," 360).

II
Sexual Norms and Ethics

JEROME NEU

Freud and Perversion

The first of Freud's *Three Essays on the Theory of Sexuality* is entitled "The Sexual Aberrations." Why should Freud begin a book the main point of which is to argue for the existence of infantile sexuality with a discussion of adult perversions (after all, the existence of the adult aberrations was not news)? While many answers might be suggested with some plausibility (e.g., to ease the shock of the new claim; or, medical texts typically begin with pathology), I think Freud's beginning can be usefully understood as part of a brilliant argumentative strategy to extend the notion of sexuality by showing how extensive it already was. Freud himself (in the Preface to the Fourth Edition) describes the book as an attempt "at enlarging the concept of sexuality" ([11], p. 134). The extension involved in the notion of perversion prepares the way for the extension involved in infantile sexuality.

The book begins, on its very first page, with a statement of the popular view of the sexual instinct: "It is generally understood to be absent in childhood, to set in at the time of puberty in connection with the process of coming to maturity and to be revealed in the manifestations of an irresistible attraction exercised by one sex upon the other, while its aim is presumed to be sexual union, or at all events actions leading in that direction ([11], p. 135)." But it quickly becomes obvious that this will not do as a definition of the sphere of the sexual. Sexuality is not confined to heterosexual genital intercourse between adults, for there are a number of perversions, and even popular opinion recognizes these as sexual in their nature. Popular opinion might wish to maintain a narrow conception of what is to count as *normal* sexuality, thus rais-

ing a problem about how one is to distinguish between normal and abnormal sexuality, but the more interesting and immediate problem is to make clear in virtue of what the perversions are recognized as sexual at all. And it is here that Freud makes an enormous conceptual advance. He distinguishes the object and the aim of the sexual instinct (decomposing what might have seemed an indissoluble unity), and he introduces the notion of erotogenic zones (thus extending sexuality beyond the genitals), and is thus able to show that the perversions involve variations along a number of dimensions (source, object, and aim) of a single underlying instinct. Heterosexual genital intercourse is one constellation of variations, and homosexuality is another. Homosexuality, or inversion, involves variation in object, but the sexual sources (erotogenic zones, or bodily centers of arousal) and aims (acts, such as intercourse and looking, designed to achieve pleasure and satisfaction) may be the same. Thus what makes homosexuality recognizably sexual, despite its distance from what might be presented as the ordinary person's definition of sexuality, is the vast amount that it can be seen to have in common with "normal" sexuality once one comes to understand the sexual instinct as itself complex, as having dimensions.

Freud makes the complexity of the sexual instinct compelling by drawing on the researches of the tireless investigators of sexual deviation such as Krafft-Ebing and Havelock Ellis. He makes the complexity intelligible by distinguishing the few dimensions (source, object, and aim) of the underlying instinct that are needed to lend order to the vast variety of phenomena, providing an illuminating new classi-

From E. E. Shelp, ed., *Sexuality and Medicine*, vol. I Dordrecht, The Netherlands: D. Reidel, 1987, pp. 153–184. Copyright © 1987 by D. Reidel Publishing Company. Reprinted with permission of Kluwer Academic Publishers.

ficatory scheme. Once each of the perversions is understood as involving variation along one or more dimensions of a single underlying instinct, Freud is in a position to do at least two extraordinary things: First, to call into question the primacy of one constellation of variations over another. And second, to show that other phenomena that might not appear on the surface sexual (e.g., childhood thumbsucking) share essential characteristics with obviously sexual activity (e.g., infantile sensual sucking involves pleasurable stimulation of the same erotogenic zone, the mouth, stimulated in adult sexual activities such as kissing), and can be understood as being earlier stages in the development of the same underlying instinct that expresses itself in such various forms in adult sexuality. Freud is in a position to discover infantile sexuality. To briefly retrace the steps to this point: Perversions are regarded as sexual because they can be understood as variations of an underlying instinct along three dimensions (somatic source, object, and aim). The instinct has components, is complex or "composite" ([11], p. 162). If adult perversions can be understood in terms of an underlying instinct with components that can be specified along several dimensions, then many of the activities of infancy can also be so understood, can be seen as earlier stages in the development of those components. But now I wish to focus on the newly problematic relation of normal and abnormal sexuality. Is one set of variations better or worse than another? The mere fact of difference, variation in content, is no longer enough once one cannot say one set of variations is somehow natural and others are not. Once one sees sexuality as involving a single underlying instinct, with room for variation along several dimensions, new criteria for pathology are needed. Moreover, insofar as variation is thought-dependent, rather than a matter of biological aberration, the question arises of whether there is such a thing as a pathology of sexual thought. Is there room for a morality of desire and phantasy alongside the ordinary morality governing action?

HOMOSEXUALITY

Freud initially distinguishes inversion from perversion. Inversion involves displacement of the sexual object from members of the opposite sex to members of the same sex. Inversion includes male homosexuality and lesbianism. Insofar as it involves variation in object only, it may appear less deviant than other sexual aberrations. But insofar as the point of singling out inversion is to contrast it with aberrations involving displacement in aim rather than object, it might as well include a wider range of aberrations, aberrations where displacement is to someone or something other than members of the same sex. From that point of view, bestiality, necrophilia, etc. are more like inversion than like the other aberrations—and Freud in fact treats them together as "deviations in respect of the sexual object" ([11], p. 136). If we include these less common and more troubling variations in object, inversion may no longer seem a less problematical form of sexual aberration. Moreover, the distinction between inversion and perversion tends to collapse as Freud discusses fetishism (is the deviation in object? in aim?—[11], p. 153). And it should be remembered that homosexuality is itself (like heterosexuality) internally complex, encompassing many different activities and attitudes. I shall use "perversion" broadly, as Freud himself usually does, so that homosexuality counts as perversion within Freud's classificatory scheme.

Is that a reproach? In the *Three Essays,* Freud states explicitly that it is inappropriate to use the word perversion as a "term of reproach" ([11], p. 160). But that is in the special context of exploring the implications of his expanded conception of sexuality. In the case of Dora, published in the same year (1905) as the *Three Essays,* he refers to a phantasy of fellatio as "excessively repulsive and perverted" ([10], p. 52). A reproach seems built into the reference. It could be argued that Freud is forced to use the vocabulary of the view he wishes to overthrow, and that it carries its unwelcome connotations with it. Indeed, he in the same place argues that "We must learn to speak without indignation of what we call the sexual perversions—instances in which the sexual function has extended its limits in respect either to the part of the body concerned or to the sexual object chosen" ([10], p. 50). Perhaps Freud's own feelings, about the term if not the specific acts referred to, are ambivalent. The important question is what the appropriate attitude is and whether Freud's theory offers any light. So, again, let us consider homosexuality. Supposing it is a perversion, is that a reproach? Is the fact that it counts as a perversion a reason for disapproving of it in others or avoiding it oneself?

One could take the high ground and claim that it is pointless to disapprove what is not in a person's control, and then argue that choice of sexual object or sexual orientation is not in a person's control. But this does not really take one very far. Perhaps one has no or only marginal control over whether one contracts diabetes, but this does not stop us from recognizing that diabetes is a bad thing (while it does compel us to treat diabetes patients as victims). Even if we had an aetiological theory that assured us that homosexuality is not a matter of choice, and so perhaps not properly disapproved, that would not settle the question of whether it is a good or a bad thing (something we should avoid if we could). Moreover, even if sexual orientation is a given, outside the individual's control, what is given is a direction to desire. There remains the question of whether the individual should seek to control and suppress, or act on and express, the given desires.[1] Freud does not in fact take the high ground. His own aetiological views seem to leave open the extent of biological and other dispositional factors in leading to homosexuality. Whether homosexuality is innate or acquired is for him an open and a complex question ([11], p. 140). And, to whatever extent it is acquired, the conditions of its acquisition are also complex ([11], pp. 144f.). The so-called "choice" of a sexual object is thus multiply obscure, and it is unclear to what extent the relevant causal conditions are within the individual's control (though one might also question whether and when control should be regarded as a condition of responsibility—see [43] and [36]). Freud nonetheless argues, on other grounds, that the "perversity" of homosexuality gives no reason to condemn it:

The uncertainty in regard to the boundaries of what is to be called normal sexual life, when we take different races and different epochs into account, should in itself be enough to cool the zealot's ardour. We surely ought not to forget that the perversion which is the most repellent to us, the sensual love of a man for a man, was not only tolerated by a people

so far our superiors in cultivation as were the Greeks, but was actually entrusted by them with important social functions. The sexual life of each one of us extends to a slight degree—now in this direction, now in that—beyond the narrow lines imposed as the standard of normality. The perversions are neither bestial nor degenerate in the emotional sense of the word. They are a development of germs all of which are contained in the undifferentiated sexual disposition of the child, and which, by being suppressed or by being diverted to higher, asexual aims—by being "sublimated"—are destined to provide the energy for a great number of our cultural achievements. ([10], p. 50)

This passage actually contains at least two different types of argument. One is an appeal to universality across individuals, another an appeal to diversity across cultures. There is no doubt that sexual standards are culturally relative: different societies approve and disapprove of different sexual activities. But one might still wonder whether some societies are perverse in a pejorative sense. There is no avoiding direct consideration of the question of the criteria for perversion. Do they allow for something more than culturally relative, or even individually relative (whatever pleases one), judgments of sexual value?

CRITERIA OF PERVERSION

Once one accepts Freud's view of the complexity of the underlying sexual instinct, the old content criterion for perversion and pathology must be abandoned. As Freud writes, "In the sphere of sexual life we are brought up against peculiar and, indeed, insoluble difficulties as soon as we try to draw a sharp line to distinguish mere variations within the range of what is physiological from pathological symptoms" ([11], pp. 160–161).

It might seem simple enough to provide a sociological or statistical specification of perversion, but there are difficulties. For what precisely would the statistics reflect? One's questionnaires or surveys might seek to discover what the majority regards as perverse, but that would leave one wanting to know what perversion is (after all, members of the majority might in fact be applying very various standards). One might try to avoid direct circularity by, without mentioning the concept perversion, trying to elicit information revealing of which sexual desires the majority disapproves. But circularity re-emerges on this approach because there might be all sorts of different grounds for disapproval (aesthetic, moral, religious, political, biological, medical . . .), and what one wants is to single out those desires and practices which are disapproved of as (specifically) perverse. It appears one's questions and evidence would have already to be applying some standard of perversion in order to achieve that singling out. Parallel and further problems would apply to surveys of actual sexual practices. (Are perversions necessarily rare? If a practice became popular, would it therefore cease to be perverse? And if a practice were rare, e. g., celibacy or adultery, would that necessarily make it perverse?) Surely perversion is meant to mark only a certain kind of deviation from a norm. And there is another difficulty. For whatever method one uses, it will turn out that what counts as perversion will vary from society to society, will vary over time and place, in short, will be culturally relative. So insofar as one's concern is wider than the views of a particular society or group, insofar as it is a concern with general psychological theory, with the nature of human nature, no sociological approach will do. Moreover, insofar as one's concern is personal, or perhaps even therapeutic (unless one's standards of therapy are simply adaptation to local and contemporary prevailing norms), that is, if one is concerned to know how one ought to live one's life (including one's sexual life), a sociological approach will not do. For one's society may be wrong-headed, prejudiced, misguided, or in other ways mistaken. One has only one life to live. It might be necessary to resist one's society's demands or even to leave it. So one must look further.

Perhaps perversion can still be defined in terms of content if we are willing to start (again) with the popular view of normal sexuality as consisting of heterosexual genital intercourse between adults: then, any sexual desire or practice which goes beyond the body parts intended for sexual union, or that devotes too exclusive attention to a form of interaction normally passed through on the way to the final sexual aim, or which is directed at an object other than an adult member of the opposite sex, might be regarded as perverse.[2] One might insist on this stand independently of what the members of any particular society happen to think. But as we have seen, once one accepts Freud's analysis of the sexual in terms of a single, but complex, underlying instinct, while it becomes clear why the sexual perversions count as sexual, it becomes unclear why they are perverse. What privileges heterosexual genital intercourse between adults? Is there some further criterion that transcends individual societal views?

One might consider disgust. That is, we might try to pick out sexual activities to be condemned as perverse on the basis of a, presumably natural, reaction of disgust. So fellatio and cunnilingus might count as perverse because of disgust felt at oral–genital contact. Extensions of sexual activity beyond the genitals, alternative sources of sexual pleasure, would be perverse if disgust at them were sufficiently widespread. But disgust is itself generally culturally variable and often purely conventional. As Freud points out, "a man who will kiss a pretty girl's lips passionately, may perhaps be disgusted at the idea of using her toothbrush, though there are no grounds for supposing that his own oral cavity, for which he feels no disgust, is any cleaner than the girl's" ([11], pp. 151–152). Nonetheless, Freud seems to think that a content criterion can be preserved in certain extreme cases "as, for instance, in cases of licking excrement or of intercourse with dead bodies" ([11], p. 161). Perhaps some things, such as licking excrement, are thought to be objectively, universally disgusting. But perverse practices reveal that is not true, and Freud should know better.

Developmentally, children must learn to be disgusted at feces. This fact may not be obvious, but Freud was well aware of it. During the period of his earliest speculations about anal erotism, Freud wrote a fascinating letter to his friend Fliess: "I wanted to ask you, in connection with excrement-eating . . . and animals, when disgust first appears in small children and whether there is a period in early infancy when no disgust is felt. Why do I not go to the nursery and—experiment? Because with twelve-and-a-half hours' work I have no time, and because the womenfolk do not back me in my investigations. The answer would be interesting theoretically" ([29], p. 192, Letter 58 of February 8, 1897). (This letter reminds us of how little Freud's theories about infantile sexuality were based on the direct observation of children. Which, to my mind, far from undermining his achievement—given its substantial confirmation by subsequent observations—makes it all the more remarkable.) The answer to his question was well known to Freud by the time he wrote the *Three Essays*. Children will play quite happily with their little turds, and as Freud writes, the contents of the bowels "are clearly treated as a part of the infant's own body and represent his first 'gift': by producing them he can express his active compliance with his environment and, by witholding them, his disobedience" ([11], p. 186). And Freud elsewhere develops the analogy between feces and other valued possessions, such as gold [12].[3] Disgust at the excremental is itself in need of explanation:

Where the anus is concerned . . . it is disgust which stamps that sexual aim as a perversion. I hope, however, I shall not be accused of partisanship when I assert that people who try to account for this disgust by saying that the organ in question serves the function of excretion and comes in contact with excrement—a thing which is disgusting in itself—are not much more to the point than hysterical girls who account for their disgust at the male genital by saying that it serves to void urine. ([11], p. 152)

It is true that Freud singles out disgust as one of the triumvirate of "forces of repression" (disgust, shame and morality—[11], pp. 162, 178), and it may be that the forces of repression are ultimately instinctual and so present in every society, but that need not fix the content of the reaction. That is, it *may be* that everyone is necessarily (meaning biologically) bound to feel disgust at something, while still leaving room for variation in the objects of disgust. It should be no more surprising that the objects of disgust (as an instinct) are variable, than that the objects of sexual desire (as an instinct) are variable. So if the objects of sexual desire have no fixed or determinate content, neither do the objects of sexual disgust. We must look elsewhere if we are to find usable criteria for perversion and pathology.

Before looking elsewhere, we should note that there is another problem in a content criterion for perversion, which stems not from the variations we have been emphasizing, but from the universality we have mentioned only in passing. Freud points out that we can find apparently perverse desires not only in (otherwise admirable) other societies, but also within ourselves. In the case of homosexuality, he points out that our desires are responsive to external circumstances. Many will turn to homosexual pleasures given the appropriate favorable or inhibiting circumstances (e.g., "exclusive relations with persons of their own sex, comradeship in war, detention in prison . . . "—[11], p. 140). And even more strongly Freud concludes: "Psycho-analytic research is most decidedly opposed to any attempt at separating off homosexuals from the rest of mankind as a group of a special character. By studying sexual excitations other than those that are manifestly displayed, it has found that all human beings are capable of making a homosexual object-choice and have in fact made one in their unconscious" ([11], p. 145n.). There is a sense in which all human beings are bisexual. Moreover, the universality of perversions other than homosexuality is exhibited in the role they play in foreplay ([11], pp. 210, 234). The prevalence of perversion (and the "negative" of perversion, neurosis) receives its theoretical underpinning in terms of the universality of polymorphously perverse infantile sexuality. But for now the point is to see that a simple content criterion for perversion will not do. Given the facts of variety in cultural practice and of uniformity in individual potential, it is difficult to see how any particular object-choice (to focus on one dimension) can be singled out as necessarily abnormal. The nature of the sexual instinct itself sets no limit, for as Freud concludes, "the sexual instinct and the sexual object are merely soldered together" ([11], p. 148).

An alternative criterion for perversion and pathology emerges in connection with Freud's discussion of fetishism. Freud characterizes fetishism in general in terms of those cases "in which the normal sexual object is replaced by another which bears some relation to it, but is entirely unsuited to serve the normal sexual aim" ([11], p. 153). (Note that the variation seems to affect both object and aim.) But he shows that it has a point of contact with the normal through the sort of overvaluation of the sexual object, and of its aspects and of things associated with it, that seems quite generally characteristic of love. He continues:

The situation only becomes pathological when the longing for the fetish passes beyond the point of being merely a necessary condition attached to the sexual object and actually *takes the place* of the normal aim, and, further, when the fetish becomes detached from a particular individual and becomes the *sole* sexual object. These are, indeed, the general conditions under which mere variations of the sexual instinct pass over into pathological aberrations. ([11], p. 154).

Freud spells out the general conditions in terms of "exclusiveness and fixation":

In the majority of instances the pathological character in a perversion is found to lie not in the *content* of the new sexual aim but in its relation to the normal. If a perversion, instead of appearing merely *alongside* the normal sexual aim and object, and only when circumstances are unfavourable to *them* and favourable to *it*—if, instead of this, it ousts them completely and takes their place in *all* circumstances—if, in short, a perversion has the characteristics of exclusiveness and fixation—then we shall usually be justified in regarding it as a pathological symptom. ([11], p. 161)

But this really will not do as a general criterion either, for reasons provided by Freud himself in a note a few pages earlier:

[P]sycho-analysis considers that a choice of an object independently of its sex—freedom to range equally over male and female objects—as it is found in childhood, in primitive states of society and early periods of history, is the original basis from which, as a result of restriction in one direction or the other, both the normal and the inverted types develop. Thus from the point of view of psycho-analysis the exclusive sexual interest felt by men for women is also a problem that needs elucidating and is not a self-evident fact based upon an attraction that is ultimately of a chemical nature. ([11], p. 146n.)

Once it is recognized that the instinct is merely soldered to its object, that there are wide possibilities of variation in the choice of object, then every choice of object becomes equally problematical, equally in need of explanation. Exclusiveness and fixation cannot be used to mark off homosexuality as perverse without marking off (excessively strong) commitments to heterosexuality as equally perverse. Thus, exclusiveness and fixation are no help if the point of a criterion for perversion is to distinguish the abnormal from the normal, and if heterosexual

genital intercourse between adults is to be somehow privileged as the paradigm of the normal. We need some norm for sexuality if the notion of perversion is to take hold. From where can we get it? Is there any reason to suppose that it will take the form of the popular view of normal sexuality?

DEVELOPMENT AND MATURATION

Freud in fact, as we have seen, operates with multiple criteria for perversion and pathology. We have also seen that his own views provide materials for a critique of those criteria if one attempts to generalize them. But there emerges from within his theory yet another criterion, a criterion which is meant to be ultimately biological and so not culturally relative. As Freud puts it at the start of the third of his *Three Essays:* "Every pathological disorder of sexual life is rightly to be regarded as an inhibition in development" ([11], p. 208). Perverse sexuality is, ultimately, infantile sexuality. While consideration of the adult perversions prepares the way for the extension of our understanding of sexuality to infantile activities in the course of Freud's book, infantile sexuality prepares the way for both normal and perverse sexuality in the development of the individual.[4] It is through arrests in that development, or through regression to earlier points of fixation when faced by later frustration, that an adult comes to manifest perverse sexual activity. We can pick out sexual desires and activities which count as perverse if we have an ideal of normal development and maturation.

Freud's theory of psychosexual development, with its central oral–anal–genital stages, provides such an ideal. The dynamic is at least partly biological. At first, the infant has control of little other than its mouth, and in connection with its original need for taking nourishment it readily develops independent satisfaction in sensual sucking ([11], p. 182). That the anus in due course becomes the center of sexual pleasure and wider concerns ("holding back and letting go") is not surprising in the light of a variety of biological developments: as the infant gets older, the feces are better formed, there is more sphincter control (so the child begins to have a choice about when and where to hold back or let go), and with teething there is pressure for the mother to wean.[5] Finally, there comes puberty and the possibility of reproduction and increased interest in the genitals. But one should not totally biologize what is at least in part a social process. There may be a confusion between the ripening of an organic capacity with the valuation of one form of sexuality as its highest or only acceptable form. The subordination of sexuality to reproduction, and the importance attached to heterosexual genital activity, is after all, a social norm. Freud does not claim that there is a biological or evolutionary *preference* for reproduction; the individual preference, if any, is simply for end-pleasure. Even if the preference for end-pleasure or orgasm over fore-pleasure ([11], pp. 210-212) is biologically determined, the conditions for such pleasure are not. Whether end-pleasure takes place under conditions that might lead to reproduction depends on a wide range of factors, and whether it *should* take place under such conditions is subject to both circumstance and argument. Even if one attaches supreme importance to the survival of the species, other things, including sexual pleasure (which may in turn depend on a certain degree of variety) may be necessary to the survival of the species. And for most of recent history, over-population and unwanted conception have been of greater concern than maximizing the reproductive effects of sexual activity. Under certain circumstances homosexuality might have social advantages.[6]

In terms of Freud's instinct theory (not to be confused with standard biological notions of hereditary behavior patterns in animals), every instinct involves an internal, continuously flowing source of energy or tension or pressure. Freud adds, however: "Although instincts are wholly determined by their origin in a somatic source, in mental life we know them only by their aims" ([21], p. 123). Given Freud's fundamental hypotheses concerning the mechanisms of psychic functioning, the aim is in every case ultimately discharge of the energy or tension. And given Freud's discharge theory of pleasure (or tension theory of un-pleasure), the aim must ultimately be understood in terms of pleasure. Freud is well aware of the problems of a simple discharge theory of pleasure, especially in relation to sexuality (where, after all, the subjective experience of increasing tension is typically as pleasurable as the experience of

discharge). (See [11], pp. 209f., and [26].) The point here, however, is that on Freud's view the essential aim of sexual activity (as instinctual activity) must be pleasure, achievable by a wide variety of particular acts (under a wider variety of thought-dependent conditions). Sexuality may serve many other purposes and have many other functions and aims from a range of different points of view. Among these are reproduction, multi-level interpersonal awareness, interpersonal communication, bodily contact, love, money. . . .[7] Within Freud's theory, perversion is to be understood in terms of infantile, that is non-genital, forms of pleasure. This approach has its problems. For one thing, homosexuality, in some ways the paradigm of perversion for Freud, is not necessarily non-genital and so not obviously perverse by this criterion. Moreover, insofar as other perversions, such as fetishism, aim at genital stimulation and discharge, they too are not purely infantile. (Cf. [22], p. 321.) In practice, of course, Freud collapses the individual's experienced concern for genital pleasure together with the biological function of reproduction, so that the development and maturation criterion for perversion reduces to the question of the suitability of a particular activity for reproduction.

One should not confuse the (or a) biological function of sexuality, namely reproduction, with sexuality as such. Freud is at pains to point out that sexuality has a history in the development of the individual that precedes the possibility of reproduction. The reproductive function emerges at puberty ([22], p. 311). An ideal of maturation that gives a central role to that function makes all earlier sexuality of necessity perverse. The infant's multiple sources of sexual pleasure make it polymorphously perverse. And the connection works both ways. Sexual perversions can be regarded as in their nature infantile. As Freud puts it:

[I]f a child has a sexual life at all it is bound to be of a perverse kind; for, except for a few obscure hints, children are without what makes sexuality into the reproductive function. On the other hand, the abandonment of the reproductive function is the common feature of all perversions. We actually describe a sexual activity as perverse if it has given up the aim of reproduction and pursues the attainment of pleasure as an aim independent of it. So . . . the breach and turning-point in the development of sexual life lies in its becoming subordinate to the purposes of reproduction. Everything that happens before this turn of events and equally everything that disregards it and that aims solely at obtaining pleasure is given the uncomplimentary name of "perverse" and as such is proscribed. ([22], p. 316)

I believe Freud may well provide an accurate account of the link in our language between perversion and non-reproductive sex. On the other hand, I don't believe Freud's theory is committed to maintaining that link (the theoretically necessary aim is pleasure, not reproduction). Moreover, even if detachment from the possibility of reproduction is a necessary condition of regarding a practice as perverse, it cannot be sufficient: otherwise sterile heterosexual couples or those who use contraceptives would have to be regarded as perverse. (More on these matters in a moment.)

In privileging heterosexual genital intercourse between adults, if only for the purpose of classifying the perversions, one is making a choice based on norms. Freud's discussion of reproduction reflected existing social norms, and so the fact that they were norms was perhaps concealed. The norms of the sexual liberationists, such as Herbert Marcuse and Norman O. Brown, are in some ways perhaps continuous with the standards built into Freud's model. Does polymorphous perversion include sadism? Should it? Contemporary debates over the appropriate ideals of sexuality cannot be decided by simple appeals to biology. "Regression" is doubtless an empirical concept, but it gets its sense against a background provided by social norms of development (not purely biological norms of development). In picking out the perversions we apply an external standard to sexuality. Which is not to say that we should not. It is to say only that we should be self-conscious about what we are doing and why. Calling perversions "infantile" may in fact describe them, but the immature is usually regarded as inferior. And if that judgment is to follow, one needs more grounds than those provided by biology. After all, if we live long enough, we eventually decay. Later does not necessarily mean better.

MORE ON HOMOSEXUALITY

Is homosexuality a perversion? On a content criterion, whether ultimately based on a reac-

tion of disgust or something else, the answer will vary over time and place, and it is arguable that the reaction of disgust is at least as malleable as the desire to which it is a reaction. On a criterion of exclusiveness and fixation, it is no more or less a perversion than heterosexuality of equivalent exclusivity. On a criterion of development and maturation, or arrest and regression, the answer is less clear. Many say that homosexuality is a developmentally immature stage or phase. I do not see where Freud says that. In the *Three Essays,* Freud notes that homosexuality "may either persist throughout life, or it may go into temporary abeyance, or again it may constitute an episode on the way to a normal development." He goes on, "It may even make its first appearance late in life after a long period of normal sexual activity" ([11], p. 137). In this case, it is heterosexuality that is the earlier phase. In passing, in the lecture on anxiety in the *New Introductory Lectures on Psycho-Analysis,* Freud indicates that "in the life of homosexuals, who have failed to accomplish some part of normal sexual development, the vagina is" represented by the anus ([28], p. 101) and presumably therefore avoided. But this must refer to only one type of homosexual (and surely not the kind that prefers sodomy).[8] Freud does say that infantile sex is characteristically auto-erotic ([11], p. 182), that, is involves no sexual object. In that respect, homosexuality is clearly not infantile. But then foot fetishism and bestiality also involve objects. Would one want to conclude that they are also not infantile, also not perverse? The presence of a whole person as object in the case of homosexuality doubtless makes a significant difference. (Inversion as such may, after all, be importantly different from perversion as such.)

The closest Freud comes to referring to homosexuality as an immature form of sexuality is in a letter in response to a mother who wrote him about her homosexual son. Freud wrote:

Homosexuality is assuredly no advantage, but it is nothing to be ashamed of, no vice, no degradation; it cannot be classified as an illness; we consider it to be a variation of the sexual function, produced by a certain arrest of sexual development. Many highly respectable individuals of ancient and modern times have been homosexuals, several of the greatest men among them (Plato, Michelangelo, Leonardo da Vinci, etc.). It is a great injustice to persecute homosexuality as a crime—and a cruelty, too. . . . What analysis can do for your son runs in a different line. If he is unhappy, neurotic, torn by conflicts, inhibited in his social life, analysis may bring him harmony, peace of mind, full efficiency, whether he remains homosexual or gets changed. ([7], pp. 419–420, April 4, 1935)

Without support from his theoretical writings, the "arrest of sexual development" must be presumed to refer to (the social norm of) reproduction. At a theoretical level, it is only in the case of lesbianism that there looks like there is a stage-specific point to be made about object-choice. That is, given the basic premises of psychoanalytic theory, it is not entirely clear why all women are not lesbians. Up to the genital phase, their development parallels that of little boys, and the beginnings of object relations should tie both little boys and girls to their mothers as the main supporting figure. Girls, unlike boys, are supposed to switch the gender of their love objects in the course of going through their Oedipal phase. The incest taboo is supposed to lead boys to exclude their mothers, but not all women, as possible sexual objects. Under pressure of the castration complex, and through identification with their father, boys are supposed to search for "a girl just like the girl who married dear old dad." Girls, on the other hand, are supposed to switch from a female to a male love object. Why they do this is open to various accounts: Some in terms of penis envy (which needs more elaboration than can be provided here—in any case, biological accounts in terms of a switch in interest from clitoris to vagina will not work). Some in terms of rivalry with the same-gender parent (something girls have in common with boys—it is just that their same-gender parent happened previously to have been the primary object of dependence and so love). Some in terms of a desire to please the mother (involving getting a penis for her). Whatever the account one gives of female psychosexual development, there is little reason to regard male homosexuality as involving arrest at or regression to an earlier phase of development, and so as infantile and (on that criterion) perverse.[9]

Still, perhaps something further can be extracted from Freud's general theory of development. It might be argued that there is a sense in which the basic mechanism of homosexual object-choice is more primitive than the mechanism involved in heterosexual choice. Freud distinguishes two basic types of object-choice: anaclitic and narcissistic ([20], pp. 87–88). On the anaclitic (or attachment) model, just as the sexual component instincts are at the outset attached to the satisfaction of the ego-instincts, the child's dependence on the parents provides the model for later relationships. On the narcissistic model, the individual chooses an object like himself. It might seem obvious that homosexual object-choice is narcissistic, and that narcissistic object-choice is more primitive than the other type. Neither point is correct. While the homosexual certainly has an object that is in at least one respect (gender or genitals) like himself, there are many other aspects of the individual, and in terms of those other aspects even heterosexual object-choice can be importantly narcissistic. Moreover, the mechanisms of homosexual object-choice are various (e.g., Freud sometimes gives emphasis to the avoidance of rivalry with the father or brothers), and the similarity of the object to oneself may not be crucial in all cases—indeed, an anaclitic-type dependence on the object may be much more prominent.[10] That narcissism as a stage, in the sense of taking oneself as a sexual object, may be more primitive than object-choice, in the sense of taking someone else as a sexual object, does not make the narcissistic type of object-choice more primitive than the anaclitic type. In both cases, unlike primitive narcissism, someone else is the object, it is just that on one model similarity matters most, on the other dependence matters most. Even if narcissism is considered the first form of object-choice (after auto-erotism), dependence is present from the very beginning (and a whole school of psychoanalysis would argue object relations are present from the very beginning). Freud himself wrote:

At a time at which the first beginnings of sexual satisfaction are still linked with the taking of nourishment, the sexual instinct has a sexual object outside the infant's own body in the shape of his mother's breast. It is only later that the instinct loses that object, just at the time, perhaps, when the child is able to form a total idea of the person to whom the organ that is giving him satisfaction belongs. As a rule the sexual instinct then becomes auto-erotic, and not until the period of latency has been passed through is the original relation restored. There are thus good reasons why a child sucking at his mother's breast has become the prototype of every relation of love. The finding of an object is in fact the refinding of it. ([11], p. 222)

Homosexuality is no *more* a return to earlier modes of relationship than any other attempt at love.[11]

The American Psychiatric Association has struggled with the question of the classification of homosexuality. The classification is not without practical implications, and it is not surprising that the debate has taken political turns.[12] Nosology is not simply a matter of aetiological theories in any case. At the minimum, classification sometimes takes account of symptomatic patterns and treatment possibilities as well as aetiology. The argument against classifying homosexuality as a disease could well include the notion that it *should not* be treated (whatever its origin) as well as the political claim that the disease classification contributes to inappropriate discrimination (e.g., in jobs—should homosexuality be grounds for dismissal? should schizophrenia?) In 1973, the Board of Trustees of the American Psychiatric Association voted to remove homosexuality (as such) from the list of disorders in the *Diagnostic and Statistical Manual of Mental Disorders* ([5], pp. 281–282). Nonetheless, something called "ego-dystonic homosexuality" was included. That is, if a homosexual does not desire his condition, or suffers distress at his condition, the condition is then regarded as a disorder. Clearly the criteria of mental disorder employed by the APA in this connection are not "neutral": distress and undesirability can be traced to social attitudes (what produces distress and is therefore undesired in Iowa may be very different from what produces distress and is undesired in San Francisco—so homosexuality might be a "disorder" in Iowa but not San Francisco).[13] In any case, it does not follow from the aetiological and developmental theories of psychoanalysis that homosexuality must produce distress and so be undesired.

It must be acknowledged, however, that even if homosexuality involves no developmental arrest or inhibition, even if homosexuality is as "genital" and mature as heterosexuality, it is, as things currently are, detached from the possibility of reproduction and in *that* sense perverse. Any sexual activity which must be detached in its effect from reproduction can be, and has been, regarded as perverse. (Note the relevant detachment is in effect, not in purpose. If the purpose of the persons engaged in the activity was what mattered, most heterosexual genital intercourse would have to be regarded as perverse.) Granting this sense to perversion, however, one should be careful what one concludes about people whose activities are in this sense perverse. For one thing, reproduction would in fact be excluded only if their activities were exclusively perverse. For another, whether it is socially beneficial to *bear* children (the care and upbringing of children is not excluded by perverse—that is, non-reproductive —activity) depends on circumstances (other features of the parents, and social circumstances such as over-population). Moreover, new reproductive technologies may make the reproductive limitations of perverse activity of lesser concern, just as new contraceptive technologies have made the dangers of unwanted conception of lesser concern in "normal" sexual activity. Whatever the biological place of reproduction in human sexual life, it cannot settle the appropriate attitude to non-reproductive human sexual activity. After all, normal sex, that is, heterosexual genital intercourse between adults, can be multiply defective. There can be failures of reciprocity and mutuality, or interactive completeness (private sexual phantasies may make intercourse closer to masturbation in its experience, even if not in its possible effects). And even sex normal in the present sense, that is, of the kind that could in appropriate circumstances lead to reproduction, may fail in its actual effects (most intercourse does not lead to pregnancy, and intercourse between sterile partners or involving the use of contraceptives is most unlikely to). Does detachment from reproductive concerns in one's sexual activity make an individual defective? There is no reason to believe so. Freud frequently points out the great social contributions of homosexuals in history, sometimes even tying the contributions to the sexual orientation, deriving social energies from homosexual inclinations.[14] Not that Freud is blind to defects; he does not assume all homosexuals are mainstays of civilization: "Of course they are not . . . an 'elite' of mankind; there are at least as many inferior and useless individuals among them as there are among those of a different sexual kind" ([22], p. 305). Whether homosexuals contribute to society may be relevant to the question of the appropriate attitude to take towards homosexuality, but the same can be said for heterosexuals and those of mixed inclinations; there is no reason to expect uniformity of contributions within such groupings. It remains unclear whether homosexuality should be regarded as a perversion: it depends on which criterion for perversion is adopted (e.g., content, with disgust the marker; exclusiveness and fixation; or development and maturation, with reproduction the marker), and given certain criteria, on which developmental and aetiological theories are believed. But it does seem clear that even if homosexuality is regarded as a perversion, that in itself gives no ground for condemning it or thinking it worse than heterosexuality; no reason to disapprove it in others or avoid it in oneself.

FOOT FETISHISM

If anything is a perversion according to prevailing attitudes, foot fetishism is, and Freud's discussion of exclusiveness and fixation helps us understand why.[15] But other criteria of perversion (content, maturation, reproduction, completeness . . .) would doubtless yield the same result—indeed, it might be a condition of adequacy on such criteria that they yield that result. Classification is not the problem. Understanding the source and point of this sort of unusual interest in feet is.

Usually, when confronted with a desire one does not share, one can sympathize with the unshared desire at least to the extent of having a sense of what is desirable about the object. Part of the mystery of fetishism is making sense of the extraordinary value and importance attached to the object. Bringing out the link of fetishism to more ordinary overvaluation of sexual objects (which can in turn be tied to narcissism—[20], pp. 88–89, 91, 94, 100–101) goes some way towards making fetishism intelligible ([11], pp. 153–154), but it still leaves us wanting to know why desires should take such peculiar directions. Partly this is a question about the mechanism of object-choice, but more importantly it is a question about the meaning of object-choice. What is it about a foot that makes it so attractive? Why are some particular feet more attractive than others? How can they come to satisfy (or be

seen to satisfy) needs? Psychoanalysis offers answers. In the central cases, "the replacement of the object by a fetish is determined by a symbolic connection of thought, of which the person concerned is usually not conscious" ([11], p. 155). In the case of foot fetishism, in condensed form, psychoanalysis argues (among other things) that "the foot represents a woman's penis, the absence of which is deeply felt" ([11]), p. 155n.) Thus condensed the answer may seem wildly implausible. But in his paper on fetishism [27] Freud traces a chain of experience, phantasy, and association, that suggests how a foot might come to provide reassurance about castration fears, and so become the focus for sexual interests. Thus filled in, the story may still seem implausible. But notice that the question of plausibility enters at two levels: one is the plausibility of the beliefs ascribed to the fetishist (how could anyone believe anything as implausible as that a foot is the mother's missing penis?), and the second is the plausibility of the ascription of the (implausible) beliefs. The genius of the psychoanalytic account is not that it seeks to make bizarre or ad hoc beliefs plausible, but it takes beliefs that it gives us other reasons for ascribing to people and shows how in certain cases they persist and give direction to desire.

Some of the relevant beliefs (e.g., in the ubiquity of the male genital) are to be found in infantile sexual theories. Much of the evidence for such beliefs, as well as for symbolic equations, comes from the study of neurotics; which is as it should be, for, as Freud repeatedly points out, "neuroses are . . . the negative of perversions" ([11], p. 165). We should perhaps pause for a moment on this point. The sexual instinct, we have seen, is complex, has several dimensions ([11], p. 162). It is not the simple, "qualityless" energy of much of Freud's earliest theorizing ([11], pp. 168, 217). It is thus possible to reidentify the "same" instinct in different contexts because variation in (for example) object may leave the source clearly the same. Instincts, unlike qualityless energy, meet one of the conceptual restrictions on "displacement": a change in object can be seen as "displacement" (rather than mere change) only against a background of continuity. One of the things that may have concealed the underlying continuity between infantile and adult sexuality is that the infant is "polymorphously perverse"

([11], p. 191)—and the tie to adult sexuality is clearest in relation to perverse sexuality (not heterosexual genital intercourse). Similarly, the role of sexuality in the neuroses was concealed partly because the sexuality involved is typically perverse: as Freud puts it, *"neuroses are, so to say, the negative of perversions"* ([11], p. 165)—so the sexual nature of neuroses tends to be hidden. What Freud means by the famous formula is spelled out a bit more fully in a note: "The contents of the clearly conscious phantasies of perverts (which in favourable circumstances can be transformed into manifest behaviour), of the delusional fears of paranoics (which are projected in a hostile sense on to other people) and of the unconscious phantasies of hysterics (which psycho-analysis reveals behind their symptoms)—all of these coincide with one another even down to their details" ([11], p. 165 N. 2). To make this claim persuasive, one must bring out the content of the unconscious phantasies of hysterics, but this is made simpler by the fact that, in the case of neurotics, "the symptoms constitute the sexual activity of the patient" ([11], p. 163), and "at least *one* of the meanings of a symptom is the representation of a sexual phantasy" ([10], p. 47). Thus Dora's hysterical cough could be analyzed in terms of an unconscious phantasy of fellatio ([10], pp. 47–52). None of this is very surprising if one remembers that neurotic sexuality, like perverse sexuality, is infantile ([11], p. 172)—whatever shape the sexual instinct eventually takes, it inevitably has its roots in infantile sexuality.

Returning to foot fetishism, whatever one thinks of the psychoanalytic story, it is clear that some story is needed. The attachment is, without further explanation, too peculiar. It is hard for one who does not share the desire to see what is desirable. With suitable hidden significances, the desire at least becomes intelligible as desire. And to understand all may here be to forgive all, if forgiveness is needed. By the standard of exclusiveness and fixation, fetishism is doubtless perverse. We have argued that the criterion of exclusiveness and fixation is itself inadequate if applied quiet generally. Nonetheless, there is something peculiar about fetishism, and insofar as psychoanalysis can help us understand that peculiarity, it may help us understand the appropriate attitude towards perversions in general. In the case of fetishism, while we might not share the beliefs, we can

see how given certain beliefs, certain objects and activities might become desirable. It does not follow that all desires become equally uncriticizable once understood. The beliefs may have wider implications and having the beliefs and desires may have wider effects. So some perversions may be objectionable. Our ordinary standards for judging human action and human interaction do not lapse in the face of perversions; but the mere fact of perversion is not an independent ground for moral criticism.

Again, foot fetishism demands some explanation. Those who wish to reject the psychoanalytic account of foot fetishism have the burden of supplying an alternative. I believe that a simple stimulus generalization account will not do. Psychoanalysis readily includes the standard associationist points, though sometimes adding less standard associative connections as well; for example, Freud notes:

In a number of cases of foot-fetishism it has been possible to show that the scopophilic instinct, seeking to reach its object (originally the genitals) from underneath, was brought to a halt in its pathway by prohibition and repression. For that reason it became attached to a fetish in the form of a foot or shoe, the female genitals (in accordance with the expectations of childhood) being imagined as male ones." ([11], p. 155 N. 2; cf. [27] p. 155)

But Freud is also properly wary of attributing too much to early sexual impressions, as though they were the total determinant of the direction of sexuality:

All the observations dealing with this point have recorded a first meeting with the fetish at which it already aroused sexual interest without there being anything in the accompanying circumstances to explain the fact. . . . The true explanation is that behind the first recollection of the fetish's appearance there lies a submerged and forgotten phase of sexual development. The fetish, like a "screen-memory," represents this phase and is thus a remnant and precipitate of it. ([11], p. 154 N. 2).[16]

The connections Freud emphasizes are typically meaningful, rather than mere casual associations. The more general problem with simple stimulus generalization is that it tends to explain both too little and too much. Why do other people exposed to the same stimuli not develop fetishistic attachments? (Psychoanalysis may also have trouble with this question. See [27], p. 154.) Why do fetishists often attach special conditions (such as smell) to their preferred objects? (Here psychoanalysis has some interesting suggestions. See [15], p. 247; and [11], p. 155 N. 2.) If stimulus generalization stands alone as an explanatory mechanism, it can appear able to explain actual particular outcomes of an association only at the expense of appearing equally able to explain any other outcome of a given early impression. The factors pointed to by the conditioning theorists are simply too pervasive and nondiscriminating. Something that would explain everything explains nothing. (See [37], pp. 126–127.)

The desires of the fetishist are typically highly thought-dependent. He sees the fetish object as of a certain kind, as having certain connections. (This "seeing as" is another aspect of the situation generally neglected by behaviorist approaches. See [42].) Psychoanalysis seeks to trace out these connections (some of them hidden from the individual himself) and their history. It seeks to understand their compulsive force and to enable the individual to specify more fully what it is that he desires in relation to the object. The thought of the object (including the thought of the reason for the desire or of the feature that makes the object desired desirable) specifies the desire. A proper understanding of the relevant thoughts may be a necessary condition of freedom, of the possibility of altering desire via reflective self-understanding. A too exclusive attention to the behavior involved in perverse sexuality may neglect the thought and so the desire behind the behavior. Since people may do observably the same thing for very different reasons (sometimes one person wants to, while another person might be paid to; the different meanings of the same behavior may be revealed in associated phantasies, conscious and unconscious, and other thoughts), behaviorist specifications of perverse activity, like sociological accounts of perverse activity, may inevitably miss the point. If we are to understand perverse (and also "normal") sexual desires (and activities) we must look to the thoughts behind them.[17]

THE MENTAL AND THE PHYSICAL

Plato draws a line between physical love and spiritual love, thinking the latter higher than the former.

The line between the physical and the mental does not correspond to the line between the sexual and the spiritual. For whatever one thinks of spirituality and mentality, sexuality is not purely physical. Indeed, if it were, one might expect the objects and aims of sexual desire to be fixed by biology. But while human biology is relatively uniform, the objects and aims of sexual desire are as various as the human imagination. There are psychological conditions of sexual satisfaction. Sex is as much a matter of thought as of action. While the machinery of reproduction, the sexual organs themselves, the genitals, have determinate structures and modes of functioning, sexual desire takes wildly multifarious forms. Sexuality is as much a matter of thought or the mind as of the body. To think one can get away from sexuality via the denial of the body is to mistake the half for the whole.

While it would be an exaggeration to say sex is all in the mind, it would be less of a mistake than the common notion that sex is purely physical. Freud came closest to the truth in locating sexuality at the borderland or bridge between the mental and the physical. Writing of instincts in general, Freud explained his meaning: "By an 'instinct' is provisionally to be understood the psychical representative of an endosomatic, continuously flowing source of stimulation, as contrasted with a 'stimulus,' which is set up by *single* excitations coming from *without*. The concept of instinct is thus one of those lying on the frontier between the mental and the physical" ([11], p. 168). Thus the sexual instinct is not to be equated with neutral energy (as in Freud's earlier theorizing, e. g., in [8]). It has direction (aim and object) as well as a somatic source and impetus (or strength). The instinct involves both biologically given needs and thought-dependent desires. It is our thoughts that specify the objects of our desire (however mistaken we may be about whether they will satisfy our real needs). Via transformations and displacements of various sorts, our sexual instinct takes various directions. As Freud at one place puts it, "In psycho-analysis the concept of what is sexual . . . goes lower and also higher than its popular sense. This extension is justified genetically . . . " ([17], p. 222; cf. the discussion of "The Mental Factor" at [11], pp. 161–162). The analysis of sexual desires starts with an instinctual need derived from a somatic source. But the psychical representatives of this instinctual need develop in the history of the individual, attracting him to a variety of objects and aims (modes of satisfaction). Given different vicissitudes, our original instinctual endowment develops into neurosis, perversion, or the range of normal sexual life and character. Our character is among those (perhaps "higher") attributes that Freud traces back to sexuality. In his essay on "Character and Anal Erotism" Freud says we can "lay down a formula for the way in which character in its final shape is formed out of the constituent instincts: the permanent character-traits are either unchanged prolongations of the original instincts, or sublimations of those instincts, or reaction-formations against them" ([12], p. 175). I cannot pursue the puzzles raised by these alleged transformations, and by the psychoanalytic explanation of the normal, here (I make a start in [37], esp. pp. 191–192), but it should be clear that our sexual character in large measure determines our character, who we are: whether directly, as suggested in the formula, or indirectly, as the model for our behavior and attitudes in other spheres.[18]

There are lessons in multiplicity to be learned from Freud. At a minimum, I would have us take the following from this essay on Freud's *Three Essays*:

First. Sexuality, far from being unified, is complex. The sexual instinct is made up of components which can be specified along several dimensions (source, object, aim). It is a composite that develops and changes, and

can readily decompose. In particular, the instinct is "merely soldered" to its object.

Second. The criteria for perversion are multiple, and no one of them is truly satisfactory if one is searching for a cross-cultural standard founded in a common human nature. Not that there are not ideals of sexuality (with corresponding criteria for perversion), but they too are multiple, and must be understood in connection with more general ideals for human interaction.

Third. The purposes, functions, and goals of sexuality are multiple. It is not a pure bodily or biological function. There is a significant mental element that emerges perhaps most clearly in relation to the perversions, where the psychological conditions for sexual satisfaction are dramatically emphasized. Here we might find the beginnings of a defensible (Spinozist–Freudian) ideal in the sphere of the sexual: health and maturity involve coming to know what we really want and why we want it. Further, since what we want depends on what we think, if we wish to change what we want, we may have to change how we think.

Who we are is revealed in who or what and how we love. The structure of our desires emerges in the course of the transformation of the sexual instinct as we learn to live in a world full of internal and external pressures and constraints, as we learn to live with others and ourselves.

NOTES

1. While I here emphasize that the existence of some causal story does not render all evaluation out of place, I should perhaps also emphasize that some evaluations are almost always out of place. Whether homosexuality is the result of nature or nurture, it makes little sense to condemn homosexuality as "unnatural." For one thing, nature, or at least human nature, includes conditions of nurture: all humans must be somehow nurtured in order to survive and develop. The "somehow" of course allows for variations. The real point of the contrast of nature and nurture, two types of causes, may ultimately simply be in terms of uniformity versus nonuniformity. In terms of individual responsibility, nature and nurture may both be viewed as "external" causes (the individual does not choose them, and so does not control the result). For another thing, nature in general includes more than many would like to admit (one of the constant lessons of the Marquis de Sade). Insofar as charges of perversion are based on notions of unnaturalness, they may always be inapplicable. (See Michael Slote, "Inapplicable Concepts and Sexual Perversion" [40].) The various contrasts between the natural and the unnatural, and the historical development of the charge of unnaturalness against homosexuality, are interestingly traced by John Boswell in his *Christianity, Social Tolerance, and Homosexuality* [4]. In the coroner's verdict, "death by natural causes," the contrast is with other types of causes, basically causes involving the intervention of human intentions. Whatever the causes of homosexuality and homosexual desires they must be of the same *type* as the causes of heterosexuality and heterosexual desires. This point is reflected in Aristophanes' myth in Plato's *Symposium*. Incidentally, one might note that if Freud had this myth in his discussion at the start of the *Three Essays* ([11], p. 136), his account there is somewhat misleading. Freud speaks as if the "poetic fable" is supposed to explain only heterosexuality, and as if the existence of homosexuality and lesbianism therefore comes as a surprise. In fact, Aristophanes' story of the division of the original human beings into two halves, and their subsequent quest

to reunite in love, allows for all three alternatives: Aristophanes starts with three original sexes. Thus the myth offers an explanation (the same explanation) of homosexuality and lesbianism as well as heterosexuality. (One should perhaps also note that there is an Indian version of the myth that may conform better to Freud's account, and Freud refers to it explicitly later in *Beyond the Pleasure Principle*.) From the point of view of psychoanalytic theory, heterosexual object-choice and homosexual object-choice are equally problematic, equally in need of explanation ([11], p. 146n.).

Freud himself, in his published writings, only used the term "unnatural" three times in connection with perverse desires or practices. In each of the three instances ([9], p. 265; [22], p. 302; and [23], p. 149), in context, the term refers to the views of others.

2. Freud spells out the content criterion for deviations in respect of source and aim: "Perversions are sexual activities which either (a) extend, in an anatomical sense, beyond the regions of the body that are designed for sexual union, or (b) linger over the intermediate relations to the sexual object which should normally be traversed rapidly on the path towards the final sexual aim" ([11], p. 150). The question remains, what is so objectionable about "extending" and "lingering"?

3. Freud summarizes his views on the child and feces in Introductory Lecture XX: "To begin with . . . He feels no disgust at his faeces, values them as a portion of his own body with which he will not readily part, and makes use of them as his first 'gift,' to distinguish people whom he values especially highly. Even after education has succeeded in its aim of making these inclinations alien to him, he carries on his high valuation of faeces in his estimate of 'gifts' and 'money.' On the other hand he seems to regard his achievements in urinating with peculiar pride" ([22], p. 315).

4. "Not only the deviations from normal sexual life but its normal form as well are determined by the infantile manifestations of sexuality" ([11], p. 212).

5. Hence, as Erikson suggests, the infant is expelled from the oral paradise of an earlier stage ([6], p. 79). Erikson is in general very helpful on the social contribution to and meaning of the psychosexual stages.

6. There has been some speculation on the possible evolutionary advantages of homosexuality in terms of altruistic and social impulses. (See, e. g., [44], pp. 142f.)

7. The multiplicity of ends and essences for sexuality, and the corresponding multiplicity of criteria for perversion, is amply evidenced in a growing philosophical literature on sexual perversion (much of it collected in two anthologies: [1] and [41]). The authors tend to vacillate between on the one hand explicating the concept of perversion in a way which captures our ordinary classifications of particular practices, and on the other providing a sustained rationale for a defensible ideal of sexuality (with its attendant, sometimes revisionary, implications for what counts as a perversion). Here, as elsewhere, a "reflective equilibrium" between our intuitions and principles may be desirable. Perhaps most interesting from the point of view of the issues considered in this essay are Thomas Nagel's "Sexual Perversion" [35] and Sara Ruddick's "Better Sex" [39]. Nagel finds the essence of sexuality in multi-leveled personal interaction and awareness, a dialectic of desire and embodiment that makes desires in response to desires central to sexuality. Hence the criterion for perversion that emerges is in terms of interactive incompleteness—according to which homosexuality need not be perverse, foot fetishism must be, and heterosexual intercourse with personal phantasies might be. While the form of incompleteness is different, the emphasis on incompleteness might be suggestively connected with the sort of unification or totalization of components in Freud's final genital organization of sexuality—in terms of which perversions might be understood as component (or "incomplete") instincts, (Cf. Freud's statement, echoed often elsewhere, that the perversions are "on the one hand inhibitions, and on the other hand dissociations, of normal development" [11], p. 231.) In any case, Nagel's emphasis on a full theory of the nature of sexual desire seems to me right-headed. Also of special interest is Ruddick's "Better Sex," which, among other things, sorts out clearly the relation of reproduction to perversion in ordinary language and understanding.

Freud's emphasis on the role of pleasure (or discharge) in sexuality should be complicated by his emphasis on the psychological conditions of pleasure (thought-dependent conditions of discharge). Pleasure, as Freud well understood, is not itself simply bodily or otherwise simple. When the question shifts from sexuality and pleasure to the larger questions of love and falling in love, a whole range of additional factors has to be taken into account. Love and the family bring the Oedipal complex back to the center of the picture, and love relationships (whether the object is of the same or opposite gender) have to be understood in terms of transference, ego ideals, and the splitting of the ego [24]. The coming together of the sexual and affectionate currents in a mature love relationship raises all sorts of difficulties, but failures in this coming together tend to result in what might more properly be called "neurotic" love than "perverse" love (e.g., Oepidal dependence or triangles are recreated, or needs for degraded or forbidden objects with accompanying patterns of psychical impotence emerge—see [11], p. 200 and reference at 200 N. 2).

8. Or is the point (at [28], p. 101) that for heterosexuals the anus is represented by the vagina (that is, heterosexual intercourse involves displaced anal erotism)? It might for some purposes be helpful to maintain the distinction between inversion and perversion. For it then becomes easier to ask whether it is their inversion (in object) that makes some individuals perverse (in aim), or whether it is their perversion (in aim) that makes some individuals inverted (in their choice of object). Or, to put it slightly differently, the question of perversion may be relatively independent of the question of choice of object (of homosexuality or heterosexuality).

9. Indeed, some analysts, such as Michael Balint, insist that many forms of homosexuality "are definitely not survivals of infantile forms of sexuality but later developments" ([21], p. 136). But it must be noted that many of Balint's views are insupportable, or at any rate not provided with support. In particular, of homosexuals he claims "they all know—that, without normal intercourse, there is no real contentment" (p. 142).

The deeper problem raised by lesbianism (presuming that everyone starts with a female primary love object) may be how anyone (female or male) can love a man. Is it the sameness or the maleness of the object that matters for a homosexual? Again, how does maleness matter for women? For anyone?

10. Among the mechanisms of homosexual object-choice considered by Freud, the main one involves identification with the mother ([11], p. 145n.; [16], pp. 98–101; [24], p. 108; [25], pp. 230–231) and a secondary one involves reaction-

formation against sibling rivalry ([25], pp. 231–232). Freud speaks elsewhere, in connection with a case of lesbianism, of "retiring in favour of someone else" ([23], p. 159n.).

11. Nonetheless, at the risk of redundancy, it should perhaps be noted that there remains one difficult early passage in which Freud connects homosexuality with a transitional phase of narcissism. Writing in 1911 of the psychotic Dr. Schreber: "Recent investigations have directed our attention to a stage in the development of the libido which it passes through on the way from auto-erotism to object-love. This stage has been given the name of narcissism. What happens is this. There comes a time in the development of the individual at which he unifies his sexual instincts (which have hitherto been engaged in auto-erotic activities) in order to obtain a love-object; and he begins by taking himself, his own body, as his love-object, and only subsequently proceeds from this to the choice of some person other than himself as his object. This half-way phase between auto-erotism and object-love may perhaps be indispensable normally; but it appears that many people linger unusually long in this condition, and that many of its features are carried over by them into the later stages of their development. What is of chief importance in the subject's self thus chosen as a love-object may already be the genitals. The line of development then leads on to the choice of an external object with similar genitals—that is, to homosexual object-choice—and thence to heterosexuality. People who are manifest homosexuals in later life have, it may be presumed, never emancipated themselves from the binding condition that the object of their choice must possess genitals like their own; and in this connection the infantile sexual theories which attribute the same kind of genitals to both sexes exert much influence" ([18], pp. 60–61).

This may account for *one* type of homosexual object-choice (perhaps characteristic of Leonardo—see Freud's study ([16], pp. 98–101), but, again, narcissism should not be confused with homosexuality. Loving oneself is not the same as loving someone else of the same gender, even if the first may in some cases lead to the second. So even if narcissism is a stage in development, homosexual object choice is not thereby reduced to such a stage.

There is a perhaps more troubling reading of the passage. Laplanche and Pontalis write: "In his first attempts to work out the idea of narcissism, Freud makes the homosexual narcissistic choice into an interim stage between narcissism and heterosexuality: the child is said to choose an object initially whose genital organs resemble its own" ([33], p. 259).

While the description in the passage may apply to some homosexuals (such as Schreber), who go on to become heterosexuals, there is no suggestion that homosexuality is a step in the standard route to heterosexuality; and Freud certainly makes no such suggestion elsewhere. Moreover, as Laplanche and Pontalis argue, "the idea of the narcissistic choice is not a straightforward one even in the case of homosexuality: the object is chosen on the model of the little child or adolescent that the subject once was, while the subject identifies with the mother who used to take care of him" ([33], p. 259).

And Freud suggests that the initial heterosexual object-love may be preserved in the process of identification: "By repressing his love for his mother he preserves it in his unconscious and from now on remains faithful to her" ([16], p. 100). And finally, as Laplanche and Pontalis conclude, "it is doubtful whether an antithesis between the narcissistic and the anaclitic object-choices, even as ideal types, is tenable. It is in 'complete object-love of the attachment type' that Freud observes 'the marked sexual over-valuation which is doubtless derived from the child's original narcissism and thus corresponds to a transference of that narcissism to the sexual object'" ([20], p. 88). Conversely, he describes the case of "narcissistic women" in the following terms: "Strictly speaking, it is only themselves that such women love with an intensity comparable to that of the man's love for them. Nor does their need lie in the direction of loving, but of being loved; and the man who fulfils this condition is the one who finds favour with them" ([20], p. 89). It may be asked whether a case such as this, described here as *narcissistic*, does not display a subject seeking to reproduce the child's relationship to the mother who feeds it—an aim which according to Freud is a defining characteristic of the *anaclitic* object-choice" ([33], p. 259).

12. The basic facts are recounted in [34]. A more detailed journalistic account is available in [3].

13. This may conflict with the APA's own general characterization of a mental disorder: "a mental disorder is conceptualized as a clinically significant behavioral or psychologic syndrome or pattern that occurs in an individual and that typically is associated with either a painful symptom (distress) or impairment in one or more important areas of functioning (disability). In addition, there is an inference that there is a behavioral, psychologic, or biologic dysfunction, and that the disturbance is not only in the relationship between the individual and society. When the disturbance is limited to a conflict between an individual and society, this may represent social deviance, which may or may not be commendable, but is not by itself a mental disorder" ([5], p. 363).

C. Culver and B. Gert [30] raise difficulties of their own with the APA definitions and classifications of mental disorders, but they are less troubled than they ought to be about the category of "ego-dystonic homosexuality." They write: "[t]he primary reason why certain recurring sexual behaviors are maladies is that they are ego-dystonic. The person engaging in the behavior is distressed by it. Of course, such behavior is probably also a manifestation of a volitional disability, but even if it is not, the distress, if significant, is sufficient to make it count as a malady. Note that neither in the case of distress nor of a volitional disability is the sexual condition a malady because it is sexual, but rather because of some other characteristic attached to the condition. Thus, we believe that when homosexuality qualifies as a malady it is because of the distress the person experiences, not because of the person's homosexual phantasies or desires" ([30], p. 104).

But I believe that by their own criteria for what counts as a "malady" they should be more equivocal. They argue ([30], pp. 95–98) that grief should not be regarded as a disease because it has a "distinct sustaining cause" (namely, an external loss—if the sufferer came to believe the loss was not real, grief and suffering would cease). And so it would seem that it is unclear whether "ego-dystonic homosexuality" is, in their terms, a "malady." Doesn't the suffering (and even the putative "volitional disability") have a "distinct sustaining cause"? After all, if society changed its attitude, the suffering might disappear and there might be no need to overcome desires. Culver and Gert at one point write: "If a person is suffering or at increased risk of suffering evils principally because of conflict with his social environment, then his social environment would be a distinct sustaining cause of his suffering and he would not have a malady" ([30], p. 94). A theory of the source of suffering is needed if suffering is to be the sign of a malady. Even supposing a change in social attitudes would not in a given case remove suffering, when a desire is ego-dystonic, it may be because the individual has internalized mistaken standards. Is the problem then in the desire or in the standards (it is the two together that produce the distress)? Which should be changed? An individual can suffer from an unjustified (but perhaps socially encouraged) self-loathing.

14. For example: "It is well known that a good number of homosexuals are characterized by a special development of their social instinctual impulses and by their devotion to the interests of the community. . . . the fact that homosexual object-choice not infrequently proceeds from an early overcoming of rivalry with men cannot be without a bearing on the connection between homosexuality and social feeling" ([25], p. 232).

The more usual connection that Freud makes is, of course, between social feeling and sublimated homosexuality (rather than active homosexuality): "After the stage of heterosexual object-choice has been reached, the homosexual tendencies are not, as might be supposed, done away with or brought to a stop: they are merely deflected from their sexual aim and applied to fresh uses. They now combine with portions of the ego-instincts and, as 'attached' components, help to constitute the social instincts, thus contributing an erotic factor to friendship and comradeship, to *esprit de corps* and to the love of mankind in general. How large a contribution is in fact derived from erotic sources (with the sexual aim inhibited) could scarcely be guessed from the normal social relations of mankind. But it is not irrelevant to note that it is precisely manifest homosexuals, and among them again precisely those that set themselves against an indulgence in sensual acts, who are distinguished by taking a particularly active share in the general interests of humanity—interests which have themselves sprung from a sublimation of erotic instincts" ([18], p. 61).

15. Foot fetishism is not generally regarded as disgusting. What is disturbing or troubling about it is the idea that someone might be (sexually) interested *only* in feet. However much such focus might simplify life, it does seem to leave out other valuable possibilities.

16. The problem here is rather like the problem with certain other behaviorist attempts to explain complex psychological phenomena. For example, Wolpe and Rachman suggest, in relation to Freud's case of Little Hans, "that the incident to which Freud refers as merely the exciting cause of Hans' phobia was in fact the cause of the entire disorder" ([45], p. 216). The incident involved was Hans' witnessing the fall of a horse that was drawing a bus. Aside from other problems with their account (see [37], pp. 124–135), Freud had pointed out fifty years before: "Chronological considerations make it impossible for us to attach any great importance to the actual precipitating cause of the outbreak of Hans' illness, for he had shown signs of apprehensiveness long before he saw the bus-horse fall down in the street" ([14], p. 136).

Later additions to the psychoanalytic theory of fetishism (including emphasis on phases of development earlier than the phallic stage) are traced in Phyllis Greenacre, "Fetishism" [31].

17. I, like Nagel [35], wish to give special emphasis to the role of desires in perversion. For whether a particular activity or practice as engaged in by a particular individual should be regarded as perverse typically depends on the desires that inform his practice (though the force of this point might vary with alternative criteria for perversion and for sexuality). Description, here as elsewhere, is theory-laden. Whether a particular observable action counts as "neurotic" depends on why it was done, on its meaning. A person who washes his hands fifteen times a day need not be obsessive-compulsive, he may be a surgeon. Similarly, a "golden shower" performed out of sexual interest has a very different significance in respect to the question of "perversion" than one done as an emergency measure to treat a sea urchin wound. Of course, actions can be over-determined, motives can be mixed, and motives can be hidden. In any case, the full description of what a person is doing typically depends on what he thinks (whether consciously or unconsciously) he is doing and why. Underlying thoughts and desires are essential in characterizing the nature of activities and practices.

And again, in understanding the nature of desires themselves, the role of thoughts can scarcely be overemphasized. As Stuart Hampshire concludes in the course of a discussion of the role of thought in desire: "the traditional scheme, which distinguishes the lusts from thoughtful desires, may turn out to be much too simple, and to reflect too grossly simple moral ideas. Any study of sexuality shows that thought, usually in the form of fantasy, enters into a great variety of sexual desires, which are normally also associated with physical causes. The traditional equation of physical desire, or lust, with unthinking desire is not warranted by the evidence. Nor is it true the more reflective and fully conscious desires, which are in this sense rational, are necessarily or always the most complex. On the contrary, there can be pre-conscious and unconscious desires which are shown to have developed from very complex processes of unreflective and imaginative thought" ([32], p. 137).

18. As Freud puts it in discussing the case of the Rat Man: "A man's attitude in sexual things has the force of a model to which the rest of his reactions tend to conform" ([15], p. 241). The thought also forms the basis for Freud's main doubt about masturbation: "injury may occur through the laying down of a *psychical pattern* according to which there is no necessity for trying to alter the external world in order to satisfy a great need" ([19], pp. 251–252; cf. [13], pp. 198–200). We should perhaps note that he continues: "Where, however, a far-reaching reaction against this pattern develops, the most valuable character-traits may be initiated."

BIBLIOGRAPHY

[1] Baker, R. and Elliston, F. (eds.): 1975, *Philosophy and Sex*, Prometheus Books, Buffalo.
[2] Balint, M.: 1965, "Perversions and Genitality," *Primary Love and Psycho-analytic Technique*, Tavistock Publications, London.
[3] Bayer, R.: 1981, *Homosexuality and American Psychiatry: The Politics of Diagnosis*, Basic Books, New York.
[4] Boswell, J.: 1980, *Christianity, Social Tolerance, and Homosexuality*, University of Chicago Press.
[5] DSM-III: 1980, *Diagnostic and Statistical Manual of Mental Disorders*, 3rd ed., American Psychiatric Association, Washington, D. C.
[6] Erikson, E.: 1963, *Childhood and Society*, 2nd ed., W. W. Norton and Company, New York.

[7] Freud, E. L. (ed.): 1961, *Letters of Sigmund Freud: 1873–1939*, The Hogarth Press, London.
[8] Freud, S.: 1895, *Project for a Scientific Psychology*, Standard Edition I.
[9] Freud, S.: 1898, *Sexuality in the Aetiology of the Neuroses*, Standard Edition III.
[10] Freud, S.: 1905, *Fragment of an Analysis of a Case of Hysteria*, Standard Edition VII.
[11] Freud, S.: 1905, *Three Essays on the Theory of Sexuality*, Standard Edition VII.
[12] Freud, S.: 1908, *Character and Anal Erotism*, Standard Edition IX.
[13] Freud, S.: 1908, *"Civilized" Sexual Morality and Modern Nervous Illness*, Standard Edition IX.
[14] Freud, S.: 1909, *Analysis of a Phobia in a Five-Year-Old Boy*, Standard Edition X.
[15] Freud, S.: 1909, *Notes upon a Case of Obsessional Neurosis*, Standard Edition X.
[16] Freud, S.: 1910, *Leonardo da Vinci and a Memory of His Childhood*, Standard Edition XI.
[17] Freud, S.: 1910, *"Wild" Psycho-Analysis*, Standard Edition XI.
[18] Freud, S.: 1912, *Psycho-Analytic Notes on an Autobiographical Account of a Case of Paranoia*, Standard Edition XII.
[19] Freud, S.: 1912, *Contributions to a Discussion on Masturbation*, Standard Edition XII.
[20] Freud, S.: 1914, *On Narcissism*, Standard Edition XIV.
[21] Freud, S.: 1915, *Instincts and their Vicissitudes*, Standard Edition XIV.
[22] Freud, S.: 1917, *Introductory Lectures on Psycho-Analysis*, Standard Edition XVI.
[23] Freud, S.: 1920, *The Psychogenesis of a Case of Homosexuality in a Woman*, Standard Edition XVIII.
[24] Freud, S.: 1921, *Group Psychology and the Analysis of the Ego*, Standard Edition XVIII.
[25] Freud, S.: 1922, *Some Neurotic Mechanisms in Jealousy, Paranoia and Homosexuality*, Standard Edition XVIII.
[26] Freud, S.: 1924, *The Economic Problem of Masochism*, Standard Edition XIX.
[27] Freud, S.: 1927, *Fetishism*, Standard Edition XXI.
[28] Freud, S.: 1933, *New Introductory Lectures on Psycho-Analysis*, Standard Edition XXII.
[29] Freud, S.: 1954, *The Origins of Psycho-Analysis: Letters to Wilhelm Fliess, Drafts and Notes, 1887–1902*, Imago, London.
[30] Gert, B. and Culver, C.: 1982, *Philosophy in Medicine: Conceptual and Ethical Issues in Medicine*, Oxford University Press.
[31] Greenacre, P.: 1979, "Fetishism," in I. Rosen (ed.), *Sexual Deviation*, 2nd ed., Oxford University Press, pp. 79–108.
[32] Hampshire, S.: 1975, *Freedom of the Individual*, 2nd ed., Chatto and Windus, London.
[33] Laplanche, J. and Pontalis, J. B.: 1973, *The Language of Psycho-Analysis*, The Hogarth Press, London.
[34] Marmor, J.: 1980, "Epilogue: Homosexuality and the Issue of Mental Illness," in J. Marmor (ed.), *Homosexual Behavior: A Modern Reappraisal*, Basic Books, New York, pp. 390–401.
[35] Nagel, T.: 1969, "Sexual Perversion," *The Journal of Philosophy*, 66, pp. 5–17. Included in his *Mortal Questions*, Cambridge University Press, 1979, and in [1] and [41].
[36] Nagel, T.: 1976, "Moral Luck," *Proceedings of the Aristotelian Society*, vol. Supp. L, pp. 137–151. Included in his *Mortal Questions*, Cambridge University Press, 1979.
[37] Neu, J.: 1977, *Emotion, Thought, and Therapy*, Routledge & Kegan Paul, London.
[38] Neu, J.: 1981, "Getting Behind the Demons," *Humanities in Society* IV, 171–196.
[39] Ruddick, S.: "Better Sex," in [1], pp. 83–104.
[40] Slote, M.: "Inapplicable Concepts and Sexual Perversion," in [1], pp. 261–267.
[41] Soble, A. (ed.): 1980, *The Philosophy of Sex: Contemporary Readings*, Littlefield, Adams and Co.
[42] Taylor, C.: 1964, *The Explanation of Behaviour*, Routledge & Kegan Paul, London.
[43] Williams, B.: 1976, "Moral Luck," *Proceedings of the Aristotelian Society*, vol. Supp. L, pp. 115–135. Included in his *Moral Luck*, Cambridge University Press, 1981.
[44] Wilson, E. O.: 1978, *On Human Nature*, Harvard University Press.
[45] Wolpe, J. and Rachman, S.: 1963, "Psychoanalytic Evidence: A Critique Based on Freud's Case of Little Hans," in S. Rachman (ed.), *Critical Essays on Psychoanalysis*, Pergamon, Oxford, pp. 198–220.

THOMAS NAGEL

Sexual Perversion

There is something to be learned about sex from the fact that we possess a concept of sexual perversion. I wish to examine the concept, defending it against the charge of unintelligibility and trying to say exactly what about human sexuality qualifies it to admit of perversions. But let me make some preliminary comments about the problem before embarking on its solution.

Some people do not believe that the notion of sexual perversion makes sense, and even those who do, disagree over its application. Nevertheless, I think it will be widely conceded that if the concept is viable at all, it must meet certain general conditions. First, if there are any sexual perversions, they will have to be sexual desires or practices that can be plausibly described as in some sense unnatural, though the explanation of this natural/unnatural distinction is, of course, the main problem. Second, certain practices, such as shoe fetishism, bestiality, and sadism will be perversions if anything is; other practices, such as unadorned sexual intercourse, will not be; and about still others there is controversy. Third, if there are perversions, they will be unnatural sexual *inclinations* rather than merely unnatural practices adopted not from inclination but for other reasons. I realize that this is at variance with the view, maintained by some Roman Catholics, that contraception is a sexual perversion. But although contraception may qualify as a deliberate perversion of the sexual and reproductive functions, it cannot be significantly described as a *sexual* perversion. A sexual perversion must reveal itself in conduct that expresses an unnatural *sexual* preference. And although there might be a form of fetishism focused on the employment of contraceptive devices, that is not the usual explanation for their use.

I wish to declare at the outset my belief that the connection between sex and reproduction has no bearing on sexual perversion. The latter is a concept of psychological, not physiological interest, and it is a concept that we do not apply to the lower animals, let alone to plants, all of which have reproductive functions that can go astray in various ways (think, for example, of seedless oranges). Insofar as we are prepared to regard higher animals as perverted, it is because of their psychological, not their anatomical similarity to humans. Furthermore, we do not regard as a perversion every deviation from the reproductive function of sex in humans: sterility, miscarriage, contraception, abortion.

Another matter that I believe has no bearing on the concept of sexual perversion is social disapprobation or custom. Anyone inclined to think that in each society the perversions are those sexual practices of which the community disapproves should consider all of the societies that have frowned upon adultery and fornication. These have not been regarded as unnatural practices, but have been thought objectionable in other ways. What is regarded as unnatural admittedly varies from culture to culture, but the classification is not a pure expression of disapproval or distaste. In fact it is often regarded as a *ground* for disapproval, and that suggests that the classification has an independent content.

I am going to attempt a psychological account of sexual perversion, which will depend on a specific psychological theory of sexual desire and human sexual interactions. To approach

From *Journal of Philosophy* LXVI (1969): 5–17. Copyright © 1969 by The Journal of Philosophy, Inc. Reprinted with permission of the author and publisher.

this solution I wish first to consider a contrary position, one that provides a basis for skepticism about the existence of any sexual perversions at all, and perhaps about the very significance of the term. The skeptical argument runs as follows:

Sexual desire is simply one of the appetites, like hunger and thirst. As such it may have various objects, some more common than others perhaps, but none in any sense "natural." An appetite is identified as sexual by means of the organs and erogenous zones in which its satisfaction can be to some extent localized, and the special sensory pleasures that form the core of that satisfaction. This enables us to recognize widely divergent goals, activities, and desires as sexual, since it is conceivable in principle that anything should produce sexual pleasure and that a nondeliberate, sexually charged desire for it should arise (as a result of conditioning, if nothing else). We may fail to empathize with some of these desires, and some of them, like sadism, may be objectionable on extraneous grounds, but once we have observed that they meet criteria for being sexual, there is nothing more to be said on *that* score. Either they are sexual or they are not: sexuality does not admit of imperfection, or perversion, or any other such qualification—it is not that sort of affection.

This is probably the received radical position. It suggests that the cost of defending a psychological account may be to deny that sexual desire is an appetite. But insofar as that line of defense is plausible, it should make us suspicious of the simple picture of appetites on which the skepticism depends. Perhaps the standard appetites, like hunger, cannot be classed as pure appetites in that sense either, at least in their human versions.

Let us approach the matter by asking whether we can imagine anything that would qualify as a gastronomical perversion. Hunger and eating are importantly like sex in that they serve a biological function and also play a significant role in our inner lives. It is noteworthy that there is little temptation to describe as perverted an appetite for substances that are not nourishing. We should probably not consider someone's appetites as perverted if he liked to eat paper, sand, wood, or cotton. Those are merely rather odd and very unhealthy tastes: they lack the psychological complexity that we

expect of perversions. (Coprophilia, being already a sexual perversion, may be disregarded.) If, on the other hand, someone liked to eat cookbooks or magazines with pictures of food in them, and preferred these to ordinary food—or if when hungry he sought satisfaction by fondling a napkin or ashtray from his favorite restaurant—then the concept of perversion might seem appropriate (in fact it would be natural to describe this as a case of gastronomical fetishism). It would be natural to describe as gastronomically perverted someone who could eat only by having food forced down his throat through a funnel, or only if the meal were a living animal. What helps in such cases is the peculiarity of the desire itself, rather than the inappropriateness of its object to the biological function that the desire serves. Even an appetite, it would seem, can have perversions if in addition to its biological function it has a significant psychological structure.

In the case of hunger, psychological complexity is provided by the activities that give it expression. Hunger is not merely a disturbing sensation that can be quelled by eating; it is an attitude toward edible portions of the external world, a desire to relate to them in rather special ways. The method of ingestion—chewing, savoring, swallowing, appreciating the texture and smell—is an important component of the relation, as is the passivity and controllability of the food (the only animals we eat live are helpless mollusks). Our relation to food depends also on our size: we do not live upon it or burrow into it like aphids or worms. Some of these features are more central than others, but any adequate phenomenology of eating would have to treat it as a relation to the external world and a way of appropriating bits of that world, with characteristic affection. Displacements or serious restrictions of the desire to eat could then be described as perversions, if they undermined the direct relation between man and food that is the natural expression of hunger. This explains why it is easy to imagine gastronomical fetishism, voyeurism, exhibitionism, or even gastronomical sadism and masochism. Indeed, some of these perversions are fairly common.

If we can imagine perversions of an appetite like hunger, it should be possible to make sense of the concept of sexual perversion. I do not wish to imply that sexual desire is an appetite

—only that being an appetite is no bar to admitting of perversions. Like hunger, sexual desire has as its characteristic object a certain relation with something in the external world; only in this case it is usually a person rather than an omelet, and the relation is considerably more complicated. This added complication allows scope for correspondingly complicated perversions.

The fact that sexual desire is a feeling about other persons may tempt us to take a pious view of its psychological content. There are those who believe that sexual desire is properly the expression of some other attitude, like love, and that when it occurs by itself it is incomplete and unhealthy—or at any rate subhuman. (The extreme Platonic version of such a view is that sexual practices are all vain attempts to express something they cannot in principle achieve: this makes them all perversions, in a sense.) I do not believe that any such view is correct. Sexual desire is complicated enough without having to be linked to anything else as a condition for phenomenological analysis. It cannot be denied that sex may serve various functions—economic, social, altruistic—but it also has its own content as a relation between persons, and it is only by analyzing that relation that we can understand the conditions of sexual perversion.

It is very important that the object of sexual attraction is a particular individual, who transcends the properties that make him attractive. When different persons are attracted to a single person for different reasons—eyes, hair, figure, laugh, intelligence—we feel that the object of their desire is nevertheless the same, namely, that person. There is even an inclination to feel that this is so if the lovers have different sexual aims, if they include both men and women, for example. Different specific attractive characteristics seem to provide enabling conditions for the operation of a single basic feeling, and the different aims all provide expressions of it. We approach the sexual attitude toward the person through the features that we find attractive, but these features are not the objects of that attitude.

This is very different from the case of an omelet. Various people may desire it for different reasons, one for its fluffiness, another for its mushrooms, another for its unique combination of aroma and visual aspect; yet we do not enshrine the transcendental omelet as the true common object of their affections. Instead we might say that several desires have accidentally converged on the same object: any omelet with the crucial characteristics would do as well. It is not similarly true that any person with the same flesh distribution and way of smoking can be substituted as object for a particular sexual desire that has been elicited by those characteristics. It may be that they will arouse attraction whenever they recur, but it will be a new sexual attraction with a new particular object, not merely a transfer of the old desire to someone else. (I believe this is true even in cases where the new object is unconsciously identified with a former one.)

The importance of this point will emerge when we see how complex a psychological interchange constitutes the natural development of sexual attraction. This would be incomprehensible if its object were not a particular person, but rather a person of a certain *kind*. Attraction is only the beginning, and fulfillment does not consist merely of behavior and contact expressing this attraction, but involves much more.

The best discussion of these matters that I have seen is in part three of Sartre's *Being and Nothingness*.[1] Since it has influenced my own views, I shall say a few things about it now. Sartre's treatment of sexual desire and of love, hate, sadism, masochism, and further attitudes toward others, depends on a general theory of consciousness and the body that we can neither expound nor assume here. He does not discuss perversion, partly because he regards sexual desire as one form of the perpetual attempt of an embodied consciousness to come to terms with the existence of others, an attempt that is as doomed to fail in this form as it is in any of the others, which include sadism and masochism (if not certain of the more impersonal deviations) as well as several nonsexual attitudes. According to Sartre, all attempts to incorporate the other into my world as another subject, that is, to apprehend him as at once an object for me and a subject for whom I am an object, are unstable and doomed to collapse into one or the other of the two aspects. Either I reduce him entirely to an object, in which case his subjectivity escapes the possession or appropriation I can extend to that object; or I become merely an object for him, in which case I am no longer in a position to appropriate his subjectivity. Moreover, neither of these aspects is stable: each is continually in danger of giving way to the other. This has the consequence that there can be no such thing as a successful sexual relation, since the deep aim of sexual desire cannot in principle be accomplished. It seems likely, therefore, that this view will not permit a basic distinction between successful, or complete, and unsuccessful, or incomplete, sex and therefore cannot admit the concept of perversion.

I do not adopt this aspect of the theory, nor many of its metaphysical underpinnings. What interests me is Sartre's picture of the attempt. He says that the type of possession that is the object of sexual desire is carried out by "a double reciprocal incarnation" and that this is accomplished, typically in the form of a caress, in the following way: "I make myself flesh in order to impel the Other to realize *for-herself* and *for me* her own flesh, and my caresses cause my flesh to be born for me in so far as it is for the Other *flesh causing her to be born as flesh.*"[2] The incarnation in question is described variously as a clogging or troubling of consciousness, which is inundated by the flesh in which it is embodied.

The view I am going to suggest—I hope in less obscure language—is related to Sartre's, but differs in allowing sexuality to achieve its goal on occasion and thus in providing the concept of perversion with a foothold.

Sexual desire involves a kind of perception, but not merely a single perception of its object, for in the paradigm case of mutual desire there is a complex system of superimposed mutual perceptions—not only perceptions of the sexual object, but perceptions of oneself. Moreover, sexual awareness of another involves considerable self-awareness to begin with— more than is involved in ordinary sensory perception. The experience is felt as an assault on oneself by the view (or touch, or whatever) of the sexual object.

Let us consider a case in which the elements can be separated. For clarity we will restrict ourselves initially to the somewhat artificial case of desire at a distance. Suppose a man and a woman, whom we may call Romeo and Juliet, are at opposite ends of a cocktail lounge with many mirrors on its walls, permitting un-

observed observation and even mutual unobserved observation. Each of them is sipping a martini and studying other people in the mirrors. At some point Romeo notices Juliet. He is moved, somehow, by the softness of her hair and the diffidence with which she sips her martini, and this arouses him sexually. Let us say that X *senses* Y whenever X regards Y with sexual desire. (Y need not be a person, and X's apprehension of Y can be visual, tactile, olfactory, and so on, or purely imaginary. In the present example we shall concentrate on vision.) So Romeo senses Juliet, rather than merely noticing her. At this stage he is aroused by an unaroused object; so he is more in the sexual grip of his body than she of hers.

Let us suppose, however, that Juliet now senses Romeo in another mirror on the opposite wall, though neither of them yet knows that he is seen by the other (the mirror angles provide three-quarter views). Romeo then begins to notice in Juliet the subtle signs of sexual arousal: heavy-lidded stare, dilating pupils, a faint flush. This of course renders her much more bodily, and he not only notices but senses this as well. His arousal is nevertheless still solitary. But now, cleverly calculating the line of her stare without actually looking her in the eyes, he realizes that it is directed at him through the mirror on the opposite wall. That is, he notices, and moreover senses, Juliet sensing him. This is definitely a new development, for it gives him a sense of embodiment, not only through his own reactions, but also through the eyes and reactions of another. Moreover, it is separable from the initial sensing of Juliet, for sexual arousal might begin with a person's sensing that he is sensed and being assailed by the perception of the other person's desire rather than merely by the perception of the person.

But there is a further step. Let us suppose that Juliet, who is a little slower than Romeo, now senses that he senses her. This puts Romeo in a position to notice, and be aroused by, her arousal at being sensed by him. He senses that she senses that he senses her. This is still another level of arousal, for he becomes conscious of his sexuality through his awareness of its effect on her and of her awareness that this effect is due to him. Once she takes the same step and senses that he senses her sensing him, it becomes difficult to state, let alone imagine, further iterations, though they may be logically distinct. If both are alone, they will presumably turn to look at each other directly, and the proceedings will continue on another plane. Physical contact and intercourse are perfectly natural extensions of this complicated visual exchange, and mutual touch can involve all the complexities of awareness present in the visual case, but with a far greater range of subtlety and acuteness.

Ordinarily, of course, things happen in a less orderly fashion—sometimes in a great rush—but I believe that some version of this overlapping system of distinct sexual perceptions and interactions is the basic framework of any full-fledged sexual relation and that relations involving only part of the complex are significantly incomplete. The account is only schematic, as it must be to achieve generality. Every real sexual act will be psychologically far more specific and detailed, in ways that depend not only on the physical techniques employed and on anatomical details but also on countless features of the participants' conceptions of themselves and of each other, which become embodied in the act. (It is a familiar enough fact, for example, that people often take social roles and the social roles of their partners to bed with them.)

The general schema is important, however, and the proliferation of levels of mutual awareness it involves is an example of a type of complexity that typifies human interactions. Consider aggression, for example. If I am angry with someone, I want to make him feel it, either to produce self-reproach by getting him to see himself through the eyes of my anger and to dislike what he sees, or to produce reciprocal anger or fear by getting him to perceive my anger as a threat or attack. What I want will depend on the details of my anger, but in either case it will involve a desire that the object of that anger be aroused. This accomplishment constitutes the fulfillment of my emotion through domination of the object's feelings.

Another example of such reflexive mutual recognition is to be found in the phenomenon of meaning, which appears to involve an intention to produce a belief or other effect in another by bringing about his recognition of one's intention to produce that effect. (That result is due to H. P. Grice,[3] whose position I shall not attempt to reproduce in detail.) Sex has a related structure: it involves a desire that one's partner be aroused by the recognition of one's desire that he or she be aroused.

It is not easy to define the basic types of awareness and arousal of which these complexes are composed, and that remains a lacuna in this discussion. I believe that the object of awareness is the same in one's own case as it is in one's sexual awareness of another, although the two awarenesses will not be the same, the difference being as great as that between feeling angry and experiencing the anger of another. All stages of sexual perception are varieties of identification of a person with his body. What is perceived is one's own or another's *subjection* to or *immersion* in his body, a phenomenon that has been recognized with loathing by St. Paul and St. Augustine, both of whom regarded "the law of sin which is in my members" as a grave threat to the dominion of the holy will.[4] In sexual desire and its expression the blending of involuntary response with deliberate control is extremely important. For Augustine, the revolution launched against him by his body is symbolized by erection and the other involuntary physical components of arousal. Sartre too stresses the fact that the penis is not a prehensile organ. But mere involuntariness characterizes other bodily processes as well. In sexual desire the involuntary responses are combined with submission to spontaneous impulses: not only one's pulse and secretions but one's actions are taken over by the body; ideally, deliberate control is needed only to guide the expression of those impulses. This is to some extent also true of an appetite like hunger, but the takeover there is more localized, less pervasive, less extreme. One's whole body does not become saturated with hunger as it can with desire. But the most characteristic feature of a specifically sexual immersion in the body is its ability to fit into the complex of mutual perceptions that we have described. Hunger leads to spontaneous interactions with food; sexual desire leads to spontaneous interactions with the other persons, whose bodies are asserting their sovereignty in the same way, producing involuntary reactions and spontaneous impulses in *them*. These reactions are perceived, and the perception of them is perceived, and that perception is in turn perceived;

at each step the domination of the person by his body is reinforced, and the sexual partner becomes more possessible by physical contact, penetration, and envelopment.

Desire is therefore not merely the perception of a preexisting embodiment that in turn enhances the original subject's sense of himself. This explains why it is important that the partner be aroused, and not merely aroused, but aroused by the awareness of one's desire. It also explains the sense in which desire has unity and possession as its object: physical possession must eventuate in creation of the sexual object in the image of one's desire, and not merely in the object's recognition of that desire or in his or her own private arousal. (This may reveal a male bias. I shall say something about that later.)

To return, finally, to the topic of perversion: I believe that various familiar deviations constitute truncated or incomplete versions of the complete configuration and may therefore be regarded as perversions of the central impulse.

In particular, narcissistic practices and intercourse with animals, infants, and inanimate objects seem to be stuck at some primitive version of the first stage. If the object is not alive, the experience is reduced entirely to an awareness of one's own sexual embodiment. Small children and animals permit awareness of the embodiment of the other, but present obstacles to reciprocity, to the recognition by the sexual object of the subject's desire as the source of his (the object's) sexual self-awareness.

Sadism concentrates on the evocation of passive self-awareness in others, but the sadist's engagement is itself active and requires a retention of deliberate control that impedes awareness of himself as a bodily subject of passion in the required sense. The victim must recognize him as the source of his own sexual passivity, but only as the active source. De Sade claimed that the object of sexual desire was to evoke involuntary responses from one's partner, especially audible ones. The infliction of pain is no doubt the most efficient way to accomplish this, but it requires a certain abrogation of one's own exposed spontaneity. All this, incidentally, helps to explain why it is tempting to regard as sadistic an excessive preoccupation with sexual technique, which does not permit one to abandon the role of agent at any stage of

the sexual act. Ideally one should be able to surmount one's technique at some point.

A masochist on the other hand imposes the same disability on his partner as the sadist imposes on himself. The masochist cannot find a satisfactory embodiment as the object of another's sexual desire but only as the object of his control. He is passive not in relation to his partner's passion but in relation to his nonpassive agency. In addition, the subjection to one's body characteristic of pain and physical restraints is of a very different kind from that of sexual excitement: pain causes people to contract rather than dissolve.

Both of these disorders have to do with the second stage, which involves the awareness of oneself as an object of desire. In straightforward sadism and masochism other attentions are substituted for desire as a source of the object's self-awareness. But it is also possible for nothing of that sort to be substituted, as in the case of a masochist who is satisfied with self-inflicted pain or of a sadist who does not insist on playing a role in the suffering that arouses him. Greater difficulties of classification are presented by three other categories of sexual activity: elaborations of the sexual act, intercourse of more than two persons, and homosexuality.

If we apply our model to the various forms that may be taken by two-party heterosexual intercourse, none of them seem clearly to qualify as perversions. Hardly anyone can be found these days to inveigh against oral–genital contact, and the merits of buggery are urged by such respectable figures as D. H. Lawrence and Norman Mailer. There may be something vaguely sadistic about the latter technique (in Mailer's writings it seems to be a method of introducing an element of rape), but it is not obvious that this has to be so. In general, it would appear that any bodily contact between a man and a woman that gives them sexual pleasure is a possible vehicle for the system of multilevel interpersonal awareness that I have claimed is the basic psychological content of sexual interaction. Thus a liberal platitude about sex is upheld.

About multiple combinations the least that can be said is that they are bound to be complicated. If one considers how difficult it is to carry on two conversations simultaneously, one may appreciate the problems of multiple simultaneous interpersonal perception that can arise in even a small-scale orgy. It may be inevitable that some of the component relations should degenerate into mutual epidermal stimulation by participants otherwise isolated from each other. There may also be a tendency toward voyeurism and exhibitionism, both of which are incomplete relations. The exhibitionist wishes to display his desire without needing to be desired in return; he may even fear the sexual attentions of others. A voyeur, on the other hand, need not require any recognition at all by his object, certainly not a recognition of the voyeur's arousal.

It is not clear whether homosexuality is a perversion if that is measured by the standard of the described configuration, but it seems unlikely. For such a classification would have to depend on the possibility of extracting from the system a distinction between male and female sexuality; and much that has been said so far applies equally to men and women. Moreover, it would have to be maintained that there was a natural tie between the type of sexuality and the sex of the body and that two sexualities of the same type could not interact properly.

Certainly there is much support for an aggressive–passive distinction between male and female sexuality. In our culture the male's arousal tends to initiate the perceptual exchange; he usually makes the sexual approach, largely controls the course of the act, and of course penetrates whereas the woman receives. When two men or two women engage in intercourse they cannot both adhere to these sexual roles. The question is how essential the roles are to an adequate sexual relation. One relevant observation is that a good deal of deviation from these roles occurs in heterosexual intercourse. Women can be sexually aggressive and men passive, and temporary reversals of role are not uncommon in heterosexual exchanges of reasonable length. If such conditions are set aside, it may be urged that there is something irreducibly perverted in attraction to a body anatomically like one's own. But alarming as some people in our culture may find such attraction, it remains psychologically unilluminating to class it as perverted. Certainly if homosexuality is a perversion, it is so in a very different sense from that in which shoe-fetishism is a perversion, for some version of the full range of interpersonal perceptions

seems perfectly possible between two persons of the same sex.

In any case, even if the proposed model is correct, it remains implausible to describe as perverted every deviation from it. For example, if the partners in heterosexual intercourse indulge in private heterosexual fantasies, that obscures the recognition of the real partner and so, on the theory, constitutes a defective sexual relation. It is not, however, generally regarded as a perversion. Such examples suggest that a simple dichotomy between perverted and unperverted sex is too crude to organize the phenomena adequately.

I shall close with some remarks about the relation of perversion to good, bad, and morality. The concept of perversion can hardly fail to be evaluative in some sense, for it appears to involve the notion of an ideal or at least adequate sexuality that the perversions in some way fail to achieve. So, if the concept is viable, the judgment that a person or practice or desire is perverted will constitute a sexual evaluation, implying that better sex, or a better specimen of sex, is possible. This in itself is a very weak claim since the evaluation might be in a dimension that is of little interest to us. (Though, if my account is correct, that will not be true.)

Whether it is a moral evaluation, however, is another question entirely, one whose answer would require more understanding of both morality and perversion than can be deployed here. Moral evaluation of acts and of persons is a rather special and very complicated matter and by no means are all of our evaluations of persons and their activities moral evaluations. We make judgments about people's beauty or health or intelligence that are evaluative without being moral. Assessments of their sexuality may be similar in that respect.

Furthermore, moral issues aside, it is not clear that unperverted sex is necessarily *preferable* to the perversions. It may be that sex that receives the highest marks for perfection *as sex* is less enjoyable than certain perversions, and if enjoyment is considered very important, that might outweigh considerations of sexual perfection in determining rational preference.

That raises the question of the relation between the evaluative content of judgments of perversion and the rather common *general* distinction between good and bad sex. The latter distinction is usually confined to sexual acts, and it would seem, within limits, to cut across the other: even someone who believed, for example, that homosexuality was a perversion could admit a distinction between better and worse homosexual sex, and might even allow that good homosexual sex could be better *sex* than not very good unperverted sex. If this is correct, it supports the position—if judgments of perversion are viable at all—that they represent only one aspect of the possible evaluation of sex, even *qua sex*. Moreover it is not the only important aspect: certainly sexual defi-

ciencies that evidently do not constitute perversions can be the object of great concern.

Finally, even if perverted sex is to that extent not so good as it might be, bad sex is generally better than none at all. This should not be controversial: it seems to hold for other important matters, like food, music, literature, and society. In the end, one must choose from among the available alternatives, whether their availability depends on the environment or on one's own constitution. And the alternatives have to be fairly grim before it becomes rational to opt for nothing.

NOTES

1. Trans. Hazel E. Barnes (New York: Philosophical Library, 1956).
2. Ibid., p. 391. Sartre's italics.
3. "Meaning," *Philosophical Review* 66, no. 3 (July 1957): 377–88.
4. See Romans 7:23, and the *Confessions,* Book 8, v.

MICHAEL RUSE

Is Homosexuality Bad Sexuality?

MODERN ETHICAL PHILOSOPHIES

Let us turn now to the modern era, the time after the scientific revolution. There are two major, secular moral philosophies, those of the German thinker, Immanuel Kant (1949, 1959), and of the (primarily) British utilitarians. Both groups thought their views threw light on the status of homosexual behaviour (again, feelings get short shrift). Let us take them in turn.

Kant thought humans are subject to an overriding and necessary moral law, a supreme directive, the "categorical imperative." It is this law which tells us what we ought to do; wherein lies our duty. There are various ways in which Kant formulated his maxim (Körner 1955 gives a readable introduction). At one point he suggested that the key lies in the need to be able to *universalize* our actions: never do anything which you would not want to say that anybody and everybody should be able to do in a similar situation. Wanton cruelty is therefore wrong because one would not want to give people licence to do it to oneself. Another formulation of the categorical imperative is that one should always treat people as ends and not as means. In other words, one ought not simply use people for one's own benefit or for the benefit of others. People must be treated as subjective worthy beings in their own right.

As Kant (1963) himself recognized, at a quite general level sex and the categorical imperative have a rather uneasy relationship. The starting point to sex is the sheer desire of a person for the body of another. One wants to feel the skin, to smell the hair, to see the eyes—one wants to bring one's own genitals into contact with those of the other, and to reach orgasm. This gets dangerously close to treating the other as a means to the fulfillment of one's own sexual desire—as an object, rather than as an end. And this, according to the categorical imperative, is immoral. To escape from this dilemma, and one surely must if the end of the human race is not to be advocated on moral grounds, one must go on to treat the object of one's sexual advances as an end. One does this by broadening one's feelings, so that the personhood of the object of one's desire is brought within one's attraction, and by giving oneself reciprocally—by yielding oneself, body and soul, one shows respect for the other as an end, and not just as a means.

But what about a sincere commitment between two people of the same sex, the sort of homosexual equivalent of heterosexual marriage? At this point Kant invokes the notion of a *crimina carnis,* an abuse of one's sexuality. There are two kinds. First, there are acts which are contrary to sound reason, *crimina carnis secundum naturam.* These are immoral acts which go against the moral code imposed upon us as humans, and include such things as adultery. Second, there are acts contrary to our animal nature, *crimina carnis contra naturam.* These include masturbation, sex with animals, and homosexuality. They are the lowest and most disgusting sort of vice, worse in a sense even than suicide, and they are practices that we hesitate to mention. In fact, Kant found himself in something of a dilemma: mention the vices and you draw people's attention to them; fail to mention them and you do not warn people of them.

From Michael Ruse, *Homosexuality.* Oxford: Basil Blackwell, 1988. Reprinted with permission of the publisher.

On balance, though, because they involve so great a violation of the categorical imperative, something must be said:

A second *crimen carnis contra naturam* is intercourse between *sexus homoginii,* in which the object of sexual impulse is a human being but there is homogeneity instead of heterogeneity of sex, as when a woman satisfies her desire on a woman, or a man on a man. This practice too is contrary to the ends of humanity; for the end of humanity in respect of sexuality is to preserve the species without debasing the person; but in this instance the species is not being preserved (as it can be by a *crimen carnis secundum naturam*), but the person is set aside, the self is degraded below the level of the animals, and humanity is dishonoured. (Kant 1963: 170)

Contrasting with Kantian ethics is that of the utilitarians, the most prominent of whom were Jeremy Bentham and the two Mills, James (father) and John Stuart (son). For them, the key to ethical theory is happiness. "The creed which accepts as the foundation of morals utility or the greatest happiness principle holds that actions are right in proportion as they tend to promote happiness; wrong as they tend to produce the reverse of happiness" (Mill 1910: 6). Of course, there is a lot more to the theory than this, particularly revolving around what one might mean by "happiness" and "pleasure." To the more intellectually robust Bentham, "quantity of pleasure being equal, pushpin is as good as poetry" (Bentham 1834). To the more sensitive (and greater) John Stuart Mill, "better to be Socrates dissatisfied than a fool satisfied" (Mill 1910: 9). But the important point is that to evaluate a moral action, one simply judges its consequences in terms of happiness (or pleasure) and unhappiness. And one action is better than another, and consequently that which one ought to do or approve, if it leads to greater happiness and to less unhappiness than the other.

Like Kant, Bentham applied his ethical theory to homosexual behaviour. Yet although they were writing at the same time, and although Bentham's language is frequently uncomplimentary, they might as well have been in different worlds. Bentham thinks homosexual interactions as acceptable morally as Kant finds them pernicious. Such interactions give pleasure to the people engaged in them, and so by

the greatest happiness principle they ought to be valued. "As to any primary mischief, it is evident that [a homosexual interaction] produces no pain in anyone. On the contrary it produces pleasure . . ." (Bentham 1978: 390). Bentham is not advocating homosexual behaviour for everyone, only for those who want to so indulge. Then, there will be no harm. Nor is there any real problem stemming from the possibility that homosexual practices might incline or influence others into similar behaviour. People who indulge homosexual appetites seem to enjoy themselves; so at most one is inclining others to enjoyable practices.

What of the claim that homosexual behaviour runs one down physically, thus as it were reducing one's long-term pleasure in life? Bentham's conclusion is that there is no evidence to this effect. In any case, being in line with medical opinion of the time, and accepting that masturbation is physically debilitating, Bentham pointed out the injustice of trying to eliminate homosexuality through the law, when one did (and obviously could) do nothing about self-abuse. What of the claim that homosexuality is a threat to the keeping of population numbers up to an acceptable level? (Bentham had no doubts that a sizeable population is a good thing.) Again Bentham saw no danger on this score. Men's sexual appetites and capabilities far exceed those of females, particularly in the sense that a man can fertilize many more times than a fertilized female can give birth. Hence, for homosexuality to be a threat to population numbers "the nature of the human composition must receive a total change" (Bentham 1978: 396). Indeed, suggested Bentham rather tongue in cheek, with more homosexuality we should need fewer (heterosexual) prostitutes. These women, who rarely give birth, would therefore be freed for child-bearing purposes.

What about the idea that homosexuality among men deprives women of sex and marriage? Here, Bentham shows that what he is concerned to defend is the right of anyone to have homosexual relations, including those people chiefly of a heterosexual bent.

Were the prevalence of this taste to rise to ever so great a height the most considerable part of the motives to marriage would remain entire. In the first place, the desire of having children, in the next place the desire of forming alliances between families, thirdly the convenience of having a domestic companion whose company will continue to be agreeable throughout life, fourthly the convenience of gratifying the appetite in question at any time when the want occurs and without the expense and trouble of concealing it or the danger of a discovery. (p. 400)

I take it that Bentham's concern with the right of heterosexuals to indulge homosexuality was (in part) a function of the fact that he was dealing with a society much like the Ancient Greeks', where upper-class young men were segregated from members of the opposite sex.

Bentham does incidentally make brief acknowledgement of the fact of lesbianism, but although noting that "where women contrive to procure themselves the sensation by means of women, the ordinary course of nature is as much departed from as when the like abomination is practised by men with men" (p. 100), he says nothing at all about its moral status. Presumably, he considered lesbian behaviour as no more immoral than male homosexual behaviour. It should be noted that Bentham's failure to discuss lesbianism in detail was not sexist bias. In writing on male homosexuality he was trying to show that it did not merit the very severe legal penalties to which it was then subject. There were no such laws against lesbianism in England at the time that he was writing.

Bentham never published his ideas—perhaps out of prudence. We never therefore got public debate and opposition between the great ethical philosophers. But, with respect to homosexual activity, the difference is about as great as one could get. And this being so, we have reached a good point to stop and take stock.[1]

IS HOMOSEXUAL BEHAVIOUR BIOLOGICALLY UNNATURAL?

I take it that the switch we have now encountered, from the focus on sexual orientation to the present concern with homosexual activity, is understandable and relatively uncontroversial. Homosexual orientation is something thrust upon you. You have no choice or freedom in the matter. Consequently, in this respect you are not a moral agent. Homosexual behav-

iour, however, is a question of choice. Here you do have the power to make decisions, to act rationally. Here, therefore, it is appropriate to make value judgements.

Turning now to discussion, as a philosopher I shall not presume to judge the purely religious input to the question of the moral status of homosexual behaviour. I shall use my exposition primarily to ferret out religious themes which sneak into ostensibly philosophical theses, and conversely. Indeed, with respect to homosexual activity it seems to me as an outsider that the religious position is thoroughly ambiguous. On the one hand, however much reinterpretation you may do, the Biblical prohibitions really are explicit. On the other hand, does the Christian truly have to take as literal everything in Leviticus or in the epistles of St. Paul? You simply cannot make a reasonable decision about the moral status of homosexual activity, without some philosophical input—a conclusion which is supported by the fact that there are as many different stands on the homosexual question as there are religious denominations. (Batchelor 1980 carries an excellent survey of the various [American] church positions on homosexuality.)

We turn to philosophy, and as always we turn back to Plato, for it was he who introduced the argument which has had the greatest influence on western thought about the worth of homosexuality. Plato stated categorically that homosexuality (the behaviour at least) is wrong because it is unnatural—it is not something done by the animals. "Our citizens should not be inferior to birds and many species of animals . . . " (Plato, Laws, 840de, tr. Dover 1978: 166). And this is an argument which repeats itself through history. There are some things which ought not to be done because they go against nature in some way, and homosexual acts must be included. Our bodies are "designed" for proper functioning, and the genitalia specifically are designed for heterosexual relations, which are themselves the beginning step on the way to reproduction and thence to the creation of new humans. A penis in a vagina is doing what it was intended to do; a penis in an anus is not; and this is all there is to the matter. We learn this fact directly from the non-human world where, uncorrupted by perverted lusts, animals behave in their proper

fashion, that is to say where they behave het-
erosexually. Homosexuality is unnatural, because it goes against our biology. Therefore it
is immoral. Christian philosophers like Aquinas (1968) sing the theme; Kant (1963) finds
homosexuality worse than suicide because of
this; and there are loud echoes of it today. Undoubtedly the average (heterosexual!) woman
or man would condemn homosexuality because
it "goes against nature."

At least, now, we can see fully why so many
radical thinkers were so hostile to biology, especially to a biology being applied to the understanding of homosexuality. It is biology which
is the strongest plank in the barrier against the
permissibility to same-gender sex. But should
we condemn homosexual behaviour as immoral
because it is unnatural, in the sense of being
against biology? Should we say that animals do
not behave homosexually; therefore humans
should not behave homosexually? Is it true that
genitals were "designed" for heterosexual ends
and that all other uses are a wicked corruption?
We must try to answer these questions for ourselves, and to this end a number of points must
be raised.

First, it is simply not true, if by "unnatural"
one means "not performed by animals" or even
"not commonly performed by animals," that
homosexuality is unnatural. We know that in
species after species, right through the animal
kingdom, students of animal behaviour report
unambiguous evidence of homosexual attachments and behaviour—in insects, fish, birds,
and lower and higher mammals (reviewed in
Weinrich 1982). Of course, you can always
maintain that animal homosexual behaviour is
not really homosexual behaviour. But granting
that talk of animal homosexuality is not a conceptual confusion—and I have said all I have
to say on that topic in the context of Dörner's
rats—there are the kinds of behaviour and
bonds occurring in nature that fully fit the description. There is evidence of anal penetration
of one male by another and emission of semen
(Denniston 1980), and one cannot go further
than that. Whatever the moral implications of
homosexuality and naturalness may be, it is
false that homosexuality is immoral because it
does not exist amongst animals. It has taken
people a long time to realize how universal
animal homosexual behaviour really is, or perhaps we should say that it has taken a long time

for those knowledgeable about animal homosexuality (such as farmers and naturalists) to
pass on their knowledge to those interested in
the possibility of animal homosexuality (such
as philosophers and theologians). But it does
exist nevertheless, and we cannot pretend otherwise.

A second point is that, if by "unnatural" we
mean "going against our biology"—and this is
the sense of "unnatural" we are considering in
this section—then if there is any truth at all in
the sociobiological hypotheses, much human
homosexuality (no doubt like much animal
homosexuality) has a solid biological basis. It
is something maintained by natural selection.
To say, for example, that vaginas were designed for penises and that anuses were not so
designed is simply not relevant. If, as a consequence of putting his penis in another man's
anus, or allowing his own anus to be so used, a
man better replicates his genes than if he were
to devote his attention to seeking out vaginas,
then biologically speaking this is perfectly
proper or natural. Admittedly, anuses are also
for defecating; but then, penises are also for
urinating. There is a popular joke amongst gay
men: "If God had meant us to be homosexuals,
then he would have given us all anuses."

A third point against the thesis that homosexuality is biologically unnatural is that humans are not mere animals. This remains true
even after Darwin. Humans have a social and
cultural realm to a degree virtually inconceivable, by comparison with animals (Boyd and
Richerson 1985). I see, therefore, no reason
why things as important to our social and general life as our sexual emotions and attachments should be judged by animal standards. I
do not condemn the male walrus for being po-
lygamous; but neither do I suggest that therefore humans have the universal right to be po-
lygamous (Barash 1977). Why should the male
walrus be a standard for me? Or why should the
(supposedly) heterosexual birds be a standard?

I think, in fact, that one can take this argument a little further. One sociobiological claim
which does seem reasonably uncontentious is
that humans, because they need so much parental care, have evolved sexual habits somewhat
different from the rest of the animal world. In
particular, unlike most mammals the male human must get involved in child rearing (Hrdy
1981). One way in which the female keeps the

male in attendance is by being continuously sexually receptive. This means that much human sexual intercourse—the heterosexual variety—does not have the direct biological end of reproduction, in the sense of insemination. Hence, the whole set of arguments that any kind of sex that could not potentially lead to conception is unnatural is simply based on bad biology. Even if humans were physiologically like monkeys or rats in their reproductive mechanisms (and we have seen that in some respects they certainly are not), still at the non-cultural biological level humans differ essentially from monkeys and rats (Meyer-Bahlburg 1984). What is natural for others is not necessarily natural for us, nor do all human organs have simple, obvious uses.

A fourth and perhaps related point is that, even if it turns out that some kinds of sexual behaviour have nothing to do with straight biology, even if it turns out that the homosexual is doing him/herself a biological disservice and perhaps even his/her race or species a similar disservice, this does not as such imply that anything sexual, including homosexual, is immoral. What moral obligation has the individual got to reproduce (Ruse 1984)? What moral obligation has the individual got to help his/her species reproduce?[2] It might be argued that any behaviour which is so disruptive of society that society itself fails to reproduce is immoral; but this is a contingent claim and one must justify it (Gray 1978). One has to show first that any such behaviour is in fact so disruptive of society, and secondly either that society's reproduction is a morally good thing, or that the disruption in itself causes so much trouble as to be a bad thing.

But, in reply, first of all it is obvious that homosexual activity today is not so disruptive of society as to prevent overall reproduction. Second, the moral importance of society's reproduction is not that obvious. We may have an obligation to future generations not so to pollute our planet that life for them becomes depressingly difficult, but do we have an obligation to produce future generations? I confess that I see no straightforward reasons to suggest that we do. Of course, if people want society to continue, then that is reason enough, and I think most people do want the human race to continue. But if enough of us felt otherwise, then why should their wish be wrong? (I am not saying that it would be moral to destroy all living people.) Third, even if homosexual activity were reducing population numbers, it would hardly be that disruptive of heterosexuals. No one is arguing that heterosexuals must be castrated, merely that those who do not want to reproduce need not.

The morality of homosexuality, therefore, must be judged on grounds other than those of biological naturalness. If what is natural is judged by what occurs in the animal world, then homosexuality is not unnatural. If what is natural is what is biologically advantageous to do, then homosexuality is not obviously unnatural. And even if one agreed that naturalness for humans could be defined in terms of biological advantage, and even if one also agreed (which I do not) that homosexuality is unnatural, then it still would not necessarily be immoral. Its wrongness would have to be judged on other grounds. I am not denying that there is any concept of naturalness which is appropriate for humans; nor am I denying that violations of this concept might be, or be considered, bad things. When you have an argument with the ongoing appeal that the one we are now considering obviously has, it would be rash to pretend that there is nothing to it. Indeed, I shall be suggesting shortly that there may well be something to a notion of naturalness which is connected to value—although where this will leave homosexual behaviour is another matter. What I am saying is that one cannot tease out the moral status of human homosexual behaviour on grounds of *biological* naturalness. (This whole argument about biological unnaturalness strikes me as being a conceptual sibling of many of the arguments for evolutionary ethics; and with about as much validity. See Flew 1967; Ruse 1986.)

Obviously, one might try to resurrect the argument by appealing to additional premises. One possible way in which one could keep defending the thesis that homosexuality is immoral because it is biologically unnatural is along the lines suggested by Aquinas, where that which is biologically natural is seen as the rationale of boundaries that God wants us to respect. But apart from the fact that we still have the problem of explicating what is biologically natural for humans, we have also got to prove that it is God's will that we stay within bounds. Of course, Aquinas thinks he can do this and sets about the task with much subtlety and brilliance. But here, clearly, we move again from the philosophical to the theological. I can respect the Catholic doctrine of natural law, but it is not my job to believe it, defend it, or attack it. The fact remains that, on its own, the argument that homosexuality is biologically unnatural and hence immoral, fails. And with it goes much of the mainstay of the traditional critique of homosexual activity.

HOMOSEXUALITY AND THE MODERN PHILOSOPHERS

We come to the present. Some radical thinkers would have us jettison all established moral principles, relying merely on intuitions and feelings. Thus, Jeffrey Weeks writes: "If we endorse the radical approach that no erotic act has any intrinsic meaning this suggests that, though they may not be the conclusive factors, subjective feelings, intentions and meanings are vital elements in deciding on the merits of an activity. The decisive factor is an awareness of context, of the situation in which choices are made." (Weeks 1985: 219). But this leaves you quite powerless. Both Adolf Hitler and Mother Teresa were aware in their different ways; yet we must evaluate their actions differently. Throwing out moral principles sacrifices integrity on the altar of subjectivity.

We would do better to stay with the great ethical theories of the modern era, Kantianism and utilitarianism. We have seen how Kant and the major utilitarian thinker Jeremy Bentham reached almost diametrically opposed positions on the morality of homosexual behaviour. Given that both thinkers explicitly and (I think) genuinely referred to their ethical foundations to justify their conclusions, one may conclude that this is all there is to the matter. I am not sure, however, that this is quite so. I suspect that the Kantian position is, if anything, somewhat more conservative than the utilitarian position, or at least some versions of the position, but I remain unconvinced that (as moral philosophies) they lead to totally different conclusions on the question of homosexual behaviour. On neither scheme will the Greek admiration for personal restraint be entirely lost.

Speaking of sexuality generally, Kant (1963) argued that the danger in any erotic encounter lies in the using of one's partner simply as an end to one's own (orgasmic) ends. Only through marriage can one achieve sex without violation of the categorical imperative. Here, one enters into an agreement to let another have complete rights over oneself, in return for equal rights over that person: "[I]f I yield myself completely to another and obtain the person of the other in return, I win myself back; I have given myself up as the property of another, but in turn I take that other as my property, and so win myself back again in winning the person whose property I have become" (p. 167). I get myself back as an end and treat my partner as an end in some way, because I have given myself absolutely to another who has given him/herself absolutely to me.

Now, putting matters this way, legal questions about marriage aside, I simply cannot see that a homosexual relationship is any less a potentially full, moral encounter than is a heterosexual relationship. There is no reason why homosexuals should not reach out in a loving and giving relationship any less than do heterosexuals. At this level, whatever Kant himself says to the contrary, homosexuality is quite compatible with the categorical imperative—it is a good, even. Kant himself, as we saw, speaks of the self being "degraded" and of humanity being "dishonoured," and I am sure that he thought that in homosexual acts people—including oneself—were being used as means rather than ends. Again, he spoke of "the species not being preserved" and, considering the categorical imperative as a demand that actions be universalizable, no doubt, he thought that if we were all homosexual then humankind would come to a rapid halt. But if you remove the biology-as-unnatural-therefore-immoral element, then nothing remains to Kant's objections. We are no longer degraded by being lower than the animals, and even if we were different—breaking from the "naturalness" of animals—then so what? Humans uniquely cook their meat. Does this debase us? And, in any case, preservation of the species is not an ultimate, either in biology or morality. Of course, I would like the human species to continue. Kant would like the species to continue. But these desires do not stem from the categorical imperative.

I expect there will be those Kantians who try a different tack, arguing on empirical grounds that full, loving homosexual relationships are impossible. . . .[3] I am not, of course, arguing that homosexuality is a good above heterosexuality, and ought therefore to be practised by heterosexuals. For the sake of argument, at this point, I am prepared even to accept a conservative claim that, perhaps if there are not children, a homosexual relationship will be less fulfilled than a heterosexual relationship. My point simply is that for those whose inclinations tend to homosexuality, and who can and would enter into full relationships that way, it is a good on Kantian grounds. It is certainly morally superior to the alternatives, which are either that homosexuals enter into heterosexual relationships or that they suffer an imposed celibacy. . . .

Nevertheless, all of this talk of intense, one-to-one relationships, does rather raise the question of casual sexual encounters. These, heterosexual as well as homosexual, are far more difficult to justify within a Kantian framework (despite what some modern interpreters have implied to the contrary: Elliston 1975). It is true that, however casual an encounter, one can give one's body reciprocally to one's partner; but one is caught in a situation where people are treating each other as objects to such an extent that I doubt that this giving fully compensates. Obviously, this is a matter of degrees: not all casual sex is as impersonal as fellatio with a stranger through a hole in the wall in a public lavatory. But generally speaking, in a transient sexual encounter one seems not to be involved with the other person as a person. If nothing else, the case can surely be made that in casual sex one is sexually desensitizing oneself, so the full-blown sexual relationship—precious precisely because it is unique—is made that much more difficult. Hence, I suspect that the promiscuous lifestyles of so many male homosexuals transgress the categorical imperative. (I will take as given all of the qualifications one must now make in this era of AIDS. Even if "safe sex" is, or becomes, possible, the Kantian has trouble with promiscuity —although, I confess that the thought of several hundred men, in an abandoned warehouse, clad in nothing but gym-shoes, engaging in group masturbation, strikes me as more ludicrous than positively evil. I assume that if one is knowingly engaging in any sex that might infect others, this is wrong to the Kantian—or

to any other moral theorist, for that matter. Whether running a risk for oneself is immoral is a nice point. Kant would have thought it is. Since none of us is Robinson Crusoe, I would myself probably argue likewise, if not for the same reasons.)

Turning to the utilitarian position, Bentham (1978) is surely right in concluding that, judged by the criterion of pleasure, there is nothing immoral in homosexuality per se. If people who indulge in such activities get pleasure from the activities, then so be it. It may be objected that homosexuals on average are less happy than heterosexuals. However, even if this objection were true . . . , it would hardly be all that relevant. The point is whether people of homosexual inclination get more pleasure from homosexual activities than they would from enforced heterosexual activities, and there is no question about the answer to this. They are happier in freely chosen homosexual activity than they would be in compulsory heterosexuality. Nor is it plausible that the discomfort caused to heterosexuals by homosexuals' practices alters the overall calculus of pleasure. Letting homosexuals behave after their inclinations increases the total pleasure. Therefore homosexual activity is not a moral evil. It is a positively good thing, in fact. . . .

I suspect that the Benthamite version of the greatest happiness principle most probably extends to an endorsement of fairly casual sexual affairs as well as long-term, deep, loving relationships. If people get pleasure from casual sex acts at whatever level, then they are acceptable. "Push-pin is as good as poetry." The only qualifications would come from the above mentioned dangers of disease. However, in this context of casual sex one really ought to mention the views of John Stuart Mill (1910) and his distinction between qualities of pleasures. Mill certainly does not want to rule out sex entirely. He himself was for years deeply in love with Harriet Taylor, finally marrying her. But his position, borne out by his own relationship with Mrs. Taylor, is that a sexual relationship must be part of an overall relationship: a union demanding intellect and emotions, if it is to achieve true happiness and be morally worthwhile. I see nothing in any of this which would bar a homosexual relationship from reaching just such a desirable state as a heterosexual relationship. However, I really cannot imagine that Mill would rate casual encounters very high on the happiness scale. Quite apart from the pleasure-destroying risks that such encounters carry, he would surely think that the efforts expended on them could be better employed elsewhere. For Mill, physical pleasures are far outweighed by pleasures which involve the intellect or meaningful interaction between people: "Human beings have faculties more elevated than the animal appetites, and when once made conscious of them, do not regard anything as happiness which does not include their gratification" (1910: 7). Undoubtedly, this eliminates casual encounters as objects of moral desirability—certainly casual encounters which do not go beyond the level of physical animal sex.

My conclusions, therefore, are that once you strike out fallacious arguments about biological naturalness, and bring forward modern realizations of the possibilities for homosexuals of meaningful relationships, the Kantian and utilitarian positions come very much closer together. Certainly, at a minimum, there is moral worth in the close-coupled relationships of the Second Kinsey study, and probably more. Yet, Benthamite utilitarianism excepted, there simply has to be concern at total sexual promiscuity. To radicals, this may sound like retreat. But moral philosophies, if they are to have any bite, have to draw the line somewhere—and I believe they draw the line here.

I have no wish, myself, to hide behind the great names of the past. I have elsewhere argued for the central worth of both Kantian and (Millian) utilitarian moral philosophies (Ruse 1986). I see no reason now to back off from what I take to be their consequences qua homosexual behaviour. Homosexuality within a loving relationship is a morally good thing. Casual promiscuity threatens us all, heterosexual and homosexual. One qualification must be added, however. It is a great deal easier to avoid wrongdoing, if you are not tempted. Thinking now especially of the average heterosexual male, to sleep with 1003 women would truly demand the charm and dedication of Don Giovanni, not to mention the assistance of Leporello. For the average homosexual male, the opportunities are readily available and the numbers easily passed (qualifications about AIDS, and so forth, taken as read). Also—whether the reasons be biological or cultural—the actual

harm done in 1003 homosexual encounters might be much, much less than the harm done in 1003 heterosexual encounters (Symons 1979). I defy anyone to have 1003 heterosexual encounters without an extraordinary amount of cheating and lying—even if you do not end by killing a Commandatore. For these and like reasons, I think the moral philosopher—Kantian or utilitarian—should be very wary of rushing in and, although allowing the ideal of a homosexual relationship, denying the reality as it affects many (if not most) homosexual males. (Since lesbians apparently are far less promiscuous than male homosexuals, these qualifying words hardly apply to them.)

SEXUAL PERVERSION

In theory, this should conclude our discussion at this point. Once you have strained out religious elements, once you have dropped outmoded scientific claims, once you have sorted through the proper relationship between "is" and "ought," once you have discovered a little bit about what homosexuals are really like rather than what you think they might be like, moral conclusions start to fall fairly readily into place. Yet there is something about homosexual activity—and, indeed, the whole overt homosexual life style—that other people find disturbing and threatening; something which drives people to conclude that, for all of the fancy arguments of the philosophers, homosexual activity is a wrong: a moral evil. (The feeling is particularly strong of males, by males—an asymmetry to which I shall return.)

What is it about homosexuality—what is it about male homosexuality in particular—that brings forth such negative judgements? One thing, above all else, comes across. Listen to the eminent theologian Karl Barth (1980): "[Homosexuality] is the physical, psychological and social sickness, the phenomenon of perversion, decadence and decay, which can emerge when man refuses to admit the validity of the divine command in the sense in which we are now considering it" (p. 49). Forget about the sickness part of the complaint. God does not condemn the diabetic. What troubles Barth and his God—what troubles virtually all of those who hate homosexuality—is that they see it as a *perversion*. It is the epitome of wrongdoing, and therefore must be censored in the strongest possible way.

Obviously, from our perspective, we have seen a paradox. Homosexual behaviour seems not so very morally pernicious; yet, through the notion of perversion, this is precisely how it appears to many people—in our society, at least. How can we resolve it? Fortunately, some help is at hand, for the notion of perversion has been much discussed by analytic philosophers in recent years.[4] Typical in many respects, certainly in that which ties in best with our previous discussion, is an analysis by Sara Ruddick (1975). Trying to capture the concept, she turns to traditional arguments, claiming that what people have been arguing about down through the ages is less a moral question and more one of perversity. She suggests that the natural end of sex is reproduction: that all and only acts which tend to lead to reproduction are natural, and that all unnatural acts are perverted.

The ground for classifying sexual acts as either natural or unnatural is that the former type serve or could serve the evolutionary and biological function of sexuality—namely, reproduction. "Natural" sexual desire has as its "object" living persons of the opposite sex, and in particular their postpubertal genitals. The "aim" of natural sexual desire—that is, the act that "naturally" completes it—is genital intercourse. Perverse sex acts are deviations. . . . (p. 91)

Clearly, on her criterion, Ruddick finds homosexual acts perverse. However, unlike many, Ruddick sees nothing morally inferior about perverted sex acts. Indeed she goes so far as to say that, all other things being equal, "perverted sex acts are preferable to natural ones if the latter are less pleasurable or less complete" (p. 96).

As Ruddick's proposal stands, it obviously will not do. Apart from the difficulties with the notion of "biological naturalness," how do you deal with non-obviously sexual perversions? I should say that a man who spreads his sheets with faeces before he hops into bed is perverse. Yet Ruddick's analysis tells us nothing of it. Conversely, are we supposed to believe that such non-reproductive sex as using a condom is perverse? And, in any case, although I agree that homosexuality per se is not immoral, Ruddick—in what one critic has called the

"over-intellectualized-approach" typical of philosophers (Goldman 1977)—surely misses what is most central to the notion of perversion: the very strong emotional reaction that perverse acts raise in us. To most people, to say "perverted sex acts are preferable to natural ones" is virtually a contradiction in terms. Perversion *is* a value concept. (Weeks 1985 is quite right in connecting judgements of perversion with political commitments—the latter are value notions also.)

So, how does one do better? Naturalness keeps coming up. Perhaps the time has come to make it work for us, rather than against us. And indeed, this is a reasonable move, for people like Ruddick are surely right in thinking naturalness important. The pervert who spreads faeces all over his bedsheets is unnatural. And, because he is unnatural, he is a pervert. Yet a biological definition will not do. Perhaps the time has come to make a break. We are human beings: that means we live in a cultural realm, unlike animals who are fundamentally trapped down at the level of pure biology. What I argue, therefore, is that naturalness ought to be defined in terms of culture and not simple biology. What is unnatural, and what is consequently in some important sense perverse, is what goes against or breaks with our culture. It is what violates the ends or aims that human beings think are important or worth striving for. This may include reproduction, but extends to all the things we hold dear, the things that make us happy and make life worth living generally. And this is why perversity is indeed a value laden term, because a perversion puts itself against human norms and values. (In invoking culture to define perversion, I am with Gray 1978, and Margolis 1975, although I doubt they would agree with all that I would claim.)

We have to go a little bit further than just referring to culture to define perversion, however. Stealing or murder go against western culture's rules, but one would not want to say that the thief qua thief or the murderer qua murderer was a pervert. It is true indeed that some who break society's moral rules are perverts, but I suspect that the breaking of the rules and the perversity are not quite logically identical, even though they may coincide. Reginald Halliday Christie used to get a sexual thrill from murdering women while having intercourse with them (Kennedy 1960). He was a pervert. But his perversity lay not in the murder per se but in his sexual propensities. Conversely, not all perversities violate moral rules, at least not in a straightforward way. A person who eats 10 kg of chocolates per day, and then vomits them up, is close to perversion—even though there may not be much immoral about the action. Had Christie confined his activities to copulating with (suitably hollowed) cabbages, tearing them to shreds at the point of orgasm, he would still have been a pervert, although his actions would not have been immoral.

This is the key to perversions: what I like to call the "Ugh! factor." A perversion involves a breaking not of a moral rule, but more of an aesthetic rule. We find perversions disgusting, revolting. But why is this? I would suggest the following reason. A perversion involves going against one of culture's values or ends or things considered desirable, and other members of society cannot understand why one would want to go against the value. People cannot empathize with the pervert or understand why he/she has done what he/she has (Stoller 1975). One may not approve of what the murderer has done, but at least one can understand the action. We have all felt hate for others, even wishing that people were dead. Very few of us have felt the urge to strangle our partner during copulation, or think we or anyone else could enjoy it.

Put matters this way: in the *Republic* (11. 359–60), Plato tells the story of Gyges, who found a magic ring which would make him invisible at will. Hence, he had full power to do and get whatever he wanted. Gyges in fact killed the king, and seduced the queen, and set himself up in power. We may not approve: we can understand. Were Gyges to have stolen 10 kg of chocolates per day, or copulated with cabbages, we simply would not have understood. Nor would we have understood had he wanted to strangle the queen during intercourse. (By understand here, I do not mean "understand causally"; I mean "feel an empathy with a fellow human being." Of course, causal understanding may lead to empathy.) My point, therefore, is that a perversion is something which goes against the very things we hold worthwhile: that we could not imagine wanting to do, even if we could.

Note that a perversion does not necessarily involve doing something that one does not want to do. I may not want to become a celibate monk, but such a monk is not therefore a pervert. I can understand a monk's feelings well enough to empathize. I simply cannot so empathize with a child molester. Note also that although a perversion is not immoral because it is a perversion, often its perversity lies in that which makes it immoral. We find it so alien to use a person as Christie used his victims that we think his actions perverse. This explains why many perversions are not merely aesthetically revolting but also morally pernicious.

We have come back to the original Platonic position—but with crucial shifts. Unnaturalness is connected to culture, not biology. (As a Darwinian, though, I would never deny that the former comes from and is moulded by the latter. That is why many perversions do involve biologically unsavoury acts—like eating faeces.) And the values involved are not so much moral as aesthetic. So what about homosexuality? Are homosexual acts perverse acts, and is the inclination to such acts a perverse inclination? Acknowledging that I am trying to offer a descriptive rather than prescriptive analysis, I do not think there is any straightforward answer to these questions. But I look upon this as a strength of my analysis, not a weakness! I think the question of the perversity of homosexuality is to a great extent an empirical matter. How do people feel about homosexual behaviour? Can they in some sense relate to it, whether or not they want to do it themselves and whether or not they have homosexual inclinations? The answer surely is that some people can—homosexuals themselves and some heterosexuals. Many others, like Karl Barth, cannot—they find it totally alien and disgusting. Hence, I suggest that for some people in our society homosexuality is not a perversion and for some it is. Some other societies have seen homosexuality totally as a perversion. Some other societies have not seen it as a perversion at all (Churchill 1967; Bullough 1976; Blackwood 1985).

What I am arguing, therefore, is that, faced with divided opinion in our society about the perverted nature of homosexuality (inclination and behaviour), neither side is absolutely right and neither side is absolutely wrong. There is a crucial element of subjectivity at work here, as with liking or disliking spinach. Perversion, especially as it applies to homosexuality, is a relative concept. But this does not mean that people's minds on the subject cannot be changed, or that one has no obligation to change people's minds. If one agrees that homosexuality is not immoral, then surely one ought to persuade people not to regard homosexuals and their habits with loathing. Certainly, one ought to persuade people not to confuse their disgust at a perversion with moral indignation. This does not mean that one should try to turn everyone or anyone into a homosexual; but, given that feelings of loathing are hurtful to people in a society, if there is no good reason for the feelings (that is, if they do not reinforce moral norms), then they are simply divisive, and one should try to end them. And not simply for the sake of those despised. Homophobics are not paradigmatically happy people (De Cecco 1984).

CONCLUSION

This brings this part of the discussion to an end. If you need further argument to convince you of the truth of what I have been saying, let me remind you of the curious phenomenon of lesbianism and the law. Morally, I defy you to find any difference between a male homosexual act and a lesbian act. Yet western law, as enforcer of morals, has always been more strict against the former than against the latter. It has not been from the reluctance of the (almost invariably) male legislators to judge female morality—the laws against adultery usually fall more heavily on women than on men. The answer lies in the fact that the average male heterosexual can regard lesbianism without strong counter-emotions. He finds it erotic, even. Thus, he does not stand in danger of confusing disgust at perversion with moral outrage. . . .

For men, it is otherwise. Many people have strongly negative feelings about male homosexuality. What I suggest is that they mistake the nature of their emotions. In their disgust, they make moral judgements whereas (at most) they should admit to aesthetic judgements. This is not to say that people cannot back up their feelings with moral arguments. But if these latter can be dismissed—and I have given my opinion on this—then we should work on our feelings. Not to do so is morally wrong. Indeed, it is important that this chapter end with this point resonating in your mind. Heterosexuals are only too ready to make moral judgements about homosexuals. Unrestrained homophobia is far worse sin than two or twenty homosexuals grappling together.

NOTES

1. Since the eighteenth century, there has been comparatively little written on the topic of homosexuality by professional philosophers. One who does touch on the subject is the French existentialist, Jean-Paul Sartre; but he is mainly interested in using the refusal to accept homosexual identity as an example of bad faith ("*mauvais fois*"). See Sartre 1965; also 1947, 1962.

2. Already, here, with the emphasis on the group we are going beyond biology, but let it pass. Today's evolutionists emphasize that natural selection works for, and only for, the species. Anyone who says that the homosexual is letting down the side, biologically speaking, is twenty years out of date, biologically speaking.

3. An interesting Kantian-like suggestion from Scruton (1986) is that perhaps homosexual relationships fail to measure with heterosexual relationships because, being narcissus-like, they do not involve the same level of mystery (and consequent need to risk oneself) as is required when dealing with a person of the other gender. Perhaps paradoxically, given that I am more sympathetic to the significance of human biology than is Scruton, I would claim that any relationship with another requires such a self-transcending commitment.

4. The classic article in this field is by Thomas Nagel (1969). But I agree with his critics that he speaks less of the sexually perverse and more of the sexually complete or incomplete. I take it that the Freudian notion of "perversion" . . . is a technical term, with no immediate connection to the general sense being discussed here.

REFERENCES

Aquinas, T. (1968). *Summa Theologiae,* 43, *Temperance* (2a, 2ae, 141–54). Trans. T. Gilby. London: Blackfriars.
Barash, D. P. (1977). *Sociobiology and Behaviour.* New York: Elsevier.
Barth, K. (1980). Church dogmatics. In E. Batchelor (ed.), *Homosexuality and Ethics.* New York: Pilgrim, 48–51.
Batchelor, E. (1980). *Homosexuality and Ethics.* New York: Pilgrim.

Bentham, J. (1834). *Deontology*. Ed. J. Bowring. London: Longman.

———. (1978) Offences against one's self: paederasty. *Journal of Homosexuality,* 3 (4), 383-405; 1 (4), 91–107.

Blackwood, E. (1985). *Antrhopology and Homosexual Behaviour*. New York: Haworth Press.

Boyd, R. and Richerson, P. (1985). *Culture and the Evolutionary Process*. Chicago: University of Chicago Press.

Bullough, V. L. (1976). *Sexual Variance in Society and History*. New York: Wiley.

Churchill, W. (1967). *Homosexual Behaviour Among Males; A Cross-Cultural and Cross-Species Investigation*. New York: Hawthorn Books.

De Cecco, J. P. (ed.) (1984). *Homophobia: An Overview*. New York: Haworth Press.

Denniston, R. M. (1980). Ambisexuality in animals. In J. Marmor (ed.), *Homosexual Behaviour: A Modern Reappraisal*. New York: Basic Books.

Elliston, F. (1975). In defense of promiscuity. In R. Baker and F. Elliston (eds.), *Philosophy and Sex*. Buffalo, N.Y.: Prometheus, 222–46.

Flew, A. G. N. (1967). *Evolutionary Ethics*. London: Macmillan.

Goldman, A. H. (1977). Plain Sex. *Philosophy and Public Affairs*, 6, 267–88.

Gray, R. (1978). Sex and sexual perversion. *Journal of Philosophy*, 75, 189–99.

Hrdy, S. (1981). *The Woman that Never Evolved*. Cambridge, Mass.: Harvard University Press.

Kant, I. (1949). *Critique of Practical Reason*. Trans. L. W. Beck. Chicago: University of Chicago Press.

———. (1959). *Foundations of the Metaphysics of Morals*. Trans. L. W. Beck. Indianapolis: Bobbs-Merrill.

———. (1963). *Lectures on Ethics*. Trans. L. Infield. New York: Harper and Row.

Kennedy, L. (1960). *Ten Rillington Place*. London: Gollancz.

Körner, S. (1955). *Kant*. Harmondsworth, Eng.: Penguin.

Margolis, J. (1975). The question of homosexuality. In R. Baker and F. Elliston (eds.), *Philosophy and Sex*. Buffalo, N.Y.: Prometheus Books, 288–302.

Meyer-Bahlburg, F. L. (1984). Psychoendocrine research on sexual orientation. Current status and future options. In G. J. De Vries, et al. (eds.), *Progress in Brain Research*. Amsterdam: Elsevier, vol. 61, 375–98.

Mill, J. S. (1910). *Utilitarianism*. London: Dent.

Nagel, T. (1969). Sexual perversion. *Journal of Philosophy*, 66, 1–17.

Ruddick, S. (1975). Better sex. In R. Baker and F. Elliston (eds.), *Philosophy and Sex*. Buffalo, N.Y.: Prometheus Books, 83–104.

Ruse, M. (1984). The sociobiology of human sexuality. In D. M. Brock and A. Harward (eds.), *The Culture of Biomedicine*. Newark: University of Delaware Press, vol. 1, 98–123.

———. (1986). *Taking Darwin Seriously*. Oxford: Blackwell.

Sartre, J.-P. (1947). *The Age of Reason*. London: Hamish Hamilton.

———. (1962). *Saint Genet*. Paris: Gallimard.

———. (1965). *The Humanism of Existentialism*. In W. Baskin (ed.), *The Philosophy of Existentialism*. New York: Philosophical Library, 31–62.

Scruton, R. (1986). *Sexual Desire*. London: Weidenfeld.

Stoller. R. (1975). *Perversion: The Erotic Form of Hatred*. New York: Pantheon.

Symons, D. (1979). *The Evolution of Human Sexuality*. New York: Oxford University Press.

Weeks, J. (1985). *Sexuality and Its Discontents*. London: Routledge.

Weinrich, J. D. (1982). Is homosexuality biologically natural? In W. Paul, et al. (eds.), *Homosexuality: Social, Psychological, and Biological Issues*. Beverly Hills, Calif.: Sage, 197–208.

J. ROGER LEE

Sadomasochism: An Ethical Analysis

I have been asked to address a topic that many people will find repugnant to consider. To confront this reality, I will start by presenting a detailed account of the psychological factors that are at the root of a desire for sadomasochistic sexual activity among its most committed practitioners. Next I will describe, in a general and summary way, the structure of situations in which sadomasochistic sexual activity is most often organized and show how the situations' "themes" and activities are products of the underlying psychology.

I present this psychological account for two reasons. First, once equipped with this account, even those who have no empathy with or sympathy for the sadomasochist and his activities will presumably have a less repugnantly charged cognitive grasp of what is happening in sadomasochistic sexual activity. Second, any ethical analysis of sadomasochistic sexual activity must be informed by the relevant facts of what sadomasochistic sexual activity is. Then I will turn to the ethical analysis of sadomasochistic sexual activity.

The ethical analysis proceeds on the model of a "virtues approach" to the ethical analysis of issues. This style of ethical analysis is the one that Aristotle exemplified in his *Nicomachean Ethics*. It is the approach to ethical analysis, through consideration of the excellences people can have in character and manifest in action and feeling, that many recent moral theorists consciously sought to revive in the later half of the twentieth century.

Sadomasochism is a psychological dynamic at the level of character. Sadomasochistic activity is motivated by underlying psychology in complex and nonobvious ways. Some sadomasochistic behavior is sexual, some is not. This paper aims to evaluate sadomasochistic sexual activity as a putatively potential constituent of the moral excellence of morally excellent people.

The result of the analysis offered here is that sadomasochistic activity, and by inclusion sadomasochistic sexual activity, is not constitutive per se of the moral excellence of a morally excellent person. The best that can be said for sadomasochistic sexual activity is that not all occasions of its practice are incompatible with moral excellence, and that in some situations a sadomasochistic sexual activity may be the best act that a morally excellent person should choose, or that a person who is stuck in an inferior state should take.

Before proceeding with the discussion just outlined, I must note a serious topic in passing. This paper assumes without argument that some cases of sadomasochistic sexual activity are consensual. I adopt this position because, if there were no consensual sadomasochistic sexual activity, the question of the moral status of sadomasochistic sexual activity would be too easily answered. One would say: "Sadomasochistic sexual activity is always morally impermissible because, first, sadomasochistic sexual activity involves the infliction of pain on someone who does not deserve algetic punishment and who has not consented to it, and second, the infliction of undeserved pain, without consent, is impermissible." That would be all to be said about the moral status of sadomasochistic sexual activity. In order to engage in a more fine-grained discussion of the moral status of sadomasochistic sexual activity I make the facilitating, unargued assumption that *all* sadomasochistic sexual activity discussed here is consented to by *all* parties involved.

PSYCHOLOGY

A definition performs the function of offering a precise summary of the role that a concept plays in a theory. Sadomasochism is defined as a collection of psychological traits, desires,

and beliefs focused on the infliction or suffering of pain, as a mode of attempting to realize
the impossibly grandiose demands of a Narcissistic Personality Disorder. The theory that definition summarizes is as follows.

In the course of normal development the first
psychological achievement of the child is to
develop a sense of its own self as a functioning
entity distinct from, first Mother, and then
from the other objects[1] presented in experience. This is a huge achievement, not usually
completed until the age of two-and-a-half to
three years.

Not all children succeed in pulling this off.
Sadomasochism arises out of such a failure.[2] It
emerges from an inaccurate differentiation of
self and object called Narcissistic Personality
Disorder.[3] The usual causal mechanism for narcissism to emerge in early self–object differentiation in the infant is the infant's perception of
lack of mirroring and of lack of supportive,
loving feedback, all of which are needed for
the child to identify her own desires, feelings,
capacities, and autonomy.[4] Given the child's
inherent need of and desire for love, support,
and nurturing, the absence of these desiderata
will itself be painful because needs are not being met. Regrettably, the further pains of objective abuse also will afflict some unfortunate
children. An accurate perception of self will
not develop in this environment. Social reinforcement is as essential to the development of
accuracy in this area as it is for any other developmental achievements of children.

Failure of *accurate* self-other differentiation
does not entail failure of *effective* self-other differentiation that yields an *inaccurate* conception of the self. In Narcissistic Personality Disorder, a self-representation is attained in these
privative circumstances. It represents the self
as being an impossibly dramatic, grandiose
self, capable of almost boundless achievement
and perfection in virtue of its being. Such a
self-image is illusory, of course, regardless of
its usefulness as a short-term, infantile means
of denying unpleasant reality.

The cost of this deliciously dramatic illusion, however, is *ignorance* of the condition of
the real self.[5] The developing child does not
have accurate experience of its own capacities
and efficacy. It is important and not redundant
to note that as a result, the child has little sense
of its own efficacy and feels inadequate to deal

with the reality of its actual situation in the
world. In fact, for the narcissist, genuine self-
awareness, and so accurate awareness of the
place of the self in the world, is fled as an
impossibly trying danger. The narcissist lives a
life of constant self-deceit, of constant fictional
adaptation of what facts are glimpsed, to the
service of a false appearance of her inherent,
larger-than-life excellence. All the while, the
narcissist remains in a state of undeveloped ego
that does not provide personal strength. The
narcissist remains objectively inadequate to the
ordinary demands of life and happiness.

Narcissism is often noted as a potent engine
of creativity. Examples are cited of people who
exploited some talent in service of the grandiosity that was felt to be requisite in life. But the
history that is replete with tales of great creators who have enriched humanity is also the
history of the same great creators leading personally impoverished lives in which the simple
demands of faithful friendship, family, or even
of a minimally adequate sex life remained outside their greatly undeveloped personal abilities.[6]

While creativity is *an* excellence, it can
hardly be *the sole* excellence of an excellent
life. And while we, their posterity, may well be
better off for having Beethoven's music or
Wittgenstein's philosophical writings among
our cultural resources, one cannot think that it
was *good for* either Beethoven or Wittgenstein
to have led the largely sad lives they led.[7]

Sadomasochism is a mode of narcissism[8]
availed of by some who react in a specific way
to the pains of neglect or abuse during self–
other differentiation in early childhood. The
child who needs and desires loving, nurturing,
and mirroring feedback, and who instead gets
pain from others, may opt to develop a fictional
theory of a world in which it really is loved and
cared for, or alternatively, it may try to develop
a fictional theory of a world in which it is
(grandiosely) self-sufficient and able to incorporate and transcend the pain of its actual condition, and by so doing attain excellence.[9]

If the first fiction is used, the child thinks of
himself as somehow *deserving* of the pain that
flows from "genuinely loving" others; the child
thinks of himself as somehow *responsible* for
the pain that the loving parents are *forced* to
give him though they would rather love him, as
is shown by hasty generalization from the few

guarded actions they take that could be called affectionate. Abused children often create a myth of being loved, not abused.[10] The cost of this myth is that the child sees himself as the pain-bringer, the responsible agent who blocks the parent's love and defeats the benign intentions of the parent.

If the second false picture is resorted to, the child creates a fictional world in which the truth of parental nonsupport is acknowledged, but in which the child elevates herself to a status of premature and unrealistic self-sufficiency. The child says to herself, "They don't love me, but that's OK, I don't need their love and support. I can take care of myself!"[11]

Whichever fiction is deployed, the psychological effect on self-concept comes down to the same thing: the self is viewed fictitiously on an unrealistically very grand level. Under the first fiction, a person is so harm generating that for the person to function at all successfully in the world, the person must have (unrealistically) awesome qualities of self-monitoring, self-control to attain hoped-for avoidance of the *seemingly natural* pains and harms that will beset him. Further, having monitored and controlled so wonderfully, he must then engage in awesome self-abdication to others who will have to be the only possible good-bringers to life.[12] Relative to the second fictional weltanschauung, the person must be (unrealistically) asocial and self-generating, self-sufficient; he must be remarkably sui generis. Both fictions present an unrealistically enlarged picture of the self, its capacities, and its resources that is the characteristic defining feature of narcissism.

For the child who resorts to narcissism under either of these fictions, a pseudofact is accommodated by the child's fictional picture of the world. The whole point of creating the fiction was to treat what is a central, terrible falsehood as if it were true, and then allow for optimism about the self and its prospects. If either of these fictions is adopted by the child, the child accepts and accommodates the terrible falsehood that the *painfulness* of the position the child was born into is a *natural given,* a fact about the nature of the world that is not to be avoided by a person who has any regard for the objectivity of fact.[13] If one resorts to either fiction, one does so as a way of adopting and accommodating a false metaphysics: that the

world, including oneself, works in such a way that pain and alienated nonsupport naturally flow to one; any hope one could have for a joyous life must have first accommodated that fact and second must indicate how that fact is to be worked on to allow some, perhaps very small success, joy, and love into one's life.[14]

Both of these fictional, narcissistic adaptations to pain are sadomasochistic. If one is sadomasochistic, one shows one's grandiosity by accepting and acknowledging the painfulness of life and going on anyway. Therein lies masochism. But sadism is the other side of the same psychological dynamic.

The sadist will feel that if others do not acknowledge the painfulness dimension of an excellent life, they should have it brought to their attention. The sadomasochist, like many other people, thinks that it is proper to hold people to a minimum standard of responsibility: the requirement that they face facts. Someone working under a sadomasochistic fiction will think that appreciation and accommodation of the "naturally very painful" character of life is a fact that others should be called on to face up to. The sadist reasons that if others are ever going to meet this minimal condition for excellence, let alone realize excellence, they must face this "fact." The sadist reasons that people should have the painfulness of life brought to their attention if they are ever going to integrate it into their life in the requisite way for excellence.[15] The sadist will enjoy the response of someone who is pain-accommodating in this way. After all, from the sadist's point of view, that person will be behaving admirably, responsibly. The sadomasochist will enjoy the shared project of pain manipulation that makes for so much of the excellence of a person, including the masochistic pain recipient. This all makes sense to the sadist. But, in fact, drawing people's attention to pain, to require that they make submission to pain central to their lives, is sadistic.

The sadomasochist attempts to make the pains of life central to a grandiose sense of self and of human excellence. The masochist seeks to make her own pain, no matter how intense, something that she transcends, carrying on well anyway. The sadist is the teacher,[16] the leader, who holds people responsible for feeling the pains of life, and if they accept her direction, carrying on anyway. The sadist either views herself as offering a necessary condition for excellence or views herself as an agent of truth, showing people the requirement of the acceptance of pains as an extensive, natural given in life.[17]

To a person who is not sadomasochistic, both the sadist and the masochist will seem to present unintelligible demands. The masochist presents a request for a muting of normal joyousness and other-regard. The sadist will seem to be pointlessly offensive, rude, and threatening.

To a sadomasochist, the normal person will seem to be inauthentic. The normal person will strike the sadomasochist as being a foolishly optimistic person who is inadequate to face the traumas of the world.

In fact, the sadomasochist is wrong. In fact, it is the normal, nonnarcissistic, nonsadomasochistic people who function best in the world, making achievements in a broad range of the dimensions of life, and who are capable of coping with a broad range of the challenges and opportunities of everyday life. That this is so is explained by the fact that only the nonnarcissistic person can have an accurate sense of his capabilities in a situation and so of the objective conditions for action in a given situation. The narcissist has to flee the facts of the situation—both inner and outer facts—and retreat into illusion and delusion. Narcissism is not an efficient strategy for success in the world.

SEX AND SADOMASOCHISM

Sex is a powerful drive, with powerful associated feelings, that engages a person at puberty and may never let go. Puberty occurs quite later in life than the self–other differentiation phase of self formation in infancy. By the time puberty begins, the child will have established a style of self—a character or personality type. So, at puberty, one's sexuality with its intensity of drive and feeling will have to be integrated into the style of person one already is.

If one has developed a personality structure in which the narcissistic, sadomasochistic awareness of pain is central to the sense one has of one's self at its full, intense, most excellent functioning, then the all-consuming intensity of feeling and drive that come with sexu-

ality and sexual activity will feel off, not right, unacceptably disconcerting without a phenomenology of pain as a component part.[18]

Sadomasochistic integration of sexuality into one's life will require the infliction or acceptance of pain phenomena as part of sexual activity. Sadomasochism requires intentionality to pain as part of any interaction as intense as a sexual interaction if that intensity of feeling is to be integrated acceptably as a feeling of the perceived grandiose-through-pain-administration self. In some cases, the integration of pain into the intensity of drive and feeling of sexuality may be so dominant a feeling as to *eclipse* what would normally be taken to be realization, culmination, or resolution of the sexual experience through the attainment of arousal or orgasm.[19]

People tend to repeat objectively failed interactions, regardless of the subjective gloss that has been put on them, be it positive or negative. People tend to do so in an attempt to get the interaction right, once and for all, and to get the failure behind them through final success.[20] Sadomasochistic sexual activity is resorted to in the intense atmosphere of sex in order to provide a repetition of the central failed adjustment of childhood, accommodation of painful inputs from what should have been the earliest necessarily nurturing environment during the pre-oedipal period.

The sadomasochist who has adopted the false metaphysical thesis that painfulness is an essential feature of life and its successes as a displacement of the initial disappointment in parenting, will be engaged in repetition behavior of pain accommodation in most areas of life. The metaphysical thesis broadens the base of frustration. So, by broadening the base of frustration, it is open to the parents to be recast in contrast to the world as a whole, counterfactually, as *relatively* loving and supporting sources of nurture. While this tactic diminishes the disappointment in family, it does so by providing more occasions for a felt need for suffering and for its successful accommodation.

Intense areas of life like sex and art are so deeply engaging of ourselves and of our feelings that the pain-oriented pseudoself of the sadomasochist must find itself in there. Elaborate procedures involving whips, ropes, clothespins, and the like, together with slaps, bites, pinches, restraints, tickles, penetrations and so on, routinely are described in sado-masochistic pornography, in social studies accounts of the activities of prostitutes who have a sadomasochistic clientele, in accounts of voluntary sadomasochistic interactions, and among the discussants on the Internet discussion group, alt/sex/bondage.[21] Seemingly responsible people (given accounts of them reported in the secondary literature, and given some of the impressive academic and corporate return addresses that show up on contributions to discussion on the Internet) contribute accounts of their use of such devices and practices in intimate activity.

Common features emerge from a review of this material. Usually sadomasochistic sexual activity occurs in the context of a firm contractual precommitment of all parties to parameters on what can be expected to happen in sadomasochistic sexual activity. The only exception to this involves descriptions of established friends/lovers who have established trust in a history of caretaking or limit observance. "Safe words" are agreed to beforehand so the masochistic participant (often called a "bottom") can signal the end of sadomasochistic sexual activity if the pain he is accepting becomes too much to take.

The bottom, assured by these elements of context, can abandon himself to a feeling of helplessness in the administration of pain by a sadist (often called a "top"). The top also functions as the hoped-for good provider or teacher through the pain she brings to the transaction and through her supposed authority regarding the meaning and acceptable limits of pain manipulation that are good for both the top and the bottom.

Although the top demands attention through the administering of pain that is commanding in its presence, the bottom is *the center of attention,* just as she was as an infant. Everything that occurs in the sadomasochistic sexual activity interaction (usually called a "scene") either is or has its purpose in and takes its meaning from *what the bottom feels* and how *she* behaves in response to the felt pain. All other parties focus their attention on that.

Resolution of a sadomasochistic sexual activity scene is attained in one of a number of ways: when a top brings a bottom to a newer level of pain acceptance than had been attained

before and the bottom is congratulated or comforted; when the bottom passes out and awakens outside the scene; when the bottom attains orgasm or when the top uses the bottom to attain orgasm and leaves the bottom without orgasmic relief and in a suspended scene of ongoing pain, to be resumed later, at the pleasure of the top.

The themes are always the same. The top brings the bottom to a supposedly elevated level by getting him to accept, endure, and relish pain. The bottom, by being pain receptive, improves himself and is elevated to a transcendence of the pain.

The theme is always the repetition of the sadomasochistic narcissistic solution to the helpless pain reception of the abused child and its transcendence of the pain-bringing parent through masochistic narcissism.[22]

Throughout this paper I write of pain. But very different things function as modes of pain in sadomasochistic sexual activity. One is the restraint that a bound person, incapable of movement or defense, will feel. Another is the sensory deprivation that the gagged, the blindfolded, the auditorially muted person would feel. Other forms of pain include ridicule, embarrassment, subjugation to harsh authority, fear, exposure, defenselessness, and humiliation. All of these "pains" function to leave the bottom with a feeling of powerlessness and lack of defense in the presence of the top. Slavery is even enshrined as a mutual desideratum in some of this literature.

I have called all this "painfulness" because these are the pains that abused, neglected, and dependent-for-nurturing children will feel in child-abuse situations. The pains that are embraced in sadomasochistic sexual activity scenes are repetitions of the painful interactions of childhood. Pathetically, a sadomasochist is trying to repeat and (finally) get right the painful interactions of infancy. This is pathetic, because the procedure of the sadomasochistic sexual activity scene will reinforce failed solutions rather than advance the participant to success. Raising pain in intensity of feeling to the level one can take and still be able to carry on leads to reinforcement of narcissistic grandiosity of pain manipulation, not the refutation of grandiosity that has to be achieved in going beyond childhood failure. The sadomasochistic scene mirrors and thus reinforces the false, grandiose self of pain transcendence of the narcissistic participants.[23]

ETHICS

Ethics is the attempt to discover ideals for humans to realize in themselves and in their actions. These ideals should be realistic, because they should be realized. Minimally, the ideals should be such that humans *could* realize the ideals. In a stronger sense, the ideals of ethics should be realistic in the sense that essential facts about human nature, accidental facts about the history and involvements of an individual human, and accidental facts about the environment calling for action each partially inform the ideals that ethics describes and their application to action by that person, in that situation. The thought is that if the facts were to be different than they are, then either the ideals described by ethics would be different or the character of the particular instantiation of the ideals in a particular situation would be different than it is.

Sexual ethics is the attempt to discover ideals in the areas of sexual activity that will integrate sexual activities (or their avoidance) into the ideals of a human life. Thus the task of this paper is to describe the place (if any) that sadomasochistic sexual activity will have in a person's life that manifests human ideals.

Many recent ethicists have found it worthwhile to adopt a classical fourth- and fifth-century B.C.E. Greek way of describing ethical ideals, as virtues, and of describing actions in keeping with those ideals as actions in keeping with the virtues. The Greek word that we translate as "virtue" is "*aretē*," a word that conveys more of our sense of the word "excellence."[24] For the classical tradition represented by Socrates, Plato, and Aristotle, ethics prescribed a life in which human excellences were constitutive of the person and were lived up to in action.

One learns the excellences through the training offered by parents, and by others who care for one, all of whom hopefully have practical wisdom to impart. One acquires excellences by having one's actions and feelings habituated to patterns that conform to the excellences and by having one's rational faculty trained to be sensitive to judgments of proportion that track what is fine, noble, or beautiful and by doing so will track what actions, what action outcomes, and what states of an acting person are in keeping with the excellences.[25] Someone who has honed all these skills and tendencies for action will select fine and noble actions and goals in situations and will be repelled by actions and goals that are repugnant, base, or ignoble. Someone who is so disposed to act, and further has the practical wisdom (*phronēsis*) to reason to the selection of actions and goals in her life, will have the excellences of an ideal person and will select actions and goals in keeping with the ideal in situations calling for action.

A person who develops the excellences and acts in terms of them, Aristotle said, attains *eudaimonia,* which he defined as living well (*eu zēn*) and acting well (*eu prattein*) (1095a19). The person with the excellences who has *eudaimonia* will have command of his functions and will use them to select the right act, at the right time, about the right things, in the right way, to the right extent, with the right people (1106b24), with a sensitivity to, and a goal to conform to, what is fine and noble.

According to Aristotle, some people will attain the highest state of development of the excellences: nobility-and-goodness (*kalokagathia*).[26] This is the state of someone who both has the excellences and is sensitive to the fine and noble in such a way that the good-things-for-humans can be good-things-for-her. Put another way, a point of having the excellences is not only to live well and act well, but to make it possible that the good things of life can be integrated into one's life in such a way as to be good-for-oneself.

Put negatively, someone who is without the excellences and who has not developed aspects of nobility-and-goodness, will not be able to integrate the good things of life, like pleasure, honor, money, or sex, into her life in a way that would be good-for-her. Frequently such a person will attempt to weave a good into her life but is frustrated because she finds that the good thing cannot be good-for-her. She finds that the good thing can be incorporated into her life only in a way that is destructive to *eudaimonia,* to living well and doing well.

I endorse and embrace all of these aspects of

an outline of Aristotle's moral philosophy. The theses I advance in sexual ethics and in these reflections on sadomasochistic sexual activity, are arrived at and play their intellectual roles in an ethical theory executed in terms of these Aristotelian theses.[27]

NORMAL SEX

Human beings have a drive for, a natural desire for, and tendency to seek out sexual activities. Sexual activities are diverse and multityped, and the sex drive itself could be analyzed into a set of drives such that satisfaction of some will activate others. Some of the strivings are for psychological goals such as for nurturing support, for acceptance, for mirroring, and for bonding. Some of the strivings of the sex drive are for a complex of physical sensations of soothing and of irritative sorts. Some strivings are for a mixture of the physical and the psychological. Good sexual activity triggers shared feelings of physical immediacy, in complex sequences that are otherwise inaccessible and that contribute elements of or cause constitutive elements of the psychological goods that come from sexual activity.

To access and satisfy a good mix of these drives is exaltedly life expressing and reinforcing. Thus accessing and satisfying a good mix of these drives is a constitutive element of a human's living fully and well, and of a human's *being aware* of living fully and well. Accessing and satisfying these drives is a constitutive element of a person's *eudaimonia,* of living well and functioning well.

Further, sexual activity promotes effects that are goods for the sexually active person. It promotes bonding with one's sexual partner, through shared passion, intimacy, and rewarded trust. Trust itself is reinforced in good sexual activity. Good sexual activity offers felt support for one's most immediate feelings, unguardedly exhibited. Such support is strength generating. Good sexual activity is also fun, and its satisfactions are reinforcing to the drives. Sexual activity, by being done well, focuses the drives and makes their frequent satisfaction more likely. Last, children can be generated through heterosexual sex if birth control is waived. This result will be appealing to those who feel their progenerative drives, and who judge their situation to be sufficient for undertaking the responsibilities of children and family. Progenerative goods will flow from only a small percentage of sexual activities, however, while the other goods that flow from good sexual activity do so at a high level of frequency.

The administration of pain, its infliction and its enjoyment, have little to no function in this natural set of drives called "human sexuality." To the extent that one is intentional to pain during sexual activity one is distracted from access to desires and tendencies the working through of which is sexuality.

ETHICAL CONSIDERATION OF SADOMASOCHISTIC SEXUAL ACTIVITY

Can sadomasochistic sexual activity play a legitimate role in a happy life of living well and doing well? Can it be integrated into a life of someone who manifests the excellences of character, the virtues?

Insofar as sadomasochistic sexual activity integrates into a life as a manifestation of a sadomasochistic mode of Narcissistic Personality Disorder, it is clear that the answer is "No; it does not integrate into a life of living well and doing well through the human excellences." This judgment is rendered because nothing that is expressive of, or supportive of, a Narcissistic Personality Disorder is expressive of or a manifestation of living well and doing well. A person living to the demands of Narcissistic Personality Disorder is not noble-and-good.

The proof that a person living to the demands of Narcissistic Personality Disorder is not noble-and-good is the following. If living to the demands of the Narcissistic Personality Disorder were noble-and-good, then, in virtue of fulfilling narcissism, the narcissist would make it possible that things that are objectively good would be good-for-her. The narcissist, as is shown above, is made *unable* to make an objective good—knowledge of herself and of her place in the world—be good-for-her. So it follows that actions that function as a manifestation of or that support narcissism are *not* noble-and-good, and so are not aspects of living well and doing well, of a happy, commendable life at its highest level of achievement.

The substantive claims that function in the

proof just concluded are the facts of psychology that were reported above, along with one evaluative claim. The evaluative claim is: "Knowledge of oneself and of one's place in the world is an objective good." The evaluative claim is uncontroversial since such knowledge is required for and helps in our accurate planning of action to secure whatever else are goods and to integrate those goods into our lives. Further, knowledge of one's self and of one's place in the world is not merely an instrumental good, but has its own intrinsic worth.

The rest of the proof is the working out of the logical implications of the substantive claims. The proof establishes its conclusion: actions, including sadomasochistic sexual activity, manifesting or sustaining Narcissistic Personality Disorder do not exhibit nobility-and-goodness and so are not manifestations of living well and acting well through the excellences.

This result, referring as it does to the underlying causal and substantive basis of sadomasochism and of the broadest class of sadomasochistic sexual activities, is obtained at a fundamental level of description: "manifestation of narcissism." It is obtained independently of talk about pain, enslavement, domination, humiliation, and so on, that ordinarily dominate discussions of sadomasochistic sexual activity. In most cases of sadomasochistic sexual activity, those in which narcissism is being manifested, the putative evil of any or all of these is superficial and ancillary to a deeper evil: the goodness of a full life is being denied by, thwarted by, inferior conditions.

Close discussion of the place of pain administration in sadomasochistic sexual activity is important to another weighing of sadomasochistic sexual activity which proceeds as follows. To a sadomasochist, pain administration plays an essential role in the feeling that the self is living fully and well. But, as I detailed above, this is a deceptive view of the self. It is a view of the self that disallows knowledge of and development of enjoyment of the real self. The sadomasochist in particular and the narcissist in general cannot make many of the goods of self-knowledge good-for-him.

But sadomasochistic sexual activity tries to subsume the complexities of sexual drive satisfaction under the perceived central dynamic of pain administration. Not all of sexual drive satisfaction fits into this literally infantile drama of the pseudoself. Even elements that can be translated lose complexity of or completeness of realization "in the translation."

The good of knowledge is not all that is lost to the sadomasochistic narcissist. Many goods of sexual activity cannot be accessed either. Further, some goods, associated with what the sadomasochist thinks is a false picture of unconflicted trustworthy, unconditional support, are perceived as being threatening and are fled from, if ever glimpsed on a possibility horizon. Not only *won't* they be available goods for the sadomasochist, but qua sadomasochist, she *cannot* even imagine having them be goods-for-her. Many of the goods of sex cannot be goods-for-her.

Sometimes practices are denounced as sadomasochistic unfairly and inaccurately. One should not call most gentle bites, pinches, slaps, and holdings that may infrequently occur in some people's sexual improvisations, sadomasochistic. Some activities that people integrate into their sexual activities, even if they are instances of typical activities in sadomasochistic scenes, do not manifest narcissism or even sadomasochism. It would be inaccurate to call people sadomasochistic or their sexual activity sadomasochistic sexual activity if their sexual activities that might otherwise be described as sadomasochistic play an infrequent and never psychologically central role for those people.

In the cases of nonsadomasochistic nibbling, holding, and so on, in sex that I have in mind, pain administration is not a causal explainer of what is going on. Rather, because normal sexual activity involves a complex physiology of excitation and release of nervous and affective energies and states through alternate irritation and soothing of sensitive areas of the organism, it works out that occasional, nonthreatening, nonpainful, constructive irritation of the organism can be obtained by biting, scratching, holding, or slapping, when integrated with other stimulations in a nondistracting way.

In fact, since irritation in normal sex is not limited to the physiological but can be psychological too, a slap or a bite that has psychological–social overtones of meaning and associated affect can be a more intense irritation than those irritations that arise as by-products of organisms rubbing against each other in sexual activity. But it is precisely because of overtones of affect and meaning that bites, slaps, and the like, must be used very sparingly in sexual activity, for danger of distracting the participant, away from awareness necessary in sexual activity, to some other negatively reacting frame of mind.

Some constructive neural irritants in the complex of irritation and soothing that takes place in sexual activity can be provided by slapping, biting, and so on, that in other contexts could bear the description "the administration of pain and abuse." But they do not bear that description in the context of good sex.

Too much can be made of this fact by people who would take the fact to license a hasty generalization to the claim that a pain-restraint-centered sadomasochistic sexual activity scene can be licensed as a normal sexual activity.[28] For those who pay attention to the details cited above, no such hasty generalization will be tempting.

The conceptual geography for our current best theory of sexual activity in human psychology and physiology and of human excellences should present the fact that the wrongness of bites, slaps, and so on, in sadomasochistic sexual activity does not arise from the nature of, or even from the social–affective associated meanings of, biting, slapping, and the like, but from some other source.

One way that biting, slapping, and the like, can be wrong in sexual activity has been presented above: insofar as those activities manifest or perpetuate an underlying sadomasochistic mode of narcissism, they are ruled out of the domain of human excellence and should be rejected by morality. Subject to one minor qualification below, the subject of underlying sadomasochistic modes of narcissism underlying almost all cases of sadomasochistic sexual activity, have been fully discussed. There are, however, further considerations for and against sadomasochistic sexual activity.

Between the extremes of the morally innocuous slaps and tickles and the morally odious sadomasochistic sexual activity scenes as celebrations of a destructive and false self-image, there is a continuum of degrees of involvement of symbolic irritants as progressively more permeating of, and more central to, the intentional states in one's sexual activities. As with all such continuums, there is a vague "borderline"

region in which the criteria for the application of terms like "moral" and "immoral" to points on the continuum do not yield determinate results. The criterion for the application of "moral" and "immoral" to points of the continuum is: "To what extent does this proportion count as enhanced sexual activity, as opposed to a theater of pain manipulation in lieu of, or displacing, aspects of the realization of one's sexuality in sexual activity?" Enhanced guidance is rendered by consideration of the psychological phenomenon of distraction. We say: x is a distraction of y from z if and only if y is consciously aware of z or z is a teleology which y is undertaking, and on the occasion of x for y, either y ceases to be (or is diminished in the extent of being) consciously aware of z or y ceases to be (or is diminished in the extent of being) involved in undertaking teleology z.

If and to the extent that the slaps, bites, and so on, that could be elements that constitute a sadomasochistic sexual activity scene *distract* one from the emerging complex teleology of the unfolding manifestations of sexual drive, then, to that extent, the domain of *pain* is at work, *not the domain of sexuality*. From the standpoint of sexual morality, the activity is then not part of what is endorsed as morally approved sexual activity.

The criterion—for evaluation of activities that could either be part of good sexual activity or part of a morally rejected sadomasochistic sexual activity scene—that has just been produced and amplified will yield clear results at the extremes of the continuum and not at some intermediate points. However, as a practical matter for one's ethics, since one's sexuality can be impaired by actions that are wrong in the manner at issue, one should restrict oneself to clear cases of good sexual activity rather than gamble in the border region.

ETHICAL CONSIDERATION OF SADOMASOCHISTIC SEXUAL ACTIVITY FOR LESS THAN OPTIMAL CASES

Some people are unlucky: the condition that fate has given them does not allow for full human functioning for happiness. Aristotle knew this. He gave a list of defeating factors for *eudaimonia* that looks cold and superficial to readers today. Being ill-born was on Aristotle's list of defeating factors and he probably meant some offensively class-oriented sense of being "ill-born." Nonetheless, we frequently speak of another sense of someone's being ill-born as destroying the capacity for *eudaimonia,* for living well and doing well. Our sense of "ill-born" is "being born into a child-abuse situation." Parental neglect and abuse can defeat the development of capacities in children. These undeveloped capacities, in turn, leave the otherwise developed adult who emerges from that childhood unable to function as a human who is fully capable of *eudaimonia* should. The narcissistic sadomasochist is such a person. Sadomasochism arises in an environment of earliest child–parent interaction. The sadomasochistic narcissist is inhibited in her capacity for action developing and manifesting excellences that track what is fine.

While ethics should address the typical and normal case (1094b20–25), the ideals that ethics discovers should be realized in a person's life, not as theoretically fixed points to which the person aspires, but as dimensions of a person's life that are set contextually by prior states of the agent. Morality does not call on us to coerce our frame into an externally set mold, but describing states of the condition in which we find ourselves, indicates how, and to what extent, those states should be reinforced or changed in action. Ethics should have something to say to many persons who have blocked capacities. Ethics should at least have something to say to the narcissistic sadomasochist.

There are, of course, psychodynamic therapies that can recapture the lost capacities of the sadomasochistic narcissist. In the context of such therapy we are told that sadomasochistic sexual activity is counterindicated.[29] These therapies, however, take much time, are expensive, and are not available in some locales. So therapy and its required suspension of sadomasochistic sexual activity, while ideal for such cases, may not be possible for others. What of those cases?

If nothing reconstructive can be done, then the sadomasochist will not function sexually without sadomasochistic sexual activity. For some such sadomasochists, relationship among themselves, involving safely executed and considerate sadomasochistic sexual activity may be the best they can hope to have, given an accidental impossibility of personality recon-

struction to a character that supports more optimal sexual functioning. Such sadomasochists should be brought to an awareness that their sex life is not optimal, that it really is not even much of a *sex life* because satisfaction of *sexual drive* is minimized. But what these people are doing should not be morally censured, unless contrary to hypothesis therapeutic adjustment back to the norm becomes realistic.

What should a nonsadomasochistic person who loves a non-therapy-possible sadomasochist do? Should he engage in sadomasochistic sexual activity to meet the sadomasochist's need for such? Were love in our control I would advise such a person to find someone else to love, because his sexuality is at risk for frustration or for destructive change in such a relationship.

Love, however, is not always in our control, and it is theoretically possible that a genuine connection of love would be established between a sadomasochist who had no realistic hope of therapy and a normal person. As an expression of love, sadomasochistic sexual activity that did not offend or upset the normal lover could properly be agreed to, so long as the sexual needs of the normal lover could also be met, perhaps on other occasions. I would think that relationships formed along these lines are unstable and will tend to develop in one of two ways or to rupture. First, there is a danger that an attraction to a sadomasochist may be a function of an underlying inadequacy in the normally functioning partner's sense of self. If present, such an inadequacy can leave an opening for the exotic character of sadomasochistic sexual activity to inspire and be an organizational theme for the construction of a grandiose self-substitute. A realistic sense of self can thus be partially obstructed and made inaccessible to the formerly normally functioning person. The damaged, progressively alienated self will in turn create a vacuum for more reliance on a grandiose self-substitute. In short, there is a genuine danger that the normal sexual partner would lose his normality, and so lose the accessibility of satisfaction of his sexual drives.

The second development that a relationship between a normally functioning person and a sadomasochist may take would be for the sadomasochist to develop toward normality. I stipulated that path to be not readily available to the sadomasochist prior to the relationship. That stipulation was made to provide a necessary condition for envisioning any permissibility of sadomasochistic sexual activity in the relationship. It should be noted, however, that a loving relationship with a normal person is itself a psychological resource. In cases at the margin, the psychological resources that flow from such a relationship may make a difference to the sadomasochist's capacity, or willingness, to make budgetary adjustments to accommodate the possible development toward normality in therapy. The direction of development would be toward the normality of both parties.

Of these two possible developmental paths, the development of the normal person toward sadomasochism is more likely than that of the development of the sadomasochist toward normality. The development of the normal person toward sadomasochism is more likely because it is the development that takes the least effort for change. It is a progressive decay of the self occasioned through sadomasochistic sexual activity in a context of pre-existing weakness. The contrary development of the sadomasochist toward normality takes *much* effort and has been hypothesized to be an unrealistic possibility, for these cases, to start with.

Most relations between sadomasochists and normal lovers will take neither of these developmental paths but will rupture in an extinction of love. Strains arise in a relationship from two people pursuing different ends in joint activity: the sadomasochist will be working the pain

dynamic drama, while the normal-functioning person will be trying to bond, in part through engaging a teleology of (would-be) shared, complex sexual drive satisfaction.

Sadomasochistic sexual activity is psychologically dangerous both for the sadomasochist and for the normally functioning person. The danger to the sadomasochist is that weakening delusions will be reinforced. The danger to the more normal party is that personal resourcefulness can be undermined. So, while permissible in some cases, sadomasochistic sexual activity between a normally functioning person and a sadomasochist is always dangerous and should be approached very guardedly. Where, and to the extent that they are available, mutually satisfying alternative sexual behaviors that do access and satisfy the sex drives should be pursued instead.

For the sadomasochist, outside a loving relationship, abstinence from pseudosexual sadomasochistic sexual activity may be preferable to indulgence in some cases. Abstinence is also destructive to or deforming of the sexual drives. But at some point, perhaps this one, we are reduced from talking about nonoptimal possibilities for ethical action for ideals, to talking about what people should do who do not have the resources to do much if anything of the things they should do. At this point it is not surprising that there are few if any things that can be said clearly and with good reason about what these people should do.

NOTES

1. Psychologists have the initially disconcerting practice of referring to all non-self entities, including other *people,* and even *family members,* as "objects." While odd, this terminology is not a mark of insensitivity to a humanistic perspective. I adopt their terminological practice in the use of "object" in this essay.

2. Susanne P. Schad-Somers, *Sadomasochism: Etiology and Treatment* (New York: Human Sciences Press, 1982), 129–31.

3. I shall use "Narcissistic Personality Disorder" and "Narcissism" as synonymous in this essay, and refer to the person who is inhibited by Narcissistic Personality Disorder as a narcissist. Theoretical room should be left for someone to be narcissistic in some dimension(s) of their life without having a Narcissistic Personality Disorder. My move for terminological convenience in this essay is not meant to deny this fact.

4. Nathan Schwartz-Salant, *Narcissism and Character Transformation: The Psychology of Narcissistic Character Disorders* (Toronto: Inner City Books, 1982), 45–50; James F. Masterson, *The Real Self: A Developmental, Self, and Object Relations Approach* (New York: Brunner/Mazel, 1985), 24–29, 31, 32; N. Gregory Hamilton, *Self and Others: Object Relations Theory in Practice* (London: Jason Aronson, 1988), 165; Heinz Kohut, *The Search for the Self: Selected Writings of Heinz Kohut: 1950–1978* vol. 2, ed. Paul H. Ornstein (New York: International Universities Press, 1978), 629–630, 649.

5. Schwartz-Salant, *Narcissism,* 67.

6. The examples of the Ludwigs, Beethoven and Wittgenstein, come quickly to mind. Should Wittgenstein's self-imposed "minimalist" style of life seem not sufficiently grandiose for narcissism, consider that even the *smallest* number in an ordered number sequence is the *greatest* extent in *one* direction. Concerning the debate about W. W. Bartley's claim that Wittgenstein engaged in sadomasochistic sexual activity, it does not matter who is right between Bartley and Monk, who offers the more

guarded claim that Wittgenstein only had voyeuristic excitement from and was tempted by the boys of the Prater. Even if Monk is right, the very feeling of attraction would have been shameful and threatening to Wittgenstein's demanding sense of his ideal self (grandiosity). See W. W. Bartley, *Wittgenstein* (LaSalle, Ill.: Open Court, 1985), and Ray Monk, *Ludwig Wittgenstein: The Duty of Genius* (New York: Penguin, 1991), Appendix.

7. Norman Malcolm, in his memoir on Wittgenstein, remarked on Wittgenstein's last words: "Tell them I've had a wonderful life." He thought that Wittgenstein must have been so unhappy that the suggestion was implausible if not incredible; see Norman Malcolm, *Ludwig Wittgenstein: A Memoir* (Oxford: Oxford University Press, 1984), 81. In his second thoughts on the matter (84), Malcolm allows that Wittgenstein must have had some moments of intense joy and so his life may well have been happy or at least wonderful. I find these second thoughts unconvincing. His first reaction seems more likely—moments of joy amidst "plenty of pain" do not a happy life make. Last, it is worthy of note that in young adulthood, Wittgenstein praised Beethoven's way of living.

8. Arnold M. Cooper, "The Narcissistic–Masochistic Character," in *Masochism: Current Psychoanalytic Perspectives,* ed. Robert A. Glick and Donald I. Meyers (Hillsdale, N. J.: Analytic Press, 1988), 291, 126; Schad-Somers, *Sadomasochism,* 53.

9. "[O]ne may consider that the infant, out of the need to maintain some vestiges of self-esteem in situations of more than ordinary pain, displeasure, failure of reward, and diminished self esteem, will still attempt to salvage pleasure by equating the familiar with the pleasurable. Survival in infancy undoubtedly depends on retaining some capacity for receiving pleasurable impressions from the self and object. We may theorize that the infant makes the best adaptation he can—familiar pains may be the best available pleasure." ; see Cooper, Narcissistic-Masochistic Character, 127–28.

10. Narcissistic-Masochistic Character, 128.

11. Schwartz-Salant, *Sadomasochism,* 68. Intermediate positions are also possible. For example, many people will not think themselves to be the cause of their own pain but will come to accept pain endurance and degradation anyway as a supposedly necessary means for accessing perceived parental love and repair (see Schwartz-Salant, *Sadomasochism,* 57). They may not feel responsible for having caused the pain, but they feel responsible for willingly accepting and coping with it in order to make parental manifestations of love possible.

12. Cooper, "Narcissistic–Masochistic Character," 128; Schad-Somers, *Sadomasochism,* 49–53.

13. Theo L. Dorpat states that "in masochistic patients the central dynamic involves the introjection of the parents' sadism"; see "An Object-Relations Perspective on Masochism," in *Essential Papers on Character Neurosis and Treatment,* ed. Ruth F. Lax (New York: New York University Press, 1989), 281.

14. Jill D. Montgomery, "The Hero as Victim: The Development of a Masochistic Life," in *Masochism: The Treatment of Self-Inflicted Suffering,* ed. Jill D. Montgomery and Ann C. Greiff (Madison, Conn.: International Universities Press, 1989), 75–77; James L. Stacksteder, "Thoughts on the Positive Value of a Negative Identity," in Montgomery and Greiff, eds., *Masochism,* 106–7; Dorpat, "An Object-Relations Perspective on Masochism," 281–2.

15. Jerzy Kosinski's pre-oedipal development may (or may not) have been orthodox, but his World War II experiences, starting at age six, rivaled the abusive horrors he depicted in *Painted Bird.* Kosinski was a novelist who used strong sadomasochistic elements in his fiction and who thought that horror was widespread in the world; see Tom Teicholz, ed., *Conversations with Jerzy Kosinski* (Jackson: University Press of Mississippi, 1993), 12–13. Kosinski, teaching at Princeton during the period of American involvement in the war in Vietnam, had a student who said something devaluing about Kosinski's tendency to write about violence and death. Kosinski described his sadistic reply to the student, as follows: "I apologized for being a member of the non realistic school of fiction, and said, 'you know, the very first time I saw you I got the strange feeling that you were going to die young.' My student was dumbfounded: 'I'm only twenty-two. That's a terrible thing to tell a man!' he said, with real tears in his eyes. ' . . . To tell a man? But I'm talking about *you.* Didn't you say that *you'd* be going to Vietnam?' 'Yes,' he answered. In reality, of course, I had no such premonition of his death. I had simply wanted to shock him, to get an intense personal reaction out of him by making him aware of the one individual experience he could not escape: his own death"; see Jerzy Kosinski, "Dead Souls on Campus," in his *Passing By: Selected Essays, 1962–1991* (New York: Random House, 1992), 145. Of course, one can intensely be aware of pleasurable or warm experiences too. Presumably this young man may well have had such intense feelings in his past, without Kosinski's intervention. What Kosinski wanted to do was to make this "pain-denying" person feel real, inescapable fear, horror, and pain.

16. Consider the often ill-advised but frequently presented line of dialogue, "That'll teach him!," after some harm has been administered. Also it should be noted that in much sadomasochistic fiction, the sadist is presented in the role of the masochist's instructive guide to pain administration.

17. Of course, on a simpler level, sadism can be seen as an expression of narcissistic rage; see Kohut, *The Search for the Self,* 637–38.

18. Not everyone with a sadomasochistic personality will embrace sadomasochistic sexual activity. The actual practices may never occur to people living in isolated social environments who may never hear of such practices. For others, who may hear of sadomasochistic sexual activities, the socially endorsed negative affect associated with sadomasochistic sexual activities may be an overriding message, trumping any feeling of psychic fit that they might have had. Thus some people with sadomasochistic personality structures may not fall into sadomasochistic sexual practices when they integrate sexuality into their lives at puberty. However, the integration of purely nonsadomasochistic sexual activities into such a personality structure will be incomplete and unstable; there will remain a potential for satisfied adoption of sadomasochistic sexual activity. Chasseguet-Smirgel presents the example of a patient, involved in an intense sadomasochistic sexual relationship, but who prior to that relationship had led a normal life with sadomasochism only latent. Married, with three children, her sexual life had been acceptable to her till age thirty-five: "Then she met a pervert . . . "; see Janine Chasseguet-Smirgel, *Creativity and Perversion* (New York: W. W. Norton, 1984); 93, 131, 134. At any point of life, a sadomasochistic person may register a datum of sadomasochistic sexual activity and note the psychic fit between her sadomasochistic personality and sadomasochis-

tic sexual activity. From that point on, the strong allure of sadomasochistic sexual activity becomes a large psychic fact to be dealt with in that person's sex life.

19. Leonard's remarks, quoted in Gloria G. Brame, William D. Brame, and Jon Jacobs, *Different Loving: An Exploration of the World of Sexual Dominance and Submission* (New York: Villard Books, 1993), 62.

20. Not surprisingly, psychologists call this fact about people the "repetition phenomenon."

21. Schad-Somers, *Sadomasochism*, 61; see the Internet publication by Rob Jellinghaus (robertj@Autodesk.COM), The alt.sex.bondage FAQ List, Message-ID: ⟨17610@autodesk.COM⟩, Date: 15 Sep 92 07:04:33 GMT.

22. Schad-Somers, *Sadomasochism*, 61.

23. Schad-Somers, *Sadomasochism*, 62.

24. For ease of quick exposition, I shall use "excellence" instead of the interchangeable "virtue" in most places in this essay.

25. "Actions expressing excellence are fine and aim at what is fine" (*Hai de kat aretēn praxeis kalai kai tou kalou heneka*); Aristotle, *Nicomachean Ethics*, 1120a24). Unless otherwise noted, all subsequent quotations from Aristotle are from his *Nicomachean Ethics*. The Greek word *kalos*, here translated as "fine," is ambiguous between "fine," "noble," and "beautiful." It is in fact a "common feature of the excellences" (*koinon . . . tais aretais*; 1122b7) that they track the fine in the way that Aristotle indicates at 1120a24. See: 1115b11–14, 1115b20–23, 1116a28, 1116b2-3, 1117b9, 1117b14, 1119a18, 1119b16, 1121b1, 1123a24–25, 1124a4, 1125b11–12.

26. "Nobility and goodness then is perfect excellence" (*Estin oun kalokagathia aretē teleios*; *Eudemian Ethics*, 1249a17). Aristotle's discussion of nobility-and-goodness occurs in *Eudemian Ethics*, viii, 3, 1248b8–1249a18, and in *Magna Moralia* 1207b20–1208a4. See also Troels Engenberg-Pedersen, *Aristotle's Theory of Moral Insight* (Oxford: Clarendon Press, 1983), 51.

27. There is much in Aristotle's moral philosophy and particular ethical analyses that I cannot endorse, notably his thoughts regarding women, artisans, money, and slaves.

28. Alex Comfort, "Sauces and Pickles," in *The Joy of Sex: A Cordon Bleu Guide to Lovemaking* (New York: Simon and Schuster, 1972).

29. Schad-Somers, *Sadomasochism*, 124.

DAVID HUME

Of Chastity and Modesty

If any difficulty attend this system concerning the laws of nature and nations, 'twill be with regard to the universal approbation or blame, which follows their observance or transgression, and which some may not think sufficiently explain'd from the general interests of society. To remove, as far as possible, all scruples of this kind, I shall here consider another set of duties, *viz.* the *modesty* and *chastity* which belong to the fair sex: And I doubt not but these virtues will be found to be still more conspicuous instances of the operation of those principles, which I have insisted on.

There are some philosophers, who attack the female virtues with great vehemence, and fancy they have gone very far in detecting popular errors, when they can show, that there is no foundation in nature for all that exterior modesty, which we require in the expressions, and dress, and behavior of the fair sex. I believe I may spare myself the trouble of insisting on so obvious a subject, and may proceed, without farther preparation, to examine after what manner such notions arise from education, from the voluntary conventions of men, and from the interest of society.

Whoever considers the length and feebleness of human infancy, with the concern which both sexes naturally have for their offspring, will easily perceive, that there must be an union of male and female for the education of the young, and that this union must be of considerable duration. But in order to induce the men to impose on themselves this restraint, and undergo chearfully all the fatigues and expences, to which it subjects them, they must believe, that the children are their own, and that their natural instinct is not directed to a wrong object, when they give a loose to love and tenderness. Now

if we examine the structure of the human body, we shall find, that this security is very difficult to be attain'd on our part; and that since, in the copulation of the sexes, the principle of generation goes from the man to the woman, an error may easily take place on the side of the former, tho' it be utterly impossible with regard to the latter. From this trivial and anatomical observation is deriv'd that vast difference betwixt the education and duties of the two sexes.

Were a philosopher to examine the matter *a priori,* he wou'd reason after the following manner. Men are induc'd to labour for the maintenance and education of their children, by the persuasion that they are really their own; and therefore 'tis reasonable, and even necessary, to give them some security in this particular. This security cannot consist entirely in the imposing of severe punishments on any transgressions of conjugal fidelity on the part of the wife; since these public punishments cannot be inflicted without legal proof, which 'tis difficult to meet with in this subject. What restraint, therefore, shall we impose on women, in order to counter-balance so strong a temptation as they have to infidelity? There seems to be no restraint possible, but in the punishment of bad fame or reputation; a punishment, which has a mighty influence on the human mind, and at the same time is inflicted by the world upon surmizes, and conjectures, and proofs, that wou'd never be receiv'd in any court of judicature. In order, therefore, to impose a due restraint on the female sex, we must attach a peculiar degree of shame to their infidelity, above what arises merely from its injustice, and must bestow proportionable praises on their chastity.

But tho' this be a very strong motive to fidel-

From L. A. Selby-Bigge, ed., *A Treatise of Human Nature,* 3d ed., rev. P. H. Nidditch. New York: Oxford University Press, 1978.

ity, our philosopher wou'd quickly discover, that it wou'd not alone be sufficient to that purpose. All human creatures, especially of the female sex, are apt to over-look remote motives in favour of any present temptation: The temptation is here the strongest imaginable: Its approaches are insensible and seducing: And a woman easily finds, or flatters herself she shall find, certain means of securing her reputation, and preventing all the pernicious consequences of her pleasures. 'Tis necessary, therefore, that, beside the infamy attending such licences, there shou'd be some preceding backwardness or dread, which may prevent their first approaches, and may give the female sex a repugnance to all expressions, and postures, and liberties, that have an immediate relation to that enjoyment.

Such wou'd be the reasoning of our speculative philosopher: But I am persuaded, that if he had not a perfect knowledge of human nature, he wou'd be apt to regard them as mere chimerical speculations, and wou'd consider the infamy attending infidelity, and backwardness to all its approaches, as principles that were rather to be wish'd than hop'd for in the world. For what means, wou'd he say, of persuading mankind, that the transgressions of conjugal duty are more infamous than any other kind of injustice, when 'tis evident they are more excusable, upon account of the greatness of the temptation? And what possibility of giving a backwardness to the approaches of a pleasure, to which nature has inspir'd so strong a propensity; and a propensity that 'tis absolutely necessary in the end to comply with, for the support of the species?

But speculative reasonings, which cost so much pains to philosophers, are often form'd by the world naturally, and without reflection: As difficulties, which seem unsurmountable in theory, are easily got over in practice. Those, who have an interest in the fidelity of women, naturally disapprove of their infidelity, and all the approaches to it. Those, who have no interest, are carried along with the stream. Education takes possession of the ductile minds of the fair sex in their infancy. And when a general rule of this kind is once establish'd, men are apt to extend it beyond those principles, from which it first arose. Thus batchelors, however debauch'd cannot chuse but be shock'd with any instance of lewdness or impudence in women. And tho' all these maxims have a plain reference to generation, yet women past child-bearing have no more privilege in this respect, than those who are in the flower of their youth and beauty. Men have undoubtedly an implicit notion, that all those ideas of modesty and decency have a regard to generation; since they impose not the same laws, *with the same force,* on the male sex, where that reason takes not place. The exception is there obvious and extensive, and founded on a remarkable difference, which produces a clear separation and disjunction of ideas. But as the case is not the same with regard to the different ages of women, for this reason, tho' men know, that these notions are founded on the public interest, yet the general rule carries us beyond the original principle, and makes us extend the notions of modesty over the whole sex, from their earliest infancy to their extremest old-age and infirmity.

Courage, which is the point of honour among men, derives its merit, in a great measure, from artifice, as well as the chastity of women; tho' it has also some foundation in nature, as we shall see afterwards.

As to the obligations which the male sex lie under, with regard to chastity, we may observe, that according to the general notions of the world, they bear nearly the same proportion to the obligations of women, as the obligations of the law of nations do to those of the law of nature. 'Tis contrary to the interest of civil society that men shou'd have an *entire* liberty of indulging their appetites in venereal enjoyment: But as this interest is weaker than in the case of the female sex, the moral obligation, arising from it, must be proportionably weaker. And to prove this we need only appeal to the practice and sentiments of all nations and ages.

IMMANUEL KANT

Duties Towards the Body in Respect of Sexual Impulse

Amongst our inclinations there is one which is directed towards other human beings. They themselves, and not their work and services, are its Objects of enjoyment. It is true that man has no inclination to enjoy the flesh of another—except, perhaps, in the vengeance of war, and then it is hardly a desire—but none the less there does exist an inclination which we may call an appetite for enjoying another human being. We refer to sexual impulse. Man can, of course, use another human being as an instrument for his service; he can use his hands, his feet, and even all his powers; he can use him for his own purposes with the other's consent. But there is no way in which a human being can be made an Object of indulgence for another except through sexual impulse. This is in the nature of a sense, which we can call the sixth sense; it is an appetite for another human being. We say that a man loves someone when he has an inclination towards another person. If by this love we mean true human love, then it admits of no distinction between types of persons, or between young and old. But a love that springs merely from sexual impulse cannot be love at all, but only appetite. Human love is good-will, affection, promoting the happiness of others and finding joy in their happiness. But it is clear that, when a person loves another purely from sexual desire, none of these factors enter into the love. Far from there being any concern for the happiness of the loved one, the lover, in order to satisfy his desire and still his appetite, may even plunge the loved one into the depths of misery. Sexual love makes of the loved person an Object of appetite; as soon as that appetite has been stilled, the person is cast aside as one casts away a lemon which has been sucked dry. Sexual love can, of course, be combined with human love and so carry with it the characteristics of the latter, but taken by itself and for itself, it is nothing more than appetite. Taken by itself it is a degradation of human nature; for as soon as a person becomes an Object of appetite for another, all motives of moral relationship cease to function, because as an Object of appetite for another a person becomes a thing and can be treated and used as such by every one. This is the only case in which a human being is designed by nature as the Object of another's enjoyment. Sexual desire is at the root of it; and that is why we are ashamed of it, and why all strict moralists, and those who had pretensions to be regarded as saints, sought to suppress and extirpate it. It is true that without it a man would be incomplete; he would rightly believe that he lacked the necessary organs, and this would make him imperfect as a human being; none the less men made pretence on this question and sought to suppress these inclinations because they degraded mankind.

Because sexuality is not an inclination which one human being has for another as such, but is an inclination for the sex of another, it is a principle of the degradation of human nature, in that it gives rise to the preference of one sex to the other, and to the dishonouring of that sex through the satisfaction of desire. The desire which a man has for a woman is not directed towards her because she is a human being, but because she is a woman; that she is a human being is of no concern to the man; only her sex is the object of his desires. Human nature is

From Immanuel Kant, *Lectures on Ethics*, trans. Louis Infield. London: Methuen, 1930. Reprinted with permission of the publisher.

thus subordinated. Hence it comes that all men and women do their best to make not their human nature but their sex more alluring and direct their activities and lusts entirely towards sex. Human nature is thereby sacrificed to sex. If then a man wishes to satisfy his desire, and a woman hers, they stimulate each other's desire; their inclinations meet, but their object is not human nature but sex, and each of them dishonours the human nature of the other. They make of humanity an instrument for the satisfaction of their lusts and inclinations, and dishonour it by placing it on a level with animal nature. Sexuality, therefore, exposes mankind to the danger of equality with the beasts. But as man has this desire from nature, the question arises how far he can properly make use of it without injury to his manhood. How far may persons allow one of the opposite sex to satisfy his or her desire upon them? Can they sell themselves, or let themselves out on hire, or by some other contract allow use to be made of their sexual faculties? Philosophers generally point out the harm done by this inclination and the ruin it brings to the body or to the commonwealth, and they believe that, except for the harm it does, there would be nothing contemptible in such conduct in itself. But if this were so, and if giving vent to this desire was not in itself abominable and did not involve immorality, then any one who could avoid being harmed by them could make whatever use he wanted of his sexual propensities. For the prohibitions of prudence are never unconditional; and the conduct would in itself be unobjectionable, and would only be harmful under certain conditions. But in point of fact, there is in the conduct itself something which is contemptible and contrary to the dictates of morality. It follows, therefore, that there must be certain conditions under which alone the use of the *facultates sexuales* would be in keeping with morality. There must be a basis for restraining our freedom in the use we make of our inclinations so that they conform to the principles of morality. We shall endeavour to discover these conditions and this basis. Man cannot dispose over himself because he is not a thing; he is not his own property; to say that he is would be self-contradictory; for in so far as he is a person he is a Subject in whom the ownership of things can be vested, and if he were his own property, he would be a thing over which he could have ownership. But a person cannot be a property and so cannot be a thing which can be owned, for it is impossible to be a person and a thing, the proprietor and the property.

Accordingly, a man is not at his own disposal. He is not entitled to sell a limb, not even one of his teeth. But to allow one's person for profit to be used by another for the satisfaction of sexual desire, to make of oneself an Object of demand, is to dispose over oneself as over a thing and to make of oneself a thing on which another satisfies his appetite, just as he satisfies his hunger upon a steak. But since the inclination is directed towards one's sex and not towards one's humanity, it is clear that one thus partially sacrifices one's humanity and thereby runs a moral risk. Human beings are, therefore, not entitled to offer themselves, for profit, as things for the use of others in the satisfaction of their sexual propensities. In so doing they would run the risk of having their person used by all and sundry as an instrument for the satisfaction of inclination. This way of satisfying sexuality is *vaga libido,* in which one satisfies the inclinations of others for gain. It is possible for either sex. To let one's person out on hire and to surrender it to another for the satisfaction of his sexual desire in return for money is the depth of infamy. The underlying moral principle is that man is not his own property and cannot do with his body what he will. The body is part of the self; in its togetherness with the self it constitutes the person; a man cannot make of his person a thing, and this is exactly what happens in *vaga libido.* This manner of satisfying sexual desire is, therefore, not permitted by the rules of morality. But what of the second method, namely *concubinatus*? Is this also inadmissible? In this case both persons satisfy their desire mutually and there is no idea of gain, but they serve each other only for the satisfaction of sexuality. There appears to be nothing unsuitable in this arrangement, but there is nevertheless one consideration which rules it out. Concubinage consists in one person surrendering to another only for the satisfaction of their sexual desire whilst retaining freedom and rights in other personal respects affecting welfare and happiness. But the person who so surrenders is used as a thing; the desire is still directed only towards sex and not towards the person as a human being. But it is obvious that to surrender part of oneself is to surrender the whole, because a human being is a unity. It is not possible to have the disposal of a part only of a person without having at the same time a right of disposal over the whole person, for each part of a person is integrally bound up with the whole. But concubinage does not give me a right of disposal over the whole person but only over a part, namely the *organa sexualia*. It presupposes a contract. This contract deals only with the enjoyment of a part of the person and not with the entire circumstances of the person. Concubinage is certainly a contract, but it is one-sided; the rights of the two parties are not equal. But if in concubinage I enjoy a part of a person, I thereby enjoy the whole person; yet by the terms of the arrangement I have not the rights over the whole person, but only over a part; I, therefore, make the person into a thing. For that reason this method of satisfying sexual desire is also not permitted by the rules of morality. The sole condition on which we are free to make use of our sexual desire depends upon the right to dispose over the person as a whole—over the welfare and happiness and generally over all the circumstances of that person. If I have the right over the whole person I have also the right over the part and so I have the right to use that person's *organa sexualia* for the satisfaction of sexual desire. But how am I to obtain these rights over the whole person? Only by giving that person the same rights over the whole of myself. This happens only in marriage. Matrimony is an agreement between two persons by which they grant each other equal reciprocal rights, each of them undertaking to surrender the whole of their person to the other with a complete right of disposal over it. We can now apprehend by reason how a *commercium sexuale* is possible without degrading humanity and breaking the moral laws. Matrimony is the only condition in which use can be made of one's sexuality. If one devotes one's person to another, one devotes not only sex but the whole person; the two cannot be separated. If, then, one yields one's person, body and soul, for good and ill and in every respect, so that the other has complete rights over it, and if the other does not similarly yield himself in return and does not extend in return the same rights and privileges, the arrangement is one-sided. But if I yield myself completely to another and obtain the person of the other in return, I win myself

back; I have given myself up as the property of another, but in turn I take that other as my property, and so win myself back again in winning the person whose property I have become. In this way the two persons become a unity of will. Whatever good or ill, joy or sorrow befall either of them, the other will share in it. Thus sexuality leads to a union of human beings, and in that union alone its exercise is possible. This condition of the use of sexuality, which is only fulfilled in marriage, is a moral condition. But let us pursue this aspect further and examine the case of a man who takes two wives. In such a case each wife would have but half a man, although she would be giving herself wholly and ought in consequence to be entitled to the whole man. To sum up: *vaga libido* is ruled out on moral grounds; the same applies to concubinage; there only remains matrimony, and in matrimony polygamy is ruled out also for moral reasons; we, therefore, reach the conclusion that the only feasible arrangement is that of monogamous marriage. Only under that condition can I indulge my *facultas sexualis*. We cannot here pursue that subject further.

But one other question arises, that of incest. Incest consists in intercourse between the sexes in a form which, by reason of consanguinity, must be ruled out; but are there moral grounds on which incest, in all forms of sexual intercourse, must be ruled out? They are grounds which apply conditionally, except in one case, in which they have absolute validity. The sole case in which the moral grounds against incest apply absolutely is that of intercourse between parents and children. Between parents and children there must be a respect which should continue throughout life, and this rules out of court any question of equality. Moreover, in sexual intercourse each person submits to the other in the highest degree, whereas between parents and their children subjection is one-sided; the children must submit to the parents only; there can, therefore, be no equal union. This is the only case in which incest is absolutely forbidden by nature. In other cases incest forbids itself, but is not incest in the order of nature. The state prohibits incest, but at the beginning there must have been intermarriage between brothers and sisters. At the same time nature has implanted in our breasts a natural opposition to incest. She intended us to combine with other races and so to prevent too great a sameness in one society. Too close a connection, too intimate an acquaintance produces sexual indifference and repugnance. But this propensity must be restrained by modesty; otherwise it becomes commonplace, reduces the object of the desire to the commonplace and results in indifference. Sexual desire is very fastidious; nature has given it strength, but it must be restrained by modesty. It is on that account that savages, who go about stark-naked, are cold towards each other; for that reason, too, a person whom we have known from youth evokes no desire within us, but a strange person attracts us much more strongly. Thus nature has herself provided restraints upon any desire between brother and sister.

Crimina Carnis

Crimina carnis are contrary to self-regarding duty because they are against the ends of humanity. They consist in abuse of one's sexuality. Every form of sexual indulgence, except in marriage, is a misuse of sexuality, and so a *crimen carnis*. All *crimina carnis* are either *secundum naturam* or *contra naturam*. *Crimina carnis secundum naturam* are contrary to sound reason; *crimina carnis contra naturam* are contrary to our animal nature. Among the former we reckon *vaga libido*, which is the opposite of matrimony and of which there are two kinds: *scortatio* and *concubinatus*. *Concubinatus* is indeed a *pactum*, but a *pactum inaequale*, in which the rights are not reciprocal. In this pact the woman surrenders her sex completely to the man, but the man does not completely surrender his sex to the woman. The second *crimen carnis secundum naturam* is *adulterium*. Adultery cannot take place except in marriage; it signifies a breach of marriage. Just as the engagement to marry is the most serious and the most inviolable engagement between two persons and binds them for life, so also is adultery the greatest breach of faith that there can be, because it is disloyalty to an engagement than which there can be none more important. For this reason adultery is cause for divorce. Another cause is incompatibility and inability to be at one, whereby unity and concord of will between the two persons is impossible. Next comes the question whether incest is incest *per se*, or whether it is by the civil law that it is made a *crimen carnis*, natural or unnatural. The question might be answered either by natural instinct or by reason. From the point of view of natural instinct incest is a *crimen carnis secundum naturam*, for it is after all a union of the sexes; it is not *contra naturam animalium*, because animals do not differentiate in this respect in their practices. But on the judgment of the understanding incest is *contra naturam*.

Uses of sexuality which are contrary to natural instinct and to animal nature are *crimina carnis contra naturam*. First amongst them we have onanism. This is abuse of the sexual faculty without any object, the exercise of the faculty in the complete absence of any object of sexuality. The practice is contrary to the ends of humanity and even opposed to animal nature. By it man sets aside his person and degrades himself below the level of animals. A second *crimen carnis contra naturam* is intercourse between *sexus homogenii*, in which the object of sexual impulse is a human being but there is homogeneity instead of heterogeneity of sex, as when a woman satisfies her desire on a woman, or a man on a man. This practice too is contrary to the ends of humanity; for the end of humanity in respect of sexuality is to preserve the species without debasing the person; but in this instance the species is not being preserved (as it can be by a *crimen carnis secundum naturam*), but the person is set aside, the self is degraded below the level of the animals, and humanity is dishonoured. The third *crimen carnis contra naturam* occurs when the object of the desire is in fact of the opposite sex but is not human. Such is sodomy, or intercourse with animals. This, too, is contrary to the ends of humanity and against our natural instinct. It degrades mankind below the level of animals, for no animal turns in this way from its own species. All *crimina carnis contra naturam* degrade human nature to a level below that of animal nature and make man unworthy of his humanity. He no longer deserves to be a person. From the point of view of duties towards himself such conduct is the most disgraceful and the most degrading of which man is capable. Suicide is the most dreadful, but it is not as dishonourable and base as the *crimina carnis contra naturam*. It is the most abominable conduct of which man can be guilty. So abominable are these *crimina carnis contra naturam* that they are unmentionable, for the very mention of them is nauseating, as is not the case with suicide. We all fight shy of mentioning these vices; teachers refrain from mentioning them, even when their intention is unobjectionable and they only wish to warn their charges against them. But as they are of frequent occurrence, we are in a dilemma: are we to name them in order that people should know and prevent their frequent occurrence, or are we to keep them dark in order that people should not learn of them and so not have the opportunity of transgressing? Frequent mention would familiarize people with them and the vices might as a result cease to disgust us and come to appear more tolerable. Hence our modesty in not referring to them. On the other hand, if we mention them only circumspectly and with disinclination, our aversion from them is still apparent. There is also another reason for our modesty. Each sex is ashamed of the vices of which its members are capable. Human beings feel, therefore, ashamed to mention those things of which it is shameful for humanity to be capable. These vices make us ashamed that we are human beings and, therefore, capable of them, for an animal is incapable of all such *crimina carnis contra naturam*.

FREDERICK ELLISTON

In Defense of Promiscuity

The Western tradition has been remarkably conservative in its reflections on sexual morality.[1] Whether this conservatism is due to the fact that practically every major philosopher before Hegel was a bachelor male dedicated to the pursuit of some form of reason is a moot point on which I shall not speculate. Whatever the explanation, most philosophers have tended to formulate and resolve sexual issues in favor of the status quo. Perhaps because sexual promiscuity (the only type I shall consider) has usually been a practice widely at variance with prevalent norms, it has scarcely arisen as an issue at all—much less been criticized or defended. Today, however, sexual norms have changed—at least for an increasingly significant number of society's members. This change challenges the philosophers to question the assumptions on which the conventions that regulate our sex lives are based, much as recent political changes have provided the motive for a radical critique of social practices and institutions.[2] My purpose here is to take up this challenge by offering a defense of promiscuity: first, I shall criticize current notions of promiscuity as inadequate and provide my own definition; second, I shall rebut some traditional arguments against promiscuity; and third, I shall defend it in terms of three sexual paradigms. I shall conclude with some reflections on the limits of my defense.

LINGUISTIC FORAYS

What is meant by "promiscuity"? It may be that the word has no descriptive content, but only emotive and/or hortatory force. On this view, to condemn a practice or person as promiscuous is simply to express feelings of disapproval, or to issue a prohibitive "Stop!" This position attempts to resolve the issue of meaning by limiting "promiscuity" to its emotional or prescriptive force.[3] Even this restriction, though, does not eliminate all of the problems. For not all people oppose promiscuity, and hence the intended overtones are not always negative. And this position leaves an important question unanswered: To what kinds of persons or actions does the term apply? Only when this question has been answered are we in a position to ask how we should feel about, act toward, or react to promiscuous people or behavior.

The *Oxford English Dictionary* defines "promiscuous" as: "without distinction, discrimination or order." *Webster's New Twentieth Century Dictionary* adds: "engaging in sexual intercourse indiscriminately or with many persons." The root notion operative in these definitions is *indiscriminate,* sometimes signified quantitatively, according to *Webster's.*

But this definition is too broad and begs the question at hand. For the promiscuous person clearly does draw *some* distinctions: typically he or she does not derive sexual satisfaction from a lover's shoe or copulate with a dead body or a sibling. In such cases more precise terminology is applied—fetishism, necrophilia, or incest. Even a promiscuous person usually discriminates between things and persons, between living people and dead people, between people who are members of the family and those who are not. Since some distinctions are operative, the suggestion that a promiscuous person is *completely indiscriminate* is too strong.

Similar difficulties arise with *Webster's* nu-

From Robert Baker and Frederick Elliston, eds., *Philosophy and Sex.* Buffalo, N.Y.: Prometheus Books, 1975. Copyright © 1975 by Prometheus Books. Reprinted with permission of the publisher.

merical criterion: How many liaisons must a person engage in before he or she is promiscuous? Clearly more than one is required; anyone who has made love to only one person cannot (logically) be labeled "promiscuous." But is two enough? Perhaps a person who carries on two affairs would be called "promiscuous." But imagine someone who married at twenty and who remarried at forty, two years after his wife died. Clearly, under these conditions he is not promiscuous. If two is not enough, then increase the number to three and repeat the scenario: married at twenty, forty, and sixty, two years after each wife died. This twice-widowed "Romeo" satisfies *Webster's* numerical criterion, for he has engaged in sex with many (that is, three) people; and yet he is clearly not promiscuous. As more marriages are added it still remains uncertain at what point a person becomes promiscuous. And even if a clear line could be drawn, the question would immediately arise: Why draw it there, for what is the criterion for assessing the number of liaisons that suffice to justify the judgment "promiscuous"? This is a further legitimate question raised by *Webster's* definition but left unanswered.

Of course these examples deal with sequential liaisons, which may be more problematic than their simultaneous counterparts. But I think the basic problem remains: Is a person who carries on two serious loving affairs that endure for a lifetime promiscuous? I think not. Then again, if two are not enough, how many are required and on what grounds?

By these two counterattacks I am suggesting that it is *false* that a promiscuous person is indiscriminate and *facile* to assess promiscuity numerically. But what is it, then, that invites this judgment? More likely the condemnation arises not because such people do not discriminate *at all,* but because they fail to discriminate *according to the prevalent sexual code.* Promiscuous behavior challenges our sexual conventions, thereby giving this label its emotive force and prescriptive overtones.[4]

More precisely, promiscuity violates a very special principle that regulates our erotic life: "Sexual relations shall be exclusively heterosexual and . . . no sexual activity shall take place outside monogamous unions which are, intentionally at least, life-long."[5] It is this "Western norm," as Ronald Atkinson terms it,

that prescribes the *distinctions* to be drawn, the *discriminations* to be made, and the *order* to be upheld in our sex lives, to which the definition in the *Oxford English Dictionary* alludes.

But to say that promiscuity violates the Western norm is still too broad, for so does coprophilia. Though many people use the term in this vague sense, a more precise definition is needed.

Promiscuity is sometimes identified with "free love." This persuasive definition (or redefinition) may induce some to accept this sexual pattern because freedom, like motherhood, is a good everyone is supposed to espouse. But what exactly is the sexual freedom in question? If it means freedom from *all* sexual prohibitions (including, for example, those against perversions), then this rephrasing is again too broad. And if it means freedom from just the Western norm (which would allow perverted sex within marriage), then it is no improvement. Moreover "free love" is a misleading expression: like everything else, sex has its price—assessed in terms of time, effort, emotional tensions, and a trade off of other benefits and burdens.

Promiscuity may be identified with recreational sex—intercourse just for the fun of it. But this definition is disquieting because of what might be hidden under the adverb "just"; and the term "fun" would align the defenders of promiscuity with that "vulgar hedonism" that some may want to reject in favor of a broader conception of the good life. Though when it harms no one promiscuity may be defensible simply on the grounds that it provides pleasure, this justification should not be built into the definition. A more neutral definition is preferable in order to avoid this commitment at the outset and thereby leave open the question of its justification.

Neither the definitions of the *Oxford English Dictionary* nor *Webster's New Twentieth Century Dictionary,* nor any of the current philosophic or popular notions is satisfactory. In view of the failure of these linguistic forays to uncover a viable definition I shall offer my own. In so doing I cross a thin but significant boundary between linguistic analysis and linguistic revision. And conceding Wittgenstein's insight that language is a form of life, the dispute over the definition of promiscuity cannot be regarded as merely semantic.

With these caveats (or concessions), I shall offer the following definition, or redefinition: "promiscuity" means sex with a series of other adults, not directly related through marriage, with no commitments. Let me explain each component in turn.

First, promiscuity demands *copulation*—its *telos* is sexual intercourse. Someone who engages in the rituals of seduction without this goal is perhaps a flirt or a "tease"—but is not promiscuous. Of course not every seduction succeeds. But at least the intention to consummate the relation must be present on all occasions and realized on some. Whether the sex is "straight" or perverted is irrelevant, for these are two different phenomena. One can be perverted and not promiscuous, or promiscuous and not perverted: a lifelong incestuous relation renders a person perverted but not promiscuous; and many promiscuous liaisons accord with the paradigm of natural sex—"the two-minute emissionary missionary male-superior ejaculation service."[6]

Second, *repetition* is essential—the pursuit of a new partner must recur. Promiscuity on only one occasion is logically impossible. If someone is remarkably casual about his or her one affair, he or she may be labeled "superficial" or "unfeeling," but cannot be called promiscuous. Different partners on several occasions must be sought. The *number* of affairs per se does not suffice to delineate promiscuity (the mistake of *Webster's* definition); plurality is a necessary but not a sufficient condition of promiscuity.

Third, both partners must be *adults*. If one partner is a child, then their behavior is pedophilia. If the child is a son or daughter, it is incest. In neither case is it promiscuity. Adulthood cannot be fixed chronologically; it signifies a degree of maturity some teen-agers have and some elderly people lack. The other adult need not be of the opposite sex. Homosexuals and lesbians per se are not necessarily promiscuous. Some make significant personal sacrifices to maintain their relationship; though their behavior violates the Western norm, it is not promiscuous, because of the commitment their sacrifices signify.

Fourth, the couple cannot be directly related through *marriage*. It is logically impossible for husband and wife to engage in promiscuity with one another, though of course their sex play may sometimes bear a "family resemblance" to it. Similarly, sex between a brother and sister, even when they are adults, is a different phenomenon. It is possible to be promiscuous with distant cousins to whom one is not *directly* related through marriage; different societies draw the lines for incest in different ways.[7]

Finally and most decisively, promiscuity is *noncommittal* sex. It defies the traditional connection between sex and marriage—not just as a social institution, but as a symbol of a serious, loving, and intentionally lifelong relation. Promiscuity asserts a freedom from the obligation within or without marriage to "love, honor, and obey" and a freedom to engage in sex with any peer who agrees. These refusals to issue promissory notes for affection and support throughout an indefinite future and to issue a guarantee of sexual exclusivity are promiscuity's most significant departures from the traditional sexual norm.

Is such behavior defensible? I shall now turn to some familiar arguments against it.

REBUTTALS AND REJOINDERS

Several arguments can be offered in defense of the Western norm and hence in opposition to promiscuity. As I shall try to demonstrate in my rejoinders, none are sound.

The Western Norm and Technology

At one time a strong argument might have been made in defense of the Western norm by invoking the causal connection between sex and reproduction: unless the natural processes are interrupted, intercourse leads to procreation; for the sake of children, on whom society's future depends, promiscuity is rightly prohibited in order to confine sex to marriage, as that secure and loving context within which children can best be raised. As stated, this argument relies on two claims, the first factual and the second normative.

The first premise has been falsified by technology: the advances of medicine have made available reliable birth-control devices and reasonably safe techniques for sterilization and abortion, thereby making sex possible without the risk of conception or birth. Second, the absolute value of the nuclear family as the *only* context for child rearing is at least problematic: experiments in communal living and the increasing number of single parents provide some evidence that the needs of the child can be met either through a plurality of parent figures or through just one individual. Moreover, even granting the risk of pregnancy, despite precautions, and the value of the nuclear family, despite alternatives, the prohibitions against promiscuity would not follow. First, pregnancies can be terminated. With the exception of the Roman Catholic Church, many concede the legitimacy of abortion, at least during the first trimester. Second, even if this option is disregarded, it should be emphasized that promiscuity is *logically* compatible with *some* commitments to one's partner in the event of pregnancy and to the child in the event of its birth. Promiscuity does not preclude such contingent agreements; it rules out only emotional and sexual commitments as a precondition of sex—the promise to love the other exclusively and to share a life completely.

This rejoinder asserts that available technology should be used as a safeguard against undesirable consequences. But "can" does not always entail "ought": not everything science is capable of doing should be done. Some, notably Roman Catholics, have argued strongly against the use of such means.

The Inseparability Premise and Promiscuity

The Roman Catholic position is that the sex act[8] has two inseparable functions: to foster the physical, emotional, and spiritual union of man and woman, and to reproduce the species. If this claim were true, then the use of birth-control devices or sterilization and abortion techniques would be prohibited. Promiscuity would then become more hazardous since without contraceptives the risk of pregnancy would be much greater; and it would become less frequent since only *coitus interruptus* and the rhythm method could be practiced to avoid conception. Of course abstinence and masturbation would be alternatives; but to practice them is to cease to be promiscuous.

The most recent defense of this inseparability premise is found in Pope Paul VI's *Humanae Vitae*: to violate the inseparability of the unitive and procreative aspect of sex is "to contradict the nature of both man and woman and of their most intimate relationship, and therefore it is to contradict also the plan of God and His will."[9]

Carl Cohen contends that this inseparability premise is false.[10] First, it has no basis in scripture or natural law, but rests only on a fallacious *argumentum ad verecundiam*. Second, the entailed prohibition against birth control would cause overpopulation and hunger. Third, the fear of pregnancy and the ensuing inhibitions thwart the conjugal love that the Church promulgates. Fourth, the assumption that all sexual processes must be completed is erroneous, for we recognize acts with erotic overtones that rightly remain unconsummated (for example, a father's love for his daughter). Fifth, the integrity of the spiritual and natural is frequently denied without transgressing a divine (or moral) command—for example, eating for pleasure rather than nourishment. And finally, if the Church sanctions drugs to promote physical health, it should permit drugs (for example, oral contraceptives) to promote sexual health.

Though Cohen's six points may not persuade all Catholics,[11] they do provide an impressive list of reasons for legitimizing birth control. Though admittedly his purpose is to defend their use within marriage, this limitation is not demanded by his logic. They serve to justify the use of the technology that severs the causal tie on which the earlier rebuttal of promiscuity depended.

Promiscuity as a Threat to Monogamy

Like adultery, promiscuity may be judged immoral on the grounds that it endangers one of our society's central and sacred institutions—monogamous marriage:[12] allowing people to achieve sexual gratification while escaping long-term commitments undermines this basic institution in a way that threatens the stability of our society; in self-defense, society rightly imposes social sanctions against the threatening promiscuous behavior.

This argument rests on two assumptions: first, that promiscuity has adverse effects on monogamy; and second, that monogamy is socially superior to the alternatives.

The first assumption is a questionable causal claim. For despite the recent weakening of sexual taboos, marriage continues to be a popular practice. Even conceding the high divorce rate does not weaken this claim, for many who are divorced remarry—thereby testifying to the value they accord this institution. Consequently, the so-called new morality is not clearly harming marriage. Indeed, two alternative hypotheses about the causal relation between promiscuity and monogamy are equally plausible: by providing for a broader range of sex partners from which to select a spouse promiscuity increases the probability of sexual compatibility within marriage, and hence the probability of a more "successful" marriage (at least according to this one criterion of success—the satisfaction of one need); and by eliminating the need to marry *merely* for sexual gratification (and hence to disregard those other factors that contribute to successful marriages, such as respect, considerateness, shared values, love, and compassion), promiscuity again increases the likelihood of a successful marriage. Perhaps the trouble with premarital unions, trial marriage, and open marriage is that they have not been tried, for the strong presumption that monogamy is the only way to institutionalize our sex life works against such experiments. Freeing sex of the monopoly of marriage could provide for new institutions that might satisfy more effectively the emotional and physical needs of society's members and offer greater scope for the exercise of personal freedom and initiative in creating new lifestyles. Though society once had the right to insist that its members have a "license to procreate," to use Michael Bayles's expression, with the development of new contraceptives it no longer has the right to insist on a license to copulate. Abolishing the demand for such a license by permitting promiscuity may ease the unnecessary and spurious pressures on monogamy, so as to promote rather than prevent healthy changes within this institution.

Lying, Deceiving, and Exploiting

According to the popular prototype, promiscuous people are unfaithful and unreliable: they break promises, say things that are not true, and use others for their own sexual gratification. If this prototype were true, promiscuity would indeed be wrong, because it would violate familiar moral rules: people are supposed to keep their promises, tell the truth, and not deceive or exploit others. But does promiscuity *necessarily* involve these forms of immorality?

At one time these subterfuges may have been necessary in order to obtain sex and yet avoid commitments. To circumvent the Western norm, which was justified when copulation entailed procreation, those who wanted *only* the "joys of sex" were forced to tease, tempt, and manipulate. Under these circumstances promiscuity is wrong—*not* because it is promiscuity, but because it violates well-established ethical principles. The moral fault lies not in noncommittal sex but in the lies, deceptions, and exploitation to which some *happen* to have recourse in order to have intercourse. Such immoral behavior is only contingently associated with promiscuity; logically, rather than empirically, it is not necessary. In some groups or societies openly promiscuous behavior is tolerated, if not encouraged. When the threat of pregnancy is minimized, sex for its own sake becomes possible, enjoyable, and desirable—thereby making many of the earlier reasons for lying, deceiving, and exploiting invalid. That promiscuity must involve immoral behavior then becomes an anachronism, an empirical claim that is no longer true. Promiscuity per se or prima facie is not wrong. At most, it is the immoral things promiscuous people sometimes happen to do that are wrong.

This defense is complicated by the fact that a double standard is operative within large segments of society: men are allowed to "sow their wild oats," whereas women are denigrated as "loose" or "fallen" for the same behavior. Though this sexual inequality may once have served to protect women who had more to lose through such "sins" (for it is women who become pregnant, and not men), now it discriminates against them. Because of this double standard, promiscuity is to the advantage of males and to the disadvantage of females. Consequently it becomes exploitive in a more subtle fashion: men receive sexual gratification; women receive social condemnation.

This argument invites the initial rejoinder that it is not promiscuity that is wrong, but the double standard. In this case it is not promiscuity that we should abandon, but the double standard that places promiscuous women at a disadvantage in comparison to promiscuous men. However, this response may be too facile, too theoretical in its disregard for the reality of the social inequality of the sexes. Yet, even conceding the inadequacy of this initial rejoinder, this argument against promiscuity on the grounds that it exploits women would not apply to all cases: women immune or indifferent to social reprobation and members of groups without a double standard could still be promiscuous and yet not necessarily exploit others or be exploited by them. Since promiscuity cannot be shown to be wrong in all cases, the charge that it necessarily violates generally accepted moral principles is false.

Personal Emotional Security and Growth

Peter Bertocci argues against premarital sex, and by implication against promiscuity, on the grounds that it threatens "personal emotional security."[13] He contends that the demand for sex outside marriage exhibits a lack of self-discipline in people who cannot control their desires, and a failure to show respect and consideration for those on whom the demand is placed. Such undisciplined and inconsiderate behavior places needless strain on the relationship, threatening to destroy whatever values it embodies.

Is it true that a promiscuous person is completely lacking in self-discipline? The ritual of seduction frequently has its own carefully observed logic in the selection of a suitable consort, the finesse of the "first approach," and the rhythms of attracting and repulsing, until the ceremony reaches its *telos*.[14] What Bertocci perceives as incoherent or irrational behavior is really a self-conscious refusal to be directed by the Western norm. But promiscuous people should not be faulted for failing to regulate their actions according to a principle they reject.

Does promiscuity entail inconsiderateness? The rejoinder here parallels the earlier refutation of the charge that promiscuity is necessarily exploitive. The fact that some promiscuous people are rude, brusque, or selfish does not establish this logical tie, any more than the fact that some doctors collect stamps establishes a logical tie between medicine and philately. Only if respect is defined in terms of the Western norm is promiscuity necessarily disrespectful. Though such a definition is possible, it would beg the question at hand, which must remain empirical. Acknowledging the other's freedom to engage or not engage in noncommittal sex demonstrates some degree of respect. And at each subsequent stage of the battle of the sexes, its dialectical impetus arises through the joint effort to preserve the other's freedom.[15] The reciprocity of initiatives whereby each person asserts his or her selfhood, presided over by moral rules that embody recognition for "man as an end in himself" (to use Kant's somewhat chauvinistic phrase), provides further testimony for respect.

Does promiscuity threaten what is valuable in the relation? Of course the answer depends in part on what is considered valuable; pleasure, freedom, and respect certainly *need not* be endangered. Bertocci believes that the emotional tensions and guilt feelings that arise from violating the taboos against nonmarital sex corrode the relation. But this harm can alternatively be eliminated by abolishing the taboos instead, so that promiscuity would no longer count as an infraction and hence no longer generate the strain that it now does. Since the traditional supports for these taboos have collapsed through an advancing technology, abolishing the Western norm is the more rational solution.

It is not promiscuity that is bad, but the arguments that purport to rebut it. These rejoinders to those arguments, though, do not prove that promiscuity itself is morally good, for I have not considered all possible arguments against it. And even if I had, the conclusion would not follow logically: promiscuity could still be bad although no one has formulated a good argument to prove it.

Perhaps promiscuity is neither good nor bad in any moral sense, but purely a matter of individual taste. To categorize it as an aesthetic rather than ethical issue concedes its normative status, but removes it from the sphere of other-regarding virtues. But even granting this move, some critical issues would remain: Is promiscuity in good taste or bad taste, and how does one decide?

Alternatively, promiscuity might be dismissed as neither a moral nor an aesthetic issue but a prudential one—a question of what is to the advantage of the agent within the sphere of actions that affect only him or her. This approach too leaves critical issues unresolved: Is promiscuity to my advantage or disadvantage, and how do I decide? Moreover this reduction of the normative to the prudential seems to disregard the fact that it takes two people (minimally) to be promiscuous—that is, others are involved.

Such attempts to categorize promiscuity presuppose a clarity and consensus on the nature of good taste and personal advantage that is altogether lacking in the literature. So I shall eschew these ways of demonstrating that promiscuity is positively a good thing in favor of a less traditional defense.

PARADIGMS AND ARCHETYPES

Development of a satisfactory sexual philosophy is hindered in part by lack of knowledge: Just what are the contingent ties between sexual intercourse, love, marriage, and the things or activities we find valuable? This difficulty is further compounded by linguistic confusions: the language at our disposal is notoriously vague and radically ambiguous. Moreover these two shortcomings are aggravated by a third: the absence of accepted paradigms for conceptualizing our sex life and of corresponding archetypes to give substance to our ideals. I shall now turn to three descriptive and normative models for understanding and directing sexual activities. In each case, I shall argue, promiscuity plays a legitimate role.

A Classical Liberal Defense

According to John Stuart Mill's principle of liberty, "the sole end for which mankind are warranted, individually or collectively, in interfering with the liberty of action of any of their number is self-protection. That the only purpose for which power can be rightfully exercised over any member of a civilized community, against his will, is to prevent harm to others. His own good, either physical or moral, is not a sufficient warrant."[16]

Promiscuity falls within this domain of individual liberty provided those who engage in it satisfy two conditions: they must observe some traditional moral rules, and they must exercise extreme care to avoid unwanted births. The conventional prohibitions against lying, deceit, and exploitation serve to prevent harm to others—most immediately to the person exploited or deceived and less immediately, but

no less importantly, to others indirectly affected. The second proviso is designed to avoid illegitimacy, abortion, adoption, and forced marriage—not to mention the social stigma of an unwanted pregnancy, unmarried motherhood, or bastardy. Assuming then that promiscuity (as defined earlier) satisfies these two negative conditions, what can be said in its defense?

For at least some of the people some of the time sex is fun. Whatever else may be true of it, at the barest level sex remains an intensely pleasing physical activity. Like the satisfaction of an appetite (such as eating) or the release of tension (such as a good drive in golf), sex is physically enjoyable. Midst the mystification of sex it should not be forgotten that sex is and continues to be sensual; the erotic appeal of another engages all of our senses in a way equaled by few (if any) other physical activities. One paradigm that must be acknowledged by all is that sex is a type of bodily interaction that can be intensely pleasing. Granted the two earlier provisos, sex is good for this reason, if no other.

This defense does not entail that pleasure alone is good. The underlying hedonism is not "vulgar," to use Michael Bayles's term, for no attempt need be made to reduce sex merely to a sensation of pleasure.[17] A variety of things good in themselves can be acknowledged while still insisting that pleasure as "the joy of sex" is one of them. Insofar as promiscuity maximizes the pleasures that can be derived from sex, it is good; and insofar as the prohibition against promiscuity is a limitation on the pleasures to be derived from sex, it is unwarranted—in a word, "bad."

Despite his insistence that pleasure and pleasure alone is good in itself,[18] Mill himself gives evidence that he is not a vulgar hedonist. In defending his principle of liberty he suggests that happiness is not so much a sensation of pleasure as the full development of an individual's "higher faculties." Quoting Wilhelm von Humbolt with enthusiastic agreement, Mill asserts that the end of man is "the highest and most harmonious development of his powers to a complete and consistent whole."[19] This remark suggests a second defense of promiscuity within classical liberalism: the freedom to be promiscuous can contribute to the full growth of the human personality.

In many areas, such as clothing, vocation, and recreation, the need for experimentation and diversity is recognized and conceded. Mill defends his principle of liberty, not just in the intellectual arena by arguing for freedom of thought and discussion, but in the practical domain with his insistence on the individual's right to form and carry out his own "plan of life."[20] The lack of commitment that characterizes promiscuity is a freedom to explore patterns of sexual behavior at variance with the tradition. This exploration can engage one's "higher faculties" of reason, judgment, and good taste.[21] Promiscuity opens up to each person a broader range of sex partners and practices.

From the standpoint of classical liberalism, then, promiscuity may increase the pleasures of individuals, enhance the cultivation of their higher faculties (happiness in the eudaemonian sense) and enrich society with the ensuing institution.

Sex as Body Language

The sexual paradigm operative in the liberal defense of promiscuity has its limitations. For though sex is admittedly a form of bodily interaction that leads to pleasure, it is clearly more than that in some sense. In his papers "Sexual Paradigms" and "Sex and Perversion,"[22] Robert Solomon suggests what this "more" might be: As body language, sex has "meaning" that goes beyond its physical dimensions.

Just as words are more than marks and sounds, sex is more than thrusts and moans, caresses and sighs. Just as verbal language has a dimension of meaning beyond phonemes and morphemes,[23] so body language has a significance beyond the intertwining of two bodies. The sentences and words of verbal languages have their analogues in the gestures and particular movements of body language. As in all language, these latter are subject to rules that demarcate well-formed formulae. Body language has its own semantics and syntax.

This type of language can serve to express feelings, to state intentions, and to issue commands or invitations. An embrace can express genuine affection. A nod toward the bedroom door conjures up a familiar series of events. A sly glance may frequently initiate the rituals of seduction. Of course not all body language is sexual. Canadian Prime Minister Pierre Trudeau's infamous shrug communicates political indifference.[24] A policeman's hand signal issues a legal command. And holding open an elevator door is an invitation to enter something far more prosaic than what a coy smile offers. Meaning here as elsewhere depends on context. What imparts sexual significance to body language is the kind of possibility intimated —namely, intercourse, or some incomplete moment in the dialectical movement toward it.

Promiscuity has instrumental value in that it can facilitate the mastery of one kind of body language. To be in command of a language is to possess an extensive vocabulary, clear diction, and rhetorical devices for conveying meaning. These verbal skills are acquired through social interaction. Sexual body language is learned through sexual interaction.

Sexual experiences enable an individual to develop a repertoire of gestures for communicating desire and affection and of decisive movements that clearly state intentions of love or amusement. People can be moved not only by the things we *say* but by the things we *do*— with them, for them, or to them. Desire and satisfaction can be communicated not only through verbal exchanges such as "please" and "thank you," but through a lingering look and an appreciative caress. To a shattered ego a physical embrace may express far more reassurance than its verbal counterparts, and a kiss may convey desire more eloquently than pleas or poems. The subjectivity of another, their autonomy and individuality, is confirmed in the dialectics of sex: in the reversals of their roles as the initiator and the initiated, the aggressor and the pursued, the lover and the loved, each can experience his or her own incarnate freedom and acknowledge that of the other. Like verbal etiquette, the sexual rituals of flirtation and seduction are subject to rules that prohibit interruption while another is "speaking," that prescribe that each be allowed to participate fully in the conversation, and that exclude insults, attacks, and abuses. The observance of this etiquette is an acknowledgement of the selfhood of the other. The acquisition of it is one of the opportunities promiscuity provides.

Strict adherence to the Western norm places our sex lives in a straightjacket that curtails body language to "I love you," the *only* message to be delivered, to just *one* person, with *fixed* diction and intonation—until the disillusioned pair have become bored by the repetition.

Sex and eating are frequently compared, since both are appetites whose satisfaction is socially regulated. Consider a society where the following etiquette is operative. Each man is allowed to dine with only one woman. Before their first meal begins, each receives a solemn injunction: "Thou shalt dine with none other, so long as you both shall live." Their partnership is exclusive; no one may be invited to the meal ("three is a crowd"). Only the utensils already provided and accepted by others may be used; bringing a new gadget to the meal is an innovation attempted by many, though (curiously) condemned by all. Throughout the remaining meals the menu is fixed on the grounds that meat and potatoes are the most nourishing foods. The ways in which these meals are prepared and consumed is subject to strict regulation: one is not supposed to touch the food with one's hands; everyone must keep an upright position (it is considered an insult, for one to stand while the other lies). Interaction is drastically curtailed: one is not allowed to exchange dishes; one must feed only oneself (for a man to place his spoon in his partner's mouth is a mortal sin). These rules prescribe that each person gratify his own appetite, but in the company of a select other (to eat alone is forbidden, though many do).[25] During the meal a typical conversation consists of compliments —how good the meal is and how agreeable the company—regardless of their truthfulness.

If food and sex were only the satisfaction of appetites, these restrictions might be defensible —though the prohibitions against some changes would still be contentious. However, some innovations, at least for some people, not only could enhance the efficiency of such practices, but could add to their *meaning* as well. To "dine" with several different people can make eating not only more pleasant, but more enlightening too. To vary the "menu" is a safeguard against boredom that not only expands the topic of conversation, but also has nutritional value. To invite a guest similarly intensifies the conversation, which need not dissolve into monologues if considerateness is shown by all.[26] People should be allowed to get their fingers sticky (sex is wet) and to eat alone (masturbation makes neither your eye-

sight grow dim nor your hair fall out). Sometimes it may be more convenient to eat standing up or lying down: the exceptions of one society may elsewhere be the rule. More interaction can make the experience more significant; for example, switching dishes when the desires are different (to the dismay of many, they frequently only *look* different) provides variety that, after all, is still "the spice of life." If the food is not well-cooked and the company is no longer mutually attractive, admit these shortcomings; such honesty may lead to better meals. Only recently have the stereotypes that determined who issued the invitations, and who prepared the meal and did the serving, begun to dissolve. Exchanging traditional sex roles by allowing the woman to show greater initiative (if not aggression) can enhance mutual understanding and respect by dramatizing what it is to be in the other person's place.

Loosening the restrictions of the Western norm in these ways is tantamount to permitting, if not promulgating, promiscuity. The ensuing changes promise to make our sex lives not only physically more satisfying, but also more meaningful. This second defense of promiscuity has expanded the model of sexual behavior from mere bodily interaction for pleasure to a form of corporeal dialogue. With the third defense, to be offered next, these models are expanded further, to envelop man in the totality of his concrete existence.

Authentic Sexuality: An Existential Defense of Promiscuity

Heidegger's insistence that Being-with (*Mitsein*) is an essential structure of existence correctly stresses that the human personality is always situated within a social matrix.[27] My world includes others to whom I relate in various modes of solicitude. To this Heideggerian insight Merleau-Ponty adds that sexuality is an irreducible dimension of the being of the self as body subject: the erotic contours of the world reflect my incarnate being as sexual within that *gestalt* that is my existence taken as a whole.[28] Conjoining these two insights yields *eros* as a dimension of all modalities of social existence.

Among the three basic ways to be with others—against them, for them, or indifferently passing them by—Heidegger distinguishes two positive modes of "solicitude"

(*Fürsorge*): to leap-in (*einspringen*) is to perform some task for another; to leap-ahead (*vorausspringen*) is to prepare another for their genuine or authentic (*eigentlich*) possibilities.[29] This authenticity stands in contrast to the inauthenticity of everyday life, which is lived under the domination of the "they-self" (*das Man*) and distinguished by a lack of distinction in public, anonymous ways of thinking and acting.[30]

This everyday immersion in the commonplace, with its uncritical assimilation of the traditional, is disrupted by the call of conscience,[31] which summons the self (*Dasein*) to the recognition and acceptance of its finitude, or what Heidegger somewhat misleadingly calls "guilt."[32] My choices (*Existenz*) are finite: in pursuing one path I must forego its alternatives. My power over the world into which I am thrown (*geworfen*) is finite: some aspects of my situation remain forever beyond my control. And finally, my genuine existence, even when attained, is bounded by inauthenticity: the accommodating and tranquilizing ruses of the mediocre (*durchschnittlich*), leveled-down public life constantly tempt me to abandon personal initiative and responsibility.[33] This finitude is also temporal: my death is the ever-present possibility of my no longer having a world in which to reside, an eventuality certain to overcome me, though the moment always remains indefinite.[34] Authenticity (*Eigentlichkeit*) arises as a resolve (*Entschluss*) to remain open (*Erschliessen*) to this finitude—to be responsive to the summons to guilt and to anticipate (*vorlaufen*) death.[35] In their everyday lives, and indeed throughout a philosophical tradition, people have closed themselves off (a kind of ontological untruth for Heidegger[36]) from guilt and death, hence from that reality that they are and from that totality of entities (*Ganzheit des Seienden*) to which they are inextricably bound.

Authentic sexuality—admittedly a rather un-Heideggerian conjunction—requires a similar openness to others. Commitments are chains that bind us to some and exclude us from others, blinders that narrow down the field of social praxis to a privileged one (monogamy) or few (friendship). To elicit the many facets of the human personality requires a dynamic network of social interaction. Full sexual growth similarly requires a receptivity to the many erotic dimensions of social existence. Promiscuity provides this openness through its freedom from emotional and sexual commitments.

In the Western tradition love has been mistakenly treated as exclusive because it is erroneously thought of as possessive (compare, to "have" a woman), or that in which I have invested my will, in Hegelian terms.[37] But another person (*Mitdaseiende*) is neither a tool (*Zuhandene*) to be appropriated to my ends, nor a mere object of cognition (*Vorhandene*) to be explored. Rather, others are entities like me, with whom I share a world. Consequently love should be construed in Heideggerian terms as a leaping-ahead that affirms another's genuinely human possibilities, or in R. D. Laing's terms, as the confirmation of that which is true and good in another.[38]

The tradition has reversed the relation between sex and love—for reasons that once applied but, as previously pointed out, that are now anachronistic. The nakedness of sexual intercourse is not only physical, but psychological and emotional too: by laying bare not just our bodies, but our thoughts and feelings, two people can achieve a privileged moment from which they may *then* decide what kinds of commitments subsequently to make to one another. Promiscuity prepares for this moment through its "lack of commitment." To insist on an emotional involvement that closes off the future as a condition of this sexual self-revelation to others is, ironically, to frustrate the growth of the very love that such commitments are intended to cultivate. And to insist that this commitment as love can be made to only one other person is to succumb to the ontological fallacy of confusing people with things.

With its freedom from emotional and sexual restrictions promiscuity can play an important role in the achievement of authentic sexuality. This negative freedom-from is a positive freedom-for a genuinely human mode of social and sexual interaction.

CONCLUDING UNSCIENTIFIC POSTSCRIPT

My remarks might suggest that I believe promiscuity is *always* right. But this conclusion overstates my position. The claim I have sought to defend is more modest: for some of the people some of the time promiscuity is a good thing. Such behavior is curtailed by moral obligations to tell the truth, to be honest, and to respect others. It is also limited in time: for some, on occasion, promiscuity may not yet, or no longer, be good. To put my defense in perspective I shall conclude with a nod to Kierkegaard.

Kierkegaard's refutation of the Don Juan complex locates promiscuity as one stage on life's way.[39] Aping the Hegelian dialectic, of which he is both master and critic, he notes that the cause of its ultimate demise is boredom: despite the novelty achieved through the rotation method (varying the fields on which one's "seed" is sown), the full pursuit of the life of the senses ultimately succumbs to a cycle of sameness from which it can be rescued only by advancing to a higher mode of existence—the principled life of the ethical stage.[40]

Applied to the preceding sexual paradigms, Kierkegaard's insight suggests three corresponding resolutions of promiscuity. First, the good sex life cannot be achieved through physical gratification alone. The moral commitment represented by the Western norm is an attempt to achieve the advance Kierkegaard extols: wedded love regulated by reason seeks to overcome and yet to preserve (*aufheben*) the fleeting pleasures of the body. To deny this dialectical movement is to deny one's full humanity, to be arrested at a lower level of existence. Second, it may be noted that what the dialogue carried on through the body achieves in breadth it may lose in depth: having talked with many, we may discover that our most meaningful dialogue can be carried on with one. The commitment to this one person becomes, henceforth, a "natural" way to safeguard and foster this corporeal dialogue. The prohibitions against multiple dialogues were overthrown at the earlier stage so that this one person might be found and now they serve only as superfluous restrictions that need not be enforced to be observed. Finally, the openness of authentic sexuality may likewise achieve a moment at which a full commitment to a single other is its natural fruition; through its own catharsis the promiscuous life may discover a completion in Buber's I-Thou relation.[41] On such occasions promiscuity ceases to be of value in the sexual life of the individual. Indeed, from this point on not to abandon it would be as wrong as the prohibitions against it were at the earlier stage.

From this temporal perspective promiscuity has definite but limited value in the movement toward a sexual ideal. Michael Bayles is correct in his insistence that the intentionally life-long relationship is intrinsically more valuable, but wrong in his (implicit) suggestion that intentionally temporary relations are of no value.[42] The principled life represented by the traditional commitment "to love, honor, and obey" signifies a higher mode of existence that partially transcends the vicissitudes of time. Whether this ideal is expressed in Platonic terms, as the longing for a love that is eternal,[43] or in Buber's terms, as a full awareness of the other in their unity, totality, and uniqueness, it must be wrung from man's historical existence. The value of promiscuity is located in the pursuit of just such ideals.

NOTES

1. I am grateful to Professors Willard Enteman and Jan Ludwig for suggestions and criticisms that helped to rescue this paper from some of its more egregious errors and confusions.

2. See, for example, Robert Paul Wolff's *In Defense of Anarchism* (New York: Harper & Row, 1970). Though I shall not pursue the parallels between political and sexual life, I believe anarchy represents a moment in Wolff's account of political obligation analogous to the promiscuous moment in sexual morality: each is marked by a radical freedom that serves as the transcendental ground for subsequent commitments and obligations.

3. This thesis was advanced by A. J. Ayer in *Language, Truth and Logic* (New York: Dover, 1946), chap. 6, in order to account for the nonscientific (that is, nondescriptive) character of moral discourse. See C. L. Stevenson, *Ethics and Language* (New Haven: Yale University Press, 1944) and R. M. Hare, *The Language of Morals* (London: Oxford University Press, 1952) for subsequent refinements of this thesis.

4. What is true of promiscuity is also true of perversion: violations of the operative code tend to make our adrenalin flow. For one explanation of this emotional reaction to unnatural sexual acts see Michael Slote, "Inapplicable Concepts and Sexual Perversion," in R. Baker and F. Elliston, eds., *Philosophy and Sex* (Buffalo, N.Y.: Prometheus Books, 1925).

5. Ronald Atkinson, *Sexual Morality* (London: Hutchinson, 1965), p. 45.

6. See Robert Solomon, "Sex and Perversion," in Baker and Elliston, p. 271.

7. The boundaries of incest vary from society to society and, indeed, between groups within society. Freud sought to account for these differences in the incest taboo in terms of myth, Darwinism, and anthropology. See *Totem and Taboo* (New York: New Republic, 1931), pp. 249ff. Some have tried to show it is instinctive (see Robert H. Lowrie, *Primitive Society* [New York: Liveright, 1920]). Others explain the prohibition as a safeguard against biological degeneration due to inbreeding (see Lewis H. Morgan, *Ancient Society* [New York, 1877], pp. 69, 378, 424), or as a way of expanding and hence protecting the tribe (E.B. Tylor, "On a Method of Investigating the Development of Institutions: Applied to Laws of Marriage & Descent," *Journal of the Anthropological Institute* 18 [1888]: 245–69), or as a consequence of the prohibition against shedding the blood of one's own totemic group (Émile Durkheim, "La prohibition de l'incest et ses origins," *L'Annee Sociologique* 1 [1898]: 1–70). For a more recent treatment see S. Kirson Weinberg, *Incest Behavior* (New York: Citadel, 1955).

8. To refer to this as the "conjugal act," as the Roman Catholic Church does, is to beg the question of sex outside marriage. This restriction has a long and venerable tradition within Roman Catholicism, beginning with St. Paul's warning that it is better to marry than to burn in hell. See the following: Augustine, *De Genesi ad Litteram*, Book IX, cap. 7, n. 12; Thomas Aquinas, *On the Truth of the Catholic Faith*, Book 3, parts 1 and 2; Pope Leo XIII, *Rerum Novarum* (1891); and Pope Pius XI, *Casti Connubii* (1930).

9. Pope Paul VI, *Humanae Vitae*, "Faithfulness to God's Design," in Baker and Elliston.

10. Carl Cohen, "Sex, Birth Control, and Human Life," *Ethics* 79 (1969): 251–62.

11. See, for example, E. D. Watt, "Professor Cohen's Encyclical," *Ethics* 80 (1970): 218–21.

12. Richard Wasserstrom considers this point in his article "Is Adultery Immoral?" in Baker and Elliston.

13. See Peter Bertocci, *The Human Venture in Sex, Love and Marriage* (New York: Associated Press, 1949), chap. 2, and his *Sex, Love and the Person* (New York: Sheed & Ward, 1967).

14. For an entertaining description of this ritual see Soren Kierkegaard, *Diary of a Seducer*, trans. K. Fick (Ithaca, N. Y.: The Dragon Press, 1935).

15. In *Being and Nothingness* (Part 3, chap. 3) Sartre transmutes the celebrated Hegelian dialectical battle for prestige between the master and slave of *The Phenomenology of Mind* (pp. 228–40) into the notorious battle of the sexes. The intervening link between Sartre and Hegel is Alexander Kojève; see his *Introduction to the Reading of Hegel*, trans. J. H. Nichols (New York: Basic Books, 1969), pp. 31–70.

16. *The Essential Works of John Stuart Mill*, ed. Max Lerner (New York: Bantam, 1961), p. 263.

17. See Michael Bayles, "Marriage, Love, and Procreation," in Baker and Elliston.

18. Mill, *The Essential Works*, pp. 193ff.

19. Ibid., p. 306.

20. Ibid., p. 307. Mill's insistence on the freedom to create one's own mode of life and his emphasis on individuality and the cultivation of human facilities align him with the existential tradition of Sartre ("condemned to be free"; "fundamental project") and Heidegger (*Seinkönnen*—"potentiality for Being") more than Mill's interpreters have yet recognized. I quoted Wilhelm von Humbolt earlier because he (and Aristotle) may provide the historical link.

21. Mill, *The Essential Works*, p. 323.

22. R. C. Solomon, "Sexual Paradigms," *Journal of Philosophy* 71 (1974): 336–45; and "Sex and Perversion."

23. Max Black, *The Labyrinth of Language* (New York: Praeger, 1968), chap. 2, provides one explanation of this terminology.

24. Those less familiar with the gallic (and galling) tendencies of Canadian politics should consult Walter Stewart, *Shrug: Trudeau in Power* (New York: Outerbridge, 1971).

25. Lest the analogy seem far-fetched by this point, it is worth recalling that Kant was one respected moral philosopher who regarded sex as mutual masturbation, salvaged only by the sanctity of matrimony. See Immanuel Kant, *Lectures on Ethics*, trans. Louis Infield (London: Methuen, 1930), pp. 162–71.

26. The conclusion that group sex is necessarily dissatisfying may be a faulty inference from the failures of its unskilled practitioners who have not yet mastered the complexities of multi-person corporeal conversations.

27. See Martin Heidegger, *Being and Time*, trans. J. Macquarrie and E. Robinson (New York: Harper & Row, 1962), sec. 27.

28. Maurice Merleau-Ponty, *The Phenomenology of Perception*, trans. Colin Smith (New York: Humanities Press, 1962), Part 1, chap. 6.

29. *Being and Time*, sec. 26. R. Weber, in "A Critique of Heidegger's Concept of 'Solicitude,'" *New Scholasticism* 42 (1965): 537–60, misinterprets mineness (*Jemeinigkeit*) and the nonrelational character of death, thereby generating her spurious paradoxes. For a more faithful but less direct account see J. Macquarrie's excellent book, *Existentialism* (Baltimore: Penguin, 1973), chap. 5. "Existence and Others."

30. *Being and Time*, sec. 27. For an explication of inauthenticity see Ernest H. Freund, "Man's Fall in Martin Heidegger's Philosophy," *The Journal of Religion* 24 (1944): 180–87.

31. *Being and Time*, secs. 54–57.

32. Ibid., sec. 58. On Heidegger's existential notion of guilt see Michael Gelven, *Winter Friendship and Guilt* (New York: Harper & Row, 1972); D. V. Morano, *Existential Guilt: A Phenomenological Study* (Assen, The Netherlands: Van Gorcum, 1973); C. O. Schrag, *Existence and Freedom* (Evanston, Ill.: Northwestern University Press, 1961), chap. 6

33. *Being and Time*, secs. 25–27, 35–38.

34. Ibid., division C, chap. 1.

35. On Heidegger's existential notion of death see J. G. Gray, "Martin Heidegger: On Anticipating My Own Death," *Personalist* 46 (1965): 439–58; R. Hinners, "Death as Possibility," *Continuum* 5 (1967): 470–82; and B. E. O'Mahoney, "Martin Heidegger's Existential Death," *Philosophical Studies* (Ireland) 18 (1969): 58–75.

36. Heidegger explicates his ontological notion of truth and relates this to the epistemological concepts in section 44 of

Being and Time and in his essay "On the Essence of Truth," in *Being and Existence,* ed. W. Brock (Chicago: Gateway, 1949). This central concept has attracted much discussion. Ernst Tugendhat's *Der Wahrheitsbegriff bei Husserl und Heidegger* (Berlin: W. de Gruyter, 1970) is perhaps the most noteworthy.

37. G. W. F. Hegel, *The Philosophy of Right,* trans. T. M. Knox (London: Oxford University Press, 1942), pp. 40–56.

38. R. D. Laing, *Self and Others* (Baltimore: Penguin, 1971), chap. 7.

39. See Søren Kierkegaard, "The Rotation Method" (reprinted from *Either/Or*), in *A Kierkegaard Anthology,* ed. R. Bretall (New York: Modern Library, 1946), pp. 21–32.

40. In his recourse to the rational to overcome the sensual (or the "aesthetic," as Kierkegaard somewhat misleadingly terms it), Kierkegaard's solution to the morality of sex resembles Kant's (see note 23).

41. I have not tried to develop a notion of authentic sexuality on the model of Buber's I–Thou, though such an interpretation could be provided, because what I find lacking in Buber but present in Heidegger is a fuller recognition of the historicity of such ideals. For a Buberian interpretation of sexuality see M. Friedman, "Sex in Sartre and Buber," in *Sexuality and Identity,* ed. H. Ruitenbeek (New York: Bantam, 1970), pp. 84–99.

42. See p. 197. Though Bayles does not quite say they are of no value whatsoever, he believes that they are not sufficiently valuable to warrant legal protection.

43. See D. P. Verene, "Sexual Love and Moral Experience," in Baker and Elliston; and his *Sexual Love and Western Morality* (New York: Harper & Row, 1972), pp. 10–47.

RICHARD A. WASSERSTROM

Is Adultery Immoral?

Many discussions of the enforcement of morality by the law take as illustrative of the problem under consideration the regulation of various types of sexual behavior by the criminal law. It was, for example, the Wolfenden Report's recommendations concerning homosexuality and prostitution that led Lord Devlin to compose his now famous lecture, "The Enforcement of Morals." And that lecture in turn provoked important philosophical responses from H. L. A. Hart, Ronald Dworkin, and others.

Much, if not all, of the recent philosophical literature on the enforcement of morals appears to take for granted the immorality of the sexual behavior in question. The focus of discussion, at least, is whether such things as homosexuality, prostitution, and adultery ought to be made illegal even if they are immoral, and not whether they are immoral.

I propose in this paper to think about the latter, more neglected topic, that of sexual morality, and to do so in the following fashion. I shall consider just one kind of behavior that is often taken to be a case of sexual immorality—adultery. I am interested in pursuing at least two questions. First, I want to explore the question of in what respects adulterous behavior falls within the domain of morality at all: For this surely is one of the puzzles one encounters when considering the topic of sexual morality. It is often hard to see on what grounds much of the behavior is deemed to be either moral or immoral, for example, private homosexual behavior between consenting adults. I have purposely selected adultery because it seems a more plausible candidate for moral assessment than many other kinds of sexual behavior.

The second question I want to examine is that of what is to be said about adultery, without being especially concerned to stay within the area of morality. I shall endeavor, in other words, to identify and to assess a number of major arguments that might be advanced against adultery. I believe that they are the chief arguments that would be given in support of the view that adultery is immoral, but I think they are worth considering even if some of them turn out to be nonmoral arguments and considerations.

A number of the issues involved seem to me to be complicated and difficult. In a number of places I have at best indicated where further philosophical exploration is required without having successfully conducted the exploration myself. The paper may very well be more useful as an illustration of how one might begin to think about the subject of sexual morality than as an elucidation of important truths about the topic.

Before I turn to the arguments themselves there are two preliminary points that require some clarification. Throughout the paper I shall refer to the immorality of such things as breaking a promise, deceiving someone, etc. In a very rough way, I mean by this that there is something morally wrong that is done in doing the action in question. I mean that the action is, in a strong sense of "*prima facie*," *prima facie* wrong or unjustified. I do not mean that it may never be right or justifiable to do the action; just that the fact that it is an action of this description always does count against the rightness of the action. I leave entirely open the question of what it is that makes actions of this kind immoral in this sense of "immoral."

The second preliminary point concerns what is meant or implied by the concept of adultery.

I mean by "adultery" any case of extramarital sex, and I want to explore the arguments for and against extramarital sex, undertaken in a variety of morally relevant situations. Someone might claim that the concept of adultery is conceptually connected with the concept of immorality, and that to characterize behavior as adulterous is already to characterize it as immoral or unjustified in the sense described above. There may be something to this. Hence the importance of making it clear that I want to talk about extramarital sexual relations. If they are always immoral, this is something that must be shown by argument. If the concept of adultery does in some sense entail or imply immorality, I want to ask whether that connection is a rationally based one. If not all cases of extramarital sex are immoral (again, in the sense described above), then the concept of adultery should either be weakened accordingly or restricted to those classes of extramarital sex for which the predication of immorality is warranted.

One argument for the immorality of adultery might go something like this: what makes adultery immoral is that it involves the breaking of a promise, and what makes adultery seriously wrong is that it involves the breaking of an important promise. For, so the argument might continue, one of the things the two parties promise each other when they get married is that they will abstain from sexual relationships with third persons. Because of this promise both spouses quite reasonably entertain the expectation that the other will behave in conformity with it. Hence, when one of the parties has sexual intercourse with a third person he or she breaks that promise about sexual relationships which was made when the marriage was entered into, and defeats the reasonable expectations of exclusivity entertained by the spouse.

In many cases the immorality involved in breaching the promise relating to extramarital sex may be a good deal more serious than that involved in the breach of other promises. This is so because adherence to this promise may be of much greater importance to the parties than is adherence to many of the other promises given or received by them in their lifetime. The breaking of this promise may be much more hurtful and painful than is typically the case.

Why is this so? To begin with, it may have been difficult for the nonadulterous spouse to have kept the promise. Hence that spouse may

feel the unfairness of having restrained himself or herself in the absence of reciprocal restraint having been exercised by the adulterous spouse. In addition, the spouse may perceive the breaking of the promise as an indication of a kind of indifference on the part of the adulterous spouse. If you really cared about me and my feelings—the spouse might say—you would not have done this to me. And third, and related to the above, the spouse may see the act of sexual intercourse with another as a sign of affection for the other person and as an additional rejection of the nonadulterous spouse as the one who is loved by the adulterous spouse. It is not just that the adulterous spouse does not take the feelings of the spouse sufficiently into account, the adulterous spouse also indicates through the act of adultery affection for someone other than the spouse. I will return to these points later. For the present, it is sufficient to note that a set of arguments can be developed in support of the proposition that certain kinds of adultery are wrong just because they involve that breach of a serious promise which, among other things, leads to the intentional infliction of substantial pain by one spouse upon the other.

Another argument for the immorality of adultery focuses not on the existence of a promise of sexual exclusivity but on the connection between adultery and deception. According to this argument, adultery involves deception. And because deception is wrong, so is adultery.

Although it is certainly not obviously so, I shall simply assume in this paper that deception is always immoral. Thus the crucial issue for my purposes is the asserted connection between extramarital sex and deception. Is is plausible to maintain, as this argument does, that adultery always does involve deception and is on that basis to be condemned?

The most obvious person on whom deceptions might be practiced is the nonparticipating spouse; and the most obvious thing about which the nonparticipating spouse can be deceived is the existence of the adulterous act. One clear case of deception is that of lying. Instead of saying that the afternoon was spent in bed with A, the adulterous spouse asserts that it was spent in the library with B, or on the golf course with C.

There can also be deception even when no

lies are told. Suppose, for instance, that a person has sexual intercourse with someone other than his or her spouse and just does not tell the spouse about it. Is that deception? It may not be a case of lying if, for example, the spouse is never asked by the other about the situation. Still, we might say, it is surely deceptive because of the promises that were exchanged at marriage. As we saw earlier, these promises provide a foundation for the reasonable belief that neither spouse will engage in sexual relationships with any other persons. Hence the failure to bring the fact of extramarital sex to the attention of the other spouse deceives that spouse about the present state of the marital relationship.

Adultery, in other words, can involve both active and passive deception. An adulterous spouse may just keep silent or, as is often the fact, the spouse may engage in an increasingly complex way of life devoted to the concealment of the facts from the nonparticipating spouse. Lies, half-truths, clandestine meetings, and the like may become a central feature of the adulterous spouse's existence. These are things that can and do happen, and when they do they make the case against adultery an easy one. Still neither active nor passive deception is inevitably a feature of an extramarital relationship.

It is possible, though, that a more subtle but pervasive kind of deceptiveness is a feature of adultery. It comes about because of the connection in our culture between sexual intimacy and certain feelings of love and affection. The point can be made indirectly at first by seeing that one way in which we can, in our culture, mark off our close friends from our mere acquaintances is through the kinds of intimacies that we are prepared to share with them. I may, for instance, be willing to reveal my very private thoughts and emotions to my closest friends or to my wife, but to no one else. My sharing of these intimate facts about myself is from one perspective a way of making a gift to those who mean the most to me. Revealing these things and sharing them with those who mean the most to me is one means by which I create, maintain, and confirm those interpersonal relationships that are of most importance to me.

Now in our culture, it might be claimed, sexual intimacy is one of the chief currencies through which gifts of this sort are exchanged.

One way to tell someone—particularly someone of the opposite sex—that you have feelings of affection and love for them is by allowing to them or sharing with them sexual behaviors that one doesn't share with the rest of the world. This way of measuring affection was certainly very much a part of the culture in which I matured. It worked something like this. If you were a girl, you showed how much you liked someone by the degree of sexual intimacy you would allow. If you liked a boy only a little, you never did more than kiss—and even the kiss was not passionate. If you liked the boy a lot and if your feeling was reciprocated, necking, and possibly petting, was permissible. If the attachment was still stronger and you thought it might even become a permanent relationship, the sexual activity was correspondingly more intense and more intimate, although whether it would ever lead to sexual intercourse depended on whether the parties (and particularly the girl) accepted fully the prohibition on nonmarital sex. The situation for the boy was related, but not exactly the same. The assumption was that males did not naturally link sex with affection in the way in which females did. However, since women did, males had to take this into account. That is to say, because a woman would permit sexual intimacies only if she had feelings of affection for the male and only if those feelings were reciprocated, the male had to have and express those feelings, too, before sexual intimacies of any sort would occur.

The result was that the importance of a correlation between sexual intimacy and feelings of love and affection was taught by the culture and assimilated by those growing up in the culture. The scale of possible positive feelings toward persons of the other sex ran from casual liking at the one end to the love that was deemed essential to and characteristic of marriage at the other. The scale of possible sexual behavior ran from brief, passionless kissing or hand-holding at the one end to sexual intercourse at the other. And the correlation between the two scales was quite precise. As a result, any act of sexual intimacy carried substantial meaning with it, and no act of sexual intimacy was simply a pleasurable set of bodily sensations. Many such acts were, of course, more pleasurable to the participants because they were a way of saying what the participants' feelings were. And sometimes they were less pleasurable for the same reason. The point is, however, that in any event sexual activity was much more than mere bodily enjoyment. It was not like eating a good meal, listening to good music, lying in the sun, or getting a pleasant back rub. It was behavior that meant a great deal concerning one's feelings for persons of the opposite sex in whom one was most interested and with whom one was most involved. It was among the most authoritative ways in which one could communicate to another the nature and degree of one's affection.

If this sketch is even roughly right, then several things become somewhat clearer. To begin with, a possible rationale for many of the rules of conventional sexual morality can be developed. If, for example, sexual intercourse is associated with the kind of affection and commitment to another that is regarded as characteristic of the marriage relationship, then it is natural that sexual intercourse should be thought properly to take place between persons who are married to each other. And if it is thought that this kind of affection and commitment is only to be found within the marriage relationship, then it is not surprising that sexual intercourse should only be thought to be proper within marriage.

Related to what has just been said is the idea that sexual intercourse ought to be restricted to those who are married to each other as a means by which to confirm the very special feelings that the spouses have for each other. Because the culture teaches that sexual intercourse means that the strongest of all feelings for each other are shared by the lovers, it is natural that persons who are married to each other should be able to say this to each other in this way. Revealing and confirming verbally that these feelings are present is one thing that helps to sustain the relationship; engaging in sexual intercourse is another.

In addition, this account would help to provide a framework within which to make sense of the notion that some sex is better than other sex. As I indicated earlier, the fact that sexual intimacy can be meaningful in the sense described tends to make it also the case that sexual intercourse can sometimes be more enjoyable than at other times. On this view, sexual intercourse will typically be more enjoyable where the strong feelings of affection are pres-

ent than it will be where it is merely "mechanical." This is so in part because people enjoy being loved, especially by those whom they love. Just as we like to hear words of affection, so we like to receive affectionate behavior. And the meaning enhances the independently pleasurable behavior.

More to the point, moreover, an additional rationale for the prohibition on extramarital sex can now be developed. For given this way of viewing the sexual world, extramarital sex will almost always involve deception of a deeper sort. If the adulterous spouse does not in fact have the appropriate feelings of affection for the extramarital partner, then the adulterous spouse is deceiving that person about the presence of such feelings. If, on the other hand, the adulterous spouse does have the corresponding feelings for the extramarital partner but not toward the nonparticipating spouse, the adulterous spouse is very probably deceiving the nonparticipating spouse about the presence of such feelings toward that spouse. Indeed, it might be argued, whenever there is no longer love between the two persons who are married to each other, there is deception just because being married implies both to the participants and to the world that such a bond exists. Deception is inevitable, the argument might conclude, because the feelings of affection that ought to accompany any act of sexual intercourse can only be held toward one other person at any given time in one's life. And if this is so, then the adulterous spouse always deceives either the partner in adultery or the nonparticipating spouse about the existence of such feelings. Thus extramarital sex involves deception of this sort and is for this reason immoral even if no deception vis-à-vis the occurrence of the act of adultery takes place.

What might be said in response to the foregoing arguments? The first thing that might be said is that the account of the connection between sexual intimacy and feelings of affection is inaccurate. Not inaccurate in the sense that no one thinks of things that way, but in the sense that there is substantially more divergence of opinion than that account suggests. For example, the view I have delineated may describe reasonably accurately the concept of the sexual world in which I grew up, but it does not capture the sexual *weltanschauung* of today's youth at all. Thus, whether or not adultery implies deception in respect to feelings depends very much on the persons who are involved and the way they look at the "meaning" of sexual intimacy.

Second, the argument leaves to be answered the question of whether it is desirable for sexual intimacy to carry the sorts of messages described above. For those persons for whom sex does have these implications, there are special feelings and sensibilities that must be taken into account. But it is another question entirely whether any valuable end—moral or otherwise —is served by investing sexual behavior with such significance. That is something that must be shown and not just assumed. It might, for instance, be the case that substantially more good than harm would come from a kind of demystification of sexual behavior: one that would encourage the enjoyment of sex more for its own sake and one that would reject the centrality both of the association of sex with love and of love with only one other person.

I regard these as two of the more difficult, unresolved issues that our culture faces today in respect to thinking sensibly about the attitudes toward sex and love that we should try to develop in ourselves and in our children. Much of the contemporary literature that advocates sexual liberation of one sort or another embraces one or the other of two different views about the relationship between sex and love.

One view holds that sex should be separated from love and affection. To be sure sex is probably better when the partners genuinely like and enjoy each other. But sex is basically an intensive, exciting sensuous activity that can be enjoyed in a variety of suitable settings with a variety of suitable partners. The situation in respect to sexual pleasure is not different from that of the person who knows and appreciates fine food and who can have a very satisfying meal in any number of good restaurants with any number of congenial companions. One question that must be settled here is whether sex can be so demystified; another, more important question is whether it would be desirable to do so. What would we gain and what might we lose if we all lived in a world in which an act of sexual intercourse was no more or less significant or enjoyable than having a delicious meal in a nice setting with a good friend? The answer to this question lies beyond the scope of this paper.

The second view seeks to drive the wedge in a different place. It is not the link between sex and love that needs to be broken; rather, on this view, it is the connection between love and exclusivity that ought to be severed. For a number of the reasons already given, it is desirable, so this argument goes, that sexual intimacy continue to be reserved to and shared with only those for whom one has very great affection. The mistake lies in thinking that any "normal" adult will only have those feelings toward one other adult during his or her lifetime—or even at any time in his or her life. It is the concept of adult love, not ideas about sex, that, on this view, needs demystification. What are thought to be both unrealistic and unfortunate are the notions of exclusivity and possessiveness that attach to the dominant conception of love between adults in our and other cultures. Parents of four, five, six, or even ten children can certainly claim and sometimes claim correctly that they love all of their children, that they love them all equally, and that it is simply untrue to their feelings to insist that the numbers involved diminish either the quantity or the quality of their love. If this is an idea that is readily understandable in the case of parents and children, there is no necessary reason why it is an impossible or undesirable ideal in the case of adults. To be sure, there is probably a limit to the number of intimate "primary" relationships that any person can maintain at any given time without the quality of the relationship being affected. But one adult ought surely be able to love two, three, or even six other adults at any time without that love being different in kind or degree from that of the traditional, monogamous, lifetime marriage. And as between the individuals in these relationships, whether within a marriage or without, sexual intimacy is fitting and good.

The issues raised by a position such as this one are also surely worth exploring in detail and with care. Is there something to be called "sexual love" which is different from parental love or the nonsexual love of close friends? Is there something about love in general that links it naturally and appropriately with feelings of exclusivity and possession? Or is there something about sexual love, whatever that may be, that makes these feelings especially fitting here? Once again the issues are conceptual, empirical, and normative all at once: What is love? How could it be different? Would it be a good thing or a bad thing if it were different?

Suppose, though, that having delineated these problems we were now to pass them by. Suppose, moreover, we were to be persuaded to the possibility and the desirability of weakening substantially either the links between sex and love or the links between sexual love and exclusivity. Would it not then be the case that adultery could be free from all of the morally objectionable features described so far? To be more specific, let us imagine that a husband and wife have what is today sometimes characterized as an "open marriage." Suppose, that is, that they have agreed in advance that extramarital sex is—under certain circumstances—acceptable behavior for each to engage in. Suppose, that as a result there is no impulse to deceive each other about the occurrence or nature of any such relationships, and that no deception in fact occurs. Suppose, too, that there is no deception in respect to the feelings involved between the adulterous spouse and the extramarital partner. And suppose, finally, that one or the other or both of the spouses then have sexual intercourse in circumstances consistent with these understandings. Under this description, so the argument might conclude, adultery is simply not immoral. At a minimum, adultery cannot very plausibly be condemned either on the ground that it involves deception or on the ground that it requires the breaking of a promise.

At least two responses are worth considering. One calls attention to the connection between marriage and adultery; the other looks to more instrumental arguments for the immorality of adultery. Both issues deserve further exploration.

One way to deal with the case of the "open marriage" is to question whether the two persons involved are still properly to be described as being married to each other. Part of the meaning of what it is for two persons to be married to each other, so this argument would go, is to have committed oneself to have sexual relationships only with one's spouse. Of course, it would be added, we know that that commitment is not always honored. We know that persons who are married to each other often do commit adultery. But there is a difference between being willing to make a commitment to marital fidelity, even though one may

fail to honor that commitment, and not making the commitment at all. Whatever the relationship may be between the two individuals in the case described above, the absence of any commitment to sexual exclusivity requires the conclusion that their relationship is not a marital one. For a commitment to sexual exclusivity is a necessary although not a sufficient condition for the existence of a marriage.

Although there may be something to this suggestion, as it is stated it is too strong to be acceptable. To begin with, I think it is very doubtful that there are many, if any, *necessary* conditions for marriage; but even if there are, a commitment to sexual exclusivity is not such a condition.

To see that this is so, consider what might be taken to be some of the essential characteristics of a marriage. We might be tempted to propose that the concept of marriage requires the following: a formal ceremony of some sort in which mutual obligations are undertaken between two persons of the opposite sex; the capacity on the part of the persons involved to have sexual intercourse with each other; the willingness to have sexual intercourse only with each other; and feelings of love and affection between the two persons. The problem is that we can imagine relationships that are clearly marital and yet lack one or more of these features. For example, in our own society, it is possible for two persons to be married without going through a formal ceremony, as in the commonlaw marriages recognized in some jurisdictions. It is also possible for two persons to get married even though one or both lacks the capacity to engage in sexual intercourse. Thus, two very elderly persons who have neither the desire nor the ability to have intercourse can, nonetheless, get married, as can persons whose sexual organs have been injured so that intercourse is not possible. And we certainly know of marriages in which love was not present at the time of the marriage, as, for instance, in marriages of state and marriages of convenience.

Counterexamples not satisfying the condition relating to the abstention from extramarital sex are even more easily produced. We certainly know of societies and cultures in which polygamy and polyandry are practiced, and we have no difficulty in recognizing these relationships as cases of marriages. It might be objected, though, that these are not counterexamples because they are plural marriages rather than marriages in which sex is permitted with someone other than with one of the persons to whom one is married. But we also know of societies in which it is permissible for married persons to have sexual relationships with persons to whom they were not married; for example, temple prostitutes, concubines, and homosexual lovers. And even if we knew of no such societies, the conceptual claim would still, I submit, not be well taken. For suppose all of the other indicia of marriage were present: suppose the two persons were of the opposite sex, suppose they participated in a formal ceremony in which they understood themselves voluntarily to be entering into a relationship with each other in which substantial mutual commitments were assumed. If all these conditions were satisfied, we would not be in any doubt about whether or not the two persons were married even though they had not taken on a commitment of sexual exclusivity and even though they had expressly agreed that extramarital sexual intercourse was a permissible behavior for each to engage in.

A commitment to sexual exclusivity is neither a necessary nor a sufficient condition for the existence of a marriage. It does, nonetheless, have this much to do with the nature of marriage: like the other indicia enumerated above, its presence tends to establish the existence of a marriage. Thus, in the absence of a formal ceremony of any sort, an explicit commitment to sexual exclusivity would count in favor of regarding the two persons as married. The conceptual role of the commitment to sexual exclusivity can, perhaps, be brought out through the following example. Suppose we found a tribe which had a practice in which all the other indicia of marriage were present but in which the two parties were *prohibited* ever from having sexual intercourse with each other. Moreover, suppose that sexual intercourse with others was clearly permitted. In such a case we would, I think, reject the idea that the two were married to each other and we would describe their relationship in other terms, for example, as some kind of formalized, special friendship relation—a kind of heterosexual "blood-brother" bond.

Compare that case with the following. Suppose again that the tribe had a practice in which all of the other indicia of marriage were present, but instead of a prohibition on sexual intercourse between the persons in the relationship there was no rule at all. Sexual intercourse was permissible with the person with whom one had this ceremonial relationship, but it was no more or less permissible than with a number of other persons to whom one was not so related (for instance, all consenting adults of the opposite sex). Although we might be in doubt as to whether we ought to describe the persons as married to each other, we would probably conclude that they were married and that they simply were members of a tribe whose views about sex were quite different from our own.

What all of this shows is that *a prohibition* on sexual intercourse between the two persons involved in a relationship is conceptually incompatible with the claim that the two of them are married. The *permissibility* of intramarital sex is a necessary part of the idea of marriage. But no such incompatibility follows simply from the added permissibility of extramarital sex.

These arguments do not, of course, exhaust the arguments for the prohibition on extramarital sexual relations. The remaining argument that I wish to consider—as I indicated earlier—is a more instrumental one. It seeks to justify the prohibition by virtue of the role that it plays in the development and maintenance of nuclear families. The argument, or set of arguments, might, I believe, go something like this.

Consider first a farfetched nonsexual example. Suppose a society were organized so that after some suitable age—say, 18, 19, or 20—persons were forbidden to eat anything but bread and water with anyone but their spouse. Persons might still choose in such a society not to get married. Good food just might not be very important to them because they have underdeveloped taste buds. Or good food might be bad for them because there is something wrong with their digestive system. Or good food might be important to them, but they might decide that the enjoyment of good food would get in the way of the attainment of other things that were more important. But most persons would, I think, be led to favor marriage in part because they preferred a richer, more varied, diet to one of bread and water. And they might remain married because the family was the only legitimate setting within which good food was obtainable. If it is important to have society organized so that persons will both get married and stay married, such an arrangement would be well suited to the preservation of the family, and the prohibitions relating to food consumption could be understood as fulfilling that function.

It is obvious that one of the more powerful human desires is the desire for sexual gratification. The desire is a natural one, like hunger and thirst, in the sense that it need not be learned in order to be present within us and operative upon us. But there is in addition much that we do learn about what the act of sexual intercourse is like. Once we experience sexual intercourse ourselves—and in particular once we experience orgasm—we discover that it is among the most intensive, short-term pleasures of the body.

Because this is so, it is easy to see how the prohibition upon extramarital sex helps to hold marriage together. At least during that period of life when the enjoyment of sexual intercourse is one of the desirable bodily pleasures, persons will wish to enjoy those pleasures. If one consequence of being married is that one is prohibited from having sexual intercourse with anyone but one's spouse, then the spouses in a marriage are in a position to provide an important source of pleasure for each other that is unavailable to them elsewhere in the society.

The point emerges still more clearly if this rule of sexual morality is seen as of a piece with the other rules of sexual morality. When this prohibition is coupled, for example, with the prohibition on nonmarital sexual intercourse, we are presented with the inducement both to get married and to stay married. For if sexual intercourse is only legitimate within marriage, then persons seeking that gratification which is a feature of sexual intercourse are furnished explicit social directions for its attainment; namely marriage.

Nor, to continue the argument, is it necessary to focus exclusively on the bodily enjoyment that is involved. Orgasm may be a significant part of what there is to sexual intercourse, but it is not the whole of it. We need only recall the earlier discussion of the meaning that sexual intimacy has in our own culture to begin to see some of the more intricate ways in which sexual exclusivity may be connected with the establishment and maintenance of marriage as the primary heterosexual, love relationship.

Adultery is wrong, in other words, because a prohibition on extramarital sex is a way to help maintain the institutions of marriage and the nuclear family.

Now I am frankly not sure what we are to say about an argument such as this one. What I am convinced of is that, like the arguments discussed earlier, this one also reveals something of the difficulty and complexity of the issues that are involved. So, what I want now to do—in the brief and final portion of this paper—is to try to delineate with reasonable precision what I take several of the fundamental, unresolved issues to be.

The first is whether this last argument is an argument for the *immorality* of extramarital sexual intercourse. What does seem clear is that there are differences between this argument and the ones considered earlier. The earlier arguments condemned adulterous behavior because it was behavior that involved breaking of a promise, taking unfair advantage, or deceiving another. To the degree to which the prohibition on extramarital sex can be supported by arguments which invoke considerations such as these, there is little question but that violations of the prohibition are properly regarded as immoral. And such a claim could be defended on one or both of two distinct grounds. The first is that things like promise-breaking and deception are just wrong. The second is that adultery involving promise-breaking or deception is wrong because it involves the straightforward infliction of harm on another human being—typically the non-adulterous spouse—who has a strong claim not to have that harm so inflicted.

The argument that connects the prohibition on extramarital sex with the maintenance and preservation of the institution of marriage is an argument for the instrumental value of the prohibition. To some degree this counts, I think, against regarding all violations of the prohibition as obvious cases of immorality. This is so partly because hypothetical imperatives are less clearly within the domain of morality than are categorical ones, and even more because instrumental prohibitions are within the domain of morality only if the end they serve or the way they serve it is itself within the domain of morality.

What this should help us see, I think, is the fact that the argument that connects the prohibition on adultery with the preservation of marriage is at best seriously incomplete. Before we ought to be convinced by it, we ought to have reasons for believing that marriage is a morally desirable and just social institution. And this is not quite as easy or obvious a task as it may seem to be. For the concept of marriage is, as we have seen, both a loosely structured and a complicated one. There may be all sorts of intimate, interpersonal relationships which will resemble but not be identical with the typical marriage relationship presupposed by the traditional sexual morality. There may be a number of distinguishable sexual and loving arrangements which can all legitimately claim to be called *marriages*. The prohibitions of the traditional sexual morality may be effective ways to maintain some marriages and ineffective ways to promote and preserve others. The prohibitions of the traditional sexual morality may make good psychological sense if certain psychological theories are true, and they may be purveyors of immense psychological mischief if other psychological theories are true. The prohibitions of the traditional sexual morality may seem obviously correct if sexual intimacy carries the meaning that the dominant culture has often ascribed to it, and they may seem equally bizarre when sex is viewed through the perspective of the counterculture. Irrespective of whether instrumental arguments of this sort are properly deemed moral arguments, they ought not to fully convince anyone until questions like these are answered.

JOHN H. BOGART

On the Nature of Rape

The legal and social responses to rape in the United States have been in upheaval for nearly 20 years. Despite vast changes in the criminal law and other social institutions, despite a burgeoning scholarly and popular literature, there has been comparatively little attention paid to defining rape.[1] My aim here is to provide a discussion of the nature of rape and thereby provide a sounder foundation for both analysis and reform.

The article is divided into several sections. In the first I develop and discuss four distinct conceptions of rape found in legal and other scholarly discussions of rape. I then argue for the superiority of a particular, and very powerful, conception of rape which focuses upon a person's voluntary and effective consent and not upon force or will. In the third section I consider some objections to my account of rape. I have left for another time the discussion of implications for reform of the account defended in this article.

DEFINITIONAL ACCOUNTS OF THE CONCEPT OF RAPE

There seem to me to be four major alternatives with respect to defining rape: as forcible, coerced, nonvoluntary, or nonconsensual sex.[2] In each of these accounts, the emphasis, in the present circumstances, is on the first element. Although necessary for a complete account of rape, I will not attempt to delineate the sexual content required for an act to be rape (or attempted rape). I should also note that the following accounts are to be understood as nested, such that each successive account includes within its scope each of the previous accounts. The scope of the force account, for example, is a proper subset of the scope of the coercion account.

The first possibility for an account of rape is that it is constituted by forcible sex.[3] Sexual intercourse is forcible if procured by means of force or the threat of force against the victim. It involves violence or the threat of violence, and the force is such that it overcomes resistance on the part of the victim.

By rape we might instead mean coerced sex.[4] What this means, in addition to what is encompassed by the concept of forcible sex, is that the sex may be obtained by means of serious threats of other kinds. The threat may be directed at a third party, or may be deprivation of livelihood, or any of a number of other serious harms. Again the threat is sufficiently serious that it overcomes resistance on the part of the victim. The victim acts in a way she otherwise would not have acted, and does so only because of the threat, but the threat is not necessarily of personal bodily harm to the rape victim.[5]

Nonvoluntary sex is the third option.[6] I mean by that to include not only what falls under both forcible and coerced sex, but also to cooperation due to compelling circumstantial pressures. When resistance is possible only at the cost of serious inconvenience or substantial harm (or to harms which fall under the preceding accounts), the action may be nonvoluntary. I would be inclined to include here such things as exchanges of sex for employment, or an exchange of sex for not being abandoned in a remote location.

The fourth possibility is to understand rape

From *Public Affairs Quarterly* 5 (1991): 117–36. Copyright © 1991 by *Public Affairs Quarterly*. Reprinted with permission of the author and publisher.

as nonconsensual sex. This account is distinguished from the other three by counting as instances of rape all cases of sexual intercourse which occur without the consent of at least one of the participants. Where participation is not willing, not chosen freely, not chosen without the application or presence of external pressures, the sexual interaction will count as a form of rape.[7]

Much of the traditional discussion of rape is in terms of consent, but this is extremely misleading because in such discussions it is not consent that is actually the definitional standard. Rather, nonconsent is equated with various standards of resistance (often "utmost" resistance).[8] The nonconsent account I have set out above, however, is not properly identified with resistance standards.[9]

GROUNDS FOR CHOOSING AMONG THE DEFINITIONS

There are three main grounds on which to prefer one of the preceding accounts over the others. The first ground for preference is a better fit with a variety of relevant cases (standard of scope). In this case, the domain consists of a number of types or categories of events which intuitively seem to be instances of rape despite significant variation in means and context.

The second ground of preference is that one account provides a sounder basis for an explanation of the harm intrinsic to rape (harm standard). I indicate below what I believe the intrinsic harms of rape are (and for the remainder of the essay I shall speak of these four linked harms as the harm of rape). Part of the case for the harm as I have identified it lies in the discussion of the domain of rape. Part of the claim for the superiority of the nonconsent account is that what I have suggested as the nature of the harm of rape is best captured by accepting that account of the nature of rape. The arguments should be seen, therefore, as interdependent.

The third basis for preference is superiority of fit with related background theories (background theory standard). Background theories should be understood in a wide and full sense. I include among the background theories matters which are not at all in the background of the social problem of rape.

Scope

There are a number of categories of cases that belong within the (core) domain of rape. Any adequate account of the nature of rape must yield an appropriate explanation of the inclusion of such cases within the domain. The categories I will consider are these:

Case 1: Sexual relations brought about by means of force or threat of force against the victim.

Case 2: Sex obtained by means of threats against a third party.

Case 3: Relations during a period in which the victim is incapacitated.

Case 4: Sexual relations obtained by means of fraud.

Case 5: Sex involving a child.[10]

The first thing to be noticed is that the first account of rape, forcible sex, comfortably accounts for only one of the five kinds of cases being considered, Case 1. The coercion account fares somewhat better. It does handle at least some cases beyond the reach of the force account. For example, under a coercion theory we may count as instances of rape those cases involving induced intoxication and a portion of child cases. But the coercion account is not adequate. It does not properly handle such cases as incapacity, or fraud. Merely exploiting a dependency relationship is insufficient for coercion, although such cases will surely constitute some significant portion of incestuous rapes. This is plain enough in cases where the victim is too young properly to understand the events, or is otherwise incapacitated.

The choice between the two wider accounts is reflected in differences at the edges of their respective domains. The nonvoluntary account requires treating as rape all those cases in which sexual contact is nonvoluntary. Acceptable sexual contact is voluntary sexual contact. This means that in instances of Case 5 we will need separate explanatory and justificatory accounts for prohibitions on sexual contacts. While many such cases will fail to be voluntary, certainly not all can be so characterized. A six or eight year old is certainly capable of voluntary action. Indeed, children are capable of voluntary action much earlier than that. It is not, after all, necessary for an act to be voluntary that the agent understand the *full* nature of the action or the consequences of the action.[11] The action is voluntary when not coerced or compelled by external forces.

Voluntariness and consent diverge in at least two other areas important to the present topic, those involving intoxication or fraud. Suppose a woman[12] becomes quite intoxicated. Indeed, she becomes sufficiently intoxicated that she can no longer be said fully to understand her actions or to be more than dimly cognizant of her surroundings and companions. In such a state she is no longer capable of consenting to anything, although she is still able to act voluntarily. Thus she may voluntarily enter a car, or voluntarily fall into bed with someone. No one forces her to do so, and she is not acting under an impulse we would normally call irresistible. But she does not consent. She cannot consent because her understanding is too deeply impaired. In such a case, although sex may be voluntary, it is not consensual. In important ways, this sort of case stands as a bridge to the dependency case discussed above. What links the two is the incapacity to give consent. As we should not think that a seriously intoxicated person could consent to a financial contract, so she could not consent to a sexual arrangement. In the case of intoxication, the incapacity is temporary. But the incapacity may be permanent as well and in such instances too there is no consent.

Fraud provides the final sort of case which I want to use to distinguish nonvoluntary from nonconsensual sex. Among the kinds of cases to be counted under this category, are those where sexual access is gained under false pretenses. If a woman accedes to sexual requests under the mistaken belief that it is a medical treatment, it would count as a case of rape.[13] So too would cases where the victim does not realize before the fact that what she is agreeing to is sexual intercourse. Other sorts of cases would include those where there is consent to sex with one party and it is another who actually engages in sexual relations.[14] Where a person relies on a mistake as to identity to gain sexual favors, that too would be an instance under this category.[15]

The nonconsensual model of rape will cover these cases, while none of the other accounts will. In these cases, the action is voluntary, or there would be no fraud. Because the beliefs underlying the action are false, although the action itself is voluntary, there is no effective consent. Consequently, the cases may be termed instances of rape under the nonconsent model. Under the nonvoluntary model, these are cases of simple seduction.

The Harm Standard

Part of the argument in favor of the nonconsent account of rape is that it provides a better explanation of the harm of rape, and in particular the continuity and identity of harm across distinct categories of rape. On the assumption that all five cases do in fact mark distinct categories of rape, then any adequate account must display the cases as instantiating a like harm (or set of harms). That standard can be met by the nonconsent account, and it can be met by that account because of the abstract, formal, nature of harm under the account.

The case which characterizes the common image of rape involves ordinary adults and the use of force to effect the rape. Consider the following sort of case (Case 1). A is accosted by B who demands that A perform sexual intercourse with B. B's demand is backed by an explicit threat of force against A in the event A does not cooperate. A performs the requested acts. This, I take it, is a paradigmatic case of rape.

With respect to the rape itself, A has suffered four kinds of harm:

1. There has been a violation of A's interest in sexual self-determination.
2. There has been a violation of A's interest in bodily integrity.
3. A's autonomy has been violated.
4. A has suffered from alienation.

It is very likely that in addition to the rape, A has been harmed in a number of other related, collateral, and consequent ways. But it is just these four kinds of harm which characterize what A suffers insofar as we consider only the rape itself.

Of course, merely asserting that certain

harms capture rape is insufficient. It is also necessary to explain why that is so. We begin with a commonplace observation, valuable despite its apparent triviality. Rape involves sex.[16] The way in which it involves sex is important. It is quite common, as in the example above, for a rape to occur in the midst of a physical attack on the victim. The aggressor may rely on force, or the threat of the use of a weapon, and the attack may include other humiliating or degrading events. These aspects of the action are conceptually distinct from that which constitutes the rape. Insofar as A is the victim of a physical attack, rape is not distinct from a mugging or other beating. We need to be careful here to disentangle the many related harms suffered by a rape victim and to focus on only those which constitute the event as an instance of rape, to focus on those which are peculiar to rape.[17]

Physical assault is not peculiar to rape, however closely related in practice. By the same reasoning we can see that the harm of rape does not lie in a physical attack directed at sexual organs. A beating which included blows to sex organs would not constitute a form of rape, nor an attempt at rape. It is not rape to attack a person because of their sex, however common that may be as motivating rape.

What it means to say that rape involves sex is that rape is an attack on a person as a sexual being, it is an attack on a person through their sexuality. For that reason, in order for a rape to occur, it is necessary for there to be contact with the victim and for that contact to implicate the victim's body as sexualized, even if the contact need not take a definite and predetermined form.[18]

It is not obvious that rape is properly characterized as an abstract harm. Talk of set-backs to interests does seem to miss something rather important: the experiences of victims. Loss of autonomy is an odd way to refer to what is often a form of torture. Is there an experiential element intrinsic to rape? If there were such an element, it would matter very much to the choice of the proper account of the nature of rape.

I do not think there is an experiential element intrinsic to the harm of rape notwithstanding the factual connection between that harm and often seriously destructive experiences of vic-

tims.[19] Requiring an experiential element leads to serious problems. It requires that there in fact be *an* experience common to all cases of rape. It is clear that there is no common experience temporally extensional with the rape. A looser temporal connection will not remedy the lack. The experiences of rape victims vary significantly. Some victims are in states which preclude relevant experiences (the unconscious, for example). We should also have to exclude those cases where the victim does not have disfavored experiences.[20] Further, the experiential requirement raises serious barriers to a proper understanding of sexual oppression on a multicultural and historical basis.[21]

A focus on experience also leads to legal snares. If rape has an experiential core, then it is natural for evidentiary inquiries to permit, indeed encourage, investigation of a putative victim's experiences. The place in an inquiry into "how it felt" is then assured.[22]

Not placing an experiential element within the essential harm of rape should not be interpreted as discounting the importance of the experiences undergone in being raped. Rape can be, and often is, devastating. When we turn to the wrong of rape, we are turning, in part, to the harms as experienced. Experiences play a pivotal role in determining the moral status of cases and classes of rape, and are important in determining the appropriate assessment of the social role of rape.

A different aspect of the abstract nature of the harm of rape is that it is immune to inconsequentiality. That the victim does not suffer does not deny the rape. The harm accrues whether or not it is recognized by the victim or by others. In that sense, it is like a violation of political rights. The seriousness of the violation does not turn solely on how the violation is perceived, experienced, felt. There may be a serious violation despite a general failure of recognition or concern.

Several important things follow if victim experience is not intrinsic to rape. First, it means that we should expect that the social response to rape and to victims of rape, along with the psychology of the victims, will be variable. Second, it means that much of what makes rape, understood as social phenomena, wrong will depend on things other than the intrinsic nature of rape. In other words, the seriousness of instances of rape will vary. The background theories matter very much to how we evaluate instances and classes of cases of rape.

It may be helpful at this point to provide a fuller explanation of the nature of the four harms, and then to explain how it is they are so linked as to constitute rape.

Every person has an interest in determining for themselves, insofar as that is practically possible, certain substantive relations in and aspects of their lives. Among the relations are those concerned with sexual expression and experience. Sexuality, after all, is an important element in the formation of individual personality. In speaking of sexual self-determination, we assign to each person some substantial control over the means of and partners (if any) in that person's sexual life. Plainly in cases of rape, the interest in sexual self-determination is severely compromised.

Many will think sexual self-determination (as well as bodily integrity) no more than a partial and limited specification of the claims of autonomy. Doubtless self-determination is part of what is meant by autonomy. An autonomous agent is self-determining, but not merely. Autonomy requires the agent's choices to be consonant with and expressive of a rational and reasonable personality. An autonomous agent, for example, is not merely subject to her desires and preferences, but is able to shape those desires and preferences. Autonomy requires an active second order set of preferences.[23]

One way to understand the difference between autonomy and sexual self-determination is to notice that self-determination is consonant with (virtually) any set of sexual preferences and practices, while autonomy is not. Self-determination and autonomy need not be harmonious, and because there is the possibility of conflict, there is a need to understand separately the role each plays in rape. Sexual self-determination gives no grounds on which to question a choice to assume the role of a sexual slave, provided that the person in question in fact has the requisite set of desires and preferences. On the basis of autonomy, in contrast, there are grounds on which the legitimacy of such a choice may be doubted.

The interest in bodily integrity is, I think, relatively transparent. It is a precondition for autonomy, but is not itself a mere specification of autonomy. Alienation is the final sort of harm to be considered. In the present context, alienation takes the form of objectification, the reduction of an individual to what is only a fragment of their being.[24] The starkest form of alienation involved in such a case of rape is the treatment of the victim as a sexual body at the disposal of the aggressor. In this sort of case the victim is appropriated as a body (for a period of time), and hence reduced to a piece of property available for appropriation. There is, of course, a great deal more to be said about alienation, as there is about autonomy and sexual self-determination. But it is not necessary at this point to provide any more elaborate discussion.

These harms are inherent in rape in the sense that it is the presence of these harms which characterizes the generalizable core content of the act such that it is an instance of the class of rapes. Yet these harms are not what directly characterize the experience of rape. However, although they do not characterize the experience of rape, they lie at the conceptual basis of those experiences. The paradigmatic case of rape invokes thoughts of invasion, humiliation, degradation, loss of control. These are just the sorts of psychological results to be expected when there are serious compromises of the interests listed above. Incurring the harms is indicative of being subject to a more or less serious assault, and an assault characterized as sexual. The confluence of the harms distinguishes rape from (simple) assault, on the one side, and nonphysical sexual harassment on the other side. So the elements identified as the harms of rape are what may be thought of as abstract structural features of rape.

This account of the harm of rape is certainly congruent with the core cases of rape described earlier. The cases involving force or coercion will fall under this account without difficulty. The incomplete discussion lay in the difference between an account of rape as nonvoluntary sexual relations and as nonconsensual sexual relations. Consider again the case of intoxication. For the nonvoluntary account, rape occurs at a point much closer to unconsciousness. It is plain that much action undertaken while the agent is in the grip of strong intoxicants will count as voluntary.[25] But the action will not count as consensual. It cannot so count because the agent is unable to appreciate the nature of action or the risk of the conduct. Present capacity to reason and full appreciation of available relevant information is required for consensual activity. The difference here is in where the line is drawn.

In cases where the key factor is one of status (Case 5) the consensual model provides a better explanation of the prohibition and more accurately captures the harm involved. The important claim is that the individuals involved may all be capable of voluntary action without defeating the charge of rape. Children are not automatons who suddenly blossom at age 18 (or 14, etc.) into rational agents. They are quite capable of voluntary action at a very early age. This is reflected in a host of behavior patterns and attitudes directed at children. But the capacity for voluntary action is not the same as a capacity for consensual activity. It is also important to notice that under the approach I am suggesting we need not treat these as special cases.[26] The theoretical explanation of and justification for the treatment of these cases as cases of rape is organic and relatively straightforward. That is not so under alternative approaches.

The harm of rape is present as well in cases of fraud. The reasons for treating such cases as inconsistent with, or compromises of, the autonomy interests are somewhat different than in the preceding cases. These cases involve an agent exploiting misinformation, or purveying misinformation, with the aim of obtaining what would otherwise be unavailable. The fraud is in a certain way like inducing intoxication. In both cases the cognitive state of the victim is "impaired" in order to prevent an accurate assessment and expression of self-determination. The victim's interests are overridden for the benefit of another agent. In the case of fraud, what is gained is gained against the expected desires, intentions, wishes of the victim. The failure of effective consent is a way of expressing the determination to lodge control of these aspects of one's life in one's own hands, as far as that is possible. Clearly fraud defeats that aim. In defeating that aim, fraud conflicts with autonomy interests. Consequently we may say that such cases constitute a sort of case in which the harm of rape occurs. But this claim only follows from accepting effective consent as the guarantor of autonomy in sexual matters.

It may help to consider the differences among the accounts of rape on the basis of the protection of relevant interests: what interests are protected, and how well, by each of the accounts? Assume the four interests identified by the harms intrinsic to rape are the relevant interests (at least from the perspective of the victim). The first two accounts do afford some protection of those interests, but only rather weak protection because so narrowly circumscribed. With respect to the second two accounts, nonvoluntary and nonconsent, the choice may be framed by asking what interests the nonvoluntary account better provides for. It does not protect the interests noted in the harm discussion as well as the nonconsent account does. If it is to be recommended on this basis it would be because it better protects some *other* interests. But what might they be? An interest in obtaining sex through deception? An interest in exploiting others, or in taking advantage of naivete or vulnerability? An interest in encouraging mystification of sex and dishonesty in social relations? So not only does a nonvoluntary account afford less protection of (and hence demonstrate less concern for) the interests of victims, but does so by promoting interests of a rather dubious sort.

Background Theories Standard

A consent-based account of rape yields the best fit with relevant background theories. The relation between rape, in particular the harm of rape, and morality is discussed at some length in the next section of the paper and so has been set to one side for the moment. There are several other bases for establishing fit with background theories, and in each case a nonconsent model seems superior.

A nonconsent model of rape is consistent with two relevant aspects of legal theory and development. First, with respect to the history of Anglo-American rape law, an admittedly parochial standard, a consent-based account of rape works quite well. The development of rape law appears consistent with an interpretation of it as developing sophistication about the conditions of effective consent over sexual affairs. The shift of rape from a form of property crime to a crime against the person of the victim may be read in light of the improved legal status of women, the extension to women of full standing to control their own affairs.[27] The introduction of sex-neutral rape laws may be seen as recognition of the dependence of rape on issues of autonomy, self-determination, etc., which are themselves sex-neutral. More recent reforms with respect to limitations on defenses to charges of rape, introduction of explicit language making consent central to the crime of rape, and abandonment of the marital exemption, among others, can be understood in the same light.

Second, the emphasis on consent reflects a pervasive shift in legal doctrines.[28] In both civil and criminal law, there has been a marked shift away from a concern with effective consent in only special circumstances. Merely voluntary action no longer serves as the paradigm for action subject to legal constraint. Again, these are changes in only some legal systems, and the question of fit is limited as a result.

The consent-based account yields a reasonably good fit with the sociology of rape and important segments of the public response to issues of rape. For example, accurate surveys of the prevalence of rape (and related sexual wrongs) reflect a nonconsent conception.[29] Rape education programs not only rely explicitly on such an approach, but require it. A nonconsent standard is what is required to make sense of the need for (and effectiveness of) educating victims to the fact of victimization.

Theories of politics and social oppression, in particular as relevant to women, provide confirmation of the nonconsent account of rape.[30] A consent approach integrates effectively into a philosophical political liberalism, which places at the center of justificatory theory the autonomy of the individual.[31] Political legitimacy depends on consent of the governed, and hence the legitimacy of social institutions and practices are conditioned on the degree of effective consent the affected may be thought to have given (even if hypothetically). Assuming the interests protected are important, consensual control of sexual activities enhances autonomy. But it is not merely political liberalism that supports a nonconsent account of rape. The values which, as central parts of liberal political theory, assure fit with the suggested account of rape also play important roles in competing political theories. Marxist theory aims at the creation of a society of human flourishing and autonomy[32] which must surely place consen-

sual standards near the center of acceptable personal relations. Similar sorts of claims legitimately may be advanced with respect to a number of other approaches to political theory.[33]

RAPE, HARM, MORALITY

One unusual feature of the account of rape I have advanced is that there is not a straightforward identification of rape as an egregious evil. However, nothing I have said supports the inference that rape is not a very pressing social problem or the inference that normally rape is not a very serious evil. There are conceptually important reasons for identifying the nature of rape in a way which allows for the possibility described. But we cannot understand rape without attending to the relation between rape and morality, the relation between the harm which constitutes rape and a moral assessment of that harm.

There are four elements to the determination of the evil of rape. The first element concerns the assignment of answerability. The second element is the nature of the related violations of duties and commission of immoralities. The collateral duties violated in the course of the rape matter. The third element is that of felt harms. What are the psychological and physical effects of rape on the victim? The fourth element for assessing the evil of rape is the nature of systemic effects of the presence and pervasiveness of rape, and the ideological commitments which make sexual assault of particular significance. These elements require more detailed individual discussion.

Answerability

Briefly, answerability can be thought of as a measure of the degree of wrong involved in an act determined by the degree to which the wrong was intended by the agent involved. It is not that it is *only* wrong if the agent intended the act (under the description as wrong). The wrongness of the act is amplified by the degree to which the act was undertaken intentionally or deliberately. So deliberate rape shows a higher degree of moral corruption than does an accidental case. The wrong is greater because, in part, the agent displays a greater disregard for the victim and the demands of morality (as a general matter).

This is not to suggest that responsibility is simply a function of intent. The theory is that an agent may also be responsible for proceeding with risky conduct,[34] or failing to attend to context in appropriate ways.[35] But what I wish to emphasize here is just that consideration of the different ways in which we assign responsibility reflects differences in the degree of immorality. The agent may be more or less evil even where the harm is invariant.

The influence of established social norms is an important example here. It is clear that an act of rape may not violate behavioral norms; that is a contingent matter. Indeed, it may be that some norms encourage rape, at least as I have defined it. The presence of such norms will have an effect on the assessment of the particular acts related to it. Where it is not the case that women are (normally) accorded control over access to their bodies, we should have a different view of the responsibility of men for the rapes they commit than in social contexts in which women are accorded control over sexual access to their bodies.[36] The import may lie in another area, i. e., the systemic effect of rapes, their political content. In this light we may then see that social norms may both excuse (or mitigate the responsibility of) actors in particular instances of rape and yet exacerbate the problem of individual security (among other political issues).

Collateral Obligations

The second element which affects the nature of the evil of rape is the nature and degree of related obligations violated in the course of the rape. These are of various and quite distinct sorts. In some instances what is involved is the conduct by means of which the rape is effected. Obligations to refrain from attacks on others are commonly violated in the course of committing rape. These sorts of duties are stringent, and the evil of the rape is commensurately raised with the gravity of such violations. In addition to the wrongs involved in physical attacks on others, we should also include here constraints on infliction of psychological distress or trauma. There are, of course, various ways of expressing and cataloguing the host of wrongs of these sorts which may be involved.

Their implications seem, in any case, fairly plain.

But there are other quite important sorts of wrongs which may occur that are not likely to be captured under the constraints on inflicting pain or serious harms. There are, for example, also duties of information. Ignorance may be culpable after all.[37] We may do wrong when we act without appropriate inquiries regarding information or risk, or when we are insufficiently attentive to the information available to us. These wrongs have an independent status. They often play a role in the creation of serious risks or serious harms. They certainly play a complicating role in the assignment of responsibility for actions and outcomes. In the present circumstance, they take the form of a duty to inquire as to consent of sexual partners, or a duty to make reasonable efforts to assess claims or information.

I am not suggesting that this is a complete list of related duties. The point is rather that the importance and stringency of related duties has an effect on the assessment of the seriousness of the rape as it is confronted in life. The degree of evil of the rape is affected by the nature of wrongs committed in the course of the commission. As more stringent duties are violated, the rape rises in seriousness. In part this is so because these sorts of issues are indicia of the degree of moral corruption of the agent. Its place in a web of wrongdoing is therefore important, and these factors help measure that.

Experience

The third factor in assessing the evil of rape is what I have termed the consequences as felt harms. This is a somewhat misleading rubric, for there are three individualizable elements considered here. The first is such things as the psychological harms of the experience of rape. The fragmentation of personality, the creation of lasting fear, anxiety, etc., are measures of the seriousness of the consequences of the rape. As the causal nexus from which these debilitating effects flow, the rape may be judged by the import of these effects. As the victim's personality is deformed, the seriousness of the rape rises. These effects are constituted by the way in which the rape is experienced by the victim. I should also point out, once again, that some of these effects flow from the rape itself and some flow from the means used to effect the rape. We need not, and cannot, separate them at this stage because the victim need not separate them as experiential elements.

The second part of this factor in the seriousness of rape concerns the harms of autonomy. I have already discussed these harms in a fashion which indicated that I did not think of them as necessarily being wrongs. I do not wish to withdraw that characterization. I want instead to supplement it. Consider for a moment the somewhat different issue of exploitation and work. Work processes inevitably involve some exploitation of those who perform the work. I think this true of all work processes presently feasible. But I need not therefore hold that work *always* involves moral wrong. Exploitation is not a proper subset of immorality. The degree of exploitation matters to an assessment of the wrongness of the work process. Where the exploitation is trivial (or perhaps relatively so), there is no wrong. Wrong comes once the level of exploitation is serious.

The third element is that of the physical costs inflicted on the victim. The bruises, contusions, broken bones, mutilation, the further complications of possible pregnancy or contraction of sexually transmitted diseases (among other sorts of infections), etc., all constitute further substantial harms of moral significance.

Systemic Effects

The final element to be discussed is that of systemic effects of rape. Up to this point the discussion has proceeded on the basis of consideration of particular instances. But patterns of conduct are important as well as the individual acts which constitute the patterns. The systemic effects of rape, and responses to rape, are quite important and play an informative and valuable role in analyses of systems of social domination, especially as related to systems of gender or sex domination. Part of the evil of rape is its political role. The question is not just how particular acts, considered in isolation, are responded to, but also the nature and extent of protection or respect accorded to individual sexual autonomy. It is a different social world when there are isolated cases of rape from the world where rape is prevalent or within accepted social norms of interaction. The patterns

of treatment and action have conditioning effects on the persons in the context of consideration.

Rape, like most forms of interactions, has social content beyond the individuals involved in particular instances, and the overall pattern generates effects autonomous of the individual acts of the pattern. So women and men may be conditioned to respond to only certain sorts of cases as legitimate cases of rape, and to consider other cases of rape as acceptable forms of sexual interaction. Such patterns matter in two ways. They affect assessments of individual participants, and guide the assessment of the social system as a whole. The two levels of assessment are distinct.

It is attention to patterns of conduct in addition to the particular instances that allows us to talk sensibly about such matters as institutional racism and sexism.[38] In the present case, the pattern of rape will itself play an important part in understanding the nature and degree of sexism embedded in the organizational core of a society. Further, such patterns play a very important role in shaping responses to the problems of controlling rape and in improving responses to victims.

Thus the assessment of the evil of rape proceeds on two levels. On the one hand, we have various factors to be considered in speaking of the evil of particular cases of rape. On the other hand, we also must attend to the social context of the occurrence of rape, the systemic role and effects of practices which control or encourage rape. It is both personal and political corruption that is involved in rape, and our knowledge of the evil is similarly doubled.

SOME IMPLICATIONS AND OBJECTIONS

The account of rape advanced here has a number of implications which are likely to cause resistance. The nonconsent account of rape clearly entails some disturbing descriptions of many ordinary sexual relationships. Intoxication, for example, plays a large and widely accepted part in seduction and courtship. Under the present account, where there is intoxication, the capacity to give effective consent is compromised and, consequently, we may pass over from seduction to rape.[39] Indeed, on this account, it is entirely proper to speak of mutual rape where (at least) two individuals engage in sexual relations while intoxicated.[40] I can see no way to avoid such an outcome, but neither does it seem to me particularly bothersome. In the first place, the claim is not, in such cases, that there must have been some terrible evil done.[41] These are cases of rape, but ones of much diminished significance. Indeed, it is such cases as these that illustrate the value of separating the nature of rape from the moral assessment of rape. There is no need to consider this sort of case as a candidate for legal intervention.

In the second place, it is important to see that there is a natural path that links rape to other sexual activities.[42] There is no doubt that adoption of a nonconsent view of rape opens very serious debates about acceptable conduct, excusable conduct, and the like. But is identification of risky conduct as risky really objectionable? A failure to see the continuum here complicates the task of identifying the socially systemic workings of sexual differentiations and domination. It makes seeing the connections between kinds of rape and other forms of sexual interactions far more difficult. That is an obscurity which we are only beginning to dissipate, and of which the failure to notice has perpetuated serious harms.[43]

On first look, it would also appear that in widening the scope of rape, we would be condemning a proportionately large segment of the population for committing what is usually a fairly serious wrong. The complaint is that there are too many wrongdoers. The idea behind the complaint is that we would end up condemning unduly large numbers of men and women (although mainly the former I would expect) for committing the crime of rape when they lacked the requisite intentional states for the claim of responsibility to be justified. This complaint is the result of a misunderstanding. Because the scope of instances of rape is expanded, it does not follow that the range of those fully responsible (those to be punished by law, e. g.) must also expand.

Delineating the conditions of responsibility is a difficult task, and one that is properly sensitive to a number of factors in addition to causal roles. One factor that assignments of responsibility depend on is the purpose of the assignment (we should have different concerns when the point is imprisonment of wrongdoers than when the point is verbal admonition or is statistical analysis). Another set of factors concern the evidence available about a particular case, and the reasonableness of the beliefs and actions of the relevant agents. It is worth emphasizing that answerability and responsibility are not univocal concepts, but rather matters of complex and subtle gradations and kinds.

It may also be objected that the case developed here is not for a nonconsent account of rape as much as it is a case for multiple concepts of rape. That objection might be put in the following way. Grant that the only account of rape that covers all six categories of cases is the nonconsent account. Nevertheless the nonconsent account itself has some surprising and troublesome implications (e.g., the mutual rape case discussed above). The reason for this is that the net is being cast too widely. We can do better by admitting that there are several concepts of rape. By splitting the categories of cases we may more fully and accurately account for both our present intuitions and social practices regarding rape without including the problematic implications of the nonconsent account.

The distinctiveness, according to the objector, of rape as a crime turns on its experience by victims. The experiences are most clearly captured in thinking of rape as sex occurring against the will of the victim. This "against the will" concept of rape is the fundamental concept underlying the law.[44] There are acceptable counterfactual extensions available sufficient to provide coverage of cases of incapacity. The cases left out are handled by development of a status concept, one which takes the prohibitions on sexual activities involving children (and certain others) as manifesting a distinct set of concerns—partly paternalistic, partly prohibitions on seriously exploitive conduct.

This approach misconceives the nature of rape. Placing an experiential element at the center of the concept of rape has pernicious consequences, as I have already argued. Furthermore, maintaining such an experiential element requires treating rape in an anomalous fashion. There is no similar experiential element to homicide or theft or even battery. More importantly, the experiential claim is grounded in a parochial understanding of the nature and problems of rape. It presumes a set of deeply ahistorical human reactions and psychology. It reifies present social relations and their effects.

What seems to be occurring in the effort to identify rape with how it is experienced is a conflation of cause and effect. There is no doubting that rape occasions seriously disfavored experiences on a regular basis. But those are effects of the rape in a given historical context. The significance of rape changes with the context.

Rape understood as sex against the will of the victim is a notion ambiguous in several ways. First, acts against the will fall across the distinct categories of coercion, nonvoluntary, and nonconsensual acts. In the archaic language of will, what seems to be invoked is the idea of (at least internal) resistance.[45] Indeed, the idea of the against the will account leads to standards of resistance as relevant to the question of the occurrence of a rape. It should not be necessary to detail the reasons why that is a defect.

The will account must be understood so as to provide for counterfactual cases if it is to be at all plausible. The thought is that just as there is a sense in which surgery on an unconscious or intoxicated person may be (counterfactually) against the will of the person, so too may sex. Thus many cases of rape relying on incapacity can be accommodated by the will account. However, this effort to extend the will account fails because it demonstrates a confusion at its heart. The difficulty is that the counterfactual

analogies are properly formed only with respect to consent and not will. The medical cases concern questions of consent, not questions of will. The development of proxy and implied consent theories in medicine are not disguised theories of proxy will or implied will. The counterfactual analysis simply adopts that of consent, renaming it along the way. So in those cases which rely on a counterfactual analysis, the nonconsent account of rape is to be preferred on grounds of simplicity.

Insofar as rape involves compromise of interests in sexual self-determination, it is logically independent of victim will. Consider the case where the victim lacks independence. On the will account, this person cannot be raped. There is no counterfactual extension to this sort of case. It is not like intoxication cases where we may sensibly speak of what the person would have desired had she not been intoxicated. In the present example, it is susceptible to counterfactual analysis by substituting for the victim. But then, what is the sense of adhering to the language of will? What we are concerned with is the victim's consent, a matter which is free of experiential requirements. In fact, attending to the way in which the counterfactual cases must all be handled under the will account displays the degree to which it is parasitic on a nonconsent theory. The conclusion we should draw is that the language of will hinders understanding rape. It is best thought of as a stand-in for an analysis of rape as nonconsensual sex. Rape is nonconsensual sex.[46]

NOTES

1. E.g., Susan Estrich, *Real Rape* (Cambridge: Harvard University Press, 1986), discusses and criticizes current legal treatment of rape, but does not offer an analysis of the nature of rape. At 8 Estrich offers a traditional common law definition which is ambiguous among force, coercion, and involuntary accounts (discussed below . . .), but at 102–3 relies on a nonconsent account. See also, e. g., Vivian Berger, "Man's Trial, Woman's Tribulation: Rape Cases in the Courtroom," *Columbia Law Review,* vol. 77 (1977), pp. 1–104; Leigh Beinen, "Mistake," *Philosophy and Public Affairs,* vol. 7 (1978), pp. 224–45; Leigh Beinen and Hubert Field, *Jurors and Rape* (Lexington: Lexington Books, 1980); Toni Pickard, "Culpable Mistake and Rape: Relating Mens Rea to Crime," *University of Toronto Law Journal,* vol. 30 (1980), pp. 75–98.

In the nonlegal literature the situation is similar. Susan Brownmiller, *Against Our Will: Men, Women and Rape* (New York: Simon & Schuster, 1975), has no explicit discussion of the topic (although she seems to have a nonconsent model in mind; pp. 8 & 301). See also Diana E. H. Russell, *The Politics of Rape* (New York: Stein & Day, 1975) and *Rape in Marriage* (New York: Macmillan, 1982); Susan Griffin, "Rape: The All-American Crime," and Pamela Foa, "What's Wrong with Rape," both in Mary Vetterling-Braggin *et al.* (eds.), *Feminism and Philosophy* (Totowa: Roman & Littlefield, 1977), pp. 313–32 and 347–59 respectively.

2. The facts about enforcement of rape laws support the idea that there are those four possible accounts. See Estrich, *op. cit.,* for an excellent discussion of current legal standards regarding rape. The traditional common law definition is "a man commits rape when he engages in intercourse . . . with a woman not his wife, by force or threat of force, against her will and without her consent." Such a definition is ambiguous among all four definitions canvassed here. As Estrich and others have shown, the operative definition is usually force, or sometimes coercion.

3. Force remains the usual definitional requirement in U.S. jurisdictions. See Leigh Beinen and Hubert Field, *op. cit.*

4. The Model Penal Code defines rape as sexual intercourse where a man "compels [a woman] to submit by force or threat of imminent death, serious bodily injury, extreme pain or kidnapping, to be inflicted on anyone." MPC sec. 213.1.

5. See Alan Wertheimer, *Coercion* (Princeton: Princeton University Press, 1987), and Joel Feinberg, *Harm to Self* (New York: Oxford University Press, 1986), Chapters 23 and 24, for general discussions.

6. This view may lie behind the common use of "against the will" language in legal definitions of rape. See Cal. Pen. Code Section 261.(1), (3), (4). See also Feinberg, *Harm to Self,* Chapter 20.

7. See Cal. Pen. Code 261.6. See also Feinberg, *op cit.*, Chapter 22, for general discussion of consent in criminal law context.

8. See Estrich, *op cit.*

9. For examples of such substitution, see *Reidhead v. State* 31 Ariz. 70, 250 P. 366 (1926); *Salerno v. State* 162 Neb. 99, 75 N. W. 2d 362 (1956).

10. In particular the argument below assumes that instances of Case 5 concern children (up to about age 12), rather than adolescents.

11. That is not a requirement even for adults. In many cases, it is clear that normal adults act without full understanding of action and are properly held responsible for their conduct.

12. Although the account of rape I urge is sex-neutral, realism about social facts leads me to identify perpetrators as male and victims as female.

13. *State v. Ely* 114 Wash. 185, 194 N. W. 988 (1921); *Eberhardt v. State* 134 Ind. 651, 34 N. E. 637 (1893).

14. *Crosswell v. People* 13 Mich. 427 (1865); *State v. Shephard* 7 Conn. 54 (1828); *Regina v. Dee* 15 Cox C. C. 579 (1884); MPC section 213.1(2).

15. *State v. Williams* 128 N. C. 573, 37 S. E. 952 (1901).

16. See also Catharine MacKinnon, *Feminism Unmodified* (Cambridge: Harvard University Press, 1987), pp. 87–88.

17. The other related harms are discussed . . . below.

18. I do not think a requirement of penetration is necessary for rape. See Janice Moulton, "Sexual Behavior: Another Position," in Alan Soble (ed.), *The Philosophy of Sex* (Totowa: Rowman & Littlefield, 1980), pp. 110–18.

19. For a contrary view, see MacKinnon, *op. cit.*, at 82.

20. Peculiarities of individual psychology should not stand as an obstacle to understanding and properly identifying whether the person has been raped. It is instructive to consider the lives of Celine and Foucault here.

21. I have in mind particularly cases of effective and extensive socialization such that, e. g., women are considered and consider themselves primarily as sexual and reproductive property, hence finding nothing objectionable in treatment amounting to systematic and continuous rape. See Paola Tabet, "Hands, Tools, Weapons," *Feminist Issues,* vol. 2 (1982), pp. 3–62, and "Imposed Reproduction: Maimed Sexuality, " *Feminist Issues,* vol. 7 (1987), pp. 3–31; Nicole-Claude Mathieu, "Biological Paternity, Social Maternity," *Feminist Issues,* vol. 4 (1984), pp. 63–71; Colette Guillaumin, "The Practice of Power and Belief in Nature, Part I: The Appropriation of Women," *Feminist Issues,* vol. 1 (1981), pp. 3–28.

22. Leaving experience outside the core account of rape would not constitute a legal anomaly. After all, it is not *experience* which defines the core harms of homicide, theft, battery, slavery (peonage). Mistreatment and disfavored experiences certainly aggravate the evil of slavery, but they are not essential to the nature of slavery.

23. See John Christman, "Constructing the Inner Citadel: Recent Work on Autonomy," *Ethics,* vol. 99 (Fall 1988), pp. 109–24.

24. See Sandra Bartky, "Narcissism, Femininity and Alienation," *Social Theory and Practice,* vol. 8 (1982), pp. 127–44; Alison Jaggar, *Feminist Politics and Human Nature* (Totowa: Rowman & Allenheld, 1983).

25. At least that is the entrenched view in U. S., U. K., and related jurisdictions. *D.P.P. v. Majewski* 2 A11 E. R. 142 (1976); Cal. Pen. Code Section 22. See also Jerome Hall, *General Principles of Criminal Law* (Indianapolis: Bobbs-Merrill, 1960), p. 537; George Fletcher, *Rethinking Criminal Law* (Boston: Little, Brown, 1980), Section 10.4.5; Douglas Husak, *Philosophy of Criminal Law* (Totowa: Rowman & Littlefield, 1987), pp. 53–56.

26. See also John Crewdson, *By Silence Betrayed* (Boston: Little, Brown, 1988), on child sexual abuse. There are interesting differences in the language commonly used in describing child cases. "Rape" seems largely confined to post-pubescent (female) victim cases, and other cases are called "molestation" despite the fact that identical conduct is involved.

27. The importance of consent can also be seen by considering American laws regarding interracial sex in historical perspective. See A. Leon Higginbotham, Jr., and Barbara K. Kopytoff, "Racial Purity and Interracial Sex in the Law of Colonial and Antebellum Virginia," *The Georgetown Law Journal,* vol. 77 (1989), pp. 2007–2029.

28. See Lucinda Vandervoort, "Social Justice in the Modern Regulatory State: Duress, Necessity, and the Consensual Model in Law," *Law and Philosophy,* vol. 6 (1987), pp. 205–25.

29. See Diana Russell, *Rape in Marriage; Secret Trauma: Incest in the Lives of Girls and Women* (New York: Basic Books, 1986), e. g., p. 23; *Sexual Exploitation: Rape, Child Abuse, and Workplace Harassment* (Beverly Hills: Sage Publications, 1984).

30. See, e. g., Monique Wittig, "Social Contract," *Feminist Issues,* vol. 9 (1989), pp. 3–12.

31. See, among others, John Rawls, *A Theory of Justice* (Cambridge: Harvard University Press, 1973).

32. See Jon Elster, *Making Sense of Marx,* Chapter 9; Allen Buchanan, *Marx and Justice* (Totowa: Rowman & Littlefield, 1982); Paul Hughes, *Marx and Morality* (Ph.D. Dissertation, University of Illinois at Chicago, 1985).

33. See, e. g., John Finnis, *Natural Law and Natural Rights* (Oxford: Oxford University Press, 1980); David Miller, *Anarchism* (London: J. W. Dent, 1984); John Stuart Mill, *On Liberty* (Indianapolis: Hackett Publishing Company, 1978).

34. Model Penal Code Sect. 2.02(2) (c). See George Fletcher, *Rethinking Criminal Law,* Sections 4.3, 6. 6.6, and 8.3; Alan White, *Grounds of Liability* (Oxford: Clarendon Press, 1984), Chapter 7 (especially 105–11, 94–99).

35. See Alan White, *op. cit.*, Chapter 7; Toni Pickard, *op. cit.*, and "Culpable Mistake and Rape: Harsh Words on Pappajohn," *University of Toronto Law Journal*, vol. 30 (1980), pp. 415–20; Holly Smith "Culpable Ignorance," *The Philosophical Review*, vol. 92 (1983), pp. 543–72; Douglas Husak, *op. cit.*, p. 54.

36. This does not entail claiming the rape is less important for prevalence of occurrence, but that we should assess differently the actions of particular individuals in light of prevailing social norms. I iterate that victims of rape may be of either sex, and so too the perpetrators. In fact, nevertheless, men are disproportionately perpetrators.

37. See Holly Smith, *op. cit.*, and A. D. Woozley, "Negligence and Ignorance," *Philosophy*, vol. 53 (1978), pp. 293–306.

38. See Richard Wasserstrom, "Racism and Sexism" and "Preferential Treatment" in *Philosophy and Social Issues* (Notre Dame: University of Notre Dame Press, 1980).

39. Where the intoxicants are used as performance enhancers, it is likely still seduction. Where the use replaces judgment we move towards rape.

40. But no odder than the possibility for mutual battery or mutual homicide, to name two.

41. An account of rape is *not* an account of bad sex. Cf. Lois Pineau, "Date Rape: A Feminist Analysis," *Law and Philosophy*, vol. 8 (1989), pp. 217–43. I also do not think that it is psychological states of participants that determine whether or not there has been a rape. There is nothing wrong, after all, in speaking of a person as not knowing that they were raped although conscious at the relevant times.

42. A point stressed by MacKinnon, among others. See Catharine MacKinnon, "Sexuality, Pornography, and Method," *Ethics*, vol. 99 (1989), pp. 314–46, esp. 335–41.

43. Part of the difficulties associated with intelligent discussion of child sexual abuse lies here. Freud's failure with respect to the "child seduction" theory (which is not about seduction anyway) is instructive. See J. M. Masson, *The Assault on Truth: Freud's Suppression of the Seduction Theory* (New York: Farrar, Straus & Giroux, 1984); J. Herman, *Father–Daughter Incest* (Cambridge: Harvard University Press, 1981).

44. This approach treats rape as fundamentally a violent, rather than a sexual act. See MacKinnon, "Sexuality, Pornography, and Method," p. 323.

45. See *People v. Berschneider* 89 Daily Journal D.A.R. 7208, where the requirement is met by an apparently effortless movement of the victim's hand. In such cases, it is the clear lack of consent rather than anything about the victim's will that constitutes the rape.

46. I am grateful to Carola Mone for enlightening conversations and comments on earlier versions of this work. I also owe thanks to Sandra Bartky, John Christman, Jeffrey Murphy, Karen Snell, and Monique Wittig. I have benefited from comments by the audience when this material was presented at the Central Division of the APA, University of Colorado, Florida State, Indiana University, San Francisco State, UC Davis, and USC.

III

Erotic Love

PLATO

Symposium

In your oration, my dear Agathon, I think that you were certainly right in proposing to speak of the nature of Love first and afterwards of his works—that is a way of beginning which I very much approve. And as you have set forth his nature with such stately eloquence, may I ask you further, Whether Love is by his nature the love of something or of nothing? And here I must explain myself: I do not want you to say that Love is the love of a father or the love of a mother—that would be ridiculous; but to answer as you would, if I asked, Is a father a father of something? to which you would find no difficulty in replying, of a son or daughter: and the answer would be right.

Very true, said Agathon.

And you would say the same of a mother?

He assented.

Yet let me ask you one more question in order to illustrate my meaning: Is not a brother to be regarded essentially as a brother of something?

Certainly, he replied.

That is, of a brother or sister?

Yes, he said.

And now, said Socrates, I will ask about Love:—Is Love of something or of nothing?

Of something, surely, he replied.

Keep in mind what this is, and tell me what I want to know—whether Love desires that of which love is.

Yes, surely.

And does he possess, or does he not possess, that which he loves and desires?

Probably not, I should say.

Nay, replied Socrates, I would have you consider whether "necessarily" is not rather the word. The inference that he who desires something is lacking in that thing, and that he who does not desire a thing is not in lack of it, is in my judgement, Agathon, absolutely and necessarily true. What do you think?

I agree with you, said Agathon.

Very good. Would he who is great, desire to be great, or he who is strong, desire to be strong?

That would be inconsistent with our previous admissions.

True. For he who has those qualities cannot be lacking in them?

Very true.

Suppose that a man being strong desired to be strong, or being swift desired to be swift, or being healthy desired to be healthy,—since in that case he might be thought to desire something which he already has or is, I refer to the point in order that we may not be led astray—you will see on reflection that the possessors of these qualities must have their respective advantages at the time, whether they choose or not; and who can desire that which he has? Therefore, when a person says, I am well and wish to be well, or I am rich and wish to be rich, and I desire to have exactly what I have—to him we shall reply: "You, my friend, having wealth and health and strength, want to have the continuance of them; for at this moment, whether you choose or no, you have them. And when you say, I desire that which I have and nothing else, is not your meaning that you want to have in the future what you have at present?" He must agree with us—must he not?

He must, replied Agathon.

Then, said Socrates, he desires that what he has at present may be preserved to him in the future, which is equivalent to saying that he desires something which is non-existent to him, and which as yet he has not got?

Very true, he said.

Then he and everyone who desires, desires

From *The Dialogues of Plato*, trans. Benjamin Jowett. Oxford: Oxford University Press, 1920.

that which he has not already, and which is future and not present, and which he has not, and is not, and which he lacks;—these are the sort of things which love and desire seek?

Very true, he said.

Then now, said Socrates, let us recapitulate the argument. First, is not love of something, and of something too which is wanting to a man?

Yes, he replied.

Remember further what you said in your speech, or if you like I will remind you: you said that the love of the beautiful set in order the empire of the gods, for that of deformed things there is no love—did you not say something of that kind?

Yes, said Agathon.

Yes, my friend, and the remark was a just one. And if this is true, love is the love of beauty and not of deformity?

He assented.

And the admission has been already made that love is of something which one lacks and has not?

True, he said.

Then Love lacks and has not beauty?

Certainly, he replied.

And would you call that beautiful which lacks beauty and does not possess it in any way?

Certainly not.

Then would you still say that Love is beautiful?

Agathon replied: I fear that I said what I did without understanding.

Indeed, you made a very good speech, Agathon, replied Socrates; but there is yet one small question which I would fain ask:—Is not the good also the beautiful?

Yes.

Then in lacking the beautiful, love lacks also the good?

I cannot refute you, Socrates, said Agathon:—Be it as you say.

Say rather, beloved Agathon, that you cannot refute the truth; for Socrates is easily refuted.

And now, taking my leave of you, I will rehearse a tale of love which I heard from Diotima of Mantinea,[1] a woman wise in this and many other kinds of knowledge, who in the days of old, when the Athenians offered sacrifice before the coming of the plague, delayed the disease ten years. She was my instructress in the art of love, and I shall try to repeat to you what she said to me, beginning with the propositions on which Agathon and I are agreed; I will do the best I can do without any help.[2] As you, Agathon, suggested,[3] it is proper to speak first of the being and nature of Love, and then of his works. (I think it will be easiest for me if in recounting my conversation with the wise woman I follow its actual course of question and answer.) First I said to her in nearly the same words which he used to me, that Love was a mighty god, and likewise fair; and she proved to me, as I proved to him, that by my own showing Love was neither fair nor good. "What do you mean, Diotima," I said, "is Love then evil and foul?" "Hush," she cried; "must that be foul which is not fair?" "Certainly," I said. "And is that which is not wise, ignorant? do you not see that there is a mean between wisdom and ignorance?" "And what may that be?" I said. "Right opinion," she replied; "which, as you know, being incapable of giving a reason, is not knowledge (for how can knowledge be devoid of reason?) nor again ignorance (for neither can ignorance attain the truth), but is clearly something which is a mean between ignorance and wisdom." "Quite true," I replied. "Do not then insist," she said, "that what is not fair is of necessity foul, or what is not good evil; or infer that because Love is not fair and good he is therefore foul and evil; for he is in a mean between them." "Well," I said, "Love is surely admitted by all to be a great god." "By those who know or by those who do not know?" "By all." "And how, Socrates," she said with a smile, "can Love be acknowledged to be a great god by those who say that he is not a god at all?" "And who are they?" I said. "You and I are two of them," she replied. "How can that be?" I said. "It is quite intelligible," she replied; "for you yourself would acknowledge that the gods are happy and fair—of course you would—would you dare to say that any god was not?" "Certainly not," I replied. "And you mean by the happy, those who are the possessors of things good and things fair?" "Yes." "And you admitted that Love, because he was in want, desires those good and fair things of which he is in want?" "Yes, I did." "But how can he be a god who has no portion in what is good and fair?" "Impossible." "Then you see that you also deny the divinity of Love."

"What then is Love?" I asked; "Is he mortal?" "No." "What then?" "As in the former instance, he is neither mortal nor immortal, but in a mean between the two." "What is he, Diotima?" "He is a great spirit ($\delta\alpha\iota\mu\omega\nu$), and like all spirits he is intermediate between the divine and the mortal." "And what," I said, "is his power?" "He interprets between gods and men, conveying and taking across to the gods the prayers and sacrifices of men, and to men the commands of the gods and the benefits they return; he is the mediator who spans the chasm which divides them, and therefore by him the universe is bound together, and through him the arts of the prophet and the priest, their sacrifices and mysteries and charms, and all prophecy and incantation, find their way. For God mingles not with man; but through Love all the intercourse and converse of gods with men, whether they be awake or asleep, is carried on. The wisdom which understands this is spiritual; all other wisdom, such as that of arts and handicrafts, is mean and vulgar. Now these spirits or intermediate powers are many and diverse, and one of them is Love." "And who," I said, "was his father, and who his mother?" "The tale," she said, "will take time; nevertheless I will tell you. On the day when Aphrodite was born there was a feast of all the gods, among them the god Poros or Plenty, who is the son of Metis or Sagacity. When the feast was over, Penia or Poverty, as the manner is on such occasions, came about the doors to beg. Now Plenty, who was the worse for nectar (there was no wine in those days), went into the garden of Zeus and fell into a heavy sleep; and Poverty considering that for her there was no plenty, plotted to have a child by him, and accordingly she lay down at his side and conceived Love, who partly because he is naturally a lover of the beautiful, and because Aphrodite is herself beautiful, and also because he was begotten during her birthday feast, is her follower and attendant. And as his parentage is, so also are his fortunes. In the first place he is always poor, and anything but tender and fair, as the many imagine him; and he is rough and squalid, and has no shoes, nor a house to dwell in; on the bare earth exposed he lies under the open heaven, in the streets, or at the doors of houses, taking his rest; and like his mother he is always in distress. Like his father too, whom he also partly resembles, he is always plotting

against the fair and good; he is bold, enterprising, strong, a mighty hunter, always weaving some intrigue or other, keen in the pursuit of wisdom, fertile in resources; a philosopher at all times, terrible as an enchanter, sorcerer, sophist. He is by nature neither mortal nor immortal, but alive and flourishing at one moment when he is in plenty, and dead at another moment in the same day, and again alive by reason of his father's nature. But that which is always flowing in is always flowing out, and so he is never in want and never in wealth; and, further, he is in a mean between ignorance and knowledge. The truth of the matter is this: No god is a philosopher or seeker after wisdom, for he is wise already; nor does any man who is wise seek after wisdom. Neither do the ignorant seek after wisdom; for herein is the evil of ignorance, that he who is neither a man of honour nor wise is nevertheless satisfied with himself: there is no desire when there is no feeling of want." "But who then, Diotima," I said, "are the lovers of wisdom, if they are neither the wise nor the foolish?" "A child may answer that question," she replied; "they are those who are in a mean between the two; Love is one of them. For wisdom is a most beautiful thing, and Love is of the beautiful; and therefore Love is also a philosopher or lover of wisdom, and being a lover of wisdom is in a mean between the wise and the ignorant. And of this, too, his birth is the cause; for his father is wealthy and wise, and his mother poor and foolish. Such, my dear Socrates, is the nature of the spirit Love. The error in your conception of him was very natural; from what you say yourself, I infer that it arose because you thought that) Love is that which is loved, not that which loves; and for that reason, I think, Love appeared to you supremely beautiful. For the beloved is the truly beautiful, and delicate, and perfect, and blessed; but the active principle of love is of another nature, and is such as I have described."

I said: "O thou stranger woman, thou sayest well; but, assuming Love to be such as you say, what is the use of him to men?" "That, Socrates," she replied, "I will attempt to unfold: of his nature and birth I have already spoken; and you acknowledge that love is of the beautiful. But someone will say: What does it consist in, Socrates and Diotima?—or rather let me put the question more clearly, and ask: When a man loves the beautiful, what does his love desire?" I answered her "That the beautiful may be his." "Still," she said, "the answer suggests a further question: What is given by the possession of beauty?" "To what you have asked," I replied, "I have no answer ready." "Then," she said, "let me put the word 'good' in the place of the beautiful, and repeat the question once more: If he who loves loves the good, what is it then that he loves?" "The possession of the good." "And what does he gain who possesses the good?" "Happiness," I replied; "there is less difficulty in answering that question." "Yes," she said, "the happy are made happy by the acquisition of good things. Nor is there any need to ask why a man desires happiness; the answer is already final." "You are right," I said. "And is this wish and this desire common to all? and do all men always desire their own good, or only some men?—what say you?" "All men," I replied; "the desire is common to all." "Why, then," she rejoined, "are not all men, Socrates, said to love, but only some of them? whereas you say that all men are always loving the same things." "I myself wonder," I said, "why this is." "There is nothing to wonder at," she replied; "the reason is that one part of love is separated off and receives the name of the whole, but the other parts have other names." "Give an illustration," I said. She answered me as follows: "There is creative activity which, as you know, is complex and manifold. All that causes the passage of non-being into being is a 'poesy' or creation, and the processes of all art are creative; and the masters of arts are all poets or creators." "Very true." "Still," she said, "you know that they are not called poets, but have other names; only that one portion of creative activity which is separated off from the rest, and is concerned with music and metre, is called by the name of the whole and is termed poetry, and they who possess poetry in this sense of the word are called poets." "Very true," I said. "And the same holds of love. For you may say generally that all desire of good and happiness is only the great and subtle power of love; but they who are drawn towards him by any other path, whether the path of money-making or gymnastics or philosophy, are not called lovers—the name of the whole is appropriated to those whose desire takes one form only—they alone are said to love, or to be lovers," "I dare say," I

replied, "that you are right." "Yes," she added, "and you hear people say that lovers are seeking for their other half; but I say that they are seeking neither for the half of themselves, nor for the whole, unless the half or the whole be also a good; men will cut off their own hands and feet and cast them away, if they think them evil. They do not, I imagine, each cling to what is his own, unless perchance there be someone who calls what belongs to him the good, and what belongs to another the evil; for there is nothing which men love but the good. Is there anything?" "Certainly, I should say, that there is nothing." "Then," she said, "the simple truth is, that men love the good." "Yes," I said. "To which must be added that they love the possession of the good?" "Yes, that must be added." "And not only the possession, but the everlasting possession of the good?" "That must be added too." "Then love," she said, "may be described generally as the love of the everlasting possession of the good?" "That is most true."

"Then if this be always the nature of love, can you tell me further," she went on, "what is the manner of the pursuit? what are they doing who show all this eagerness and heat which is called love? and what is the object which they have in view? Answer me." "Nay, Diotima," I replied, "if I knew, I should not be wondering at your wisom, neither should I come to learn from you about this very matter." "Well," she said, "I will teach you:—The object which they have in view is birth in beauty, whether of body or soul." "I do not understand you" I said; "The oracle requires an explanation." "I will make my meaning clearer," she replied. "I mean to say, that all men are bringing to the birth in their bodies and in their souls. There is a certain age at which human nature is desirous of procreation—procreation which must be in beauty and not in deformity. The union of man and woman is a procreation; it is a divine thing, for conception and generation are an immortal principle in the mortal creature, and in the inharmonious they can never be. But the deformed is inharmonious with all divinity, and the beautiful harmonious. Beauty, then, is the destiny or goddess of parturition who presides at birth, and therefore, when approaching beauty, the procreating power is propitious, and expansive, and benign, and bears and produces fruit: at the sight of ugliness she frowns and contracts and has a sense of pain, and turns away, and shrivels up, and not without a pang refrains from procreation. And this is the reason why, when the hour of procreation comes, and the teeming nature is full, there is such a flutter and ecstasy about beauty whose approach is the alleviation of the bitter pain of travail. For love, Socrates, is not, as you imagine, the love of the beautiful only." "What then?" "The love of generation and of birth in beauty." "Yes," I said. "Yes, indeed," she replied. "But why of generation? Because to the mortal creature, generation is a sort of eternity and immortality, and if, as has been already admitted, love is of the everlasting possession of the good, all men will necessarily desire immortality together with good: whence it must follow that love is of immortality."

All this she taught me at various times when she spoke of love. And I remember her once saying to me, "What is the cause, Socrates, of love, and the attendant desire? See you not how all animals, birds as well as beasts, in their desire of procreation, are in agony when they take the infection of love, which begins with the desire of union and then passes to the care of offspring, on whose behalf the weakest are ready to battle against the strongest even to the uttermost, and to die for them, and will let themselves be tormented with hunger, or make any other sacrifice, in order to maintain their young. Man may be supposed to act thus from reason; but why should animals have these passionate feelings? Can you tell me why?" Again I replied that I did not know. She said to me: "And do you expect ever to become a master in the art of love, if you do not know this?" "But I have told you already, Diotima, that my ignorance is the reason why I come to you, for I am conscious that I want a teacher; tell me then the cause of this and of the other mysteries of love." "Marvel not," she said, "if you believe that love is of the immortal, as we have several times acknowledged; for here again, and on the same principle too, the mortal nature is seeking as far as is possible to be everlasting and immortal: and this is only to be attained by generation, because generation always leaves behind a new and different existence in the place of the old. Nay, even in the life of the same individual there is succession and not absolute uniformity: a man is called the same, and yet in the interval between youth and age, during which every animal is said to have life and identity, he is undergoing a perpetual process of loss and reparation—hair, flesh, bones, blood, and the whole body are always changing. Which is true not only of the body, but also of the soul, whose habits, tempers, opinions, desires, pleasures, pains, fears, never remain the same in any one of us, but are always coming and going. What is still more surprising, it is equally true of science; not only do some of the sciences come to life in our minds, and others die away, so that we are never the same in regard to them either: but the same fate happens to each of them individually. For what is implied in the word 'recollection', but the departure of knowledge, which is ever being forgotten, and is renewed and preserved by recollection, and appears to be the same although in reality new, according to that law by which all mortal things are preserved, not absolutely the same, but by substitution, the old worn-out mortality leaving another new and similar existence behind—unlike the divine, which is wholly and eternally the same? And in this way, Socrates, the mortal body, or mortal anything, partakes of immortality; but the immortal in another way. Marvel not then at the love which all men have of their offspring; for that universal love and interest is for the sake of immortality."

I was astonished at her words, and said: "Is this really true, O most wise Diotima?" And she answered with all the authority of an accomplished sophist: "Of that, Socrates, you may be assured;—think only of the ambition of men, and you will wonder at the senselessness of their ways, unless you consider how they are stirred by the passionate love of fame. They are ready to run all risks, even greater than they would have run for their children, and to pour out money and undergo any sort of toil, and even to die, 'if so they leave an everlasting name.' Do you imagine that Alcestis would have died to save Admetus, or Achilles to avenge Patroclus, or your own Codrus in order to preserve the kingdom for his sons, if they had not imagined that the memory of their virtues, which still survives among us, would be immortal? Nay," she said, "I am persuaded that all men do all things, and the better they are the more they do them, in hope of the glorious fame of immortal virtue; for they desire the immortal."

"Those who are pregnant in the body only, betake themselves to women and beget children—this is the character of their love; their offspring, as they hope, will preserve their memory and give them the blessedness and immortality which they desire for all future time. But souls which are pregnant—for there certainly are men who are more creative in their souls than in their bodies, creative of that which is proper for the soul to conceive and bring forth: and if you ask me what are these conceptions, I answer, wisdom, and virtue in general—among such souls are all creative poets and all artists who are deserving of the name inventor. But the greatest and fairest sort of wisdom by far is that which is concerned with the ordering of states and families, and which is called temperance and justice. And he who in youth has the seed of these implanted in his soul, when he grows up and comes to maturity desires to beget and generate. He wanders about seeking beauty that he may get offspring—for from deformity he will beget nothing—and naturally embraces the beautiful rather than the deformed body; above all, when he finds a fair and noble and well-nurtured soul, he embraces the two in one person, and to such a one he is full of speech about virtue and the nature and pursuits of a good man, and he tries to educate him. At the touch and in the society of the beautiful which is ever present to his memory, even when absent, he brings forth that which he had conceived long before, and in company with him tends that which he brings forth; and they are married by a far nearer tie and have a closer friendship than those who beget mortal children, for the children who are their common offspring are fairer and more immortal. Who, when he thinks of Homer and Hesiod and other poets, would not rather have their children than ordinary human ones? Who would not emulate them in the creation of children such as theirs, which have preserved their memory and given them everlasting glory? Or who would not have such children as Lycurgus left behind him to be the saviours, not only of Lacedaemon, but of Hellas, as one may say? There is Solon, too, who is the revered father of Athenian laws; and many others there are in many other places, both among Hellenes and barbarians, who have given to the world many noble works, and have been the parents of virtue of every kind; and

many temples have been raised in their honour for the sake of children such as theirs; which were never raised in honour of anyone, for the sake of his mortal children.

"These are the lesser mysteries of love, into which even you, Socrates, may enter; to the greater and more hidden ones which are the crown of these, and to which, if you pursue them in a right spirit, they will lead, I know not whether you will be able to attain. But I will do my utmost to inform you, and do you follow if you can. For he who would proceed aright in this matter should begin in youth to seek the company of corporeal beauty; and first, if he be guided by his instructor aright, to love one beautiful body only—out of that he should create fair thoughts; and soon he will of himself perceive that the beauty of one body is akin to the beauty of another; and then if beauty of form in general is his pursuit, how foolish would he be not to recognize that the beauty in every body is one and the same! And when he perceives this he will abate his violent love of the one, which he will despise and deem a small thing, and will become a steadfast lover of all beautiful bodies. In the next stage he will consider that the beauty of the soul is more precious than the beauty of the outward form; so that if a virtuous soul have but a little comeliness, he will be content to love and tend him, and will search out and bring to the birth thoughts which may improve the young, until he is compelled next to contemplate and see the beauty in institutions and laws, and to understand that the beauty of them all is of one family, and that personal beauty is a trifle; and after institutions his guide will lead him on to the sciences, in order that, beholding the wide region already occupied by beauty, he may cease to be like a servant in love with one beauty only, that of a particular youth or man or institution, himself a slave mean and narrowminded; but drawing towards and contemplating the vast sea of beauty, he will create many fair and noble thoughts and discourses in boundless love of wisdom, until on that shore he grows and waxes strong, and at last the vision is revealed to him of a single science, which is the science of beauty everywhere. To this I will proceed; please to give me your very best attention:

"He who has been instructed thus far in the things of love, and who has learned to see the beautiful in due order and succession, when he comes toward the end will suddenly perceive a nature of wondrous beauty (and this, Socrates, is the final cause of all our former toils)—a nature which in the first place is everlasting, knowing not birth or death, growth or decay; secondly, not fair in one point of view and foul in another, or at one time or in one relation or at one place fair, at another time or in another relation or at another place foul, as if fair to some and foul to others, or in the likeness of a face or hands or any other part of the bodily frame, or in any form of speech or knowledge, or existing in any individual being, as for example, in a living creature, whether in heaven, or in earth, or anywhere else; but beauty absolute, separate, simple, and everlasting, which is imparted to the ever growing and perishing beauties of all other beautiful things, without itself suffering diminution, or increase, or any change. He who, ascending from these earthly things under the influence of true love, begins to perceive that beauty, is not far from the end. And the true order of going, or being led by another, to the things of love, is to begin from the beauties of earth and mount upwards for the sake of that other beauty, using these as steps only, and from one going on to two, and from two to all fair bodily forms, and from fair bodily forms to fair practices, and from fair practices to fair sciences, until from fair sciences he arrives at the science of which I have spoken, the science which has no other object than absolute beauty, and at last knows that which is beautiful by itself alone. This, my dear Socrates," said the stranger of Mantinea, "is that life above all others which man should live, in the contemplation of beauty absolute; a beauty which if you once beheld, you would see not to be after the measure of gold, and garments, and fair boys and youths, whose presence now entrances you; and you and many a one would be content to live seeing them only and conversing with them without meat or drink, if that were possible—you only want to look at them and to be with them. But what if a man had eyes to see the true beauty—the divine beauty, I mean, pure and clear and unalloyed, not infected with the pollutions of the flesh and all the colours and vanities of mortal life—thither looking, and holding converse with the true beauty simple and divine? Remember how in that communion only, beholding beauty with that by which it can be beheld, he will be enabled to bring forth, not images of beauty, but realities (for he has hold not of an image but of a reality), and bringing forth and nourishing true virtue will properly become the friend of God and be immortal, if mortal man may. Would that be an ignoble life?"

Such, Phaedrus—and I speak not only to you, but to all of you—were the words of Diotima; and I am persuaded of their truth. And being persuaded of them, I try to persuade others, that in the attainment of this end human nature will not easily find a helper better than Love. And therefore, also, I say that every man ought to honour him as I myself honour him, and walk in his ways, and exhort others to do the same, and praise the power and spirit of Love according to the measure of my ability now and ever.

The words which I have spoken, you, Phaedrus, may call an encomium of Love, or anything else which you please.

NOTES

1. Cf. *Alcibiades* I.
2. Cf. *Gorg.* 505 e.
3. *Supra,* 195 a.

ARTHUR SCHOPENHAUER

The Metaphysics of the Love of the Sexes

We are accustomed to see poets principally occupied with describing the love of the sexes. This is as a rule the chief theme of all dramatic works, tragical as well as comical, romantic as well as classical, Indian as well as European. Not less is it the material of by far the largest part of lyrical and also of epic poetry, especially if we class with the latter the enormous piles of romances which for centuries every year has produced in all the civilised countries of Europe as regularly as the fruits of the earth. As regards their main contents, all these works are nothing else than many-sided brief or lengthy descriptions of the passion we are speaking of. Moreover, the most successful pictures of it—such, for example, as Romeo and Juliet, *La Nouvelle Héloïse,* and *Werther*—have gained immortal fame. Yet, when Rochefoucauld imagines that it is the same with passionate love as with ghosts, of which every one speaks, but which no one has seen; and Lichtenberg also in his essay, "Ueber die Macht der Liebe," disputes and denies the reality and naturalness of that passion, they are greatly in error. For it is impossible that something which is foreign and contrary to human nature, thus a mere imaginary caricature, could be unweariedly represented by poetic genius in all ages, and received by mankind with unaltered interest; for nothing that is artistically beautiful can be without truth:

Rein n'est beau que le vrai; le vrai seul est aimable." [Boil]

Certainly, however, it is also confirmed by experience, although not by the experience of every day, that that which as a rule only appears as a strong yet still controllable inclination may rise under certain circumstances to a passion which exceeds all others in vehemence, and which then sets aside all considerations, overcomes all obstacles with incredible strength and perseverance, so that for its satisfaction life is risked without hesitation, nay, if that satisfaction is still withheld, is given as the price of it. Werthers and Jacopo Ortis exist not only in romance, but every year can show at least half a dozen of them in Europe: *Sed ignotis perierunt mortibus illi;* for their sorrows find no other chroniclers than the writers of official registers or the reporters of the newspapers. Yet the readers of the police news in English and French journals will attest the correctness of my assertion. Still greater, however, is the number of those whom the same passion brings to the madhouse. Finally, every year can show cases of the double suicide of a pair of lovers who are opposed by outward circumstances. In such cases, however, it is inexplicable to me how those who, certain of mutual love, expect to find the supremest bliss in the enjoyment of this, do not withdraw themselves from all connections by taking the extremest steps, and endure all hardships, rather than give up with life a pleasure which is greater than any other they can conceive. As regards the lower grades of that passion, and the mere approaches to it, every one has them daily before his eyes, and, as long as he is not old, for the most part also in his heart.

So then, after what has here been called to mind, no one can doubt either the reality or the importance of the matter; and therefore, instead of wondering that a philosophy should also for once make its own this constant theme of all poets, one ought rather to be surprised that a thing which plays throughout so important a

From Arthur Schopenhauer, *The World as Will and Idea,* trans. by R. B. Haldane and J. Kemp. London: Routledge and Kegan Paul, 1883.

part in human life has hitherto practically been disregarded by philosophers altogether, and lies before us as raw material. The one who has most concerned himself with it is Plato, especially in the *Symposium* and the *Phædrus*. Yet what he says on the subject is confined to the sphere of myths, fables, and jokes, and also for the most part concerns only the Greek love of youths. The little that Rousseau says upon our theme in the "Discours sur l'inégalité" (p. 96, ed. Bip.) is false and insufficient. Kant's explanation of the subject in the third part of the essay, "Ueber das Gefühl des Schönen und Erhabenen" (p. 435 seq. of Rosenkranz's edition), is very superficial and without practical knowledge, therefore it is also partly incorrect. Lastly, Platner's treatment of the matter in his *Anthropology* (§ 1347 *seq.*) every one will find dull and shallow. On the other hand, Spinoza's definition, on account of its excessive naïveté, deserves to be quoted for the sake of amusement: "*Amor est titillatio, concomitante idea causae externae*" (*Eth.* iv., prop. 44, *dem.*) Accordingly I have no predecessors either to make use of or to refute. The subject has pressed itself upon me objectively, and has entered of its own accord into the connection of my consideration of the world. Moreover, least of all can I hope for approbation from those who are themselves under the power of this passion, and who accordingly seek to express the excess of their feelings in the sublimest and most ethereal images. To them my view will appear too physical, too material, however metaphysical and even transcendent it may be at bottom. Meanwhile let them reflect that if the object which to-day inspires them to write madrigals and sonnets had been born eighteen years earlier it would scarcely have won a glance from them.

For all love, however ethereally it may bear itself, is rooted in the sexual impulse alone, nay, it absolutely is only a more definitely determined, specialised, and indeed in the strictest sense individualised sexual impulse. If now, keeping this in view, one considers the important part which the sexual impulse in all its degrees and nuances plays not only on the stage and in novels, but also in the real world, where, next to the love of life, it shows itself the strongest and most powerful of motives, constantly lays claim to half the powers and thoughts of the younger portion of mankind, is the ultimate goal of almost all human effort, exerts an adverse influence on the most important events, interrupts the most serious occupations every hour, sometimes embarrasses for a while even the greatest minds, does not hesitate to intrude with its trash interfering with the negotiations of statesmen and the investigations of men of learning, knows how to slip its love letters and locks of hair even into ministerial portfolios and philosophical manuscripts, and no less devises daily the most entangled and the worst actions, destroys the most valuable relationships, breaks the firmest bonds, demands the sacrifice sometimes of life or health, sometimes of wealth, rank, and happiness, nay, robs those who are otherwise honest of all conscience, makes those who have hitherto been faithful, traitors; accordingly, on the whole, appears as a malevolent demon that strives to pervert, confuse, and overthrow everything;—then one will be forced to cry, Wherefore all this noise? Wherefore the straining and storming, the anxiety and want? It is merely a question of every Hans finding his Grethe.[1] Why should such a trifle play so important a part, and constantly introduce disturbance and confusion into the well-regulated life of man? But to the earnest investigator the spirit of truth gradually reveals the answer. It is no trifle that is in question here; on the contrary, the importance of the matter is quite proportionate to the seriousness and ardour of the effort. The ultimate end of all love affairs, whether they are played in sock or cothurnus, is really more important than all other ends of human life, and is therefore quite worthy of the profound seriousness with which every one pursues it. That which is decided by it is nothing less than *the composition of the next generation.* The *dramatis personae* who shall appear when we are withdrawn are here determined, both as regards their existence and their nature, by these frivolous love affairs. As the being, the *existentia,* of these future persons is absolutely conditioned by our sexual impulse generally, so their nature, *essentia,* is determined by the individual selection in its satisfaction, *i.e.,* by sexual love, and is in every respect irrevocably fixed by this. This is the key of the problem: we shall arrive at a more accurate knowledge of it in its application if we go through the degrees of love, from the passing inclination to the vehement passion, when we shall also recognise that the difference of these grades arises from the degree of the individualisation of the choice.

The collective love affairs of the present generation taken together are accordingly, of the whole human race, the serious *meditatio compositionis generationis futurae, e qua iterum pendent innumerae generationes.* This high importance of the matter, in which it is not a question of individual weal or woe, as in all other matters, but of the existence and special nature of the human race in future times, and therefore the will of the individual appears at a higher power as the will of the species;—this it is on which the pathetic and sublime elements in affairs of love depend, which for thousands of years poets have never wearied of representing in innumerable examples; because no theme can equal in interest this one, which stands to all others which only concern the welfare of individuals as the solid body to the surface, because it concerns the weal and woe of the species. Just on this account, then, is it so difficult to impart interest to a drama without the element of love, and, on the other hand, this theme is never worn out even by daily use.

That which presents itself in the individual consciousness as sexual impulse in general, without being directed towards a definite individual of the other sex, is in itself, and apart from the phenomenon, simply the will to live. But what appears in consciousness as a sexual impulse directed to a definite individual is in itself the will to live as a definitely determined individual. Now in this case the sexual impulse, although in itself a subjective need, knows how to assume very skilfully the mask of an objective admiration, and thus to deceive our consciousness; for nature requires this strategem to attain its ends. But yet that in every case of falling in love, however objective and sublime this admiration may appear, what alone is looked to is the production of an individual of a definite nature is primarily confirmed by the fact that the essential matter is not the reciprocation of love, but possession, *i.e.,* the physical enjoyment. The certainty of the former can therefore by no means console us for the want of the latter; on the contrary, in such a situation many a man has shot himself. On the other hand, persons who are deeply in love, and can obtain no return of it, are con-

tented with possession, *i.e.,* with the physical enjoyment. This is proved by all forced marriages, and also by the frequent purchase of the favour of a woman, in spite of her dislike, by large presents or other sacrifices, nay, even by cases of rape. That this particular child shall be begotten is, although unknown to the parties concerned, the true end of the whole love story; the manner in which it is attained is a secondary consideration. Now, however loudly persons of lofty and sentimental soul, and especially those who are in love, may cry out here about the gross realism of my view, they are yet in error. For is not the definite determination of the individualities of the next generation a much higher and more worthy end than those exuberant feelings and supersensible soap bubbles of theirs? Nay, among earthly aims, can there be one which is greater or more important? It alone corresponds to the profoundness with which passionate love is felt, to the seriousness with which it appears, and the importance which it attributes even to the trifling details of its sphere and occasion. Only so far as this end is assumed as the true one do the difficulties encountered, the infinite exertions and annoyances made and endured for the attainment of the loved object, appear proportionate to the matter. For it is the future generation, in its whole individual determinateness, that presses into existence by means of those efforts and toils. Nay, it is itself already active in that careful, definite, and arbitrary choice for the satisfaction of the sexual impulse which we call love. The growing inclination of two lovers is really already the will to live of the new individual which they can and desire to produce; nay, even in the meeting of their longing glances its new life breaks out, and announces itself as a future individuality harmoniously and well composed. They feel the longing for an actual union and fusing together into a single being, in order to live on only as this; and this longing receives its fulfilment in the child which is produced by them, as that in which the qualities transmitted by them both, fused and united in one being, live on. Conversely, the mutual, decided and persistent aversion between a man and a maid is a sign that what they could produce would only be a badly organised, in itself inharmonious and unhappy being. Hence there lies a deeper meaning in the fact that Calderon, though he calls the atrocious Semiramis the daughter of the air, yet introduces her as the daughter of rape followed by the murder of the husband.

But, finally, what draws two individuals of different sex exclusively to each other with such power is the will to live, which exhibits itself in the whole species, and which here anticipates in the individual which these two can produce an objectification of its nature answering to its aims. This individual will have the will, or character, from the father, the intellect from the mother, and the corporisation from both; yet, for the most part, the figure will take more after the father, the size after the mother,—according to the law which comes out in the breeding of hybrids among the brutes, and principally depends upon the fact that the size of the fœtus must conform to the size of the uterus. Just as inexplicable as the quite special individuality of any man, which is exclusively peculiar to him, is also the quite special and individual passion of two lovers; indeed at bottom the two are one and the same: the former is *explicite* what the latter was *implicite*. The moment at which the parents begin to love each other—to fancy each other, as the very happy English expression has it—is really to be regarded as the first appearance of a new individual and the true *punctum saliens* of its life, and, as has been said, in the meeting and fixing of their longing glances there appears the first germ of the new being, which certainly, like all germs, is generally crushed out. This new individual is to a certain extent a new (Platonic) Idea; and now, as all Ideas strive with the greatest vehemence to enter the phenomenal world, eagerly seizing for this end upon the matter which the law of causality divides among them all, so also does this particular Idea of a human individuality strive with the greatest eagerness and vehemence towards its realisation in the phenomenon. This eagerness and vehemence is just the passion of the two future parents for each other. It has innumerable degrees, the two extremes of which may at any rate be described as Αφροδιτη πανδημος and ουρανια; in its nature, however, it is everywhere the same. On the other hand, it will be in degree so much the more powerful the more *individualised* it is; that is, the more the loved individual is exclusively suited, by

virtue of all his or her parts and qualities, to satisfy the desire of the lover and the need established by his or her own individuality. What is really in question here will become clear in the further course of our exposition. Primarily and essentially the inclination of love is directed to health, strength, and beauty, consequently also to youth; because the will first of all seeks to exhibit the specific character of the human species as the basis of all individuality: ordinary amorousness (Αφροδιτη πανδημος) does not go much further. To these, then, more special claims link themselves on, which we shall investigate in detail further on, and with which, when they see satisfaction before them, the passion increases. But the highest degrees of this passion spring from that suitableness of two individualities to each other on account of which the will, *i.e.*, the character, of the father and the intellect of the mother, in their connection, make up precisely that individual towards which the will to live in general which exhibits itself in the whole species feels a longing proportionate to this its magnitude, and which therefore exceeds the measure of a mortal heart, and the motives of which, in the same way, lie beyond the sphere of the individual intellect. This is thus the soul of a true and great passion. Now the more perfect is the mutual adaptation of two individuals to each other in each of the many respects which have further to be considered, the stronger will be their mutual passion. Since there do not exist two individuals exactly alike, there must be for each particular man a particular woman—always with reference to what is to be produced—who corresponds most perfectly. A really passionate love is as rare as the accident of these two meeting. Since, however, the possibility of such a love is present in every one, the representations of it in the works of the poets are comprehensible to us. Just because the passion of love really turns about that which is to be produced, and its qualities, and because its kernel lies here, a friendship without any admixture of sexual love can exist between two young and good-looking persons of different sex, on account of the agreement of their disposition, character, and mental tendencies; nay, as regards sexual love there may even be a certain aversion between them. The reason of this is to be sought in the fact that a child produced by them would have physical or mental qualities which were inharmonious; in short, its existence and nature would not answer the ends of the will to live as it exhibits itself in the species. On the other hand, in the case of difference of disposition, character, and mental tendency, and the dislike, nay, enmity, proceeding from this, sexual love may yet arise and exist; when it then blinds us to all that; and if it here leads to marriage it will be a very unhappy one.

Let us now set about the more thorough investigation of the matter. Egoism is so deeply rooted a quality of all individuals in general, that in order to rouse the activity of an individual being egoistical ends are the only ones upon which we can count with certainty. Certainly the species has an earlier, closer, and greater claim upon the individual than the perishable individuality itself. Yet when the individual has to act, and even make sacrifices for the continuance and quality of the species, the importance of the matter cannot be made so comprehensible to his intellect, which is calculated merely with regard to individual ends, as to have its proportionate effect. Therefore in such a case nature can only attain its ends by implanting a certain illusion in the individual, on account of which that which is only a good for the species appears to him as a good for himself, so that when he serves the species he imagines he is serving himself; in which process a mere chimera, which vanishes immediately afterwards, floats before him, and takes the place of a real thing as a motive. This illusion is instinct. In the great majority of cases this is to be regarded as the sense of the species, which presents what is of benefit to *it* to the will. Since, however, the will has here become individual, it must be so deluded that it apprehends through the sense of the individual what the sense of the species presents to it, thus imagines it is following individual ends while in truth it is pursuing ends which are merely general (taking this word in its strictest sense). The external phenomenon of instinct we can best observe in the brutes where its rôle is most important; but it is in ourselves alone that we arrive at a knowledge of its internal process, as of everything internal. Now it is certainly supposed that man has almost no instinct; at any rate only this, that the new-born babe seeks for

and seizes the breast of its mother. But, in fact, we have a very definite, distinct, and complicated instinct, that of the selection of another individual for the satisfaction of the sexual impulse, a selection which is so fine, so serious, and so arbitrary. With this satisfaction in itself, *i.e.*, so far as it is a sensual pleasure resting upon a pressing want of the individual, the beauty or ugliness of the other individual has nothing to do. Thus the regard for this which is yet pursued with such ardour, together with the careful selection which springs from it, is evidently connected, not with the chooser himself—although he imagines it is so—but with the true end, that which is to be produced, which is to receive the type of the species as purely and correctly as possible. Through a thousand physical accidents and moral aberrations there arise a great variety of deteriorations of the human form; yet its true type, in all its parts, is always again established: and this takes place under the guidance of the sense of beauty, which always directs the sexual impulse, and without which this sinks to the level of a disgusting necessity. Accordingly, in the first place, every one will decidedly prefer and eagerly desire the most beautiful individuals, *i.e.*, those in whom the character of the species is most purely impressed; but, secondly, each one will specially regard as beautiful in another individual those perfections which he himself lacks, nay, even those imperfections which are the opposite of his own. Hence, for example, little men love big women, fair persons like dark, &c. &c. The delusive ecstasy which seizes a man at the sight of a woman whose beauty is suited to him, and pictures to him a union with her as the highest good, is just the *sense of the species,* which, recognising the distinctly expressed stamp of the same, desires to perpetuate it with this individual. Upon this decided inclination to beauty depends the maintenance of the type of the species: hence it acts with such great power. We shall examine specially further on the considerations which it follows. Thus what guides man here is really an instinct which is directed to doing the best for the species, while the man himself imagines that he only seeks the heightening of his own pleasure. In fact, we have in this an instructive lesson concerning the inner nature of all instinct, which, as here, almost always sets the individual in motion for the good of the species. For clearly the pains with which an insect seeks out a particular flower, or fruit, or dung, or flesh, or, as in the case of the ichneumonidae, the larva of another insect, in order to deposit its eggs there only, and to attain this end shrinks neither from trouble nor danger, is thoroughly analogous to the pains with which for his sexual satisfaction a man carefully chooses a woman with definite qualities which appeal to him individually, and strives so eagerly after her that in order to attain this end he often sacrifices his own happiness in life, contrary to all reason, by a foolish marriage, by love affairs which cost him wealth, honour, and life, even by crimes such as adultery or rape, all merely in order to serve the species in the most efficient way, although at the cost of the individual, in accordance with the will of nature which is everywhere sovereign. Instinct, in fact, is always an act which seems to be in accordance with the conception of an end, and yet is entirely without such a conception. Nature implants it wherever the acting individual is incapable of understanding the end, or would be unwilling to pursue it. Therefore, as a rule, it is given only to the brutes, and indeed especially to the lowest of them which have least understanding; but almost only in the case we are here considering it is also given to man, who certainly could understand the end, but would not pursue it with the necessary ardour, that is, even at the expense of his individual welfare. Thus here, as in the case of all instinct, the truth assumes the form of an illusion, in order to act upon the will. It is a voluptuous illusion which leads the man to believe he will find a greater pleasure in the arms of a woman whose beauty appeals to him than in those of any other; or which indeed, exclusively directed to a single individual, firmly convinces him that the possession of her will ensure him excessive happiness. Therefore he imagines he is taking trouble and making sacrifices for his own pleasure, while he does so merely for the maintenance of the regular type of the species, or else a quite special individuality, which can only come from these parents, is to attain to existence. The character of instinct is here so perfectly present, thus an action which seems to be in accordance with the conception of an end, and yet is entirely without such a conception, that he who is drawn by that illusion often abhors the end which alone guides it, procreation, and would like to hinder it; thus it is in the case of almost all illicit love affairs. In accordance with the character of the matter which has been explained, every lover will experience a marvellous disillusion after the pleasure he has at last attained, and will wonder that what was so longingly desired accomplishes nothing more than every other sexual satisfaction; so that he does not see himself much benefited by it. That wish was related to all his other wishes as the species is related to the individual, thus as the infinite to the finite. The satisfaction, on the other hand, is really only for the benefit of the species, and thus does not come within the consciousness of the individual, who, inspired by the will of the species, here served an end with every kind of sacrifice, which was not his own end at all. Hence, then, every lover, after the ultimate consummation of the great work, finds himself cheated; for the illusion has vanished by means of which the individual was here the dupe of the species. Accordingly Plato very happily says: "ἡδονη ἁπαντων αλαζονεστατον" (*voluptas omnium maxime vaniloqua*), *Phileb.* 319. . . .

Now that an instinct entirely directed to that which is to be produced lies at the foundation of all sexual love will receive complete confirmation from the fuller analysis of it, which we cannot therefore avoid. First of all we have to remark here that by nature man is inclined to inconstancy in love, woman to constancy. The love of the man sinks perceptibly from the moment it has obtained satisfaction; almost every other woman charms him more than the one he already possesses; he longs for variety. The love of the woman, on the other hand, increases just from that moment. This is a consequence of the aim of nature which is directed to the maintenance, and therefore to the greatest possible increase, of the species. The man can easily beget over a hundred children a year; the woman, on the contrary, with however many men, can yet only bring one child a year into this world (leaving twin births out of account). Therefore the man always looks about after other women; the woman, again, sticks firmly to the one man; for nature moves her, instinctively and without reflection, to retain the nourisher and protector of the future offspring. Accordingly faithfulness in marriage is with the man artificial, with the woman it is natural, and thus adultery on the part of the woman is much less pardonable than on the part of the man, both objectively on account of the consequences and also subjectively on account of its unnaturalness.

NOTE

1. I have not ventured to express myself distinctly here: the courteous reader must therefore translate the phrase into Aristophanic language.

SØREN KIERKEGAARD

Don Juan's Secret

Never before in the world has sensuousness been conceived as it is in *Don Juan*—as a principle: for this reason the erotic is here defined by another predicate: the erotic here is *seduction*. Strangely enough, the idea of a seducer was entirely wanting among the Greeks. It is by no means my intention, because of this, to wish to praise the Greeks, for, as everybody knows, gods as well as men were indiscreet in their love affairs; nor do I censure Christianity, for, after all, it has the idea only as something external to itself. The reason that the Greeks lacked this idea lay in the fact that the whole of the Greek life was posited as individuality. The psychical is thus the predominant or is always in harmony with the sensuous. Greek love, therefore, was psychical, not sensuous, and it is this which inspires the modesty which rests over all Greek love. They fell in love with a girl, they set heaven and earth in motion to get her; when they succeeded, then they perhaps tired of her, and sought a new love. In this instability they may, indeed, have had a certain resemblance to Don Juan. To mention only one instance, Hercules might surely produce a goodly list, when one considers that he sometimes took whole families numbering up to fifty daughters, and like a family son-in-law, according to some reports, had his way with all of them in a single night. Nevertheless, he is still essentially different from a Don Juan, he is no seducer. When one considers Greek love, it is, in accordance with its concept, essentially faithful, just because it is psychical; and it is some accidental factor in the particular individual that he loves many, and with regard to the many he loves, it is again accidental every time he loves a new one; when he is in love with one, he does not think of the next one. Don

Juan, on the contrary, is a seducer from the ground up. His love is not psychical but sensuous, and sensuous love, in accordance with its concept, is not faithful, but absolutely faithless; it loves not one but all, that is to say, it seduces all. It exists only in the moment, but the moment, in terms of its concept, is the sum of moments, and so we have the seducer.

Chivalrous love is also psychical and, therefore, in accordance with its concept, is essentially faithful; only sensuous love, in terms of its very concept, is essentially faithless. But this, its faithlessness, appears also in another way; it becomes in fact only a constant repetition. Psychical love has the dialectic in it in a double sense. For partly it has the doubt and unrest in it, as to whether it will also be happy, see its desire fulfilled, and be requited. This anxiety sensuous love does not have. Even a Jupiter is doubtful about his victory, and this cannot be otherwise; moreover, he himself cannot desire it otherwise. With Don Juan this is not the case; he makes short work of it and must always be regarded as absolutely victorious. This might seem an advantage to him, but it is precisely poverty. On the other hand, psychical love has also another dialectic, it is in fact different in its relation to every single individual who is the object of love. Therein lies its wealth, its rich content. But such is not the case with Don Juan. For this, indeed, he has not time; everything for him is a matter of the moment only. To see her and to love her, that was one and the same. One may say this in a certain sense about psychical love, but in that there is only suggested a beginning. With regard to Don Juan it is valid in another way. To see her and to love her is the same thing; it is in the moment, in the same moment everything is over, and the same thing repeats itself end-lessly. If one imagines a psychical love in Don Juan, it becomes at once ridiculous and a self-contradiction, which is not even in accord with the idea of positing 1,003 in Spain. It becomes an over-emphasis which acts disturbingly, even if one imagined oneself considering him ideal-ly. Now if we had no other medium for describing this love than language, we should be up against it, for as soon as we have abandoned the naïveté which in all simplicity can insist that there were 1,003 in Spain, then we require something more, namely, the psychical indi-vidualization. The aesthetic is by no means sat-isfied that everything should thus be lumped together, and is astonished at the number. Psy-chical love does not exactly move in the rich manifold of the individual life, where the nu-ances are really significant. Sensuous love, on the other hand, can lump everything together. The essential for it is woman in the abstract, and at most is a more sensuous difference. Psy-chical love is a continuance in time, sensuous love a disappearance in time, but the medium which exactly expresses this is music. Music is excellently fitted to accomplish this, since it is far more abstract than language, and therefore does not express the individual but the general in all its generality, and yet it expresses the general not in reflective abstraction, but in the immediate concrete.

As an example of what I mean, I shall dis-cuss a little more carefully the servant's second aria: the List of the Seduced. This number may be regarded as the real epic of Don Juan. Con-sequently, make this experiment, if you are sceptical about the truth of my assertion! Imag-ine a poet more happily endowed by nature than anyone before him; give him vigor of ex-pression, give him mastery and authority over the power of language, let everything wherein there is the breath of life be obedient unto him, let his slightest suggestion be deferred to, let everything wait, ready and prepared for his word of command; let him be surrounded by a numerous band of light skirmishers, swift-footed messengers who overtake thought in its most hurried flight; let nothing escape him, not the least movement; let nothing secret, nothing unutterable be left behind him in the whole world—give him, after all this, the task of singing Don Juan as an epic, of unrolling the list of the seduced. What will the result be? He

will never finish! The epic has the fault, if one wishes to call it that, of being able to go on as long as you will. His hero, the improviser, Don Juan, can go on indefinitely. The poet may now enter into the manifold, there will always be enough there which will give pleasure, but he will never achieve the effect which Mozart has obtained. For even if he finally finishes, he will still not have said half of what Mozart has ex-pressed in this one number. Mozart has not even attempted the manifold; he deals only with certain great formations which are set in motion. This finds its sufficient explanation in the medium itself, in the music which is too abstract to express the differences. The musical epic thus becomes something comparatively short, and yet it has in an inimitable manner the epic quality that it can go on as long as it will, since one can constantly let it begin again from the beginning, and hear it over and over again, just because it expresses the general in the con-creteness of immediacy. Here we do not hear Don Juan as a particular individual, nor his speech, but we hear a voice, the voice of sensu-ousness, and we hear it through the longing of womanhood. Only in this manner can Don Juan become epic, in that he constantly fin-ishes, and constantly begins again from the be-ginning, for his life is the sum of repellent mo-ments which have no coherence, his life as moment is the sum of the moments, as the sum of the moments is the moment.

In this generality, in this floating between being an individual and being a force of nature, lies Don Juan; as soon as he becomes individu-al the aesthetic acquires quite other categories. Therefore it is entirely proper, and it has a pro-found inner significance, that in the seduction which takes place in the play, Zerlina, the girl, should be a common peasant girl. Hypocritical aestheticists who, under the show of under-standing poets and composers, contribute ev-erything to their being misunderstood, will per-haps instruct us that Zerlina is an unusual girl. Anyone who believes this shows that he has totally misunderstood Mozart, and that he is using wrong categories. That he misunder-stands Mozart is evident enough; for Mozart has purposely made Zerlina as insignificant as possible, something Hotho has also called at-tention to, yet without seeing the real reason for it. If, for instance, Don Juan's love were qualified as other than sensuous, if he were a seducer in an intellectual sense (a type which we shall consider presently), then it would have been a radical fault in the play for the heroine in the seduction which dramatically engages our attention to be only a little peasant girl. Then the aesthetic would require that Don Juan should have been set a more difficult task. To Don Juan, however, these differences mean nothing. If I could imagine him making such a speech about himself, he might perhaps say: "You are wrong. I am no husband who requires an unusual girl to make me happy; every girl has that which makes me happy, and therefore I take them all." In some such way we have to understand the saying I earlier referred to: "even sixty-year coquettes"—or in another place: *pur chè porti la gonella, voi sapete quel chè fà.* To Don Juan every girl is an ordinary girl, every love affair an everyday story. Zerlina is young and pretty, and she is a woman; this is the uncommon which she has in common with hundreds of others; but it is not the uncommon that Don Juan desires, but the common, and this she has in common with every woman. If this is not the case, then Don Juan ceases to be absolutely musical, and aesthetics requires speech, dialogue, while now, since it *is* the case, Don Juan is absolutely musical.

From another point of view I may throw some additional light upon this by analyzing the inner structure of the play. Elvira is Don Juan's mortal enemy; in the dialogue for which the Danish translator is responsible, this is frequently emphasized. That it is an error for Don Juan to make a speech is certain enough, but because of this it does not follow that the speech might not contain an occasional good observation. Well then, Don Juan fears Elvira. Now probably some aestheticist or other believes that he can profoundly explain this by coming forward with a long disquisition about Elvira's being a very unusual girl and so on. This altogether misses the mark. She is dangerous to him because she has been seduced. In the same sense, exactly in the same sense, Zerlina becomes dangerous to him when she is seduced. As soon as she is seduced, she is elevated to a higher sphere, to a consciousness which Don Juan does not have. Therefore, she is dangerous to him. Hence, it is not by means of accidental but by means of the general that she is dangerous to him.

Don Juan, then, is a seducer; in him the erotic takes the form of seduction. Here much is well said when it is rightly understood, little when it is understood with a general lack of clarity. We have already noted that the concept, a seducer, is essentially modified with respect to Don Juan, as the object of his desire is the sensuous, and that alone. This is of importance in order to show the musical in Don Juan. In ancient times the sensuous found its expression in the silent stillness of plastic art; in the Christian world the sensuous must burst forth in all its impatient passion. Although one may say with truth that Don Juan is a seducer, this expression, which can work so disturbingly upon the weak brains of certain aestheticians, has often given rise to misunderstandings, as they have scraped this and that together that could be said about such a one, and have at once applied it to Don Juan. At times they have exposed their own cunning in tracking down Don Juan's, at times they talk themselves hoarse in explaining his intrigues and his subtlety; in short, the word *seducer* has given rise to the situation that everybody has been against him to the limit of his power, has contributed his mite to the total misunderstanding. Of Don Juan we must use the word *seducer* with great caution—assuming, that is, that it is more important to say something right than simply to say something. This is not because Don Juan is too good, but because he simply does not fall under ethical categories. Hence I should rather not call him a deceiver, since there is always something more ambiguous in that word. To be a seducer requires a certain amount of reflection and consciousness, and as soon as this is present, then it is proper to speak of cunning and intrigues and crafty plans. This consciousness is lacking in Don Juan. Therefore, he does not seduce. He desires, and this desire acts seductively. To that extent he seduces. He enjoys the satisfaction of desire; as soon as he has enjoyed it, he seeks a new object, and so on endlessly. Therefore, I suppose he is a deceiver, but yet not so that he plans his deceptions in advance; it is the inherent power of sensuousness which deceives the seduced, and it is rather a kind of Nemesis. He desires, and is constantly desiring, and constantly enjoys the satisfaction of the desire. To be a seducer, he lacks time in advance in which to lay his plans, and time afterward in which to become conscious of his act. A seducer, therefore, ought to be in possession of a power Don Juan does not have, however well equipped he may otherwise be—the power of eloquence. As soon as we grant him eloquence he ceases to be musical, and the aesthetic interest becomes an entirely different matter.

Achim v. Arnim tells somewhere of a seducer of a very different style, a seducer who falls under ethical categories. About him he uses an expression which in truth, boldness, and conciseness is almost equal to Mozart's stroke of the bow. He says he could so talk with a woman that, if the devil caught him, he could wheedle himself out of it if he had a chance to talk with the devil's grandmother. This is the real seducer; the aesthetic interest here is also different, namely: how, the method. There is evidently something very profound here, which has perhaps escaped the attention of most people, in that Faust, who reproduces Don Juan, seduces only one girl, while Don Juan seduces hundreds; but this one girl is also, in an intensive sense, seduced and crushed quite differently from all those Don Juan has deceived, simply because Faust, as reproduction, falls under the category of the intellectual. The power of such a seducer is speech, i. e., the lie. A few days ago I heard one soldier talking to another about a third who had betrayed a girl; he did not give a long-winded description, and yet his expression was very pithy: "He gets away with things like that by lies and things like that." Such a seducer is of quite a different sort from Don Juan, is essentially different from him, as one can see from the fact that he and his activities are extremely unmusical, and from the aesthetic standpoint come within the category of the interesting. The object of his desire is accordingly, when one rightly considers him aesthetically, something more than the merely sensuous.

But what is this force, then, by which Don Juan seduces? It is desire, the energy of sensuous desire. He desires in every woman the whole of womanhood, and therein lies the sensuously idealizing power with which he at once embellishes and overcomes his prey. The reaction to this gigantic passion beautifies and develops the one desired, who flushes in enhanced beauty by its reflection. As the enthusiast's fire with seductive splendor illuminates even those who stand in a casual relation to

him, so Don Juan transfigures in a far deeper sense every girl, since his relation to her is an essential one. Therefore all finite differences fade away before him in comparison with the main thing: being a woman. He rejuvenates the older woman into the beautiful middle age of womanhood; he matures the child almost instantly; everything which is woman is his prey (*pur chè porti la gonella, voi sapete quel chè fà*). On the other hand, we must by no means understand this as if his sensuousness were blind; instinctively he knows very well how to discriminate and, above all, he idealizes. If for a moment I here think back to the Page in a preceding stage, the reader will perhaps remember that once when we spoke of the Page, I compared a speech of his with one of Don Juan's. The mythical Page I left standing, the real one I sent away to the army. If I now imagined that the mythical Page had liberated himself, was free to move about, then I would recall here a speech of the Page which is appropriate to Don Juan. As Cherubino, light as a bird and daring, springs out of the window, it makes so strong an impression upon Susanne that she almost swoons, and when she recovers, she exclaims: "See how he runs! My, won't he make conquests among the girls!" This is quite correctly said by Susanne, and the reason for her swoon is not only the idea of the daring leap, but rather that he had already "got around her." The Page is really the future Don Juan, though without this being understood in a ridiculous way, as if the Page by becoming older became Don Juan. Now Don Juan can not only have his way with the girls, but he makes them happy and—unhappy, but, curiously enough, in such wise that that's the way they want it, and a foolish girl it would be who would not choose to be unhappy for the sake of having once been happy with Don Juan. If I still continue, therefore, to call him a seducer, I by no means imagine him slyly formulating his plans, craftily calculating the effect of his intrigues. His power to deceive lies in the essential genius of sensuousness, whose incarnation he really is. Shrewd sober-mindedness is lacking in him; his life is as effervescent as the wine with which he stimulates himself; his life is dramatic like the strains which accompany his joyous feast; always he is triumphant. He requires no preparation, no plan, no time; for he is always prepared. Energy is always in him and also desire, and only when he desires is he rightly in his element. He sits feasting, joyous as a god he swings his cup—he rises with his napkin in his hand, ready for attack. If Leporello rouses him in the middle of the night, he awakens, always certain of his victory. But this energy, this power, cannot be expressed in words, only music can give us a conception of it. It is inexpressible for reflection and thought. The cunning of an ethically determined seducer I can clearly set forth in words, and music will try in vain to solve this problem. With Don Juan, the converse holds true. What is this power?—No one can say. Even if I questioned Zerlina about it before she goes to the dance: "What is this power by which he captivates you?"—she would answer: "No one knows," and I would say: "Well said, my child! You speak more wisely than the sages of India; *richtig, das weiss man nicht;* and the unfortunate thing is that I can't tell you either."

This force in Don Juan, this omnipotence, this animation, only music can express, and I know no other predicate to describe it than this: it is exuberant joy of life. When, therefore, Kruse lets his Don Juan say, as he comes upon the scene at Zerlina's wedding: "Cheer up, children, you are all of you dressed as for a wedding," he says something that is quite proper and also perhaps something more than he is aware of. He himself brings the gaiety with him, and no matter whose wedding it is, it is not unimportant that everyone be dressed as for a wedding; for Don Juan is not only husband to Zerlina, but he celebrates with sport and song the wedding of all the young girls in the parish. What wonder, then, that they crowd about him, the happy maidens! Nor are they disappointed, for he has enough for them all. Flattery, sighs, daring glances, soft handclasps, secret whispers, dangerous proximity, alluring withdrawal—and yet these are only the lesser mysteries, the gifts before the wedding. It is a pleasure to Don Juan to look out over so rich a harvest; he takes charge of the whole parish, and yet perhaps it does not cost him as much time as Leporello spends in his office.

By these considerations we are again brought to the main subject of this inquiry, that Don Juan is absolutely musical. He desires sensuously, he seduces with the daemonic power of sensuousness, he seduces everyone. Speech, dialogue, are not for him, for then he would be at once a reflective individual. Thus he does not have a stable existence at all, but he hurries in a perpetual vanishing, precisely like music, about which it is true that it is over as soon as it has ceased to sound, and only comes into being again, when it again sounds.

JEAN-PAUL SARTRE

First Attitude Toward Others: Love, Language, Masochism

Everything which may be said of me in my relations with the Other applies to him as well. While I attempt to free myself from the hold of the Other, the Other is trying to free himself from mine; while I seek to enslave the Other, the Other seeks to enslave me. We are by no means dealing with unilateral relations with an object-in-itself, but with reciprocal and moving relations. The following descriptions of concrete behavior must therefore be envisaged within the perspective of *conflict*. Conflict is the original meaning of being-for-others.

If we start with the first revelation of the Other as a *look*, we must recognize that we experience our inapprehensible being-for-others in the form of a *possession*. I am possessed by the Other; the Other's look fashions my body in its nakedness, causes it to be born, sculptures it, produces it as it *is*, sees it as I shall never see it. The Other holds a secret—the secret of what I am. He makes me be and thereby he possesses me, and this possession is nothing other than the consciousness of possessing me. I in the recognition of my object-state have proof that he has this consciousness. By virtue of consciousness the Other is for me simultaneously the one who has stolen my being from me and the one who causes "there to be" a being which is my being. Thus I have a comprehension of this ontological structure: I am responsible for my being-for-others, but I am not the foundation of it. It appears to me therefore in the form of a contingent given for which I am nevertheless responsible; the Other founds my being in so far as this being is in the form of the "there is." But he is not responsible for my being although he founds it in complete

freedom—in and by means of his free transcendence. Thus to the extent that I am revealed to myself as responsible for my being, I *lay claim to* this being which I am; that is, I wish to recover it, or, more exactly, I am the project of the recovery of my being. I want to stretch out my hand and grab hold of this being which is presented to me as *my being* but at a distance—like the dinner of Tantalus; I want to found it by my very freedom. For if in one sense my being-as-object is an unbearable contingency and the pure "possession" of myself by another, still in another sense this being stands as the indication of what I should be obliged to recover and found in order to be the foundation of myself. But this is conceivable only if I assimilate the Other's freedom. Thus my project of recovering myself is fundamentally a project of absorbing the Other.

Nevertheless this project must leave the Other's nature intact. Two consequences result: (1) I do not thereby cease to assert the Other—that is, to deny concerning myself that I am the Other. Since the Other is the foundation of my being, he could not be dissolved in me without my being-for-others disappearing. Therefore if I project the realization of unity for the Other, this means that I project my assimilation of the Other's Otherness as my own possibility. In fact the problem for me is to make myself be by acquiring the possibility of taking the Other's point of view on myself. It is not a matter of acquiring a pure, abstract faculty of knowledge. It is not the pure *category* of the Other which I project appropriating to myself. This category is not conceived nor even conceivable. But on the occasion of concrete experi-

From Jean-Paul Sartre, *Being and Nothingness,* trans. Hazel Barnes. New York: Philosophical Library, 1956; London: Methuen, 1956. Reprinted with permission of the publishers.

ence with the Other, an experience suffered and realized, it is this concrete Other as an absolute reality whom in his otherness I wish to incorporate into myself. (2) The Other whom I wish to assimilate is by no means the Other-as-object. Or, if you prefer, my project of incorporating the Other in no way corresponds to a recapturing of my for-itself as myself and to a surpassing of the Other's transcendence toward my own possibilities. For me it is not a question of obliterating my object-state by making an object of the Other, which would amount to *releasing* myself from my being-for-others. Quite the contrary, I want to assimilate the Other as the Other-looking-at-me, and this project of assimilation includes an augmented recognition of my being-looked-at. In short, in order to maintain before me the Other's freedom which is looking at me, I identify myself totally with my being-looked-at. And since my being-as-object is the only possible relation between me and the Other, it is this being-as-object which alone can serve me as an instrument to effect my assimilation of the *other freedom*.

Thus as a reaction to the failure of the third ekstasis, the for-itself wishes to be identified with the Other's freedom as founding its own being-in-itself. To be other to oneself—the ideal always aimed at concretely in the form of being *this Other* to oneself—is the primary value of my relations with the Other. This means that my being-for-others is haunted by the indication of an absolute-being which would be itself as other and other as itself and which, by freely giving to itself its being-itself as other and its being-other as itself, would be the very being of the ontological proof—that is, God. This ideal can not be realized without my surmounting the original contingency of my relations to the Other; that is, by overcoming the fact that there is no relation of internal negativity between the negation by which the Other is made other than I and the negation by which I am made other than the Other. We have seen that this contingency is insurmountable; it is the *fact* of my relations with the Other, just as my body is the *fact* of my being-in-the-world. Unity with the Other is therefore *in fact* unrealizable. It is also unrealizable *in theory,* for the assimilation of the for-itself and the Other in a single transcendence would necessarily involve the disappearance of the characteristic of otherness in the Other. Thus the condition on which

I project the identification of myself with the Other is that I persist in denying that I am the Other. Finally this project of unification is the source of *conflict* since while I experience myself as an object for the Other and while I project assimilating him in and by means of this experience, the Other apprehends me as an object in the midst of the world and does not project identifying me with himself. It would therefore be necessary—since being-for-others includes a double internal negation—to act upon the internal negation by which the Other transcends my transcendence and makes me exist for the Other; that is, *to act upon the Other's freedom.*

This unrealizable ideal which haunts my project of myself in the presence of the Other is not to be identified with love in so far as love is an enterprise; *i.e.,* an organic ensemble of projects toward my own possibilities. But it is the ideal of love, its motivation and its end, its unique value. Love as the primitive relation to the Other is the ensemble of the projects by which I aim at realizing this value.

These projects put me in direct connection with the Other's freedom. It is in this sense that love is a conflict. We have observed that the Other's freedom is the foundation of my being. But precisely because I exist by means of the Other's freedom, I have no security; I am in danger in this freedom. It moulds my being and *makes me be,* it confers values upon me and removes them from me; and my being receives from it a perpetual passive escape from self. Irresponsible and beyond reach, this protean freedom in which I have engaged myself can in turn engage me in a thousand different ways of being. My project of recovering my being can be realized only if I get hold of this freedom and reduce it to being a freedom subject to my freedom. At the same time it is the only way in which I can act on the free negation of interiority by which the Other constitutes me as an Other; that is the only way in which I can prepare the way for a future identification of the Other with me. This will be clearer perhaps if we study the problem from a purely psychological aspect. Why does the lover want to be *loved?* If Love were in fact a pure desire for physical possession, it could in many cases be easily satisfied. Proust's hero, for example, who installs his mistress in his home, who can see her and possess her at any hour of the day, who has been able to make her completely dependent on him economically, ought to be free from worry. Yet we know that he is, on the contrary, continually gnawed by anxiety. Through her consciousness Albertine escapes Marcel even when he is at her side, and that is why he knows relief only when he gazes on her while she sleeps. It is certain then that the lover wishes to capture a "consciousness." But why does he wish it? And how?

The notion of "ownership," by which love is so often explained, is not actually primary. Why should I want to appropriate the Other if it were not precisely that the Other makes me be? But this implies precisely a certain mode of appropriation; it is the Other's freedom as such that we want to get hold of. Not because of a desire for power. The tyrant scorns love, he is content with fear. If he seeks to win the love of his subjects, it is for political reasons; and if he finds a more economical way to enslave them, he adopts it immediately. On the other hand, the man who wants to be loved does not desire the enslavement of the beloved. He is not bent on becoming the object of passion which flows forth mechanically. He does not want to possess an automaton, and if we want to humiliate him, we need only try to persuade him that the beloved's passion is the result of a psychological determinism. The lover will then feel that both his love and his being are cheapened. If Tristan and Isolde fall madly in love because of a love potion, they are less interesting. The total enslavement of the beloved kills the love of the lover. The end is surpassed; if the beloved is transformed into an automaton, the lover finds himself alone. Thus the lover does not desire to possess the beloved as one possesses a thing; he demands a special type of appropriation. He wants to possess a freedom as freedom.

On the other hand, the lover can not be satisfied with that superior form of freedom which is a free and voluntary engagement. Who would be content with a love given as pure loyalty to a sworn oath? Who would be satisfied with the words, "I love you because I have freely engaged myself to love you and because I do not wish to go back on my word." Thus the lover demands a pledge, yet is irritated by a pledge. He wants to be loved by a freedom but demands that this freedom as freedom should no longer be free. He wishes that the Other's

freedom should determine itself to become love—and this not only at the beginning of the affair but at each instant—and at the same time he wants this freedom to be captured *by itself,* to turn back upon itself, as in madness, as in a dream, so as to will its own captivity. This captivity must be a resignation that is both free and yet chained in our hands. In love it is not a determinism of the passions which we desire in the Other nor a freedom beyond reach; it is a freedom which *plays the role of* a determinism of the passions and which is caught in its own role. For himself the lover does not demand that he be the *cause* of this radical modification of freedom but that he be the unique and privileged occasion of it. In fact he could not want to be the cause of it without immediately submerging the beloved in the midst of the world as a tool which can be transcended. That is not the essence of love. On the contrary, in Love the Lover wants to be "the whole World" for the beloved. This means that he puts himself on the side of the world; he is the one who assumes and symbolizes the world; he is a *this* which includes all other *thises.* He is and consents to be an *object.* But on the other hand, he wants to be the object in which the Other's freedom consents to lose itself, the object in which the Other consents to find his being and his *raison d'être* as his second facticity—the object-limit of transcendence, that toward which the Other's transcendence transcends all other objects but which it can in no way transcend. And everywhere he desires the circle of the Other's freedom; that is, at each instant as the Other's freedom accepts this limit to his transcendence, this acceptance is *already* present as the motivation of the acceptance considered. It is in the capacity of an end already chosen that the lover wishes to be chosen as an end. This allows us to grasp what basically the lover demands of the beloved; he does not want to *act* on the Other's freedom but to exist *a priori* as the objective limit of this freedom; that is, to be given at one stroke along with it and in its very upsurge as the limit which the freedom must accept in order to be free. By this very fact, what he demands is a limiting, a gluing down of the Other's freedom by itself; this limit of structure is in fact a *given,* and the very appearance of the given as the limit of freedom means that the freedom *makes itself exist* within the given by being its own prohibition against surpassing it. This prohibition is envisaged by the lover *simultaneously* as something lived—that is, something suffered (in a word, as a facticity) and as something freely consented to. It must be freely consented to since it must be effected only with the upsurge of a freedom which chooses itself as freedom. But it must be only what is lived since it must be an impossibility always present, a facticity which surges back to the heart of the Other's freedom. This is expressed psychologically by the demand that the free decision to love me, which the beloved formerly has taken, must slip in as a magically determining motivation *within* his present free engagement.

Now we can grasp the meaning of this demand: the facticity which is to be a factual limit for the Other in my demand to be loved and which is to result in being *his own* facticity—this is *my* facticity. It is in so far as I am the object which the Other makes come into being that I must be the inherent limit to his very transcendence. Thus the Other by his upsurge into being makes me be as unsurpassable and absolute, not as a nihilating For-itself but as a being-for-others-in-the-midst-of-the-world. Thus to want to be loved is to infest the Other with one's own facticity; it is to wish to compel him to re-create you perpetually as the condition of a freedom which submits itself and which is engaged; it is to wish both that freedom found fact and that fact have preeminence over freedom. If this end could be attained, it would result in the first place in my being *secure* within the Other's consciousness. First because the motive of my uneasiness and my shame is the fact that I apprehend and experience myself in my being-for-others as that which can always be surpassed toward something else, that which is the pure object of a value judgment, a pure means, a pure tool. My uneasiness stems from the fact that I assume necessarily and freely that being which another makes me be in an absolute freedom. "God knows what I am for him! God knows what he thinks of me!" This means "God knows what he makes me be." I am haunted by this being which I fear to encounter someday at the turn of a path, this being which is so strange to me and which is yet *my being* and which I know that I shall never encounter in spite of all my efforts to do so. But if the Other loves me then I become the *unsurpassable,* which means that I

must be the absolute end. In this sense I am saved from *instrumentality.* My existence in the midst of the world becomes the exact correlate of my transcendence-for-myself since my independence is absolutely safeguarded. The object which the Other must make me be is an object-transcendence, an absolute center of reference around which all the instrumental-things of the world are ordered as pure *means.* At the same time, as the absolute limit of freedom—*i.e.,* of the absolute source of all values—I am protected against any eventual devalorization. I am the absolute value. To the extent that I assume my being-for-others, I assume myself as value. Thus to want to be loved is to want to be placed beyond the whole system of values posited by the Other and to be the condition of all valorization and the objective foundation of all values. This demand is the usual theme of lovers' conversations, whether as in *La Porte Etroite,* the woman who wants to be loved identifies herself with an ascetic morality of self-surpassing and wishes to embody the ideal limit of this surpassing—or as more usually happens, the woman in love demands that the beloved in his acts should sacrifice traditional morality for her and is anxious to know whether the beloved would betray his friends for her, "would steal for her," "would kill for her," *etc.*

From this point of view, my being must escape the *look* of the beloved, or rather it must be the object of a look with another structure. I must no longer be seen on the ground of the world as a "this" among other "thises," but the world must be revealed in terms of me. In fact to the extent that the upsurge of freedom makes a world exist, I must be, as the limiting-condition of this upsurge, the very condition of the upsurge of a world. I must be the one whose function is to make trees and water exist, to make cities and fields and other men exist, in order to give them later to the Other who arranges them into a world, just as the mother in matrilineal communities receives titles and the family name not to keep them herself but to transfer them immediately to her children. In one sense if I am to be loved, I am the object through whose procuration the world will exist for the Other; in another sense I am the world. Instead of being a "this" detaching itself on the ground of the world, I am the ground-as-object on which the world detaches itself. Thus I am reassured; the Other's look no longer paralyzes me with finitude. It no longer fixes my being in *what I am*. I can no longer be *looked at* as ugly, as small, as cowardly, since these characteristics necessarily represent a factual limitation of my being and an apprehension of my finitude as finitude. To be sure, my possibles remain transcended possibilities, dead-possibilities; but I possess all possibles. I am all the dead-possibilities in the world; hence I cease to be the being who is understood from the standpoint of other beings or of its acts. In the loving intuition which I demand, I am to be given as an absolute totality in terms of which all its peculiar acts and all beings are to be understood. One could say, slightly modifying a famous pronouncement of the Stoics, that "the beloved can fail in three ways."[1] The ideal of the sage and the ideal of the man who wants to be loved actually coincide in this, that both want to be an object-as-totality accessible to a global intuition which will apprehend the beloved's or the sage's actions in the world as partial structures which are interpreted in terms of the totality. Just as wisdom is proposed as a state to be attained by an absolute metamorphosis, so the Other's freedom must be absolutely metamorphosed in order to allow me to attain the state of being loved.

Up to this point our description would fall into line with Hegel's famous description of the Master and Slave relation. What the Hegelian Master is for the Slave, the lover wants to be for the beloved. But the analogy stops here, for with Hegel the Master demands the Slave's freedom only laterally and, so to speak, implicitly, while the lover wants the beloved's freedom *first and foremost*. In this sense if I am to be loved by the Other, this means that I am to be freely chosen as beloved. As we know, in the current terminology of love, the beloved is often called *the chosen one*. But this choice must not be relative and contingent. The lover is irritated and feels himself cheapened when he thinks that the beloved has chosen him *from among others*. "Then if I had not come into a certain city, if I had not visited the home of so and so, you would never have known me, you wouldn't have loved me?" This thought grieves the lover; his love becomes one love among others and is limited by the beloved's facticity and by his own facticity as well as by the contingency of encounters. It becomes *love in the world*, an object which presupposes the world and which in turn can exist for others. What he is demanding he expresses by the awkward and vitiated phrases of "fatalism." He says, "We were made for each other," or again he uses the expression "soul mate." But we must translate all this. The lover knows very well that "being made for each other" refers to an original choice. This choice can be God's, since he is the being who is absolute choice, but God here represents only the farthest possible limit of the demand for an absolute. Actually what the lover demands is that the beloved should make of him an absolute choice. This means that the beloved's being-in-the-world must be a being-as-loving. The upsurge of the beloved must be the beloved's free choice of the lover. And since the Other is the foundation of my being-as-object, I demand of him that the free upsurge of his being should have his choice of *me* as his unique and absolute end; that is, that he should choose to be for the sake of founding my object-state and my facticity.

Thus my facticity is *saved*. It is no longer this unthinkable and insurmountable given which I am fleeing; it is that for which the Other freely makes himself exist; it is as an end which he has given to himself. I have infected him with my facticity, but as it is in the form of freedom that he has been infected with it, he refers it back to me as a facticity taken up and consented to. He is the foundation of it in order that it may be his end. By means of this love I then have a different apprehension of my alienation and of my own facticity. My facticity—as for-others—is no longer a fact but a right. My existence *is* because it is *given a name*. I am because I give myself away. These beloved veins on my hands exist—beneficently. How good I am to have eyes, hair, eyebrows and to lavish them away tirelessly in an overflow of generosity to this tireless desire which the Other freely makes himself be. Whereas before being loved we were uneasy about that unjustified, unjustifiable protuberance which was our existence, whereas we felt ourselves "*de trop*," we now feel that our existence is taken up and willed even in its tiniest details by an absolute freedom which at the same time our existence conditions and which we ourselves will with our freedom. This is the basis for the joy of love when there is joy; we feel that our existence is justified.

By the same token if the beloved can love

us, he is wholly ready to be assimilated by our freedom; for this being-loved which we desire is already the ontological proof applied to our being-for-others. Our objective essence implies the existence of the Other, and conversely it is the Other's freedom which founds our essence. If we could manage to interiorize the whole system, we should be our own foundation.

Such then is the real goal of the lover in so far as his love is an enterprise—*i.e.*, a project of himself. This project is going to provoke a conflict. The beloved in fact apprehends the lover as one Other-as-object among others; that is, he perceives the lover on the ground of the world, transcends him, and utilizes him. The beloved is a *look*. He can not therefore employ his transcendence to fix an ultimate limit to his surpassings, nor can he employ his freedom to captivate itself. The beloved can not will to love. Therefore the lover must seduce the beloved, and his love can in no way be distinguished from the enterprise of seduction. In seduction I do not try to reveal my subjectivity to the Other. Moreover I could do so only by *looking at* the other; but by this look I should cause the Other's subjectivity to disappear, and it is exactly this which I want to assimilate. To seduce is to risk assuming my object-state completely for the Other; it is to put myself beneath his look and to make him look at me; it is to risk the danger of *being-seen* in order to effect a new departure and to appropriate the Other in and by means of my object-ness. I refuse to leave the level on which I make proof of my object-ness; it is on this level that I wish to engage in battle by making myself a *fascinating object*. In Part Two we defined fascination as a *state*. It is, we said, the non-thetic consciousness of being *nothing* in the presence of being. Seduction aims at producing in the Other the consciousness of his state of nothingness as he confronts the seductive object. By seduction I aim at constituting myself as a fullness of being and at making myself *recognized as such*. To accomplish this I constitute myself as a meaningful object. My acts must *point* in two directions: On the one hand, toward that which is wrongly called subjectivity and which is rather a depth of objective and hidden being; the act is not performed for itself only, but it points to an infinite, undifferentiated series of other real and possible acts which I give as constituting my objective, unperceived being.

Thus I try to guide the transcendence which transcends me and to refer it to the infinity of my dead-possibilities precisely in order to be the unsurpassable and to the exact extent to which the only unsurpassable is the infinite. On the other hand, each of my acts tries to point to the great density of possible-world and must present me as bound to the vastest regions of the world. At the same time I *present* the world to the beloved, and I try to constitute myself as the necessary intermediary between her and the world; I manifest by my acts infinitely varied examples of my power over the world (money, position, "connections," *etc.*). In the first case I try to constitute myself as an infinity of depth, in the second case to identify myself with the world. Through these different procedures I propose myself as unsurpassable. This proposal could not be sufficient in itself; it is only a besieging of the Other. It can not take on value as fact without the consent of the Other's freedom, which I must capture by making it recognize itself as nothingness in the face of my plenitude of absolute being.

Someone may observe that these various attempts at expression *presuppose* language. We shall not disagree with this. But we shall say rather that they *are* language or, if you prefer, a fundamental mode of language. For while psychological and historical problems exist with regard to the existence, the learning and the use of *a particular* language, there is no special problem concerning what is called the discovery or invention of language. Language is not a phenomenon added on to being-for-others. It *is* originally being-for others; that is, it is the fact that a subjectivity experiences itself as an object for the Other. In a universe of pure objects language could under no circumstances have been "invented" since it presupposes an original relation to another subject. In the intersubjectivity of the for-others, it is not necessary to invent language because it is already given in the recognition of the Other. I *am* language. By the sole fact that whatever I may do, my acts freely conceived and executed, my projects launched toward my possibilities have outside of them a meaning which escapes me and which I experience. It is in this sense—and in this sense only—that Heidegger is right in declaring that *I am what I say*.[2] Language is not an instinct of the constituted human creature, nor is it an invention of our subjectivity. But neither does it need to be referred to the pure "being-outside-of-self" of the *Dasein*. It forms part of the *human condition;* it is originally the proof which a for-itself can make of its being-for-others, and finally it is the surpassing of this proof and the utilization of it toward possibilities which are my possibilities; that is, toward my possibilities of being this or that for the Other. Language is therefore not distinct from the recognition of the Other's existence. The Other's upsurge confronting me as a look makes language arise as the condition of my being. This primitive language is not necessarily seduction; we shall see other forms of it. Moreover we have noted that there is another primitive attitude confronting the Other and that the two succeed each other in a circle, each implying the other. But conversely seduction does not presuppose any earlier form of language; it is the complete realization of language. This means that language can be revealed entirely and at one stroke by seduction as a primitive mode of being of expression. Of course by language we mean all the phenomena of expression and not the articulated word, which is a derived and secondary mode whose appearance can be made the object of an historical study. Especially in seduction language does not *aim* at *giving to be known* but at causing to experience.

But in this first attempt to find a fascinating language I proceed blindly since I am guided only by the abstract and empty form of my object-state for the Other. I can not even conceive what effect my gestures and attitudes will have since they will always be taken up and founded by a freedom which will surpass them and since they can have a meaning only if this freedom confers one on them. Thus the "meaning" of my expressions always escapes me. I never know exactly if I signify what I wish to signify nor even if I *am* signifying anything. It would be necessary that at the precise instant I should read in the Other what on principle is inconceivable. For lack of knowing what I actually express for the Other, I constitute my language as an incomplete phenomenon of flight outside myself. As soon as I express myself, I can only guess at the meaning of what I express—*i.e.,* the meaning of what I am— since in this perspective to express and to be are one. The Other is always there, present and experienced as the one who gives to language its meaning. Each expression, each gesture,

each word is on my side a concrete proof of the alienating reality of the Other. It is only the psychopath who can say, "someone has stolen my thought"—as in cases of psychoses of influence, for example.[3] The very fact of expression is a stealing of thought since thought needs the cooperation of an alienating freedom in order to be constituted as an object. That is why this first aspect of language—in so far as it is I who employ it for the Other—is *sacred.* The sacred object is an object which is in the world and which points to a transcendence beyond the world. Language reveals to me the freedom (the transcendence) of the one who listens to me in silence.

But at the same moment I remain for the Other a meaningful object—that which I have always been. There is no path which departing from my object-state can lead the Other to my transcendence. Attitudes, expressions, and words can only indicate to him other attitudes, other expressions, and other words. Thus language remains for him a simple property of a magical object—and this magical object itself. It is an action at a distance whose effect the Other exactly knows. Thus the word is *sacred* when I employ it and *magic* when the Other hears it. Thus I do not know my language any more than I know my body for the Other. I can not hear myself speak nor see myself smile. The problem of language is exactly parallel to the problem of bodies, and the description which is valid in one case is valid in the other.

Fascination, however, even if it were to produce a state of being-fascinated in the Other could not by itself succeed in producing love. We can be fascinated by an orator, by an actor, by a tightrope-walker, but this does not mean that we love him. To be sure we can not take our eyes off him, but he is still raised on the ground of the world, and fascination does not posit the fascinating object as the ultimate term of the transcendence. Quite the contrary, fascination *is* transcendence. When then will the beloved become in turn the lover?

The answer is easy: when the beloved projects being loved. By himself the Other-as-object never has enough strength to produce love. If love has for its ideal the appropriation of the Other qua Other (*i.e.,* as a subjectivity which is looking at an object) this ideal can be projected only in terms of my encounter with the Other-as-subject, not with the Other-as-object. If the Other tries to seduce me by means of his object-state, then seduction can bestow upon the Other only the character of a *precious* object "to be possessed." Seduction will perhaps determine me to risk much to conquer the Other-as-object, but this desire to appropriate an object in the midst of the world should not be confused with love. Love therefore can be born in the beloved only from the proof which he makes of his alienation and his flight toward the Other. Still the beloved, if such is the case, will be transformed into a love only if he projects being loved; that is, if what he wishes to overcome is not a body but the Other's subjectivity as such. In fact the only way that he could conceive to realize this appropriation is to make himself be loved. Thus it seems that to love is in essence the project of making oneself be loved. Hence this new contradiction and this new conflict: each of the lovers is entirely the captive of the Other inasmuch as each wishes to make himself loved by the Other to the exclusion of anyone else; but at the same time each one demands from the other a love which is not reducible to the "project of being-loved." What he demands in fact is that the Other without originally seeking to make himself be loved should have at once a contemplative and affective intuition of his beloved as the objective limit of his freedom, as the ineluctable and chosen foundation of his transcendence, as the totality of being and the supreme value. Love thus exacted from the other could not *ask for* anything; it is a pure engagement without reciprocity. Yet this love can not exist except in the form of a demand on the part of the lover.

The lover is held captive in a wholly different way. He is the captive of his very demand since love is the demand to be loved; he is a freedom which wills itself a body and which demands an outside, hence a freedom which imitates the flight toward the Other, a freedom which qua freedom lays claim to its alienation. The lover's freedom, in his very effort to make himself be loved as an object by the Other, is alienated by slipping into the body-for-others; that is, it is brought into existence with a dimension of flight toward the Other. It is the perpetual refusal to posit itself as pure selfness, for this affirmation of self as itself would involve the collapse of the Other as a look and the upsurge of the Other-as-object—hence a state of affairs in which the very possibility of being loved disappears since the Other is reduced to the dimension of objectivity. This re-fusal therefore constitutes freedom as dependent on the Other; and the Other as subjectivity becomes indeed an unsurpassable limit of the freedom of the for-itself, the goal and supreme end of the for-itself since the Other holds the key to its being. Here in fact we encounter the true ideal of love's enterprise: alienated freedom. But it is the one who wants to be loved who by the mere fact of wanting someone to love him alienates his freedom.

My freedom is alienated in the presence of the Other's pure subjectivity which founds my objectivity. It can never be alienated before the Other-as-object. In this form in fact the beloved's alienation, of which the lover dreams, would be contradictory since the beloved can found the being of the lover only by transcending it on principle toward other objects of the world; therefore this transcendence can constitute the object which it surpasses both as a transcended object and as an object limit of all transcendence. Thus each one of the lovers wants to be the object for which the Other's freedom is alienated in an original intuition; but this intuition which would be love in the true sense is only a contradictory ideal of the for-itself. Each one is alienated only to the exact extent to which he demands the alienation of the other. Each one wants the other to love him but does not take into account the fact that to love is to want to be loved and that thus by wanting the other to love him, he only wants the other to want to be loved in turn. Thus love relations are a system of indefinite reference—analogous to the pure "reflection-reflected" of consciousness—under the ideal standard of the *value* "love"; that is, in a fusion of consciousness in which each of them would preserve his otherness in order to found the other. This state of affairs is due to the fact that consciousnesses are separated by an insurmountable nothingness, a nothingness which is both the internal negation of the one by the other and a factual nothingness between the two internal negations. Love is a contradictory effort to surmount the factual negation while preserving the internal negation. I demand that the Other love me and I do everything possible to realize my project; but if the Other loves me, he radically deceives me by his very love. I demanded of him that he should found my being as a privileged object by maintaining himself as pure subjectivity confronting me; and as soon as he loves me he experiences me as subject and is swallowed up in his objectivity confronting my subjectivity.

The problem of my being-for-others remains therefore without solution. The lovers remain each one for himself in a total subjectivity; nothing comes to relieve them of their duty to make themselves exist each one for himself; nothing comes to relieve their contingency nor to save them from facticity. At least each one has succeeded in escaping danger from the Other's freedom—but altogether differently than he expected. He escapes not because the Other makes him be as the object-limit of his transcendence but because the Other experiences him as subjectivity and wishes to experience him only as such. Again the gain is perpetually compromised. At the start, each of the consciousnesses can at any moment free itself from its chains and suddenly contemplate the other as an *object*. Then the spell is broken; the Other becomes one mean among means. He is indeed an object for others as the lover desires but an object-as-tool, a perpetually transcended object. The illusion, the game of mirrors which makes the concrete reality of love, suddenly ceases. Later in the experience of love each consciousness seeks to shelter its being-for-others in the Other's freedom. This supposes that the Other is beyond the world as pure subjectivity, as the absolute by which the world comes into being. But it suffices that the lovers should be *looked at* together by a third person in order for each one to experience not only his own objectivation but that of the other as well. Immediately the Other is no longer for me the absolute transcendence which founds me in my being; he is a transcendence-transcended, not by me but by another. My original relation to him—*i.e.*, my relation of being the beloved for my lover, is fixed as a dead-possibility. It is no longer the experienced relation between a limiting object of all transcendence and the freedom which founds it; it is a love-as-object which is wholly alienated toward the third. Such is the true reason why lovers seek solitude. It is because the appearance of a third person, whoever he may be, is the destruction of their love. But factual solitude (*e.g.*, we are alone in my room) is by no means a theoretical solitude. Even if nobody sees us, we exist for *all* consciousnesses and we are conscious of existing for all. The result is that love as a fundamental mode of being-for-others holds in

its being-for-others the seed of its own destruction.

We have just defined the triple destructibility of love: in the first place it is, in essence, a deception and a reference to infinity since to love is to wish to be loved, hence to wish that the Other wish that I love him. A pre-ontological comprehension of this deception is given in the very impulse of love—hence the lover's perpetual dissatisfacton. It does not come, as is so often said, from the unworthiness of being loved but from an implicit comprehension of the fact that the amorous intuition is, as a fundamental-intuition, an ideal out of reach. The more I am loved, the more I lose my *being,* the more I am thrown back on my own responsibilities, on my own power to be. In the second place the Other's awakening is always possible; at any moment he can make me appear as an object—hence the lover's perpetual insecurity. In the third place love is an absolute which is perpetually *made relative* by others. One would have to be alone in the world with the beloved in order for love to preserve its character as an absolute axis of reference— hence the lover's perpetual shame (or pride— which here amounts to the same thing).

Thus it is useless for me to have tried to lose myself in objectivity; my passion will have availed me nothing. The Other has referred me to my own unjustifiable subjectivity—either by himself or through others. This result can provoke a total despair and a new attempt to realize the identification of the Other and myself. Its ideal will then be the opposite of that which we have just described; instead of projecting the absorbing of the Other while preserving in him his otherness, I shall project causing myself to be absorbed by the Other and losing myself in his subjectivity in order to get rid of my own. This enterprise will be expressed concretely by the *masochistic* attitude. Since the Other is the foundation of my being-for-others, if I relied on the Other to make me exist, I should no longer be anything more than a being-in-itself founded in its being by a freedom. Here it is my own subjectivity which is considered as an obstacle to the primordial act by which the Other would found me in my being. It is my own subjectivity which above all must be denied by *my own freedom.* I attempt therefore to engage myself wholly in my being-as-object. I refuse to be anything more than an object. I rest upon the Other, and as I experience this being-as-object in shame, I will and I love my shame as the profound sign of my objectivity. As the Other apprehends me as object by means of *actual desire,* I wish to be desired, I make myself in shame an object of desire.[4]

This attitude would resemble that of love if instead of seeking to exist for the Other as the object-limit of his transcendence, I did not rather insist on making myself be treated as one object among others, as an instrument to be used. Now it is *my* transcendence which is to be denied, not his. This time I do not have to project capturing his freedom; on the contrary I hope that this freedom may *be* and *will* itself to be radically free. Thus the more I shall feel myself surpassed toward other ends, the more I shall enjoy the abdication of my transcendence. Finally I project being nothing more than an *object;* that is, radically an *in-itself.* But inasmuch as a freedom which will have absorbed mine will be the foundation of this in-itself, my being will become again the foundation of itself. Masochism, like sadism, is the assumption of guilt.[5] I am guilty due to the very fact that I am an object, I am guilty toward myself since I consent to my absolute alienation. I am guilty toward the Other, for I furnish him with the occasion of being guilty—that is, of radically missing my freedom as such. Masochism is an attempt not to fascinate the Other by means of my objectivity but to cause myself to be fascinated by my objectivity-for-others; that is, to cause myself to be constituted as an object by the Other in such a way that I nonthetically apprehend my subjectivity as a *nothing* in the presence of the in-itself which I represent to the Other's eyes. Masochism is characterized as a species of vertigo, vertigo not before a precipice of rock and earth but before the abyss of the Other's subjectivity.

But masochism is and must be itself a failure. In order to cause myself to be fascinated by my self-as-object, I should necessarily have to be able to realize the intuitive apprehension of this object such as it is *for the Other,* a thing

which is on principle impossible. Thus I am far from being able to be fascinated by this alienated Me, which remains on principle inapprehensible. It is useless for the masochist to get down on his knees, to show himself in ridiculous positions, to cause himself to be used as a simple lifeless instrument. It is *for the Other* that he will be obscene or simply passive, for the Other that he will *undergo* these postures; for himself he is forever condemned to *give them to himself.* It is in and through his transcendence that he disposes of himself as a being to be transcended. The more he tries to taste his objectivity, the more he will be submerged by the consciousness of his subjectivity—hence his anguish. Even the masochist who pays a woman to whip him is treating her as an instrument and by this very fact posits himself in transcendence in relation to her.

Thus the masochist ultimately treats the Other as an object and transcends him toward his own objectivity. Recall, for example, the tribulations of Sacher Masoch, who in order to make himself scorned, insulted, reduced to a humiliating position, was obliged to make use of the great love which women bore toward him; that is, to act upon them just in so far as they experienced themselves as an object for him. Thus in every way the masochist's objectivity escapes him, and it can even happen—in fact usually does happen—that in seeking to apprehend his own objectivity he finds the Other's objectivity, which in spite of himself frees his own subjectivity. Masochism therefore is on principle a failure. This should not surprise us if we realize that masochism is a "vice" and that vice is, on principle, the love of failure. But this is not the place to describe the structures peculiar to the vice. It is sufficient here to point out that masochism is a perpetual effort to *annihilate* the subject's subjectivity by causing it to be assimilated by the Other; this effort is accompanied by the exhausting and delicious consciousness of failure so that finally it is the failure itself which the subject ultimately seeks as his principal goal.[6]

NOTES

1. Tr. Literally, "can tumble three times."

2. This formulation of Heidegger's position is that of A. de Waehlens. *La philosophie de Martin Heidegger.* Louvain, 1942, p. 99. *Cf.* also Heidegger's text, which he quotes: "Diese Bezeugung meint nicht hier einen nachträglichen und beiher

laufenden Ausdruck des Menschseins, sondern sie macht das Dasein Menschen mit usw. (*Hölderlin und das Wesen der Dichtung*, p.6).

("This affirmation does not mean here an additional and supplementary expression of human existence, but it does in the process make plain the existence of man." Douglas Scott's translation. *Existence and Being*, Chicago: Henry Regnery. 1949, p. 297.)

3. Furthermore the psychosis of influence, like the majority of psychoses, is a special experience translated by myths, of a great metaphysical fact—here the fact of alienation. Even a madman in his own way realizes the human condition.

4. *Cf.* following section.

5. *Cf.* following section.

6. Consistent with this description, there is at least one form of exhibitionism which ought to be classed among masochistic attitudes. For example, when Rousseau exhibits to the washerwomen "not the obscene object but the ridiculous object." *Cf. Confessions*, Chapter III.

SIMONE DE BEAUVOIR

The Woman in Love

The word *love* has by no means the same sense for both sexes, and this is one cause of the serious misunderstandings that divide them. Byron well said: "Man's love is of man's life a thing apart; 'Tis woman's existence." Nietzsche expresses the same idea in *The Gay Science:*

The single word love in fact signifies two different things for man and woman. What woman understands by love is clear enough; it is not only devotion, it is a total gift of body and soul, without reservation, without regard for anything whatever. This unconditional nature of her love is what makes it a *faith,*[1] the only one she has. As for man, if he loves a woman, what he *wants*[1] is that love from her; he is in consequence far from postulating the same sentiment for himself as for woman; if there should be men who also felt that desire for complete abandonment, upon my word, they would not be men.

Men have found it possible to be passionate lovers at certain times in their lives, but there is not one of them who could be called "a great lover";[2] in their most violent transports, they never abdicate completely; even on their knees before a mistress, what they still want is to take possession of her; at the very heart of their lives they remain sovereign subjects; the beloved woman is only one value among others; they wish to integrate her into their existence and not to squander it entirely on her. For woman, on the contrary, to love is to relinquish everything for the benefit of a master. As Cécile Sauvage puts it: "Woman must forget her own personality when she is in love. It is a law of nature. A woman is nonexistent without a master. Without a master, she is a scattered bouquet."

The fact is that we have nothing to do here with laws of nature. It is the difference in their situations that is reflected in the difference men and women show in their conceptions of love. The individual who is a subject, who is himself, if he has the courageous inclination toward transcendence, endeavors to extend his grasp on the world: he is ambitious, he acts. But an inessential creature is incapable of sensing the absolute at the heart of her subjectivity; a being doomed to immanence cannot find self-realization in acts. Shut up in the sphere of the relative, destined to the male from childhood, habituated to seeing in him a superb being whom she cannot possibly equal, the woman who has not repressed her claim to humanity will dream of transcending her being toward one of these superior beings, of amalgamating herself with the sovereign subject. There is no other way out for her than to lose herself, body and soul, in him who is represented to her as the absolute, as the essential. Since she is anyway doomed to dependence, she will prefer to serve a god rather than obey tyrants—parents, husband, or protector. She chooses to desire her enslavement so ardently that it will seem to her the expression of her liberty; she will try to rise above her situation as inessential object by fully accepting it; through her flesh, her feelings, her behavior, she will enthrone him as supreme value and reality: she will humble herself to nothingness before him. Love becomes for her a religion.

As we have seen, the adolescent girl wishes at first to identify herself with males; when she gives that up, she then seeks to share in their masculinity by having one of them in love with her; it is not the individuality of this one or that one which attracts her; she is in love with man in general.³ "And you, the men I shall love, how I await you!" writes Irène Reweliotty. "How I rejoice to think I shall know you soon: especially You, the first." Of course the male is to belong to the same class and race as hers, for sexual privilege is in play only within this frame. If man is to be a demigod, he must first of all be a human being, and to the colonial officer's daughter the native is not a man. If the young girl gives herself to an "inferior," it is for the reason that she wishes to degrade herself because she believes she is unworthy of love; but normally she is looking for a man who represents male superiority. She is soon to ascertain that many individuals of the favored sex are sadly contingent and earthbound, but at first her presumption is favorable to them; they are called on less to prove their worth than to avoid too gross a disproof of it—which accounts for many mistakes, some of them serious. A naïve young girl is caught by the gleam of virility, and in her eyes male worth is shown, according to circumstances, by physical strength, distinction of manner, wealth, cultivation, intelligence, authority, social status, a military uniform; but what she always wants is for her lover to represent the essence of manhood.

Familiarity is often sufficient to destroy his prestige; it may collapse at the first kiss, or in daily association, or during the wedding night. Love at a distance, however, is only a fantasy, not a real experience. The desire for love becomes a passionate love only when it is carnally realized. Inversely, love can arise as a result of physical intercourse; in this case the sexually dominated woman acquires an exalted view of a man who at first seemed to her quite insignificant.

But it often happens that a woman succeeds in deifying none of the men she knows. Love has a smaller place in woman's life than has often been supposed. Husband, children, home, amusements, social duties, vanity, sexuality, career, are much more important. Most women dream of a *grand amour,* a soul-searing love. They have known substitutes, they have been close to it; it has come to them in partial, bruised, ridiculous, imperfect, mendacious forms; but very few have truly dedicated their lives to it. The *grandes amoureuses* are most often women who have not frittered themselves away in juvenile affairs; they have first accepted the traditional feminine destiny: husband, home, children; or they have known pitiless solitude; or they have banked on some enterprise that has been more or less of a failure. And when they glimpse the opportunity to salvage a disappointing life by dedicating it to some superior person, they desperately give themselves up to this hope. Mlle Aïssé, Juliette Drouet, and Mme d'Agoult were almost thirty when their love-life began, Julie de Lespinasse not far from forty. No other aim in life which seemed worth while was open to them, love was their only way out.

Even if they can choose independence, this road seems the most attractive to a majority of women: it is agonizing for a woman to assume responsibility for her life. Even the male, when adolescent, is quite willing to turn to older women for guidance, education, mothering; but customary attitudes, the boy's training, and his own inner imperatives forbid him to content himself in the end with the easy solution of abdication; to him such affairs with older women are only a stage through which he passes. It is man's good fortune—in adulthood as in early childhood—to be obliged to take the most arduous roads, but the surest; it is woman's misfortune to be surrounded by almost irresistible temptations; everything incites her to follow the easy slopes; instead of being invited to fight her own way up, she is told that she has only to let herself slide and she will attain paradises of enchantment. When she perceives that she has been duped by a mirage, it is too late; her strength has been exhausted in a losing venture.

The psychoanalysts are wont to assert that woman seeks the father image in her lover; but it is because he is a man, not because he is a father, that he dazzles the girl child, and every man shares in this magical power. Woman does not long to reincarnate one individual in another, but to reconstruct a situation: that which she experienced as a little girl, under adult protection. She was deeply integrated with home and family, she knew the peace of quasi-passivity. Love will give her back her mother as well as her father, it will give her back her childhood. What she wants to recover is a roof over her head, walls that prevent her from feeling her abandonment in the wide world, authority that protects her against her liberty. This childish drama haunts the love of many women; they are happy to be called "my little girl, my dear child"; men know that the words: "you're just like a little girl," are among those that most surely touch a woman's heart. We have seen that many women suffer in becoming adults; and so a great number remain obstinately "babyish," prolonging their childhood indefinitely in manner and dress. To become like a child again in a man's arms fills their cup with joy. The hackneyed theme: "To feel so little in your arms, my love," recurs again and again in amorous dialogue and in love letters. "Baby mine," croons the lover, the woman calls herself "your little one," and so on. A young woman will write: "When will he come, he who can dominate me?" And when he comes, she will love to sense his manly superiority. A neurotic studied by Janet illustrates this attitude quite cleary:

All my foolish acts and all the good things I have done have the same cause: an aspiration for a perfect and ideal love in which I can give myself completely, entrust my being to another, God, man, or woman, so superior to me that I will no longer need to think what to do in life or to watch over myself . . . Someone to obey blindly and with confidence . . . who will bear me up and lead me gently and lovingly toward perfection. How I envy the ideal love of Mary Magdalen and Jesus: to be the ardent disciple of an adored and worthy master; to live and die for him, my idol, to win at last the victory of the Angel over the beast, to rest in his protecting arms, so small, so lost in his loving care, so wholly his that I exist no longer.

Many examples have already shown us that this dream of annihilation is in fact an avid will to exist. In all religions the adoration of God is combined with the devotee's concern with personal salvation; when woman gives herself completely to her idol, she hopes that he will give her at once possession of herself and of the universe he represents. In most cases she asks her lover first of all for the justification, the exaltation, of her ego. Many women do not abandon themselves to love unless they are loved in return; and sometimes the love shown them is enough to arouse their love. The young girl dreamed of herself as seen through men's eyes, and it is in men's eyes that the woman believes she has finally found herself. Cécile Sauvage writes: "To walk by your side, to step forward with my little feet that you love, to feel

them so tiny in their high-heeled shoes with felt tops, makes me love all the love you throw around me. The least movements of my hands in my muff, of my arms, of my face, the tones of my voice, fill me with happiness."

The woman in love feels endowed with a high and undeniable value; she is at last allowed to idolize herself through the love she inspires. She is overjoyed to find in her lover a witness. This is what Colette's *Vagabonde* declares: "I admit I yielded, in permitting this man to come back the next day, to the desire to keep in him not a lover, not a friend, but an eager spectator of my life and my person. . . . One must be terribly old, Margot said to me one day, to renounce the vanity of living under someone's gaze."

In one of her letters to Middleton Murry, Katherine Mansfield wrote that she had just bought a ravishing mauve corset; she at once added: "Too bad there is no one to *see* it!" There is nothing more bitter than to feel oneself but the flower, the perfume, the treasure, which is the object of no desire: what kind of wealth is it that does not enrich myself and the gift of which no one wants? Love is the developer that brings out in clear, positive detail the dim negative, otherwise as useless as a blank exposure. Through love, woman's face, the curves of her body, her childhood memories, her former tears, her gowns, her accustomed ways, her universe, everything she is, all that belongs to her, escape contingency and become essential: she is a wondrous offering at the foot of the altar of her god.

This transforming power of love explains why it is that men of prestige who know how to flatter feminine vanity will arouse passionate attachments even if they are quite lacking in physical charm. Because of their lofty positions they embody the Law and the Truth: their perceptive powers disclose an unquestionable reality. The woman who finds favor in their sight feels herself transformed into a priceless treasure. D'Annunzio's success was due to this, as Isadora Duncan explains in the introduction to *My Life:*

When D'Annunzio loves a woman, he lifts her spirit from this earth to the divine region where Beatrice moves and shines. In turn he transforms each woman to a part of the divine essence, he carries her aloft until she believes herself really with Beatrice. . . .

He flung over each favorite in turn a shining veil. She rose above the heads of ordinary mortals and walked surrounded by a strange radiance. But when the caprice of the poet ended, this veil vanished, the radiance was eclipsed, and the woman turned again to common clay. . . . To hear oneself praised with that magic peculiar to D'Annunzio is, I imagine, something like the experience of Eve when she heard the voice of the serpent in Paradise. D'Annunzio can make any woman feel that she is the centre of the universe.

Only in love can woman harmoniously reconcile her eroticism and her narcissism; we have seen that these sentiments are opposed in such a manner that it is very difficult for a woman to adapt herself to her sexual destiny. To make herself a carnal object, the prey of another, is in contradiction to her self-worship: it seems to her that embraces blight and sully her body or degrade her soul. Thus it is that some women take refuge in frigidity, thinking that in this way they can preserve the integrity of the ego. Others dissociate animal pleasure and lofty sentiment. In one of Stekel's cases the patient was frigid with her respected and eminent husband and, after his death, with an equally superior man, a great musician, whom she sincerely loved. But in an almost casual encounter with a rough, brutal forester she found complete physical satisfaction, "a wild intoxication followed by indescribable disgust" when she thought of her lover. Stekel remarks that "for many women a descent into animality is the necessary condition for orgasm." Such women see in physical love a debasement incompatible with esteem and affection.

But for other women, on the contrary, only the esteem, affection, and admiration of the man can eliminate the sense of abasement. They will not yield to a man unless they believe they are deeply loved. A woman must have a considerable amount of cynicism, indifference, or pride to regard physical relations as an exchange of pleasure by which each partner benefits equally. As much as woman—and perhaps more—man revolts against anyone who attempts to exploit him sexually;[4] but it is woman who generally feels that her partner is using her as an instrument. Nothing but high admiration can compensate for the humiliation of an act that she considers a defeat.

We have seen that the act of love requires of woman profound self-abandonment; she bathes in a passive languor; with closed eyes, anonymous, lost, she feels as if borne by waves, swept away in a storm, shrouded in darkness: darkness of the flesh, of the womb, of the grave. Annihilated, she becomes one with the Whole, her ego is abolished. But when the man moves from her, she finds herself back on earth, on a bed, in the light; she again has a name, a face: she is one vanquished, prey, object.

This is the moment when love becomes a necessity. As when the child, after weaning, seeks the reassuring gaze of its parents, so must a woman feel, through the man's loving contemplation, that she is, after all, still at one with the Whole from which her flesh is now painfully detached. She is seldom wholly satisfied even if she has felt the orgasm, she is not set completely free from the spell of her flesh; her desire continues in the form of affection. In giving her pleasure, the man increases her attachment, he does not liberate her. As for him, he no longer desires her; but she will not pardon this momentary indifference unless he has dedicated to her a timeless and absolute emotion. Then the immanence of the moment is transcended; hot memories are no regret, but a treasured delight; ebbing pleasure becomes hope and promise; enjoyment is justified; woman can gloriously accept her sexuality because she transcends it; excitement, pleasure, desire are no longer a state, but a benefaction; her body is no longer an object; it is a hymn, a flame.

NOTES

1. Nietzsche's italics.
2. In the sense that a woman may sometimes be called "une grande amoureuse."—Tr.
3. Haenigsen's newspaper comic strip "Penny" gives never flagging popular expression to this truth.—Tr.
4. Lawrence, for example, in Lady Chatterley's Lover, expresses through Mellors his aversion for women who make a man an instrument of pleasure.

IRVING SINGER

Appraisal and Bestowal

I start with the idea that love is a way of valuing something. It is a positive response *toward* the "object of love"—which is to say, anyone or anything that is loved. In a manner quite special to itself, love affirms the goodness of this object. Some philosophers say that love *searches* for what is valuable in the beloved; others say that love *creates* value in the sense that it makes the beloved objectively valuable in some respect. Both assertions are often true, but sometimes false; and, therefore, neither explains the type of valuing which is love.

In studying the relationship between love and valuation, let us avoid merely semantical difficulties. The word "love" sometimes means liking very much, as when a man speaks of loving the food he is eating. It sometimes means desiring obsessively, as when a neurotic reports that he cannot control his feelings about a woman. In these and similar instances the word does not affirm goodness. Liking something very much is not the same as considering it good; and the object of an obsessive desire may attract precisely because it is felt to be bad. These uses of the word are only peripheral to the concept of love as a positive response toward a valued object. As we generally use the term, we imply an act of prizing, cherishing, caring about—all of which constitutes a mode of valuation.

But what is it to value or evaluate? Think of what a man does when he sets a price upon a house. He establishes various facts—the size of the building, its physical condition, the cost of repairs, the proximity to schools. He then weights these facts in accordance with their importance to a hypothetical society of likely buyers. Experts in this activity are called appraisers; the activity itself is appraisal or appraising. It seeks to find an objective value that things have in relation to one or another community of human interests. I call this value "objective" because, although it exists only insofar as there are people who want the house, the estimate is open to public verification. As long as they agree about the circumstances— what the house is like and what a relevant group of buyers prefer—all fair-minded appraisers should reach a similar appraisal, regardless of their own feelings about this particular house. In other words, appraising is a branch of empirical science, specifically directed toward the determining of value.

But now imagine that the man setting the price is not an appraiser, but a prospective buyer. The price that he sets need not agree with the appraiser's. For he does more than estimate objective value: he decides what the house is worth to *him*. To the extent that his preferences differ from other people's, the house will have a different value for him. By introducing such considerations, we relate the object to the particular and possibly idiosyncratic interests of a single person, his likings, his needs, his wants, his desires. Ultimately, all objective value depends upon interests of this sort. The community of buyers whose inclinations the appraiser must gauge is itself just a class of individuals. The appraiser merely predicts what each of them would be likely to pay for the house. At the same time, each buyer must be something of an appraiser himself; for he must have at least a rough idea of the price that other buyers will set. Furthermore, each person has to weigh, and so appraise, the relative importance of his own particular interests; and he must estimate whether the house can satisfy them. In principle these judgments are

From Irving Singer, *The Nature of Love*, vol. I. Chicago: University of Chicago Press, 1966. Copyright © 1966 by The University of Chicago. Reprinted with permission of the author and publisher.

verifiable. They are also liable to mistake: for instance, when a man thinks that certain desires matter more to him than they really do, or when he expects greater benefits from an object than it can provide. Deciding what something is worth to *oneself* we may call an "individual appraisal." It differs from what the appraiser does; it determines a purely individual value, as opposed to any objective value.

Now, with this in mind, I suggest that love creates a new value, one that is not reducible to the individual or objective value that something may also have. This further type of valuing I call bestowal. Individual and objective value depend upon an object's ability to satisfy prior interests—the needs, the desires, the wants, or whatever it is that motivates us toward one object and not another. Bestowed value is different. It is created by the affirmative relationship *itself*, by the very act of responding favorably, giving an object emotional and pervasive importance regardless of its capacity to satisfy interests. Here it makes no sense to speak of verifiability; and though bestowing may often be injurious, unwise, even immoral, it cannot be erroneous in the way that an appraisal might be. For now it is the valuing alone that *makes* the value.

Think of what happens when a man comes to love the house he has bought. In addition to being something of use, something that gratifies antecedent desires, it takes on special value for him. It is now *his* house, not merely as a possession or a means of shelter but also as something he *cares about,* a part of his affective life. Of course, we also care about objects of mere utility. We need them for the benefits they provide. But in the process of loving, the man establishes another kind of relationship. He gives the house an importance beyond its individual or objective value. It becomes a focus of attention and possibly an object of personal commitment. Merely by engaging himself in this manner, the man bestows a value the house could not have had otherwise.

We might also say that the homeowner acts as if his house were valuable "for its own sake." And in a sense it is. For the value that he bestows does not depend upon the house's capacity to satisfy. Not that love need diminish that capacity. On the contrary, it often increases it by affording opportunities for enjoyment that would have been impossible without the pecu-

liar attachment in which bestowal consists. Caring about the house, the man may find new and more satisfying ways of living in it. At the same time, the object achieves a kind of autonomy. The house assumes a presence and attains a dignity. It makes demands and may even seem to have a personality, to have needs of its own. In yielding to these "needs"—restoring the house to an earlier condition, perhaps, or completing its inherent design—the homeowner may not be guided by any other considerations.

In love between human beings something similar happens. For people, too, may be appraised; and they may be valued beyond one's appraisal. In saying that a woman is beautiful or that a man is handsome, or that a man or woman is good in any other respect, we ascribe objective value. This will always be a function of *some* community of human interests, though we may have difficulty specifying which one. And in all communities people have individual value for one another. We are means to each other's satisfactions, and we constantly evaluate one another on the basis of our individual interests. However subtly, we are always setting prices on other people, and on ourselves. But we also bestow value in the manner of love. We then respond to another as something that cannot be reduced to *any* system of appraisal. The lover takes an interest in the beloved as a *person*, and not merely as a commodity—which she may also be. (The lover may be female, of course, and the beloved may be male; but for the sake of brevity and grammatical simplicity I shall generally retain the old convention of referring to lovers as "he" and beloveds as "she.") He bestows importance upon *her* needs and *her* desires, even when they do not further the satisfaction of his own. Whatever her personality, he gives it a value it would not have apart from his loving attitude. In relation to the lover, the beloved has become valuable for her own sake.

In the love of persons, then, people bestow value upon one another over and above their individual or objective value. The reciprocity of love occurs when each participant receives bestowed value while also bestowing it upon the other. Reciprocity has always been recognized as a desired outcome of love. Since it need not occur, however, I define the lover as one who bestows value, and the beloved as one who receives it. The lover makes the beloved valuable merely by attaching and committing himself to her. Though she may satisfy his needs, he refuses to use her as just an instrument. To love a woman as a person is to desire her for the sake of values that appraisal might discover, and yet to place one's desire within a context that affirms her importance regardless of these values. Eventually the beloved may no longer matter to us as one who is useful. Treating her as an end, we may think only of how we can be useful to *her*. But still it is we who think and act and make this affirmative response. Only in relation to *our* bestowal does another person enjoy the kind of value that love creates.

In saying that love bestows value, I am not referring to the fact that lovers shower good things upon those they love. Gifts may sometimes symbolize love, but they never prove its existence. Loving is not synonymous with giving. We do speak of one person "giving love" to another, but what is given hardly resembles what we usually mean by a gift. Even to say that the lover gives himself is somewhat misleading. Love need not be self-sacrificial. In responding affirmatively to another person, the lover creates something and need lose nothing to himself. To bestow value is to augment one's own being as well as the beloved's. Bestowal generates a new society by the sheer force of emotional attachment, a society that enables the lovers to discard many of the conventions that would ordinarily have separated them. But such intimacy is only one of the criteria by which bestowal may be identified.

The bestowing of value shows itself in many different ways, not all of which need ever occur at the same time or in equal strength: by caring about the needs and interests of the beloved, by wishing to benefit or protect her, by delighting in her achievements, by encouraging her independence while also accepting and sustaining her dependency, by respecting her individuality, by giving her pleasure, by taking pleasures with her, by feeling glad when she is present and sad when she is not, by sharing ideas and emotions with her, by sympathizing with her weaknesses and depending upon her strength, by developing common pursuits, by allowing her to become second nature to him—"her smiles, her frowns, her ups, her downs"—by having a need to increase their society with other human beings upon whom they can jointly bestow value, by wanting children who may perpetuate their love. These are not necessary and sufficient conditions; but their occurrence would give us reason to think that an act of bestowal has taken place.

Through bestowal lovers have "a life" together. The lover accords the beloved the tribute of expressing *his* feelings by responding to *hers*. If he sends her valuable presents, they will signify that he too appreciates what she esteems; if he makes sacrifices on her behalf, he indicates how greatly her welfare matters to him. It is as if he were announcing that what is real for her is real for him also. Upon the sheer personality of the beloved he bestows a framework of value, emanating from himself but focused on her. Lovers linger over attributes that might well have been ignored. Whether sensuous or polite, passionate or serene, brusque or tender, the lover's response is variably fervent but constantly gratuitous. It dignifies the beloved by treating her as *someone,* with all the emphasis the italics imply. Though independent of our needs, she is also the significant object of our attention. We show ourselves receptive to her peculiarities in the sense that we readily respond to them. Response is itself a kind of affirmation, even when it issues into unpleasant emotions such as anger and jealousy. These need not be antithetical to love; they may even be signs of it. Under many circumstances one cannot respond to another person without the unpleasant emotions, as a parent cannot stay in touch with a wayward child unless he occasionally punishes him. It is when we reject the other person, reducing him to a nothing or expressing our indifference, that love disappears. For then instead of bestowing value, we have withdrawn it.

In general, every emotion or desire contributes to love once it serves as a positive response to an independent being. If a woman is *simply* a means to sexual satisfaction, a man may be said to want her, but not to love her. For his sexual desire to become a part of love, it must function as a way of responding to the character and special properties of this particular woman. Desire wants what it wants for the sake of some private gratification, whereas love demands an interest in that vague complexity we call another person. No wonder lovers sound like metaphysicians, and scientists are more comfortable in the study of desire. For love is an attitude with no clear objective. Through it one human being affirms the significance of another, much as a painter highlights a figure by defining it in a sharpened outline. But the beloved is not a painted figure. She is not static: she is fluid, changing, indefinable—*alive*. The lover is attending to a *person*. And who can say what that is?

In the history of philosophy, bestowal and appraisal have often been confused with one another, perhaps because they are both types of valuation.[1] Love is related to both; they interweave in it. Unless we appraised we could not bestow a value that goes beyond appraisal; and without bestowal there would be no love. We may speak of lovers accepting one another, or even taking each other as is. But this need not mean a blind submission to some unknown being. In love we *attend* to the beloved, in the sense that we respond to what *she* is. For the effort to succeed, it must be accompanied by justifiable appraisals, objective as well as individual. The objective beauty and goodness of his beloved will delight the lover, just as her deficiencies will distress him. In her, as in every other human being, these are important properties. How is the lover to know what they are without a system of appraisals? Or how to help her realize her potentialities—assuming that is what she wants? Of course, in bestowing value upon this woman, the lover will "accentuate the positive" and undergo a kind of personal involvement that no disinterested spectator would. He will feel an intimate concern about the continuance of good properties in the beloved and the diminishing of bad ones. But none of this would be possible without objective appraisals.

Even more important is the role of individual appraisal. The person we love is generally one who satisfies our needs and desires. She may do so without either of us realizing the full extent of these satisfactions; and possibly all individual value is somehow based upon unconscious effects. Be this as it may, our experience of another person includes a large network of individual evaluations continually in progress and available to consciousness. At each moment our interests are being gratified or frustrated, fulfilled or thwarted, strengthened or weakened in relation to the other person.

Individual value is rarely stable. It changes in accordance with our success or failure in getting what we want. And as this happens, our perception of the beloved also changes. Though the lover bestows value upon the woman as a separate and autonomous person, she will always be a person in *his* experience, a person whom he needs and who may need him, a person whose very nature may eventually conform to his inclinations, as well as vice versa. The attitude of love probably includes more, not fewer, individual appraisals than any other. How else could a lover, who must respond from his own point of view, really care about the beloved?

Love would not be love unless appraising were accompanied by the bestowing of value. But where this conjunction exists, *every* appraisal may lead on to a further bestowal. By disclosing an excellence in the beloved, appraisal (whether individual or objective) makes it easier for us to appreciate her. By revealing her faults and imperfections, it increases the importance of acting on her behalf. Love may thus encompass all possible appraisals. Once bestowal has occurred, a man may hardly care that his beloved is not deemed desirable by other men. Given a choice, he may prefer her to women who are sexually more attractive. His love is a way of compensating for and even overcoming negative appraisals. If it were a means of repaying the object for value received, love would turn into gratitude; if it were an attempt to give more than the object has provided, it would become generosity or condescension. These are related attitudes, but love differs from them in bestowing value without calculation. It confers importance no matter *what* the object is worth.

When appraisal occurs alone, our attitude develops in the direction of science, ambition, or morality. To do "the right thing" we need not bestow value upon another person; we need only recognize the truth about his character and act appropriately. Admiring a woman's superiority, we may delight in her as an evidence of the good life. We feel toward her what Hume calls "the sense of approbation." We find her socially useful or morally commendable, which is not to say that she excites our love. If she has faults, they offend our moral sensibility or else elicit our benevolence. In short, we respond to this woman as an abstraction, as a something that may be better or worse, an opportunity for judgment or for action, but not a person whom we love. Appraisal without bestowal may lead us to change other people regardless of what they want. As moralists or legislators, or as dutiful parents, we may even think that this is how we *ought* to behave. The magistrate will then enforce a distance between himself and the criminal, whose welfare he is quite prepared to sacrifice for the greater good of society. The parent will discipline his child in the hope of molding him "in the most beneficial manner." On this moral attitude great institutions are often built. But it is not a loving attitude. We are not responding affirmatively toward others. We are only doing what is (we hope) in their best interests, or else society's.

When love intervenes, morality becomes more personal but also more erratic. It is almost impossible to imagine someone bestowing value without caring about the other person's welfare. To that extent, love implies benevolence. And yet the lover does not act benevolently for the sake of doing the right thing. In loving another person, we respect *his* desire to improve himself. If we offer to help, we do so because *he* wants to be better than he is, not because *we* think he ought to be. Love and morality need not diverge, but they often do. For love is not *inherently* moral. There is no guarantee that it will bestow value properly, at the right time, in the right way. Through love we enjoy another person as he is, including his moral condition; yet this enjoyment may itself violate the demands of morality. Ethical attitudes must always be governed by appraisal rather than bestowal. They must consider the individual in his relations to other people, as one among many who have equal claims. Faced with the being of a particular person, morality tells us to pick and choose those attributes that are most desirable. It is like a chef who makes an excellent stew by bringing out one flavor and muffling another. The chef does not care about the ingredients as unique or terminal entities, but only as things that are good to eat. In loving another person, however, we enact a nonmoral *loyalty*—like the mother who stands by her criminal son even though she knows he is guilty. Her loyalty need not be *im*moral; and though she loves her son, she may realize that he must be punished. But what if the value she has bestowed upon her child

blinds her to the harm he has done, deters her from handing him over to the police, leads her to encourage him as a criminal? Her love may increase through such devotion, but it will be based on faulty appraisals and will not be a moral love.

Possibly the confusion between appraisal and bestowal results from the way that lovers talk. To love another person is to *treat* him with great regard, to confer a new and personal value upon him. But when lovers describe their beloved, they sometimes sound as if she were perfect just in being herself. In caring about someone, attending to her, affirming the importance of her being what she is, the lover resembles a man who has appraised an object and found it very valuable. Though he is bestowing value, the lover *seems* to be declaring the objective goodness of the beloved. It is *as if* he were predicting the outcome of all possible appraisals and insisting that they would always be favorable.

As a matter of fact, the lover is doing nothing of the sort. His superlatives are expressive and metaphoric. Far from being terms of literal praise, they betoken the magnitude of his attachment and say little about the lady's beauty or goodness. They may even be accompanied by remarks that diminish the beloved in some respect—as when a man lovingly describes a woman's funny face or inability to do mathematics. If he says she is "perfect" that way, he chooses this ambiguous word because it is used for things we refuse to relinquish. As in appraisal we may wish to accept nothing less than perfection, so too the lover calls perfect whatever he accepts despite its appraisal. The lover may borrow appraisive terminology, but he uses it with a special intent. His language signifies that love alone has bestowed incalculable worth upon this particular person. Such newly given value is not a good of the sort that appraisal seeks: it is not an attribute that supplements her other virtues, like a dimple wrought by some magician to make a pretty woman prettier. For it is nothing but the importance that one person assigns to another; and in part at least, it is created by the language. The valuative terms that lovers use—"wonderful," "marvelous," "glorious," "grand," "terrific"— bestow value in themselves. They are scarcely capable of describing excellence or reporting on appraisals.

If we have any doubts about the lover's use of language, we should listen to the personal appendages he usually adds. He will not say "That woman is perfect," but rather "To *me* she is perfect" or "*I* think she is wonderful." In talking this way, he reveals that objective appraisal does not determine his attitude. For objective appraisal puts the object in relation to a community of valuers, whereas love creates its own community. The men in some society may all admire an "offical beauty"—as Ortega calls her. Every male may do homage to her exceptional qualities, as if the lady were a great work of art; and some will want to possess her, as they would want to steal the crown jewels. But this is not the same as love, since that involves a different kind of response, more intimate, more personal, and more creative.

For similar reasons it would be a mistake to think that the lover's language articulates an individual appraisal. If he says that to him the woman is perfect, the lover does not mean that she is perfect *for* him. Unless the beloved satisfied in some respect, no man might be able to love her. For *she* must find a place in *his* experience; she must come alive for him, stimulate new and expansive interests; and none of this is likely to happen unless she has individual value to him. But though the beloved satisfies the lover, she need not satisfy perfectly. Nor does the lover expect her to. In saying that to him she is perfect, he merely reiterates the fact that he loves this woman. Her perfection is an honorific title which he, and only he, bestows. The lover is like a child who makes a scribble and then announces "This is a tree." The child could just as easily have said "This is a barn." Until he tells us, the scribble represents nothing. Once he tells us, it represents whatever he says—as long as his attitude remains consistent.

In being primarily bestowal and only secondarily appraisal, love is never elicited by the object in the sense that desire or approbation is. We desire things or people for the sake of what will satisfy us. We approve of someone for his commendable properties. But these conditions have only a causal tie to love: as when a man loves a woman *because* she is beautiful, or *because* she satisfies his sexual, domestic, and social needs, or *because* she resembles his childhood memory of mother. Such facts indicate the circumstances under which people love one another; they explain why this particular man loves this particular woman; and if the life sciences were sufficiently developed, the facts could help us to predict who among human beings would be likely to love whom. But explaining the occurrence of love is not the same as explicating the concept. The conditions for love are not the same as love itself. In some circumstances the bestowing of value will happen more easily than in others; but *whenever* it happens, it happens as a new creation of value and exceeds all attributes of the object that might be thought to elicit it. Even if a man loves only a woman who is beautiful and looks like his mother, he does not *love* her for these properties in the same sense in which he might *admire* her for being objectively valuable or *desire* her for satisfying his needs.

For what then does a man love a woman? For being the person she is, for being herself? But that is to say that he loves her for nothing at all. Everyone is himself. Having a beloved who is what she is does not reveal the nature of love. Neither does it help us to understand the saint's desire to love all people. They are what they are. Why should they be loved for it? Why not pitied or despised, ignored or simply put to use? Love supplements the human search for value with a capacity for bestowing it gratuitously. To one who has succeeded in cultivating this attitude, *anything* may become an object of love. The saint is a man whose earthly needs and desires are extraordinarily modest; in principle, every human being can satisfy them. That being so, the saint creates a value-system in which all persons fit equally well. This disposition, this freely given response, cannot be elicited from him: it bestows itself and happens to be indiscriminate.

To the man of common sense it is very upsetting that love does not limit itself to some prior value in the object. The idea goes against our purposive ways of thinking. If I wish to drink the best wine, I have reason to prefer French champagne over American. My choice is dictated by an objective goodness in the French champagne. If instead I wish to economize, I act sensibly in choosing a wine I value less highly. We act this way whenever we use purposive means of attaining the good life, which covers a major part of our existence. But love, unlike desire, is not wholly purposive. Within the total structure of a human life it may serve as a lubricant to purposive attitudes, furthering their aims through new interests that promise new satisfactions; but in creating value, bestowing it freely, love introduces an element of risk into the economy. Purposive attitudes are safe, secure, like money in the bank; the loving attitude is speculative and always dangerous. Love is not *practical,* and sometimes borders on madness. We take our life in our hands when we allow love to tamper with our purposive habits. Without love, life might not be worth living; but without purposiveness, there would be no life.

No wonder, then, that the *fear* of love is one of the great facts of human nature. In all men and women there lurks an atavistic dread of insolvency whenever we generate more emotion than something has a right to demand of us. In everyone there is the country bumpkin who giggles nervously at an abstract painting because it looks like nothing on earth. Man finds the mere possibility of invention and spontaneous originality disquieting, even ominous. We are threatened by any new bestowal. Particularly when it means the origination of feelings, we are afraid to run the usual risks of failure and frustration, to expose ourselves in a positive response that can be easily thwarted. As a character in D. H. Lawrence says of love: "I am almost more afraid of this touch than I was of death. For I am more nakedly exposed to it."[2] Even Pascal, who spoke of the heart's having reasons whereof reason does not know, seemed to think that love adheres to a secret, mysterious quality within the object that only feeling can discern. But Pascal was wrong. Love is sheer gratuity. It issues from the lover like hairs on his head. It can be stimulated and developed, but it cannot be derived from outside.

Love is like awakened genius that chooses its materials in accordance with its own creative requirements. Love does not create its object; it merely responds to it creatively. That is why one can rarely convince a man that his beloved is unworthy of him. For his love is a creative means of *making* her more worthy—in the sense that he invests her with greater value, not in making her a better human being. That may also happen. But more significantly, the lover changes *himself.* By subordinating his purposive attitudes, he transforms himself into a being who enjoys the act of bestowing. There

is something magical about this, as we know from legends in which the transformations of love are effected by a philter or a wand. In making another person valuable by developing a certain disposition within oneself, the lover performs in the world of feeling something comparable to what the alchemist does in the world of matter.

The creativity of love is thus primarily a self-creation. Lovers create within themselves a remarkable capacity for affective response, an ability to use their emotions, their words, their deeds for bestowing as well as appraising value. Each enhances the other's importance through an imaginative play within valuation itself. Indeed, love may be best approached as a subspecies of the imagination. Not only does the lover speak in poetic metaphors, but also he behaves like any artist. Whatever his "realistic" aspirations, no painter can duplicate reality. The scene out there cannot be transferred to a canvas. The painter can only *paint* it: i.e., give it a new importance in human life by presenting his way of seeing it through the medium of his art and the techniques of his individual talent. These determine the values of his painting, not the external landscape that may have originally inspired him. The artist may vary the scene to his heart's content, as El Greco did when he rearranged the buildings of Toledo. What matters is his way of seeing as a function of the imagination, not the disposition in space of stones and mortar. Similarly, a lover sees a woman not as others might, but through the creative agency of bestowing value. He need not change her any more than El Greco changed the real Toledo. But he renews her personality by subsuming it within the imaginative system of his own positive responses. Through her he expresses the variety of feelings that belong to love. Artists, even the most abstract, do not create out of nothing: they re-create, create anew. So too, the lover re-creates another person. By deploying his imagination in the art of bestowing value, by caring about the independent being of another person, the lover adds a new dimension to the beloved. In relation to him, within his loving attitude, she becomes the object of an affirmative interest, even an aesthetic object. She is, as we say, "*ap*preciated"— made more valuable through the special media and techniques in which love consists.

Treating love as an aspect of the imagination enables us to confront problems I have thus far ignored. For instance, I said it was *as if* the lover were predicting that no appraisal would discover any significant fault. If we now inquire into the meaning of these "as ifs," I can only remind you how they operate in other situations involving the imagination. Think of yourself as a spectator in the theater, watching an engrossing drama. The hero dies, and you begin to weep. Now for whom are you crying? Surely not for the actor: you know that as soon as the curtain falls, he will scramble to his feet and prepare for a great ovation. Is it then the character in the play? But there is no such person. You are fully aware that Hamlet (at least Shakespeare's Hamlet) never existed. How can his death, which is purely fictional, sadden you? Yet it does, more so perhaps than the death of real people you may have known. What happens, I think, is that you respond *as if* the actor were really Hamlet and *as if* Hamlet really existed. The "as if" signifies that although you *know* the actor is only acting and Hamlet only fictitious, your imaginative involvement causes you to express feelings appropriate to real people. At no point are you deluded. The "illusion" of the theater is not an illusion at all. It is an act of imagination—nothing like a mistake of judgment, nothing like the derangement that causes Don Quixote to smash the cruel puppet show in order to save the unfortunate heroine. On entering the theater, you have entered the dramatic situation. You have allowed your imagination to engage itself in one specific channel. With the assistance of the realistic props, the surrounding darkness, the company of other people doing the same imagining, you have invested the actors and the characters they represent with a capacity to affect your feelings as real persons might.

In love the same kind of thing occurs. The as ifs of love are imaginative, not essentially delusional. Of course, the lover *may* be deluded about his beloved. That is the familiar joke about lovers: they live in constant illusion, Cupid is blinded by emotion, etc. That this often happens I do not care to deny. But that this should be the essence of love, that by its very nature love should be illusory, seems to me utterly absurd. Even if people frequently clambered on stage and acted like Don Quixote, we

would not say that their behavior revealed what it is to be a theatrical spectator. We would say they did not know how to look at a play. Likewise, it is not in the acting out of illusions that people become lovers. Though lovers do commit errors of judgment and are sometimes carried away by their feelings, love itself is not illusory. Emotional aberrations are adventitious to it, not definitive. As love is not primarily a way of knowing, neither is it a way of making mistakes. Appraisal is a way of knowing, and emotions may always interfere with its proper employment. But love is an imaginative means of bestowing value that would not exist otherwise. To the extent that a man is a lover, rather than a person seeking knowledge or yielding to self-delusion (which he may also be), he accords his beloved the courtesy of being treated affirmatively regardless of what he knows about her. In refusing to let his appraisive knowledge deflect his amorous conduct, he bestows a tribute which can only be understood as an imaginative act. As one of Rousseau's characters says: "Love did not make me blind to your faults, but it made those faults dear to me."[3] It is this kind of valuative gesture that the imagination uses for courtesy as a whole. A courteous man—what used to be called a "gentleman"—may show respect to all women alike, whatever their social rank. He does so as a loving gift to the female sex, the worst as well as the best, the lowest as well as the highest. He is not normally deluded about differences in society or among human beings. He does not think that women are all the same. Yet by means of his imaginative response he acts as if there were a universal excellence in them, regardless of what they actually merit.

There is another respect in which the analogy from the theater elucidates the lover's imagination. I refer to the phenomenon of *presence*. The spectator responds to the fictional character as if it were a real person. He can do so, in part, because the character has been *presented* to him by a real person. Talking, laughing, shouting, the actor *makes present* to the spectator the reality of a human being. The very artificiality of his surroundings—his being in a "play," a fiction, his being placed on a stage so that everyone can see and hear, his giving a performance scheduled for a particular time, in a particular building—all this accentuates the fact that the actor himself is not artificial, but alive. The spectator makes his imaginative leap by seeing the actor as a present reality framed within the aesthetic contrivances of the theater. The greater the actor's "stage presence," the more he facilitates the spectator's feat. But ultimately the phenomenon depends upon the spectator himself, upon his dramatic sensibility, his creative capacity to infuse a fictional character with the reality of the human being right there before him. As the Prologue to Shakespeare's *Henry V* tells the audience: "And let us, ciphers to this great accompt, / On your imaginary forces work. / . . . For 'tis your thoughts that now must deck our kings."

In a similar fashion the lover's attention fixes upon the sheer presence of the beloved. In that extreme condition sometimes called "falling in love," such attentiveness often approaches self-hypnosis. Freud was one of the first to recognize the kinship between hypnosis and certain types of love; but his analysis neglects the philosophical import of these occurrences, their linkage to valuation. For me the loving stare of one human being visually glued to another signifies an extraordinary bestowal of value, an imaginative (though possibly excessive) response to the presence of another person. The lover's glance illuminates the beloved. He celebrates her as a living reality to which he attends. As in celebration of any sort, his response contributes something new and expressive. He introduces the woman into the world of his own imagination—as if, through some enchantment, she were indeed his work of art and only he could contemplate her infinite detail. As long as they intensify her presence, the lover will cherish even those features in the beloved that appraisal scorns. Does the lady have a facial blemish? To her lover it may be more fascinating than her baby blue eyes: it makes her stand out more distinctly in his memory. Does she have a sharp tongue and a biting temper? Her lover may come to relish these traits, not generally but in this particular woman. They make the image of her vivid and compelling. Even the ludicrous banalities of Odette are endearing to Swann. They show him with unmistakable clarity what she is; and though he loathes the banal, as Proust himself hated the everyday world, he obviously enjoys this opportunity to compensate for his loathing by the imaginative bestowal of unmerited value.

Speaking of suitable subjects for literature, Flaubert said: "Yvetot [a provincial town in Northern France] is as good as Constantinople." Likewise, one might say that everything that distinguishes the beloved, even her lack of distinction, may contribute to the lover's art. For that consists of taking a woman as she is, in opening oneself to the impact of her presence, at the same time that one invokes aesthetic categories that give her a new significance. By his affirmative response alone, the lover places an ordinary stone within the costliest of settings. The amorous imagination bestows value upon a person as the dramatic imagination bestows theatrical import upon an actor. If, as sometimes happens, the beloved is put on a pedestal, this is comparable to the actor being put on stage: not necessarily for purposes of adoration, but in order to concentrate, in the most imaginative way, upon the suggestive reality of her presence. The lover knows the woman is not objectively perfect, as the audience knows the actor is not Hamlet; but in attending to her as she is, he imaginatively treats her as the presentation of (what is to him) incomparable Venus.

I am sure that the similarity between love and the theater could be pushed much further. Love is the art of enjoying another person, as theater is the art of enjoying dramatic situations. Because it inevitably suggests the possibility of *enjoyment,* love is the most frequent theme in all entertainments based on human relations: it is the only subject that interests everyone. Nevertheless, the analogy between love and the theater can also be misleading. The actor portrays a character; the beloved does not portray anything, though she may symbolize a great deal. The beloved is not an *image* of perfection in the sense in which an actor is an image or representation of Hamlet. The lover uses his imagination to appreciate the beloved as she is, to accept her in herself; but the audience uses the actor as a vehicle for the fiction. That is why an actor can only rarely look his audience in the eye. In so direct a communication his presence crowds out his aesthetic function, and we respond to him as the person he happens to be, not as the character he represents. On the other hand, lovers may well be stereotyped (as they are often photographed or painted) in a joint posture of immediate confrontation, face to face, each searching for the other's personality, each peer-ing into the other's eyes: "Our eyebeams twisted, and did thread / Our eyes, upon one double string."[4]

This fundamental difference between love and the theater may help to explain some of the emotional difficulties actors often feel. Like ev-eryone else the actor wants to be loved for him-self; but his audiences know him only through the roles he portrays. He senses that what they "love" is really the characters or at best his characterizations, certainly no more than that part of himself which goes into making the characters present. Succeeding as an actor, he may even identify with the type of character he best portrays. That may give him an oppor-tunity to express much of his own personality, but the role he lives will often mask his deepest inclinations and make it difficult for anyone to respond to him as a person. For similar rea-sons, . . . I fail to see how Plato could be talk-ing about the love of persons when he says that the lover sees in the beloved an "image" or "representation" of absolute beauty. Plato uses this idea to argue that all lovers are really in love with the absolute. Might we not also say that the lovers he has in mind are simply inca-pable of loving another person?

In love, as in the theater, imagination mani-fests itself in a particular set or disposition. A carpenter who happens to overhear a rehearsal may surely know that the man on stage is play-ing Hamlet.But he does not respond to the ac-tor *as if* he were Hamlet. Preoccupied with his own work, the carpenter is not an audience: he has not put himself into a dramatic channel. Neither does an experimenter affirm the being of a person whom he observes with scientific detachment. He devotes himself to the experi-ment, not to the individual under observation. He may take the subject as is, but only in the sense of being impartial about his data. By de-taching himself, the scientist refuses to enter into the relationship required for love. Through love one person *attaches* himself to another, and in ways that reveal his own personality as well as the other's. The reality of the beloved glows with a sense of importance that emanates from the lover and increases dynamically when love is reciprocal. Or is glow too vibrant a word? Love is not always ecstatic; and even its poetry is often prosaic. There are quiet, com-fortable, humdrum loves as well as the rhapso-dic ones that seem to accompany inexperience. Love has infinite modulations, all possible de-grees of intensity, and endless variety in its means of imaginative expression.

It is even through the amorous imagination that one person becomes sexually attractive to another. Our instincts alone would not enable us to love or even to lust in the way that human beings do. At least not the *obvious* instincts, e. g., the mechanism of genital excitement. Pos-sibly the bestowing of value is itself instinc-tive. It need not be learned, and it would seem to be universal in man. Everyone feels the need for some loving relationship. All people crave a society of their own making, different from the one to which they were born. That is why love is always a threat to the status quo, and some-times subversive. Lovers create their own af-fective universe. When the amorous imagina-tion ricochets back and forth—each person seeing himself as both lover and beloved—a new totality results, an interacting oneness. The human species could survive without the art of the theater, or of painting, or of litera-ture, or of music; but man would not be man without the art of mutual love. In that sense, the amorous imagination, more than any other, shows us both what we are and what, ideally, we may become.

NOTES

This chapter in particular (though others as well) benefited from the extensive criticism of Jason Epstein and Alice Mayhew. I have also used suggestions of Stephen N. Thomas.

1. Though not of "evaluation." That word is usually reserved for appraisal.
2. *The Man Who Died* (New York: Vintage Books, 1960), p. 202.
3. *La Nouvelle Héloïse,* vol. 2 (Philadelphia, 1796), p.90.
4. John Donne, "The Ecstasy."

ALAN SOBLE

Reconciling Eros and Agape

Accounts of personal love in the agape tradition are prevalent among contemporary philosophers. For example, at the beginning and end of his three-volume history of the idea of love, Irving Singer presents his own theory of love.[1] In arriving at his view about the nature of love, Singer embraces the metaphilosophical principle that "explaining the occurrence of love is not the same as explicating the concept. The conditions for love are not the same as love itself" (vol. 1, p. 13). Hence, the causal antecedents of love are not to be mentioned while "explicating the concept" of love. Clearly, I am metaphilosophically at odds with Singer: I have distinguished the two views of love by their different outlooks on the basis of love; a thesis about the explanatory ground of love is central to these accounts of personal love and must figure, therefore, into their respective concepts. Eros-style loves are not merely contingently based on the merits of the object; love's being property-based is part of the concept of erosic love. Similarly, love's not being property-based is part of the concept of agapic love. The point is that Singer's metaphilosophical principle rules out the eros tradition in advance as an adequate theory of personal love. How could erosic love ever be defined if the conditions of love must be kept distinct from love itself?

In Singer's analysis, all love includes, as a necessary condition, the bestowal of value (vol. 3, p. 390). "In the love of persons," Singer writes, "people bestow value upon one another over and beyond their . . . objective value" (vol. 1, p. 6). And even more strongly, "love bestow[s] value without calculation. It confers importance no matter *what* the object is worth" (vol. 1, p. 10). Further, "loving another

as a person means bestowing value upon his personality even if it is not virtuous" (vol. 1, p. 94); "love is a way of . . . overcoming negative appraisals" (vol. 1, p. 10).[2] This love sounds like agape or neighbor-love: for Singer, x bestows value on y even if y is not meritorious, or x bestows value on a meritorious y but not in virtue of that merit. Indeed, when Singer writes, "That love might be a way of bestowing value *upon* the object, taking an interest in it regardless of how good or bad it may be—this conception is as foreign to Aristotle as it was to Plato" (vol. 1, p. 90), he is in effect repeating Gregory Vlastos' criticism of the erosic loves of Aristotle and Plato,[3] the Vlastos who advances agapic love as the correct alternative (see 13.5). One might suspect that Singer is simply explicating agape and not offering an account of personal love. But he is certainly attempting primarily to shed light on that phenomenon: "Through [love] one human being affirms the significance of another. . . . But the beloved . . . is not static: she is fluid, changing, undefinable—*alive*" (vol. 1, p. 8). "To love a woman . . . is to desire her for the sake of values that appraisal might discover, and yet to place one's desires within a context that affirms her importance regardless of these values" (vol. 1, p. 6).

The preceding sentence suggests that Singer is analyzing personal love not as purely agapic, but as a reconciliation of eros and agape: personal love involves both a response to perceived value and a bestowal of value that occurs independently of perceived value. He writes, "Love is related to both [bestowal and appraisal]; they interweave in it. Unless we appraised we could not bestow a value that goes beyond appraisal; and without bestowal there would be no love" (vol. 1, p. 9). But to claim that appraisal is necessary for bestowal, and therefore for love, seems to contradict Singer's assertion that the lover bestows value "without calculation [and] no matter *what* the object is worth." How can appraisal be necessary if love, by including bestowal, can exist when the object has no merit or when the object's merit is irrelevant? "Love is a bestowal of value which supplements, and sometimes overrides, our attitudes of appraisal," he says (vol. 3, p. 393). In another passage Singer does claim that love is "primarily bestowal and only secondarily appraisal" (vol. 1, p. 13), but this is vague and hardly looks like a reconciliation of eros and agape. The issue is, in what way is appraisal, for Singer, operative in love? There are, based on what Singer has written, three different interpretations.

Singer comments on the song "Because You're You" by Henry Blossom:

> Not that you are fair, dear
> Not that you are true,
> Not your golden hair, dear,
> Not your eyes of blue.
> When we ask the reason,
> Words are all too few!
> So I know I love you, dear,
> Because you're you.

Singer rejects the reason offered in the last line (reminiscent of Montaigne's): "[The song] seems to assert that the sheer *identity* of the beloved brings love into being. And this, I think, is highly implausible" (vol. 1, p. 150).[4] Loving "the lady *because* she's she" is "quite different" from the "bestowal over and beyond appraisal" (vol. 1, p. 149) that is a necessary component of love. For our purposes, Singer's remark about the last line of the song is important: it "makes it sound as if the delicacy of her complexion . . . had nothing to do with his loving her, which is most unlikely." He continues: "If all these endearing young charms were to vanish and fade away, would not the greatest of human loves vanish with them? We have every reason to think so, unless the lover cultivated new needs and desires." This amounts to saying (the first interpretation) that appraisal— finding valuable properties in the object—is essential for personal love, a necessary condition for humans to bestow value: "Wholly non-

appraisive love is foreign to human nature" (vol. 3, p. 391). Apparently, Singer agrees with the eros tradition about the ground of love even though he insists again (among these passages) that the explication of the concept of love must not mention this fact. Yet, as we have seen, claiming that x bestows value on y only if x already perceives value in y contradicts the claim that the bestowal of value is independent of such evaluations. The very idea of agape is the idea of a love that is not grounded in the attractiveness of its object; hence claiming that appraisal is necessary for human personal love is not to reconcile the two traditions.

Perhaps this is why Singer occasionally claims (the second interpretation) that positive appraisal plays a facilitatory role in the genesis of bestowal: "For most men it is easier to bestow value upon a beautiful rather than an ugly woman" (vol. 1, p. 23); "by disclosing an excellence . . . appraisal . . . makes it easier for us to appreciate" the other person (vol. 1, p. 10).[5] His point might be that bestowal does not strictly require antecedent positive appraisal; bestowal after such an appraisal is merely psychologically "easier," and bestowals without positive appraisal are not impossible but only "unlikely" (vol. 1, p. 149). But to attempt to reconcile agape and eros by claiming that appraisal plays a facilitatory but not essential role in love is not convincing. If appraisal sometimes plays a role this means at best that some cases of personal love are erosic while other cases are agapic, not that personal love is a reconciliation in all its cases.

The third interpretation is that the bestowal of value occurs without positive appraisal. "In some circumstances the bestowing of value will happen more easily than in others; but *whenever* it happens, it happens as a new creation of value and exceeds all attributes of the object that might be thought to elicit it" (vol. 1, p. 13). The "whenever" here suggests that love can arise independently of any positive appraisal. Indeed, Singer seems to advance seriously this radical thesis: "Nothing can elicit bestowals" (vol. 1, p. 154). He continues, "Either [bestowals] come or they don't. This is the spontaneity in love, as it is in persons. Both defy our rational calculations." In this third interpretation, Singer's account of love is squarely within the second view of personal love. God, we can suppose, loves humans for no reason; His love is a sheer gift. And this is precisely what love's bestowal of value is, even when done by humans: "Love is sheer gratuity" (vol. 1, p. 15), hence love has no erosic basis. "It issues from the lover like hairs on his head." If so, love is a "sheer gratuity" and "spontaneous" in whatever sense hairs grow gratuitously and spontaneously. Nothing, apparently, about either the subject or the object figures into the ground of love, except that the lover's nature is to grow hair. Does this help us to understand these statements: "We instinctively bestow value upon persons . . . regardless of their utility" (vol. 2, p. 339), and "the act of bestowing is neither rational nor irrational. It is nonrational, and probably instinctual" (vol. 3, p. 158)? Consider how Singer describes God's love in similar terms: "Agapē is . . . spontaneous. It simply radiates, like the glorious sun or the universe at large, giving forth energy for no apparent reason" (vol. 1, p. 275).[6]

However, because Singer so often insists that appraisal plays a role in love ("appraisal may lead on to a further bestowal" [vol. 1, p. 10]), perhaps we should propose an account of love within the eros tradition that incorporates Singer's notion of bestowal. Love, in this proposal, would be defined as the property-based bestowal of value (this love is erosic, not a reconciliation), which is consistent with Singer's claim that "love would not be love unless appraising were accompanied by the bestowing of value" (vol. 1, p. 10). Singer should be open to the suggestion that "a property-based bestowal of value" is superior (as an account of personal love) to "an ungrounded bestowal of value" given his frequent assertions about the human psychological tendency to bestow value only after positive appraisal. Indeed, because he eventually asserts that "appraisal [is] a major ingredient within love, and not merely . . . a *causal* condition. . . . [T]he appraisive element [is] an ever-present constituent of love" (vol. 3, p. 394), Singer apparently agrees that love should be understood erosically as "a property-based bestowal of value." He refuses, however, to recognize the implications of his now calling appraisal a "constituent" of personal love, for he still insists that "in its mere definition love is not bound by any degree of worth in the object" (vol. 3, p. 402). But remember that Singer's metaphilosophical

principle leads him to exclude only causal conditions from the analysis of love, but not its constituents; and he has just claimed that appraisal is "not merely . . . a causal condition." What would keep Singer from including this constituent of love, appraisal, in its definition? His argument seems to be that even though "human beings do not have this capacity," nevertheless "it is logically possible for love to bestow itself on an object that has no other worth" (vol. 3, p. 402), for we can imagine a being (the Christian God) that bestows value independently of appraisal.[7] But, then, appraisal is not a "constituent" of love after all, or it is a constituent only of personal love.

There is a deeper point to be made about Singer's claim that "in its mere definition love is not bound by any degree of worth in the object," that is, his insistence that appraisal is not part of the definition of love because "it is logically possible" to bestow independently of appraisal. His account of love amounts, as a result, to the thesis that all love involves, as a necessary common denominator, the bestowal of value (and not necessarily anything more than this). Hence, it is not unreasonable to think of God's agape for humans—the love that motivates Singer to exclude appraisal from the definition of love—as the paradigm case of love in Singer's view. Further, the claim that all love necessarily involves bestowal can be seen, because of its generality, as an umbrella account of love that applies to all cases. Thus, we could employ this umbrella account to analyze other loves, for example, parental love, the love of chocolate, patriotism; if these are genuine loves, they will all exhibit a bestowal of value even though they will be distinguishable by different causal conditions and, perhaps, by different effects. (In loving chess, the chess lover bestows value on the game beyond its perceived merit.) Singer's treatment of the human love for God confirms this interpretation: "God bestows value in loving man despite his imperfections. Man bestows value [on God] in recognizing the infinite goodness of God and delighting in it. They reciprocate within a community of bestowals" (vol. 1, p. 215). Again: "The Christians, who say God is perfect, believe that his being the creator gives a sufficient reason for man to love him. But creativity is no more reason than anything else. If the pious man loves God, he does so by bestowing a gratuitous value—as love always does" (vol. 1, p. 246). "As love always does" demonstrates that Singer, having analyzed all love as necessarily including the bestowal of value, must claim that even the human love for God includes bestowal.

Singer, then, runs into the same trouble that Plato does. The story about Plato usually goes like this: Plato's umbrella definition is that love is the desire to possess eternally the Good and the Beautiful. That is, love for a *thing*—the Form of the Good or the Beautiful—is the paradigm case of love. Hence, Plato must analyze even personal love as a case of loving only a thing. Thus, for Plato, when x loves y, x is loving only the beautiful properties (things) of y. Personal love is assimilated to the love of things, as being not essentially different from loving beautiful laws and theorems. The story concludes: to conceive of personal love in this way is to make a ghastly mistake. Singer, by analogy, is stuck with the disastrous result that the human love for God must be conceived of as including the bestowing of value on God by humans. But is it coherent to speak of humans bestowing value on God? . . . Consider again: "Man bestows value [on God] in recognizing the infinite goodness of God." Shouldn't Singer have written here, "Man positively appraises God in recognizing his infinite goodness"? "Recognizing the infinite goodness of God" becomes, for Singer, not an appraisal but a bestowal. But this expands unmercifully the notion of bestowal.

Singer eventually claims that he has driven too wide a wedge between bestowal and appraisal: "All appraisals must ultimately depend on bestowal since [appraisals] presuppose that human beings give importance to the satisfying of their needs and desires. Without such bestowal nothing could take on value of any sort. As a result, the two categories are not wholly separable" (vol. 3, p. 393). Thus, in personal love, x bestows value on y, the cause of x's love for y normally being x's positive appraisal of y; and x's positive appraisal of y depends on x's antecedent bestowal of value on x's desires that are satisfiable by these positively appraised properties in y. Hence, the bestowal of value occurs at two places in love—x bestows value on y (the top level), and x bestows value on x's desires (the deep level)—with appraisal sandwiched between.[8] Note that in this complex picture, the top-level bestowal is erosically grounded, while the deeper bestowal is ungrounded. (Singer never claims that the deeper bestowal is somehow dependent on a deeper appraisal. Hence, it must be spontaneous.) I believe Singer is right that an ungrounded bestowal of value must occur somewhere in love, but I will argue . . . that (1) x's bestowal of value on y is not the ungrounded bestowal of love, and (2) at the deepest level x bestows value on y's properties, not on x's desires. Claim (1) denies that personal love is best understood as an agapic phenomenon; the goal, then, is to explain how claim (2) is consistent with the eros tradition.

NOTES

1. Singer, *The Nature of Love,* vol. 1, "Appraisal and Bestowal," pp. 3–22; vol. 3, "Toward a Modern Theory of Love, " pp. 389–406.

2. Singer's distinction between appraisal and bestowal had earlier been made by Emil Brunner (*Justice and the Social Order,* 1945). See Outka, *Agape,* pp. 81–83, 157–158.

3. Vlastos, "The Individual as an Object of Love in Plato," p. 33.

4. Singer, then, here distances himself in this regard from the second view of personal love. He rejects Montaigne's reason also on p. 14 of vol. 1: "For what then does a man love a woman? For being the person she is, for being herself? But that is to say that he loves her for nothing at all. Everyone is himself. Having a beloved who is what she is does not reveal the nature of love." (See n. 6, below.)

5. See also vol. 3, p. 399: "Persons we appraise highly . . . are easier to love."

6. If bestowal is ungrounded, then love is, after all, "for nothing at all" (see n. 4, above). Indeed, in vol. 3 Singer asserts, rather than repudiates, Montaigne's reason: "A person acquires this gratuitous value [of bestowal] by being whatever he is. Therein lies the rich absurdity of love; for everyone . . . is what he is" (p. 393).

7. See vol. 1, chap. 13, "Agapē: The Divine Bestowal."

8. The bestowal that occurs in the human love for God, then, is apparently only the deep-level bestowal. Hence, x's bestowing value in loving God is quite different from x's bestowing value on a human—which is a top-level bestowal.

ROBERT NOZICK

Love's Bond

The general phenomenon of love encompasses romantic love, the love of a parent for a child, love of one's country, and more. What is common to all love is this: Your own well-being is tied up with that of someone (or something) you love. When a bad thing happens to a friend, it happens to her and you feel sad for her; when something good happens, you feel happy for her. When something bad happens to one you love, though, something bad also happens *to you*. (It need not be exactly the same bad thing. And I do not mean that one cannot also love a friend). If a loved one is hurt or disgraced, you are hurt; if something wonderful happens to her, you feel better off. Not every gratification of a loved one's preference will make you feel better off, though; her well-being, not merely a preference of hers, has to be at stake. (Her well-being as who perceives it, she or you?) When love is not present, changes in other people's well-being do not, in general, change your own. You will be moved when others suffer in a famine and will contribute to help; you may be haunted by their plight, but you need not feel you yourself are worse off.

This extension of your own well-being (or ill-being) is what marks all the different kinds of love: the love of children, the love of parents, the love of one's people, of one's country. Love is not necessarily a matter of caring equally or more about someone else than about yourself. These loves are large, but love in some amount is present when your well-being is affected to whatever extent (but in the same direction) by another's. As the other fares, so (to some extent) do you. The people you love are included inside your boundaries, their well-being is your own.[1]

Being "in love," infatuation, is an intense state that displays familiar features: almost always thinking of the person; wanting constantly to touch and to be together; excitement in the other's presence; losing sleep; expressing one's feelings through poetry, gifts, or still other ways to delight the beloved; gazing deeply into each other's eyes; candlelit dinners; feeling that short separations are long; smiling foolishly when remembering actions and remarks of the other; feeling that the other's minor foibles are delightful; experiencing joy at having found the other and at being found by the other; and (as Tolstoy depicts Levin in *Anna Karenina* as he learns Kitty loves him) finding *everyone* charming and nice, and thinking they all must sense one's happiness. Other concerns and responsibilities become minor background details in the story of the romance, which becomes the predominant foreground event of life. (When major public responsibilities such as commanding Rome's armies or being king of England are put aside, the tales engross.) The vividness of the relationship can carry artistic or mythic proportions—lying together like figures in a painting, jointly living a new tale from Ovid. Familiar, too, is what happens when the love is not equally reciprocated: melancholy, obsessive rumination on what went wrong, fantasies about its being set right, lingering in places to catch a glimpse of the person, making telephone calls to hear the other's voice, finding that all other activities seem flat, occasionally having suicidal thoughts.

However and whenever infatuation begins, if given the opportunity it transforms itself into continuing romantic love or else it disappears. With this continuing romantic love, it feels to the two people that they have united to form

From Robert Nozick, *The Examined Life*. New York: Simon and Schuster, 1989. Copyright © 1989 by Robert Nozick. Reprinted by permission of Simon and Schuster, Inc., and Georges Borchardt, Inc.

and constitute a new entity in the world, what might be called a *we*.[2] You can be in romantic love with someone, however, without actually forming a *we* with her or him—that other person might not be in love with you. Love, romantic love, is *wanting* to form a *we* with that particular person, feeling, or perhaps wanting, that particular person to be the right one for you to form a *we* with, and also wanting the other to feel the same way about you. (It would be kinder if the realization that the other person is not the right one with whom to form a *we* always and immediately terminated the desire to form it.) The desire to form a *we* with that other person is not simply something that goes along with romantic love, something that contingently happens when love does. That desire is intrinsic to the nature of love, I think; it is an important part of what love intends.

In a *we*, the two people are not bound physically like Siamese twins; they can be in distant places, feel differently about things, carry on different occupations. In what sense, then, do these people together constitute a new entity, a *we*? That new entity is created by a new web of relationships between them which makes them no longer so separate. Let me describe some features of this web; I will begin with two that have a somewhat cold and political-science sound.

First, the defining feature we mentioned which applies to love in general: Your own well-being is tied up with that of someone you love romantically. Love, then, among other things, can place you at risk. Bad things that happen to your loved one happen to you. But so too do good things; moreover, someone who loves you helps you with care and comfort to meet vicissitudes—not out of selfishness although her doing so does, in part, help maintain her own well-being too. Thus, love places a floor under your well-being; it provides insurance in the face of fate's blows. (Would economists explain some features of selecting a mate as the rational pooling of risks?)

People who form a *we* pool not only their well-being but also their autonomy. They limit or curtail their own decision-making power and rights; some decisions can no longer be made alone. Which decisions these are will be parceled differently by different couples: where to live, how to live, who friends are and how to see them, whether to have children and how

many, where to travel, whether to go to the movies that night and what to see. Each transfers some previous rights to make certain decisions unilaterally into a joint pool; somehow, decisions will be made together about how to be together. If your well-being so closely affects and is affected by another's, it is not surprising that decisions that importantly affect well-being, even in the first instance primarily your own, will no longer be made alone.[3]

The term *couple* used in reference to people who have formed a *we* is not accidental. The two people also view themselves as a new and continuing unit, and they present that face to the world. They want to be perceived publicly as a couple, to express and assert their identity as a couple in public. Hence those homosexual couples unable to do this face a serious impediment.

To be part of a *we* involves having a new identity, an additional one. This does *not* mean that you no longer have any individual identity or that your sole identity is as part of the *we*. However, the individual identity you did have will become altered. To have this new identity is to enter a certain psychological stance; and each party in the *we* has this stance toward the other. Each becomes psychologically part of the other's identity. How can we say more exactly what this means? To say that something is part of your identity when, if that thing changes or is lost, you feel like a different person, seems only to reintroduce the very notion of identity that needs to be explained. Here is something more helpful: To love someone might be, in part, to devote alertness to their well-being and to your connection with them. (More generally, shall we say that something is part of your identity when you continually make it one of your few areas of special alertness?) There are empirical tests of alertness in the case of your own separate identity—for example, how you hear your name mentioned through the noise of a conversation you were not consciously attending to; how a word that resembles your name "jumps out" from the page. We might find similar tests to check for that alertness involved in loving someone. For example, a person in a *we* often is considerably more worried about the dangers of traveling—air crashes or whatever—when the other is traveling alone than when both travel together or when he himself or she herself is traveling alone; it seems plausible that a person in a *we* is alert, in general, to dangers to the other that would necessitate having to go back to a single individual identity, while these are made especially salient by a significant physical separation. Other criteria for the formation of a joint identity also might be suggested, such as a certain kind of division of labor. A person in a *we* might find himself coming across something interesting to read yet leaving it for the other person, not because he himself would not be interested in it but because the other would be more interested, and one of them reading it is sufficient for it to be registered by the wider identity now shared, the *we*. If the couple breaks up, they then might notice themselves reading all those things directly; the other person no longer can do it *for them*. (The list of criteria for the *we* might continue on to include something we discuss later, not seeking to "trade up" to another partner.) Sometimes the existence of the *we* can be very palpable. Just as a reflective person can walk along the street in friendly internal dialogue with himself, keeping himself company, so can one be with a loved person who is not physically present, thinking what she would say, conversing with her, noticing things as she would, for her, because she is not there to notice, saying things to others that she would say, in her tone of voice, carrying the full *we* along.[4]

If we picture the individual self as a closed figure whose boundaries are continuous and solid, dividing what is inside from what is outside, then we might diagram the *we* as two figures with the boundary line between them erased where they come together. (Is that the traditional heart shape?) The unitive aspects of sexual experience, two persons flowing together and intensely merging, mirror and aid the formation of the *we*. Meaningful work, creative activity, and development can change the shape of the self. Intimate bonds change the boundaries of the self and alter its *topology*—romantic love in one way and friendship (as we shall see) in another.

· The individual self can be related to the *we* it identifies with in two different ways. It can see the *we* as a very important *aspect* of itself, or it can see itself as part of the *we,* as contained within it. It may be that men more often take the former view, women the latter. Although both see the *we* as extremely important for the self,

most men might draw the circle of themselves containing the circle of the *we* as an aspect *within* it, while most women might draw the circle of themselves within the circle of the *we*. In either case, the *we* need not consume an individual self or leave it without any autonomy. ·

Each person in a romantic *we* wants to possess the other completely; yet each also needs the other to be an independent and nonsubservient person. Only someone who continues to possess a nonsubservient autonomy can be an apt partner in a joint identity that enlarges and enhances your individual one. And, of course, the other's well-being—something you care about—requires that nonsubservient autonomy too. Yet at the same time there is the desire to possess the other *completely.* This does not have to stem from a desire to dominate the other person, I think. What you need and want is to possess the other as completely as you do your own identity. This is an expression of the fact that you *are* forming a new joint identity with him or her. Or, perhaps, this desire just *is* the desire to form an identity with the other. Unlike Hegel's description of the unstable dialectic between the master and the slave, though, in a romantic *we* the autonomy of the other and complete possession too are reconciled in the formation of a joint and wondrous enlarged identity for both.

The heart of the love relationship is how the lovers view it from the inside, how they feel about their partner and about themselves within it, and the particular ways in which they are good *to* each other. Each person in love delights in the other, and also in giving delight; this often expresses itself in being playful together. In receiving adult love, we are held worthy of being the primary object of the most intense love, something we were not given in the childhood oedipal triangle.[5] Seeing the other happy with us and made happy through our love, we become happier with ourselves.

To be englowed by someone's love, it must be we ourselves who are loved, not a whitewashed version of ourselves, not just a portion. In the complete intimacy of love, a partner knows us as we are, fully. It is no reassurance to be loved by someone ignorant of those traits and features we feel might make us unlovable. Sometimes these are character traits or areas of incompetence, clumsiness, or ignorance; sometimes these are personal bodily features.

Complex are the ways parents make children uncomfortable about sites of pleasure or elimination, and these feelings can be soothed or transformed in the closest attentive and loving sexual intimacy. In the full intimacy of love, the full person is known and cleansed and accepted. And healed.

To be made happy with yourself by being loved, it must be you who is loved, not some feature such as your money. People want, as they say, to be loved "for themselves." You are loved for something else when what you are loved for is a peripheral part of your own self-image or identity. However, someone for whom money, or the ability to make it, was central to his identity, or for whom good looks or great kindness or intelligence was, might not be averse to love's being prompted by these characteristics. You can fall in love with someone because of certain characteristics and you can continue to delight in these; but eventually you must love the person himself, and not *for* the characteristics, not, at any rate, for any delimited list of them. But what does this mean, exactly?

We love the person when being together with that person is a salient part of our identity as we think of it: "being with Eve," "being with Adam," rather than "being with someone who is (or has) such-and-such. . . ." How does this come about? Characteristics must have played some important role, for otherwise why was not a different person loved just as well? Yet if we continue to be loved "for" the characteristics, then the love seems conditional, something that might change or disappear if the characteristics do. Perhaps we should think of love as like imprinting in ducks, where a duckling will attach itself to the first sizable moving object it sees in a certain time period and follow that as its mother. With people, perhaps characteristics set off the imprint of love, but then the person is loved in a way that is no longer based upon retaining those characteristics. This will be helped if the love is based at first upon a wide range of characteristics; it begins as conditional, contingent upon the loved person's having these desirable characteristics, yet given their range and tenacity, it is not insecure.[6]

However, love between people, unlike imprinting with ducks, is not unalterable. Though no longer dependent upon the particular char-

acteristics that set it off, it *can* be overcome over time by new and sufficiently negative other characteristics. Or perhaps by a new imprinting onto another person. Yet this alteration will not be sought by someone within a *we*. If someone were loved "for" certain desirable or valuable characteristics, on the other hand, then if someone else came along who had those characteristics to a greater extent, or other even more valuable characteristics, it seems you should love this new person more. And in that case, why merely wait for a "better" person to turn up; why not actively seek to "trade up" to someone with a "higher score" along valuable dimensions? (Plato's theory is especially vulnerable to these questions, for there it is the Form of Beauty that is the ultimate and appropriate object of love, any particular person serves merely as a bearer of characteristics that awaken in the lover a love of the Form, and hence any such person should be replaceable by a better awakener.[7]

A readiness to trade up, looking for someone with "better" characteristics, does not fit with an attitude of love. An illuminating view should explain why not, yet why, nevertheless, the attitude of love is not irrational. One possible and boring explanation is economic in form. Once you have come to know a person well, it would take a large investment of time and energy to reach the comparable point with another person, so there is a barrier to switching. (But couldn't the other person promise a greater return, even taking into account the new costs of investment?) There is uncertainty about a new person; only after long time and experience together, through arguments and crises, can one come to know a person's trustworthiness, reliability, resiliency, and compassion in hardships. Investigating another candidate for coupledom, even an apparently promising one, is likely eventually to reach a negative conclusion and it probably will necessitate curtailing or ending one's current coupled state. So it is unwise to seek to trade up from a reasonably satisfactory situation; the energy you'd expend in search might better be invested in improving your current *we*.

These counsels of economic prudence are not silly—far from it—but they are external. According to them, nothing about the nature of love itself focuses upon the particular individual loved or involves an unwillingness to substitute another; rather, the likelihood of losses from the substitution is what militates against it. We can see why, if the economic analysis were so, we would welcome someone's directing an attitude of love toward us that includes commitment to a particular person, and we can see why we might have to trade the offering or semblance of such an attitude in order to receive it. But why would we want actually to give such a commitment to a particular person, shunning all other partners? What special value is reached through such a love relationship committed to particularism but in no other way? To add that we care about our partners and so do not want to cause them hurt by replacing them is true, yet does not answer the question fully.

Economic analysis might even provide somewhat more understanding.[8] Repeated trading with a fixed partner with special resources might make it rational to develop in yourself specialized assets for trading with that partner (and similarly on the partner's part toward you); and this specialization gives some assurance that you will continue to trade *with that party* (since the invested resources would be worth much less in exchanges with any third party). Moreover, to shape yourself and specialize so as to better fit and trade with that partner, and therefore to do so less well with others, you will want some commitment and guarantee that the party will continue to trade with you, a guarantee that goes beyond the party's own specialization to fit you. Under some conditions it will be economically advantageous for two such trading firms to combine into *one* firm, with all allocations now becoming internal. Here at last we come to something like the notion of a joint identity.

The intention in love is to form a *we* and to identify with it as an extended self, to identify one's fortunes in large part with its fortunes. A willingness to trade up, to destroy the very *we* you largely identify with, would then be a willingness to destroy your self in the form of your own extended self. One could not, therefore, intend to link into another *we* unless one had ceased to identify with a current one—unless, that is, one had already ceased to love. Even in that case, the intention to form the new *we* would be an intention to *then* no longer be open to trading up. It is intrinsic to the notion of love, and to the *we* formed by it, that there is

not that willingness to trade up. One is no more willing to find another partner, even one with a "higher score," than to destroy the personal self one identifies with in order to allow another, possible better, but discontinuous self to replace it. (This is not to say one is unwilling to improve or transform oneself.) Perhaps here lies one function of infatuation, to pave and smooth the way to uniting in a *we;* it provides enthusiasm to take one over the hurdles of concern for one's own autonomy, and it provides an initiation into *we*-thinking too, by constantly occupying the mind with thoughts of the other and of the two of you together. A more cynical view than mine might see infatuation as the temporary glue that manages to hold people together until they are stuck.

Part of the process by which people soften their boundaries and move into a *we* involves repeated expression of the desire to do so, repeatedly telling each other that they love each other. Their statement often will be tentative, subject to withdrawal if the other does not respond with similar avowals. Holding hands, they walk into the water together, step by step. Their caution may become as great as when two suspicious groups or nations—Israel and the Palestinians might be an example—need to recognize the legitimacy of one another. Neither wants to recognize if the other does not, and it also will not suffice for each to announce that it will recognize if the other one does also. For each then will have announced a conditional recognition, contingent upon the other's unconditional recognition. Since neither one has offered this last, they haven't yet gotten started. Neither will it help if each says it will recognize conditional upon the other's conditional recognition: "I'll recognize you if you'll recognize me if I'll recognize you." For here each has given the other a three-part conditional announcement, one which is contingent upon, and goes into operation only when there exists, a two-part conditional announcement from the other party; so neither one has given the other exactly what will trigger that other's recognition, namely a two-part announcement. So long as they both symmetrically announce conditionals of the same length and complexity, they will not be able to get started. Some asymmetry is needed, then, but it need not be that either one begins by offering unconditional recognition. It would be enough for the first to offer the three-part recognition (which is contingent upon the other's simple two-part conditional recognition), and for the second to offer the two-part conditional recognition. The latter triggers the first to recognize outright and this, in turn, triggers the second to do the same. Between lovers, it never becomes this complicated explicitly. Neither makes the nested announcement "I will love you if you will love me if I will love you," and if either one did, this would not (to put it mildly) facilitate the formation of a *we*. Yet the frequency of their saying to each other, "I love you," and their attention to the other's response, may indicate a nesting that is implicit and very deep, as deep as the repeated triggering necessary to overcome caution and produce the actual and unconditional formation of the *we*.

Even after the *we* is formed, its motion is Aristotelian rather than Newtonian, maintained by frequent impetus. The avowals of love may not stop, and neither may romantic gestures, those especially apt actions, breaking the customary frame, that express and symbolize one's attachment to the *we* or, occurring earlier, the desire to form it.

Granting that a willingness to trade up is incompatible with love and with the formation of a *we* with a particular person, the question becomes one of whether it is rational to love in that particular way. There is the alternative of serious and significant personal ties without a joint identity, after all—friendships and sexual relationships, for instance. An answer could be given by the long and obvious list of the things and actions and emotions especially made possible and facilitated by the *we*. It is not unreasonable to want these, hence not irrational to enter into a *we* including forgoing the option of trading up. Yet it distorts romantic love to view it through the lens of the egoistic question "What's in it for me?" What we want when we are in love is to be with that person. What we want is to be with her or him—not *to be someone who is with her or him*. When we are with the other person, to be sure, we are someone who is with that person, but the object of our desire is not being that kind of someone. We want to make the other person happy, and also, but less so, to be the kind of person who makes her or him happy. It is a question of the emphasis, of how we describe what we want and seek—to use the philosophers' language, a question of the intentional object of our desire.

The way the egoistic question distorts romantic love is by switching the focus of attention from the relation between the lovers to the way each lover in the relation is. I do not mean that the way they are then is unimportant; how good reciprocated romantic love is for us is part of the reason why we desire and value it. But the central fact about love is the relation between the lovers. The central concern of lovers, as lovers, what they dwell upon and nurture, is the other person, and the relation between the two of them, not their own state. Of course, we cannot completely abstract a relation from whatever stands in it. (Contemporary extensional logic treats a relation simply as a set of the ordered pairs of things that—as we would say—stand in the relation.) And in fact, the particularity of a romantic relation does arise from the character of the lovers and then enhances that. Yet what is most salient to each is the other person and what holds between the two of them, not themselves as an endpoint of the relation. There is a difference between wanting to hug someone and using them as an opportunity for yourself to become a hugger.

The desire to have love in one's life, to be part of a *we* someday, is not the same as loving a particular person, wanting to form a *we* with that person in particular. In the choice of a particular partner, reasons can play a significant role, I think. Yet in addition to the merits of the other person and her or his qualities, there also is the question of whether the thought of forming a *we* with that person brings excitement and delight. Does that identity seem a wonderful one for you to have? Will it be *fun*? Here the answer is as complicated and mysterious as your relation to your own separate identity. Neither case is completely governed by reasons, but still we might hope that our choices do meet what reasoned standards there are. (The desire to continue to feel that the other is the right partner in your *we* also helps one surmount the inevitable moments in life together when that feeling itself becomes bruised.) The feeling that there is just "one right person" in the world for you, implausible beforehand—what lucky accident made that one unique person inhabit your century?—becomes true after the *we* is formed. Now your identity is wrapped up in that particular *we* with that particular person, so for the particular *you* you now are, there *is* just one other person who is right.

In the view of a person who loves someone

romantically, there couldn't be anyone else who was better as a partner. He might think that person he is in love with could be better somehow—stop leaving toothpaste in the sink or whatever—but any description he could offer of a better mate would be a description of his mate changed, not one of somebody *else*. No one else would do, no matter what her qualities. Perhaps this is due to the particularity of the qualities you come to love, not just a sense of humor but that particular one, not just some way of looking mock-stern but that one. Plato got the matter reversed, then; as love grows you love not general aspects or traits but more and more particular ones, not intelligence in general but that particular mind, not kindness in general but those particular ways of being kind. In trying to imagine a "better" mate, a person in romantic love will require her or him to have a very particular constellation of very particular traits and—leaving aside various "science fiction" possibilities—no other person *could* have precisely those traits; therefore, any imagined person will be the same mate (perhaps) somewhat changed, not somebody else. (If that same mate actually alters, though, the romantic partner may well come to love and require that new constellation of particulars.) Hence, a person in romantic love *could not* seek to "trade up"—he would have to seek out the very same person. A person not in love might seek someone with certain traits, yet after finding someone, even (remarkably) a person who has the traits sought, if he loves that person she will show those traits in a particularity he did not initially seek but now has come to love—her particular versions of these traits. Since a romantic mate eventually comes to be loved, not for any general dimensions or "score" on such dimensions—that, if anything, gets taken for granted—but for his or her own particular and nonduplicable way of embodying such general traits, a person in love could not make any coherent sense of his "trading up" to *another*.

This does not yet show that a person could not have many such different focused desires, just as she might desire to read this particular book and also that one. I believe that the romantic desire is to form a *we* with that particular person *and* with no other. In the strong sense of the notion of identity involved here, one can no more be part of many *we's* which constitute one's identity than one can simul-

taneously have many individual identities. (What persons with multiple personality have is not many identities but not quite one.) In a *we,* the people *share* an identity and do not simply each have identities that are enlarged. The desire to share not only our life but our very identity with another marks our fullest openness. What more central and intimate thing could we share?

The desire to form a *we* with that person and no other includes a desire for that person to form one with you yourself and with no other; and so after sexual desire links with romantic love as a vehicle for its expression, and itself becomes more intense thereby, the mutual desire for sexual monogamy becomes almost inevitable, to mark the intimacy and uniqueness of forming an identity with that one particular person by directing what is the most intense physical intimacy toward her or him alone.

It is instructive here to consider friendship, which too alters and recontours an individual's boundaries, providing a distinct shape and character to the self. The salient feature of friendship is *sharing*. In sharing things—food, happy occasions, football games, a concern with problems, events to celebrate—friends especially want these to be had together; while it might constitute something good when each person has the thing separately, friends want that it be had or done by both (or all) of them *together*. To be sure, a good thing does get magnified for you when it is shared with others, and some things can be more fun when done together—indeed, fun, in part, is just the sharing and taking of delight in something together. Yet in friendship the sharing is not desired simply to enlarge our individual benefits.

The self, . . . can be construed as an appropriative mechanism, one that moves from reflexive awareness of things to *sole* possession of them. The boundaries between selves get constituted by the specialness of this relation of possession and ownership—in the case of psychological items, this generates the philosophical "problem of other minds." Things shared with friends, however, do not stand in a unique and special relationship to any one self as its sole possession; we join with friends in having them and, to that extent at least, our selves and theirs overlap or the boundaries between them are less sharp. The very same things—experiences, activities, conversations, problems, objects of focus or of amusement—are

part of us both. We each then are related closely to many things that another person also has
an equally close relationship to. We therefore
are not separate selves—not so separate anyway. (Should we diagram friendship as two cir-
cles that overlap?)

A friendship does not exist *solely* for further
purposes, whether a political movement's larger goals, an occupational endeavor, or simply
the participants' separate and individual benefits. Of course, there can be many further benefits that flow within friendship and from it,
benefits so familiar as not to need listing. Aristotle held one of these to be most central; a
friend, he said, is a "second self" who is a
means to your own self-awareness. (In his listing of the virtuous characteristics one should
seek in a friend, Aristotle takes your parents'
view of who your friends should be.) Nevertheless, a relationship is a friendship to the extent
that it shares activities for no further purpose
than the sharing of them.

People seek to engage in sharing beyond the
domain of personal friendship also. One important reason we read newspapers, I think, is not
the importance or intrinsic interest of the news;
we rarely take action whose direction depends
upon what we read there, and if somehow we
were shipwrecked for ten years on an isolated
island, when we returned we would want a
summary of what had happened meanwhile,
but we certainly would not choose to peruse the
back newspapers of the previous ten years.
Rather, we read newspapers because we want
to *share* information with our fellows, we want
to have a range of information in common with
them, a common stock of mental contents. We
already share with them a geography and a language, and also a common fate in the face of
large-scale events. That we also desire to share
the daily flow of information shows how very
intense our desire to share is.

Nonromantic friends do not, in general,
share an *identity*. In part, this may be because
of the crisscrossing web of friendships. The
friend of your friend may be your acquaintance, but he or she is not necessarily someone
you are close to or would meet with separately.
As in the case of multiple bilateral defense
treaties among nations, conflicts of action and
attachment can occur that make it difficult to
delineate any larger entity to which one safely
can cede powers and make the bearer of a larger identity. Such considerations also help ex-

plain why it is not feasible for a person simultaneously to be part of multiple romantic
couples (or of a trio), even were the person to
desire this. Friends want to share the things
they do *as* a sharing, and they think, correctly,
that friendship is valuable partly *because* of its
sharing—perhaps specially valuable because,
unlike the case of romantic love, this valued
sharing occurs *without* any sharing of identity.

We might pause over one mode of sharing
that, while it is not done primarily for its own
sake, produces a significant sense of solidarity.
That is participating with others in joint action
directed toward an external goal—perhaps a
political cause or reform movement or occupational project or team sport or artistic performance or scientific endeavor—where the
participants feel the pleasures of joint and
purposeful participation in something really
worthwhile. Perhaps there is a special need for
this among young adults as they leave the family, and that in part constitutes youth's "ideal-
ism." Linked with others toward a larger joint
purpose, *joined* with them at the same node of
an effectual causal chain, one's life is no longer
simply private. In such a way citizens might
think of themselves as creating together, and
sharing, a memorable civilization.

We can prize romantic love and the formation of a *we,* without denying that there may be
extended times, years even, when an adult
might best develop alone. It is not plausible,
either, to think that every single individual, at
some or another time in his life, would be most
enhanced as part of a romantically loving *we*—
that Buddha, Socrates, Jesus, Beethoven, or
Gandhi would have been. This may be, in part,
because the energy necessary to sustain and
deepen a *we* would have been removed from
(thereby lessening) these individuals' activities. But there is more to say. The particular
vivid way these individuals defined themselves
would not fit easily within a romantic *we;* their
special lives would have had to be very different. Of course, a *we* often falls short of its best,
so a prudent person might seek (or settle for)
other modes of personal relationship and connection. Yet these extraordinary figures remind
us that even at its best a *we* constitutes a particular formation of identity that involves forgoing some extraordinary possibilities. (Or is it
just that these figures needed equally extraordinary mates?)

Just as the identity of the self continues over

an extended period of time, so too is there the desire for the *we* to continue; part of identifying fully with the *we* is intending that it continue. Marriage marks a full identification with that *we*. With this, the *we* enters a new stage, building a sturdier structure, knitting itself together more fully. Being a couple is taken as given though not for granted. No longer focusing upon whether they *do* constitute an enduring *we*, the partners now are free confidently to build together a life with its own focus and directions. The *we* lives their life together. As egg and sperm come together, two biographies have become one. The couple's first child is their union—their earlier history was prenatal.

A *we* is not a new physical entity in the world, whether or not it is a new ontological one. However, it may want to give its web of love relationships a physical incarnation. That is one thing a home is about—an environment that reflects and symbolizes how the couple feel (and what they do) together, the spirit in which they are together; this also, of course, makes it a happy place for them to be. In a different way, and to a much greater extent, children can constitute a physical realization of the parents' love, an incarnation in the world of the valuable extended self the two of them have created. And children might be loved and delighted in, in part as this physical representation of the love between the parents. However, of course and obviously, the children are not merely an adjunct to the parents' love, as either a representation of it or a means of heightening it; they primarily are people to be cared for, delighted in, and loved for themselves.

Intimate bonds change the contours and boundaries of the self, altering its topology: in love, as we have seen, in the sharings of friendship, in the intimacy of sexuality. Alterations in the individual self's boundaries and contours also are a goal of religious quest: expanding the self to include all of being (Indian Vedanta), eliminating the self (Buddhism), or merging with the divine. There also are modes of general love for all of humanity, often religiously enjoined—recall how Dostoyevsky depicts Father Zossima in *The Brothers Karamazov*— that greatly alter the character and contours of the self, now no longer so appropriately referred to as "individual."

It may not be an accident that people rarely do simultaneously combine building a romantic *we* with a spiritual quest. It seems impossible to proceed full strength with more than one major alteration in the self's topology at a time. Nevertheless, it may well be important at times to be engaged in *some* or another mode of change in the boundaries and topology of the self, different ones at different times. Any such change need not be judged solely by how it substantively feeds back into the individual self, though. The new entity that is created or contoured, with its own boundaries and topology, has its own evaluations to make. An individual self justifiably might be proud to be supple enough to enter into these changes and exfoliate them, yet its perspective before the changes does not provide the only relevant standard. It *is* in the interests of an individual sperm or egg cell to unite to form a new organism, yet we do not continue to judge the new life by that gamete's particular interests. In love's bond, we metamorphose.

NOTES

1. A somewhat sharper criterion can be formulated of when another's well-being is *directly* part of your own. This occurs when (1) you say and believe your well-being is affected by significant changes in hers; (2) your well-being is affected in the same *direction* as hers, an improvement in her well-being producing an improvement in your own, a decrease, a decrease; (3) you not only judge yourself worse off, but feel some emotion appropriate to that state; (4) you are affected by the change in *her* well-being directly, merely through knowing about it, and not because it symbolically represents to you something else about yourself, a childhood situation or whatever; (5) (and this condition is especially diagnostic) your *mood* changes: you now have different occurrent feelings and changed dispositions to have particular other emotions; and (6) this change in mood is somewhat enduring. Moreover, (7) you have this general tendency or disposition toward a person or object, to be thus affected; you *tend* to be thus affected by changes in that person's well-being.

2. For a discussion of love as the formation of a *we*, see Robert Solomon, *Love* (Garden City, N. Y.: Anchor Books, 1981).

3. This curtailment of unilateral decision-making rights extends even to a decision to end the romantic love relationship. This decision, if any, you would think you could make by yourself. And so you can, but only in certain ways at a certain pace. Another kind of relation might be ended because you feel like it or because you find it no longer satisfactory, but in a love relationship the other party "has a vote." This does not mean a permanent veto; but the other party has a right to have his or her say, to try to repair, to be convinced. After some time, to be sure, one party may insist on ending the relationship even without the other's consent, but what they each have forgone, in love, is the right to act unilaterally and swiftly.

4. When two people form a *we,* does this *we* constitute an added entity in the world, something in addition to the people involved and their web of relationships? (Might there be times we want to say that in addition to the two people, the *we* also feels an emotion?) This resembles the question of whether a whole society is an additional entity in the world or merely the sum of the web of the various people's relationships. Is a human body an additional entity in the world or simply those constituent physical parts in a web of relationships? Like a body or a society, a *we* maintains itself and adapts in the face of (a wide range of) new circumstances. Unlike a society or a body, it does not continue existing as the same entity while there is replacement of some constituent parts. However, the two people in a *we* relationship often do interact with the outside world as a unit, one with a distinctive well-being and decision-making locus. Noticing the multifarious features of the *we* and the new activities and value it makes possible is more important than deciding whether it constitutes a new item of ontological furniture in the world. The latter would be an apt marker, though, for that familiar phenomenological experience of contentedly just being together in the space the two make and constitute. (For an extremely detailed and illuminating discussion of the nature of a "we" and of a plural subject, one that appeared after this book was complete, see Margaret Gilbert, *On Social Facts* [London: Routledge, 1989], pp. 146–236.)

5. Another Greek tale, that of Telemachus at home with Penelope while Odysseus wanders, provides a different picture of the family triangle's character. A father is a needed protector, not just someone to compete with for the mother's love. If the mother is as attractive as the child thinks, in the absence of the father other suitors will present themselves before her. And unlike the father, who will not kill the competitive child or maim him (despite what the psychoanalytic literature depicts as the child's anxieties), these suitors *are* his enemies. Telemachus *needs* his father—to maintain the *safe* triangle—and so he sets out to find him.

6. Being loved *for* characteristics seems to go with the notion of love being deserved, the characteristics being the basis of the desert. This notion of love's being deserved is a strange one; no one deserves non-love because they fall short of high standards. We do sometimes say someone is "unworthy" of another's love, but by this we mean that person cannot respond appropriately to being (romantically) loved, cannot respond in a loving way. (The person need not love romantically in return but the genuine love that was offered must at least be turned away in a loving way.) To be worthy of (romantic) love, then, is simply to have the capacity to love in return. Yet if that capacity is not evident beforehand in a person, might it not be created or evoked by that person's being loved? Such is the hope of those who love, convinced that the depth and nobility of their own love will awaken love in the other; it takes a certain experience of the world to discover that this is not always so.

7. See Gregory Vlastos, "The Individual as an Object of Love in Plato," in his *Platonic Studies* (Princeton: Princeton University Press, 1973), pp. 3–34.

8. This paragraph was suggested by the mode of economic analysis found in Oliver Williamson, *The Economic Institutions of Capitalism* (New York: The Free Press, 1986).

ROBERT C. SOLOMON

The Virtue of (Erotic) Love

In a famous—or infamous—passage, Kant off-handedly dismisses one of the most essential elements in ethics: "Love out of inclination cannot be commanded; but kindness done from duty—although no inclination impels us, and even although natural and unconquerable disinclination stands in our way—is *Practical,* and not *Pathological* love, residing in the will and not of melting compassion."[1] In the *Symposium,* on the other hand, Phaedrus offers us one of many contrasting comments by Plato in honor of *erōs:* "That is why I say Love is the eldest of the gods and most honored and the most powerful for acquiring virtue and blessedness, for men both living and dead."[2] This paper has two aims: to understand erotic (romantic, "pathological") love as itself a virtue, and to broaden our view of ethics.

ERŌS AND ETHICS

It [love] does not hesitate to intrude with its trash. . . . It knows how to slip its love-notes and ringlets even into ministerial portfolios and philosophical manuscripts. Every day it brews and hatches the worst and most perplexing quarrels and disputes, destroys the most valuable relationships and breaks the strongest bonds. . . . Why all this noise and fuss? . . . It is merely a question of every Jack finding his Jill. (The gracious reader should translate this phrase into precise Aristophanic language.) Why should such a trifle play so important a role?

Arthur Schopenhauer, *The World as Will and Representation*[3]

Love as a virtue? Well, hardly. Motherly love, certainly; patriotism, perhaps. The love of humanity, to be sure, but romantic love? Erotic

love? The passion that makes fools of us all and has led to the demise of Anthony, Cleopatra, young Romeo, Juliet, and King Kong? Love is nice, but it is not a virtue. Maybe it is not even nice. Hesiod in the *Theogony* warned against *erōs* as a force contrary and antagonistic to reason. Sophocles and Euripides both denounced *erōs, in Antigone* and *Hippolytus* respectively, and even Virgil had his doubts. Schopenhauer, much more recently, thought all love to be sexual and damnable, and today we are much more likely to invoke the cynical wit of Oscar Wilde or Kingsley Amis than the saccharine pronouncements of our latter-day love pundits. Indeed, running through the history of ideas in the West one cannot but be struck by the ambivalence surrounding this central and celebrated concept. It is cursed as irrational and destructive and praised as the origin of everything. *Erōs* is famous for its foolishness and at the same time elevated and venerated as a god, albeit at first a rather minor one, but by the time of early Christianity, nothing less than God as such.

Today, we find ourselves torn between such mundane considerations as dependency and autonomy, security and the dubious freedom to remain "uncommitted." It is hard to remind ourselves, therefore, that the history of love is intellectual warfare between bestiality on one side and divinity on the other. The word "love" has so often functioned as a synonym for lust that it is hard to take it seriously as a virtue. It has just as long been raised to cosmological status, by Parmenides, Empedocles, and Plotinus, for example, and it therefore seems somewhat small-minded to reduce it to a mere source of human relationships. Most

From *Midwest Studies in Philosophy,* vol. XIII, *Ethical Theory,* ed. P. French, T. Uehling, Jr., and H. Wettstein. Notre Dame, Ind.: University of Notre Dame Press, 1988. Copyright © 1988 by The University of Notre Dame Press. Reprinted with permission.

modern philosophers have, accordingly, ignored it, Schopenhauer here as elsewhere being a bit eccentric, while moralists have had a field day playing the one side (lust) against the other (divine grace, piety, and contempt for all bodily functions, but particularly those that are best when shared).

In any discussion of love as a virtue, it is necessary, if by now routine, to mention some different "kinds" of love. (The notion of "kinds" may already be question begging here, for the more difficult issue may be what links, rather than distinguishes, e. g., friendship, sexual love, and parental affection.) In particular, it is essential that we distinguish *erōs* and *agapé*, the former usually translated as sexual love, the latter as selfless and certainly sexless love for humanity. The distinction is often drawn crudely. For instance, *erōs* is taken to be purely erotic and reduced to sexual desire, which it surely is not. Or *agapé* is characterized as selfless giving, opposed by *erōs* which thus becomes selfish taking (or at least craving). *Agapé* is idealized to the point where it becomes an attitude possible only to God, thus rendering it virtually inapplicable to common human fellow-feelings. *Erōs* by contrast is degraded to the profanely secular and denied any hint of spirituality. To think of love as a virtue, therefore, is first of all to expand (once again) the domain of *erōs*. (Romantic love, I am presuming, is one historical variant of *erōs*.) One need not deny the desirability (or the possibility) of altruistic *agapé* to insist that erotic *erōs* shares at least some of its virtues.

Erōs, and what we now call "romantic love," should also be distinguished (carefully) from other forms of particular affection—for example, motherly, fatherly, brotherly, or sisterly love and friendship. I think that Schopenhauer was partly right when he suggested (with Freud following him) that all love is to some extent sexual. But to make this point one obviously needs a generously enlarged conception of sex and sexual desire, and I often fear that this insight is motivated as much by its titillating implications as by the impulse to clarify the nature of human bonding. A more modest thesis is that *erōs* (not sex) encompasses almost all intimate, personal affections. What characterizes *erōs* in general, we might then suggest, is an intense quasi-physical, even "grasping," affection for a particular person, a Buscaglian

"urge to hug" if you will. (Plato often uses such desire-defined language in talking about *erōs*, even when he is reaching for the Forms.) In romantic love, sexual desire is undeniably a part of this affection, though it is not at all clear whether this is the source of the affection or rather its vehicle. *Erōs* differs from *agapé* in the prevalence of self-interested desire, but it is not thereby selfish and the desire is not just sexual. It also includes a much more general physical desire to "be with," such personal desires as "to be appreciated" and "to be happy together," such inspirational desires as "to be the best for you," and such "altruistic" desires as "to do anything I can for you." As la Rochefoucauld once put it, "in the soul . . . a thirst for mastery; in the mind sympathy; in the body, nothing but a delicately hidden desire to possess, after many mysteries."[4]

It is a common mistake to think of the other person in sex as a mere "object" of desire, which leads to the idea that *erōs* too is degrading and seeks only its own satisfaction. Consider Kant on the matter: "Because sexuality is not an inclination which one human being has for another as such, but is an inclination for the sex of another, it is a principle of the degradation of human nature, in that it gives rise to the preference of one sex to the other, and to the dishonoring of that sex through the satisfaction of desire."[5] But surely the question (as Plato raised it 2300 years earlier) is *what* one desires when one sexually desires another person. In the *Symposium*, Aristophanes suggested that one desires not sex but permanent (re-)unification with the other; Socrates insisted that one really wants the Forms. Even if we consider such goals too fantastic for *erōs*, it is clear that the Greeks—as opposed to Kant and many moderns—saw that sexual desire was much, much more than desire for sex and not at all opposed to virtuous desire. At the very least, it is clear that sexual desire is some sort of powerful desire *for* the other person *through* sex. The question is: a desire *for what?* And by no means should we assume from the outset that the answer to this question has anything to do with sexual *objects*. Indeed, taking our clue from Hegel and Sartre, we might suggest rather that it has everything to do with sexual *subject*, and subjects by their very nature cannot be wholly sexual.

The most obvious difference between erotic

(romantic) and other particular forms of love is the centrality of sexual (do not read "genital") desire, but there are two other differences that, philosophically, are much more illuminating. The first, though quite controversial, is the prerequisite of *equality* between lovers. This may seem odd in the light of modern accusations against love as a vehicle for the degradation and oppression of women (Shulamith Firestone, Marilyn French), but in historical perspective it becomes clear that—however far we may be from real equality—romantic love emerges only with the relative liberation of women from traditional subservient social and economic roles. Romantic love emerges only when women begin to have more of a choice about their lives—and about their lovers and husbands in particular. One thinks of John Milton's Adam, created early in the era of romantic love, who specifically requested from God not a mere playmate or companion or a mirror image of himself but an *equal,* for "among unequals what society / Can sort, what harmony or true delight?[6] Or, paraphrasing Stendhal, we might say that love tends to create equals even where it does not find them, for equality is as essential to romantic love as authority is to parenthood—whether or not this is adequately acknowledged or acted upon.

One other difference between *erōs* and other loves is that romantic love, unlike familial love, for example, is unprescribed and often spontaneous. ("Romantic friendships" are especially worth noting in this context.) Critical to erotic, romantic love is the sense of *choice.* Family love, in this sense, is always prescribed. The love between husband and wife, or what such authors as de Rougemont call "conjugal love," might be considered prescribed in this sense too, including its sexuality. This is emphatically not to say that married love cannot be romantic, or that romantic love is characterized only by its novelty or by the excitement and anxiety consequent to that novelty. It is a common mistake to take the exhilaration of love as love—without asking what that exhilaration is *about.* Love and marriage often begin together even if they do not always remain together, and to separate them is just to say that love can be unhitched just as horses can, while carriages sit unmoving.

What could be virtuous about *erōs?* One might rationalize sexual love as the slippery slope to marriage, but this faint praise only reinforces our image of romantic love as something in itself childish, foolish, and a kind of conspiracy of nature and society to trick self-consciously rebellious adolescents into maturity. One might celebrate *erōs* as the often unrecognized source of many of our most beautiful creations, from Dante's poetry to the Taj Mahal, but this too is to demean love as a virtue and see it merely as a means, as Freud once saw anal retention as a means to great art. But it seems to me that *erōs* is not considered a virtue for three general sorts of reasons:

1. *Erōs* is reduced to mere sexuality, and philosophers, insofar as they deign to dirty their minds with sex at all (*qua* philosophers, of course), tend to see sexuality as vulgar and not even a candidate for virtue. Part of this is the common perception of sex as either a form of recreation or a means to procreation, but in any case a set of desires constrained by ethics but hardly of ethical value in themselves.

2. Love is an emotion and emotions are thought to be irrational, beyond our control, merely episodic instead of an essential aspect of character, products of "instinct" and intractable in the face of all evidence and objective consideration. Even Aristotle, one of the few friends of the passions in the history of philosophy, insisted that only states of character, not passions, can count as virtues.

3. *Erōs* even insofar as it is not just sexual is self-love and the self-indulgence of desire, while an essential characteristic of the virtues is, in Hume's phrase, their utility, their being pleasing to others and based on such sentiments as compassion and sympathy. Romantic love, far from being "pleasing to others," tends to be embarrassing and sometimes harmful to others and self-destructive. It tends to be possessive, jealous, obsessive, antisocial, even "mad." Such drama is not the stuff of which virtue is made.

I obviously believe that each of these objections to erotic love as a virtue is just plain wrong, but it will take most of this paper to spell out an alternative view. Simply, for now, let me state that these objections demean and misunderstand the nature of sexuality, the nature of emotions, and the nature of love in particular. So that I do not appear overly irrationalist and romantic here, let me draw Plato to my side. He clearly saw *erōs* as a virtue, and every one of the speakers in the *Symposium* agrees with this. Even Socrates, by far the most effete of the speakers, celebrates *erōs* not as the disinterested appreciation of beauty and wisdom (as many Oxford commentaries would make it seem) but rather as a "grasping" sensuality, perhaps of the mind rather than the body, but erotic none the less for that. (Why did he so distrust beauty in art but yet celebrate it in *erōs?*) In Plato's thinking, *erōs* was a virtue just because it was (in part) a passion, filled with desire and—in that peculiarly noble Socratic sense—self-obsessed as well.

ETHICS AND SUBJECTIVITY

> One more word against Kant as a *moralist*. A virtue must be *our own* invention, *our* most necessary self-expression and self-defense; any other kind of virtue is a danger. . . . "Virtue," "duty," the "good in itself," the good which is impersonal and universally valid—chimeras and expressions of decline, of the final exhaustion of life. . . . The fundamental laws of self-preservation and growth demand the opposite—that everyone invent *his own* virtue, his *own* categorical imperative.
>
> Friedrich Nietzsche, *The Antichrist.*[7]

A single paradigm of rationality has retained hegemony in ethics since the Enlightenment. In the shadow of this paradigm, there is less difference than similarity between Kant and the utilitarians: moral philosophy is nothing if not objective, rational, based on principles, and exclusive of particular self-reference and mere personal perspectives. What is shocking is what the paradigm leaves out: most emotions and love in particular (except insofar as these might motivate duty or serve "the greatest good for the greatest number"). The persistence of this paradigm (which I will call "Kantian") has turned the most exciting subject in philosophy—or so it would seem from novels, the newspapers, soap operas, and ordinary gossip—into the dry quasi-legal tedium that we find in some philosophy journals. And worse, it has proved to many people—including many philosophers—that ethics has little to do with the intricate realities of human behavior. The elegant observations of Hume are shunted aside in favor of *policy* decisions. The neglect of personal inclinations in favor of legalistic universal principles leaves out the substance of the ethical, which is not principles but feelings.

Bernard Williams points out that it would be "insane" to prefer an act of kindness born of principle rather than personal affection, as Kant recommends.[8] When one thinks of the myriad delights, affections, and felt obligations in love, one cannot help but decide that, given a choice between insisting that love is amoral (at best) and retaining the Kantian paradigm, one's preference is quite clear. Kant's line that we quoted from the *Groundwork* about "pathological love," even on the most generous interpretation (as "pathos" rather than "diseased"), dismisses romantic affection as wholly irrelevant to moral worth, and with this eliminates most of what we—and most of Kant's more romantic colleagues—take to be the very heart of morality.

Richard Taylor once wrote that he found Kantian ethics basically offensive, so much so that he insisted that he would have the same attitude toward a true Kantian that he would toward a person who "regularly drowned children just to see them squirm."[9] This is extreme, and it ignores many recent attempts to "humanize" Kant,[10] but the Kantian position is offensive, and one of the reasons for this is its resistance, if not rejection, of any inclusion of personal, particular feelings in moral evaluation. We find similar resistance in many modern Kantians, for instance, in Bernard Gert's *The Moral Rules* where he dismisses feelings as morally worthless and insists instead that "feelings are morally important only insofar as they lead to morally good actions."[11] It seems to me, on the contrary, that nothing is more important to our evaluation of a person's moral character than feelings, and not just because of our reasonable expectation that actions generally follow feelings. The worth of our feelings is not parasitic on the desirability of our actions. In love, the worthiness of our actions depends on the feelings they express. Generous and even heroic actions may follow from love, but the virtue of love stands quite on its own, even without such consequences (Socrates' criticism of Phaedrus in the *Symposium*). We may think Othello foolish and tragic but we still admire the motive, while Victorian literature is filled with Kantian gentlemen acting on their principles who are utterly repulsive (for instance, Mr. Collins in Jane Austen's *Pride and Prejudice*). Not only is it desirable to love, but those who have not loved (if not lost), or fear they cannot, rightly worry not only about their character but about their completeness as human beings—quite apart from any questions about action or performance. Love itself is admirable, quite apart from its effects and consequences.

Why is the tradition so opposed to love and other feelings as essential, even primary ingredients, in morality? The opposition is all the more surprising given the heavy emphasis on love (though as *agapé*) as the supreme virtue in the New Testament—and it is just this oddity that Kant is trying to explain away in the passage quoted. There seem to be several reasons for Kant's antagonism to feelings in moral evaluation. First and foremost, he seems to believe that only that which can be "commanded" is morally obligatory, and love as a passion cannot be commanded. This particular claim has been admirably disputed in Ed Sankowski's 1978 paper on "Love and Moral Obligation," where, in particular, he argues that we at least hold people responsible for fostering or evading the conditions that breed love.[12] One might challenge as well the claim that only that which can be commanded is moral; much of what goes into "good character," while it can be cultivated, cannot be commanded. One might also argue—as I have often—that the emotions are far more voluntaristic and under our control than we normally believe, and not just in the sense that we can foster or avoid the conditions in which they typically emerge. This is not to say that an emotion such as love can simply be produced, by an act of will or volition, as one might now produce a thought or a movement of one's finger. There may be, in Danto-esque phrase, no "basic action" where love is concerned. But there are lots of intentional actions of both mind and body that are not basic, and to insist that love can be produced *de nihilo* by a volition is surely to place an unreasonable demand on its moral virtue.

Second, on the Kantian paradigm, it is always the universal that is in question, never the particular. Here Kant is once again in agreement with New Testament ethics, for *agapé* could be argued to be universal (or, one might also say, indiscriminate) love, and not love for any particular person. (It is worth noting that Christian psychology did hold people responsible for their feelings, did believe that love could be commanded, and, in just the phrase

disputed by Kant, demanded it.) But on many interpretations Christian love, as love, is emphatically the love of particulars—even if of every particular and not just of the universal (God, humanity) as such. Love—especially erotic or romantic love—is wholly particular. It is the elevation of one otherwise ordinary person to extraordinary heights with extraordinary privileges. The idea of a categorical imperative in such instances is laughable. On the Kantian model, the particularity of love would seem to be a form of irrationality—comparable to our tendency to make "exceptions" of ourselves, in this case, making exceptions of persons close to us. In love the particular is everything. The virtue of love is and ought to be entirely preferential and personal. The lover who gives special preference to his love (though not, of course, in a bureaucratic or departmental position) is virtuous. A lover who insisted on treating everyone including his or her lover the same would strike us as utterly repulsive.

Third, because morality is a matter of reason, the irrationality of the emotions (in general) is good enough reason not to make them central to ethics. The alleged irrationality of emotions is something more than their supposed involuntariness and particularity. Kant thinks that emotions are irrational, Bernard Williams suggests, because they are capricious. One might add that they also seem to be intrusive, disruptive, stubborn, stupid, and pointless. These are very different accusations, but they are often levied together against emotions in general and love in particular. As "feelings," it is often said that emotions are *non*rational (not even smart enough to be *ir*rational.) Or, granting emotions a modicum of aims and intelligence, it is insisted that emotions (*sui generis*) have limited ends and (at best) inefficient means. Against the "disruptive" view of emotions it should be argued that they do not always intrude or disrupt life but often (always?) define it and define the ultimate ends of rationality as well. Against the view that emotions are stupid, one could argue at length how emotional "intuition" is often more insightful and certainly more strategic than many of the ratiocinations of abstract moralizing, and against the view that emotions are aimless it should be said that all emotions have their aims, even if rather odd and sometimes limited. On the other hand, it should be commented that some emotions—among them love—have the most grandiose aims, far grander than the surely limited desire to be "reasonable." Consider Hegel: "Love neither restricts nor is restricted; it is not finite at all . . . love completely destroys objectivity and thereby annuls and transcends reflection, deprives man's opposite of all foreign character, and discovers life itself without any further defect."[13]

The most common accusation against the emotions, and love in particular, is that they confuse or distort our experience (Leibniz called them "confused perceptions"). What is in question here is the infamous resistance of emotions to canons of consistency and evident facts, their alleged lack of "common sense" and tendency to bias perception and judgment, their apparent tolerance of contradiction (which Freud made one of the hallmarks of "the Unconscious"), their refusal to conform to obvious considerations of objectivity. In love, this is embarrassingly obvious. A homely lover looks longingly at his equally plain love and declares, "You are the most beautiful woman in the world." How are we to understand this? Self-deception? Insanity? Surely not "blindness" (which would be plain ignorance), for the problem is not that he cannot see. Indeed, he might well claim to see much *more* than we do, or more deeply. Impolitely pressed, our enraptured lover may resentfully concede the point, perhaps doing a phenomenological retreat to, "Well, she's the most beautiful woman in the world *to me!*," but we know how such qualifications are treated in philosophy—with proper epistemological disdain. In love one makes a claim, and it is a claim that is demonstrably false. Beauty is not in the eye of the beholder, perhaps, but is this an argument against love?

Consider in the same light the accusation of "intractability" that is thrown at the emotions as a charge, supposedly separating them from reason and rationality. (Amelie Rorty, for example, develops this charge at length in her "Explaining Emotions."[14]) It is worth noting that Kant rejected the emotions not because they were stubborn but because they were capricious, even though such a suggestion goes against the obvious—that emotions can be durable and devoted, even stubborn and intractable. In love, in particular, it is notoriously difficult, when one has been in love, to purge

that emotion, even though it now has become an intolerable source of pain and not at all a source of pleasure. But is this an accusation against the emotions, or is it rather part of their virtue? It is passing fancy that we criticize, not unmovable devotion. It is sudden anger that we call irrational, not long-motivated and well-reasoned animosity (which is not to say, of course, that sudden anger is always improper or inappropriate, or that long-term outrage is not sometimes irrational and even insane). It is true that the emotions are stubborn and intractable, but this—as opposed to much less dependable action in accordance with principle—is what makes them so essential to ethics. Principles can be easily rationalized and reinterpreted. One trusts a person fighting in accordance with his passions far more than one fighting for abstract principles. (It is remarkable how principles can always admit convenient exceptions and emendations.) Intractability is a virtue of the emotions as rationalization is to reason a vice. Indeed we might even say that the "truth" of emotions is their intractability, their resistance to every attempt to change them.

Objectively, what love sees and thinks is mostly nonsense, and what it values is quite contrary to everything that philosophical ethics likes to emphasize—objectivity, impersonality, disinterestedness, universality, respect for evidence and arguments, and so on. And yet, it seems to me that such irrationality is among our most important and charming features. We care about each other prior to any evidence or arguments that we ought to. We find each other beautiful, charming, and desirable, seemingly without reference to common standards. We think less of a lover if his or her love alters when it alteration finds, or if one bends to the opinions of friends. Love *ought* to be intractable, we believe, even if this same stubbornness causes considerable pain once the love is over. We are thoroughly prejudiced, to use a jaundiced word, thoroughly unreasonable. "Why do you love *her?!*" is a question that need not be answered or even acknowledged. Indeed, we even think it admirable, if also foolish, to love someone totally undeserving (from someone else's point of view). Love itself is the virtue, a virtue so important that rationality itself pales in importance.

Ultimately, the charge against the emotions—

and against love in particular—is that of "subjectivity." Subjectivity is a notoriously slippery notion in philosophy which is often opposed to contrastingly tidy concepts of rationality and objectivity. The charge of "subjectivity" typically turns into an accusation of bias and unreasonableness. But, on the other hand, there is a complementary charge against objectivity, against impersonal, merely abstract ratiocination. There is that sense of "objectivity"—pursued by Camus and Thomas Nagel, for example—in which we are all infinitesimal specks in the galaxy, our lives no more significant than the lives of trees or sea polyps, our bodies nothing but the stuff of physiology, our sex a dubious advancement of the reproduction of bacteria, our speech nothing but noise, our lives meaningless. It is what Nagel calls "the view from nowhere," and in its extreme forms it is as undesirable as it is impossible. But such a viewpoint tends to dominate ethics and value theory as well, if in a more humane or anthropocentric scope. Most of contemporary ethics is still framed not as personal but as policy—to be applied, one suspects, by some imagined philosopher-king. The emphasis is not on being a "good person" but rather a just and fair administrator (being a good person is presumably the same). The model, thinly disguised by the evasive logic of "universalizability," is the bureaucrat, who treats everyone the same and has no relevant personality of his or her own. Love is thus unethical, for against all principles of ethics it has the audacity to view one other person as someone very special and does not, as Mill insisted, count "everyone as one and only one" at all.

ON LOVE'S VIRTUES: PLATO'S SYMPOSIUM REVISITED

It is, in fact, just a love story. . . . Alcibiades, asked to speak about erōs, cannot describe the passion or its object in general terms, because his experience of love is an experience that happened to him only once, and in connection with an individual who is seen by him to be like nobody else in the world.

Martha Nussbaum,
"The Speech of Alcibiades"[15]

The classical text on the virtue(s) of erotic love is, of course, Plato's *Symposium,* and Plato (not Socrates) provides us with a portrait of *erōs* as a virtue which is quite appropriate to our modern concept of romantic love. Let us begin by saying very quickly that the concept of *erōs* there discussed is not the same as our concept of romantic love, that Greek love is asymmetrical love between man and youth rather than our symmetrical romance between man and woman, that Plato is doing much in that dialogue which is by no means evident or easily comprehensible to the modern nonclassicist reader. That said, we can remind ourselves that the subject of the dialogue is the nature and the virtues of love. Each of the various speeches can be interpreted as a substantial theory. It is worth noting that Socrates objects to Phaedrus' speech, in particular, because he stresses only the virtues of love—we might say love's good social consequences—instead of the emotion itself, while Aristophanes would give us an account of the nature of love without giving us an adequate account of its virtues. I think that Socrates is right on both counts: virtues are not virtues by virtue of their consequences (against Hume, for example), and an analysis of love that does not tell us how important it is—not just why we are obsessed with it—is inadequate. But we might also note that the usual characterization of the dialogue is extremely misleading, that is, as a ladder of relatively forgettable speeches leading up to a culmination—the speech by Socrates that tells us exactly what love is. The usual assumption that Socrates acts here as the spokesman for Plato's own view seems utterly unsupportable. In this dialogue, even the minor speeches portray essential aspects of love. For example, the banal speech of Eryximachus the physician clumsily captures today's obsession with love as a physiological phenomenon with health as its virtue. Most important, however, is the fact that in this dialogue, Socrates does not have the last or the best word. Martha Nussbaum, Michael Gagarin, and others have shown, convincingly, I believe, that Alcibiades' tragicomic description of Socrates at the end of the dialogue is essential, if not the key, to the *Symposium.*[16] Indeed, one might even make the case that Plato is partially opposed to Socrates and uses Alcibiades as his argument. Socrates' speech makes love virtuous but only by ignoring or denying most of its essential features—its sexual passion, its interpersonality, its particularity, and its apparent irrationality. *Erōs,* in short, becomes excitement about philosophy. It is impersonal, indifferent to any particular person, "above" bodily desire. In contrast, Alcibiades emphasizes the very personal, passionate, irrational, physical aspect of love, the love for a particular, incomparable human being, not a desexed universal. A similar foil for Socrates is the delightful story by Aristophanes, once he has gotten over his hiccups, in which we are all imagined to be the offspring of perfect (spherical) ancestral beings, split in two by Zeus, twisted around and now desperately looking for our other halves. This explains the "infinite longing" that every lover knows, which includes the longing for sexual union but by no means can be satisfied just with that. Aristophanes is about to continue his story near the end of the dialogue—perhaps completing the account by telling us about virtue—when he is interrupted by Alcibiades, wholly drunk, who launches into his paean for Socrates, contradicting everything Socrates has just been arguing. Socrates is sandwiched between Aristophanes and Alcibiades and it must be said that the conclusion of the debate is that Socrates is weird. Here, I think, is Plato's own voice, not as Socrates *via* Diotima, but as Alcibiades, presenting love as it is against the perhaps admirable but admittedly inhuman efforts of Socrates to say what it should be ideally. I think that this is important for our concern here, because the problem with understanding love as a virtue is not just its undervaluation as sex and emotion: it is also its excessive idealization as something more—or completely different from—sexuality and personal passion. If we think that the virtue of love is nothing less than the virtues of divinity itself, then love may be virtuous but it will have little to do with us and our petty particular affections. If love is a virtue in the sense that I want to defend here, it must apply to Alcibiades as well as Socrates. Socrates gives us a noble sense of the idealization that is part and parcel of *erōs* but I think that we can safely say that he goes too far in abandoning the eroticism of the particular.

THE HISTORY OF LOVE

Having said all this, we may now agree that the Western concept of love (in its heterosexual and humanistic aspects) was—if not "invented" or "discovered"—at least developed in the twelfth century as never before. Only at that late date was man able to begin thinking consecutively about ways of harmonizing sexual impulses with idealistic motives, of justifying amorous intimacy not as a means of preserving the race, or glorifying God, or attaining some ulterior metaphysical object but rather as an end in itself that made life worth living.

Irving Singer, *The Nature of Love*[17]

The virtues, according to Alasdair MacIntyre, are historical. They perform different functions in different societies, and one would not expect the virtues of a warrior in Homeric Greece to be similar to those of a gentleman in Jane Austen's England. Love as a virtue is also functional and historical. Sexuality "fits" into different societies in different ways, and conceptions of love and marriage vary accordingly. However "obvious" the universal function of uninterrupted and unhampered heterosexual intercourse may be in the preservation of every society, sexual desire is virtually never limited to this end, and the myriad courtship rituals, mores, and emotions invented by human cultures attest to the variety of ends to which this basic *ur-lust* can be employed. The virtues of love, accordingly, are the intrinsic ends which *erōs* serves, one of which may be, as Stendhal used to argue, its existence for its own sake.

Sexual desire may seem like something of a constant through history, but the objects of desire (obviously) and the source, nature, and vicissitudes of that desire vary as much as societies and their philosophies. Love is defined not primarily by sex or the libido but by ideas, and romantic love, which is a very modern (eighteenth century) concept, involves certain specific ideas about sex, gender, marriage, and the meaning of life as well as the perennial promptings of biology. Strictly speaking, there is nothing in the *Symposium* (or anywhere else before the seventeenth century) about romantic love. Romantic love is part and parcel of Romanticism, a distinctively modern movement. It presupposes an unusually strong conception of privacy and individual autonomy, a relatively novel celebration of the emotions for their own sake, and a dramatic metaphysics of unity—of which sexual unity in love is a particularly exciting and tangible example. (Compare Hegel, "In love the separate does still remain, but as something united and no longer as something separate," or Shelley, "one soul of interwoven flame.") The speakers in Plato's *Symposium* praised courage, education, and wisdom as the virtues of love, but they had little to say of the virtues of heterosexuality (apart, of course, from its function of producing more Athenians). Charity, devotion, and chastity were praised as virtues of Christian love, but there was too little to say about the joys of sexuality. (Consider the classic seventeenth-century preface: "Let virtue be rewarded, vice be punished, and chastity treated as it deserves.") Romantic love has among its virtues the metaphysical legitimization of sexual desire, the motivation for marriage, and the equalization of the sexes, surely no part of Greek love and doubtful in traditional Christian love. (Contemporary Christian concepts of love, of course, have adopted and incorporated much of the romantic ideology.) Romantic love has as its virtue the expansion of the self to include another, hardly necessary in societies in which citizenship and other memberships provided all of the shared identity one could possibly imagine. Romantic love has as a virtue the expression of what we opaquely call "the inner self," again not a virtue that would have been understood in less psychological and more socially minded societies. To put the matter bluntly (and without argument), romantic love came of age only when newly industrialized and increasingly anonymous societies fostered the economically independent and socially shrunken ("nuclear") family, when women as well as men were permitted considerable personal *choice* in their marriage partners, when romantic love novels spread the gospel to the multitude of women of the middle class (whereas courtly love had been the privilege of a few aristocratic heroines), and, philosophically most important, when the now many centuries old contrast between sacred and profane love had broken down and been synthesized in a secular mode (like so many ideas in the Enlightenment). Romantic love depended on what Robert Stone has called "affective individualism," an attitude to the individual and the importance of his or her emotions that did not and could not have arisen until modern times.

It is essential that we keep the historical character of love in mind so that we do not get seduced by an idea that might well be prompted by the seeming timelessness of the *Symposium* or the always familiar (and cynical) view that love is nothing but hormonal agitation coupled with the uncertainties and frustrations of courtship—or as Freud put it, "lust plus the ordeal

of civility." This idea is that love is itself something timeless and universal, a singular phenomenon which varies only in its culturization and interpretation but is otherwise universally the same. In fact, even the *Symposium* provides us with no fewer than half-a-dozen conceptions of love, and it is not clear to what extent these are disagreements about the true nature of *erōs* or different kinds of *erōs*. Socrates, in particular, is certainly giving us a new conception, a "persuasive definition." Historically, we find these variations played out on a grand scale, with Socrates setting the stage for an ethereal concept of love that comes of age with Christian theology, Alcibiades displaying the "languor" and its imagery that would come to characterize late medieval courtly love, and Aristophanes anticipating modern romantic love. But paganism, even in Plato, cannot begin to capture the range and complexity of romantic conceptions of love in modern times. To understand erotic love as we know it, it is necessary to appreciate the power of the long, if often antagonistic, history of Christian conceptions of love.

The history of erotic love has been determined not only by the fact that Christian thought demeaned sexual love as such but also by the Christian emphasis on the "inner" individual soul and the importance of such emotions as faith and devotion. The genius of Christianity was that it coopted erotic love and turned it into something else, still the love of one's fellow man and even perhaps the love of one's wife or husband, but no longer particularly sexual, no longer personal, no longer merely human. In its positive presentation, love became a form of idealization, even worship, an attempt to transcend not only oneself and one's own self-interests but also the limited self-interests of an *égoisme-à-deux*. It did not have to deny the sexual or the personal so much as the Christian conception of love aimed always "higher," toward not just virtue or happiness but perfection itself. On the negative side, it must be said (and often has been) that the Christian conception of love was also brutal and inhuman, denying not only our "natural" impulses but even the conception of a loving marriage as such. Saint Paul's advice, "better to marry than to burn," was one of the more generous sentiments governing this revised concept of love. Tertullian was not alone in insisting that even to look on one's wife with lust was a sin. Aristophanes' thesis that lovers experience that "infinite longing" which manifests and only momentarily satisfies itself in sex would be lost here. Indeed all such desires become antithetical to love, not an expression of it. To Nietzsche's observation that Christianity is Platonism for the masses we might add that because of Christian psychology, we now have psychoanalysis.

Christian theology may have encouraged and revered love above all else, but it was not erotic love that flourished. Alternative names for love—"*caritas*" and "*agapē*"—may have clarified the scholarship but not the phenomenology of the emotion. When one looked lovingly at another, who could say whether the feeling was divine *caritas* or nasty *erōs*, except that one knew that one *should* feel the former. An entire literature grew up, from which some of our favorite first-date dialogues are derived, distinguishing loving from sexual desire as if these were not only always distinguishable but even opposed. By the fourteenth century, this confusion had become canonized as Platonic love, for which Plato (or at least Socrates) is indeed to blame. Platonic love dispensed with Agathon, Aristophanes, and the others, took Diotima (whose name means "honor the god") at her word, and substituted Christian faith for pagan wisdom. Love had become even more idealized than Socrates had urged, but what had been gained in spirituality was more than lost in the denial of the erotic passions and the importance of happy human relationships for their own sake.

It was in reaction to this insensitivity to human desires and affections that courtly love was directed in the twelfth-century. Romantic love is often identified historically with courtly love—which is rightly recognized as its significant late medieval predecessor. But the two are quite distinct, as Irving Singer has argued in his *Nature of Love*.[18] The two are often conflated (e.g., by Denis de Rougemont, in his much celebrated but dubious study of the subject),[19] and courtly love, in particular, is often reduced to the ridiculous image of the horny troubadour singing pathetically before the (very tall) tower of some inevitably fair but also unavailable lady. The name "courtly love," it should be noted, was not employed by the participants themselves but rather was applied much later—in the romantic period—by Gaston Paris, who used it to refer to the hardly frustrated or separated couple of Lancelot and Guinevere. Indeed, the paradigm of courtly love began not as chaste and frustrated (if poetic) desire but as secret, adulterous, and all-embracing illicit love. (C. S. Lewis continues this paradigm well into this century.)

Socially, courtly love was a plaything of the upper class. It was as much talk (and crooning) as action, and, perhaps most important, it was wholly distinct from, even opposed to, marriage. (It is not surprising that the texts and theories of the male troubadours—Andreas Capellanus, especially—were typically drawn from the adulterous advice of Ovid. But their female counterparts—Eleanor of Aquitaine, for example—did not take love and marriage any more seriously, in part because they were almost always already married.) What is often said of courtly love—that it rarely resulted in consummation—is not true. Indeed, if anything, one might say that courtly love was *more* obsessed with sex than contemporary romantic love. The fact that consummation came slowly and after considerable effort does not eclipse the fact that consummation was the explicit and sometimes single end of the endeavor.

Much of the history of our changing conceptions of love has to do with the effort to bring together and synthesize the idealization suggested by Plato and Christian love with the very real demands and desires of a couple in love. The virtue of "courtly love" was its effort to carry out this synthesis and at the same time introduce some sexual and aesthetic satisfaction into a world of arranged marriages based wholly on social, political, and economic considerations (thus the separation—if not opposition—between courtly love and marriage). It is courtly love that also introduces the essential romantic conception of erotic love as good in itself, a conception that one does not find in the teleology of the *Symposium* and certainly does not find in Christian concepts of love. In his study, Singer formulates five general features of love that characterize the courtly: (1) that sexual love between men and women is *itself* an ideal worth striving for, (2) that love ennobles both lover and beloved, (3) that sexual love cannot be reduced to mere libidinal impulse, (4) that love has to do with courtship but not (necessarily) with marriage, and (5) that love involves a "holy oneness" between man and woman.[20] It should be clear, as Singer goes on to argue in great detail, how courtly love constituted an attempt to synthesize both pagan and Christian conceptions of love, incorporating both ethical ideals and sexual desire. The first feature signals a radical challenge to the traditional Christian view of love, while the third is a rebuke of the vulgar view that love is nothing but sexual desire. It is worth noting that the last feature listed is very much in tune with much of Christian theology, and indeed, the Aristophanic notion of love as a "union" would continue to be one of the central but most difficult (and therefore often "magical" or "mystical") themes of love through the romantic period. I shall try to develop this idea more literally in the following section.

The distinction between love and marriage is of particular interest in the history of love, and it is worth noting that these have not always been linked so essentially as "horse and carriage," as one popular song would have it. In Plato, for obvious reasons, the question of marriage did not even arise in considerations of *erōs* (at least, for that form of *erōs* that was worthy of philosophical consideration). Ovid considered love and marriage as opposites, although the marriage of one's intended did provide a challenging obstacle and thereby an additional source of excitement. The long history of marriage as a sacrament has little to say about sexual love and sometimes has much to say against it, and by the time of courtly love, courtship typically provided an alternative to loveless marriage rather than a prelude to marriage or—almost unheard of—the content of marriage itself. Gaston Paris and C. S. Lewis's paradigm of Lancelot and Guinevere may have represented excessive antagonism between love and all social and religious institutions and obligations, especially marriage, but courtly love cannot be conceived—whatever else it may have been—as a prelude to or a legitimate reason for marriage. Indeed, the idea that marriage is the culmination of love becomes popular only in the seventeenth century or so, as exemplified in Shakespeare's plays, especially in the comedies. And compared to the rigid ethos of Jane Austen's novels, for example, it must be said that our current understanding of love and marriage is quite in flux and confused.

Romantic love, we may now say, is the historical result of a long and painful synthesis between erotic pagan love and idealistic Christian love or, ahistorically, between Aristophanes and Alcibiades on the one hand and Socrates on the other. It is not just sexual, or even primarily sexual, but an idealistic up-dating of the pagan virtues of cultivation and sensuousness and Christian devotion and fidelity in the modern context of individual privacy, autonomy, and affectivity. To think that romantic love is without virtue is to grossly mistake romance with sexual recreation or unrealistic idealization and ignore the whole historical development that lies behind even the most ordinary love affair. But it is time to say something more about the nature of romantic love as such.

WHAT IS ROMANTIC LOVE?

Love is the expression of an ancient need, that human desire was originally one and we were whole, and the desire and the pursuit of the whole is called love.

Aristophanes, *Symposium*[21]

Romantic love, we may need to remind ourselves, is an emotion—an ordinary and very common emotion, even if it is experienced by most of us but once or twice in a lifetime. It is not a "force" or a "mystery." Like all emotions, it is largely learned, typically obsessive, peculiar to certain kinds of cultures with certain brands of philosophy. I will not here rehearse once again my usual analysis of emotion as a complex of judgments, desires, and values. Let me just claim, without argument, the weaker thesis that every emotion presupposes, if it is not composed of, a set of specifiable concepts (e.g., anger as offense, sadness as loss, jealousy as the threat of loss) and more or less specific desires and values, such as revenge in anger, care in sadness, possessiveness in jealousy. Love, accordingly, can and must be analyzed in terms of such a set of concepts and desires, some of which are obvious, the more interesting perhaps not so. It is evident enough that one set of desires in romantic love is the desire to be with, the desire to touch, the desire to caress, and here we are immediately reminded of Aristophanes' lesson: that which manifests itself as a sexual urge in love is actually something much more, a desire to be reunited with, to be one with, one's love. From this, I want to suggest what I take to be the dominant conceptual ingredient in romantic love, which is just this urge for *shared identity,* a kind of *ontological dependency.* The challenge, however, is to get beyond this familiar idea (and its kindred characterizations as a "union," "a merger of souls," etc.) and explain exactly what "identity" could possibly mean in this context. Aristophanes' wonderful metaphor is still a metaphor, and whether or not we would want Hephaestus to weld the two of us together, body and soul, the image does not do our understanding much good. Aristophanes claims that we want the impossible, indeed the unimaginable; he does not give us any indication of how we might in fact share an identity, over and above brief and not always well-coordinated unifications of the flesh.

More to the point, one might well quote Cathy's climactic revelation in *Wuthering Heights:* "I *am* Heathcliff—he's always, always in my mind—not as a pleasure, anymore than I am always a pleasure to myself—but as my own being." Here we have more than a hint of what is involved in shared identity, not a mystical union nor a frustrated physicality but a sense of presence, always "in mind," defining one's sense of self to one's self. Love is just this shared identity, and the desires of love—including especially the strong nonphysiological desire for sexual intercourse—can best be understood with reference to this strange but not at all unfamiliar concept. I cannot do justice to this challenge here, but let me at least present the thesis: Shared identity is the intention of love, and the virtues of love are essentially the virtues of this intended identity. This is not to deny or neglect sex but to give it a context. Nor does this give away too much to marriage (which is a legal identity) but it does explain how romantic love and marriage have come so close together, the latter now considered to be the culmination of the former.

Before we say any more, however, let me express a Socratic caveat: I think that it is necessary to display love as it is by itself, without confusing it with all of the other Good Things we would like and expect to go with it—companionship, great sex, friendship, someone to travel with, someone who really cares, and, ultimately, marriage. Of course we want these things, and preferably all in the same package, but love can and must be understood apart from all of them. Without being depressing, let us remind ourselves that love often goes wrong, that love can be unrequited, that love can interfere with or at least it does not assure satisfying sex, that love and friendship are sometimes opposed, that love can be very lonely, that love

can be not only obsessive but insane. Not that love must be or often is all of these, but it can be, and so let us look at the virtues of love itself, as Socrates insisted, not in terms of its consequences or its most desirable embellishments.

The nature of identity in love, briefly described, is this. (You will note, no doubt, a certain debt to Hegel and Sartre in what follows.) We define ourselves, not just in our own terms (as adolescent existentialists and pop-psychologists may argue) but in terms of each other. The virtues, in a society such as Aristotle's, are defined and assigned communally; the idea of "private" virtues would be incomprehensible. But we distinguish public and private with a vengeance, and we typically value our private, personal character more highly than our public persona, which is sometimes thought to be superficial, impersonal, "plastic," and merely manipulative, instrumental. A person's character is best determined by those who "really know him," and it is not odd to us that a person generally known as a bastard might be thought to be a good person just on the testimony of a wife, a husband, or a close friend. ("But if you knew Johnny as I do, you would see that. . . . ") In a fragmented world so built on intimate privacies, love even more than family and friendship determines selfhood. Love is just this determining of selfhood. When we talk about "the real self" or "being true to ourselves," what we often mean is being true to the image of ourselves that we share with those we love most. We say, and are expected to say, that the self we display in public performance, the self we present on the job, the self we show to acquaintances, is not real. We sometimes take great pains to prove that the self we share with our family (a historical kind of love) is no longer the self that we consider real. Nor is it any surprise that the self we would like to think of as most real is the self that emerges in intimacy, and its virtues are the typically private virtues of honesty in feeling and expression, interpersonal passion, tenderness, and sensitivity.

The idea of an Aristophanic union—the reunification of two halves that already belong together—is charming and suggestive, but it is only half of the story. The other half starts with the fact of our differences and our stubbornness, and how we may ill fit together even after years of compromise and cohabitation. The freedom of choice that allows us virtually unrestricted range for our romantic intentions also raises the possibility—which was one of the suppositions of courtly love as well—that our choice will often be difficult, if not socially prohibited. (Who was the one girl in Verona that young Romeo should not have chosen? And the one woman wholly forbidden to Lancelot?) The process of mutual self-identification runs into conflict with one of its own presuppositions—the ideal of autonomous individualism. The selves that are to merge do not have the advantage of having adjusted to and complemented each other when the self was still flexible and only partially formed—as in societies where families arrange marriages between children who have grown up together. And whatever the nostalgic popularity of "first love" and the Romeo and Juliet paradigm, the truth is that most of us fall in love well advanced in our development, even into old age, when the self is full-formed and complementarity is more often an exercise in compromise. The development of love is consequently defined by a *dialectic,* often tender but sometimes ontologically vicious, in which each lover struggles for control over shared and reciprocal self-images, resists them, revises them, rejects them. For this reason, love—unlike many other emotions—takes time. It does not make sense to say of love, as it does of anger, that one was in love for fifteen minutes but then calmed down. But neither is this to say that there is no such thing as unrequited love, or that unrequited love is not love, for the dialectic, complete with resistance and conflict, can go on just as well in one soul as in two. Granted that the drama may be a bit impoverished, but as Stendhal often argued, the imagination may be enriched thereby. Or as Goethe once said, "If I love you, what business is that of yours?"

IN PURSUIT OF A PASSION (CONCLUSION)

True love, whatever is said of it, will always be honored by men; for although its transports lead us astray, although it does not exclude odious qualities from the heart that feels it—and even produces them—it nevertheless always presupposes estimable qualities without which one would not be in a condition to feel it.

Jean-Jacques Rousseau, *Emile*[22]

Love, briefly summarized, is a dialectical process of (mutually) reconceived selfhood with a long and varied history. As such, it is much more than a feeling and it need not be at all capricious or unintelligent or disruptive. But the idea that love is concerned with selfhood might suggest that love is essentially self-love, casting love in the role of a vice rather than a virtue. And the suggestion that love is essentially the reconception and determination of oneself through another looks dangerously similar to some familiar definitions of narcissism. But self-reference entails neither cynicism nor narcissism. Although one does see oneself through the other on this analysis, and although as in narcissism the idea of "separation of subject and object" is greatly obscured, love as mutual self-defining reflection does not encourage either vicious or clinical conclusions. Unlike narcissism, love takes the other as its standard, not just as its mirror, which is why the courtly lovers called it "devotion" (as in devoting oneself to God) and why Stendhal—himself an accomplished narcissist—called "passion-love" the one wholly unselfish experience. Love is not selfless but it is nevertheless the antithesis of selfishness. It embodies an expansion of self, modest, perhaps, but what it lacks in scope it more than makes up for in motivation.

The virtues of love can be understood in terms of this sense of this limited but passionate self-expansion. In a fragmented and mobile society, romantic love allows us to forge intensive ties to others, even to strangers. There is much talk in ethics today of "communitarian" as opposed to individualistic frameworks, but the fact is that a passionately united community larger than a small circle of carefully chosen friends strikes most of us as oppressive if not dangerous. One may well lament the lack of public virtues or the priority of private virtues, but the fact is that the primacy of privacy is where we must now begin. Nor should one in Kantian enthusiasm for the universal ignore the dramatic importance of the modest move from caring only about oneself to caring about someone else. The expansion of selfhood in love may be modest but, in today's climate of personal greed and "self-fulfillment," it is for many successful citizens today one of the last virtues left standing.

Romantic love is a powerful emotional ally—far better than communal indignation and shared resentment—in breaking down the isolating individualism that has become the dubious heir of some of our favorite traditional values. But we remain staunch individualists, and the extent to which we will allow our virtues to be publicly determined remains limited indeed. But too many authors in recent years have simply dismissed such intimacies as love as not virtuous at all, when a more just judgment would seem to be that love is a particularly appropriate virtue in a society such as ours. With this it is essential to revise our concept of virtue. Some important virtues are not public, so we can no longer use Aristotle, nor even Hume, as our guide. Being virtuous does not mean for us "fitting into" the community; good character is rather privately determined

be its betters in this regard. (It was not just Iago's intelligence that made him more than a match for Othello; he had his envy to motivate him.) The inspirational qualities of love and its impulse to creativity do not just refer, of course, to those who are particularly gifted, for we find at least attempts at poetic self-expression in even the most philistine lovers. Indeed, regardless of the quality of the products of such inspiration, one might argue— following Stendhal—that the exhilaration and inspiration of love is itself its greatest virtue, a virtue that is often ignored in the age-old over-appreciation for philosophical *apatheia*. I too would want to argue that romantic love is a virtue just because it is exciting. One rarely finds philosophers taking excitement as a virtue (Nietzsche being the most obvious exception), but I think many of us do in fact take energy, ... ality, being "turned on" as virtuous, what-...er might result and however exhausting. I ...nk we ought to wonder about the frequent if ...plicit emphasis on dullness as a prominent ...ature of the virtues.

So too we might note the low esteem of sexu-lity in discussions of virtue. Romantic love is ...exual love, and here too we can appreciate the ...esistance of traditionally modest moral philos-...ophers. Sex, in the history of ethics, has been treated as a biological urge, a force (often an inhuman force) to be controlled. So treated, it is hard to see any virtue in it. Ethical questions about sex tend to focus on its restriction, and sexual love is offered at best as a legitimization of sex but still hardly a virtue. So too we should vehemently reject that picture of sex, evidently held by chaste Kant, which takes intercourse to be either a biological function (reproduction or, sanctioned by God, "procreation") or mere recreation—what Kant considered mutual masturbation. Either way, sex loses any status in ethics and, more mysteriously, loses its immediate connection with love (the conceptual problem that faced courtly love). But sex, I would argue, ought to be viewed not as an urge and neither as procreation nor recreation but rather as expression, defined neither by physiology nor by pleasure but rather circumscribed by ideas and what is expressed. In particular, sex is (or can be) an expression of love, though this is just part of the story (as Sartre in particular has gruesomely argued). But the point that should be made here is that love is a virtue in part

...*posium* and often propounded by some of the courtly troubadours. To love is to be intensely conscious of one's own "worth" and greatly concerned with one's virtues (not only charms) where being in love is already considered the first great step in the teleology of self-realization. ("Love me as I am" is not an expression or an instruction of love but rather a defensive reaction.) We might mention, too, the healthy and positive outlook on the world that often accompanies love, a form of generalized idealization that—while it might not take on the cosmic form suggested by Hegel in his early writings—nonetheless counters the cynicism and suspicion that have become the marks of wisdom in our society.

So too we might mention the fact that love is a remarkably inspirational and creative emotion—though one might somewhat cynically speculate that envy and resentment may because of and not despite its sexuality. My Nietzschean premise (though one can find a sublimated version of it in Spinoza) is that the virtues can be exhilarating, and this is (in part) what makes them virtues.

The foregoing points would be greatly misunderstood if they were taken to suggest that erotic love is some sort of "trump" virtue, more important than any others. Virtues can conflict, and any one virtue may be but a negligible exception in an otherwise wholly flawed or pathological character. To pretend that the private joys and obsessions of love raise no questions in terms of public engagement, to move from the objection that love has been neglected in ethics to the insistence that such personal emotions take the place of policy decisions in the public sphere, would be irresponsible. But the example of love makes it evident that the traditional objections to subjectivity in ethics, that appeal to emotions is whimsical, not serious and not subject to criticism, will not bear scrutiny. And against much of recent "virtue ethics" love seems to show that virtues should not be understood as traits (for no matter how "loving" one may be, the only virtue in love is actually loving), nor are all virtues instantiations of universal principles, as Frankena, for example, has argued.[23] It has too long been claimed without argument that subjectivity and emotion in ethics inevitably mean selfishness, prejudice, chaos, violence, and destruction, but the truth is that the nature of love, at least, is quite the opposite, not at all selfish, often tender, and creative. Indeed, against the obsessive emphasis on objectivity and impersonal equality in ethics, the aim of love is to *make* a single person extraordinary and to reconceptualize oneself in his or her terms, to *create* an escape from the anonymity of the Kantian moral world and thrive in a world *à deaux* of one's own. Of course, to deny that love can go wrong—against the cumulative evidence of ten thousand romantic novels—would be absurd. It can destroy as well as conjoin relationships, and it can ruin as well as enhance a life. Yes, love can be dangerous, but why have we so long accepted the idea that the virtuous life is simple and uncomplicated rather than, as Nietzsche used to say, a work of romantic art? For love is a virtue as much of the imagination as of morals.

NOTES

1. I. Kant, *The Groundwork of the Metaphysics of Morals,* trans. H. J. Paton (New York: Harper & Row, 1964), p. 67 (p. 13 of the standard German edition).

2. Plato, *The Symposium,* trans. W. Hamilton (London: Penguin Classics, 1951), p. 43.

3. A. Schopenhauer, *The World as Will and Representation,* trans. E. Payne (New York, 1958), quoted in *Sexual Love and Western Morality,* ed. D. Verene (New York: Harper & Row, 1972), p. 175.

4. La Rochefoucauld, *Maxims,* trans. J. Heayd (Boston and New York: Houghton Mifflin, 1917), no. 68.

5. I. Kant, *Lectures on Ethics,* trans. L. Infield (Indianapolis, 1963), p. 164.

6. J. Milton, *Paradise Lost* (New York: Random House, 1969), bk. 8, lines 383–85.

7. F. Nietzsche, *The Antichrist,* trans. H. Kaufmann (New York, 1954), sect. 11.

8. Bernard Williams, "Morality and the Emotions," in *Problems of the Self* (Cambridge: Cambridge University Press, 1973).

9. Richard Taylor, *Good and Evil* (New York: Macmillan, 1970), p. xii.

10. Barbara Herman, "The Practice of Moral Judgment," *Journal of Philosophy* 82, no. 8 (1985).

11. Bernard Gert, *The Moral Rules* (New York: Harper & Row, 1973), p. 143.

12. Edward Sankowski, "Love and Moral Obligation" and "Responsibility of Persons for Their Emotions," in *Canadian Journal of Philosophy* 7 (1977): 829–40.

13. G. W. F. Hegel, *Early Theological Manuscripts,* trans. T. Knox (Philadelphia: University of Pennsylvania Press, 1971), p. 305.

14. Amelie Rorty, "Explaining Emotions," in *Explaining Emotions* (Berkeley: University of California Press, 1980).

15. M. Nussbaum, "The Speech of Alcibiades," *Philosophy and Literature* 3, no. 2 (1979).

16. Ibid., and Michael Gagarin, "Socrates' Hubris and Alcibiades' Failure," *Phoenix* 31 (1977).

17. I. Singer, *The Nature of Love,* vol 2 (Chicago: University of Chicago Press, 1986), pp. 35–36.

18. Ibid.

19. Denis de Rougemont, *Love in the Western World* (New York: Harper & Row, 1974).

20. Singer, *Nature of Love,* pp. 22–23.

21. *Symposium,* 64.

22. J. J. Rousseau, *Emile,* trans. A. Bloom (New York: Basic Books, 1979), p. 214.

23. William Frankena, *Ethics* (Englewood Cliffs, N. J.: Prentice-Hall, 1973), and in a recent newsletter to University of Michigan Philosophy Department alumni.

IV
Friendship and Familial Love

ARISTOTLE

Nicomachean Ethics

After what we have said, a discussion of friendship would naturally follow, since it is a virtue or implies virtue, and is besides most necessary with a view to living. For without friends no one would choose to live, though he had all other goods; even rich men and those in possession of office and of dominating power are thought to need friends most of all; for what is the use of such prosperity without the opportunity of beneficence, which is exercised chiefly and in its most laudable form towards friends? Or how can prosperity be guarded and preserved without friends? The greater it is, the more exposed it is to risk. And in poverty and in other misfortunes men think friends are the only refuge. It helps the young, too, to keep from error; it aids[1] older people by ministering to their needs and supplementing the activities that are failing from weakness; those in the prime of life it stimulates to noble actions—"two going together"[2]—for with friends men are more able both to think and to act. Again, parent seems by nature to feel it for offspring and offspring for parent, not only among men but among birds and among most animals; it is felt mutually by members of the same race, and especially by men, whence we praise lovers of their fellow-men. We may see even in our travels how near and dear every man is to every other. Friendship seems too to hold states together, and lawgivers to care more for it than for justice; for unanimity seems to be something like friendship, and this they aim at most of all, and expel faction as their worst enemy; and when men are friends they have no need of justice, while when they are just they need friendship as well, and the truest form of justice is thought to be a friendly quality.

But it is not only necessary but also noble; for we praise those who love their friends, and it is thought to be a fine thing to have many friends; and again we think it is the same people that are good men and are friends.

Not a few things about friendship are matters of debate. Some define it as a kind of likeness and say like people are friends, whence come the sayings "like to like,"[3] "birds of a feather flock together,"[4] and so on; others on the contrary say "two of a trade never agree".[5] On this very question they inquire for deeper and more physical causes, Euripides saying that "parched earth loves the rain, and stately heaven when filled with rain loves to fall to earth",[6] and Heraclitus "it is what opposes that helps" and "from different tones comes the fairest tune" and "all things are produced through strife",[7] while Empedocles, as well as others, expresses the opposite view that like aims at like.[8] The physical problems we may leave alone (for they do not belong to the present inquiry); let us examine those which are human and involve character and feeling, e.g. whether friendship can arise between any two people or people cannot be friends if they are wicked, and whether there is one species of friendship or more than one. Those who think there is only one because it admits of degrees have relied on an inadequate indication; for even things different in species admit of degree. We have discussed this matter previously.[9]

The kinds of friendship may perhaps be cleared up if we first come to know the object of love. For not everything seems to be loved but only the lovable, and this is good, pleasant, or useful; but it would seem to be that by which some good or pleasure is produced that is useful, so that it is the good and the useful that are lovable as ends. Do men love, then, *the* good, or what is good for *them?* These sometimes clash. So

From *Nicomachean Ethics*, trans. W. D. Ross. London: Oxford University Press, 1925.

too with regard to the pleasant. Now it is thought that each loves what is good for himself, and that the good is without qualification lovable, and what is good for each man is lovable for him; but each man loves not what is good for him but what seems good. This however will make no difference; we shall just have to say that this is "that which seems lovable". Now there are three grounds on which people love; of the love of lifeless objects we do not use the word "friendship"; for it is not mutual love, nor is there a wishing of good to the other (for it would surely be ridiculous to wish wine well; if one wishes anything for it, it is that it may keep, so that one may have it oneself); but to a friend we say we ought to wish what is good for his sake. But to those who thus wish good we ascribe only goodwill, if the wish is not reciprocated; goodwill when it *is* reciprocal being friendship. Or must we add "when it is recognized"? For many people have goodwill to those whom they have not seen but judge to be good or useful; and one of these might return this feeling. These people seem to bear goodwill to each other; but how could one call them friends when they do not know their mutual feelings? To be friends, then, they must be mutually recognized as bearing goodwill and wishing well to each other for one of the aforesaid reasons.

Now these reasons differ from each other in kind; so, therefore, do the corresponding forms of love and friendship. There are therefore three kinds of friendship, equal in number to the things that are lovable; for with respect to each there is a mutual and recognized love, and those who love each other wish well to each other in that respect in which they love one another. Now those who love each other for their utility do not love each other for themselves but in virtue of some good which they get from each other. So too with those who love for the sake of pleasure; it is not for their character that men love ready-witted people, but because they find them pleasant. Therefore those who love for the sake of utility love for the sake of what is good for *themselves,* and those who love for the sake of pleasure do so for the sake of what is pleasant to *themselves,* and not in so far as the other is the person loved[10] but in so far as he is useful or pleasant. And thus these friendships are only incidental;

for it is not as being the man he is that the loved person is loved, but as providing some good or pleasure. Such friendships, then, are easily dissolved, if the parties do not remain like themselves; for if the one party is no longer pleasant or useful the other ceases to love him.

Now the useful is not permanent but is always changing. Thus when the motive of the friendship is done away, the friendship is dissolved, inasmuch as it existed only for the ends in question. This kind of friendship seems to exist chiefly between old people (for at that age people pursue not the pleasant but the useful) and, of those who are in their prime or young, between those who pursue utility. And such people do not live much with each other either; for sometimes they do not even find each other pleasant; therefore they do not need such companionship unless they are useful to each other; for they are pleasant to each other only in so far as they rouse in each other hopes of something good to come. Among such friendships people also class the friendship of host and guest. On the other hand the friendship of young people seems to aim at pleasure; for they live under the guidance of emotion, and pursue above all what is pleasant to themselves and what is immediately before them; but with increasing age their pleasures become different. This is why they quickly become friends and quickly cease to be so; their friendship changes with the object that is found pleasant, and such pleasure alters quickly. Young people are amorous too; for the greater part of the friendship of love depends on emotion and aims at pleasure; this is why they fall in love and quickly fall out of love, changing often within a single day. But these people do wish to spend their days and lives together; for it is thus that they attain the purpose of their friendship.

Perfect friendship is the friendship of men who are good, and alike in virtue; for these wish well alike to each other *qua* good, and they are good in themselves. Now those who wish well to their friends for their sake are most truly friends; for they do this by reason of their own nature and not incidentally; therefore their friendship lasts as long as they are good—and goodness is an enduring thing. And each is good without qualification and to his friend, for the good are both good without qualification and useful to each other. So too they are pleasant; for the good are pleasant both without qualification and to each other, since to each his own activities and others like them are pleasurable, and the actions of the good *are* the same or like. And such a friendship is as might be expected permanent, since there meet in it all the qualities that friends should have. For all friendship is for the sake of good or of pleasure—good or pleasure either in the abstract or such as will be enjoyed by him who has the friendly feeling—and is based on a certain resemblance; and to a friendship of good men all the qualities we have named belong in virtue of the nature of the friends themselves; for in the case of this kind of friendship the other qualities also[11] are alike in both friends, and that which is good without qualification is also without qualification pleasant, and these are the most lovable qualities. Love and friendship therefore are found most and in their best form between such men.

But it is natural that such friendships should be infrequent; for such men are rare. Further, such friendship requires time and familiarity; as the proverb says, men cannot know each other till they have "eaten salt together"; nor can they admit each other to friendship or be friends till each has been found lovable and been trusted by each. Those who quickly show the marks of friendship to each other wish to be friends, but are not friends unless they both are lovable and know the fact; for a wish for friendship may arise quickly, but friendship does not.

This kind of friendship, then, is perfect both in respect of duration and in all other respects, and in it each gets from each in all respects the same as, or something like what, he gives; which is what ought to happen between friends. Friendship for the sake of pleasure bears a resemblance to this kind; for good people too *are* pleasant to each other. So too does friendship for the sake of utility; for the good are also useful to each other. Among men of these inferior sorts too, friendships are most permanent when the friends get the same thing from each other (e.g. pleasure), and not only that but also from the same source, as happens between ready-witted people, not as happens between lover and beloved. For these do not take pleasure in the same things, but the one in seeing the beloved and the other in receiving attentions from his lover; and when the bloom of

youth is passing the friendship sometimes passes too (for the one finds no pleasure in the sight of the other, and the other gets no attentions from the first); but many lovers on the other hand are constant, if familiarity has led them to love each other's characters, these being alike. But those who exchange not pleasure but utility in their amour are both less truly friends and less constant. Those who are friends for the sake of utility part when the advantage is at an end; for they were lovers not of each other but of profit.

For the sake of pleasure or utility, then, even bad men may be friends of each other, or good men of bad, or one who is neither good nor bad may be a friend to any sort of person, but for their own sake clearly only good men can be friends; for bad men do not delight in each other unless some advantage come of the relation.

The friendship of the good too and this alone is proof against slander; for it is not easy to trust any one's talk about a man who has long been tested by oneself; and it is among good men that trust and the feeling that "he would never wrong me" and all the other things that are demanded in true friendship are found. In the other kinds of friendship, however, there is nothing to prevent these evils arising.

For men apply the name of friends even to those whose motive is utility, in which sense states are said to be friendly (for the alliances of states seem to aim at advantage) and to those who love each other for the sake of pleasure, in which sense children are called friends. Therefore we too ought perhaps to call such people friends, and say that there are several kinds of friendship—firstly and in the proper sense that of good men *qua* good, and by analogy the other kinds; for it is in virtue of something good and something akin to what is found in true friendship that they are friends, since even the pleasant is good for the lovers of pleasure. But these two kinds of friendship are not often united, nor do the same people become friends for the sake of utility and of pleasure; for things that are only incidentally connected are not often coupled together.

Friendship being divided into these kinds, bad men will be friends for the sake of pleasure or of utility, being in this respect like each other, but good men will be friends for their own sake, i.e., in virtue of their goodness. These, then, are friends without qualification; the others are friends incidentally and through a resemblance to these.

As in regard to the virtues some men are called good in respect of a state of character, others in respect of an activity, so too in the case of friendship; for those who live together delight in each other and confer benefits on each other, but those who are asleep or locally separated are not performing, but are disposed to perform, the activities of friendship; distance does not break off the friendship absolutely, but only the activity of it. But if the absence is lasting, it seems actually to make men forget their friendship; hence the saying "out of sight, out of mind".[12] Neither old people nor sour people seem to make friends easily; for there is little that is pleasant in them, and no one can spend his days with one whose company is painful, or not pleasant, since nature seems above all to avoid the painful and to aim at the pleasant. Those, however, who approve of each other but do not live together seem to be well-disposed rather than actual friends. For there is nothing so characteristic of friends as living together (since while it is people who are in need that desire benefits, even those who are supremely happy desire to spend their days together; for solitude suits such people least of all); but people cannot live together if they are not pleasant and do not enjoy the same things, as friends who are companions seem to do.

The truest friendship, then, is that of the good, as we have frequently said;[13] for that which is without qualification good or pleasant seems to be lovable and desirable, and for each person that which is good or pleasant to him; and the good man is lovable and desirable to the good man for both these reasons. Now it looks as if love were a feeling, friendship a state of character; for love may be felt just as much towards lifeless things, but mutual love involves choice and choice springs from a state of character; and men wish well to those whom they love, for their sake, not as a result of feeling but as a result of a state of character. And in loving a friend men love what is good for themselves; for the good man in becoming a friend becomes a good to his friend. Each, then, both loves what is good for himself, and makes an equal return in goodwill and in pleasantness; for friendship is said to be equality, and both of these are found most in the friendship of the good. . . .

But there is another kind of friendship, viz. that which involves an inequality between the parties, e. g. that of father to son and in general of elder to younger, that of man to wife and in general that of ruler to subject. And these friendships differ also from each other; for it is not the same that exists between parents and children and between rulers and subjects, nor is even that of father to son the same as that of son to father, nor that of husband to wife the same as that of wife to husband. For the virtue and the function of each of these is different, and so are the reasons for which they love; the love and the friendship are therefore different also. Each party, then, neither gets the same from the other, nor ought to seek it; but when children render to parents what they ought to render to those who brought them into the world, and parents render what they should to their children, the friendship of such persons will be abiding and excellent. In all friendships implying inequality the love also should be proportional, i. e. the better should be more loved than he loves, and so should the more useful, and similarly in each of the other cases; for when the love is in proportion to the merit of the parties, then in a sense arises equality, which is certainly held to be characteristic of friendship.

But equality does not seem to take the same form in acts of justice and in friendship; for in acts of justice what is equal in the primary sense is that which is in proportion to merit, while quantitative equality is secondary, but in friendship quantitative equality is primary and proportion to merit secondary. This becomes clear if there is a great interval in respect of virtue or vice or wealth or anything else between the parties; for then they are no longer friends, and do not even expect to be so. And this is most manifest in the case of the gods; for they surpass us most decisively in all good things. But it is clear also in the case of kings; for with them, too, men who are much their inferiors do not expect to be friends; nor do men of no account expect to be friends with the best or wisest men. In such cases it is not possible to define exactly up to what point friends can remain friends; for much can be taken away and friendship remain, but when one party is removed to a great distance, as God is, the possibility of friendship ceases. This is in fact the origin of the question whether friends really wish for their friends the greatest goods, e.g. that of being gods; since in that case their friends will no longer be friends to them, and therefore will not be good things for them (for friends *are* good things). The answer is that if we were right in saying that friend wishes good to friend for his sake,[14] his friend must remain the sort of being he is, whatever that may be; therefore it is for him only so long as he remains a man that he will wish the greatest goods. But perhaps not *all* the greatest goods; for it is for himself most of all that each man wishes what is good.

Most people seem, owing to ambition, to wish to be loved rather than to love; which is why most men love flattery; for the flatterer is a friend in an inferior position, or pretends to be such and to love more than he is loved; and being loved seems to be akin to being honoured, and this is what most people aim at. But it seems to be not for its own sake that people choose honour, but incidentally. For most people enjoy being honoured by those in positions of authority because of their hopes (for they think that if they want anything they will get it from them; and therefore they delight in honour as a token of favour to come); while those who desire honour from good men, and men who know, are aiming at confirming their own opinion of themselves; they delight in honour, therefore, because they believe in their own goodness on the strength of the judgement of those who speak about them. In being loved, on the other hand, people delight for its own sake; whence it would seem to be better than being honoured, and friendship to be desirable in itself. But it seems to lie in loving rather than in being loved, as is indicated by the delight mothers take in loving; for some mothers hand over their children to be brought up, and so long as they know their fate they love them and do not seek to be loved in return (if they cannot have both), but seem to be satisfied if they see them prospering; and they themselves love their children even if these owing to their ignorance give them nothing of a mother's due. Now since friendship depends more on loving, and it is those who love their friends that are praised, loving seems to be the characteristic

virtue of friends, so that it is only those in whom this is found in due measure that are lasting friends, and only their friendship that endures. . . .

Friendship and justice seem, as we have said at the outset of our discussion,[15] to be concerned with the same objects and exhibited between the same persons. For in every community there is thought to be some form of justice, and friendship too; at least men address as friends their fellow-voyagers and fellow-soldiers, and so too those associated with them in any other kind of community. And the extent of their association is the extent of their friendship, as it is the extent to which justice exists between them. And the proverb "what friends have is common property" expresses the truth; for friendship depends on community. Now brothers and comrades have all things in common, but the others to whom we have referred have definite things in common—some more things, others fewer; for of friendships, too, some are more and others less truly friendships. And the claims of justice differ too; the duties of parents to children and those of brothers to each other are not the same, nor those of comrades and those of fellow-citizens, and so, too, with the other kinds of friendship. There is a difference, therefore, also between the acts that are unjust towards each of these classes of associates, and the injustice increases by being exhibited towards those who are friends in a fuller sense; e.g. it is a more terrible thing to defraud a comrade than a fellow-citizen, more terrible not to help a brother than a stranger, and more terrible to wound a father than any one else. And the demands of justice also seem to increase with the intensity of the friendship, which implies that friendship and justice exist between the same persons and have an equal extension. . . .

The question is also debated, whether a man should love himself most, or some one else. People criticize those who love themselves most, and call them self-lovers, using this as an epithet of disgrace, and a bad man seems to do everything for his own sake, and the more so the more wicked he is—and so men reproach him, for instance, with doing nothing of his own accord—while the good man acts for honour's sake, and the more so the better he is, and acts for his friend's sake, and sacrifices his own interest.

But the facts clash with these arguments, and this is not surprising. For men say that one ought to love best one's best friend, and a man's best friend is one who wishes well to the object of his wish for his sake, even if no one is to know of it; and these attributes are found most of all in a man's attitude towards himself, and so are all the other attributes by which a friend is defined; for, as we have said,[16] it is from this relation that all the characteristics of friendship have extended to our neighbours. All the proverbs, too, agree with this, e.g. "a single soul",[17] and "what friends have is common property", and "friendship is equality", and "charity begins at home",[18] for all these marks will be found most in a man's relation to himself; he is his own best friend and therefore ought to love himself best. It is therefore a reasonable question, which of the two views we should follow; for both are plausible.

Perhaps we ought to mark off such arguments from each other and determine how far and in what respects each view is right. Now if we grasp the sense in which each school uses the phrase "lover of self", the truth may become evident. Those who use the term as one of reproach ascribe self-love to people who assign to themselves the greater share of wealth, honours, and bodily pleasures; for these are what most people desire, and busy themselves about as though they were the best of all things, which is the reason, too, why they become objects of competition. So those who are grasping with regard to these things gratify their appetites and in general their feelings and the irrational element of the soul; and most men are of this nature (which is the reason why the epithet has come to be used as it is—it takes its meaning from the prevailing type of self-love, which is a bad one); it is just, therefore, that men who are lovers of self in this way are reproached for being so. That it is those who give themselves the preference in regard to objects of this sort that most people usually call lovers of self is plain; for if a man were always anxious that he himself, above all things, should act justly, temperately, or in accordance with any other of the virtues, and in general were always to try to secure for himself the honourable course, no one will call such a man a lover of self or blame him.

But such a man would seem more than the other a lover of self; at all events he assigns to himself the things that are noblest and best, and gratifies the most authoritative element in himself and in all things obeys this; and just as a city or any other systematic whole is most properly identified with the most authoritative element in it, so is a man; and therefore the man who loves this and gratifies it is most of all a lover of self. Besides, a man is said to have or not to have self-control according as his reason has or has not the control, on the assumption that this is the man himself; and the things men have done on a rational principle are thought most properly their own acts and voluntary acts. That this is the man himself, then, or is so more than anything else, is plain, and also that the good man loves most this part of him. Whence it follows that he is most truly a lover of self, of another type than that which is a matter of reproach, and as different from that as living according to a rational principle is from living as passion dictates, and desiring what is noble from desiring what seems advantageous. Those, then, who busy themselves in an exceptional degree with noble actions all men approve and praise; and if *all* were to strive towards what is noble and strain every nerve to do the noblest deeds, everything would be as it should be for the common weal, and every one would secure for himself the goods that are greatest, since virtue is the greatest of goods.

Therefore the good man should be a lover of self (for he will both himself profit by doing noble acts, and will benefit his fellows), but the wicked man should not; for he will hurt both himself and his neighbours, following as he does evil passions. For the wicked man, what he does clashes with what he ought to do, but what the good man ought to do he does; for reason in each of its possessors chooses what is best for itself, and the good man obeys his reason. It is true of the good man too that he does many acts for the sake of his friends and his country, and if necessary dies for them; for he will throw away both wealth and honours and in general the goods that are objects of competition, gaining for himself nobility; since he would prefer a short period of intense pleasure to a long one of mild enjoyment, a twelvemonth of noble life to many years of humdrum existence, and one great and noble action to many trivial ones. Now those who die for others doubtless attain this result; it is therefore a great prize that they choose for themselves. They will throw away wealth too on condition that their friends will gain more; for while a man's friend gains wealth he himself achieves nobility; he is therefore assigning the greater good to himself. The same too is true of honour and office; all these things he will sacrifice to his friend; for this is noble and laudable for himself. Rightly then is he thought to be good, since he chooses nobility before all else. But he may even give up actions to his friend; it may be nobler to become the cause of his friend's acting than to act himself. In all the actions, therefore, that men are praised for, the good man is seen to assign to himself the greater share in what is noble. In this sense, as has been said, a man should be a lover of self; but in the sense in which most men are so, he ought not.

NOTES

1. Reading βοήθεια in l. 14 with M[b].
2. *Il.* x. 224.
3. *Od.* xvii. 218.
4. Lit. "jackdaw to jackdaw". The source is unknown.
5. Lit. "all such men (i.e. all those who resemble one another) are potters to one another", an allusion to Hes. *Op.* 25, καὶ κεραμεὺς κεραμεῖ κοτέει καὶ τέκτονι τέκτων.
6. Fr. 898.7–10 Nauck[2].
7. Fr. 8 Diels.
8. Fr. 22.5, 62.6, 90.1–2 Diels.
9. Place unknown.
10. The MS. reading seems to be sufficiently supported by E. E. 1237[b]1.
11. i.e. absolute pleasantness, relative goodness, and relative pleasantness, as well as absolute goodness.
12. Lit. "many a friendship has lack of converse broken". The source is unknown.
13. 1156[b]7, 23, 33, 1157[a]30,[b]4.
14. 1155[b] 31.
15. 1155[a] 22–28.
16. Ch. 4.
17. Eur. *Or.* 1046.
18. Lit. "the knee is nearer than the shin".

NEERA KAPUR BADHWAR

The Circumstances of Justice: Pluralism, Community, and Friendship

INTRODUCTION

Liberal political theory sees justice as the "first virtue" of a good society, the virtue that guides individuals' conceptions of their own good and protects the equal liberty of all to pursue their ends, so long as these ends and pursuits are just. But ever since Marx's declaration that "liberty as a right of man is not founded upon the relations between man and man, but rather upon the separation of man from man,"[1] liberal society has been frequently criticized for falling seriously short of the conditions of a good society.[2] A prominent recent criticism of this sort has been voiced by "communitarians," who charge that the primacy of rights in liberalism reveals a failure to appreciate the value of friendship and community, and tends to undermine their possibility.[3] My aim in this paper is to defend liberal political theory, understood as the theory that justifies a polity of individual rights and justice, against this charge.[4] My main argument will be directed at the assumption that there is an inherent tension between rights and justice, on the one hand, and familial love and friendship, on the other.

According to the communitarian, two or more individuals constitute a community when they share a common conception of the good and see this good as partly constitutive of their identities or selves.[5] Such a "constitutive community," in Michael Sandel's words, may be a close friendship or a family relationship, or an intermediate association such as a neighborhood organization, or a comprehensive political community. The communitarian charges that in making justice the first virtue of social institutions, liberalism undermines community

at all levels, and this for two reasons. First, liberalism demands that we revise or surrender our conceptions of the good—including our attachments and commitments to family and friends—if they should turn out to be unjust. But this demand, the communitarian claims, requires attitudes that are inconsistent with these attachments and commitments. Second, the political priority of justice encourages a sense of justice at the expense of a sense of community. For justice and its circumstances are inversely related to community and its circumstances: the flourishing of justice, communitarians say, discourages community, while the flourishing of community constitutes an "unsettling presence" for justice. Sandel argues for this thesis by focusing on familial love and friendship: in relations of familial love and friendship, he argues, justice is largely superfluous, but should it become predominant, it undermines these relations.[6] Sandel's argument echoes a view held by many liberals about the relationship of justice to love and friendship.[7] But since, unlike liberals, Sandel sees political community as an extended friendship or family, he sees the predominance of justice in the political realm as a threat to political community as well. Paraphrasing Allen Buchanan, I shall label the view that justice is inversely related to friendship and to community "the inverse proportionality (IP) thesis."[8]

Communitarians offer a metaphysical diagnosis for the normative priority of justice in liberal society and theory. The first step is to argue that this priority rests mainly on the fact of pluralism, in other words, that pluralism is the most important of the circumstances that make justice the first priority. A pluralistic so-

From *Journal of Political Philosophy* 1 (1993): 250–76. This version revised and abridged by the author. Reprinted with permission of the author and Basil Blackwell.

ciety is a society characterized by a variety of incompatible conceptions of the good. This incompatibility leads to conflict and a lack of mutual understanding, and the need for conflict resolution and harmony brings justice to the forefront. The second step is to argue that pluralism itself is largely based on the view that the good has no objective status,[9] and that this view of the good goes hand in hand with a conception of the self as a free and rational chooser of ends. Such a self is essentially independent of, or "unencumbered" by, its ends, its identity being wholly expressed in its ability to order, revise, and pursue these ends according to principles of justice.[10] But, according to communitarians, both this Kantian view of the self and the subjectivist theory of the good are mistaken. Once this is admitted, pluralism will be seen as a defect, and justice as merely a remedial and (normatively) secondary virtue; and only when this is recognized can community and friendship flourish.[11] In short, communitarians argue, value subjectivism and the Kantian conception of the self lead to pluralism, pluralism leads to the priority of justice, and the priority of justice undermines community and friendship.

Many liberal theorists who have responded to this critique in defense of liberalism have pointed out that neither value subjectivism nor the Kantian conception of the self as independent of its ends is essential to liberalism.[12] They have also argued that the constitutive political community favored by the communitarian is not a desirable or viable ideal, and that consequently pluralism is not a defect, much less a defect that can be overcome. And their response to the criticism that the political priority of justice tends to undermine our private commitments to friends, family, and others has been either to deny that this is true, or else to deny that this fact reveals a fault in liberalism.[13] However, Sandel's IP thesis in itself has gone unchallenged by liberals, their only argument against taking it seriously being that it is beside the point, since no society has ever been, or could or should ever be, a constitutive political community. A major task of this paper is to defend liberalism by showing that the IP thesis is false. Hence, much of my argument will be addressed to liberals no less than to communitarians.[14]

I will start by arguing that even if pluralism

could be overcome, justice would not become secondary—the circumstances of justice are far too deeply rooted for *that* (see the second section of this paper). The IP thesis rests on an inadequate conception of justice and its circumstances. On an adequate conception, justice can be seen to be crucially important not only in the political, but also in the nonpolitical, aspects of our lives, that is, those aspects not properly governed by law.[15] Sandel uses the case of friendship to argue *for* the IP thesis; I shall use friendship to argue *against* it by showing the constitutive role of justice in friendship.[16] Since a friendship is the paradigm of a relationship constituted by a shared conception of the good and a common identity, if it can be shown that justice is at least as important as other virtues in friendship, it will follow that it would be at least as important as other virtues even in a constitutive political community. But if the IP thesis is false, then the criticism that the political priority of justice undermines friendship and community cannot stand.

I shall also argue that the political priority of justice does not entail any obligations on, or require any attitudes of, individuals that are inconsistent with the obligations and commitments of friendship (see the third section of this paper). The citizen of a liberal polity can have the virtue of political justice—the sense of justice that leads him to uphold just institutions and to respect the rights of all—and also the virtue of justice in friendship. In short, the liberal citizen's commitment to "public justice" need not be inversely proportional to her commitment to "private justice."

Finally, I shall argue that the liberal political community does exhibit a degree of civic friendship, although no doubt not a sufficient degree. But the cure for its deficiencies is not the communitarians' aspiration to a constitutive political community, but rather a more just community.

THE CIRCUMSTANCES OF JUSTICE AND THE INVERSE PROPORTIONALITY THESIS

The Circumstances of Justice

Liberals from David Hume to John Rawls and David Gauthier have defended justice as the

primary virtue of any society in the circumstances of justice, that is, in the "normal
conditions under which human cooperation is
both possible and necessary."[17] These circumstances consist of both objective factors (a
moderate or relative scarcity of goods) and subjective factors (a plurality of ends and limited
benevolence or mutual disinterest). Individuals
are thought of as being roughly equal in their
physical and mental powers, with differing
conceptions of the good, and with the desire
and ability to satisfy their own ends. According
to Rawls, "the circumstances of justice obtain
whenever mutually disinterested persons put
forward conflicting claims to the division of
social advantages under conditions of moderate
scarcity. Unless these circumstances existed
there would be no occasion for the virture of
justice, just as in the absence of threats of injury to life and limb there would be no occasion
for physical courage."[18]

Presumably, then, if one or more of the circumstances of justice were to change, justice
would become either unnecessary or impossible. For example, if the world were to offer its
goods in such abundance that there was no fear
of anyone being left in want, or if our benevolence were to become so extensive and strong
that others' interests spoke to us with the same
urgency as our own, or if the divergent plans of
individuals were to be replaced by a shared
conception of the good, then there would be
little or no need for justice. In the circumstances of justice, however, justice is needed
both to *regulate* individuals' conceptions of
their good, and to *protect* them in their pursuit
of these just conceptions through a specification of their equal rights. No matter how great
the need for justice, though, justice would be
impossible if limited benevolence or mutual
disinterest were replaced by unlimited malevo-
lence, or the moderate scarcity by acute and
extensive scarcity. In the former case, justice
would fail to speak to us; in the latter, its claims
would be drowned in the clamor of our own
needs. The possibility of justice depends on our
social nature, our ability to cooperate with others to mutual advantage, and on the general
availability of the goods necessary for survival.

The critics of liberalism have concentrated
on the circumstances that make justice *necessary,* while downplaying the subjective
circumstances—in particular, our sociability—

that make it *possible.* Thus Marxist critics have
declared that communism will produce a cor-
nucopia of goods that will spell the death of
justice and rights, whereas communitarian critics have declared that a communitarian society
will produce a common conception of the good
that will reveal the limited and secondary role
of justice. Until these changes take place, justice should be seen as a necessary evil (Marxists), or as merely a remedial virtue whose
function it is to remedy defects in our society or
morality (communitarians). As Sandel puts it,
justice is "the first virtue of social institutions
not absolutely, as truth is to theories, but only
conditionally, as physical courage is to a war
zone."[19]

According to communitarians, it is pluralism
that makes for the priority of justice in liberal
theories. If this plurality of ends were replaced
by shared final ends that formed the core of
individuals' identities, justice would be replaced by these shared ends as the guide of
individual action, and the harmony among persons would make justice unnecessary as a mediator of conflict. Hence in a communitarian
society justice would lose its preeminence, and
friendship and community would flourish. But
this view is a consequence of what I have called
the IP thesis; if this thesis is false, as I believe it
is, the view is left without any visible support.
Since the IP thesis finds its clearest formulation
and defense in Sandel's writings, I will concentrate on his arguments.

The Inverse Proportionality Thesis

To make his case for this thesis, Sandel invites
us to consider

a more or less ideal family situation where relations
are governed in large part by spontaneous affection
and where, in consequence, the circumstances of
justice prevail to a relatively small degree. Individual
rights and fair decision procedures are seldom invoked, not because injustice is rampant but because
their appeal is pre-empted by a spirit of generosity in
which I am rarely inclined to claim my fair share.
Nor does this generosity necessarily imply that I receive out of kindness a share that is equal to or
greater than the share I would be entitled to under
fair principles of justice. I may get less. The point is
not that I get what I would otherwise get, only more
spontaneously, but simply that the questions of what
I get and what I am due do not loom large in the
overall context of this way of life.[20]

The presence of friendship makes justice largely *irrelevant*. Conversely, if "the harmonious family comes to be wrought with dissension," and "[i]nterests grow divergent," the circumstances of justice, and thus justice, come to the fore again.[21] Justice can also be *antagonistic* to friendship.[22] Since what is true of friendship is also true of community,[23] the IP thesis may be stated as follows:

1. When friendship or community flourish, justice retreats into the background; when friendship or community fade, justice becomes more important.
2. When justice is made the primary virtue of a political society, both community and friendship are undermined.

In short, justice and its circumstances are inversely related to friendship and community. Let us now look at the reasons given for this thesis. One reason given is that friendship and community replace mutual disinterest or limited benevolence with enhanced benevolence, another, that they replace a plurality of ends with shared ends. In either case, the result is a reduced need for justice. Each of these arguments has well-known liberal antecedents, the first in Hume, the second in Rawls. Thus Hume declares: "Encrease to a sufficient degree the benevolence of men . . . and you render justice useless, by supplying its place with much nobler virtues."[24] But Rawls rejects this claim on the grounds that benevolence itself needs the guidance of justice as long as it is directed at different persons with different ends: "Benevolence is at sea as long as its many loves are in opposition in the persons of its many objects."[25] Without justice, benevolence "is at sea" regarding *whose* good it may promote, to *what* extent, and *how*. For example, justice guides benevolence by telling A that the good she seeks to do out of benevolence for B should not violate C's rightful claim to his share or, for that matter, paternalistically violate B's own conception of his own good. In short, as long as individuals have different ends, benevolence needs the guidance of justice. However, Rawls seems to endorse the thesis that in a community of shared ends and a shared identity justice will become secondary to the good when he states that "[i]n an association of saints agreeing on a common ideal, if

such a community could exist, disputes about justice would not occur. Each would work selflessly for one end as determined by their common religion, and reference to this end (assuming it to be clearly defined) would settle every question of right."[26]

Thus, both arguments given for the IP thesis—the argument from enhanced benevolence and the argument from shared ends—have liberal antecedents. So it should not be surprising that liberals who have disagreed with communitarians in other respects have generally agreed with them here. Thus, for example, Charles Larmore states that Sandel is right to think that "among friends or family or in certain intermediate associations, there can be a shared view of the good life to which considerations of justice may be subordinated," and that "fostering abstract justice as the primary political virtue may sacrifice existing sentiments of general benevolence or fraternity.[27] Likewise, Buchanan admits that the IP thesis "may be unexceptionable."[28] Their only quarrel with Sandel on this point is that society as a whole never *has* been, and never *will* be, the kind of fraternity that would make justice a subordinate virtue. Hence, says Buchanan, "an advocate of the liberal political thesis need not deny" the IP thesis.[29] This is undoubtedly true: a liberal *need* not deny the IP thesis to defend liberalism. But since—as I shall argue—this thesis is false, and since seeing its falsity strengthens the case for liberalism, a liberal *ought* to deny it.

Let us now take a closer look at Sandel's argument for the IP thesis. Sandel agrees with Rawls that an enlarged benevolence does not in itself make justice irrelevant or secondary, for in a pluralistic society the separateness and boundedness of persons makes the content of their good "largely opaque" to one another.[30] This opacity "we may at times overcome" in the case of "a beloved individual," but hardly so in the case of "a plurality of persons whose interests may conflict."[31] Sandel claims that "[w]here for Hume we need justice because we do not *love* each other well enough, for Rawls we need justice because we cannot *know* each other well enough for even love to serve alond.[32] If this "epistemic deficit" did not obtain, justice would become a subordinate virtue. And, according to Sandel, this would be the case in a communitarian society, for there we would define ourselves in terms of shared final ends, and understand ourselves in terms of a common vocabulary. Hence, in a communitarian society justice would yield its regulative role to a common conception of the good. In short, the reason that friendship or community putatively make justice largely irrelevant is that they unite individuals through common ends and mutual understanding. Only where such unity exists does the spirit of generosity pre-empt the appeal to justice.

But how can shared final ends and mutual knowledge replace justice in guiding a person's benevolence? Shared final ends allow for a great divergence of intermediate ends, and mutual knowledge cannot tell us which ends to promote when not all can be promoted, without invoking justice. Furthermore, even when there is a complete identity of ends, both final and intermediate, there is still a plurality of *individuals* seeking those ends, each with an interest in *pursuing* his ends, and not only in seeing those ends *realized*.

Consider an ideal family of five, a family united by shared final ends and mutual love and understanding. Imagine that the family shares the dream of starting up a small commuter airline, but that doing this requires undergoing special training. Imagine, further, that the parents can afford to fund only two children's training. The third child must either raise the funds for her training herself, or else pursue some other goal. Given that each child is interested in contributing to the realization of the family dream, the parents' equal love and knowledge of their children cannot suffice to tell them how they should act—it only gives them an additional reason to act justly.

Perhaps Sandel would say that in such a family the spirit of generosity will pre-empt appeals to justice. But if the parents do not appeal to justice to decide such family matters, will not the child who gets less have cause for complaint on grounds of justice? An ideal family or friendship may wipe out all differences of ends, both final and intermediate, but it cannot wipe out "the separateness of life and experience." *Au contraire,* it would seem that it is precisely ideal familial love and ideal friendship that will appreciate the "distinction of persons," recognizing the interest of each individual in *pursuing* a shared good, and his right to do so within the constraints of justice. Reference to a common good will not, therefore, settle every question of right. It may be that in such a relationship—and therefore in a constitutive political community—the need for justice will be *reduced,* but this alone gives no reason to suppose that justice will become *subordinate,* rather than simply *equal,* to the other virtues of friendship.[33]

The view that friendship makes justice a subordinate virtue requires the stronger claim that notions of rights and justice are alien or antagonistic to love or friendship. This claim is suggested by Sandel's remark that Rawls's view that our love of persons be guided by respect for autonomous persons—that is, by respect for their rights—is a love that is "of an oddly judicial spirit."[34] But what is odd about a love with a judicial spirit? The answer cannot be that the requirements of justice and rights are legally enforceable, whereas those of love are not. For not all matters of rights and justice are enforceable—for example, most cases of truth telling or promise keeping are not. A right may be a valid moral claim without necessarily being a valid *legal* claim. Perhaps the objection to a judicial spirit in relations of love and friendship is this. The requirements of justice, it is often said, are universal and invariable, whereas those of friendship are particular and variable.[35] The "logic of rights," as Sandel puts it, is a "universalizing logic."[36] He allows that there are special obligations in friendship, but denies that they have anything to do with rights or justice, for allegiances to "family or community or nation or people . . . go beyond the obligations I voluntarily incur and the 'natural duties' I owe to human beings as such. They allow that to some I owe more than justice requires or even permits, not by reason of agreements I have made but instead in virtue of those more or less enduring attachments and commitments that, taken together, partly define the person I am."[37] What we owe to our friends goes beyond what we owe to human beings as such. But why is this characterized as going beyond justice? Surely this is a contradiction in terms: justice, at its most abstract, is *defined* as giving others their due. If more is due to our friends and others with whom we have "constitutive attachments," then, as Aristotle pointed out, justice demands more of us in such relationships.[38] Nor does the universalizing logic of justice and rights pose a problem here:

if friendship gives rise to special duties of justice, then they apply universally to all friends.

Sandel also claims, however, that "to some I owe more than justice . . . *permits*" (italics mine). He does not explain what he means by this, but it would be uncharitable to take him to be saying that we may be justified in pursuing intrinsically unjust commitments or projects, that is, those that necessarily demand injustice toward certain individuals or groups. So I shall take him to be saying simply that what we owe to those with whom we have constitutive attachments may conflict with what we owe to human beings as such, for example, the (prima facie) demands of justice in friendship may conflict with the (prima facie) demands of political justice—and that the former ought to prevail over the latter. I shall discuss this view in the third part of this paper.

Another reason for the thesis that rights and justice are alien to, and subversive of, friendship might be connected with the fact that the very concept of friendship requires that we sometimes go beyond justice and act for our friends' good even when they do not have a *right* that we so act, whereas justice informs us that the limits of others' rights are the limits of our obligations to them. Thus justice permits us to neglect the non-judicial requirements of friendship. But why should this permission threaten friendship? Is it because the permission will justify us in not fulfilling these requirements? This is surely wrong: the fact that not fulfilling them is not an injustice will "justify" us only in the sense that we will have violated no *rights,* but not in the sense that we will have committed *no wrong.* If it is part of the concept of friendship that friends sometimes go beyond justice, then the failure to do so implies the failure to act as a friend should. More generally, even in our relations with acquaintances or strangers, a complete lack of generosity, or willingness to aid, to forgive, or to comfort may be ne less wrong than a failure to respect certain rights.[39] Most moral theorists, including the deontologists who are the object of the communitarian ire, hold such a view. So, for example, Kant regards the transgression of the imperfect duty of general beneficence as a violation of the categorical imperative, and Rawls regards failure in the natural duty of mutual aid as wrong, though neither regards these cases of moral wrongness as cases of injustice.[40]

Perhaps the reason why rights are so often seen as antagonistic to bonds of love and friendship lies in a common picture of rights as weapons with which rights-bearers confront each other to demand the fulfillment of their competing claims. Widespread rights consciousness—consciousness of oneself as a rights-bearer—is then thought to undermine consciousness of oneself as a participant in a common enterprise, or as a friend. Despite its prevalence in liberal, communitarian, and Marxist literature, I think this picture of rights, and of rights-bearers as adversaries, is seriously misleading. But let us grant it for the moment, and ask if it follows that we must also grant that widespread rights consciousness undermines consciousness of oneself as a participant in a common enterprise, or as a friend.

One argument for this view might be that the "contagion" of justice in a liberal society leads people to act out of a sense of justice in inappropriate circumstances, thereby replacing friendship and commmunity with the circumstances of justice. Thus Sandel argues that "acting out of a sense of justice can be contagious," but when this sense of justice "is applied to a situation where, or in so far as, the circumstances of justice do not obtain . . . say in circumstances where the virtues of benevolence and fraternity rather than justice are relevantly engaged . . . my act and the sense of justice that informs it have the self-fulfilling effect of bringing about the conditions under which they *would* have been appropriate."[41] To illustrate this Sandel gives the example of a graceless friend who, out of a sense of justice, "insists on calculating and paying his precise share of every common expenditure, or refuses to accept any favor or hospitality except at the greatest protest and embarrassment," so that "at some point [I] may begin to wonder whether I have not misunderstood our relationship."[42] Such behavior can, indeed, subvert a friendship. But Sandel's argument and example raise two questions: (1) is the behavior of the friend of his example really an expression of an adequate sense of justice? and (2) whether or not it is, is it true that the priority of justice in liberal society actually does lead people to act like that, thereby undermining friendship and community?

Regarding the first question, I think the right answer is "no": Sandel's friend lacks an adequate understanding of justice—as well as of friendship. For having a virtue implies having an understanding of how, when, why, and where to exercise it, just as having a concept implies having an understanding of how and where to apply it. This understanding is incompatible with treating rights and justice like dogma. But this *is* how Sandel's friend treats them. He knows that justice requires that one contribute one's fair share of a cost, but he seems not to know under what circumstances the question of a fair share becomes relevant. He knows that friends have a *right* not to pay more for their share of an expenditure, but is ignorant of the fact that friends commonly *want to,* and *do,* waive this right. He knows that one should respect others' rights, but not that others' rights are theirs to waive. The narrow calculation of Sandel's ungracious friend no more displays a sense of justice than, say, stealing a stranger's wallet to give to a colleague displays generosity instead of dishonesty, or rushing in where angels fear to tread displays courage instead of foolishness. Lacking an adequate understanding of the principles of rights and justice, the friend of Sandel's example uses them like accounting principles, and manages to reveal a lack of generosity by never *giving* more than he owes, and a lack of graciousness by never *accepting* more than is owed to him. He thus also fails to understand the role of generosity in friendship.[43] In short, Sandel's calculating friend is neither a good friend nor someone with an adequate sense of rights and justice.

I should not want to claim that someone who has an adequate sense of rights and justice will *never* stand on his rights in inappropriate circumstances. This is certainly possible—just as it is possible to understand a concept, but on occasion to use it infelicitously. But someone who does this *characteristically,* like Sandel's friend, does display a deficiency in his understanding of justice—as well as of friendship.

The second question raised by Sandel's argument is whether the political priority of justice in liberal society leads to such deficiency. There are no doubt times when we invoke rights too frequently, too quickly, to the ultimate detriment of all involved. Yet the situation is nowhere as extreme as Sandel depicts. For there is also no doubt that most of us often waive our rights for the sake of preserving solidarity, expressing tolerance, or safeguarding

privacy or intimacy with friends, family, and associates. These values are given weight at the level of state policy as well, for example, by the state's refusal to recognize most civil suits among family members.[44] Indeed, there is much evidence to suggest that, despite our greater awareness of exploitative social structures, in certain relationships (especially family relationships) we—as individuals and as a society—continue to err on the side of too great tolerance of exploitation or worse rather than on the side of standing too much on our rights, or allowing too many rights claims. For example, there continues to be widespread reluctance to take action in cases of spouse or child abuse, both by the victimized spouse or the victimized child's representative (the non-abusive parent), and by the state's agents. And it is well known that the rights of homosexuals to sexual intimacy is still denied by many state legislatures and courts—with widespread public support.[45] The lesson to be drawn from the persistence of such inadequacies even in a society where justice does have political priority is that they would be even graver in a society in which justice was subordinate to some other value.

To summarize the argument thus far: even if we accept the adversarial or competitive picture of rights-bearers drawn above, there is no reason to believe that the political priority of justice in liberal society leads to such an undue emphasis on rights and justice that community and friendship are systematically undermined. I shall now argue that we should also reject this picture of rights-bearers as combatants as a distorted and incomplete picture. For it implies that rights exist only to resolve conflicts, and that consciousness of oneself and others as rights-bearers is *essentially* one of competitors or adversaries, at odds with consciousness of oneself and others as participants in a common enterprise.

An especially effective way of testing a claim about what is essential or central to a concept or viewpoint is to imagine a world lacking that concept or viewpoint. To do this is the purpose of Joel Feinberg's imaginary Nowheresville.[46] Nowheresville is a world without consciousness of rights. The inhabitants of Nowheresville have the virtues of benevolence and compassion, they act out of a sense of duty in the sense of the morally mandatory, and they have a notion of personal desert understood as a propriety of response to action or character. But they do not have the notion of a right. Hence they are *grateful* when they get what they deserve, but uncomplaining when they don't:

The most conspicuous difference, I think, between the Nowheresvillians and ourselves has something to do with the activity of *claiming*. Nowheresvillians, even when they are discriminated against invidiously, or left without the things they need, or otherwise badly treated, do not think to leap to their feet and make righteous demands against one another though they may not hesitate to resort to force and tirckery to get what they want. They have no notion of rights, so they do not have a notion of what is their due; hence they do not claim before they take.[47]

They have no notion of what is their due—or what is others' due. They do not claim—claiming something implies having a sense of a right to that thing—but they take all the same. The result is that whereas in our world a conflict of interests among members of a common enterprise may lead people to become open adversaries who appeal to common rules of justice, in Nowheresville—the world without rights consciousness—the same conflict leads poeple to become sneaky, treacherous adversaries-in-the-night. Nor would this picture change if we were to stipulate that the inhabitants of Nowheresville understand themselves as participants in a common enterprise—a family, or a sports team, or a university department, or a constitutive political community. For even participants in a common enterprise can be (illegitimately) discriminated against, or otherwise badly treated.

The case of Nowheresville suggests two things: (1) an absence of rights consciousness merely implies an absence of consciousness of oneself and others as combatants with competing *claims,* and not an absence of consciousness of oneself and others as combatants with competing *interests;* and (2) an absence of rights consciousness even *with* consciousness of oneself as a participant in a common enterprise does not suffice to diminish adversarial relations.

Feinberg's next task is to show exactly which element of moral value is missing from Nowheresville. He says:

Having rights, of course, makes claiming possible; but it is claiming that gives rights their special moral significance. This feature of rights is connected in a way with the customary rhetoric about what it is to be a human being. Having rights enables us to "stand up like men," to look others in the eye, and to feel in some fundamental way the equal of anyone. To think of oneself as the holder of rights is not to be unduly but properly proud, to have that minimal self-respect that is necessary to be worthy of the love and esteem of others. Indeed, respect for others (this is an intriguing idea) may simply be respect for their rights, so that there cannot be the one without the other; and what is called "human dignity" may simply be the recognizable capacity to assert claims. To respect a person then, or to think of him as posessed of human dignity, simply *is* to think of him as a potential maker of claims.[48]

What is missing from the moral life of the members of the enterprise called Nowheresville is a sense of human dignity.

Feinberg's picture of what is essential to seeing oneself as a rights-holder is significantly different from the traditional picture of rights-bearers confronting each other as contestants with competing claims. Whereas Feinberg's picture upholds consciousness of oneself as a rights-bearer as a positive ideal, the traditional picture suggests that it is a lamentable necessity. A better understanding of friendship and the circumstances of justice that prevail in friendship supports Feinberg's picture against the traditional one.

We saw in my depiction of the ideal family that there was potential for injustice, and hence for asserting claims, despite the family members' shared ends, common identity, and mutual knowledge. The reason for this, I suggested, was that each family member had an interest in *pursuing* her conception of the good and not merely in seeing it *realized*. In that particular case, however, another factor was also operative: a scarcity of resources. But if my suggestion is correct, there is room for rights and justice even when there is no such scarcity. Let me now clarify and support this idea.

Many claims of justice no doubt arise from our interest in protecting our conceptions of the good, or in getting our share of some scarce commodity. But there are at least three other independent interests that give rise to such claims, interests that would exist even if the world were to become a material and communal paradise. For these interests are rooted in the fact that we are numerically distinct individuals with our own perspectives and experiences, and this is not a fact that would change even if the curcumstances usually thought of as the cirumstances of justice were to change. As numerically distinct individuals we have, first, the interest already discussed in being the *agents* of our ends, in bringing about our (shared) conception of the good through our own actions, and not just in participating in the happy outcome regardless of how it is brought about.[49] Second, as distinct individuals we have an interest in being seen and judged for what we are—that is, an interest in fair judgment. And third, as distinct individuals we have an interest in a fair exchange of emotional and intellectual goods. A threat to any of these interests gives rise to claims of justice. But what could possibly threaten them in the absence of divergent ends or material scarcity? The answer is: our human finitude and fallibility.

Our fallibility and finitude manifest themselves in limited understanding, rationality, energy, memory, and attention. These limitations can lead to ignorance, or forgetfulness, or negligence, or insensitivity, or sloth, all of which are conditions whose existence (though not, indeed, extent) is independent of economic or political conditions. And these conditions can lead people to threaten each others' interests and act unjustly. So, for instance, someone may do injustice to another by forgetting—or not ascertaining—the facts, or by adopting inappropriate criteria of judgment, or by drawing unwarrented conclusions from the data, or by making excessive emotional or intellectual demands. An individual who sees himself as a rights-bearer will see himself as a potential maker of claims in any of these situations. But these situations can arise in *any* human relationship, from the most distant to the closest relations of familial love and friendship. Indeed, in some ways such situations achieve their greatest urgency in intimate relationships, suggesting that justice is not only *a* feature, but a *central* feature, of friendship. The following sketch illustrates this point.

Zoe and Aleph are close friends with a common passion for cultivating new strains of tulips. They work together as well as alone, often sharing their results and their ideas, a practice they find beneficial to their work as well as

intrinsically pleasurable. They also spend much of their leisure time together and are usually responsive to each other's emotional and intellectual needs. Sometimes, however, Zoe gets so absorbed in the task of experimenting with grafts and new techniques that she neglects her friend's legitimate expectations of companionship, and responds to his attempts to communicate with her impatiently. At other times, Aleph gets so excited by the result of a new method that he expects Zoe to adopt it uncritically, showing scant regard for her point of view or her judgment. There are also times when one or the other is sorely tempted to be paternalistic, to do what is good for the other even against the other's wishes, forgetting that a love that "recognizes the separateness of life and experience is guided by what individuals themselves would consent to."[50]

Zoe and Aleph's relationship, like most real relationships, contains certain moral failures which they rightly see as forms of injustice. Close friendships like theirs involve interactions across a whole spectrum of concerns: leisure activities, relations with other friends, emotional and physical needs, shared tasks and financial burdens, and so on. Questions of a fair distribution of tasks and responsibilities can and do arise with respect to all of these concerns. Things would not go well for their relationship if it lacked reciprocity in beneficence, or if one of them assumed a disproportionate share of the responsibility for creating mutual understanding and care, for initiating joint projects, and for thinking of new ways to enrich their intellectual and emotional life together. The appropriate description of such a friendship would be that it fell short of a fair exchange of emotional, moral, and intellectual goods.[51]

Considerations of nondistributive justice and, in particular, of justice in the frequent (implicit or explicit) judgments we make of one another, also arise with particular urgency in close friendships. Judgments of people's contributions to shared goals, or responsibility for undesirable consequences, or ability for various tasks, or of their motives or character traits, are part of normal human intercourse. The intensity and frequency of interactions among friends not only increases the frequency of such judgments, but also highlights the issue of their justice. For friends disclose intimate aspects of their selves to each other, trusting each other to see them as they are.[52] This increases their vulnerability to each others' opinions, and this greater vulnerability in turn creates a greater burden of justice. This is at least one reason why, other things being equal, the injustice of an unjust act is greater the closer the friendship.[53] And when it gets too great, the trust necessary to friendship is destroyed and the friendship falls apart.

It might be objected at this point that there is something awry about this picture of friendship, because justice and rights are inextricably linked to claims and thus to demands, and the language of demands is peculiarly ill-suited to friendship. Hence it is wrong to think of friendship as structured by justice and rights.[54] But this conclusion surrenders too much, too quickly, to save the intuition that the language of demands is ill-suited to friendship: it should be possible to keep the baby without the bathwater.

Someone may try to do this by proposing that although there is justice in friendship, such "private justice" is not a duty, and hence not correlated with rights. This response is suggested by David Heyd's construal of Aristotle's notion of private justice. Private justice, he claims, must be understood as "supererogatory justice," rather than as a duty, because it exceeds the demands of legal justice, and is up to the individual to give or not.[55] This argument, however, cannot suffice to banish duties and rights from friendship. For even though justice between friends is "*legally* supererogatory," it is not—and cannot be—*morally* supererogatory. If, as a friend, Zoe *owes* it to Aleph to be understanding of his hopes and desires, then it is morally *incumbent* upon her to give Aleph this understanding, and Aleph has a *right* to expect such understanding. Hence we cannot construe the notion of justice between friends without recourse to the notion of their mutual duties or, therefore, of their rights. In short, if there is justice in friendship, then there are duties and rights in friendship.

Yet it is true that the language of demands is ill-suited to friendship. What we must do, then, is break the link between rights and demands. Buchanan is surely right to point out that to claim something as a right is not "to request it as something one desires"; but this does not imply, as he concludes, that to claim something as a right "is to demand it as one's due."[56] Perhaps the best support for this intuition

comes from the fact that many of the things to which we have a right in friendship are things we *cannot* get in response to a demand—"cannot" in the sense that if it is only the *demand* that brings the response, what we get is not, after all, what we had a right to and wanted in the first place. For example, I have a right to expect that my friend give me more of her time than she gives to mere acquaintances, but to get it as the result of a demand would be self-defeating. For what I really want, and have a right to expect, is not simply that she give me more of her time, but that she do so *because she wants to*. And this is not something I can get simply as the result of a demand. Indeed, it may even be incoherent to suppose that emotions or attitudes can be had on demand, for their authenticity requires that they be spontaneous and "self-produced."

On the other hand, there is nothing either self-defeating or incoherent in the idea of having a *right to expect* certain emotions and desires in a friend. For if the friend really is a friend, these will already be among her dispositional properties, and the expectation will be simply that she exercise the reflective and imaginative skills that, typically, serve to actualize dispositional emotions and desires. Hence the idea that rights must—or even *can*—always be expressed as *demands* is simply false: there is a conceptual space between "requests" and "demands" that allows us to claim our rights without (unfriendly) demands or (conceptually confused) requests. So, for example, when Zoe neglects Aleph, and is brusque in her manner with him, Aleph *reminds* Zoe that as a friend he has a right to expect more friendly treatment. When Aleph rides roughshod over Zoe's judgment, Zoe *draws his attention to* the fact that their friendship does not license disrespect. Thus they make known what is due to them by making each other aware of their rightful expectations.

In short, friendship necessarily involves justice and rights, but rights may be expressed—and pressed—in different ways: sometimes as demands, sometimes even as legal threats, but in friendship, typically, merely as reminders—gentle or forceful, matter-of-fact or emotional—of legitimate expectations and entitlements.[57] A consideration of the divers ways in which rights claims arise and are satisfied in friendship suggests a richer, more nuanced conception of rights—a conception that is more sensitive to the complex contours of our moral concerns, and allows a deeper appreciation of the importance of justice in our lives than the standard conception.

The greater frequency and intimacy of interactions between friends also suggests that friendship does not lessen the *need* for justice, but merely changes its *focus* from "public" to "private" concerns. Hence if the political community were to become akin to a close friendship, it too would merely change the focus of justice, and not the amount.

In this section I have argued that the circumstances of justice are far more deeply rooted in the human condition than is generally recognized. They are rooted (1) in our human fallibility and finiteness, and (2) in our numerical distinctness which gives rise to the interests (i) in exercising our agency, (ii) in being seen and judged for what we are, and (iii) in a fair exchange of emotional and intellectual goods. These conditions exist even when individuals share all their final ends, have "the same affection and tender regard" for one another as they do for themselves, and live in a material paradise. Contrary to both the defenders and the critics of liberal justice, then, neither shared ends nor enhanced benevolence—nor both together—in a world of abundance can render justice useless or of minor importance. They would do this only if they were also to wipe out our fallibility and finiteness, or our numerical distinctness. The circumstances of justice are ubiquitous, and so justice must be of great concern to *everyone*, to friends and family no less than to strangers. Indeed, I have argued, far from rights and justice being irrelevant or antagonistic to friendship or community, they are partially constitutive of it. Hence, the IP thesis is false and communitarianism is not a cure for the undoubted malaise of liberal society.

However, a modified form of the IP thesis, based on the distinction between private and public justice, may yet be defensible. To this thesis I now turn.

THE POLITICAL PRIORITY OF JUSTICE AND PRIVATE COMMITMENTS

The basic structure of society, according to the liberal, must be just, and must be just before it is anything else. This means that justice must regulate the plans, policies, and rules of political and legal institutions. It also means that individuals must regulate their conceptions of the good by the principles of justice. This implies that conceptions of the good must be just not only toward members of some favored group—friends, family, or associates—but toward *everyone*. Thus the ideal liberal citizen must possess a developed ability for critical reflection on his conception of the good, and a willingness to revise it if it is unjust.[58] In short, the ideal liberal citizen must be autonomous and impartial. It is true, of course, that even a commitment to a friendship or association requires such an ability and willingness—I would not be much of a friend or associate if I were incapable of critical reflection on my ends or bent on pursuing them regardless of the cost to my friends or associates. But since liberalism is concerned with a wider moral constituency, commitment to liberalism requires a greater autonomy and wider impartiality than does commitment to friends or associates. The IP thesis could then be reformulated in terms of the conflict between private and public justice, between the requirements of friendship and the requirements of a liberal polity. This reformulated IP thesis would state that friendship and the political priority of justice are inversely related because the autonomy and impartiality required by the latter undercut our commitments to friends.

A liberal might respond by agreeing that autonomy and impartiality undercut our private commitments, but by denying that this is a bad thing. Thus Stephen Macedo agrees that the requirement of liberal justice that we maintain a "critical detachment" from our private commitments, subordinating them to liberal norms, will lead to affections that are "broader but less intense or deep than pre-liberal ones," yet he argues for such subordination and detachment all the same.[59] But why should the subordination of private commitments to liberal justice, and a detachment from them in the service of such justice, make our affections less intense or deep? Certainly there is no *logical* inconsistency between such detachment and impartiality on the one hand, and depth of feeling on the other hand. There is, of course, a *psychological* tension between the two when the requirements of liberal justice clash with the requirements of friendship. But psychological tensions are not unique to liberalism: *any* public commitment, including, no doubt, commitment to communitarian structures, can conflict with commitment to family and friends, thus creating a psychological tension.[60]

Communitarians might say that such a conflict would not arise in a communitarian society, because there the political community would be constitutive of the individual's very self. But even if we grant the possibility of such a community, this claim would save the day only on the obviously false assumption that there cannot be conflicts *within* the self. So the only possible remaining criticism of liberalism on this issue of public–private conflict must be that such conflict is more frequent in a liberal society than it would be in a communitarian society. But this criticism awaits some showing of what principles and measures communitarians would use to minimize such conflict. On the face of it, at least, commitment to liberal justice appears to require much less political intervention in our lives, and thus to create much less conflict, than would commitment to a constitutive political community.[61]

In any case, liberalism does not dictate that *whenever* there is a conflict the requirements of public justice—the commitment to uphold just institutions and respect the rights of all—should take precedence over the requirements of friendship, no matter how weighty the demands of the latter or how slight the claims of the former.[62] Liberalism is only a political theory, which must be justified within a comprehensive moral theory. How far, and when, public commitments should override private ones is a question for a comprehensive theory of morality to answer (although it is probably not a question that can be answered with any great specificity by any theory). What liberalism can and must do, as a component of such a comprehensive theory, is to recognize the importance of private commitments, and to show ways of minimizing conflict between public and private commitments and safeguarding the latter.

To appreciate the contributions made by liberal vis-à-vis illiberal societies in this respect, it would be instructive to remind ourselves of some social and legal structures of illiberal societies that served and serve as powerful obstacles to private commitment, for instance, interference from extended families or neighborhoods, caste and class barriers, feudal loyalties, legalized inequality between men and women, laws that allow men to divorce their wives by uttering the word "talaq" three times, or political structures that demand total allegiance to the state. By either preventing the imposition of such social and legal constraints and inequities, or diminishing or freeing us of them, liberal rights and rules have freed us from powerful constraints on private commitments. Nor is this all: they have also provided us with ways of preserving old commitments and constituting new ones. The most obvious legal device for creating a new commitment, the marriage contract, is not, of course, a quintessentially liberal device.[63] There are, however, quintessentially liberal ways of contributing to the creation of private commitments. One way is by creating social and economic conditions which, in turn, are instrumental to the creation of the psychological and moral attitudes essential to friendship. Legal equality for women, for example, can bring about a sense of equality and mutual respect, and thus friendship, between the sexes. According to Mary Shanley, Mill's fundamental concern in *The Subjection of Women* was not legal equality as such, but rather the marital friendship that it would help bring about.[64] Mill believed that marital friendship would create, in his words, "a school of genuine moral sentiment," liberating *both* men *and* women from their warped consciousness. This in turn, he argued, would lead to an enhancement of the quality of public life. Hence a liberal polity must aim, among other things, at promoting the conditions under which friendship can flourish.

Another way legal rights contribute to the creation of private commitments is by providing protection "[for] new beginnings and for moral initiatives which challenge existing affections"[65] Jeremy Waldron's fascinating discussion of *Romeo and Juliet* illustrates the tragedy that can result from living in a world that provides no such protection. The Verona the young lovers inhabit offers no safe, reliable structures for actions that defy existing affections and disaffections created by the warring Capulets and Montagues. The series of misfortunes that befalls Juliet and Romeo, culminating in their deaths, is not the work of chance or fate, but the near-inevitable result of the absence of a framework of legal rights, a framework that, in liberal societies, allows people to co-ordinate their actions and expectations and forge new commitments.[66]

There are also quintessentially liberal ways of preserving existing commitments. Consider, for instance, the spousal privilege of confidential communication, which protects private communications between spouses as intimates (but not communications made in the presence of a third party, or between spouses as business partners or criminal coconspirators). The rationale behind this privilege is that privacy of communication is essential for fostering and maintaining trust and friendship between spouses as intimates, and that public policy should be concerned to protect the conditions of trust and friendship.[67] The spousal privilege of confidential communication, like other privileges of confidential communication, may or may not be compatible with the interests of criminal justice. But it is, I think, justifiable as a recognition of the individual's legitimate interest in protecting his or her private commitments. Thus the spousal privilege of confidential communication is an expression of the quintessentially liberal impulse to limit state power to protect the individual's sphere of privacy.

Existing legal devices for protecting community and commitment also offer great potential for creative redeployments. A novel proposal for such a redeployment is Ferdinand Schoeman's proposal that the privilege of confidential communication be extended to cover private communications between *all* intimate friends.[68] If this were done, it would further reduce the incidence of moral conflict between the demands of private and public commitment, and enable friends to avoid the painful dilemma of either betraying a trust or perjuring themselves.

CIVIC FRIENDSHIP IN LIBERAL SOCIETY

Communitarians might now concede that liberal rights and limitations on state power do play a crucial creative and sustaining role for private commitments. But they might still complain that the quality of liberal *civic* friendship remains a poor thing. So, for example, Alasdair MacIntyre complains that liberal society exhibits "at best that inferior form of friendship which is founded on mutual advantage," as contrasted with the superior form of friendship envisioned by Aristotle for the ideal polis.[69] MacIntyre's dismissive attitude toward "advantage-friendship" may be motivated by his suspicion that such friendship is just mutual commerce by another name. Any friendship worth the name must involve mutual goodwill and well-wishing and, as part of this goodwill and well-wishing, *some* interest in the qualities of mind and character of the friend. And MacIntyre might think that a so-called advantage-friendship does not have these features.

But is this true? Do not the citizens of a liberal polity exhibit a general mutual goodwill and interest in the character of their fellow citizens? In "Political Animals and Civic Friendship"[70] John Cooper argues that they do because, for example, the typical American takes pride in the qualities of mind and character of American industrialists or writers or workers, and feels injured by news of a major wrongdoing by a prominent figure in government or industry or the arts.[71] On the other hand, Cooper points out, similar qualities and acts by prominent figures in foreign countries do not evoke such personal reactions.[72] Nevertheless, there is no doubt that the quality of civic friendship in the American polity leaves much to be desired. But the proper model for it cannot be the superior form of friendship that MacIntyre claims to find in the polis, at least if by "superior form" he means Aristotle's character-friendship. For such a friendship, according to Aristotle, can exist only between people of good character, whereas the polis is inhabited by individuals of all kinds of character. So a superior form of civic friendship in a polis, as in the modern liberal state, can only be an improved form of advantage-friendship. And to achieve this, what the liberal state must aspire to—if my analysis of the relationship between justice and friendship is correct—is a "more perfect" system of rights and justice, rather than a constitutive political community.

CONCLUSION

In this paper I have argued for the following claims:

1. The circumstances of justice exist in *all* human relations, from the most distant to the closest, because these circumstances are a function of our fallibility and finiteness com-

bined with the interests arising from our numerical distinctness. Contrary to the IP thesis, rights and justice are not inversely related to friendship and community but, rather, are part of their very structure. Friendship and community change the *focus* of justice from public to private concerns but do not lessen the *need* for it. Attention to the way that rights claims arise and are satisfied in friendship shows the constructive role that rights and justice play in our lives, revealing the common picture of rights-bearers as combatants with competing claims as distorted and incomplete.

2. Although commitment to liberal justice can *conflict* with our private commitments, it is not *inconsistent* with them. And even where there is a conflict, liberal theory as such does not—and cannot—dictate that the public commitment ought always to override the private. Moreover, by comparison with illiberal societies, liberalism provides impressive resources for minimizing conflict between public and private commitments, and for safeguarding the latter.

3. Modern liberal society does exhibit civic

friendship, but undoubtedly there is much room here for improvement. The way to achieve this, however, is not by driving out rights and justice, but by forging a better system of rights and justice.

I shall close by drawing attention to a little-noticed feature of liberal justice. The commitment to protecting the individual's sphere of liberty and privacy, when doing so is consistent with the commitment to just institutions, is an essential feature of liberal justice. But, as illustrated by the spousal privilege of confidential communication, one criterion for deciding when such protection *is* so consistent is the importance of the individual's private commitments themselves. In other words, the demands of public justice are themselves partly limited by the demands of private justice. In using this criterion, the practice of liberal politics shows its recognition of a truth insufficiently reflected in its theory, namely, that far from liberal justice being *indifferent* to our private commitments, an essential part of its political task is to delimit the sphere of public justice by the requirements of these very commitments.

NOTES

I am grateful to the editors of the *Journal of Political Philosophy*, Robert Goodin and Chandran Kukathas, for their helpful comments on this paper, as well as to Chris Swoyer, whose liberal comments went far beyond the requirements of justice between friends. I am also grateful to the Institute for Humane Studies (IHS) at George Mason University for supporting research on this paper with the F. Leroy Hill Summer Faculty Fellowship (1990), and to the IHS referees for their comments. Finally, I owe thanks to the Department of Philosophy at the University of Arkansas and to *The Faculty Workshop* at the University of Oklahoma for the opportunity to present and discuss this paper.

1. K. Marx, *On the Jewish Question*, in *The Marx–Engels Reader*, ed. R. C. Tucker (New York: W. W. Norton, 1972). Bourgeois rights, Marx goes on to say, are the rights of "egoistic man," of the "*circumscribed* individual" isolated from the community.

2. Like Marx, E. Fromm excoriates capiitalist-liberal societies for their fairness ethic, but for a quite different reason, namely, that the fairness ethic is antithetical to the Judeo-Christian norm of brotherly love. For the fairness ethic requires only that you not "use fraud and trickery in the exchange of commodities and services, and in the exchange of feelings, [that you] respect the rights of your neighbor," whereas the "Jewish-Christian norm of brotherly love" requires that you "love your neighbor, that is . . . feel responsible for and one with him (See *The Art of Loving* (New York: Harper and Row, 1956), 8.

3. A. MacIntyre, *After Virtue* (Notre Dame, Ind: Notre Dame University Press, 1981); M. Sandel, *Liberalism and the Limits of Justice* (New York: Cambridge University Press, 1982), hereafter cited as *Liberalism*, "The Procedural Republic and the Unencumbered Self," *Political Theory* 12 (February 1984): 81–96, hereafter cited as "Procedural Republic," and "Morality and the Liberal Ideal," *New Republic*, May 7, 1984, pp. 15–17; C. Taylor, "Atomism" and "The Nature and Scope of Distributive Justice," in *Philosophy and the Human Sciences: Philosophical Papers*, vol. 2 (Cambridge: Cambridge University Press, 1985), and "Alternative Futures: Legitimacy, Identity and Alienation in Late Twentiety-Century Canada," in *Constitutionalism, Citizenship and Society in Canada*, ed. A. Cairns and C. Williams (Toronto: University of Toronto Press, 1985), 183–229, hereafter cited as "Alternative Futures." Taylor's criticisms are usually couched not in terms of communitarianism versus liberalism, but in terms of a conflict *within* liberal societies between their "atomist" individualist rights dimensions and their communal participatory dimensions.

4. Sandel states that he is concerned to challenge deontological liberalism, the liberalism that justifies the primacy of justice without reference to any goal or good. But since he also believes that such justification is essential to a defense of the primacy of justice, and since the primacy of justice is essential to liberalism, he sees his critique of deontological liberalism as challenging liberalism as such (*Liberalism*, 1–7; "Procedural Republic," 88).

5. See, for example, Sandel, *Liberalism*, 150, and "Procedural Republic," 86–87; MacIntyre, *After Virtue*, 146, 160–61, 204–5, 213, 215, 219f; and Taylor, "Atomism," 207–8, "Alternative Futures," 211, 213–14.

6. Sandel, *Liberalism*, 34–35. Taylor explicitly endorses this thesis and Sandel's on page 301 of "The Nature and Scope of Distributive Justice." But on page 312 he seems to change his mind, when he says that "different degrees of mutual involvement . . . create different degrees of mutual obligation. So that we may have to think both of justice between individuals, as well as between communities, and also perhaps within communities."

7. There are different kinds of friendship—for example, personal and civic—as well as different degrees of friendship, but what all friendships must have in common is an active and mutual goodwill and concern. In this paper I shall use the word "friendship" only for a personal relationship of shared activities and goals, and of comparable mutual affection, concern, and understanding. Thus, as I use the term, friendship can exist between unrelated people as well as between family members. I will use the term "civic friendship" to mean the active mutual goodwill and concern that might characterize a community. By "community" I will mean any association of people who share some goals, and have some mutual concern, but who do not have the emotional bond or detailed personal knowledge of one another that characterizes a friendship. The word "community," then, will cover both the liberal and the communitarian conceptions of community.

8. Buchanan calls it "the proportionality thesis"; see page 877 of A. E. Buchanan, "Assessing the Communitarian Critique of Liberalism," *Ethics* 99 (1989): 852–82.

9. MacIntyre, *After Virtue*, 30–31, 56–57, 204–5; Sandel, *Liberalism*, 175–77.

10. Sandel, *Liberalism*, 10–11, 175–77, 179; MacIntyre, *After Virtue*, 205. In "Atomism" Taylor rejects this conception of the free individual by arguing that "since the free individual con only maintain his identity within a society/culture of a certain kind," he exercises "a fuller freedom" if he can shape his society through political means, encouraging those conceptions of life that favor freedom, discouraging [outlawing?] those that depreciate it (207–8). Among the latter he includes "those which look on originality, innovation, and diversity as luxuries" (207).

11. According to MacIntyre, the citizens of a modern liberal society "possess at best that inferior form of friendship which is founded on mutual advantage. That they lack the bond of friendship [he continues] is of course bound up with the self-avowed moral pluralism of such liberal societies" (*After Virtue*, 147). He contrasts this sorry state of affairs with Aristotle's vision of a polis, in which, supposedly, citizens enjoy the highest kind of friendship. I discuss these claims in the next-to-last section of this paper.

12. Some of the major recent defenses of liberalism against communitarianism are A. Gutmann, "Communitarian Critics of Liberalism,"*Philosophy and Public Affairs* 14, no.3 (Summer 1985): 308–22; C. Larmore, *Patterns of Moral Complexity* (Cambridge: Cambridge University Press, 1987); A. Buchanan, "Assessing the Communitarian Critique"; W. Kymlicka, *Liberalism, Community, and Culture* (Oxford: Oxford University Press, 1989); S. Macedo, *Liberal Virtues* (Oxford: Oxford University Press, 1990); and F. D. Miller and J. Paul, "Communitarian and Liberal Theories of the Good," *Review of Metaphysics* 43, no.4 (June 1990): 803–30. This last offers the only sustained defense of the compatibility of liberalism with value objectivism.

13. See Buchanan, "Assessing the Communitarian Critique," 867–72, for the former view, and Macedo, *Liberal Virtues*, 267–68, for the latter.

14. In a longer version of this paper I have argued that the metaphysics of the good is quite irrelevant to the plurality of the good and the political priority of justice (see section 2 of this paper in the *Journal of Political Philosophy*, 1, no.3 [1993]: 208–34). For even if the good is objective, its complexity ensures the kind of partial understandings and plural instantiations of it that lead to conflict. Moreover, every *plausible* conception of the good must recognize the goodness of just choices. Hence, I have argued, every viable society—every society that "instantiates" a plausible theory of the good—must be pluralistic, and every good society must treat justice as its first political virtue. (But not necessarily as *lexically* first. A lexical or absolute priority may be dictated by the kind of Kantian justification of justice employed by Rawls, but such a justification is not the only alternative to a consequentialist justification. The priority of justice can be given a nonconsequentialist, individualistic defense by reference to the nature of a political community and the limits of political authority, without it being the case that this priority must be absolute, that justice can *never* be overriden by other moral and political considerations [see, e. g., Macedo, *Liberal Virtues*, 208–10]. I understand the liberal thesis of the priority of justice in this nonconsequentialist and non-absolutist sense.)

15. Since the law constrains all actions and relationships, including marriage and family, the distinction between the political and the nonpolitical, or the legal and the nonlegal, *aspects* of our lives is clearer than the usual distinction between the public and the private, or the political and the personal, *realms*.

16. The *locus classicus* of this view is, of course, Aristotle's *Nicomachean Ethics*. I argued for it in relation to a discussion of forgiveness in my "Friendship, Justice and Supererogation" (*American Philosophical Quarterly* 22, no.2 [April 1985]: 123–31). By and large, contemporary philosophers have ignored or denied the constitutive role of justice in friendship. The only other extended defense of it that I am aware of is M. Friedman, "Justice among Friends" (paper presented at the Eastern Division Meetings of the *American Philosophical Association*, December 1986). F. Schoeman discusses the interplay and interdependence of intimacy and moral and legal rights in the parent–child relationship in "Adolescent Confidentiality and Family Privacy," in *Person to Person*, ed. G. Graham and H. LaFollette (Philadelphia: Temple University Press, 1989), 213–34. After I had completed this paper in April 1991, I heard J. Feinberg's lecture, "In Defense of Moral Rights: Their Social Importance," in which he defends the importance of rights in loving relationships in the context of a more general defense of moral rights. This lecture, entitled "The Social Importance of Moral Rights," has been published in *Philosophical Perspectives*, vol. 6: *Ethics* ed. J. E. Tomberlin and in J. Feinberg, *Freedom and Fulfillment: Philosophical Essays* (Princeton, N. J.: Princeton University Press, 1992). More recently, Jean Hampton has argued that distributive justice is required in intimate relations. See her "Feminist Contractarianism," in L.Antony and C. Witt, eds., *A Mind of Her Own* (Boulder, Col.: Westview Press, 1993).

17. J. Rawls, *A Theory of Justice* (Cambridge, Mass.: Harvard University Press, 1971), 126. Both Rawls and Gauthier state that their account of the circumstances of justice basically follows that of Hume in *A Treatise of Human Nature*, bk. III, pt. II sec. ii, and *An Enquiry Concerning the Principles of Morals,* sec. III, pt. I. See D. Gauthier, *Morals by Agreement* (Oxford: Oxford University Press, 1986), 345.

18. Rawls, *Justice,* 128.

19. Sandel, *Liberalism,* 31.

20. Sandel, *Liberalism,* 33.

21. Sandel, *Liberalism,* 33.

22. Sandel, *Liberalism,* 34–35.

23. Sandel, *Liberalism,* 173–74, "Procedural Republic," 93.

24. Hume, *Treatise,* bk. III, pt. II, sec. ii.

25. Rawls, *Justice,* 190.

26. Rawls, *Justice,* 129.

27. Larmore, *Patterns of Moral Complexity,* 126.

28. Buchanan, "Assessing the Communitarian Critique," 877.

29. Buchanan, "Assessing the Communitarian Critique," 877.

30. Sandel, *Liberalism,* 170–71.

31. Sandel, *Liberalism,* 171.

32. Sandel, *Liberalism,* 172.

33. Later I shall suggest a reason for thinking that perhaps what friendship or community do is not *reduce* the need for justice, but merely change its *focus* from the public to the private aspects of our lives.

34. Sandel, *Liberalism,* 165. Buchanan canvasses the possibility of explicating "respect" without reference to the notion of rights, but expresses doubt that such a non-judicial concept "could fulfill the basic role of structuring human relationships" (*Marx and Justice* [Totowa, N. J.: Rowman and Littlefield, 1982], 78–79).

35. L. Blum, *Friendship, Altruism and Morality* (London: Routledge & Kegan Paul, 1980), 93–94.

36. Sandel, "Procedural Republic," 94.

37. Sandel, "Procedural Republic," 90.

38. "For in every community there seems to be some sort of justice, and some type of friendship also . . . And the extent of their community is the extent of their friendship, since it is also the extent of the justice found there" (Aristotle, *Nichomachean Ethics,* tr. T. Irwin [Indianapolis: Hackett, 1985], 1159b27–31).

39. Both kinds of wrongs admit of degrees: both a failure to aid when one should and a failure to respect a right can be either a minor matter of negligence or a matter of vice. However, a complete absense of respect for rights is no doubt far worse than a complete absence of beneficience.

40. Both would recognize that the violation of these duties is usually less grave in its consequences than the violation of a duty of justice. But this fact clearly has no deontic import for Kant; and although Rawls remarks that "[f]rom the standpoint of the theory of justice, the most important natural duty is that to support and to further just institutions" (*Justice,* 334), his considered opinion seems to be that it may not be possible to formulate rules for ranking the natural duties (*Justice,* 339–40).

41. Sandel, *Liberalism,* 34–35.

42. Sandel, *Liberalism,* 34–35.

43. One of the greatest values of friendship, according to Aristotle, is that it provides an opportunity for the best kind of beneficence, beneficence toward friends (*Nichomachean Ethics,* 1155a 5–10).

44. F. Schoeman, "Adolescent Confidentiality and Family Privacy," 221.

45. At the time of the *Bowers v. Hardwick* decision (1986), in which the U. S. Supreme Court upheld the constitutionality of Georgia's law forbidding consensual sodomy, there were about twenty-five states with such laws. In all or nearly all cases, the law has been used only against homosexuals. On the other (liberal) hand, several cities have enacted "domestic partner" laws that grant legal recognition to same-sex couples. And recently, the Supreme Court of Kentucky struck down the Kentucky sodomy law as unconstitutional.

46. J. Feinberg, "The Nature and Value of Rights," in *Rights, Justice, and the Bounds of Liberty* (Princeton, N. J.: Princeton University Press, 1980), 143–55.

47. Feinberg, "Nature and Value of Rights," 148.

48. Feinberg, "Nature and Value of Rights," 151.

49. Rawls sees the significance of numerical distinctness as lying only in the fact that it gives rise to different conceptions of the good and an interest in protecting them; see "Kantian Constructivism in Moral Theory," *Journal of Philosophy* 77, no. 9 (September 1980): 515–72, 542.

50. Rawls, *Justice,* 191.

51. In "Justice among Friends," Friedman discusses both justice in exchange and rectifactory justice in friendship.

52. For an insightful discussion of intimate self-disclosure in friendship, see L. Thomas, *Living Morally: A Psychology of Moral Character* (Philadelphia: Temple University Press, 1989), 104–8.

53. Cf. Aristotle, *Nicomachean Ethics,* 1160a3–5.

54. See, for instance, J. Waldron, "When Justice Replaces Affection: The Need for Rights," *Harvard Journal of Law and Public Policy,* (Summer 1988): 625–47. Waldron states that rights are necessary as a fall-back position in the event of a breakdown of the affective bond, but are not constitutive of it. For, "[t]o stand on one's rights is to distance oneself from those to whom the claim is made; it is to announce, so to speak, an opening of hostilities; and it is to acknowledge that other warmer bonds of kinship, affection, and intimacy can no longer hold" (628). In the same spirit Buchanan talks about the support a juridicial framework needs from "deeper affective structures which are not themselves informed by conceptions of justice and

rights," and of "the bonds of mutual respect among right-bearers [as being] too rigid and cold to capture some of what is best in human relationships" (*Marx and Justice,* 178).

55. D. Heyd, *Supererogation* (Cambridge: Cambridge University Press, 1982), 43–44.

56. Buchanan, *Marx and Justice,* 163.

57. On this point, see also Feinberg, "The Value of Moral Rights," 19–22.

58. And this idea, William Galston points out, is not Cartesian or Kantian but Socratic; see his "Pluralism and Social Unity," *Ethics* 99 (1989): 711–26, at 722. See also Macedo for an illuminating discussion of the virtues of the ideal liberal citizen (*Liberal Virtues,* 254–85).

59. Macedo, *Liberal Virtues,* 244, 267–68.

60. Indeed, *any* commitment can conflict with any other: commitment to one friend with commitment to another, commitment to colleagues with commitment to country, and so on.

61. In "Assessing the Communitarian Critique of Liberalism," Buchanan concedes that some forms of attachment and community may wither in a liberal society, but argues that "liberal society offers the best feasible framework for rendering autonomy and commitment compatible" (867), and that, indeed, communitarian society may leave so little room for autonomy, that it may be unable to accomodate any genuine commitment (as distinct from blind obsession) (871–72).

62. For example, liberalism does not dictate that the right thing to do for a police officer who sees a friend shoplifting is to arrest the friend. It is perfectly consistent with commitment to liberalism to say, instead, that the police officer should quietly confront the friend and make him either replace the item or pay for it—or, if the friend needs the item desperately but cannot pay for it, that the police officer should pay for it herself.

63. See Buchanan's insightful discussion of the way the marriage contract can create a commitment that goes beyond a merely contractual commitment ("Assessing the Communitarian Critique," 868–70).

64. M. L. Shanley, "Marital Slavery and Friendship: John Stuart Mill's *The Subjection of Women,*" *Political Theory* 9, no.2 (1981): 229–47.

65. Waldron, "When Justice Replaces Affection," 631.

66. Waldron, "When Justice Replaces Affection," 632–33.

67. Ferdinand Schoeman, "Friendship and Testimonial Privileges," in *Ethics, Public Policy, and Criminal Justice,* ed. F. Elliston and N. Bowie (Cambridge, U. K.: Oelgeschlager, Gunn and Hain, 1982), 257–73.

68. Schoeman, "Friendship and Testimonial Privileges." As for the practical difficulty of determining whether two people really are intimate friends, Schoeman suggests that those who wish to claim this status and the attendant privilege may document this wish, and have the document notarized at periodic intervals.

69. See note 11. Taylor also charges that modern "society and its institutions are seen as mere instruments to our private purposes" ("The Nature and Scope of Distributive Justice," 305).

70. J. Cooper, "Political Animals and Civic Friendship," in *Proceedings of the XIth Symposium Aristotelicum,* 1990, 220–41.

71. Witness the widespread reaction of pride in the performance of the armed forces in the recent Persian Gulf War, as well as the widespread agonizing over the possible injustice of the massive casualties inflicted on the enemy in the closing days of the war.

72. Cooper, "Political Animals and Civic Friendships," 14–15.

ELLEN FOX

Paternalism and Friendship

Though much has been written about when paternalistic intervention is justified, and about how it is justified, much less has been written about who may do the intervening. This is a substantial lacuna in our understanding of the nature of justified paternalism. By examining the question of who it is that may most appropriately interfere with the course of our decision-making, we can learn something useful both about paternalism and about the nature of friendship.

In this essay I will argue that friendship and paternalistic intervention are linked. Friendship of the close, intimate variety that I will be discussing is in part constituted by the fact that one friend is morally justified in interfering with the other's (problematic) decisions. Intimate friendship involves a partial meshing of identities. This meshing of identities manifests itself in part by the liberties that one friend takes in guiding the life of the other. Paternalistic intervention between friends can thus be justified because it expresses the union of the friends, and because it preserves that union.

Finally, I will argue against the view that it is consent of any variety that justifies intervention between friends. Certainly consent justifies many types of paternalistic intervention between strangers or casual acquaintances, or between physician and patient. Though it may seem plausible to suppose that it is some version of consent which justifies the intervention between friends, this conclusion is incorrect. Consent presupposes a distance and separateness between individuals which is antithetical to intimate friendship.

To illustrate my point, let me begin with a story.

Cathy and Steve have been dating for several months; the relationship has been passionate but stormy. Cathy's company has transferred her to a branch office three states away. The couple's romance remains unresolved, and both are distracted by their unsatisfying letter-and-phone relationship. After several lengthy and acrimonious fights about whether to break up or try to find a way to live near each other again, Steve, in a fit of disgust over the whole situation, leaves a message on Cathy's answering machine telling her they are through. He then unplugs his own phone.

Cathy is frantic to find Steve's abrupt dismissal of the relationship waiting for her when she walks in the door. Agitated and overwhelmed, she impulsively starts throwing clothes into an overnight bag in preparation for the two-day drive to the city where Steve lives. This sudden decision will have drastic consequences for her career; her new supervisor and coworkers have already observed a certain emotional fragility in her manner, connected with the affair with Steve. She has an important presentation to give in the morning, and many other pressing professional responsibilities throughout the week; to abandon them will spell the end of her career at this office and will cloud her reputation within her small and gossipy profession. Under ordinary circumstances Cathy wouldn't dream of neglecting her obligations in this way; she values her professional reputation as well as her self-respect. But for now she can't think of anything except the horror of never seeing Steve again; the repercussions for her professional life and personal reputation barely impinge on her consciousness.

At this moment her close friend Elizabeth drops by. Elizabeth is horrified to see Cathy on the verge of throwing her professional life

From *Canadian Journal of Philosophy* 23 (1993): 575–94. Copyright © 1993 by the University of Calgary Press. Reprinted with permission of the author and publisher.

away; she knows how hard Cathy has worked to make a place for herself in a competitive field. Elizabeth begins with the standard means of persuasion. She tries to reason with Cathy. She points out the negative consequences of Cathy's behavior on her immediate and distant future. She reminds Cathy of the fact that she will regret her actions very deeply very soon. Cathy is beyond caring. Elizabeth argues that the relationship with Steve isn't worth pursuing; she tells Cathy that the romance has been making her crazy and that Steve obviously isn't good for her. This line only makes Cathy more agitated and hostile. Elizabeth is at her wits' end; she thinks despairingly of how sorry Cathy is going to be when she has ruined her professional life for a relationship that will probably crumble within the next several months. Rebuilding her life could take years and be terribly painful. When Cathy's back is turned, Elizabeth grabs Cathy's purse containing car keys, wallet, credit cards, checkbook, and other life essentials and throws it in the trunk of her own car. Cathy soon asks Elizabeth if she has seen the purse, but Elizabeth denies that she has. An hour later, considerably more exhausted, Cathy again asks Elizabeth if she has seen the purse. This time Elizabeth admits what she has done, refuses to return the purse, and stoically waits out Cathy's enraged demands for the purse. Eventually Cathy collapses in a chair, exhausted and crying. Elizabeth gives her a Valium from her own purse and waits until Cathy has dozed off. Then she too falls asleep at the apartment so that she will be there when Cathy wakes up in the morning, and will be able to help her pull herself together and go to work.

This story raises problems for paternalism as it has been discussed in the literature. Elizabeth's interference might well be counted as justified by the criteria set forth by such opponents of paternalism as Joel Feinberg and Donald Van De Veer, because Cathy's autonomy was impaired. But surely not just anyone could act as Elizabeth did; only a friend could intervene so forcefully. Asking only about the autonomy of the individual is inadequate; after we have determined that her autonomy is indeed impaired we still have not decided who may step in to protect an individual from herself.

There is more to the justification of pater-

nalistic interference, then, than has been addressed in the literature so far. The fundamental mistake of most writers has been to view the two individuals too atomistically. The emphasis has been on the autonomy (or lack thereof) of the subject of the intervention. Though clearly an important part of any justificatory story, the individual's autonomy is not the only consideration; the relationship between the two people plays at least as large a role in the warranting of paternalistic interference.

PATERNALISM AND THE PRIVATE REALM

Discussions about the legitimate scope of the right of autonomy are generally cast against the background of the public sphere. Often writers puzzle over which governmental or legal infringements of our right of autonomy are justified; generally, the conclusion is not many.[1] And for good reason—the vision of an overbearing, coercive government meddling in our personal affairs is alarming. There is some discussion of the limits of personal autonomy in bioethics, where the problem of paternalism is particularly troubling. There is the debate, for example, about whether physicians may lie to patients, thereby possibly subverting the patients' ability to make ideally autonomous choices. Although there is generally thought to be room for debate in this arena, nevertheless the predominant view is still that any infringement of the patients' right of autonomy calls for a pretty strong justificatory story, and that patient autonomy has a high enough value to override most competing paternalistic claims. This attitude has been the more widely adopted as the physician-patient relationship has become more anonymous and impersonal.

It is easy to appreciate why this strong presumption in favor of the value of personal autonomy should prevail in the more impersonal, public realm. Most of us shudder at the idea of some unknown individual or group interfering with our (non-criminal) important life choices. Who knows, we may reason, the person making the decision may be poorly informed, incompetent, or worse. More importantly, it is enraging to think of our life decisions being made for us this way even if the deciding person or committee is sensible and competent. It is simply not the place of an anonymous agent to step in and change the course of our lives for us.

"Who are you to tell me what to do?" is not always a rhetorical question, however. If we shift our perspective to the private sphere, the question may well have a defensible answer. "Your best friend," "your spouse," "your parent," or even "your former college roommate, that's who" may, in certain contexts, be entirely appropriate replies that carry within them the kernel of the justification for the interference.

LOVE AND AUTONOMY

Let us return to the case of Cathy and Elizabeth. It seems pretty clear that Elizabeth's actions are justified (if they are justified) by virtue of her friendship with Cathy. We certainly would not want a stranger to interfere with our lives so profoundly, even if the consequences were beneficial. Indeed, Elizabeth's actions would be completely outrageous if undertaken by a concerned passerby or a representative of the government. After all, Elizabeth did lie to Cathy, violate her property rights, and provide her with drugs without really obtaining her informed consent. These are just the kind of actions we do not want a government to try without overwhelming justification. Nor do we want our neighbors to feel free to employ such tactics. Only our closest friends would ever be justified in taking any such action, and even then only in fairly serious cases.

The nature of the relationship between the individuals has been consistently overlooked in the literature on paternalism. Beginning with the case of Cathy and Elizabeth, let us consider whether the traditional justifications for intervention would allow Elizabeth's behavior. Consider Joel Feinberg's enlightening discussion of the conditions under which we may justify paternalistic interference in the legal realm. Such interference can be permissible, Feinberg argues, when the agent's actions are not substantially voluntary. Developing a full theory of voluntariness is beyond the scope of this paper; Feinberg devotes a large section of *Harm to Self* to the discussion of factors which limit voluntariness. For our purposes, we may limit ourselves to considering whether the agitation that Cathy suffers is sufficient to call into question whether her action was suffi-

ciently involuntary to permit paternalistic interference.

Feinberg and Donald Van De Veer both develop lists of factors which circumscribe the voluntariness of actions. Intoxication, neurosis, and ignorance are paradigm cases of impairment of voluntariness. Feinberg also lists "powerful passion[s], e. g. rage, hatred, lust, or a gripping mood, e. g. depression, mania"[2] as factors which reduce the voluntariness of an action. Van De Veer's short list includes "the diminished capacities resulting from disease, injury, fainting, drunkenness, drug usage, embarrassment, fear, and so on."[3] Neither writer pays any special attention to the distorted behavior that often follows from the experience of being in love, and more particularly from the experience of being in love with someone who is not treating you well. Yet both popular and classical literature[4] are full of examples of the various lengths to which love can drive a person, and most people can think of examples from their own personal experience or that of those closest to them. Lately, it is feminists and psychologists who have provided us with the most examples of the problems for voluntary action which face those who love abusive or unstable people, but it would be a mistake to characterize the problem as purely a women's issue; though less visible in the media, the world is full of men who behave in a substantially impaired way as a consequence of being in love.

FRIENDSHIP AND CONSENT

Certainly this seems to be the case with Cathy. Her emotional state is at least as unsettled as it would be if she were suffering from rage, embarrassment, or drunkenness, and her actions are correspondingly out of character. Her behavior is not the result of her settled and considered preferences; quite the contrary. Her settled and considered preferences are that she be successful and respected at her work and that she be free of her tormenting attachment to Steve.

Nevertheless, most of us would be very uneasy at the idea of the law stepping in and requiring her to go to work, or even requiring her to wait several hours to see if her desire to see Steve persisted past the time of her most intense agitation. Nor would we be happy about an anonymous neighbor hiding our car keys for our own good. It is only Elizabeth, Cathy's closest friend, who can intervene so drastically in Cathy's life, despite the fact that Cathy's capacity for autonomy is substantially impaired.

Why should this be so?

It might be argued that some form of consent can be invoked here as justification. There are several alternatives along these lines. We might argue that the friends consented to the friendship, and in so doing consented to future interventions in each other's lives. Or perhaps they in some way signified consent to the particular act of interference. That consent might have been express, tacit, or implied. Let us break these alternatives down into stages, since the issue of friendship and consent is fairly complicated.

It is true that friendship is a voluntary relationship in our culture. Marilyn Friedman comments on this idea:

To say that something is "voluntary" is typically to say that it lacks external coercion or constraint. In the context of personal relationships, however, this definition is not wholly appropriate. On the one hand, it is too *narrow*. The sense in which we have no choice over, for example, family ties has more to do with the way in which they are ascribed to us . . . than it has to do with coercion or constraint. Thus, the voluntariness of friendship must also encompass the notion that it is not a socially *ascribed* relationship. On the other hand . . . our choices of friends are indeed constrained, both by the limited range of our acquaintances and by the responses of others to us.[5]

Thus, Friedman notes, the definition is also too broad.

In fact, there are even more constraints than Friedman remarks upon, constraints that are related to the workings of human psychology. The way we commonly picture friendships developing (when we bother to picture this process at all) is on the model of an open market. A person decides to have friends, looks around at his available options from the people in his world, makes a few overtures, and sees what response he gets. Actually, as Steven Duck has shown, whenever two people meet there is a presumption in favor of friendship, a presumption which is defeated if there is some indica-

tion that the two will not be compatible.[6] Such indications can be race, sex, or age of the acquaintance, or something in her manner or style that suggests that friendship will not be possible. The human drive towards friendship is surprisingly strong, and people are generally not free to disregard it. Thus to some extent we are also constrained by our own emotional makeup.

Nevertheless, Friedman is right to consider friendships to be substantially voluntary. Though we may, out of necessity, strike up some version of friendship with co-workers or near neighbors, or with individuals to whom we are in constant close proximity, the type of very close friendship which is the subject of this essay must be seen as considerably more voluntary than not. Very close friendships require so much planning and work that it is generally not possible to develop them non-voluntarily.

But does the fact that close friendships are largely voluntary mean that we *consent* to them? Not in any obvious way. Let us imagine how Cathy and Elizabeth's friendship might have developed.[7] Let us suppose that they were roommates in college their freshman year, and were therefore thrown into constant contact. They hit it off well and shared their opinions about the school and their fellow students, and about their families and their boyfriends; they discovered that they shared many fundamental values and attitudes. Let us further suppose that these values and attitudes were not widely shared at their school. These circumstances fostered their sense that they are fundamentally inseparable, and contribute to their sense of unity. Eventually they reach the point where each can scarcely form an opinion without a contribution from the other; experiences do not seem satisfying or complete for either until she has shared it with the other. Each puts as much faith in the other's judgment as in her own. They are as close to "one soul in two bodies" as two people can become. Though this situation arose more voluntarily than involuntarily, can we say that they *consented* to this arrangement? I will argue that they did not. Consent as it has been discussed in the recent literature is a very stringent notion, and the behavior of the two young women in this scenario does not meet the conditions set forth by most writers. Let us see why.

As Locke discovered, instances of express

consent are often hard to come by. It will be helpful to look at some of Locke's commentators who have tried to coax the notion of consent into covering cases of problematic political obligation. There are, of course, disagreements among these commentators as to exactly why consent has the moral force that it has; some analogize consent to promising, while others argue that its force derives from other sources.[8] This need not concern us here; I will assume that consent justifies a wide range of actions which would otherwise be impermissible, and that all the actions under discussion fall within that range.

So, how do we recognize consent? Weale, for instance, argues that

By consenting to another's action, I am intentionally inducing in him a reliance that I will do nothing to interfere with his performance of the action in question. . . . In more general terms, A consents to B doing beta if the following conditions obtain: (1) A induces in B a reliance upon A not interfering with B doing beta; (2) A intends to induce this reliance in B; and (3) A intends B to recognize A's intention to induce this reliance. (69)

This characterization shows at least one weakness, for our purposes, with the standard use of consent: namely, consent is generally given to a *particular act*. Becoming friends is not a particular act, though of course the process is made up of particular acts, and we can ask if each of those was consented to. We can ask if Cathy consented to Elizabeth's second or third attempts to share her feelings or if Elizabeth consented to stay up late and try to interpret Cathy's boyfriend's puzzling behavior. But becoming friends is not one act which can be consented to.

Putting that objection aside for the moment, let us suppose, for the sake of argument, that friendship is the sort of thing that can be consented to. Express consent will not correctly characterize the accord between the friends, because only a few more people ever say, "I consent to this friendship" (or even its more colloquial equivalents) than say, "I consent to the present government." So let us then consider Simmons's useful discussion of the notion of *tacit* consent. Does the beginning of a friendship fit the model of tacit consent? Simmons suggests that five conditions must be met for tacit consent to be genuine consent:

(1) The situation must be such that it is perfectly clear that consent is appropriate and that the individual is aware of this. . . . (2) There must be a definite period of reasonable duration when objections or expressions of dissent are invited or clearly appropriate. . . . (3) The point at which expressions of dissent are no longer allowable must be made clear in some way to the potential consenter. . . . (4) The means acceptable for indicating dissent must be reasonable and reasonably easily performed. (5) The consequences of dissent cannot be extremely detrimental to the potential consenter.[9]

If we strain, we can make this characterization of tacit consent fit the case of friendship; but we will be stretching it. Here again, the question of consent to *what* is a problem. Consent to have breakfast together? Certainly. Consent to *become friends?* More problematic, since the relationship may evolve in a way that does not require conscious reflection on what is happening. Is there a definite period of reasonable duration when expressions of dissent are appropriate, with the end of that period clearly known to both parties? This condition seems easier to meet, since we can end a friendship at any time, simply by saying, "I never want to see you again." Conditions 4 and 5 are met here too, since that sentence is easily (if painfully) uttered, and in general the dissent will not be extremely detrimental to the dissenter.

It should be noted, however, that "dissent" doesn't fit the scenario very well; we do not think of ourselves as 'dissenting' from a relationship. We dissent from another person's specific actions. If you refuse to be my friend, or if you terminate an ongoing friendship, you are not a dissenter or a dissident.

It should be clear from this discussion that the notion of consent does not work well when applied to the case of friendship in general; but suppose we do wrestle with some notion of tacit consent and force the evolution of friendship onto that model. What would follow?

It is instructive here to look at the case of marriage. In marriage, there genuinely is a precise moment at which both parties explicitly consent to enter into the legal status of marriage. People do not just find themselves married one day[10] (though they may find themselves expected to marry a particular person because of the way the relationship has been going). Though friends may wonder about when it was that they realized that they were close, spouses always know the exact day that their consent was given. But is there any consensus about what was consented to? One common liberal feminist critique of marriage is that it is one of the few contracts that most people sign without ever having read the terms or even discussed them with the potential partner.

The ceremony that commits them to the contractual relationship does not specify the legal duties of marriage. . . . Special effort may even be taken to obscure the fact that the marriage ceremony legally commits the couple to a contractual relationship. . . . This practice is in conflict with the standard liberal and legal principle that a contract may be void if the contractees do not have the opportunity to read it . . . since the validity of contracts depends on the free, informed consent of the contracting parties.[11]

That most young people of marriageable age do not in fact know what is legally required of them is made clear to anyone teaching the subject to college students, who are almost always shocked to learn that in many states wives are still legally required to perform domestic duties and the husbands to provide financial support.[12] Thus, as Ketchum notes, even the fact of formal legal consent is rendered problematic by the fact that the terms of the contract are not made known to the parties before they sign.

But if the legal terms of marriage are not legitimately consented to, it might next be argued that the more informal, socially determined features of marriage are widely enough known for consent to bind to those non-legal norms. On this line of argument, it might be held that since almost everybody in the culture knows what is expected of them in marriage, their consent can be considered binding because the informed consent criterion is met. But this really will not do either. Though most people probably recognize that, *ceteris paribus,* they are consenting to share a residence and to present themselves publicly as part of a new family, there is just no general agreement on exactly what the details of the marriage will be like. There is a long history of television situation comedies based on the confusion of newlyweds as to what it is exactly that they have gotten themselves into. And with the changes in the culture and economy in the last thirty years or so, whatever cultural uniformity there once might have been regarding the be-

havior of spouses has gotten lost in the upheaval. The bulk of the details of a marital relationship are worked out in accordance with the needs and preferences of the partners. And that means that consent has to be given many times within the course of the marriage—not only to the myriad details of married life which are not specified by the legal/social contract, but also to any changes in the legal/social contract that the partners want to make. This flexibility is presently regarded as a good thing; it would be very imprudent to consent to a marital contract that specified *all* of the details of married life, even if such a thing were possible (cf. Shultz). Kleinig comments,

Closely associated with the knowledge requirement is the relatively *determinate* character of consent. When X consents, X does not generally consent to anything at all, but to some determinate act a, and to what is known to be normally associated with a. This should not surprise us, since consent implies responsibility, and it is irresponsible to accept unlimited responsibility. (105)

There is not enough consensus about the nature of marriage or knowledge about the future of our own lives for there to be much that is "known to be normally associated with" marriage.

The best example of the problematic role of consent in marriage comes from the issue of marital rape. It is often (though not always) spelled out in the law that sexual intercourse is to be expected between the spouses; and regardless of the law of a particular state, there is certainly a very widespread belief that when an individual marries, he or she is expected to engage in intercourse with his or her spouse. People who are not aware of this social norm are very few and far between. So we may, for argument's sake, suppose that in consenting to marriage each individual is aware that he or she is consenting to future acts of intercourse with his or her spouse. It was historically held that marital rape was a conceptual impossibility; when the wife consented to marry, she consented to intercourse with her husband, and this was taken to mean that she consented to *all* future acts of intercourse with him. It has more recently been argued, and fairly widely accepted, that consenting to marriage does *not* imply consent to any and all future acts of intercourse. When and whether intercourse will occur must be decided on independent grounds; actual consent must be operative for each act of intercourse to be justified.

Now consider again the case of friendship. Not only is there no explicit act of consent to enter into the status of friendship; there are no legal norms and very few social ones structuring what friendship *is*. Marriage has a formal starting point and has legal and social norms structuring it, and even so it is not at all clear that we are consenting to much in the way of specific future actions when we marry. How much more problematic, then, is the case of friendship. Friedman comments,

Friendship receives far less formal recognition in our rituals and conventions, including legal conventions, than do familial relationships, and is maintained by fewer of those formalities. If kinship is a form of ascribed status, then friendship is a kind of achievement. Those who would be friends must exert themselves actively to sustain their own relationship. (4)

If the details of married life vary from couple to couple, the inner workings of friendship vary so much that, as noted in the introductions, practically any ongoing relationship between two people gets called friendship. We cannot confidently say, then, that when two people become friends, they know exactly what they are getting into and so can legitimately be said to have given each other their informed consent.

A somewhat more plausible attempt to get some notion of consent to do our work for us here comes from an appeal to what Donald Van De Veer calls subsequent consent. If two people are close friends for a period of years, then perhaps they have been through so much together that each knows clearly what the other will consent to. Long-term friendships often result in a profound understanding of the other's views. Thus we might argue that we can accurately predict what our friend will consent to on the basis of what she has previously consented to. The appeal to subsequent consent is captured in the common phrase, "you'll thank me for this later."

Van De Veer provides persuasive reasons for thinking that this approach is inadequate. He argues that there are conceptual problems with subsequent consent. It is very odd to suppose

that consent can "reach back in time" and justify actions which occurred in the past. "'Consent after the event' surely does not alter the fact that at the time of the interference, no permission had been given, no right waived, no interferers released from a duty not to interfere" (69).

In short, even though you might later approve of the intervention, or in some sense be glad it happened, that approval does not operate in the same way that actual consent does, and it is hard to see how this "backwards causation" notion of consent could really count as consent at all.

Moreover, the argument assumes that people are very consistent. Not only are people not always consistent from one day to the next, they are rarely consistent from one year to the next, and we may suppose that major life crises do not appear more than every several months or so, at most. Thus we cannot automatically suppose that what our friend consented to (or endorsed) three years ago is what she would consent to today.

Furthermore, present crises can be substantially different from previous ones; this is particularly true for friendships that develop when the friends are young and continue for many years or decades. Crises over prom dresses and insensitive parents give way to crises over career decisions and marital problems, and then to medical worries and the deaths of family members and friends. We cannot assume that the crises are so similar that one decision can be generalized over all of them. Our friend might see the circumstances as being so different from any previous ones that inferences from past behavior would seem invalid.

Finally, the argument from previous experience does not let us account for the first intervention that a friend makes after the friendship has been established. At some point after two people have been close a major crisis will inevitably arise, and one friend must simply pray that she is guessing right when she intervenes, since by hypothesis she has no previous experience of similar circumstances with this particular friend to draw on. Yet if she never makes that first attempt she will never have any previous experience to draw on.

We might nevertheless be able to invoke individualized *hypothetical* consent[13] in a particular instance to justify paternalistic interference by a friend, just as we could to justify such interference by the state or an anonymous agent. Van De Veer provides a general framework for such a justification that can be modified to account for friendly interference.

A's paternalistic interference, X, with a generally competent subject, S, is justified (morally permissible) if and only if

1. A's doing X involves no presumptive wrong toward S or others
   or
2. A's doing X does not wrong those other than A or S
      and
either 1. S has given currently operative valid consent
or   2. S would validly consent to A's doing X if
   a) S were aware of the relevant circumstances and
   b) S's normal capacities for deliberation and choice were not impaired. (Van DeVeer, 88)

Thus, to take a standard example, if I am drunk and am about to drive over a washed-out bridge, you are justified in preventing me if I *would* consent to your doing so if only (a) I knew the bridge were washed out and (b) I weren't drunk.

A crucial question for our purposes, then, is: Would Cathy validly consent to Elizabeth's hiding her purse if (a) Cathy were aware of the relevant circumstances (namely, that she will lose her job and her standing and be very remorseful); and (b) Cathy's normal capacities for deliberation and choice were not impaired?

It might here be objected that the crucial issue is the privileged epistemological position that Elizabeth occupies relative to Cathy. Elizabeth is justified in intervening because she knows all the details of Cathy's life and knows much better than a stranger would what Cathy really wants when her autonomy is not vitiated by love. Thus the reason Cathy would consent to Elizabeth's intervention and not someone else's is simply that Elizabeth knows her so much better than anyone else. But consider the following example. Suppose that there is a very quiet, watchful, reclusive man living next door to Cathy. The walls between the apartments are very thin. Our recluse is careful to make very little noise, so Cathy is unaware of the ease with which sound travels between the two

rooms. Cathy talks openly (and loudly) on the phone about her various troubles, and the recluse hears her conversations as well as all the messages left on her answering machine. After awhile his picture of Cathy, her troubles, and her goals is as clear as Elizabeth's. Is he, therefore, equally justified in hiding her purse and lying to her?[14]

Neither considerations of Cathy's ultimate welfare nor appeals to the condition of her autonomy allow us to distinguish between Elizabeth's interference and that of our helpful recluse. After all, on consequentialist grounds, anyone who prevents the bad outcome for Cathy is justified in so doing; and on the more Kantian model of respect for autonomy, either both Cathy and the recluse are justified in intervening or neither is. Yet there still seems to be a difference between the justifiability of the two cases.

What we need, and what formal models of hypothetical consent do not give us, is a way of accounting for the fact that Cathy would consent to *Elizabeth's* interference, but not to a stranger's. Again, this problem arises because the literature on paternalism focuses so heavily on either the ultimate welfare of the individual or on the preservation of the individual's autonomy.

But the hypothetical consent account of the justification of Elizabeth's action still seems to be missing a crucial point, namely, that friendship and intimacy justify paternalistic interference *independently* of considerations of consent, hypothetical or real.

CONSENT AND INDIVIDUALISM

The main problem with any use of consent in this context is that it does serious damage to the phenomenon we are discussing. The power of consent is relegated to those contexts in which we are, for heuristic or metaphorical purposes, considering human beings as highly individualistic and autonomous, or at least in those contexts where those features of human beings are most relevant. It is not coincidental that Locke, who was so individualistic in his social and political theory, leaned so heavily on consent as the moral foundation of the state. Kleinig, in criticizing a different aspect of consent theory, remarks,

A world which places high importance on the secure-ment and determination of consent is one which also places high importance on the autonomy or respon-sibility of individuals. It is not uncommon to see this in individualistic terms. Consent is seen as a free interaction between atomic individuals, who con-front one another with their self-created projects, seeking to elicit support for their implementation or advancement. (Kleinig, 111)

Though Kleinig is one of the few theorists who explicitly points this out, skimming a ran-dom selection of articles on consent theory will bear out this analysis. And this really should not surprise us, given the role consent theory plays in moral and social theory. Questions of consent are usually invoked when we are trying to get someone to do that which, by hypothe-sis, they do not want to do, e.g., obey the state. We use consent as a last line of defense against a reluctant and hostile individual, either to jus-tify our own actions or to force them to go through with their own. Consent is resorted to when we are standing not only independent from each other, but when we are positively in opposition to each other.

And this is the opposite of relationship be-tween friends. This difference can best be illus-trated with another short example, this time showing the differences between two kinds of consensual behavior.

Suppose Leah and Allison have been close friends since high school. Now in their late twenties, they still live and work near each oth-er. They are approximately the same size, and have similar taste in clothing (which is not too surprising, since their tastes were formed to-gether). The two women exchange house keys and have a standing policy that their clothes are held in common, though each knows which ones are the ones she bought. If one of them has gone to work and the other wants to wear a particular sweater, she just goes to the other's closet and gets the sweater.

Now suppose that Allison just wants a larger wardrobe available to her and is willing to take a certain amount of risk to get it. She advertises in the paper, perhaps, or asks around at work if there is someone who is willing to combine wardrobes with her. She and this other person then write up an agreement about how the trades will be made, and perhaps include some rules about responsibility for dry cleaning and

damage and so forth. They negotiate mutually acceptable terms and exchange house keys.

Why is Allison justified in using the strang-er's clothes? Because the stranger consented to it. They both approached the situation as rea-sonably atomistic individuals with pre-existing wants and contracted a deal which was to their mutual advantage, where their advantage is specified quite completely by reference to the 100 percent increase in usable clothes. This type of situation is handled quite admirably by consent theory.

Why is Allison justified in using Leah's clothes? It is perfectly true that Leah consented to this use; but this is not the complete explana-tion. Leah and Allison share their clothes *be-cause it is an expression of their shared sense of self*. Although it is true that they each benefit from having the use of more clothes than each would have independently, this is not really their reason for sharing and does not really play a large role in justifying the procedure. The sense that the clothes are "our" clothes, and not "yours" and "mine" is the major benefit that the women gain from their arrangement.

It is not that this situation cannot be forced onto the consent model; of course it can. We *can* say that Allison's use of Leah's clothes is justified because Leah consented to it, and that the two cases are morally equivalent because consent was given in each case. Some consent theorists more or less force this conclusion by allowing no intrusion of extraneous details, such as the *reason* for the consent, into the analysis of consent. See, e.g., Weale: "It is an important feature of the analysis of consent that the speech-act be defined by reference to the addressor's *intentions,* and not his *motives.* Consent is defined in terms of a complex set of intentions irrespective of the motives which lead people to form those intentions" (70).

As Weale himself notes, it follows from this analysis that coerced consent is still a case of consent, though the moral force of coerced consent is defeasible. This is itself not the most attractive conclusion, but need not concern us here. What is problematic for this analysis is that it precludes our making any moves to ex-plain what really justifies Allison and Leah in using each other's wardrobes, and makes the two cases just described exactly morally equiv-alent. But this is to do substantial violence to the phenomenon. In the second story, consent does the moral work because it is accurate to describe the two individuals as atomistic acquisitive individuals whose good is defined by reference to material possessions, which is the scenario consent presupposes. In the second the women's good is defined by reference to their shared concept of themselves as a team, so to speak, and emphasizing consent merely forces them back into a conception of themselves as individuals.

PATERNALISM AND INTIMACY

With all these arguments about the limitations of consent behind us, let us return to our two examples and see what conclusions we may reach.

As we noted, the case of Elizabeth's interference with Cathy can be accounted for by straining the notion of consent; but I have been arguing that it is arbitrary and dogmatic to try to make consent do all the work in justifying certain kinds of interventions between friends. In this example, Elizabeth is the one who is justified in preventing Cathy from doing serious harm to her own prospects not merely because of considerations of Cathy's welfare, and not merely because Cathy's autonomy is in question, but because Elizabeth is her friend. Elizabeth's intervention is justified because the two women do not consider themselves to be absolutely independent from each other, and Elizabeth's intervention is expressive of their sense of being mutually interconstituted.

The two people cannot view themselves as an "I" rather than a "we," at least not without lapsing into a psychopathology as troublesome as its reverse, that is, viewing oneself as a presocial atomistic individual. But if we are to be honest, we will acknowledge that since these relationships are fluid it will always be a matter of moral uncertainty about where to draw the lines. And not only can no one outside the relationship judge adequately about her behavior, she herself will always be uncertain, if she is a morally sensitive person.

Finally, in this section I want to ask the reader to consider the opposite point of view from the one I have been arguing. Close consideration of this view will, I think, reveal its weaknesses and will lend indirect support for the case I am making in this chapter.

Consider, for example, Sharon Bishop Hill's argument in her "Self-Determination and Autonomy."[15] She discusses a husband and wife who are at odds over whether the wife and her daughter ought to pursue certain activities and options. Bishop Hill outlines various morally unacceptable ways in which the husband might influence his wife, including physical force and financial coercion, and rightly rejects these methods. But, she continues,

The wrong is not . . . simply that someone made a conscious attempt to interfere with someone's legitimate choice, but rather that someone's selections were blocked or interfered with. In addition, the right of self-determination takes us a good way towards directly undermining John's views about women. He seemed to think that it was perfectly all right to advise adult women to engage in and stick with traditional domestic life styles on the grounds that it was efficient or natural for women to have them. (63)

Bishop Hill argues that such advice interferes with women's right of self-determination. She ends her essay by observing that "in those we care about and love . . . it will mean valuing and appreciating what they choose simply because it is their choice. This is, perhaps, one way of expressing our love. If so, then Harriet may have taken John's reticence about some of her projects as signs that he did not love her" (70).

Now, many of Bishop Hill's points are well-taken, and of course the husband/wife relationship raises many complications which do not trouble friendships, as was discussed in section I. But her argument points out the ways in which autonomy, as she characterizes it, and intimacy, are at times incompatible. John cannot even *advise* Harriet not to pursue certain activities (Bishop Hill mentions sky-diving and attending therapy as bones of marital contention). Intimacy without the acceptance of back and forth advice-giving seems a very peculiar form of intimacy. The picture of the spouses merely acknowledging and valuing the other's choices without ever objecting or advising or otherwise putting in his or her two-cents' worth is a lonely, isolated one. The image is of two independent individuals each pursuing an independent life course within the context of mutual benign neglect. Each person's individual autonomy would be preserved, but at the cost of genuine intimacy between them. Intimacy without kibitzing is hardly intimacy at all. Bishop Hill's example works as well as it does in part because sky-diving and attending therapy are not insane things to want to do, and it seems unreasonable to object to them as activities. But what about all the considerably more foolish things that we may decide to do? Should we really just value and appreciate *any* activity our friends select? That conclusion actually seems incompatible with friendship.

Intimacy requires strongly identifying with the other person. The most representative cultural metaphors have of course been about marriage, and this is problematic, as mentioned earlier. "The two shall become as one" has been rightly objected to by feminists in large part because the "one" was the husband; the culture dictated that in a heterosexual marriage the man was always to be the dominant remaining figure, with the wife absorbed into him. But the metaphor does not have to be so politically loaded. If we speak of friendship rather than marriage, and of friendship between members of the same sex, there is then less cultural pressure for the uniting of the two to be slanted to the benefit of one of them and the detriment of the other. It is possible for two people to feel "as one" without the dominant/subordinate dynamic, and that would seem to take off much of the moral onus. To think of you and your friend as one, it is necessary to de-emphasize considerations of personal autonomy (at least as Bishop Hill and various other theorists characterize it), which is inherently individuating.

There is a tension, then, between the demands of intimacy and the demands of autonomy, and the question is: how should those demands be balanced? None of the forgoing argument should be taken to imply that autonomy is of no value at all; on the contrary, autonomy is crucially constitutive of a well-lived life. This point has been made again and again by writers from various moral traditions. The problem is, intimacy is *also* crucially constitu-

tive of a well-lived life, a point that has been made much less frequently by moral theorists. And the balancing of the two values cannot be done according to any simple formula. There are going to be times when the two conflict, and it is not clear why autonomy should always be given the pride of place which many moral theorists have awarded it.

In conclusion, then, I have argued that the justification for paternalistic interference does not rest entirely on respect for the autonomy of the individual nor on utilitarian considerations of the individual's welfare. Instead, certain kinds of interference are justified by the bonds of friendship and intimacy which connect particular people. Focusing on autonomy can blind one to the fact that, in some cases, vitiated autonomy is insufficient to justify paternalistic intervention; and that in other cases, autonomy need not be vitiated for the justification to hold. The value of intimacy must also play a role in moral deliberation; and if we are honest, we will admit that there is no easy formula for determining the relative weights of autonomy and intimacy.

Moreover, the role of consent in friendship is highly problematic. I have argued that friendship is not paradigmatically the kind of thing to which the notion of consent applies. Even if we overlook that problem and postulate that we can, in theory, consent to friendship, we encounter the difficulty in finding any specific act or expression which signifies consent to the friendship. If, to evade this problem, we turn to some notion of tacit consent (which is not unproblematic in application), we find that it is not at all clear precisely what it is that we have consented to. Tacit consent to the state may obligate us to obey its laws, but friendship is a different beast. It is not like the government, or even marriage, constituted by laws and extralegal social policies which are widely publicly promulgated. Thus the notion of consent is not always well applied in the context of friendship.

NOTES

1. See, for example, Paul S. Appelbaum, et al., *Informed Consent: Legal Theory and Clinical Practice* (New York: Oxford University Press 1987); Ruth R. Faden and Tom L. Beauchamp, *A History and Theory of Informed Consent* (New York: Oxford University Press 1986); and the work of Feinberg and Van De Veer, noted below.

2. Joel Feinberg, *Harm to Self* (Oxford: Oxford University Press 1986), 115.

3. Donald Van De Veer, *Paternalistic Intervention: The Moral Bounds on Benevolence* (Princeton, N. J.: Princeton University Press 1986), 347.

4. From, e.g., *Othello* to *Fatal Attraction*. There are interesting questions about whether the lead characters in these works were really maddened by love or by its consequences when thwarted, which might lead us back to the "rage" or "gripping mood" excuses. Love is probably considerably less separable from these consequences than we would like to believe.

5. Marilyn Friedman, "Friendship, Choice, and Change," unpublished manuscript, 2.

6. Steven Duck, *Personal Relationships and Personal Constructs: A Study of Friendship Formation* (London: J. Wiley 1973).

7. Obviously this story is fictional in its particulars, but it represents a type of friendship development which is reasonably common.

8. See, e.g., Albert Weale, "Consent," *Political Studies* 27: (1978) 65–77; Harry Beran, "In Defense of the Consent Theory of Political Obligation and Authority," *Ethics* 87 (1977): 260–71; Frederick Siegler, "Plamenatz on Consent and Obligation," *Philosophical Quarterly* 18 (1968): 256–62; John Kleinig, "The Ethics of Consent," *Canadian Journal of Philosophy* Supplement 8 (1982): 91–119.

9. A. John Simmons, "Tacit Consent and Political Obligation," *Philosophy and Public Affairs* 5 (1976): 274–91.

10. The case of common law marriage does not constitute an adequate counterexample to this claim, since it is surprisingly hard to become married in this way, and intention to marry or present oneself as married is generally necessary.

11. Sarah Ketchum, "Liberalism and Marriage Law," in Sharon Bishop and Marjorie Weinzweig, eds., *Philosophy and Women* (Belmont, Calif.: Wadsworth 1979), 185.

12. Cf. also Carole Pateman, *The Sexual Contract* (Stanford: Stanford University Press 1988), esp. ch. 6; Sheila Cronan, "Marriage," in Alison M. Jaggar and Paula S. Rothenberg, eds., *Feminist Frameworks* (New York: McGraw-Hill 1984), 329–34; Marjorie Maguire Shultz, "Contractual Ordering of Marriage: A New Model for State Policy," *California Law Review* 70 (1982): 204–330.

13. This is in contrast to what Van De Veer calls Hypothetical Rational Consent, which is the principle that intervention is justified if a fully rational person would consent to it. Van De Veer argues, rightly I think, that we must rather be concerned with the question of what *this particular individual* would consent to.

14. I am indebted to John Pollock for this example.

15. Sharon Bishop Hill, "Self-Determination and Autonomy," in Richard Wasserstrom, ed., *Today's Moral Problems* (New York: Macmillan 1985), 55–70.

JAMES CONLON

Why Lovers Can't Be Friends

That one's spouse is also one's closest friend is a common claim and seems innocent enough. Often it is offered as a gentle boast—for example, by a celebrity introducing a spouse at a formal gathering. Usually, its tone is that of achievement, as if being able to combine lover and friend is the epitome of human intimacy, as desirable as it is rare.

I found myself reacting to such claims with undeniable hostility. At first, I blamed my reactions on an unhealthy cynicism, perhaps even an unconscious resentment. However, as I explored the nature of my hostility more carefully, especially in conjunction with certain texts of Plato, I realized that it was intellectually grounded. It is not that the union of friend and lover is an ideal more difficult to achieve than facile introductions would have us believe. It is, rather, that the union is impossible; its desirability is founded on an mistaken model of human intimacy. Therefore, the claim to combine lover and friend is not just a harmless exaggeration, but a seriously misguided ideal.

To show this, I must first make explicit the theory of human relationships that the claim assumes. Like most theories in Western thought, it has its roots in Plato.

On this theory, each human self is a discrete substance combining essential and unique qualities. All attraction between selves is a desire for union, for sharing these qualities, possessing them, taking part in them in some way. One can hierarchically order the various types of attraction between selves by the essential importance (reality) of the qualities shared. Thus, according to Plato's famous *scala amoris* in *The Symposium,* attraction to, and participation in, the beauties of an individual body are ranked lower than attraction to, and participation in, the beauties of an individual soul. Hence, lovers of souls "enjoy a far fuller com-

munity with each other . . . and enjoy a far surer friendship."[1]

Applying this basic approach to concrete contemporary categories of relationship yields the following analysis. Two colleagues in the same profession at the same institution have a certain closeness; they share each other's expertise, like working on specific projects together, and hope for similar goals. Suppose, as often happens, these colleagues become friends. Now, they no longer meet only for work-related tasks, but go to the movies together, have dinner at each other's houses, and participate in a variety of activities associated with friendship. What has happened, according to the standard theory, is that the relationship has moved up a notch on the scale. It has become a fuller intimacy because more is shared, both in quantity and essential quality. If these friends subsequently become lovers, this change would be interpreted in the same manner: as an increase in their degree of intimacy.

This cumulative ascent is central to the appeal of Plato's model. For him, the lover who has climbed to the apex of love and "turned to the great sea of beauty"[2] has not really left anything of consequence behind. The beauty of "face or hands or anything else that belongs to the body"[3] is included as part of loving the form of Beauty itself. Nothing of real value is lost. It is not just that the vision of the Sun is superior to other visions: it includes them in itself. There is nothing to be loved in the shadows that is not present in the Sun. Its light subsumes and completes all other experience.

Plato's notion was, of course, carried over into Christianity. Everything said of Plato's vision of the Beautiful could equally be said of Dante's vision of God at the climax of the *Divine Comedy.* Vergil and Beatrice are subsumed in God. Nothing would be lost in choosing God over these lesser intimacies.

In summary, then, the standard model of intimacy views the differences between colleague, friend, and lover as basically differences of degree. Each form of intimacy represents a level of quality sharing that can be placed somewhere along a continuum, with minimal sharing at one end and total sharing at the other.

My criticism of this model centers around the fact that it does not present an accurate account of what happens when relationships change form. Even when the change is positive, it is not simply additive, for there is an inevitable deprivation as well.

There is a revealing scene in Robertson Davies's novel of academe, *Rebel Angels*. In it Simon Darcourt, an Anglican parson and Greek scholar, asks a treasured graduate student, Maria, to marry him. She has already had an affair with another mentor and it is out of its failure that she responds to Simon.

"I love him [the mentor] the way I love you—for the splendid thing that you are, in your own world of splendid things. Like a fool I wanted him in the way you are talking about, and whether it was because I wanted him or he wanted me I don't know and never shall know, but it was a very great mistake. Because of that stupidity, which didn't amount to a damn as an experience, I think I have put something between us that has almost lost him to me. Do you think I want to do that with you? Are all men such greedy fools that they think love only comes with that special favor? . . .

Simon, you called me Sophia: the Divine Wisdom, God's partner and playmate in Creation. . . . [I]f we go to bed it will be Sophia who lies down but it will certainly be Maria—and not the best of her—who gets up, and Sophia will be gone forever. And you, Simon dear, would come into my bed as my Rebel Angel, but very soon you would be a stoutish Anglican parson, and a Rebel Angel no more."[4]

Simon's proposal clearly comes out of the standard model we have been analyzing. In his mind, it seems only logical to move the teacher–student intimacy to a higher level by adding romance. Maria, however, has been down that road and experienced something the theory did not predict: loss. For her, romantic intimacy did not augment the old; instead, it destroyed it.

But, you will say, this destruction is peculiar to the change from student to lover and not true of relational changes in general. Surely, for example, it does not apply to the change from colleague to friend. There, it is a simple case of addition. Colleagues limit their discussions to professional concerns. If they become friends, they continue to have professional discussions, but include personal and emotional concerns as well. A simple case of addition!

But a closer analysis reveals that it is too simple. Even in this change something is definitely lost. A relationship that was once purely professional (and to read "purely" as "merely" here begs the question) is so no longer. This is not to claim that the relationship now becomes shady or incompetent, but it does lose the intimacy that pure professionals have between each other and assumes another form.

Suppose, for example, two colleagues on a promotion and tenure committee meet privately to discuss a difficult applicant. They are not friends. Although they deeply admire each other's professional competence, their lives connect only through work. Thus, their conversation is "purely professional," that is, they focus primarily on the matter at hand and are unconcerned about each other's private selves. But make no mistake: there is significant intimacy here. As they dissect the pros and cons of the applicant, their own cherished ideals are an integral, if indirect, part of the discussion. Who they are as scholars, teachers, and institutional members is shared with an intensity unique to the action-focused work of "unconcerned" professionals.

Obviously, the kind of intimacy that comes with shared professional action could never exist with someone outside the profession—even with the closest of friends. Equally obvious, of course, is that a professional could share with a nonprofessional friend things she never could share with a colleague. She might, for example, explore with a friend her own jealousies toward the applicant in a way impossible to pursue in professional discussion.

But could friends in the same profession combine both types of sharing? I do not see how. Friends would be continuously conscious of, and concerned about, personal factors extending far beyond the topic at hand, They could not put these on hold while they discussed professional matters. Thus, the joys and powers of purely professional conversation would be lost to them.

But if loss is inescapable whenever relationships change form, then the standard model of human intimacy is fundamentally mistaken. It differentiates relationships according to degree, according to what level they occupy on a continuum. The reality of loss suggests that relationships actually differ not in degree, but in kind. They are not steps on the way toward anything fuller; they are just what they are, modes of relation, each possessing distinct and—sometimes—incompatible strengths and weaknesses.

What does this mean for a model of intimacy? If the standard model has its roots in Plato, perhaps a countermodel would have its roots in Nietzsche (arguably the first Western thinker to be truly non-Platonic). Nietzsche's critique of Plato's theory of knowledge, his perspectival alternative to it, provides equally effective possibilities in relation to Plato's theory of love.

On a Nietzschean model, each type of intimacy is a perspective on, creates an interpretation of, the sharing of selves. Since there are only interpretations, with no correct or complete sharing conceivable, the various types of intimacy do not accumulate toward a definitive beatific communion. Each interpretation has its distinctive mode of operation and its own individual value. In contrast to the Platonic model, however, these values are not all commmensurable. There exist some real and positive goods that are fundamentally incompatible with others.

An analogy can best illustrate the model I have in mind. Each type of relationship (colleague, friend, lover, and so on) is like a literary genre (poem, novel, play). Obviously, differences between genres do not represent steps toward a perfect and complete artistic expression (despite Hegel's efforts). Rather, they are just different ways of doing it. Although new ways may be created, they are not progressions toward a perfect way. To describe the poem as fuller or deeper than the novel makes no sense. The novel does things a poem could never do; but since the reverse is equally true, efforts to set up a hierarchy between them are clearly misguided. A poem may, in certain contexts and circumstances, be more meaningful than a novel, but this is a practical decision, not a metaphysical one. And the practical value of such a decision involves recognizing when genres are incommensurable. Although efforts to explore the limits of any genre are crucial to

the creatio
genre's d'
meaning
tries to '
So f
about
love.

my
hov
un
lieve, tw
poem and the no
Likewise, it is a mistake
er" than the other. Each is unique
limited.

Before I argue this, two clarifications are in order. First, the term "love" is often used indiscriminately to refer to all forms of attraction (one "loves" ice cream, children, and God), but I am using the term narrowly to refer specifically to passionate, romantic love—that characterized by Tristan for Isolde, Anna Karenina for Vronsky, and Swann for Odette. Second, I believe that although passionate love has an inextricable sexual component, it is not synonymous with sexual desire. Although one cannot love romantically without sexual desire, one can certainly desire sexually those one does not love.

What is it, then, about romantic love that makes it incompatible with friendship? In one sense, the answer is so obvious as to seem simplistic. Friends share each other's experience of the world; they see it in similar ways and enjoy it together. Lovers, in contrast, as the rhetoric of romance insists repeatedly, *are* each other's world. Passion for the beloved is the organizing force of the lover's life, if not in actuality, at least in desire. In love, the world happens only through the other's eyes.

A concrete example will illustrate my point. A man is visiting an art museum in a foreign land. As he marvels at its beauties, he regrets that his friend, who shares his taste in art, was not able to make the trip with him. He anticipates the dinner they have planned for next week and the pleasure his friend will take in the detailed stories of his trip.

If, however, the man is in love, his trip will be quite different. His experience of the museum will seem somehow hollow—like everything else he experiences without the beloved. In love, one does not so much delight in sharing

...as want every experience, ...e, not to be separate. This is ...therine's famous "I *am* Heath-...n in *Wuthering Heights*.[5] It is ...ce of the jealousy so foreign to ...nd so integral to romance.

...ewis, in *The Four Loves,* claims that ...re friends side by side and lovers face ...e.[6] This insight seems essentially correct ...e, and essentially the difference I am trying ...describe. Friends are fascinated primarily by ...he world (and by each other as objects in it). They delight in exchanging the world with each other. Lovers, on the other hand, are fascinated primarily by each other, and see the world only in each other's eyes. The focus and delight of friends is decidedly different from that of lovers.

In pointing out this difference, I am not claiming to have finally identified the true meaning of love or friendship—or even to have said very much about either. My intent is the minimal one of demonstrating that they are incompatible. Lewis's image is particularly helpful in this. People can stand side by side or they can stand face to face, but they obviously cannot do both at the same time.[7] Each stand has its own unique delights, but having one logically requires losing the other.

Historically, when differences were emphasized, it was usually to serve a particular hierarchical order. I want to avoid this historical tendency. While insisting that love and friendship are irreconcilably different, I also want to insist on their equality. Though circumstances may make one better than the other, this is a practical and not a metaphysical superiority. In themselves they are equal.

The overwhelming tendency of popular culture is to deny this equality and place romantic love above everything else, to view it as the most intimate relationship possible between human beings. The language of romance, with its penchant for totalizing and divine superlatives, feeds this popular hierarchy. But the "made for each other," "everything to me" rhetoric is obviously exaggerated. Romance surely unites people in a way unlike any other, but so does colleagueship. Not enough is said about romance's limits (or colleagueship's strengths). For instance, there is not the level of choice in romance that there is in other relationships. Also, its narrow focus generates and

idealized intensity detrimental to the broader context (love's proverbial blindness). Finally, it is notoriously temporary. In short, to proclaim that romance is the most important of life's offerings is simplistic at best, and has often been downright dangerous.

But in detailing the limitations of romance I am not trying, like Montaigne,[8] to invert the popular hierarchy and proclaim friendship as the height of intimacy. If the populace has tended to overrate passion, intellectuals—from Plato to Shulamith Firestone—have been too prone to vilify it. While it is true that in the purduring constancy of friendship aspects of the self get shared and enacted that would never be possible in the frenzy of passion, there are glories that exist only amidst that madness. This is the truth at the heart of Heloise's famous protestation to the intellectualizing Abelard: "The name of wife may seem more sacred or more binding, but sweeter for me will always be the word mistress, or, if you will permit me, that of concubine or whore."[9] Like any genre, passionate romance has values that only it can deliver.

At the outset of this paper I said that the claim to have united love and friendship was not merely innocent bragging, but a significant and dangerous error. This may have seemed melodramatic at the time, but I want now to reassert and explain it.

The two models of intimacy I have been contrasting reflect profoundly differing views on the meaning of human life and the possibilities inherent in it. Plato's view is marked by a radical and unbounded optimism—which is what made him so useful to Christianity. To him, all genuine goods are compatible; therefore, it is possible to "have them all," possible for the human being to achieve perfect communion with all of reality. For him, the struggle of the moral life involves discerning the narrow path toward total union and unflinchingly ascending it. When Plato has Socrates reject the passionate advances of Alcibiades, he is absolutely confident that Socrates would find nothing in the arms of Alcibiades that would not also be found in the transcendent arms of Beauty itself. Given the right choices, nothing is really lost; all tears will be wiped from our eyes. In other words, when Plato chooses, he assumes he can have it all—an inviting but dangerous assumption!

The perspectival model of intimacy that I am suggesting is more modest. There is no totalizing genre that subsumes all others in itself, no perfect communion. Since some goods, some forms of intimacy, are incompatible with others, one must choose between them. What gives this choice its poignancy is the realization that having some forms, albeit powerful and splendid, means the death of others powerful and splendid in their own right. On this model, morality is not so much an ascent to totality, but—to use a different metaphor—a kind of quilting in which one struggles to arrange as many compatible goods as one can into a significant and individual unity.

But any effective arrangement realizes that choice involves real losses, real goods eternally excluded. The drama of the moral life, its tragic edge, consists in deciding which things to let die. Yes, truth demands that we embrace and reverence and enjoy the goods we choose, but it also demands mourning for the goods our choice excludes. That Socrates chose well that cold night he slept in the arms of Beauty itself, I do not for an instant deny. His quilt works like no other. But his quilt does not include Alcibiades; it never will—and such a terrible loss demands appropriate tears. [10]

NOTES

1. Plato, *Symposium,* trans. Alexander Nehamas and Paul Woodruff (Indianapolis, Ind.: Hackett, 1989), 209c.

2. Ibid., 210d.

3. Ibid., 211a.

4. Robertson Davies, *Rebel Angels* (Penguin: New York, 1981), p. 256.

5. Emily Bronte, *Wuthering Heights* (Random House N. Y.: Literary Guild, 1943), 51.

6. C. S. Lewis, *The Four Loves* (New York: Harcourt, Brace, & World, 1960), 98.

7. It should be noted that, contrary to the logic of his own image, Lewis sees friendship and love as compatible. I take this inconsistency to be due to the overpowering force of his Christian hope.

8. Michel de Montaigne, *Essays,* trans. J. M. Cohen (New York: Penguin, 1958), 94.

9. *Letters of Abelard and Heloise,* trans. Betty Radice (New York: Penguin, 1974), 113.

10. My thoughts on Alcibiades owe a great deal to Martha Nussbaum's *The Fragility of Goodness* (Cambridge: Cambridge University Press, 1986), especially chap. 6, "The Speech of Alcibiades."

JANE ENGLISH

What Do Grown Children Owe Their Parents?

What do grown children owe their parents? I will contend that the answer is "nothing." Although I agree that there are many things that children *ought* to do for their parents, I will argue that it is inappropriate and misleading to describe them as things "owed." I will maintain that parents' voluntary sacrifices, rather than creating "debts" to be "repaid," tend to create love or "friendship." The duties of grown children are those of friends and result from love between them and their parents, rather than being things owed in repayment for the parents' earlier sacrifices. Thus, I will oppose those philosophers who use the word "owe" whenever a duty or obligation exists. Although the "debt" metaphor is appropriate in some moral circumstances, my argument is that a love relationship is not such a case.

Misunderstandings about the proper relationship between parents and their grown children have resulted from reliance on the "owing" terminology. For instance, we hear parents complain, "You owe it to us to write home (keep up your piano playing, not adopt a hippie lifestyle), because of all we sacrificed for you (paying for piano lessons, sending you to college)." The child is sometimes even heard to reply, "I didn't ask to be born (to be given piano lessons, to be sent to college)." This inappropriate idiom of ordinary language tends to obscure, or even to undermine, the love that is the correct ground of filial obligation.

FAVORS CREATE DEBTS

There are some cases, other than literal debts, in which talk of "owing," though metaphorical, is apt. New to the neighborhood, Max barely knows his neighbor, Nina, but he asks her if she will take in his mail while he is gone for a month's vacation. She agrees. If, subsequently, Nina asks Max to do the same for her, it seems that Max has a moral obligation to agree (greater than the one he would have had if Nina had not done the same for him), unless for some reason it would be a burden far out of proportion to the one Nina bore for him. I will call this a *favor*: when A, at B's request, bears some burden for B, then B incurs an obligation to reciprocate. Here the metaphor of Max's "owing" Nina is appropriate. It is not literally a debt, of course, nor can Nina pass this IOU on to heirs, demand payment in the form of Max's taking out her garbage, or sue Max. Nonetheless, since Max ought to perform one act of similar nature and amount of sacrifice in return, the term is suggestive. Once he reciprocates, the debt is "discharged"—that is, their obligations revert to the condition they were in before Max's initial request.

Contrast a situation in which Max simply goes on vacation and, to his surprise, finds upon his return that his neighbor has mowed his grass twice weekly in his absence. This is a voluntary sacrifice rather than a favor, and Max has no duty to reciprocate. It would be nice for him to volunteer to do so, but this would be supererogatory on his part. Rather than a favor, Nina's action is a friendly gesture. As a result, she might expect Max to chat over the back fence, help her catch her straying dog, or something similar—she might expect the development of a friendship. But Max would be chatting (or whatever) out of friendship, rather than in repayment for mown grass. If he did not return her gesture, she might feel rebuffed or miffed, but not unjustly treated or indignant,

From Onora O'Neill and William Ruddick, eds., *Having Children: Philosophical and Legal Reflections on Parenthood.* New York: Oxford University Press, 1979.

since Max has not failed to perform a duty. Talk of "owing" would be out of place in this case.

It is sometimes difficult to distinguish between favors and non-favors, because friends tend to do favors, for each other, and those who exchange favors tend to become friends. But one test is to ask how Max is motivated. Is it "to be nice to Nina" or "because she did x for me"? Favors are frequently performed by total strangers without any friendship developing. Nevertheless, a temporary obligation is created, even if the chance for repayment never arises. For instance, suppose that Oscar and Matilda, total strangers, are waiting in a long checkout line at the supermarket. Oscar, having forgotten the oregano, asks Matilda to watch his cart for a second. She does. If Matilda now asks Oscar to return the favor while she picks up some tomato sauce, he is obliged to agree. Even if she had not watched his cart, it would be inconsiderate of him to refuse, claiming he was too busy reading the magazines. He may have a duty to help others, but he would not "owe" it to her. But if she has done the same for him, he incurs an additional obligation to help, and talk of "owing" is apt. It suggests an agreement to perform equal, reciprocal, canceling sacrifices.

THE DUTIES OF FRIENDSHIP

The terms "owe and "repay" are helpful in the case of favors, because the sameness of the amount of sacrifice on the two sides is important; the monetary metaphor suggests equal quantities of sacrifice. But friendship ought to be characterized by *mutuality* rather than reciprocity: friends offer what they can give and accept what they need, without regard for the total amounts of benefits exchanged. And friends are motivated by love rather than by the prospect of repayment. Hence, talk of "owing" is singularly out of place in friendship.

For example, suppose Alfred takes Beatrice out for an expensive dinner and a movie. Beatrice incurs no obligation to "repay" him with a goodnight kiss or a return engagement. If Alfred complains that she "owes" him something, he is operating under the assumption that she should repay a favor, but on the contrary his was a generous gesture done in the hopes of developing a friendship. We hope that he would

not want her repayment in the form of sex or attention if this was done to discharge a debt rather than from friendship. Since, if Alfred is prone to reasoning in this way, Beatrice may well decline the invitation or request to pay for her own dinner, his attitude of expecting a "return" on his "investment" could hinder the development of a friendship. Beatrice should return the gesture only if she is motivated by friendship.

Another common misuse of the "owing" idiom occurs when the Smiths have dined at the Joneses' four times, but the Joneses at the Smiths' only once. People often say, "We owe them three dinners." This line of thinking may be appropriate between business acquaintances, but not between friends. After all, the Joneses invited the Smiths not in order to feed them or to be fed in turn, but because of the friendly contact presumably enjoyed by all on such occasions. If the Smiths do not feel friendship toward the Joneses, they can decline future invitations and not invite the Joneses; they owe them nothing. Of course, between friends of equal resources and needs, roughly equal sacrifices (though not necessarily roughly equal dinners) will typically occur. If the sacrifices are highly out of proportion to the resources, the relationship is closer to servility than to friendship.[1]

Another difference between favors and friendship is that after a friendship ends, the duties of friendship end. The party that has sacrificed less owes the other nothing. For instance, suppose Elmer donated a pint of blood that his wife Doris needed during an operation. Years after their divorce, Elmer is in an accident and needs one pint of blood. His new wife, Cora, is also of the same blood type. It seems that Doris not only does not "owe" Elmer blood, but that she should actually refrain from coming forward if Cora has volunteered to donate. To insist on donating not only interferes with the newlyweds' friendship, but it belittles Doris and Elmer's former relationship by suggesting that Elmer gave blood in hopes of favors returned instead of simply out of love for Doris. It is one of the heart-rending features of divorce that it attends to quantity in a relationship previously characterized by mutuality. If Cora could not donate, Doris's obligation is the same as that for any former spouse in need of blood; it is not increased by the fact that Elmer similarly aided her. It *is* affected by the degree to which they are still friends, which in turn may (or may not) have been influenced by Elmer's donation.

In short, unlike the debts created by favors, the duties of friendship do not require equal quantities of sacrifice. Performing equal sacrifices does not cancel the duties of friendship, as it does the debts of favors. Unrequested sacrifices do not themselves create debts, but friends have duties regardless of whether they requested or initiated the friendship. Those who perform favors may be motivated by mutual gain, whereas friends should be motivated by affection. These characteristics of the friendship relation are distorted by talk of "owing."

PARENTS AND CHILDREN

The relationship between children and their parents should be one of friendship characterized by mutuality rather than one of reciprocal favors. The quantity of parental sacrifice is not relevant in determining what duties the grown child has. The medical assistance grown children ought to offer their ill mothers in old age depends upon the mothers' need, not upon whether they endured a difficult pregnancy, for example. Nor do one's duties to one's parents cease once an equal quantity of sacrifice has been performed, as the phrase "discharging a debt" may lead us to think.

Rather, what children ought to do for their parents (and parents for children) depends upon (1) their respective needs, abilities, and resources and (2) the extent to which there is an ongoing friendship between them. Thus, regardless of the quantity of childhood sacrifices, an able, wealthy child has an obligation to help his needy parents more than does a needy child. To illustrate, suppose sisters Cecile and Dana are equally loved by their parents, even though Cecile was an easy child to care for, seldom ill, while Dana was often sick and caused some trouble as a juvenile delinquent. As adults, Dana is a struggling artist living far away, while Cecile is a wealthy lawyer living nearby. When the parents need visits and financial aid, Cecile has an obligation to bear a higher proportion of these burdens than her sister. This results from her abilities, rather than from

the quantities of sacrifice made by the parents earlier.

Sacrifices have an important causal role in creating an ongoing friendship, which may lead us to assume incorrectly that it is the sacrifices that are the source of the obligation. That the source is the friendship instead can be seen by examining cases in which the sacrifices occurred but the friendship, for some reason, did not develop or persist. For example, if a woman gives up her newborn child for adoption, and if no feelings of love ever develop on either side, it seems that the grown child does not have an obligation to "repay" her for her sacrifices in pregnancy. For that matter, if the adopted child has an unimpaired love relationship with the adoptive parents, he or she has the same obligations to help them as a natural child would have.

The filial obligations of grown children are a result of friendship, rather than owed for services rendered. Suppose that Vance married Lola despite his parents' strong wish that he marry within their religion, and that as a result, the parents refuse to speak to him again. As the years pass, the parents are unaware of Vance's problems, his accomplishments, the birth of his children. The love that once existed between them, let us suppose, has been completely destroyed by this event and thirty years of desuetude. At this point, it seems, Vance is under no obligation to pay his parents' medical bills in their old age, beyond his general duty to help those in need. An additional, filial obligation would only arise from whatever love he may still feel for them. It would be irrelevant for his parents to argue, "But look how much we sacrificed for you when you were young," for that sacrifice was not a favor but occurred as part of a friendship which existed at that time but is now, we have supposed, defunct. A more appropriate message would be, "We still love you, and we would like to renew our friendship."

I hope this helps to set the question of what children ought to do for their parents in a new light. The parental argument, "You ought to do *x* because we did *y* for you," should be replaced by, "We love you and you will be happier if you do *x*," or "We believe you love us, and anyone who loved us would do *x*." If the parents' sacrifice had been a favor, the child's reply, "I never asked you to do *y* for me," would have been relevant; to the revised parental remarks, this reply is clearly irrelevant. The child can either do *x* or dispute one of the parents' claims: by showing that a love relationship does not exist, or that love for someone does not motivate doing *x*, or that he or she will not be happier doing *x*.

Seen in this light, parental requests for children to write home, visit, and offer them a reasonable amount of emotional and financial support in life's crises are well founded, so long as a friendship still exists. Love for others does call for caring about and caring for them. Some other parental requests, such as for more sweeping changes in the child's lifestyle or life goals, can be seen to be insupportable, once we shift the justification from debts owed to love. The terminology of favors suggests the reasoning, "Since we paid for your college education, you owe it to us to make a career of engineering, rather than becoming a rock musician," This tends to alienate affection even further, since the tuition payments are depicted as investments for a return rather than done from love, as though the child's life goals could be "bought." Basing the argument on love leads to

different reasoning patterns. The suppressed premise, "If A loves B, then A follows B's wishes as to A's lifelong career" is simply false. Love does not even dictate that the child adopt the parents' values as to the desirability of alternative life goals. So the parents' strongest available argument here is, "We love you, we are deeply concerned about your happiness, and in the long run you will be happier as an engineer." This makes it clear that an empirical claim is really the subject of the debate.

The function of these examples is to draw out our considered judgments as to the proper relation between parents and their grown children, and to show how poorly they fit the model of favors. What is relevant is the ongoing friendship that exists between parents and children. Although that relationship developed partly as a result of parental sacrifices for the child, the duties that grown children have to their parents result from the friendship rather than from the sacrifices. The idiom of owing favors to one's parents can actually be destructive if it undermines the role of mutuality and leads us to think in terms of quantitative reciprocal favors.

NOTE

1. Cf. Thomas E. Hill, Jr., "Servility and Self-Respect," *Monist* 57 (1973). Thus, during childhood, most of the sacrifices will come from the parents, since they have most of the resources and the child has most of the needs. When children are grown, the situation is usually reversed.

JEFFREY BLUSTEIN

The Duties of Grown Children

THE OWING IDIOM

Parents bear the burdens of support, care, and concern for their children when they are young, and older children, it might be argued, ought to do things for their parents because they are owed for services rendered and efforts made during this period. On Aquinas's view, children are indebted to their parents for their earlier benefactions, indebted not in the sense of having a debt of repayment, i.e., a legal debt, where "the amount given is the measure of the recompense," but in the sense of having a debt of gratitude, i.e., a moral debt, where "the sentiment of the giver" is regarded "more than what he has given" (*Summa,* question 106, article 5). Alternatively, we might wish to confine the notion of indebtedness to cases where it seems appropriate to speak about some form of repayment, and to characterize gratitude as something owed to another for some other reason. Joel Feinberg takes this approach in the following passage:

Many writers speak of duties of gratitude as if they were special instances, or perhaps informal analogues, of duties of indebtedness. But gratitude, I submit, feels nothing at all like indebtedness. . . . My benefactor once freely offered me his services when I needed them. There was, on that occasion, nothing for me to do in return but express my deepest gratitude to him. (How alien to gratitude any sort of *payment* would have been!) But now circumstances have arisen in which he needs help, and I am in a position to help him. Surely, I *owe* him my services now, and he would be entitled to resent my failure to come through.[1]

On this view, it would not be inconsistent to claim that grown children owe their parents many things and yet are not indebted to them.

The expression "duty of gratitude" requires some explanation. It does not mean the duty to feel grateful, for feeling grateful cannot be an immediate result of an act of the will. Otherwise, it would be appropriate to say to an ungrateful person, "Stop that at once! Feel grateful!" At the same time, we regard the disposition to feel gratitude for favors received from another as a virtue of character and the inculcation of this virtue as an aim of moral education. One may not be to blame for having a character defect with respect to any of the choices made at a time at which one already has the defect, but it may be appropriate to hold such a person at least partially responsible for *becoming* that sort of person, for not developing the feelings and attitudes involved in gratitude. Further, gratitude is a duty in that one has a duty to *express* gratitude in words or deeds or both. Even persons who cannot be criticized for having a defect of character may need to have pointed out to them what they should do in particular circumstances. Sometimes, perhaps because we have forgotten what our benefactors did for us or how valuable it was to us at the time, or because our benefactors need our help now when it is difficult for us to help them, we may have to be reminded that we owe them our gratitude and enlightened as to what would be a fitting response to their prior services.

There are a number of differences between the moral debt of gratitude and the legal debt of repayment (to use Aquinas's terminology) or between the duty of gratitude and the duty of indebtedness (to use Feinberg's). The first concerns the motivations of those to whom these duties are owed. Duties of gratitude are owed only to those who have helped or benefited us freely, without thought of personal gain, simply out of a desire to protect or promote our well-being.[2] The givers may hope for some return, but they do not give in expectation of it. Duties of indebtedness, in contrast, can be owed to those who were motivated primarily by self-interest or by the desire to help only insofar as this was believed to involve no risk or loss to themselves. A second difference has to do with how the notion of sacrifice figures in the account of these types of duties. An important factor in determining whether gratitude is owed is the degree of sacrifice or concession or exertion made by a person who helps or benefits us, because the more a person sacrifices for us (provided the sacrifice is voluntary), the more confident we are likely to be that what the person did for us was done out of a genuine desire to help us and not in order to gain favor. The more our benefactor's actions coincide with his or her own self-interest, the less sure we may be about what lies behind the decision to help us and hence that gratitude is the appropriate response in the situation. In addition, sacrifice is an important factor in determining *what* is required in the way of specific performance. Though duties of gratitude do not necessarily presuppose sacrifice on the part of our benefactors, more is owed to one who has undergone significant personal hardship in aiding us than to one who has suffered little or not at all. In contrast, sacrifice is relevant to duties of indebtedness not because of what it tells us about the sentiments of the giver, but because of its possible relation to what is given. The person who sacrifices more may give us more as a result, so that we may have a duty to repay that person more. If, however, A has to sacrifice more than B to give us the same x (and we have consented to A's giving us x), then we have a duty to repay A for x, and only x, as well perhaps as a duty to do something extra for A as a token of our appreciation for those efforts. (In the case of filial duties of indebtedness, social customs may help define what constitutes adequate recompense.)

Another difference between duties of gratitude and indebtedness is brought out by asking the question "Do we have such duties with respect to benefits that are owed to us, that is, in situations where those providing them are fulfilling their duties to us?" If A has a duty to provide B with benefits, and this duty does not arise out of a contractual relationship or some other voluntary transaction between A and B, then B has no duty to repay A for those benefits. For example, if A promises C that he will do x for B in exchange for C's doing y for A, and C accepts, it is C, not B, who is indebted to A for x. Similarly for the so-called natural duties, i.e., the duties that obtain between all as equal moral persons, irrespective of their voluntary acts. If I am in need or jeopardy, and you can and do help me at little cost or risk to yourself, I have no duty to repay you for your service. You had a duty to help me under these circumstances, a duty that was not contingent on my performing some service in return. In contrast, I may have a duty to show *gratitude*, even though those who provided me with benefits were fulfilling duties that did not arise out of any express or tacit agreement between us. This is so for two reasons. First, gratitude "regards the sentiment of the giver more than what he has given," and though you, the giver, may have had a duty to help or benefit me in certain ways, you may not have helped or benefited me solely or primarily because you regarded this as your duty. On the contrary, you may have done so because you cared for me or loved me. Second, while you may just have been doing your duty, the fulfillment of that duty may have been onerous for you, and the fact that you undertook to perform certain duties that are in themselves exceedingly demanding, or that you did your duty in circumstances in which many of us would not, may entitle you to some expression of appreciation from the recipient of your benefits. Lifeguards, for example. are responsible for the performance of those specific duties that are attached to their office, including the rescuing of drowning swimmers, and they should not demand or even expect repayment from a rescued swimmer when they were only doing their job in rescuing him. But possibly because the job of a lifeguard is inherently dangerous, or because this lifeguard incurred more than the usual risk in this particular instance, the rescued swimmer normally feels grateful to the lifeguard, and he ought to show that gratitude in some way as well. (For simplicity's sake, I assume here that the swimmer wanted to be rescued.)

One of the factors that affect the issue of what we ought to do to demonstrate our gratitude to another is the degree of sacrifice or concession made by the one who confers a benefit upon us. Another is the value of the benefit to us. Yet sometimes grantors do not know whether we will value their services or how highly, and they may think that they do us a great service when in fact they do us no service at all (as judged by us) or their services turn out to be less valuable to us than they had thought they would. If in the first case the grantor was proceeding on the basis of reasonable (though unfortunately erroneous) assumptions about what we value, and had reason to believe that we would want the services, then it seems we ought to do something to demonstrate our appreciation for the grantor's benevolent regard, for what he or she *attempted* to do for us, though not for what was actually *done* for us. That we did not request those services does not in itself entail that we have no duty to show gratitude for them. Indeed, since gratitude is essentially a response to benevolence, it seems that we may have a duty to show gratitude (at some point) for benefits that we did not voluntarily accept but only received, and for benefits which, at the time they were provided, were judged to be benefits by the grantor alone, and not by the recipient. But if we did not want the grantor's services, and let him or her know it, a question arises as to the grantor's true motives in helping us and therefore as to the appropriateness of gratitude in this situation. In general, there is an important difference between the case where benefits are bestowed *without* the voluntary consent of the recipient, and the case where benefits are bestowed in *disregard* of the recipient's voluntary choice. When my wishes are known, but you claim that benevolence justifies you in acting contrary to those wishes, you must overcome the presumption that one is better off when one's wishes are respected; when my wishes are not known, and you perform services for me without my consent, your professed benevolence is not immediately suspect.

In contrast, merely receiving benefits or help from another does not give rise to a duty of indebtedness. I cannot create such a duty for you by going ahead and doing something without your request or knowledge. Thus, if you come back from vacation and find, to your surprise, that I have cut your lawn while you were away, it might be ungrateful of you not to do something in return. But it would not be unjust

of you to refuse to do so. This difference between gratitude and indebtedness with regard to the necessity of consent is not hard to explain. "Gratitude," according to Kant, "consists in honoring a person because of a kindness he has done for us,"[3] and to be sure, we ought to have some control over what others do for us, even out of kindness. Mature individuals have the right to refuse another's gifts, just as they have the right to turn down another's business propositions. But, I submit, it is only when we mistakenly suppose that the aim of gratitude is to rectify some moral imbalance, to restore something that rightfully belongs to another, that we feel the need to protect ourselves against others' kindnesses to the same extent as we protect ourselves against others' claims to repayment (namely, by stipulating that merely receiving benefits of others never creates a duty of gratitude to them).

With these general distinctions between gratitude and indebtedness in hand, we can proceed to consider the special case of grown children's duties to their parents. The question is this: Is it appropriate to describe the things that adult children ought to do for their parents as things *owed* to them? Blackstone, for one, thought so:

The duties of children to their parents arise from a principle of natural justice and retribution. For to those who gave us existence we naturally owe subjection and obedience during our minority, and honor and reverence ever after; they who protected the weakness of our infancy are entitled to our protection in the infirmity of their age; they who by sustenance and education have enabled their offspring to prosper ought in return to be supported by that offspring in case they stand in need of assistance.[4]

On this view, the relation between parents and grown children is not unlike the *quid pro quo* exchange of a business transaction, where equity and justice dominate. Alternatively, we might argue that though grown children do owe their parents many things and ought to requite their benefits, the monetary metaphor of repayment is fundamentally at odds with the affectionate nature of family life.

To resolve this question, let us begin by applying one of the distinctions between duties of gratitude and duties of indebtedness discussed above. In order for claims to repayment to have any moral force, it must first be established that what parents claim repayment for is something that they were morally at liberty to give to or withhold from their children. If parents have any right to repayment from their children, it can only be for that which was either above and beyond the call of parental duty, or not required by parental duty at all. Thus grown children are not indebted (in the narrow sense) to their parents for having seen to it that they received an adequate education, adequate relative to the children's capabilities and to society's needs, for this was something that the parents, as parents, had a duty to do. They may actually have had a duty to do more, if parents in general ought to provide for their children in a manner commensurate with the parents' particular means and station in life. Parents might also do things for their children which they have no duty to do, as when they continue to support them past the age of majority and they are not in such a feeble and dependent condition physically and mentally as to be unable to support themselves. The principles that govern the content and duration of parental duties serve as a reference point for assessing the validity of parents' claims to repayment from their grown children, and sometimes parents can be shown to have no right to repayment for their prior services simply by appealing to standards of parental care.

On the other hand, it is not necessary for parents to go beyond their duty, or to do things for their children that they have no duty to do, before it is appropriate to ask what the children must do to show their gratitude to the parents. For though our parents are under a duty to give us a decent upbringing and to care for us to the best of their ability, love is essential to a really good upbringing and sometimes great sacrifices have to be made to provide it, and it is the motive of the giver that gratitude regards, not the obligatoriness of the actions. Indeed, since the degree of obligation to gratitude is to be judged in part by how beneficial the service was to the obligated subject, and since the duties of parents are duties to protect and promote the child's serious interests, grown children may actually have more of a duty to show gratitude for benefits that were owed them than for those that were not.

It is not only because parents were merely discharging the duties of parenthood that their children have no duty of indebtedness to them. For it is also necessary that the benefits received be voluntarily accepted, and young children and infants are not able to choose not to accept the benefits of being born, fed, clothed, nurtured, and educated. Young children cannot exercise genuine choice with respect to the benefits of early care, and until their capacities of rationality and self-control develop sufficiently, they have a duty to cooperate with their parents in their childrearing efforts. Even when parents do what they have *no* duty to do, perhaps in expectation of some recompense from their children when they grow up, they do not thereby make it obligatory for their children to repay them. For when the children are older and have the real capacity for choice, they may quite rationally decide that they would rather not have received these benefits at all than be indebted to their parents for having bestowed them on them. They may feel that they would rather be somewhat less well off than take the lower place of the dependent in relation to their parents. Older children's refusal to accept this dependency cannot, of course, alter the fact that they did receive those nonobligatory parental benefits while young and did (possibly still do) profit from them. But the freedom to decide when, and to whom, one shall become indebted, cannot be abridged in advance by unilateral parental decisions.

Filial gratitude, in contrast, is not to be thought of as the price of parental benefits, a price that older children may not be willing to pay for benefits they could have gotten along without. It is rather an acknowledgement of the generosity of parents. As Kant puts it,

the minimum of gratitude requires one not to regard a kindness received as a burden one would gladly be rid of (since the person so favoured stands a step lower than his benefactor, and this wounds his pride), but to accept the occasion for gratitude as a moral kindness—that is, an opportunity given one . . . to combine *sensitivity* to others' benevolence . . . with the *cordiality* of a benevolent attitude of will. (*Doctrine*, p.124)

If children are sometimes afraid to allow themselves to feel grateful to their parents, it is perhaps because they are trying to break free their emotional dependency on their parents and see any admission of gratitude as an acknowledgment of their parents' superior status. To show gratitude to your parents may seem to be like asking them for a loan when you are trying to prove to yourself and to them that you can be financially self-supporting. Under these circumstances, it is not surprising to hear an older child say, "I didn't ask for your sacrifices on my behalf while I was growing up, so I owe you no gratitude for them." The denial of consent, and hence of any duty of gratitude, is the child's way of maintaining equality with the parents, as well perhaps of defending himself against their persistent accusations of ingratitude. However, the claim that I have no duty of gratitude to X (merely) because I have not consented to X's benefits or help rests on a confusion. As a general attitude, it betrays a deep-rooted suspicion about the motivations of others, an unwillingness or inability to believe that others can be motivated purely by the desire to help us, without any expectation of return from us.[5]

Assuming that grown children do have a duty of gratitude to their parents for benefits received when young, can they ever completely discharge this duty? Kant's view is that gratitude in general is a perpetual or "holy" duty, from which it follows that the duty of filial gratitude, as a special instance, is also perpetual:

Gratitude must also be considered, more especially, a *holy* duty. . . . A moral object is holy if the obligation with regard to it cannot be discharged completely by any act in conformity with the obligation (so that no matter what he does, the person who is under obligation always remains under obligation). . . . One cannot, by any requital of a kindness received, rid oneself of the obligation for this kindness, since one can never win away from the benefactor his *priority* of merit: the merit of having been the first in benevolence. (*Doctrine*, p.123)

Kant might have gone on as follows. You have a number of possible objects for your benevolence, but you select me. I ought to be grateful to you not merely because you *helped* or benefited me without expectation of reward, but because you chose *me* to benefit when there were others you might have benefited instead. Further, I am not now in the same position with respect to my benevolence as you were with respect to yours: I must benefit *you* when the circumstances demand it. No matter what I do to show you my gratitude, even if I do the same thing for you that you did for me, I cannot do enough, because I am always only responding

to your benevolence. A duty of indebtedness, in contrast, is an "ordinary duty," because repayment completely cancels the debt.

For Kant, the more beneficial your favor, and the more unselfishly you bestow it on me, the more gratitude I owe you. These factors, it seems, ought to affect the form that my gratitude should take as well as the duration of my duty. Although first in benevolence, you may only have done me a small favor at little or no personal cost, and it seems that I can compensate for being second in benevolence by doing you a great favor in return at great personal cost. The case of parents and children is particularly complicated, however, for gratitude is owed to parents when they (a) benevolently do more in their child's interest than they are morally required to do, (b) benevolently do things in their child's interest that they have no duty to do, or (c) discharge their duties at great difficulty to themselves,[6] and the fact of having been first in benevolence seems to carry more moral weight in (a) and (b) than in (c). The argument that we can never do enough to show our gratitude to our parents and are, therefore, forever obligated to them because we can never confer on them benefits like those they conferred on us, is open to the following objections: It may or may not be possible for us to give our parents the same or an equivalent benefit, but a great benefit does not entitle our benefactors to much in the way of gratitude if they had a duty to bestow it on us and did so at little personal cost. In addition, even if some form of reciprocation is required and the degree of obligation to gratitude is not slight, we do not need to give our benefactors the same or an equivalent benefit in order to fully discharge our duty of gratitude to them. To claim otherwise is once again to confuse gratitude with indebtedness.

FRIENDSHIP

The owing approach, as I conceive of it, is oriented toward past actions, in that duties of indebtedness and duties of gratitude rest on one's own previous acts and/or the previous acts of other persons. In the case of gratitude, the fact that parents have performed certain acts in the past by itself creates certain obligations for children. Grown children may not have much affection for, or be particularly fond of, their parents; they may not desire their parents' company because they do not feel that they have much in common with their parents. However, since duties of gratitude result from prior services and not from the relationship that presently exists between grown children and their parents, these facts do not in themselves show that grown children have no duties to their parents. Of course, neither is this relationship irrelevant to the duties children owe their parents, for the presence or absence of love and friendship between parents and their grown children may tell us something about the kind of upbringing they received. But there are many factors that can prevent the development of friendship between parents and children or that can undermine a friendship that already exists, and even good and loving parents may become estranged from their children when they grow up.

The duty to show gratitude to parents is not the same as the duty to treat parents as friends or the duty to become their friends. Gratitude is not properly friendliness toward benefactors, but rather respect for them, and the relationship of mutual respect between benefactor and grateful recipient is different from the relationship of mutual affection between one friend and another. The principle of gratitude regulates relations between individuals whether or not there is any intimate personal relationship between them. Moreover, while gratitude (unlike indebtedness) may sometimes lead to friendship, the element of choice necessarily enters into the latter. We choose our friends, and we do not have a duty to act on the feelings and desires that motivate actions done out of friendship unless we are already involved in an ongoing or budding friendship with someone. Even in the absence of a conscious decision to be someone's friend, friendship is still a voluntary relationship, for it would not be friendship at all if the parties involved did not endorse or consent to it.

Though gratitude toward parents can blend with and strengthen the claims that arise out of affectionate parent–child relationships themselves, friendship and benevolence are distinct sources of duty. Parents make sacrifices to give their children proper care and rearing, and chil-dren show their appreciation for what was done, but the feelings characteristic of friendship involve more than appreciation for services rendered. To be sure, if friends are indebted to one another, they will want to discharge their debts, and if they have performed kindnesses for one another, they will want to express their gratitude. But friends view these acts in the context of a broader pattern of friendly interactions, interactions that involve shared activities and interests as well as reciprocal services, and not simply as discrete, isolated incidents. They are committed to their relationship as such and seek to preserve and strengthen it as something good in itself. Out of this mutual commitment spring duties of friendship, duties that can persist after debts have been repaid and gratitude has been shown.

Friends have duties to one another because, having acknowledged and consented to their special relationship, each must do what he or she can to nourish that friendship and to work out problems and tensions that arise between them during the course of their friendship. To blame our "friends" for not acting as friends ought to act is to accuse them of a kind of breach of understanding (those who wrong others by not discharging a duty of indebtedness to them are also guilty of a breach of understanding, though of a very different kind). In Henry Sidgwick's words,

As all love is understood to include a desire for the happiness of its object, the profession of friendship seems to bind one to seek this happiness to an extent proportionate to such profession. . . . Since the profession of friendship—though the term is used to include affections of various degree—must imply a greater interest in one's friend's happiness than in that of men in general, it must announce a willingness to make more or less considerable sacrifices for him, if occasion offers. If then we decline to make such sacrifices, we do wrong by failing to fulfill natural and legitimate expectations.[7]

Duties of friendship are not essentially duties to do things in return for benefits received or sacrifices made, and hence it is inappropriate to regard them as duties *owed* to friends. Parents who say to their children, "We are friends (or at least I thought we were), and friends have the right to make certain demands of one another," are not trying to justify a claim to repayment or gratitude (indeed, gratitude does not seem to be the kind of thing that can be demanded), but are asking the children to live up to their commitment to their mutual relationship. The children can then either do what the parents want them to do, or reject one of their assumptions: that a relationship of friendship actually exists, that they (the children) at least led them to believe that such a relationship existed, or that even friends can be expected to do what the parents ask them to do.

The profession of friendship implies a willingness to do things for our friends even if our own interests are not promoted thereby or we have to make certain sacrifices for them. But a friendship would never begin, or would come to an end, if the individuals involved did not all regard their relationship as being, on balance, a good thing for them to be in (profitable, pleasurable, or valuable in some other way). Thus there can be no friendship between parents and children when parents continually expect their children to sacrifice their own interests for the sake of their friendship, or when parents act as though their friendship gives them the right to make incessant demands on their children's lifestyles. Further, while the duties of friendship are not prudential duties, they do presuppose a relationship that is on balance beneficial to all concerned. (Gratitude, in contrast, does not *presuppose* an interpersonal relationship: it *establishes* one by some form of reciprocation.) Filial duties of friendship may sometimes be quite disagreeable, but they cannot be so disagreeable so often that they stifle the affection from which those duties arise.

Though parents and adult children sometimes like to think of one another as friends, realizing this objective is often hampered by serious obstacles. There are psychological obstacles. We do not, as it were, meet our parents for the first time when we are adults. Our love for them is mingled with memories of former dependencies, and we may feel that we can never be fully the equal of those who know us so much more intimately than we can ever know them. Or we may never altogether forgive our parents for things they did or failed to do. There are also sociological obstacles. In a mobile, rapidly changing society, the child's exit from the family can lead to a loss of affection for or interest in parents and to a diversion of that affection or interest to others. If the relationship with our parents is perceived to have been an affectionate, supportive, non-manipulative, and honest one, we may make a special effort to resist our growing estrangement from our parents and to find ways of strengthening our ties to them. But sometimes, despite our best efforts, life changes, and the impact of external events preclude the intimacy that friendship demands.

Whether or not genuine friendship is possible between parents and their grown children depends in large measure on the parents' sensitivity to their children's developing capacity for friendship, and on the parents' willingness to deal with their children less and less as superiors and more and more as equals. If the relationship of the early childrearing years is to lead to friendship, it is necessary that parents not wait until their children reach adulthood before admitting them into their lives in a serious way. They must try to interest them in their affairs, confide in them, and seek their advice while they are still young and in a manner appropriate to their level of experience and understanding. As Locke puts it, as children "grow up to the use of reason, the rigour of government [should] be . . . gently relaxed, the father's brow more smoothed to them, and the distance by degrees abated. . . . Nothing cements and establishes friendship and good-will so much as confident communication of concernments and affairs".[8] Further, in a society (like ours) where the family is a tiny closed circle and family feeling is therefore particularly intense, the child's exit from the family, via change of residence, work, or marriage, may actually promote the development of friendship between the child and the parents. The child's departure from the home gives them a chance to put a little emotional distance between themselves and to find new (less authoritative, less submissive) ways of relating to one another.

Assuming that parents and older children can be friends, what does this friendship offer children?[9] Personal relationships are many and various, and they satisfy the following interdependent criteria to varying degrees: (a) the responsiveness criterion—the members of the relationship are responsive to each other's peculiarities, individual requirements, temperaments, etc.; (b) the inclusion-of-self criterion —the relationship calls upon and integrates several important parts of its members' personalities; (c) the spontaneity criterion—the members of the relationship step outside of their official roles and interact in an uninhibited and unforced way. Friendships in general score high in each of these areas, and depending on the degree of affection, intimacy, sharing, and trust involved, some friendships score higher than others.[10] As regards friendship with parents, this can be among a person's closest and most valuable. Parents and children often have very similar styles of mind or ways of thinking, and this can make for a high degree of empathy. In some cases, friends may not know exactly where they stand with one another or how far they can go with one another before putting too much of a strain on their relationship, but children who are confident of their parents' continued love feel that their relationship is resilient enough to withstand open criticism of parents' actions or beliefs, and this can strengthen the bond between them. Further, family life in the modern nuclear family is extremely introverted and private, and this exclusivity often continues long after parental authority has been relinquished, making possible special intimacies between parents and their grown children. Finally, close friendship with parents (like parenthood itself) is inclusive of self to a high degree. Friendship between parents and children is possible only if parents relinquish control and allow their adult children the independence befitting an adult. It develops as children come to terms with their prior dependency and work to integrate their past immature selves into their present mature ones. Through a deepening relationship with parents, the child's self-knowledge and self-respect are enlarged and enhanced.

One final point about friendship as an explanation of filial duty should be made. In permitting others to intervene in their children's lives, parents delegate some of their parental authority and discretion, thereby bestowing on their agents a right to command obedience from their children. However, the contacts between child and caretaker may be too brief, professional, or routine to form the basis of a lasting friendship. Children develop friendships only with those caretakers who meet their emotional needs for affection, companionship, and stimulating intimacy, and it is only this kind of parent–child relationship that can give rise to duties of friendship and their corresponding rights.

THE INTERPLAY BETWEEN GRATITUDE AND FRIENDSHIP

If a casual acquaintance unexpectedly favors me with assistance, then I ought to demonstrate my gratitude by my thanks and by means of some benefit I can give in return. In a family that is as it should be, of course, assistance is not unexpected. There is an understanding between parents and children (an understanding that need not be expressly formulated) that parents will act in the interests of their children and provide them with the things that it is good for them to have, and that children will cooperate with their parents as they attempt to do so. The children trust the parents' judgments of right and wrong and their altruistic intentions on their behalf, and count on their support and guidance as they grow in maturity. Yet the fact that growing children expect and have a right to expect certain kinds of help and assistance from their parents which they do not expect or have a right to expect from comparative strangers, in no way shows that children cannot have duties of gratitude to their parents, even for those actions that are included in the parents' moral duties.

The love and affection that normally unite parents and children in the early childrearing years is not friendship, because friendship is, on the whole, an equal partnership, and during these years parents do most of the giving and children most of the taking. Young children have a limited, though ever-growing, understanding of the contribution their own activities can make to the plans and projects of their parents. But this early relationship can perhaps lead to friendship if parents are intimate with their children as they are growing up and if external conditions are not unfavorable. Older children who do become friends with their parents do not thereby cease to owe them gratitude for benefits received and sacrifices made on their behalf while young. Older children not uncommonly do things for their parents partly out of friendship and partly out of gratitude, though it may not be until their friendship comes to an end or is temporarily on the wane that the children are able to differentiate clearly between these two motivational determinants.

A grown child does not have duties of gratitude to his or her parents *because* there is an ongoing friendship between them. Acts of gratitude and acts of friendship are not obligatory for the same reason. But the presence or absence of an ongoing friendship between older children and their parents is relevant to deciding *what* they should now do to show their gratitude to their parents. The way in which we show we care about, value, and respect our parents depends to a large extent on the kind of relationship we have with them. When our parents are also our friends, we should try to express our gratitude in ways that deepen, or do not damage, this friendship. Moreover, since some parent–child relationships are friendly,

some cool and distant, and since parent–child friendships themselves exemplify different patterns of affection and sharing, need and response, there is no one act, or specific type of act, that is invariably an appropriate expression of gratitude to parents. Some parents may not be receptive to certain kinds of help from their children, even if they are friends (e.g., financial assistance, or moving into the child's home after the death of a spouse), and children who insensitively press their services on their parents may only succeed in arousing their anger and resentment. At the same time, parents who are friends with their adult children usually want to preserve this friendship and do not ask for certain forms of assistance if they have reason to believe that meeting these requests would put a severe strain on their relationship.

NOTES

1. "Duties, Rights, and Claims," *American Philosophical Quarterly*, 3 (1966), p. 139.

2. See Fred Berger, "Gratitude," *Ethics*, 85 (1975), pp. 298–309; also Balduin V. Schwarz, "Some Reflections on Gratitude," in *The Human Person and the World of Values*, ed. Balduin V. Schwarz (New York: Fordham University Press, 1960), pp. 168–191.

3. *Doctrine of Virtue: Part II of The Metaphysics of Morals*, trans. Mary J. Gregor (New York: Harper, 1964), p. 123.

4. *Commentaries on the Laws of England*, vol.1 (Philadelphia: J. B. Lippincott and Co., 1856), bk. 1, ch. 16 section 1.

5. Individuals who lack self-respect do not believe that they are worthy of another's caring, and so cannot feel truly grateful.

6. As in economically and culturally disadvantaged families.

7. *The Methods of Ethics* (Chicago: University of Chicago Press, 1962), p. 258.

8. *John Locke on Education*, ed. Peter Gay (New York: Teachers College, 1971), pp. 30, 74.

9. I am not suggesting that the benefits children reap from friendship with their parents are among the causes of, or a basis for, this friendship.

10. If Aristotle is right that the happy man needs friends (*Nicomachean Ethics*, 1169b3–1170b19), then parents ought to give their children the kind of upbringing that is conducive to the formation of strong personal attachments later in life. Contrary to what Rousseau appears to believe, friendship is not incompatible with autonomy, and the capacity for friendship should perhaps be included among the objectives of parenting.

ANTHONY GRAYBOSCH

Parents, Children, and Friendship

Chuang Tzu tells the story of Liu Hui, a government official who was forced to flee his political enemies. Hui throws away the precious jade that symbolizes his rank, but carries his infant child away with him. Chuang Tzu asks why he would leave the jade he could sell for a small fortune, and keep the child who could only be sold for a paltry sum. Hui responds, "My bond with the jade symbol and with my office was the bond of self-interest. My bond with the child was the bond of Tao. Where self-interest is the bond, the friendship is dissolved when calamity comes. Where Tao is the bond, friendship is made perfect by calamity."[1] But many people doubt that friendship is possible between parents and their adult children. This doubt is rooted in just that aspect of parenting to which Hui appeals in explaining his action. The strength of the bond between parent and child prevents the equality and intimacy needed later for friendship to be possible.

Hui calls our attention to the permanence of a bond that cannot help but affect each individual. And to the extent that we value friendship, we may be tempted by the prospect of eventual friendship with our parents and children. Friendship with those who so intimately and monumentally affect us would add a sense of personal achievement and well-being to our lives. After all, how many friendships survive the greatest calamities?

I am going to argue that friendship between parents and adult children is both possible and desirable. The parents and children I will be considering are those who have experienced sustained relationships in a one- or two-parent family, as opposed to more communal arrangements. Since the obstacles to friendship—lingering authority, inappropriate intimacy, and inequality—are probably greater in noncommunal families, they seem to be the more crucial area to investigate.

I begin by discussing Plato's theory of love. I am particularly interested in how his account of falling in love can clarify the initial stages of love between parent and child. I also adapt his ladder of love, the notion that love ascends to higher stages as our understanding of eros increases, to the different stages of parent–child relationships leading to mutual adulthood and friendship. Then I turn to the major obstacles to parent–child friendship: inequality of benefit, lingering authority, and inappropriate intimacy. These obstacles can be removed if the parent prepares the child for friendship. And finally, I argue that friendship with adult children is not only possible, but desirable.

FALLING IN LOVE WITH CHILDREN

It is common in discussions of romantic love to distinguish the more exhilarating and exciting period of love as infatuation or falling in love. The former is shorter and usually less reliable in its perception of the beloved. Reliability is not really an issue with love of a newborn, since that love is a bestowal. I will, in any case, speak of falling in love. Falling in love occurs between the parent and the child, at least from the point of view of the parent. There are long periods of rather direct physical intimacy with the unborn and the newborn. Women enjoy nursing. Fathers gain a great deal of sensual pleasure from physical contact with their children. Feeding, hugging, kissing, rocking, and providing physical care all contribute to the development of an emotional bond. This caretaking also occasions a kind of exhilaration and a sense of worth comparable to the first stages of love between adults.

It is easy to overlook this exhilaration if we concentrate on the ethical dimensions of personal relations. For instance, Aristotle assumed that the love parents feel for children is based on a desire for biological continuity. Moreover, he argues that a mother's love is stronger because of the extra effort she expends in childbirth and her increased certainty of her parenthood.[2] The crucial element in the parent–child bond is presented as biological, and biological parenting fuels the more general care that is involved in child raising. Aristotle saw life, biological life alone, as a great gift that makes the child a permanent debtor to his father. But Aristotle nowhere mentions the physical and emotional pleasure parents derive from raising their children. Even if we accepted his emphasis on biological parenting, this omission is curious in a writer who recognized the importance of shared lives and shared pleasures for all types of friendship. The exhilaration gained from falling in love with your child is a major factor in maintaining the natural parent–child love relationship.

Parenting is a dynamic relationship. As a child matures, a parent should readjust his or her way of relating to the child to foster growth. But this platitude only describes half the relationship. The child's growth elicits responses in the parent that can foster parental growth and change the entire relationship. Both parties, parent and child, are at times active and passive participants. I want to borrow from Plato the notion of love as a progressive relationship. Plato can help us see how sensuous love grows into a rationally directed love akin to friendship. Something like Plato's ladder toward the love of the good should animate parent-and-child relationships.

In the *Symposium,* Plato's spokesperson Diotima tells Socrates that love is "giving birth in beauty, whether in body or soul."[3] Diotima offers us a vision of the lover as pregnant with beauty, as desiring to create something physical or spiritual that will embody this virtue. The lover is also able to recognize beauty in what is already created. And this recognition in turn gives birth to beauty in the lover's soul. Applied to sexual love, this image suggests that lovers are creative, and not just pursuers of pleasure.

Plato is committed to the erotic view of love. Intense, erotic, physical love is worthwhile for the pursuit of ideal beauty it inspires. Gradually, sometimes through restraint and sometimes after physical possession of the beloved,

the lover is led by reflection to the realization of the reason for loving. Plato believed that if we love a person on the basis of characteristics, if our love is basically evaluative, then it is these characteristics that are the primary objects of the desire we call love. Once the lover realizes what the characteristics are, the lover is freed from fascination with their particular embodiment and enabled to step up the ladder of love toward ideal beauty.[4] Then the lover proceeds from love of beautiful bodies to love of souls, to love of activities and laws, to love of the types of knowledge, and finally to the intuitive grasp of Beauty.[5] "One goes always upwards for the sake of this Beauty, starting out from beautiful things and using them as rising stairs.[6]

The love the Platonic lover elicits in ascending the ladder to Beauty is the love of the gods. The ascent of the ladder begins with sensuous love, specifically, the love of a male for a young boy. Gregory Vlastos claimed that Plato discovered a new form of pederastic love, "fully sensual in resonance, but denying itself consummation, transmuting physical excitement into imaginative and intellectual energy."[7] We can borrow from Plato the notion of a dramatic and exhilarating physical involvement of a parent with a newborn as the birth of love. At the end of the process, the love that is elicited is the love not of gods, but of adult children. And this love between parent and child will be embodied in their mutual friendship.

Plato's erotic concept of love is evaluative and conditional. Yet the love of parents for newborns seems closer to agape, a pure bestowal of love and value. This apparent contradiction can be resolved if we see being a child-of-mine as the property upon which parental love is initially based.[8] And those who prefer to see the initial state of parental love as a bestowal would interpret child-of-mine less biologically than those committed to erotic love. The former approach seems right to me because it acknowledges the goodwill people claim to have for children in general. And it emphasizes the importance of caring for children, psychological parenting, as opposed to biological parenting. But what way we interpret falling in love with a child matters very little because the relationship quickly becomes a fluctuating mixture of appraisal and bestowal in the cultivation of beauty in the child and the parent. And, if the result leads eventually to friendship, it will contain elements of both eros and agape.

Plato's account of love becomes conditional and impersonal, directed at the qualities that initially attracted the lover to another person: "We are to love the person so far, and only in so far, as they are good and beautiful. . . . the individual, in the uniqueness and integrity of his or her individuality will never be the object of our love."[9] Plato wanted us to use persons or bodies as vehicles to ascend the ladder to love of Beauty. He does not deny persons their individuality so much as their importance as individuals. And this is consistent with his concentration on the lover. The attribute of the beloved that is emphasized initially in parental love is a general one, for more than one child can satisfy the description child-of-mine. Parental love runs counter to Plato's vision by becoming progressively more concerned with the individuality of the child.

The final object of mature love in Plato is not a person. In parental love, the initial object of love is not yet a psychological person. But parental love plays a major part in developing the child into a person; in my view, it prepares the child for friendship with the parent. And to effectively prepare the parent and child for friendship, one thing the parent must do is place conditions on the bestowal of love. The parent must communicate to the developing child what attributes are worth loving. This, however, is not to say that parental love develops gradually from pure bestowal to pure erotic evaluation. That position is closed off philosophically because in at least one attribute, child-of-mine, erotic and agapic love seem to fuse. But, more importantly, psychologically they continue to be fused when we investigate why we would place conditions on the bestowal of signs of love. Those parents who value their children practice conditional love as part of their unconditional love in the interest of fostering increased personhood in the child. For parental love to turn into friendship, the parent must know which conditions are appropriate to institute and maintain as the child develops and when the time has come to remove such conditions.

The real question that Vlastos raised about Plato's account is whether conditional love is compatible with loving the whole person, and not just an abstract best version. Vlastos thinks Plato lacks an account of the beloved as a subject, imaginative empathy, and a notion of a father who cares for children as they are and bestows affection without regard to merit.[10]

Clearly, the care with which Plato depicts Socrates shows that he had a sense of the beloved as a subject. It also shows that he valued Socrates for good reasons, and not just for being Socrates. Plato, or anyone else, can love the whole person, warts and all, if the attractive properties outweigh the unattractive ones. We do not have to become blind to our beloved's faults in order to value both her admirable qualities and the whole person who embodies them.[11] Perhaps if Plato had considered the love of children and persons as important as we do, he would have given more emphasis to bestowal without regard to merit. I doubt that, however, given his description of parents as moral educators in the *Lysis*.[12] But placing conditions upon love does not mean that we do not regard the whole person as the object of love.

What is most valuable in Plato's account is his emphasis on the sensual genesis of love which can be redirected into a developing friendship with Beauty. We can see why this effort to ascend the ladder is worthwhile: it gives birth to beauty in both the lover and the beloved, it satisfies a divine impulse in humans to create beauty.

OBSTACLES TO THE PARENT–CHILD FRIENDSHIPS

Aristotle distinguished three kinds of friendships: pleasure, utility, and virtue. Aristotle thought that all three types of friendships would bring the friends pleasure. Our modern inclination is to equate true friendship with virtue friendships, at least to the extent that such friendships enhance the nobler aspects of human character. Some of the characteristics of friends are that they take pleasure in each other's company, they spontaneously seek out each other's company, and they are friends because of important aspects of each other's personalities. Friends are drawn to each other by virtues which they each find essential to their own lives.

Aristotle seemed to think that friends should

have identical virtues, for instance, an interest and facility in philosophy or music. We moderns are more flexible, and often have friends whose talents and interests we do not entirely share or appreciate. But we may well value these friends for their perseverance in those areas, or the extra dimension of experience our friends bring us. However, Aristotle seems to be right in noting that some overlap in important interests and talents is essential for friends. We might even say that if a friend has a keen identification with opera, for instance, we would, in so far as we are friends, attempt to cultivate our own appreciation of opera.

Equality is an important ingredient in friendship. If friendship is going to be spontaneously maintained, friends must give more-or-less equal benefits. Plato thought that love between nonequals was impossible, but Aristotle thought that it was possible if the nonequal friends had similar virtues and love was proportionate. The more perfect friend should receive more love. Their views probably embodied the suspicion that someone who is friends with a nonequal is somehow degraded or lacks a proper perspective on his own self-worth. But, practically speaking, equality in talents, education, and even finances seems undeniably to facilitate friendship.

At first glance, friendship seems to be voluntarily begun and maintained. But it is also inevitable in several ways. One is that having friends is an important part of a happy life. Another is that we initially like some people more than we like others; these initial evaluations reflect the characteristics we value, or, in a more dependent person, the characteristics we want to acquire to satisfy our needs. But still, friendship takes time to develop and requires the voluntary efforts of both friends. Yet this effort can also be involuntary since friendship is an activity more of loving another than of being loved. We seem to need friends themselves more than we need what we acquire from friendships.

So far we have found that friendship brings pleasure, that friends spend significant time together for reasons that are connected to essential parts of their personalities, that friendship is facilitated by equality, and that friendship is voluntarily maintained. Apparently, friends must have an intimate knowledge of each other to be able to relate on the basis of characteristics

that are integral to each's personality. Moreover, friendship will not only develop over time, but it will require both contact and mutual effort for its flourishing. Friends will have to be open to disclosing intimate details of their lives to facilitate each other's knowledge of their personalities. And friends will, as friends, be equal in power and authority to allow spontaneity and preserve autonomy.

Finally, the degree to which we take friendship to involve similar talents and interests will affect the sense in which friends are other selves. If we emphasize sameness of interests, then friends may be barely distinguishable from each other psychologically. If we allow more flexibility in overlapping interests, the common life of friends will be more metaphoric and psychological. What happens to my friends happens to me, and their joys and sorrows are duplicated. The second idea seems closer to our contemporary notion of a common life. And it helps explains why, although I have little interest in history, I can receive a great deal of pleasure from visiting the cruiser *Aurora* and taking photographs of it for a friend who is a historian.

If I have offered an accurate picture of friendships, we can now begin to ask what obstacles can prevent parents and adult children from becoming friends. One I already noted: children are permanently unequal to their parents because they can never repay their debt for the gift of life. Other major obstacles include a permanent inequality of authority—an unavoidable aspect of parenting—and the inappropriateness of the intimacy needed for a full friendship.

There are two primary ways in which a debt can affect friendship: the desire of the creditor to gain pleasure through reminding us of our dependency, and the desire of a debtor to avoid repayment. Aristotle thought of life as a great gift bestowed upon the child. This view always reminds me of a line from a poem. The speaker, on the gallows, muses, "When my father got me, he did not think on me."[13] Bestowing life upon a child is not always the purpose of the act that creates that child, even in a society that makes birth control and abortion readily available. I am suspicious of those who treat birth as a gift purposefully and altruistically bestowed. I guess you would have to be there to know for sure.

Less cynically, it is curious that Aristotle would remark on the need for close personal relationships in a good life and then suggest that the bestowal of life is undertaken either altruistically or to create a debt. Perhaps some parents bestow life purely to multiply or to create someone who is indebted to them, but I suspect people's motivations are more mixed. And either pure motivation for parenting would probably not be a good first step toward friendship. Most people who become parents, whether by choice or by accident, either initially believe they will benefit in some way from having a child or begin to discover actual benefits as they fall in love with their child. Here is a shared benefit based in a shared life. When one gives life it is not just to the child, but to oneself as a mother or a father.

Perhaps making a child indebted to you is a way of motivating obedience. Making the child feel indebted may be necessary in the initial stages of moral education. But if friendship is to eventuate, the debt must be de-emphasized when the child becomes old enough to question why affection exists between parent and child. It is possible to have friendships with those to whom we are indebted if they do not remind us of the debt too often. We can express gratitude only if they do not demand it, thereby allowing us to show it spontaneously.

We also no longer share Aristotle's intuition that the bestowal of life is a good in itself. Certainly we think that there are conditions in which it is irresponsible to become a parent. The ratio of abortions to births in Sarajevo switched from 1:2 in 1989 to 3:1 in 1993. We may disagree over the remedy for irresponsible sex, but there are clear cases in which one should not parent.

So, one obstacle to friendship with adult children can be removed if we keep in mind the benefits parents gain from their common life with children. Aristotle did think that friendship between nonequals was possible. So perhaps he would not think that friendships between parents and children were especially problematic if the love were proportionate to their virtues.[14] This suggests that there could be virtue friendships between parents and adult children, that they could become equal in virtue regardless of whether it is possible for a child to repay his or her parents for the gift of life. One virtue adult children could obtain is

gratitude by showing affection to those who have benefited them.

The mobility characteristic of our society can deprive families of the contact needed for friendship. The prospect of moving may demonstrate a duty we have to parents, or any friend, to maintain a friendship. When considering relocating to take a new job, we might discover that a friendship is important enough to convince us to reject the job offer. Or, if we relocate, we might have to assume a duty to find other ways to maintain contact with our friends. A major relocation might well determine how to structure family vacations for many years. Practical duties often arise within a friendship, and are not obstacles to friendship as such. Two major obstacles remain to be discussed.

Intimacy is an important element in virtue or ideal friendship. If friends are to value each other accurately, they must value each other in terms of important aspects of each other's personality. Friends should value each other in terms of those characteristics that are important to the friend. Our pleasure is greater when people want to be with us because of qualities we really do possess, and that we value ourselves. I do not want friends who value me because I have a beard—that quality is just too trivial. And I suspect that a friend who valued me for my tactfulness just did not know me very well, or had confused me with someone else. That is where the self-concept of the friend becomes so important. It determines whether you are friends with them, or a past, rejected, or transient version of the friend. Besides allowing ideal friendship, intimacy fosters the development of friendship by signaling acceptance, trust, and a willingness to progress from acquaintanceship to friendship.

So, if there are aspects of one's life that one would make available to friends but not to parents or children, this would support the view that parents and children cannot be friends. Joseph Kupfer has offered two examples of inappropriate intimacy to make this point. Kupfer believes that excursions with friends to establishments that offer sexual entertainment are not appropriate with one's parents. And I can add that disclosures regarding sexual activities, preferences, or fantasies would also be inappropriate.

Kupfer's second type of examples are complaints about one's spouse to one's children. Although he puts the case in terms of a parent making an inappropriate disclosure, such disclosures would probably be inappropriate in the other direction too. But Kupfer makes the parent the active party because he links these cases to another obstacle to friendship, leftover parental authority. It is because the parent is a permanent authority for the adult child that such disclosures are so obviously inappropriate.[15] Even when the parent becomes incompetent and dependent upon our care, authority is transformed into a respect that blocks intimacy.

So the intimacy offered by a parent who offers a revelation about a spouse is perceived by the child as an attempt to withdraw authority, something so deeply embedded in the child's psychology that it cannot be withdrawn. Instead of fostering friendship, it fosters confusion about whether to react as a child or a friend.

One problem with Kupfer's example of excursions to topless bars is that it is trivial. There are other ways to develop and maintain friendships than joint excursions to the nearest red light district. Also, it is not just parents with their adult children who do not belong in nude bars. I had a friend who was a priest. We went to a movie he had suggested, but its explicit sexual scenes made my friend extremely uncomfortable. Is it appropriate to go to sexually oriented entertainment with a priest? It probably depends on the priest. Can one have Jewish friends if you do not have a kosher kitchen? Sure, but learn their rules and do not offer them ham and cheese sandwiches. Our friends do not have to be identical to us in all their interests and values. I take tolerance to be a virtue, one I unfortunately need in friends. And the practice of respect and tolerance probably tells us something important about the nature of our friendships.

Perhaps someone might think that I have trivialized Kupfer's example, so let me change his case and focus on important revelations about sexual behavior. Should one parent tell an adult child about the other parent's sexual infidelity or impotency? Or, to use Kupfer's other example, should a parent complain to an adult child about the other parent's handling of finances or abuse of alcohol?

Here is where the analogy I drew with Plato's views on love helps. It seems to me to be entirely appropriate for a parent to make such disclosures to an adult child. The child must be an adult, and their relationship one that is well on the way to friendship. But perhaps I had better explain why such revelations are appropriate.

Parents may be permanent benefactors of their children, but there are virtues, for example, knowledge, in which children can and do excel their parents. An adult child with a Ph.D. in philosophy might excel a parent in knowledge of both logic and office politics. It is an important moment in the development of autonomy, and friendship, when the child realizes that he or she does possess some virtue to a greater degree than his or her parents. This realization allows the child not only to receive beneficial advice from the parents, but to bestow such advice in return. And it is at this point that the parental authority which Kupfer sees as permanent can begin to wither away and be replaced with friendship.

In my own case, I remember when my father told me he had met the CEO of a major corporation while on his vacation. About a week after the vacation he accepted a luncheon invitation from the CEO, whose personnel manager "just happened" to accompany them. They offered him a good job shortly thereafter. When my father told me the story he remarked, "And they never interviewed me." He had not figured out that the luncheon had been an interview in disguise. At that point, I knew he lacked a dimension of practical wisdom. Two years later, when the firm he had devoted himself to for thirty years began to progressively demote him, I was willing to convince him that he would eventually be fired. So he began to look for a job while he still had one. I like to think that I helped him avert financial disaster. It did not repay the debt I owed him for a life, but I felt as if I had managed to be a friend to him.

An important moment in the progression of a child toward autonomy occurs when that child begins to act the friend toward a parent who deserves it. It may be that this epiphany is possible only when the parent has prepared the way for friendship. But it is possible that disclosures from a parent to an adult child of sexual infidelity may be a great benefit. Certainly it enhances the child's own understanding of tensions within the family and the tendencies the child may bring to other relationships. Information about another parent's addictions are crucial to guiding an aged parent. Financial magazines regularly feature stories on the difficulties adult children have helping parents who are secretive about their finances.

Kupfer's disclosures are only inappropriate when friendship has not been allowed to develop. I would even hazard to say that it is appropriate to go to a nude bar with a widowed or a divorced parent. At the least, adult children have to learn to accept the continued sexuality of parents. And if a parent's complaints about a spouse strike the child as inappropriate, it might be because that person should be our friend also. Friends ought to confront each other directly, not gossip about each other.

The crucial factor in the development of parent–child friendship is parenting style. Kupfer is convinced that good parenting results in the parent being a lingering authority in the child's life.[16] I have argued that an inequality in authority or benefit is compatible with friendship when the superior does not wear that difference as a badge. Parents, and all friends, can be deferred-to in their areas of expertise. But I also think that the lingering authority need not be very great.

Kupfer argues that the child cannot be equally autonomous in a relationship because the parent is not shaped by the child. But parents are shaped so much by their children that they are constantly surprised by their own lack of anticipation. The child moves in the larger society and is impacted by other authority figures and other children who affect the parent through the child. A parent who raises a child to be autonomous is going to be impacted, especially as friendship develops with the adult child. It is not uncommon for children to leave the family when they begin college or a career and then to become re-acquainted with their parents when they themselves are adults. So, in contrast to Kupfer, I believe that children are less molded by parents who foster autonomy, and I also believe that children have a greater impact on molding their own parents.

Parents might also seem to have a psychological advantage in knowing how they have molded their children. But disclosures concerning the practice of parenting by those who have fostered autonomy will further enhance autonomy in the child. It would also encourage the pursuit of a similar parenting style in turn.

These two obstacles, lack of appropriate intimacy and lingering authority, reinforce each other and must be undermined jointly. Parents do need obedience from young children to be able to fulfill their duties to care and nurture them. But this obedience can become a source of confidence in the parent and lead to internalized self-discipline. The parent who monitors and recognizes this development can relax discipline and foster friendship with the emerging adult.[17]

Finally, it might be claimed that parents and children do not have to earn each other's love, that they are too similar to be friends, or that parents identify more with their children than do children with their parents. There does exist an initial bond between parent and child in unconditional love, but it is not dissimilar to the goodwill characteristic of the initial stages of friendship. And in friendship with adult children conditions are eventually placed on the developing friendship. It also will be the case that if parents foster intimacy with their children, their shared life and identification will be more nearly equal. Such identification can even help illuminate crucial events such as the choice of a career.

WHY PARENTS AND CHILDREN OUGHT TO BE FRIENDS

Suppose that I have argued successfully that parents can be friends with adult children. Someone could still maintain that there are good reasons for not parenting in the way that fosters friendship. Perhaps they believe that a strong parental authority that involves keeping an emotional distance and avoids physical and emotional intimacy is necessary for a well-ordered society. It would help to have a way of showing that friendships between parents and adult children are desirable.

Many have commented on the joy they experience caring for a dying parent. Lao Tzu wrote that it was part of the Tao to play the role of the parent to one's own parent and to become a child again in one's own turn at death. Kupfer sees an aesthetic beauty in this exchange of roles. He argues that it is one of the ways in which the parent's relationship to the adult child complements friendship while remaining a very different relationship.[18] But there is no need to look to philosophy for such testimonies, for they are found readily enough in the advice coulmns of newspapers. Such a conception of how parents and adult children should relate is extremely depressing. At best, it is a rationalization of a failed relationship. In the advice columns, these accounts always seem to be accompanied by statements about how someone finally exchanged intimate information with a dying parent, or worse, wished they had done so. It is as if the parent and child had to reach the point where death guaranteed that no awkward consequences would eventuate from their intimacy before they could begin to be friends. If friendship had an event comparable to the one-night stand, this would be it.

One of the benefits of friendship is the enhancement it can bring to our own self-understanding. And this enhancement is brought about in many different ways, some of which are not flattering. For instance, if a colleague tells me I am afraid of expressing an opinion because it is politically incorrect, I am apt to engage in denial. But the same comment from a friend will cause me to pause and seriously consider it.

Parents have two sources of information that make them the best candidates for this type of revelation and challenge. First, they have intimate knowledge of the child's life that he or she may have forgotten, repressed, or devalued. Second, given our common temperaments and genetic endowments, and the occurrence of similar crucial events in people's lives, parents have practical wisdom relevant to our own decision making. I may have helped my father find another job, but his experience taught me to always keep my resume updated.

Kupfer, following Aristotle, thinks that parents whose children care for them are presented with an embodiment of their own virtuous craft.[19] Plato might have called it a verification of the birth of beauty. All three believe that parents whose children care for them take comfort in knowing they have led a virtuous and meaningful life because of the gratitude they are shown by their children. I think it is not virtues so much as overlapping interests, intimacy, and just spending time together that is needed for friendship. In other words, your parents no more have to be saints than your other friends do. In any case, this pleasure of recognition is meaningful, and it is foolish to reserve it for the deathbed. Parents who have educated their children might enjoy their embodied virtues for many years by accompanying them to art museums, concerts, even their philosophy classes. Adult children gain a vision of what virtues are useful in their own future and gain pleasure from their parents' achievements when the common activities and intimacies of friendship are allowed.

Finally, adult children are faced with substantial economic burdens when they attempt to parent their own parents. Financial needs that occur within the best friendships can pose a serious obstacle to their maintenance. Thus, when the needs of aged parents compete with those of their adult children, people may fail to do what they can out of fear of the magnitude of their potential responsibilities. Moreover, the aged parents may hide a problem because they do not wish to become a burden to their child and risk losing contact.

I cannot at this point enter into a discussion of moral duties to parents. But it is probably clear to my readers that I would not support the notion that we have moral duties based in a natural relationship or the debt created by the gift of life. Besides moral duties, or duties of justice, there are duties of gratitude. Perhaps we have duties of gratitude to parents who either fulfilled their basic duties to children under difficult circumstances, benevolently did what went beyond their minimal duties, or benevolently went beyond their duty.[20] But unlike duties of justice, the scope of duties of gratitude is hard to define. Almost any token effort is sufficient to show gratitude.

But parents and adult children who have developed a friendship will be more aware of the extent of help each can provide, and they will be practiced in the kind of intimate conversation needed to communicate financial difficulties in a trusting environment. Since parents and adult children are friends, they are each assured that the other is committed to the maintenance of the relationship. Parents and children who can rely upon friendship are much more secure than those who must rely upon gratitude, justice, or the state.

There is, however, one duty that adult children and parents do have to each other. An example from Jane English is helpful here. English tells the story of Vance, whose parents did not approve of his choice of a spouse because of her religion. The parents unilaterally cut off contact with Vance for thirty years, but then became ill and needed his financial assistance. English thinks that Vance has no duties of gratitude to his parents. Their friendship was terminated by the parents, and when friendships end so do duties to ex-friends. She suggested, perhaps not seriously, that Vance's parents should first attempt to rebuild the friendship with Vance before asking him for financial help.[21]

English is right, in a way. Parents have such an intimate knowledge of their children, and such similar personalities, that friendship with them cannot help but enhance their children's lives through increased understanding. There may be exceptions where a history of abuse or abandonment has effectively wiped out the goodwill needed to begin a friendship. But in the absence of such conditions, I think Vance has a duty to himself to reciprocate an overture of friendship from his self-estranged parents despite their motives. After all, what kind of person would he show himself to be if he chose to hold onto the jade?[22]

NOTES

1. Thomas Merton, *The Way of Chuang Tzu* (New York: New Directions, 1965), 116.

2. Aristotle, *Nicomachean Ethics*, 1168a 25.

3. Plato, *Symposium*, trans. Alexander Nehamas and Paul Woodruff (Indianapolis: Hackett, 1989), 206 B. The point which follows about lovers as creators comes from Vlastos in the article cited below.

4. Nehamas and Woodruff, trans., *Symposium*, xxi.

5. Plato, *Symposium*, 210 B–C.

6. Plato, *Symposium*, 211 C.

7. Gregory Vlastos, "The Individual as Object of Love in Plato", in *Eros, Agape and Philia*, ed. Alan Soble, (New York: Paragon House, 1989), 105.

8. Alan Soble, *The Structure of Love* (New Haven, Conn.: Yale University Press, 1990), 14.

9. Vlastos, "The Individual," 110.

10. Vlastos, "The Individual," 111.

11. Soble, *The Structure of Love*, 311.

12. Plato, *Lysis*, 210 D.

13. A. E. Housemen, "A Shropshire Lad."

14. Aristotle, *Nicomachean Ethics*, 1158b 20–30.

15. Joseph Kupfer, "Can Parents and Children Be Friends?," *American Philosophical Quarterly* 27 (1990): 18–19.

16. Kupfer, "Can Parents and Children Be Friends," 16–17. See also Laurence Thomas, "Friendship," *Synthese* 72 (1987): 222.

17. Jeffrey Blustein, *Parents and Children* (New York: Oxford University Press, 1982), 166.

18. Kupfer, "Can Parents and Children Be Friends," 15.

19. Kupfer, "Can Parents and Children Be Friends," 15, 25.

20. Blustein, *Parents and Children*, 186.

21. Jane English, "What Do Grown Children Owe Their Parents?," in *Having Children*, ed. Onora O'Neill and William Ruddick (New York: Oxford University Press, 1979), 354–55.

22. I wish to thank Ed Romar and George Berger for their contributions.

SELECT BIBLIOGRAPHY

Anthologies

Al-Hibri, Azizah, and Margaret A. Simons, eds. *Hypatia Reborn: Essays in Feminist Philosophy.* Bloomington: Indiana University Press, 1990.

Allen, Jeffner, ed. *Lesbian Philosophies and Cultures.* Albany: State University of New York Press, 1990.

Allen, Jeffner, and Iris Marion Young, eds. *The Thinking Muse: Feminism and Modern French Philosophy.* Bloomington: Indiana University Press, 1989.

Badhwar, Neera K., ed. *Friendship: A Philosophical Reader.* Ithaca, N. Y.: Cornell University Press, 1992.

Baker, Robert, and Frederick Elliston, eds. *Philosophy and Sex.* Buffalo, N. Y.: Prometheus Books, 1975; 2d ed., 1984.

Bishop, Sharon, and Marjorie Weinzweig, eds. *Philosophy and Women.* Belmont, Calif.: Wadsworth, 1979.

Clark, Lorenne M. G., and Lynda Lange, eds. *The Sexism of Social and Political Theory: Women and Reproduction from Plato to Nietzsche.* Toronto: University of Toronto Press, 1979.

Cole, Eve Browning, and Susan Coultrap-McQuin, eds. *Explorations in Feminist Ethics: Theory and Practice.* Bloomington: Indiana University Press, 1992.

Copp, David, and Susan Wendell, eds. *Pornography and Censorship: Scientific, Philosophical and Legal Studies.* Buffalo, N. Y.: Prometheus Books, 1983.

English, Jane, ed. *Sex Equality.* Englewood Cliffs, N. J.: Prentice-Hall 1977.

Fraser, Nancy, and Sandra Lee Bartky, eds. *Revaluing French Feminism: Critical Essays on Difference, Agency, and Culture.* Bloomington: Indiana University Press, 1991.

Gaylin, Willard, and Ethel Person, eds. *Passionate Attachments: Thinking about Love.* New York: Free Press, 1988.

Gould, Carol C., and Marx W. Wartofsky, eds. *Women and Philosophy: Toward a Theory of Liberation.* New York: G. P. Putnam and Sons, 1976.

Griffiths, Morwanna, and Margaret Whitford, eds. *Feminist Perspectives in Philosophy.* Bloomington: Indiana University Press, 1988.

Holbrook, David, ed. *The Case against Pornography.* London: Tom Stacey, 1972.

Jaggar, Alison, ed. *Living with Contradictions: Controversies in Feminist Ethics.* Boulder, Colo: Westview Press, 1994.

Jaggar, Alison M., and Paula Rothenberg, eds. *Feminist Frameworks: Alternative Theoretical Accounts of the Relations between Women and Men.* 3d ed. New York: McGraw-Hill, 1994.

Mahowald, Mary Briody, ed. *Philosophy of Woman: Classical to Current Concepts.* Indianapolis, Ind.: Hackett, 1978.

Norton, David L., and Mary F. Kille, eds. *Philosophies of Love.* San Francisco: Chandler, 1971.

O'Neill, Onora, and William Ruddick, eds. *Having Children: Philosophical and Legal Reflections on Parenthood.* New York: Oxford University Press, 1979.

Osborne, Martha Lee, ed. *Woman in Western Thought.* New York: Random House, 1979.

Pakaluk, Michael, ed. *Other Selves: Philosophers on Friendship.* Indianapolis, Ind.: Hackett, 1991.

Rossi, Alice, ed. *Essays on Sex Equality: John Stuart Mill and Harriet Taylor Mill.* Chicago: University of Chicago Press, 1970.

———. *The Feminist Papers: From Adams to Beauvoir.* New York: Bantam Books, 1973.

Roszak, Theodore, and Betty Roszak, eds. *Masculine/Feminine.* New York: Harper and Row, 1969.

Sadler, Richard, ed. *Sexual Morality: Three Views.* London: Arlington Books, 1965.

Sargent, Lydia, ed. *The Unhappy Marriage of Marxism and Feminism.* Boston: Pluto, 1981.

———. *Women and Revolutions.* Boston: South End Press, 1981.

Schneir, Miriam, ed. *Feminism: The Essential Historical Writings.* New York: Random House, 1972.

Shelp, Earl E., ed. *Sexuality and Medicine*. Dordrecht, The Netherlands: D. Reidel, 1987.
Soble, Alan, ed. *Eros, Agape, and Philia: Readings in the Philosophy of Love*. New York: Paragon House, 1989.
————. *The Philosophy of Sex: Contemporary Readings* (1980). 2d rev. ed. Savage, Md.: Rowman and Littlefield, 1991.
Solomon, Robert C., and Kathleen M. Higgins, eds. *The Philosophy of (Erotic) Love*. Lawrence: University Press of Kansas, 1991.
Trebilcot, Joyce, ed. *Mothering: Essays in Feminist Theory*. Totowa, N. J.: Rowman and Allanheld, 1983.
Verene, Donald P., ed. *Sexual Love and Western Morality: A Philosophical Anthology*. New York: Harper and Row, 1972.
Vetterling-Braggin, Mary, ed. *Femininity, Masculinity, and Androgyny: A Modern Philosophical Discussion*. Totowa, N. J.: Littlefield Adams, 1982.
————. *Sexist Language: A Modern Philosophical Analysis*. Totowa, N. J.: Littlefield Adams, 1981.
Vetterling-Braggin, Mary, Frederick Elliston, and Jane English, eds. *Feminism and Philosophy*. Totowa, N. J.: Littlefield Adams,1977.

Books and Articles

Agonito, Rosemary. "The Concept of Inferiority: When Women Are Men." *Journal of Social Philosophy* 8 (1977): 8–13.
Aldridge, Alfred Owen. "The Meaning of Incest from Hutcheson to Gibbon." *Ethics* 61 (1951): 309–13.
Alexander, William M. "Sex and Philosophy in Augustine." *Augustine Studies* 5 (1974): 197–208.
Allen, Christine Garside. "Plato on Women." *Feminist Studies* 2 (1975): 131–38.
————. "Sex Identity and Personal Identity (Prolegomena to a Discussion of the Quality of Life)." In *Contemporary Issues in Political Philosophy*, edited by J. King-Farlow and W. Shea. New York: N. Watson, 1976.
Almond, Brenda. "Human Bonds." In *Applied Philosophy: Morals and Metaphysics in Contemporary Debate*, edited by Brenda Almond and Donald Hill. New York: Routledge, 1991.
Annas, Julia. "Mill and the Subjugation of Women." *Philosophy* 52 (1977): 179–94.
————. "Plato and Aristotle on Friendship and Altruism." *Mind* 86 (1977): 532–54.
Annis, David B. "Emotion, Love and Friendship." *International Journal of Applied Philosophy* 4 (1988): 1–7.
————. "The Meaning, Value, and Duties of Friendship." *American Philosophical Quarterly* 24 (1987): 349–56.
Anton, John P. "The Secret of Plato's Symposium." *Southern Journal of Philosophy* 12 (1974): 277–93.
Archard, David P. *Children: Rights and Childhood*. New York: Routledge, 1993.
Ardley, Gavin. "The Meaning of Plato's Marital Communism." *Philosophical Studies* (Ireland) 18 (1969): 36–47.
Aristotle. *De Generatione Animalium*. Books 1–4. Translated by A. L. Peck. Boston: Harvard University Press, 1943.
————. *Ethica Nicomachea*. Vol. 9, *The Works of Aristotle*. Edited and translated by W. D. Ross. Oxford: Clarendon Press, 1915.
Armstrong, Robert L. "Friendship." *Journal of Value Inquiry* 19 (1985): 211-16.
Atkinson, Ronald. *Sexual Morality*. New York: Harcourt, Brace and World, 1965.
Attig, Thomas. "Why Are You, a Man, Teaching This Course on the Philosophy of Feminism?" *Metaphilosophy* 7 (1976): 155–66.
Augustine. *City of God*. Translated by P. Levine. Cambridge, Mass.: Harvard University Press, 1966. (See Book 1, chapters 16–19; Book 12, chapter 24; Book 14, chapters 17–28; Book 15, chapter 16; Book 22, chapter 24.)
————. *Confessions*. Translated by Henry Chadwick. New York: Oxford University Press, 1991.
————. *"Continence" and "The Excellence of Widowhood."* In *Fathers of the Church*, edited by R. J. Deferrari et al., vol.14. New York: Fathers of the Church, 1948–1960; Washington, D. C.: Catholic University of America Press, 1960–1962.
————. *"The Good of Marriage" ; "Holy Virginity"; and "To Pollentius on Adulterous Marriages"*. In *Fathers of the Church*, edited by R. J. Deferrari et al., vol.15. New York: Fathers of the Church, 1948–1960; Washington, D. C.: Catholic University of America Press, 1960–1962.
Badhwar, Neera Kapur. "Friendship, Justice and Supererogation." *American Philosophical Quarterly* 22 (1985): 123–31.
Baier, Annette. "Good Men's Women: Hume on Chastity and Trust." *Hume Studies* 5 (1979): 1–19.

————. "Helping Hume to Complete the Union." *Philosophy and Phenomenological Research* 41 (1980): 167–86.

Balbus, Isaac D. *Marxism and Domination: A Neo-Hegelian, Feminist, Psychoanalytic Theory of Sexual, Political, and Technological Liberation.* Princeton, N. J.: Princeton University Press, 1983.

Barnhart, Joseph E., and Mary Anne Barnhart. "Marital Faithfulness and Unfaithfulness." *Journal of Social Philosophy* 4 (1973): 10–15.

Bartky, Sandra Lee. *Femininity and Domination.* London: Routledge, 1990.

————. "Narcissism, Femininity and Alienation." *Social Theory and Practice* 8 (1982): 127–64.

Bayles, Michael D. "Genetic Equality and Freedom of Reproduction: A Philosophic Survey." *Journal of Value Inquiry* 11 (1977): 186–207.

Bayzin, N. "The Androgynous Vision." *Women's Studies* 2 (1974): 185–215.

Beardsley, Elizabeth. "Referential Genderization." *Philosophical Forum* 5 (1973): 285–93.

Beigal, Hugo G. "Sex and Human Beauty." *Journal of Aesthetics and Art Criticism* 12 (1953): 83-92.

Belliotti, Raymond. *Good Sex: Perspectives on Sexual Ethics.* Lawrence: University Press of Kansas, 1993.

————. "A Philosophical Analysis of Sexual Ethics." *Journal of Social Philosophy* 10 (1979): 8–11.

————. "Women, Sex, and Sports." *Journal of Philosophy and Sports* 6 (1979): 67–72.

Benjamin, Jessica. "The Bonds of Love: Rational Violence and Erotic Domination." *Feminist Studies* 6 (1980): 144–74.

Bentham, Jeremy. "Offences against One's Self: Paederasty." *Journal of Homosexuality* 3 (1978): 383–405 and 4 (1978): 91–107.

Berger, Fred R. "Love, Friendship and Utility: On Practical Reason and Reductionism." In *Human Nature and Natural Knowledge*, edited by Alan Donagan, Anthony N. Perovich, and Michael V. Wedin. Dordrecht, The Netherlands: D. Reidel, 1983.

Berger, Peter, and Hansfried Kellner. "Marriage and the Construction of Reality." *Diogenes* 46 (1964): 1–24.

Bernstein, Mark. "Love, Particularity, and Selfhood." *Southern Journal of Philosophy* 23 (1986): 287–93.

Bertocci, Peter Anthony. *The Human Venture in Sex, Love, and Marriage.* New York: Association Press, 1949.

————. "The Relation between Love and Justice: A Survey of Five Possible Positions." *Journal of Value Inquiry* 4 (1970): 191–203.

————. *Sex, Love, and the Person.* New York: Sheed and Ward, 1967.

Bhattacharya, R. D. "Because He Is a Man." *Philosophy* 49 (1974): 96.

Blackstone, William T. "Freedom and Women." *Ethics* 85 (1975): 243–48.

Bloom, Allan. *Love and Friendship.* New York: Simon and Schuster, 1993.

Blum, Lawrence. *Friendship, Altruism and Morality.* London: Routledge and Kegan Paul, 1980.

Blustein, Jeffrey. *Parents and Children: The Ethics of the Family.* New York: Oxford University Press, 1982.

Boas, George. "Love," In *Encyclopedia of Philosophy*, Vol. 5. New York: Free Press, 1967.

Bouregeois, Patrick. "Kierkegaard: Ethical Marriage or Aesthetic Pleasure." *Personalist* 57 (1976): 370–75.

Boxill, Bernard R. "Sexual Blindness and Sexual Equality." *Social Theory and Practice* 6 (1980): 281-98.

Brink, Andre P. "Literature and Offence." *Philosophical Papers* 5 (1976): 53–66.

Brockriede, Wayne. "Arguers as Lovers." *Philosophy and Rhetoric* 5 (1972): 1–11.

Brown, Malcolm, and Jane Coulter, "The Middle Speech of Plato's Phaedo." *Journal of the History of Philosophy* 9 (1971): 405–23.

Bushnell, Dana E. "Love without Sex: A Commentary on Caraway." *Philosophy and Theology* 1 (1987): 369–73.

Butler, Judith P. *Gender Trouble: Feminism and the Subversion of Identity.* New York: Routledge, 1990.

Cacoullos, Ann R. "The Doctrine of Eros in Plato." *Diotima* 1 (1973): 81–99.

Calvert, Brian. "Plato and the Equality of Women." *Phoenix* 29 (1975): 231–43.

Caraway, Carol. "Romantic Love—Neither Sexist nor Heterosexist." *Philosophy and Theology* 1 (1987): 361–68.

Carson, Anne. *Eros the Bittersweet: An Essay.* Princeton, N. J.: Princeton University Press, 1986.

Clark, Lorenne M. G. "The Rights of Women: The Theory and Practice of the Ideology of Male Supremacy." In *Contemporary Issues in Political Philosophy*, edited by J. King. Farlow and W. Shea. New York: N. Watson, 1976.

Clark, Lorene M. G., and Debra J. Lewis. *Rape: The Price of Coercive Sexuality.* Toronto: Canadian Women's Educational Press, 1976.

Cohen, Howard. *Equal Rights for Children.* Totowa, N. J.: Littlefield Adams, 1980.

Collins, Margery, and Christine Pierce. "Holes and Slime: Sexism in Sartre's Psychoanalysis." *Philosophical Forum* 5 (1973): 112-27.

Cooper, W. E. "What Is Sexual Equality and Why Do They Want It?" *Ethics* 85 (1975): 256–57.

Cornford, F. M. "The Doctrine of Eros in Plato's Symposium." In *The Unwritten Philosophy and Other*

Essays. Cambridge: Cambridge University Press, 1967; reprinted in *Plato: A Collection of Critical Essays,* 2 vols., edited by Gregory Vlastos. Garden City, N. Y.: Anchor Books, 1971.

Cowburn, John. *Love and the Person: A Philosophical Theory and a Theological Essay.* London: Chapman, 1967.

Cumming, Alan. "Pauline Christianity and Greek Philosophy: A Study of the Status of Women." *Journal of the History of Ideas* 34 (1973): 517–28.

Curley, E. M. "Excusing Rape." *Philosophy and Public Affairs* 5 (1976): 325–60.

Daly, Mary. *Beyond God the Father: Toward a Philosophy of Women's Liberation.* Boston: Beacon Press, 1973.

———. *Gyn/Ecology: The Metaethics of Radical Feminism.* Boston: Beacon Press, 1978.

Dana, Richard H. "Equality in Sexual Behavior." *Journal of Thought* 15 (1980): 9–18.

Davidson, Arnold. "Sex and the Emergence of Sexuality." *Critical Inquiry* 14 (1987): 16–48.

De Beauvoir, Simone. *The Second Sex.* Translated by H. M. Parshley. New York: Knopf, 1952.

De Cew, Judith Wagner. "Violent Pornography: Censorship, Morality, and Social Alternatives." *Journal of Applied Philosophy* 1 (1984): 79–84.

Dedek, John F. *Contemporary Sexual Morality.* New York: Sheed and Ward, 1971.

De Gourmont, Remy. *The Natural Philosophy of Love.* New York: Liveright, 1932.

De Rougemont, Denis. *Love in the Western World.* New York: Harper and Row, 1974.

De Sade, Dontien Alphonse-Francois. *"Justine: Philosophy in the Bedroom"; "Eugenie de Franval" and Other Writings* (1791). Translated by R. Seaver and A. Wainhouse. New York: Grove Press, 1965.

Descartes, René. *The Passions of the Soul.* Translated by Stephen Voss. Indianapolis, Ind.: Hackett, 1989.

De Sousa, Ronald. *The Rationality of Emotions.* Cambridge, Mass.: MIT Press, 1987.

Devlin, Patrick. *The Enforcement of Morals.* New York: Oxford University Press, 1965.

Dickason, Anne. "Anatomy and Destiny: The Role of Biology in Plato's View of Women." *Philosophical Forum* 5 (1973): 45–53.

Dillon, Martin C. "Love, Death and Creation." *Research in Phenomenology* 11 (1981): 190–210.

———. "Love in *Women in Love*: A Phenomenological Analysis." *Philosophy and Literature* 2 (1978): 190-208.

———. "Toward a Phenomenology of Love and Sexuality: An Inquiry into the Limits of the Human Situation as They Condition Loving." *Soundings* 43 (1980): 341–60.

Downs, Donald Alexander. *The New Politics of Pornography.* Chicago: University of Chicago Press, 1989.

Dworkin, Andrea. *Intercourse.* New York: Free Press, 1987.

———. *Pornography: Men Possessing Women.* New York: Perigee, 1981.

———. *Right-Wing Women.* New York: Perigee, 1982.

Dworkin, Ronald. *Taking Rights Seriously.* Cambridge, Mass.: Harvard University Press, 1977.

Dyal, Robert A. "Is Pornography Good for You?" *Southwestern Journal of Philosophy* 7 (1976): 95–118.

Eames, Elizabeth R. "Sexism and Woman as Sex Object." *Journal of Thought* 11 (1976): 140–43.

Ehman, Robert. "Personal Love and Individual Value." *Journal of Value Inquiry* 10 (1976): 91–105.

Engels, Friedrich. *The Origin of the Family, Private Property and the State.* New York: International Publishers, 1942.

Engler, Barbara. "Sexuality and Knowledge in Sigmund Freud." *Philosophy Today* 13 (1969): 214–24.

English, Jane. "Sex and Equality in Sports." *Philosophy and Public Affairs* 7 (1978): 269–77.

Ericsson, Lars O. "Charges against Prostitution: An Attempt at a Philosophical Assessment." *Ethics* 90 (1980): 335–66.

Evers, Williamson M. "Rawls and Children." *Journal of Liberal Studies* 2 (1978): 109–114.

Farrell, Daniel M. "Jealousy." *Philosophical Review* 89 (1980): 527–59.

Faust, Beatrice. *Women, Sex and Pornography.* New York: Macmillan, 1981.

Feinberg, Joel. *The Idea of the Obscene.* Lawrence: University of Kansas Press, 1979.

———. "Love and Sexuality." In *Philosophy and the Human Condition,* edited by Tom L. Beauchamp, William T. Blackstone, and Joel Feinberg. Englewood Cliffs, N. J.: Prentice-Hall, 1980.

———. "Obscenity, Pornography and the Arts." In *Values and Conflicts,* Edited by Burton M. Leiser. New York: Macmillan, 1981.

———. *Offense to Others.* New York: Oxford University Press, 1985.

———. "Pornography and the Criminal Law." *University of Pittsburgh Law Review* 40 (1979): 567–604.

Ferguson, Ann. "On Compulsory Heterosexuality and Lesbian Existence: Defining the Issues." *Journal of Women in Culture and Society* 7 (1981): 158–99.

———. "Patriarchy, Sexual Identity and the Sexual Revolution." *Signs* 7 (1981): 158–72.

———. *Blood at the Root: Motherhood, Sex, and Male Domination.* London: Pandora Press, 1989.

Fichte, Johann Gottlieb. "Fundamental Principles of the Rights of the Family." In *The Science of Right* (1795). Translated by A. E. Kreger. Philadelphia: J. B. Lippincott, 1869.

Finnis, John M. "Natural Law and Unnatural Acts." *Heythrop Journal* 11 (1970): 365–87.

Firestone, Shulamith. *The Dialectic of Sex: The Case for Feminist Revolution.* New York: William Morrow, 1970.

Fisher, Mark. "Reason, Emotion and Love." *Inquiry* 20 (1978): 189–203.

Fortenbaugh, W. W. "On Plato's Feminism in *Republic* V. " *Apeiron* 9 (1975): 1–4.

Foucault, Michel. *The History of Sexuality.* 3 vols. Translated by Robert Hurley. New York: Pantheon Books, 1978–1986.

Frisbe, Sandra. "Women and the Will to Power." *Gnosis* 1 (1975): 1–10.

Fromm, Erich. *The Art of Loving.* New York: Harper, 1956.

Frye, Marilyn. *The Politics of Reality: Essays in Feminist Theory.* Freedom, Calif.: Crossing Press, 1983.

Fuchs, Jo-Ann P. "Female Eroticism in *The Second Sex.*" *Feminist Studies* 6 (1980): 304–13.

Fullbrook, Kate and Edward. *Simone de Beauvoir and Jean-Paul Sartre: The Remaking of a Twentieth-Century Legend.* N. Y.: Basic Books, 1994.

Garry, Ann. "Pornography and Respect for Women." *Social Theory and Practice* 4 (1978): 395–421.

Gastil, Raymond D. "The Moral of the Majority to Restrict Obscenity and Pornography through Law." *Ethics* 86 (1976): 231–40.

Gatens, Moira. *Feminism and Philosophy: Perspectives on Difference and Equality.* Bloomington: Indiana University Press, 1991.

Gelven, Michael. "Eros and Projection: Plato and Heidegger." *Southwestern Journal of Philosophy* 4 (1973): 125–36.

Gilbert, Paul. "Friendship and the Will." *Philosophy* 61 (1986): 61–70.

Gordon, Robert M. *The Structure of Emotions: Investigations in Cognitive Philosophy.* Cambridge: Cambridge University Press, 1987.

Govier, Trudy. "Getting Rid of the Big Bad Wolf." *Philosophy* 56 (1981): 258–61.

———. "Woman's Place." *Philosophy* 49 (1974): 303–9.

Gray, Robert. "Sex and Sexual Perversion." *Journal of Philosophy* 75 (1978): 189–99.

Graybeal, Jean. *Language and 'The Feminine' in Nietzsche and Heidegger.* Bloomington: Indiana University Press. 1990.

Graybosch, Anthony. "Which One Is the Real One?" *Philosophy and Theology* 4 (1990): 365–84.

Green, Karen. "Prostitution, Exploitation and Taboo." *Philosophy* 64 (1989): 525–34.

Greene, Andre. "Sexuality and Ideology in Marx and Freud." *Human Context* 6 (1974): 362–84.

Greene, Naomi. "Sartre, Sexuality, and *The Second Sex.*" *Philosophy and Literature* 4 (1980): 199–211.

Gregory, Paul. "Against Couples." In *Applied Philosophy: Morals and Metaphysics in Contemporary Debate,* edited by Brenda Almond and Donald Hill. New York: Routledge, 1991.

Grimshaw, Jean. *Philosophy and Feminist Thinking.* Minneapolis: University of Minnesota Press, 1986.

Gould, Thomas. *Platonic Love.* London: Routledge and Kegan Paul, 1963.

Griffin, Susan. *Pornography and Silence.* New York: Harper and Row, 1982.

Haack, Susan. "On the Moral Relevance of Sex." *Philosophy* 49 (1974): 90–95.

Halmos, Paul. "Psychologies of Love." *Philosophy* 41 (1966): 58–69.

Hamlyn, David. "The Phenomena of Love and Hate." *Philosophy* 53 (1978): 189–203.

Hansen, Linda. "Pain and Joy in Human Relationships: Jean-Paul Sartre and Simone De Beauvoir." *Philosophy Today* 23 (1979): 338–46.

Harding, Sandra. "Feminism: Reform or Revolution." *Philosophical Forum* 5 (1973): 271–84.

Hart, H.L.A. *Law, Liberty, and Morality.* Stanford, Calif.: Stanford University Press, 1963.

Hatab, Lawrence J. "Nietzsche on Woman." *Southern Journal of Philosophy* 19 (1981): 171–78.

Hegel, G.W.F. *On Christianity: Early Theological Writings.* Translated by T. M. Knox. New York: Harper and Brothers, 1948.

Hein, Hilde. "Obscenity, Politics, and Pornography." *Journal of Aesthetic Education* 5 (1971): 77–97.

———. "On Reaction and the Women's Movement." *Philosophical Forum* 5 (1973): 248–70.

———. "S-M and the Liberal Tradition." In *Against Sadomasochism: A Radical Feminist Analysis,* edited by Robin Ruth Linden et al. East Palo Alto, Calif.: Frog in the Well Publications. 1982.

Hekman, Susan J. *Gender and Knowledge: Elements of a Postmodern Feminism.* Boston: Northeastern University Press, 1992.

Held, Virginia. "Men, Women, and Equal Liberty." In *Promise and Problems of Human Equality,* edited by Walter Feinberg. Urbana: University of Illinois Press, 1976.

———. "Reasonable Progress and Self Respect." *Monist* 57 (1973): 12–27.

Hill, Judith M. "Pornography and Degradation." *Hypatia* 2 (1987): 39–54.

Holstrom, Nancy. "Do Women Have a Distinct Nature?" *Philosophical Forum* 14 (1982): 25–42.

Hughes, John C. "Sexual Harassment." *Social Theory and Practice* 6 (1980): 249–80.

Humber, James. "Sexual Perversion and Human Nature." *Philosophy Research Archives* 13 (1987–1988): 331–50.

Hume, David. "Of Polygamy and Divorces." In *Essays Moral, Political, and Literary,* 2 vols., edited by T. H. Green and T. H. Grose. London: Longmans, Green, 1875.

Hunter, J.F.M. *Thinking about Sex and Love.* Toronto: Macmillan of Canada, 1980.

Irigaray, Luce. *An Ethics of Sexual Difference.* Ithaca, N. Y.: Cornell University Press, 1993.

Jacobson, Paul. "The Return of Alcibiades: An Approach to the Meaning of Human Sexuality through the Works of Freud and Merleau-Ponty." *Philosophy Today* 22 (1978): 89–98.

Jaggar, Alison. *Feminist Politics and Human Nature.* Totowa, N. J.: Littlefield Adams, 1983.

Jarrett, James L. "On Pornography." *Journal of Aesthetic Education* 4 (1970): 61–68.

Johann, Robert O. "The Problem of Love." *Review of Metaphysics* 8 (1954–1955): 225–45.

Johnson, Edward. "Inscrutable Desires." *Philosophy of the Social Sciences* 20 (1990): 208–21.

Kaelin, Eugene F. "The Pornographic and the Obscene in Legal and Aesthetic Contexts." *Journal of Aesthetic Education* 4 (1970): 69–84.

Kainz, Howard P., Jr. "The Relationship of Dread to Spirit in Man and Woman, According to Kierkegaard." *Modern Schoolman* 47 (1969): 1–13.

Kalin, Jesse. "Lies, Secrets, and Love: The Inadequacy of Contemporary Moral Philosophy." *Journal of Value Inquiry* 10 (1976): 253–65.

Kant, Immanuel. *Lectures on Ethics: 1775–1780.* Translated by Louis Infield. Indianapolis, Ind.: Hackett, 1963.

———. *Observations on the Feeling of the Sublime and the Beautiful.* Berkeley and Los Angeles: University of California Press, 1960.

———. *The Philosophy of Law.* Translated by W. Hastie. Edinburgh, 1887. (See Part 1, sec. 1, "The Rights of the Family as a Domestic Society.")

Kappeler, Susanne. *The Pornography of Representation.* Minneapolis: University of Minnesota Press, 1986.

Kardiner, Abram. *Sex and Morality.* Indianapolis, Ind.: Bobbs-Merrill, 1954.

Keohane, Nannerl O. "Feminist Scholarship and Human Nature." *Ethics* 93 (1982): 102–13.

Ketchum, Sara Ann. "Female Culture, Woman Culture, and Conceptual Change: Toward a Philosophy of Women's Studies." *Social Theory and Practice* 6 (1980): 151–62.

Kielkopf, Charles F. "On the Structure of Chastity." *Proceedings of the Catholic Philosophical Association* 53 (1979): 164–72.

Kierkegaard, Søren. *Either/Or.* Translated by David F. Swenson. Princeton, N. J.: Princeton University Press, 1959.

———. *Works of Love: Some Christian Reflections in the Form of Discourses.* Translated by Howard and Edna Hong. London: Collins, 1962.

King-Farlow, John. "The Sartrean Analysis of Sexuality." *Journal of Existential Psychiatry* 2 (1962): 290–302.

Kleinig, John. "Censorship." *Interchange* 4 (1974): 232–240.

———. "Mill, Children and Rights." *Educational Philosophy and Theory* 8 (1976): 1–15.

———. "Reflections on Homosexuality." *Journal of Christian Education* 57 (1977): 32–57.

Kockelmans, Joseph J. "Merleau-Ponty on Sexuality." *Journal of Existentialism* 6 (1965): 9–30.

Kosok, Michael. "The Phenomenology of Fucking." *Telos* 8 (1971): 64–76.

Kraut, Richard. "The Importance of Love in Aristotle's Ethics." *Philosophical Research Archives* 1 (1975).

Kraut, Robert. "Love *De Re.*" *Midwest Studies in Philosophy* 10 (1985): 413–30.

Krell, David Farrell. "Merleau-Ponty on 'Eros' and 'Logos'." *Man and World* 7 (1974): 37—51.

Kupfer, Joseph. "Sexual Perversion and the Good." *Personalist* 59 (1978): 70–77.

———. "Can Parents and Children Be Friends?" *American Philosophical Quarterly* 27 (1990): 15–26.

La Follette, Hugh. "Licensing Parents." *Philosophy and Public Affairs* 9 (1980): 182–97.

Lange, Lynda. "The Politics of Impotence." In *Contemporary Issues in Political Philosophy,* edited by J. King-Farlow and W. Shea. New York: N. Watson, 1976.

———. "Reproduction in Democratic Theory." In *Contemporary Issues in Political Philosophy,* edited by J. King-Farlow and W. Shea. New York: N. Watson, 1976.

———. "Rousseau and Modern Feminism." *Social Theory and Practice* 7 (1981): 245–78.

Langton, Rae. "Whose Right? Ronald Dworkin, Women, and Pornographers." *Philosophy and Public Affairs* 19 (1990): 311–59.

Lear, Jonathan. *Love and Its Place in Nature: A Philosophical Interpretation of Freudian Psychoanalysis.* New York: Farrar, Straus and Giroux, 1990.

Leiser, Burton M. "Homosexuality and the 'Unnaturalness Argument.'" In *Social Ethics,* edited by Thomas Mappes and Jane Zembaty. New York: McGraw-Hill, 1982.

———. *Liberty, Justice, and Morals: Contemporary Value Conflicts.* New York: Macmillan, 1973.

LeMoncheck, Linda. *Dehumanizing Women: Treating Persons as Sex Objects.* Totowa, N. J.: Rowman and Allanheld, 1985.

Leser, Harry. "Plato's Feminism." *Philosophy* 54 (1979): 113–17.

Lesser, A. H. "Love and Lust." *Journal of Value Inquiry* 14 (1980): 51–54.

Letwin, Shirley Robin. "Romantic Love and Christianity." *Philosophy* 52 (1977): 131–45.

Levin, Michael. *Feminism and Freedom.* New Brunswick, N. J.: Transaction Books, 1987.

———. "Why Homosexuality Is Abnormal." *Monist* 67 (1984): 251–83.

Levy, Donald. "The Definition of Love in Plato's *Symposium.*" *Journal of the History of Ideas* 40 (1979): 285–91.

———. "Perversion and the Unnatural as Moral Categories." *Ethics* 90 (1980): 191–202.

Lewis, C. S. *The Allegory of Love.* Oxford: Oxford University Press, 1936.

———. *The Four Loves.* New York: Harcourt, Brace, Jovanovich, 1960.

Linton, David. "Why Is Pornography Offensive?" *Journal of Value Inquiry* 13 (1979): 75–62.

Lips, Hilary. *Women, Men, and Power.* Mountain View, Calif.: Mayfield, 1991.

Longino, Helen. "What Is Pornography." In *Take Back the Night,* edited by Laura Lederer. New York: William Morrow, 1980.

Lucas, J. R. "Because You Are a Woman." *Philosophy* 48 (1973): 161–71.

———. "The Lesbian Rule." *Philosophy* 30 (1955): 195–213.

———. "Vive La Difference." *Philosophy* 53 (1978): 363–73.

Luther, A. R. "Scheler's Interpretation of Being as Loving." *Philosophy Today* 14 (1970): 217–27.

Lyons, William. *Emotion.* Cambridge: Cambridge University Press, 1980.

MacDonald, I. A. "The 'Offence Principle' as a Justification for Censorship." *Philosophical Papers* 5 (1976): 67–84.

MacGuigan, Maryellen. "Is Woman a Question?" *International Philosophical Quarterly* 13 (1973): 485–505.

MacKinnon, Catharine A. *Feminism Unmodified: Discourses on Life and Law.* Cambridge, Mass.: Harvard University Press, 1987.

———. "Not a Moral Issue." *Yale Law and Policy Review* 2 (1984): 321–45.

———. *Only Words.* Cambridge, Mass.: Harvard University Press, 1993.

———. "Pornography as Defamation and Discrimination." *Boston University Law Review* 71 (1991): 793–815.

———. "Sexuality, Pornography, and Method: Pleasure under Patriarchy." *Ethics* 99 (1989): 314–46.

Mahowald, Mary B. "Freedom versus Happiness, and 'Women's Lib.' " *Journal of Social Philosophy* 6 (1975): 10–13.

Marcil-Lacoste, Louise. "The Consistency of Hume's Position Concerning Women." *Dialogue* 15 (1976): 415–41.

———. "The Grammar of Feminine Sexuality." *Canadian Journal of Politics and Social Theory* 4 (1980): 69-74.

———. "The Historian's Presupposition on Feminism: A Case Study." *Canadian Journal of Philosophy* 12 (1982): 185–200.

———. "The Trivialization of Equality: The Case of Feminist Writings." In *Discovering Reality,* edited by Sandra Harding and Merrill P. Hintikka. Dordrecht, The Netherlands: D. Reidel, 1982.

Marcuse, Herbert. *Eros and Civilization: A Philosophical Inquiry into Freud.* Boston: Beacon Press, 1955.

Margolis, Joseph. "Homosexuality." In *Justice for All,* edited by Tom Regan and Albert Van DeVeer. Totowa, N. J.: Littlefield Adams, 1982.

———. "Perversion." In *Negativities: The Limits of Life.* Columbus, Ohio: Charles Merrill Press, 1975.

Markus, R. A. "The Dialectic of Eros in Plato's *Symposium.*" In *Plato: A Collection of Critical Essays,* vol. 2, edited by Gregory Vlastos. Garden City, N. Y.: Anchor Books. 1971.

Marx, Karl. *On Education, Women and Children.* The Karl Marx Library, vol. 5. Translated by Saul K. Padover. New York: McGraw-Hill, 1975.

Mazis, Glen A. "Touch and Vision: Rethinking with Merleau-Ponty and Sartre on the Caress." *Philosophy Today* 23 (1979): 321–28.

Meager, R. "Obscenity: A New Danger in Literature." *British Journal of Aesthetics* 5 (1965): 57–61.

———. "The Sublime and the Obscene." *British Journal of Aesthetics* 4 (1964): 214–27.

Merleau-Ponty, Maurice. "The Body in Its Sexual Being." In *The Phenomenology of Perception.* New York: Humanities Press, 1965.

Milhaven, John Giles. "Christian Evaluations of Sexual Pleasure." In *Selected Papers.* American Society of Christian Ethics, 1976.

———. "Conjugal Sexual Love and Contemporary Moral Theology." *Theological Studies* 35 (1974): 692–710.

———. "Thomas Aquinas on Sexual Pleasure." *Journal of Religious Ethics* 5 (1977): 157–81.

Mill, Harriet Taylor. *Enfranchisement of Women.* In *Essays on Sex Equality,* edited by Alice S. Rossi. Chicago: University of Chicago Press, 1970.

Mill, John Stuart. *On the Subjection of Women.* In *Three Essays,* with an introduction by Richard Wollheim, Oxford: Oxford University Press, 1975.

Mill, John Stuart, and Harriet T. Mill. *Early Essays on Marriage and Divorce.* In *Essays on Sex Equality,* edited by Alice S. Rossi. Chicago: University of Chicago Press, 1970.

Mohr, Richard D. *Between Men—Between Women: Lesbian and Gay Cultures.* New York: Columbia University Press, 1988.

———. *Gay Ideas: Outing and Other Controversies.* Boston: Beacon Press, 1992.

———. "Gay Rights." *Social Theory and Practice* 8 (1982): 31–41.

———. *Gays/Justice.* New York: Columbia University Press, 1988.

———. "Invisible Minorities, Civic Rights, Democracy: Three Arguments for Gay Rights." *Philosophical Forum* 17 (1985): 1–24.

———. *A More Perfect Union: Why Straight America Must Stand Up for Gay Rights.* Boston: Beacon Press, 1994.

Morawski, Stefan. "Art and Obscenity." *Journal of Aesthetic Criticism* 26 (1967): 193–207.

Morgan, Douglas N. *Love: Plato, the Bible and Freud.* Englewood Cliffs, N. J.: Prentice-Hall, 1964.

Morgan, Kathryn. "The Androgynous Classroom." *Philosophy of Education: Proceedings* 36 (1980): 245–55.

———. "Androgyny: A Conceptual Critique." *Social Theory and Practice* 8 (1982): 245–83.

Nakhnikian, George. "Love in Human Reason." *Midwest Studies in Philosophy* 3 (1978): 286–317.

Neu, Jerome. "Jealous Thoughts." In *Explaining Emotions,* edited by A. Rorty. Berkeley and Los Angeles: University of California Press, 1980.

———. "What Is Wrong with Incest?" *Inquiry* 19 (1976): 27–39.

Nietzsche, Friedrich. *Beyond Good and Evil: Prelude to a Philosophy of the Future.* Translated by Walter Kaufmann. New York: Random House, 1966. (Secs. 79, 84, 85, 86, 102, 120, 123, 126, 131, 139, 144, 145, 148, 167, 168, 172.)

———. *The Gay Science.* Translated by Walter Kaufmann. New York: Random House, 1974.

———. "Morality as Anti-Nature." In *The Twilight of the Idols,* translated by R. J. Hollingdale. London: Penguin Books, 1968.

———. "On Child and Marriage" and "On Little Old and Young Women." In *Thus Spake Zarathustra,* in *The Portable Nietzsche,* translated by Walter Kaufmann. New York: Viking Press, 1954.

Nussbaum, Martha C. *Love's Knowledge: Essays in Philosophy and Literature.* Oxford: Oxford University Press, 1990.

Nygren, Anders. *Agape and Eros.* Chicago: University of Chicago Press, 1982.

Okin, Susan Moller. "Philosopher Queens and Private Wives: Plato on Woman and the Family." *Philosophy and Public Affairs* 6 (1977): 345–69.

———. "Rousseau's Natural Women." *Journal of Politics* 41 (1979): 393–416.

———. "Women and the Making of the Sentimental Family." *Philosophy and Public Affairs* 11 (1981): 65–88.

———. *Women in Western Political Thought.* Princeton, N. J.: Princeton University Press, 1979.

O'Neil, Charles. "Is Prudence Love?" *Monist* 58 (1974): 119–59.

O'Neill, Onora. "Between Consenting Adults." *Philosophy and Public Affairs* 14 (1985): 252–77.

Ortega y Gasset, José. *On Love.* Translated by Toby Talbot. New York: Meridian, 1957.

Osborne, Martha Lee. *Genuine Risk: A Dialogue on Woman.* Indianapolis, Ind.: Hackett, 1981.

———. "Plato's Unchanging View of Woman: A Denial that Anatomy Spells Destiny." *Philosophical Forum* 6 (1975): 447–52.

Outka, Gene. *Agape: An Ethical Analysis.* New Haven, Conn.: Yale University Press, 1972.

Page, Edgar. "Parental Rights." In *Applied Philosophy: Morals and Metaphysics in Contemporary Debate,* edited by Brenda Almond and Donald Hill. New York: Routledge, 1991.

Paglia, Camille. *Sex, Art, and American Culture: Essays.* New York: Vintage Books, 1992.

————. *Sexual Personae: Art and Decadence from Nefertiti to Emily Dickinson.* New Haven, Conn.: Yale University Press, 1990.

Pascal, Blaise. "Discourse on the Passion of Love." In *The Thoughts, Letters, and Opuscules of Pascal,* translated by O. W. Wight. New York: Hurd and Houghton, 1869.

Pateman, Carole. "Defending Prostitution: Charges against Ericsson." *Ethics* 93 (1983): 561–65.

————. *The Sexual Contract.* Stanford, Calif.: Stanford University Press, 1988.

Peterson, Susan Rae. "Against Parenting." In *Mothering: Essays in Feminist Theory,* edited by Joyce Trebilcot. Totowa, N. J.: Rowman and Allanheld, 1983.

Pierce, Christine. "Equality: *Republic* V. " *Monist* 57 (1973): 1–11.

Plato. "Laws," "Lysis," "Phaedrus," "Republic," and "Symposium." In *The Dialogues of Plato,* 4th ed., 4 vols., translated by Benjamin Jowett. New York and London: Clarendon Press, 1953.

Pomeroy, Sarah. "Feminism in Book V of Plato's *Republic.*" *Apeiron* 8 (1974): 33–35.

Poole, Howard. "Obscenity and Censorship." *Ethics* 93 (1982): 39–44.

Price, A. W. "Loving Persons Platonically." *Phronesis* 26 (1981): 25–34.

————. *Love and Friendship in Plato and Aristotle.* Oxford: Clarendon Press, 1989.

Price, Kingsley. "Love Yes, but Maybe not Sex." *Philosophy of Education: Proceedings* 36 (1980): 317–21.

Proudfoot, Merrill. "How Sex Can Make Us Good." *Philosophy of Education: Proceedings* 36 (1980): 307–16.

Reagan, Gerald M. "Further Questions about Androgyny." *Philosophy of Education: Proceedings* 36 (1980): 256–59.

Rettig, Salomon. "A Note on Censorship and the Changing Ethic of Sex." *Ethics* 78 (1968): 151–55.

Richards, David A. J. *Sex, Drugs, Death and the Law.* Totowa, N. J.: Rowman and Littlefield, 1982.

Richards, Janet Radcliffe. *The Skeptical Feminist: A Philosophical Enquiry.* Boston: Routledge and Kegan Paul, 1980.

Richards, Richard. *It Looks Like Love: Sometimes It Is.* Needham Hts., N.J.: Ginn Press, 1993.

————. *Love: A Philosophical Perspective.* 2d ed. Needham Hts., N.J.: Ginn Press, 1994.

Rosenthal, Abigail. "Feminism without Contradictions" *Monist* 57 (1973): 28–42.

Rousseau, Jean-Jacques. *Discourse on the Origin of Inequality.* Translated by Donald A. Cress. Indianapolis, Ind.: Hackett, 1992.

————. *Emile: or, On Education.* Translated by Allan Bloom. New York: Basic Books, 1979.

————. *Julie; or, The New Eloise.* Translated by Judith H. McDowell. University Park: Pennsylvania State University Press, 1968.

Rubenstein, Richard L. *Morality and Eros.* New York: McGraw-Hill, 1970.

Ruse, Michael. "Are Homosexuals Sick?" In *Concepts of Health and Disease,* edited by Arthur C. Caplan. New York: Addison-Wesley, 1981.

————. "Are There Any Gay Genes?" *Journal of Homosexuality* 6 (1981): 361-86.

————. *Homosexuality.* Oxford: Basil Blackwell, 1988.

Russell, Bertrand. *Bertrand Russell on Ethics, Sex, and Marriage.* Edited by Al Seckel. Buffalo, N. Y.: Prometheus Books, 1987.

————. *Marriage and Morals.* New York: Liveright, 1970.

Sankowski, Edward. "Love and Moral Obligation." *Journal of Value Inquiry* 12 (1978): 100–110.

Santas, Gerasimos. *Plato and Freud: Two Theories of Love.* Oxford: Basil Blackwell, 1988.

Saxonhouse, Arlene W. "The Net of Hephaestus: Aristophanes' Speech in Plato's *Symposium.*" *Interpretation* 13 (1985): 15–32.

————. "The Philosopher and the Female in the Political Thought Of Plato." *Political Theory* 4 (1976): 195–212.

Scheman, Naomi. *Engenderings: Constructions of Knowledge, Authority, and Privilege.* New York: Routledge, 1993.

Schopenhauer, Arthur. "On Women." In *Parerga and Paralipomena: Short Philosophical Essays,* translated by E.F.J. Payne. Oxford: Clarendon Press, 1974.

————. *The World as Will and Idea.* Translated by R. B. Haldane and J. Kemp. London: Routledge and Kegan Paul, 1883.

Scruton, Roger. *Sexual Desire: A Moral Philosophy of the Erotic.* New York: Free Press, 1986.

Shaffer, Jerome A. "Sexual Desire." *Journal of Philosophy* 75 (1978): 175–89.

Sherman, Nancy. "Aristotle on Friendship and the Shared Life." *Philosophy and Phenomenological Research* 47 (1987): 589–613.

Shrage, Laurie. "Is Sexual Desire Raced? The Social Meaning of Interracial Prostitution." *Journal of Social Philosophy* 23 (1992): 42–51.

————. *Moral Dilemmas of Feminism: Prostitution, Adultery, and Abortion.* New York: Routledge, 1994.

————. "Prostitution." In *The Encyclopedia of Bioethics,* edited by Warren T. Reich. New York: Macmillan, 1994.

Simon, G. L. "Is Pornography Beneficial?" In *Social Ethics,* edited by Thomas A. Mappes and Jane S. Zembaty. New York: McGraw-Hill, 1977.

Singer, Irving. *The Goals of Human Sexuality.* New York: W. W. Norton, 1973.

————. *The Nature of Love.* 3 vols. Chicago: University of Chicago Press, 1966–1987.

————. *The Pursuit of Love.* Baltimore, Md.: Johns Hopkins University Press, 1994.

Singer, June. *Androgyny: Toward a New Theory of Sexuality.* New York: Doubleday, 1977.

Sircello, Guy. *Love and Beauty.* Princeton, N. J.: Princeton University Press, 1989.

Slote, Michael A. "Inapplicable Concepts." *Philosophical Studies* 28 (1975): 265–71.

Soble, Alan. "Masturbation." *Pacific Philosophical Quarterly* 61 (1980): 233–44.

————. "Physical Attractiveness and Unfair Discrimination." *International Journal of Applied Philosophy* 1 (1982): 37–64.

————. "Pornography: Defamation and the Endorsement of Degradation." *Social Theory and Practice* 11 (1985): 61–87.

————. *Pornography: Marxism, Feminism, and the Future of Sexuality.* New Haven, Conn.: Yale University Press, 1986.

————. *The Structure of Love.* New Haven, Conn.: Yale University Press, 1990.

————. "The Unity of Romantic Love." *Philosophy and Theology* 1 (1987): 374–97.

Solomon, Robert C. *About Love: Reinventing Romance for Our Times.* New York: Simon and Schuster, 1988.

————. *Love: Emotion, Myth, and Metaphor.* New York: Doubleday, 1981.

————. *The Passions: Emotions and the Meaning of Life.* Indianapolis, Ind.: Hackett, 1993.

Spender, Dale. *Man-Made Language.* Boston: Routledge and Kegan Paul, 1980.

Spurrier, William A. *Natural Law and the Ethics of Love.* Philadelphia: Westminster Press, 1974.

Squadrito, Kathy. "Locke on the Equality of the Sexes." *Journal of Social Philosophy* 10 (1979): 6–11.

Stafford, J. Martin. "Love and Lust Revisited: Intentionality, Homosexuality, and Moral Education." In *Applied Philosophy: Morals and Metaphysics in Contemporary Debate,* edited by Brenda Almond and Donald Hill. New York: Routledge, 1991.

————. "On Distinguishing between Love and Lust." *Journal of Value Inquiry* 11 (1977): 292–303.

Stassinopoulos, Arianna. *The Female Woman.* New York: Random House, 1973.

Sullivan, J. P. "Philosophizing about Sexuality," *Philosophy of the Social Sciences* 14 (1984): 83–96.

Szasz, Thomas S. "Legal and Moral Aspects of Homosexuality." In *Sexual Inversion,* edited by J. Marmor. New York: Basic Books, 1965.

Taylor, Gabrielle. "Envy and Jealousy: Emotions and Vices." *Midwest Studies in Philosophy* 13 (1988): 233–49.

————. "Love." *Proceedings of the Aristotelian Society,* supplementary volume (1976–1977): 147–64. Reprinted in *Philosophy as It Is,* edited by T. Honderich and M. Burnyeat. New York: Penguin Books, 1979.

Taylor, Joan Kennedy. *Reclaiming the Mainstream: Individualist Feminism.* Buffalo, N. Y.: Prometheus Books, 1992.

Taylor, Mark C. "Love and Forms of Spirit: Kierkegaard vs. Hegel." *Kierkegaardiana* 10 (1977): 95–116.

Taylor, Richard. *Having Love Affairs.* Buffalo, N. Y.: Prometheus Books. 1982.

————. "Love and Friendship." In *Good and Evil: A New Direction.* New York: Macmillan, 1975.

————. "Love and Separation." In *With Heart and Mind.* New York: St. Martin's Press, 1973.

Teichman, Jenny. "Intention and Sex." In *Intention and Intentionality,* edited by Jenny Teichman and Cora Diamond. Ithaca, N. Y.: Cornell University Press, 1979.

Telfer, Elizabeth. "Friendship." *Proceedings of the Aristotelian Society.* 71 (1970–1971): 223–41.

Thielicke, Helmut. *The Ethics of Sex.* Translated by John Doberstein. New York: Harper and Row, 1964.

Thomas Aquinas, *On the Truth of the Catholic Faith.* Translated by Vernon J. Bourke. New York: Doubleday, 1956. (See Book 3, parts 1 and 2.)

Timmons, Mark. "Trebilcot on Androgynism." *Journal of Social Philosophy* 10 (1979): 1–4.

Tong, Rosemarie. "Feminism, Pornography and Censorship." *Social Theory and Practice* 8 (1982): 1–18.

————. *Women, Sex, and the Law.* Totowa, N. J.: Littlefield Adams, 1984.

Toon, Mark. *The Philosophy of Sex According to St. Thomas Aquinas.* Catholic University of America Philosophical Studies, no. 156. Washington, D. C.: Catholic University of America Press, 1954.

Trebilcot, Joyce. *Responsibility for Sexuality.* Berkeley, Calif.: Acacia Books, 1983.

————. "Sex Roles: The Argument from Nature." *Ethics* 85 (1975): 249–55.

————. "Two Forms of Androgynism." *Journal of Social Philosophy* 8 (1977): 4–8.

Turley, Donna. "The Feminist Debate on Pornography: An Unorthodox Interpretation." *Socialist Review* 16 (1986): 81–96.

Vadas, Melinda. "A First Look at the Pornography/Civil Rights Ordinance: Could Pornography Be the Subordination of Women?" *Journal of Philosophy* 84 (1987): 487–511.

Van de Vate, Dwight. *Romantic Love: A Philosophical Inquiry.* University Park: Penn State Press, 1981.

Vannoy, Russell. *Sex without Love: A Philosophical Exploration.* Buffalo, N. Y.: Prometheus Books, 1980.

————. "The Structure of Sexual Perversity." *Philosophy and Theology* 2 (1988): 30-44.

Vlastos, Gregory. "The Individual as an Object of Love in Plato." In *Platonic Studies*. Princeton, N. J.: Princeton University Press, 1973.

Warner, Martin. "Love, Self, and Plato's *Symposium*." *Philosophical Quarterly* 29 (1979): 329–39.

Westermarck, Edward. *Three Essays on Sex and Marriage.* London: Macmillan, 1934.

Westley, Richard J. "Justifying Infidelity." *Listening* 10 (1975): 36–44.

————. "The Maternal Instinct." *Philosophical Forum* 6 (1974–1975): 265–72.

Weston, Anthony. "Towards the Reconstruction of Subjectivism: Love as a Paradigm of Values." *Journal of Value Inquiry* 18 (1984): 181–94.

Whitbeck, Carolyn. "Theories of Sex Differences." *Philosophical Forum* 5 (1973): 54–80.

White, Stephen W. "Beautiful Losers: An Analysis of Radical Feminist Egalitarianism." *Journal of Value Inquiry* 111 (1977): 264–83.

Whiteley, C. H. "Love, Hate and Emotion." *Philosophy* 54 (1979): 235.

Wicclair, Mark R. "Is Prostitution Morally Wrong?" *Philosophical Research Archives* 7 (1981): 1429.

Willard, Duane. "Aesthetic Discrimination against Persons." *Dialogue* (Canada) 16 (1977): 676–92.

Williford, Mariam. "Bentham on the Rights of Women." *Journal of the History of Ideas* 36 (1975): 167–76.

Williston, Frank A. "A Philosophic Analysis of Pornography." *Journal of Thought* 7 (1972): 95–105.

Wilson, John. *Logic and Sexual Morality.* Baltimore, Md.: Penguin Books, 1965.

————. *Love, Sex and Feminism: A Philosophical Essay.* New York: Praeger, 1980.

Wolff, Robert Paul. "There's Nobody Here but Us Persons." *Philosophical Forum* 5 (1973): 128–44.

Wolgast, Elizabeth H. *Equality and the Rights of Women.* Ithaca, N. Y.: Cornell University Press, 1982.

Wollstonecraft, Mary. *A Vindication of the Rights of Women.* New York: W. W. Norton, 1967.

Wringe, Colin. *Children's Rights: A Philosophic Study.* Boston: Routledge and Kegan Paul, 1981.

Young, Iris Marion. *Throwing Like a Girl and Other Essays in Feminist Philosophy and Social Theory.* Bloomington: Indiana University Press, 1990.

————. "Women and Philosophy: New Anthologies." *Teaching Philosophy* 2 (1979): 172–82.

Yudkin, Marcia. "Difference Be Damned." *Philosophy* 55 (1980): 392–95.

————. "Transsexualism and Women: A Critical Perspective." *Feminist Studies* 4 (1978): 97–106.